SUPERVISION

DIVERSITY AND TEAMS IN THE WORKPLACE

E I G H T H   E D I T I O N

W. Richard Plunkett

Wright College
City Colleges of Chicago

Prentice Hall
Upper Saddle River, New Jersey 07458

Production Editor: *Julie Boddorf*
Production Manager: *Mary Carnis*
Director of Production/Manufacturing: *Bruce Johnson*
Prepress/Manufacturing Buyer: *Ed O'Dougherty*
Acquisitions Editor: *Elizabeth Sugg*
Interior Design: *Eileen Burke*
Cover Design: *Proof Positive*
Cover Illustration: *David Bishop*
Compositor: *KR Publishing Services*
Printer/Binder: *Von Hoffman*

© 1996, 1994, 1992, 1989, 1986, 1983,
1979, 1975 by Prentice-Hall, Inc.
A Simon & Schuster Company
Upper Saddle River, New Jersey 07458

Printed in the United States of America

10 9 8 7 6 5 4 3 2 1

ISBN 0-13-437955-1

Prentice-Hall International (UK) Limited, *London*
Prentice-Hall of Australia Pty. Limited, *Sydney*
Prentice-Hall Canada Inc., *Toronto*
Prentice-Hall Hispanoamericana, S.A., *Mexico*
Prentice-Hall of India Private Limited, *New Delhi*
Prentice-Hall of Japan, Inc., *Tokyo*
Simon & Schuster Asia Pte. Ltd., *Singapore*
Editora Prentice-Hall do Brasil, Ltda., *Rio de Janeiro*

Contents

YOU AND YOUR PEOPLE   145

PART III

SHAPING YOUR ENVIRONMENT   391

PART IV

SPECIAL CONCERNS 543

Preface

This eighth edition of *Supervision: Diversity and Teams in the Workplace* has been thoroughly updated, and revised in light of the many helpful comments and suggestions of adopters and reviewers of the previous edition. Special care has been taken to preserve the "how to" and the "you" approaches of the previous editions, while enriching these features with additional application materials. As before, the text emphasizes how a supervisor can apply the major concepts introduced.

Intended Readers

This new edition is intended as a primary instruction tool for those who either want to become supervisors or want to improve the present levels of their supervisory skills and knowledge. Users will find this text an excellent introduction to management functions and principles as these apply to the supervisory level of management. It is designed for use in community colleges, in various in-house industry and trade association courses, and in supervisory management programs.

The text's primary goals are to engage the students' interest; to explain management principles and theories with examples, terms, and situations that are understandable to beginners; and to translate these principles and theories into tools that can be used in the everyday practice of management. Management principles and their application to actual on-the-job situations are presented clearly and concisely.

New in This Edition

The major revisions in this seventh edition are as follows:

- The book is presented in a two-color format making the text more visually pleasing and exciting for the reader. The color has been used to maximum effect on all visuals, headings, icons and marginal notes.

- Included are three to five photographs per chapter showing more realistic applications of the major concepts.
- Themes of teamwork, quality, and ethics are highlighted throughout the text with icons and in boxed features in Chapters 3 through 16. "Supervising Teams" emphasizes the new roles being played by different types of teams in industry today. "Supervisors and Quality" highlights ways in which supervisors and their associates can influence and demonstrate quality in their performances. "Supervisors and Ethics" portrays various kinds of ethical issues confronting traditional supervisors and their counterparts—team leaders and team facilitators.
- Suggested readings have been updated to include books and periodicals available in most community and four-year colleges.
- Three major topics recur in each chapter's textual material beginning with Chapter 1: reengineering, diversity, and international applications. Each is highlighted with its own icon in the margins.
- Updated and new topics include: executing supervisory functions with and through teams, managing and getting the best from diverse individuals and groups, workforce 2000, security, computer applications and software, reengineering concepts, stretch goals, scoreboarding for results, and numerous real-world application examples from corporate America.
- Mosaic Workplace video and videodisc. Thanks to a joint venture between Allyn and Bacon and a producer of corporate training films, the Mosaic Workplace video and videodisc is available to all adopters. The six programs tie directly into major topics discussed in the text. Video users' notes that integrate the videos with the text are in the Instructor's Manual.

Program 1: Why Value Diversity?

Program 2: Understanding Our Biases and Assumptions

Program 3: Sexual Harassment

Program 4: Managing a Diverse Work Force: Recruitment and Interviewing

Program 5: Managing a Diverse Work Force: Helping New Employees Feel Valued

Program 6: Managing a Diverse Work Force: Meeting the Challenge

In addition to the new features, each chapter continues to include the following pedagogical tools to aid students in the study and retention of the chapter's major concepts:

Learning Objectives: aid the student in identifying and mastering the chapter's key concepts.

Key Terms: margin definitions within the chapter and contained in an end-of-book glossary.

Introduction: briefly highlights the chapter's theme.

All visual representations of data are now call "Exhibit," eliminating the confusion between figures and tables.

Instant Replay: lists the chapter's key concepts for review and study preparation.

Suggest Readings: suggests books and articles for further exploration of chapter topics.

Incident: an experiential exercise which asks students to apply their knowledge and experiences to the chapter's key concepts.

Cases: two case problems based on supervisors' experiences that ask students to apply each chapter's major principles.

Supplementary Material

The Instructor's Manual includes chapter outlines, three additional cases for each chapter with suggested solutions, answers to the text's questions for class discussion and its cases, a vocabulary review for each chapter's key terms, and video users' notes that integrate the Mosaic videos with chapter material. A separate test bank containing thirty true/false and thirty multiple choice questions, with answers per chapter. Those test questions are also available in either a 5-1/4" or 3-1/2" format.

Acknowledgments

Various individuals have been most helpful in the development of this eighth edition, and all previous editions. Their reviews and suggestions have provided the insight needed to update and expand this text. I would like to acknowledge the following people for their help on this edition: John C. Cox, New Mexico State University; Win Chesney, Saint Louis Community College–Meramac; Peter Vander Haeghen, Coastline Community College; WJ Waters, Central Piedmont Community College; Gloria Couch, Texas State Technical Institute; Duane Schechter, Muskingum Community College; Daniel R. Tomal, Purdue University; Smita Jain Oxford, Commonwealth College; Debbie Jansky, Milwaukee Area Tech; and Jim Mulvihill, South Central Technical College.

I would like to acknowledge the help of the following people on the previous editions: Lorraine Bassette, Prince George's Community College; Edwin A. Giermak, College of DuPage; Cheryl Macon, Butler County Community College; Jim Rassi, Paradise Valley Community College; Carl Sonntag, Pikes Peak Community College; Lynn H. Suksdorf, Salt Lake Community College; and H. Allan Tolbert, Central Texas College. Ray Ackerman, East Texas State University; Thomas Auer, Murray State

University; Richard Baker, Mohave Community College; Raymond F. Balcerzak, Jr., Ferris State University; Gregory Barnes, Purdue University; James Baskfield, North Hennepin Community College; Charles Beavin, Miami-Dade Community College; James Bishop, Arkansas State University; Frederick Blake, Bee County College; Raymond Bobillo, Purdue University; Arthur Boisselle, Pikes Peak Community College; Jerry Boles, Western Kentucky University; Terry Bordan, CUNY-Hostos Community College; Joe Breeden, Kansas Technical Institute; Robin Butler, Lakeshore Technical Institute; Leonard Callahan, Daytona Beach Community College; Donald Caruth, East Texas State University; Donald S. Carver, National University; Joseph Castelli, College of San Mateo; Joseph Chandler, Indiana-Purdue University at Fort Wayne; Win Chesney, St. Louis Community College; Jackie Conway, Lenoir Community College; Roger Crowe, State Technical Institute at Knoxville; E. Jane Dews, San Jacinto College-South; Michael Dougherty, Milwaukee Area Technical College; M. J. Duffey, Lord Fairfax Community College; C.S. "Pete" Everett, Des Moines Area Community College; Lawrence Finley, Western Kentucky University; Ethel Fishman, Fashion Institute of Technology; Jack Fleming, Moorpark College; Randall Scott Frederick, Delgado Community College; Daphne Friday, Sacred Heart College; Olene Fuller, San Jacinto College-North; Alfonso Garcia, Navajo Community College; John Geubtner, Tacoma Community College; Tommy Gilbreath, University of Texas at Tyler; Cliff Goodwin, Indiana University-Purdue University; Edward Gott, Jr., Eastern Maine Vocational Technical Institute; Luther Guynes, Los Angeles City College; Ed Hart, Elizabethtown Community College; JoAnn Hendricks, City College of San Francisco; Steven Herendeen, Indiana-Purdue University at Fort Wayne; Ron Herrick, Mesa Community College; Karen Heuer, Des Moines Area Community College; Larry Hill, San Jacinto College; Larry Holliday, Southwest Wisconsin Vocational Technical Institute; Eugene Holmen, Essex Community College; David Hunt, Blackhawk Technical Institute; Tonya Hynds, Purdue University-Kokomo; Jim Jackson, Johnston Technical College; William Jacobs, Lake City Community College; Joseph James, Jr., Lamar University-Port Arthur; Carl F. Jenks, Purdue University; F. Mike Kaufman; George Kelley, Erie Community College-City Campus; Billy Kirkland, Tarleton State University; Steve Kirman, Dyke College; Jay Knippen, University of South Florida; Thomas Leet, Purdue University; James Lewis, Gateway Technical Institute; Marvin Long, New River Community College; Doris Lux, Central Community College-Platte; Joseph Manno, Montgomery College; Manuel Mena, SUNY College at Oswego; Michael Miller, Indiana University-Purdue University at Fort Wayne; Jerry Moller, Frank Phillip's College; Sherry Montgomery, Saint Philip's College; Charles Moore, Neosho County Community College; Herff Moore, University of Central Arkansas; Jim Nestor, Daytona Beach Community College; Gerard Nistal, Our Lady of Holy Cross College; Carolyn Patton, Stephen F. Austin State University; Jean Perry, Contra Costa College;

Donald Pettit, Suffolk County Community College; Jerome Pilewski, University of Pittsburgh at Titusville; Sharon Pinebrook, University of Houston; Peter Randrup, WorWic Technical Community College; Ed Raskin, Los Angeles Mission College; William Recker, Northern Kentucky University; Robert Redick, Lincoln Land Community College; James A. Reinemann, College of Lake County; Tom Reynolds, Southside Virginia Community College; Harriett Rice, Los Angeles City College; Ralph Rice, Maryland Technical College; Shirley Rickert, Indiana University-Purdue University at Fort Wayne; Charles Roegiers, University of South Dakota; Lloyd Roettger, Indiana Vocational Technical College; Pat Rothamel, Iowa Western Community College; Robert Sedwick, Fairleigh Dickinson University; Sandra Seppamaki, Tanana Valley Community College; David Shepard, Virginia Western Community College; David Shufeldt, Clayton State College; David Smith, Dabney Lancaster Community College; Carl Sonntag, Pikes Peak Community College; Frank Sotrines, Washburn University; William Steiden, Jefferson Community College Southwest; Greg Stephens, Kansas Tech; John Stepp, Greenville Technical College; Marge Sunderland, Fayetteville Technical Institute; George Sutcliffe, Central Piedmont Community College; Wes Van Loon, Matanuske-Susitan Community College; Mike Vijuk, William Rainey Harper College; Hal Ward, Temple Junior College; Willie Weaver, Amarillo College; George White, Ohlone College; Ron Williams, Merced College; Willie Williams, Tidewater Community College; Bob Willis, Rogers State College; Ira Wilsker, Lamar University; Paul Wolff II, Dundalk Community College; Richard Wong, Olympic College; Robert Wood, Vance–Granville Community College; Charles Yauger, Arkansas State University.

Suggestions to the Students

I envy all of you for the fun and challenge you are about to experience. I congratulate you on your ambition and foresight in choosing a very fascinating course of study: the management of people.

Do not hide your talents. Share your experiences with your class, and soon you will realize how valuable your personal experiences have been to yourself—and how valuable they may be to your classmates.

You can expect to find a frequent and almost immediate use for almost everything you learn in the management course. If you are already a manager, you can apply the lessons at work. If you are not one yet, study your boss. If your boss is highly qualified, you will soon be able to see why this is so. If he or she is not, you will learn what is wrong with his or her performance. More important, you will also know what mistakes you should not make. Often the example of a poorly qualified boss can provide an excellent learning experience.

Never seek to conceal your own ignorance about the task of being a supervisor. Admit to yourself that you have a lot to learn, as we all do. Only be recognizing a void in your knowledge can you hope to fill it. And the proper way to fill it is by studying and expanding your work experience. If you ask questions in class as they occur to you, you will avoid the old problem of missing out on important pieces of information. You must take the initiative. Quite possibly, some questions that are bothering you might also concern others in the class. The more you contribute to the course, the more you will receive from it.

From now on, you should think of yourself as a supervisor. Throughout this book, I will be talking to you as one supervisor to another. In the following pages you will find many tools—the tools of supervision. Their uses are explained in detail. A skilled worker knows his or her tools and knows which one is right for each task. When you complete this course, you will have the knowledge you need to be a successful supervisor. You should put this knowledge to use as soon as possible. During the course, you will probably have a chance to present one of the case problems to your classmates. This is a fine opportunity to test yourself on how to apply the principles of supervision to a concrete situation in the world of work. You may also find other applications of these principles, both at home and on the job. Do not overlook them.

P A R T   I

THE BIG PICTURE

Part I of this text contains four chapters designed to introduce you to the supervisor's (team leader's or team facilitator's) special place in management and the concepts and functions that are essential for all managers.

Chapter 1 focuses on the unique challenges and opportunities connected with being a supervisor in any kind of organization. The skills, roles, and responsibilities required of supervisors are examined in detail.

Chapter 2 helps you assess your strengths and weaknesses and plan for the evolution of your career. It gives guidelines for personal growth and a strategy for seeking employment.

Also introduced in this part are three features that appear throughout Chapters 3–16: Supervising Teams, Supervisors and Ethics, and Supervisors and Quality. Each has been written to introduce you to various concepts and principles that will help you effectively manage your subordinates, team members, or associates, both individually and in groups.

Chapter 3 defines management as both an activity and a team of people. The concepts of authority, responsibility, accountability, and power are defined and illustrated, along with the three levels of management and the steps for rational decision making.

Chapter 4 concludes this unit with a brief look at all the functions common to all levels of management. The basic principles and tools that apply to each function are examined along with the ways in which supervisors put them to use.

The Supervisor's Special Role

OBJECTIVES

After reading and discussing this chapter, you should be able to do the following:

1. Define this chapter's key terms.

2. List and define the three management skills every supervisor must possess and apply.

3. List the three groups to whom the supervisor is responsible and what responsibilities exist toward each group.

4. Explain the concepts of effectiveness and efficiency as they apply to a supervisor's performance.

5. Discuss the possible effects on supervisors of seven current trends in U.S. business.

6. Describe the sources of supervisory personnel.

INTRODUCTION

supervisor
a manager responsible for the welfare, behaviors, and performances of nonmanagement employees (workers)

A **supervisor** is an employee (and member of the group of facilitators called *managers*) who is responsible for the welfare, behaviors, and performances of nonmanagement employees—called *workers*. (Throughout this text, the terms *worker, team member,* and *associate* will be used interchangeably with the term *subordinate.*) The supervisor is a person in the middle, positioned between the workers and higher-level managers. Supervisors' managers and subordinates differ in attitudes, values, priorities, and in the demands they make on supervisors. Workers and managers often make conflicting demands. The supervisor must cope with conflicts while gaining a sense of job satisfaction and identity in the process.

Major changes throughout both the private and public sectors of our economy are reshaping the traditional behaviors of supervisors in both large and small organizations. Organizational efforts to become more cost-effective, get closer to their customers, and tap into the creativity of all employees have created self-directing divisions and teams and pushed decision-making responsibilities into the hands of supervisors and their associates. As a result, supervisors are moving away from giving orders and commands; planning subordinates' work; rarely consulting with subordinates; and inspecting their output to leading (influencing others through words and examples), serving, coaching, counseling, guiding, consulting with, and meeting subordinates' individual and collective needs.

team leader
a supervisor working in a team and responsible for its members

team facilitator
a supervisor in charge of teams but working outside them

Supervisors are being rapidly transformed into team leaders and team facilitators: **Team leaders** serve on and lead a team; **team facilitators** nurture one or more teams of their subordinates. Both are expected to determine what human, financial, material, and informational resources are needed by their associates and to make certain that what is needed is provided. Team leaders and team facilitators exist to *support* their associates by helping to create and nurture a committed, trained, competent, and enthusiastic workforce. As the author of *Job Shift*, William Bridges (1994) puts it: The value of supervisors "…can be defined only by how they facilitate the work of…teams or how they contribute to it as a member."

Two federal laws define the supervisor. The Taft-Hartley Act of 1947 says that any person who can hire, suspend, transfer, lay off, recall, promote, discharge, assign, reward, or discipline other employees while using independent judgment is a supervisor—member of management. The Fair Labor Standards Act of 1938 states that supervisors may not use more than 20 percent of their time performing the same kind of work that their subordinates perform and that they must be paid other than an hourly wage. These distinctions prove useful in several later chapters.

foreman
a supervisor of workers in manufacturing

You may be familiar with the term **foreman.** In some organizations, it is used interchangeably with the word *supervisor* and usually refers to a supervisor of workers performing manufacturing activities.

THREE TYPES
OF MANAGEMENT SKILLS

No matter how supervisors are defined, they routinely must apply basic skills. According to Robert L. Katz, a college professor of business administration, corporate director, and management consultant, the basic **management skills** required of all managers at every level in an organization can be grouped under three headings: human, technical, and conceptual (Katz, 1975). Managers at different levels in an organization will use one or another of these skills to a greater or lesser degree, depending on the managers' positions in the organization and the particular demands of their circumstances at any given time (see Exhibit 1.1).

management skills
categories of capabilities needed by all managers at every level in an organization

Human Skills

Human skills determine the manager's ability to work effectively as a group or team member and to build cooperative effort within the group or team he or she leads and facilitates. Human skills are also needed to coordinate the interaction between that group and all the other groups with which it comes into contact.

Consider the lessons learned by team leaders in the Colorado-based XEL company. This maker of communications equipment wanted to create a quality-obsessed environment "…to become a model of workplace efficiency, dedicated to quality and teamwork" (Inc., 1994). It began with a needs assessment with team leaders asking associates what they wanted to learn and how. After trying ready-made courses and evaluating them, team leaders decided to design their own "XEL University [offering] 30 classes, on topics from soldering to problem solving" (Inc., 1994). Associates volunteer to participate, and they spend, on average, nearly five hours each month in class. Major improvements and some dozen new patents have been the result.

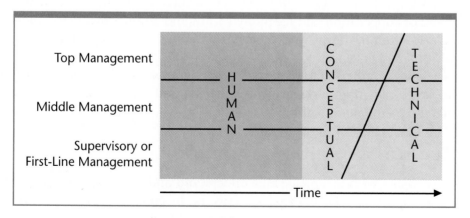

EXHIBIT 1.1
The proportions of management skills needed at the three levels of management.

Supervisors who have developed human skills know themselves well. They are tolerant and understanding of the viewpoints, attitudes, perceptions, and beliefs of others and are skillful communicators. People with human skills listen to others (XEL team leaders do), are honest and open, and possess personalities that are pleasing to others. They create an atmosphere in which others feel free to express their ideas, and they make every effort to determine how intended actions will affect others in the organization. Supervisors who once held their subordinates' jobs have empathy for them—that is, supervisors have the ability to relate to what subordinates are experiencing and feeling.

Managers at every level need human skills, but such skills are particularly important to supervisors. They must create and maintain an atmosphere of cooperation and harmony within and among the diverse individuals so often found in worker groups. Today's supervisors must contend with many challenges to both themselves and their associates, including increasing numbers of full-, part-time, and temporary subordinates, increasing workloads due to company downsizing and rightsizing, and the ever-increasing spread of technology.

Technical Skills

Supervisors with technical skills understand and are proficient in specific kinds of activity. Their expertise may be in computer programming or repair, in utilizing precision equipment and tools, or in design and drafting. Any technical skill requires its practitioner to know procedures, processes, and methods. Technical skill involves specialized knowledge, analytical ability within that specialty, and facility in the use of the tools and techniques of the specific discipline (Katz, 1975). Technical skills are the primary concern of training in industry and in vocational education programs.

Technical skills are essential to supervisors for several reasons. Supervisors' influence over subordinates comes to them in part because of their technical competence. They must thoroughly understand the work they supervise, and they must be able to train others to do it. Without an understanding of their unit's machinery, equipment, procedures, and practices, they cannot adequately evaluate performances. As with human skills, technological skills can be learned and developed. Moreover, supervisors can be expected to supervise a growing number of technical workers: "With one out of every four new jobs going to a technical worker...[they are] already the largest broad occupational category in the U.S. [and] will represent a fifth of total employment within a decade" (Richman, 1994). If you supervise technical associates, you need to create and follow a program to keep abreast of technological changes.

Practicing technical skills requires that you first possess them at a level sufficient both to apply them and to pass them along to others. Many supervisors are promoted from highly skilled jobs and then must turn around and supervise others who apply those same skills. If you are such a person, you have sound experience in skill applications. Such experience will prove quite useful to you when directing others who use those skills. But you will no longer have to execute your skills on the job as you had to when you were a worker. Your task is to get those you supervise to be as proficient as they can be in the execution of their skills. You, as a supervisor, should not do the work that your subordinates do. You are being paid to see to it that *they* do *their* jobs, with your support.

Conceptual Skills

Managers with conceptual skills view their organizations as wholes with many parts, all of which are interrelated and interdependent. Supervisors must be able to perceive themselves, their associates, teams, and sections as part of and contributors to other sections and the entire organization. Every decision made by every manager has the potential of creating a ripple effect that may influence others outside the particular decision maker's control.

Consider the lessons learned by Randy Kirk, president of AC International in California. What he and his partner, Terry Brown, felt would be the ideal arrangement for needed parts turned out to have some ugly and unanticipated surprises. Kirk and Brown created a company specializing in bicycle accessories with only themselves as employees. They relied on outside suppliers to provide needed items. Soon they began to experience customer complaints due to their suppliers' inabilities to meet commitments. Quality and quantity of bike helmets became a problem even before the supplier had a fire and stopped production for several months. A second supplier of a key product went bankrupt. A third product was made in part by two different suppliers. This led to problems in shades of color and mating the different parts. The two entrepreneurs soon learned that if they made their items themselves they would be less vulnerable to such shocks and in control of their products. Now, with the help of several dozen associates, they make most of what they sell, use outside sources for a few services and raw materials, and reap the improvements to both quality and profits that have resulted (Kirk, 1994). These entrepreneurs failed to anticipate and develop alternative plans for handling the shocks and ripple effects that they experienced. This company's experiences point out the need for conceptual thinking.

Acquiring a conceptual point of view becomes increasingly important as you climb higher on the management ladder. An employer must provide ways for you as a supervisor to know what is happening in other parts of the company and must inform you before changes are implemented. Official memos, reports, meetings, and workshops will also help keep you informed. Keeping in touch with fellow supervisors and reading the official correspondence that flows across your desk will make you a team player and help you and your people avoid unpleasant surprises.

THE SUPERVISOR'S RESPONSIBILITIES

Supervisors have responsibilities to three primary groups: their subordinates, their peers in management, and their superiors in management. They must work in harmony with all three groups if they are to be effective supervisors.

Relations with Subordinates

The responsibilities supervisors have to their subordinates are many and varied. To begin with, supervisors *must* get to know their subordinates as individual human beings. Each subordinate, like his or her supervisor, has specific needs and wants. Each has certain expectations from work, certain goals to achieve through work, and fundamental attitudes and aptitudes that influence work performances. When supervisors get to know each subordinate as an individual, they are able to tailor their approach to each. One of the first principles of good communications (see Chapter 5) is to keep your audience in mind when you attempt to communicate. If you are to be effective in your dealing with another person, you should know as much about that person as you can *before* attempting to communicate any message.

Subordinates want to know that their supervisors care about them and are prepared to do something about their problems. As Lee Ledbetter, a team leader at the Freemont, California, GM/Toyota plant puts it (Nauman, 1994),

> Back when I worked in [another] GM [plant], I worked in the group for three months, and the foreman still didn't know my name. He'd come by and show me (my paycheck), and say "Hey, is that you?" Here, everybody knows everybody by their first name, right from the plant manager on down.

A sure sign that supervisors care about their subordinates is common courtesy—using a person's name, a respectful tone of voice, personalized greetings, and sincere inquiries about the subordinate's health and well-being.

Getting to know subordinates well can be difficult. Some people are more open and outgoing than others. In addition, you can never really know your subordinates thoroughly for long because most people develop and change with the passage of time and with new experiences in life and on the job. These obstacles, however, should not be used as excuses to avoid trying to know your subordinates. Rather, such difficulties should be viewed as barriers that can be overcome through your sincere effort.

You will get to know your subordinates well only if you spend time with them and become familiar with their problems. Study each subordinate's personnel file. Talk to each person whenever you get a chance. If contacts with your people are informal, use the time for some casual conversation about them and what is going on in their lives. Your showing a sincere interest usually results in open responses from them. If contacts are formal, start out with a personal greeting, get through the formal communications, and then end on a friendly note. For example, you might say, "Well, I've had my say; is there anything you want to talk about?" Only after you have a good understanding of each subordinate can you expect to be successful in your dealings with them.

Your major responsibilities to subordinates include the following:

- Getting to know them as individuals
- Giving them the respect and trust they deserve
- Valuing their uniqueness and individuality
- Assigning subordinates work that fits their abilities
- Treating them as they want to be treated
- Providing them with adequate instruction and training
- Enabling them to do and give their best
- Encouraging them to be lifelong learners
- Handling their complaints and problems in a fair and just way
- Safeguarding their health and welfare while they are on the job
- Praising and providing constructive criticism
- Providing examples of proper conduct at work

Among the most important of these is the last one. It advises team leaders and team facilitators to walk like they talk: to make one's actions match one's words. If these obligations are met, supervisors will be perceived by their subordinates as leaders. Such supervisors gain the trust and respect of their subordinates—the keys to effective supervision and personal achievement. Your subordinates represent the most important group to whom and for whom you are responsible. Keep in mind that when the team doesn't perform, its owners fire the coach.

Relations with Peers

peer
a person on the same level of authority and status as another

Managers on the same level of management and possessing similar levels of authority and status are **peers.** As a supervisor, your peers are your fellow supervisors throughout the company. When serving as a team leader, your peers are other team leaders; when serving as a team facilitator, your peers are other team facilitators. Peers are the individuals with whom you must cooperate and coordinate if your department and theirs are to operate in harmony.

Your peers normally constitute the bulk of your friends and associates at work. If they do not, you should suspect that something is wrong with your relationships with them and take steps to correct the situation. Your peers represent an enormous pool of talent and experience that will be yours to tap and contribute to if they view you in a favorable way. For this reason alone, it is to your advantage to cultivate their friendship both on and off the job. Your peers can teach you a great deal about the company, and they are often a fine source of advice on how to handle difficult situations that may arise. They can do more to keep you out of trouble than any other group in the company. In so many ways you need each other, and both you and they stand to benefit from a partnership or alliance based on mutual respect, trust, and the need to resolve common problems. If you share your expertise with them, you can expect them to share theirs with you.

Your responsibilities to your peers include the following:

- Getting to know them as individuals
- Valuing their uniqueness and individuality
- Giving them the respect and trust they deserve
- Treating them as they want to be treated
- Fostering a spirit of cooperation and teamwork

As a supervisor, team leader, or team facilitator, you have been or will be asked or assigned to serve on peer-group teams. In such cases, your reputation is shaped by ways in which you foster a spirit of cooperation and teamwork. Your ability or inability to contribute and cooperate with peers can mean either success or failure in your career. Teams of peers are common at all organizational levels.

Chief executive officer (CEO) Jack Smith of General Motors knows the value of teaming peers. To achieve his dramatic turnaround of GM, he has organized a leadership advisory team (composed of his 100 highest-ranking executives), which meets about five times each year. "Smith describes the meetings as 'interactive—not just five guys getting up and making a speech. We take an issue apart and put it back together'" (Taylor, 1994). Smith also uses his vehicle launch center teams consisting of middle management specialists from engineering, design, and marketing to "...evaluate car and truck proposals for cost, compatibility with other GM products, and marketability" (Taylor, 1994). At the supervisory and worker levels: "GM is moving away from traditional assembly lines into smaller working units known as cells, where workers get more opportunity to design their own processes and thus improve output" (Taylor, 1994). GM's Saturn division is famous for its self-managing teams and the inclusion of customers on their teams at every level.

Supervisors off in their own little worlds and unwilling to share their know-how, are labeled uncooperative and antisocial, thus placing their careers in jeopardy. Managers in higher positions in business have no need for withdrawn or isolated managers.

Relations with Superiors

If you are a supervisor, the person you report to is a middle manager who is accountable for your actions. Your boss is similar to you in being both a follower and a member of management. He or she executes all the functions of management and is evaluated on the basis of his or her subordinates' performances. Like you, your boss must develop and maintain sound working relationships with his or her subordinates, peers, and superiors. Moreover, your boss has probably served an apprenticeship as a supervisor, so you can probably count on his or her understanding of your own situation.

Your responsibilities to your superiors, both line and staff, can be summarized as follows:

- Valuing their uniqueness and individuality
- Giving them your best effort and the support they require
- Transmitting information about problems, along with recommendations for solving them
- Operating within company policies
- Promoting the company's goals
- Striving for constant improvement
- Seeking their counsel and using it
- Using the organization's resources effectively

To your boss, you owe allegiance and respect. You must be a loyal follower if you intend to be a successful leader. To the company's team of staff specialists, you are the person through whom their recommendations are implemented. Chapter 8 has more to say about how you can get along with and cooperate with your peers and superiors in management.

Being Effective and Efficient

Managers at every level are expected to practice the skills outlined here effectively and efficiently. *Effectiveness* is defined by management author and consultant Peter Drucker (1964) as "doing the right thing." Doing the right thing means meeting deadlines. Effective supervisors work on projects today that need to be worked on today. They think ahead and schedule work so that enough resources will be available to complete it on time. Doing the right thing demands that managers at every level carefully plan their work (set goals, priorities, timetables) and stick to their plans. An *ineffective* supervisor fails to meet deadlines, falls behind on projects, and receives poor performance ratings.

Efficiency is defined as doing things right. The efficient supervisor gets the task done with a minimal expense of time, money, and other resources. The efficient supervisor avoids waste of all kinds. The *inefficient* supervisor spends too much of any resource while executing tasks. The inefficient supervisor also receives poor performance ratings and places future operations in jeopardy because the needed resources may not be available.

Clearly, a supervisor must be both effective and efficient. Effectiveness is probably the more important of the two because essential tasks will get done. Effectiveness with inefficiency can often be tolerated by organizations, at least in the short run. But efficiency without effectiveness is not tolerable, even in the short run: Essentials remain undone, and vital work is left incomplete.

SUPERVISORY ROLES

Like actors who have to learn their parts well, all supervisors are expected to learn and play specific parts or roles in order to execute their duties successfully. The precise role of individual supervisors depends on their understanding of the job, as well as on the pressures, rewards, and guidelines brought to bear on them from inside and outside the organization. What follows is a brief but important discussion of the ways in which roles are assigned to, designed for, and perceived by each supervisor in a business enterprise. The author is indebted to Robert L. Kahn and his associates (1964) and to Professor John B. Miner (1971) for much of this discussion.

Role Prescriptions

The subordinates, peers, friends, family, and superiors of supervisors help shape and define the kinds of roles the supervisors play and the way in which they play them. Demands made on the supervisors by these groups and their

Role	Description	Identifiable Activities from Study of Chief Executives
INTERPERSONAL		
Figurehead	Symbolic head; obliged to perform a number of routine duties of legal or social nature	Ceremony, status, requests, solicitations
Leader	Responsible for the motivation and activation of subordinates; responsible for staffing, training, and associated duties	Virtually all managerial activities involving subordinates
Liaison	Maintains self-developed network of outside contacts and informers who provide favors and information	Acknowledgments of mail, external board work; other activities involving outsiders
INFORMATIONAL		
Monitor	Seeks and receives wide variety of special information to develop thorough understanding of the organization and environment; emerges as nerve center of internal and external information of the organization	Handling all mail and contacts concerned primarily with receiving information
Disseminator	Transmits information received from outsiders or from subordinates to members of the organization; some information factual, some involving interpretation and integration	Forwarding mail into organization for informational purposes; verbal contacts involving information flow to subordinates

EXHIBIT 1.2
Mintzberg's ten management roles.

Source: Chart from *The Nature of Managerial Work* by Henry Mintzberg. Copyright © 1973 by Henry Mintzberg. Reprinted by permission of HarperCollins Publishers Inc.

business organization prescribe the roles (called **role prescriptions**) for them to follow. Through the expectations and demands placed on the supervisors, people help shape each supervisor's perception of his or her job. Organizational influences—such as policies, procedures, job descriptions, and the union contract—also exert influence on the roles of each supervisor. Of course, these multiple demands can and do create conflicts in the minds of supervisors: What should their roles be and how precisely should they play them?

role prescription
the collection of expectations and demands from superiors, subordinates, and others that shapes a manager's job description and perception of his or her job

Role	Description	Identifiable Activities from Study of Chief Executives
INFORMATIONAL		
Spokesman	Transmits information to outsiders on organization's plans, policies, actions, results, and so forth; serves as expert on organization's industry	Board meetings; handling mail and contacts involving transmission of information to outsiders
DECISIONAL		
Entrepreneur	Searches organization and its environment for opportunities, and initiates projects to bring about change	Strategy and review sessions involving initiation or design of improvement projects
Disturbance Handler	Responsible for corrective action when organization faces important, unexpected disturbances	Strategy and review involving disturbances and crises
Resource Allocator	Responsible for the allocation of organizational resources of all kinds—in effect the making or approving of all significant organizational decisions	Scheduling; requests for authorization; any activity involving budgeting and the programming of subordinates' work
Negotiator	Responsible for representing the organization at major negotiations	Negotiation

EXHIBIT 1.2 (cont.)

Professor and researcher Henry Mintzberg describes all management behavior with ten roles (see Exhibit 1.2). The ten roles were developed through close observations of chief executives. Mintzberg found that different managers emphasized different roles and spent varying amounts of time on each, depending on their personalities, on the job at hand, and on the situation. All supervisors play these roles on a day-to-day basis as they interact with higher-level managers, peers, associates, and people outside their organization.

Role Conflict

When conflicting and contradictory demands are made on supervisors, they find themselves in awkward or difficult positions. How they react to such pressures and what precisely they do to cope with such conflicts depend on their own values and perceptions and on the circumstances of the **role conflicts.** Consider the following incident that happened in a suburb north of Chicago. Two paramedics discovered a conflict between the instructions in their medical manual and the provisions of Illinois law about the proper method of treatment for heart-attack victims. If the paramedics followed their manual, they believed they would be in violation of state law. If they followed the law, however, they believed they would be giving incorrect or outmoded treatment to their patients. Perplexed, they asked their hospital administrator for clarification of the treatment procedures. To their surprise, they received in reply a letter that called them incompetent and suspended them from their duties as paramedics! This example highlights a common job situation, in which an employee's training in organizational procedures contradicts the demands of the immediate boss. Role conflicts can and do occur, and when they do, they create tensions and job dissatisfaction for the employees.

role conflict
a situation that occurs when contradictory or opposing demands are made on a manager

Role Ambiguity

Whenever a supervisor is not sure of the role he or she is expected to play in a given situation or how to play it, he or she is a victim of **role ambiguity.** Role conflict results from clearly contradictory demands. Role ambiguity results from unclear or nonexistent job descriptions, orders, rules, policies, or procedures. When role ambiguity exists, supervisors may do things they should not do, may fail to do things they should do, and may find it hard to distinguish where one manager's job begins and another's ends.

role ambiguity
the situation that occurs whenever a manager is uncertain about the role that he or she is expected to play

Levi Strauss is a company that recognizes and values the contributions of all its diverse employees and the need to eliminate ambiguity in its communications. It grounds its internal operations on "A set of corporate 'aspirations' written by top management, [as] a guide to all major decisions....[its communications aspiration reads in part] Management must be 'clear about company, unit, and individual goals and performances. People must know what is expected of them and receive timely, honest feedback...'" (*Business Week*, "Managing," 1994). It recognizes the need for right corporate conduct as well and further states under its "ethical management practices" aspiration the following: "Management should epitomize the stated standards of ethical behavior [walk like it talks]. We must provide clarity about our expectations and must enforce these standards throughout the corporation" (*Business Week*, "Managing," 1994).

Role Performance

Even if there is no role conflict or role ambiguity, supervisors may still fail to meet the demands of their role prescriptions for one or more of the following reasons (Miner, 1971):

1. Supervisors may not perceive their jobs in the way specified by the role prescriptions.

2. Supervisors may not want to behave in the way specified by the role prescriptions.
3. Supervisors may not have the knowledge, mental ability, or physical skills needed to behave in the way specified by the role prescriptions.

All organizations need ways to ensure that members play their roles as prescribed.

Role Sanctions

sanction
negative means, such as threats or punishments, used by superiors or the organization to encourage subordinates to play their roles as prescribed by superiors or the organization

To encourage supervisors at all levels to play their roles in accord with the role prescriptions established by their superiors, business organizations often make use of positive incentives or rewards. If the rewards for proper role playing prove to be ineffective, the superiors may use negative means to secure conformity. Such means, which may include threats or actual punishments, are known as **sanctions.** If a business organization does not provide adequate sanctions, the roles played by various supervisors and the ways in which they understand them may deviate widely from their superiors' role prescriptions. Unless people desire to play their roles as prescribed or feel that they have no real alternatives to doing so, they will usually tailor the roles they play to suit themselves.

SUPERVISORS AS LINKING PINS

linking pin
key individual who is a member of two or more formal groups in an organization, thus linking or connecting the groups

Because human beings are social animals, most business organizations contain many people who interact with one another on a regular basis, both informally and formally. The typical organizational chart shows a division of labor among individuals employed by the organization to accomplish its tasks. It also shows certain key individuals who head up and link the independent groups within the organization. These key individuals are often called **linking pins** because, as members of two or more groups, they link or lock these groups together (Likert, 1961).

A supervisor is the leader or facilitator of an organization unit but is also the subordinate of a middle manager. Each supervisor, therefore, is a member of at least two groups: a unit comprising individuals or teams and a group or team of fellow supervisors (peers) reporting to the same middle manager. In turn, the middle manager is in charge of a group of supervisors and is also a member of a group of middle management peers reporting to a higher-level manager. Linking pins play all the informational, decisional, and interpersonal roles (outlined in Exhibit 1.2) with a particular emphasis on those of figurehead, liaison, monitor, disseminator, spokesperson, disturbance handler, and negotiator.

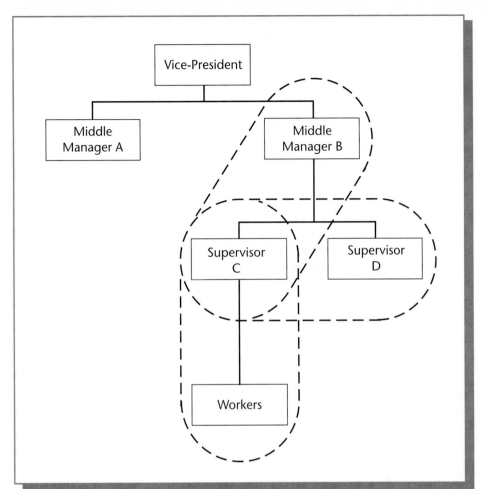

As Exhibit 1.3 shows, Supervisor C is a member of three groups: (1) Middle Manager B's department; (2) the group of B's subordinate supervisors, who are Supervisor C's peers; and (3) Supervisor C's own section. The circles that overlap Supervisor C in the figure reveal that he or she is a linking pin—that is, a manager who joins together three groups and who can serve as a communications link and coordinator between and among them.

CURRENT TRENDS AFFECTING SUPERVISORS

One thing is certain: The demands being made on today's supervisors are growing in complexity. Great changes are taking place in both our workforce and our places of work. A brief look at some major trends will indicate a few of the problems and opportunities they represent for all of us.

Information and Technology

Our economy is experiencing dramatic and fundamental changes in the ways in which business is conducted and in the ways in which people are employed. "Since 1950, the number of technical workers has increased nearly 300 percent—triple the growth rate for the workforce as a whole—to some 20 million" (Richman, 1994). Innovative technologies are freeing workers from dangerous and routine work and allowing them to focus their talents on challenging tasks requiring "...judgment and skills.... As more companies rely on technology to help eliminate quality defects, speed up product development, and improve customer service, technicians become the front-line workers [their employers] must depend on" (Richman, 1994). The majority of working Americans now earn their living by creating, processing, and distributing information. Innovations in communications and computer technology have displaced thousands of workers and opened thousands of opportunities to them. Today our homes, automobiles, offices, and factories depend on electronics and computer chips to perform their most basic functions. The power of computers is now at the fingertips of the majority of working people.

Portable laptop computers, cellular telephones, laser printers, and fax machines are the hallmarks of a modern office. Automobiles can be equipped with voice-activated telephones, computers, printers, and fax machines. Their portability frees managers from their desks and allows them to take their technology with them. Meetings are being held by cable television, eliminating many business trips and their corresponding expenses. Electronic mail links people within a building and their counterparts in different states and countries. In 1990, Wal-Mart Stores Inc., the giant discount chain, informed its suppliers that it was adopting electronic data interchange (EDI) and if they desired to continue selling their goods to Wal-Mart, they would have to adopt it too (Van, 1991). EDI allows for instantaneous transfer of electronic data between points, eliminating communication delays between suppliers and purchasers, engineers and product design teams, and professionals and clients.

The most competitive manufacturers have put the power of computers to use through CAD/CAM (computer-aided design/computer-aided manufacturing), which offers their best hope for future increases in quality, competitiveness, productivity, and profits. CAD allows draftspeople and engineers to design, analyze, and test products entirely by means of computers and their video displays. Without putting pencil to paper, researchers can put new products through the rigors of testing, thus saving great amounts of time and money that would otherwise be invested in building and testing a prototype. CAM has come to mean computer control of production tools and machines. Both can be programmed and reprogrammed to work at a variety of tasks, providing users with dependable, predictable output at speeds no skilled person can match.

Robots are CAM machines that are capable of working every hour of every day with great speed and reliability. They have been used for work that is toxic, dangerous, repetitive, boring, or extremely precise. Robots have made it possible for very small businesses to enter highly competitive and labor-intensive industries with confidence. They have become our nation's *steel collar* workers, demanding sophisticated supervision by a new breed of supervisors and workers with the latest in high-tech education and skills.

Flexible manufacturing—producing a variety of products and product variations (customization) simultaneously and in sequence using computer-integrated manufacturing (CIM)—is the current goal for many manufacturers. CIM links all the activities, materials flow, and machinery involved in manufacturing to a centralized computer control system, allowing for maximum efficiency and coordination. There is perhaps no better example of flexible manufacturing than at Nissan's newest plant at Kyushu. It is a hospital-clean factory that can "build a wide assortment of models and types of cars at high speed on one assembly line.... Inside, instead of a conveyor, is a convoy of 'intelligent motor-driven dollies,' little yellow platforms that tote cars at variable speeds down the production line, sending out a stream of computer-controlled signals to coach both robots and workers along the way" (Chandler and White, 1992).

Along with being flexible, manufacturing is becoming *lean*—using just-in-time or delivery as needed methods for supplies, simultaneously focusing on reducing costs and becoming more effective and efficient, conserving resources, and adapting operations to the latest technology. This drive to take the fat out of operations has led many companies to *outsource*—allow more cost-effective businesses to provide needed work. When companies expand their operations to new geographical areas, their suppliers follow. "...McDonald's encourages its domestic suppliers to follow the company abroad. Chicago-based meat supplier OSI Industries has joint ventures in 17 countries where it works with local companies making McDonald's hamburgers" (Serwer, 1994). These trends have led to better service for customers, exporting jobs, layoffs, and the resulting shrinkage in the size of many of America's largest companies' domestic workforces. General Motors and IBM are but two examples. As organizations shrink in both size and number of employees, fewer opportunities for promotions and careers within them are the result.

Quality and Productivity Improvement

Businesses in the United States exist and compete in a global economy. Their products and services must compete with the best that the world community has to offer. To be competitive, businesses must get and stay lean by constantly striving to improve their efficiency and effectiveness—

Dedication to teamwork resulted in Cadillac's winning the 1990 Malcolm Baldrige National Quality Award. Cadillac chose the team approach, recognizing that people are its value base. Cadillac values the opinions of its people, from top management to customers, including supervisors and factory workers.

to get more with less and to get the best results from every dollar spent or invested in order to create and sell world-class products and services. But it is not enough to simply produce efficiently. Products and services must have quality as good as, or better than, that provided by the competition. Your job and your company's survival depend on it.

Productivity may be defined as the measurement of the amount of input needed to generate a given amount of output. It is the basic measurement of the efficient use of resources and processes. By calculating how many products are produced by the investment of hours of human labor or by the use of machines over time, an organization can compare these measurements to those from the past and determine gains or losses.

Quality means different things to different people. Its result is a satisfied customer. Throughout this text, we define **quality** as the totality of features and characteristics of a product or service (or process or project) that bear on its ability to satisfy stated or implied goals (requirements of producers and customers) (Johnson and Winchell, 1989). To possess quality, products and services must be designed with the customers' needs in mind. Companies such as Chrysler, Xerox, Motorola, and Toyota consult with customers throughout the design phase of their product development to ensure that their customers' needs will be met.

Customers are the receivers and users of what is produced; they exist inside and outside the organization. Internal customers are employees who receive output from other employees. When you send your completed project to your boss, your boss becomes your customer. It is common practice today in major companies to assess employees' performances

productivity
the amount of input needed to generate a given amount of output

quality
the totality of features and characteristics of a product or service (or process or project) that bear on its ability to satisfy stated or implied goals (requirements of producers and customers)

through what is called a *360-degree* performance review. Each manager is evaluated by his or her boss, associates, and peers—all users of any outputs generated by the manager or his or her associates. Each team member is evaluated by his or her team leader, fellow team members, and the users of the team's output.

Quality and productivity improvements must go hand in hand; efforts to improve one must not interfere with efforts to improve the other. There is a definite link between a company's profitability and its quality and productivity. As efforts to improve quality yield fewer rejects, less waste, and less customer dissatisfaction, improvements in productivity result. These gains, in turn, yield higher profits. As a supervisor, you must make certain that you get the most from every resource invested by you and your associates.

As a direct result of organizations' drive toward quality and productivity improvement, a new movement and philosophy has emerged: **reengineering.** Two pioneers in this rapidly expanding field, Michael Hammer and James Champy (1993) define reengineering as follows: "The fundamental rethinking and radical redesign of business process to achieve dramatic improvements in critical, contemporary measures of performance, such as cost, quality, service, and speed." Through a reengineering approach, managers at every level ask some fundamental questions and make no assumptions. They ignore for the moment what has been and is being done to handle a problem or activity and start from scratch. "Reengineering takes nothing for granted. It ignores what *is* and concentrates on what *should be....* [I]t is about business reinvention—not business improvement, business enhancement, or business modification" (Hammer and Champy, 1993). As Richard Sullivan at Home Depot puts it: "Companies must burn themselves down and rebuild every few years" (Peters, 1994). More will be said on this issue in the following chapters.

reengineering
the total rethinking of what an organization should be doing and how it should do it

Education

According to the U.S. Census Bureau, about 75 percent of Americans over twenty-five years of age have currently completed high school, and about 25 percent of these have completed four or more years of college. "Nearly 63 percent of [1993's] high-school graduates were enrolled in college in the fall [of 1994] compared with 53 percent a decade ago.... The Department of Education [estimates] that enrollments of full- and part-time college students probably will remain steady at about 15 million for the next few years" (*The Wall Street Journal*, 1994). The growing educational level of the U.S. workforce has brought brighter, more demanding employees to the ranks of both workers and management. Increasingly, people want a voice in planning and executing their work. They bring competence and skills to the workplace, and they desire growth through challenging work and meaningful tasks. They want to be listened to and to be respected as individuals with their own specific needs and goals.

Along with the influx of more highly educated people, the U.S. work-force receives about 2.3 million illiterate adults each year. According to a study by the Southport Institute for Policy Analysis (*Chicago Tribune*, "Working," 1992),

> More than 10 million workers in small businesses have serious problems with reading, writing, mathematics, and other basic skills, causing impaired job performances.... Half of America's 5 million small businesses report skill problems that merit (training) programs, but only up to 5 percent have programs.

As a supervisor, you may find both the highly educated and the illiterate adult in your subordinate mix. Both groups present challenges that you and your organization must be prepared to deal with if you are to create quality products and productivity improvements.

Increasingly, we are becoming a lifetime learning society. No longer can any of us rely on one employer or one career during our working lives. Because of organizations' downsizing and merging, people are expected to make several job and career changes within their lifetimes. "According to a survey...by the executive search firm of Robert Half International Inc., [it isn't until] a worker [makes] five job changes in a 10-year period [that he or she] is at risk of being labeled a job-hopper" (*Chicago Tribune*, "How," 1994).

Foreign Ownership of American Businesses

Each year foreign businesses invest billions of dollars both to acquire existing companies and to establish their own in the United States. According to federal government estimates, one out of every twenty U.S. workers owes his or her job to a foreign-owned company, more than at any time in the past. Consider Japanese businesses for a moment. Japan's Bridgestone recently acquired Firestone's tire business. When Hitachi, Toyota, and Mitsubishi built their manufacturing facilities in the United States, their Japanese suppliers followed, building their facilities nearby to offer reliable delivery of needed parts. In 1992, Japanese companies owned 10 percent or more of nearly 1,600 manufacturing facilities in the United States that employed about 350,000 American citizens (*Business Week*, "Japan's," 1992).

Foreign owners often bring different philosophies, methods, and traditions to the workplace. Supervising in a foreign-owned business may require changes in the attitudes, roles, and skills derived from training in the United States and abroad. Supervisors may have to adapt to different methods and values that come from a different cultural background.

Valuing Diversity

Nearly all nations today are a mix of peoples with different origins, values, and traditions. Americans differ in race, age, gender, sexual orientation, religious beliefs, language, nation of birth, education, physical characteristics, and more. This **diversity** in individuals can both unite and separate. People of similar heritage, backgrounds, traits, and values tend to come together, forming groups that have a unique identity. These groups, therefore, serve to bind people together through a sense of common identity and kinship, and to distinguish their members from those in dissimilar groups.

diversity
differences in people and groups that serve to both unite and separate them from others

People and organizations have *cultures:* systems of shared values, beliefs, experiences, habits, norms, and expectations that give them a distinct identity. An organization usually has a dominant culture that shapes and is shaped by its members' attitudes and behaviors. The greatest influence comes from the people in charge—their values, norms, beliefs, and so on. But an organization has *subcultures* as well. Shared by groups of employees, these influence and are influenced by the organization's culture. Thus organizations nearly always have diverse cultures. **Cultural diversity** exists when two or more cultures co-exist within an organization.

cultural diversity
the co-existence of two or more cultural groups within an organization

Motorola has an outstanding reputation for world-class products and is truly a global business. "But the key to Motorola's success is a culture that fosters candid internal debate, the vigorous competition of ideas and individual business autonomy. [Its] fast-growing cellular business was devised by one Motorola sector even though it might compete with the lucrative pagers produced by another. Yet both businesses are thriving in the clash of ideas" (Lee, 1994).

Valuing diversity in people and their diverse cultures is a relatively recent development in business. Today, businesses such as Motorola, Digital, Du Pont, Avon, and Levi Strauss are realizing that employees have a right to their own identity, within and separate from that of the organization. Diversity is increasingly viewed as a source of strength—providing pools of people with different and complementary skills, competencies, and beliefs that should be valued and can be drawn on to provide what an organization needs. As Levi Strauss' "diversity" aspiration puts it: Levi's "values a diverse workforce (age, sex, ethnic group, etc.) at all levels of the organization.... Differing points of view will be sought; diversity will be valued and honestly rewarded, not suppressed." (*Business Week* "Managing," 1994).

Businesses—like the United States as a whole—now realize that they are not melting pots through which people and cultures fuse and lose their identities. They are mosaics, tapestries, and salad bowls in which individuals and groups retain their identities but work with others to yield something greater than the pieces could yield on their own. The supervisor's role in valuing diversity is discussed in each of this text's remaining chapters.

Work Schedules

According to the U.S. Bureau of Labor Statistics, about 75 percent of all jobs in the United States are in the service sector, such as managerial and professional positions and jobs in sales, administrative support, repair, security, hospitality, and finance. By the year 2000, women will account for over 50 percent of the workforce. African Americans, Hispanics, and Asians will account for over one-fourth of employed Americans by that year. Today's workforce is mobile, middle aged, and increasingly made up of other than full-time workers. About 25 percent of our nation's workforce (over 34 million people) consists of *contingent* workers—freelancers, temporaries, independent contractors, consultants, and part-timers (Smith, 1994). Several trends are in evidence: flextime, job sharing, job splitting, permanent part-time workers, telecommuting, and employee leasing. All present unique challenges and opportunities for supervisors.

Flextime allows people to vary their starting and ending times. A company may require all employees to be on the job from 10:00 A.M. until 1:00 P.M., but some may start as early as 6:00 A.M. or as late as 10:00 A.M. Some may go home as early as 1:00 P.M. Flexible scheduling appeals to working parents with school-age children and to a growing number of self-managing information workers. But such work schedules make it difficult for one supervisor to manage people who work over a span of ten or more hours. As a result, supervisors have opted for flextime too. Such work schedules make weeks of four ten-hour days possible and help individual employees meet their needs.

The Bechtel Group, a construction and engineering firm, has 27,800 employees worldwide. It offers a flexible schedule to its employees in

Your job as a supervisor is to help all of your people reach their potential. Allowing your biases to rule your judgment will not only hurt your subordinates' performance, it will reflect badly on you as a supervisor.

Houston, Texas. Under the plan, employees work nine-hour days, Monday through Thursday each week. Each Friday, about half the employees work eight hours, and the other half have the day off. All employees work eighty hours in nine days. Management initially feared that longer work days would mean lower productivity, but productivity has improved. Employees seemed to be scheduling more of their personal business for their off time.

Job sharing allows two or more people to work at one full-time job. Businesses have used job sharing with both management and worker positions. A growing number of people want to work part time, and a growing number of businesses want more part-time employees. The employer benefits in several ways. It gets double the creativity for each shared job. It cuts benefit costs, which often add 30 to 40 percent to an employee's salary. People come to work refreshed and eager to perform. Workers experience less fatigue and stress. Boring jobs can be more attractive when performed for fewer than forty hours each week.

Job splitting takes a job and cuts it in half. One part-time worker does one half, and another part-time worker does the other half. There is no overlapping of duties. In supermarkets, one person, usually of high school age, is hired to stock shelves in the morning, and another is hired to stock in the evening. The two stock different merchandise in different aisles. Another approach involves one worker who replaces stock and another who prices it. All work fewer than forty hours each week.

Permanent part-time workers usually work for small companies that do not have enough work for a full-timer to perform. Part-time work may be for any number of hours and days per week, up to thirty-five hours. In 1994, over 1.5 million jobs were filled each day in America by temporaries—people employed by a temporary help service, which assigns its people to work part time for its clients who need temporary help. Most come well trained for their jobs and work in skilled areas such as computer services, secretarial services, manufacturing, and accounting. From mid-1993 to mid-1994, temporary employment agencies filled "...one-sixth of the net new jobs in private business" (Brownstein, 1994). Sharon Canter of Manpower Inc. points out that "'more companies are using our temps as a first resource for permanent hires.' ... 38 percent of Manpower's temps were offered career positions [in 1993]" (Brownstein, 1994).

Telecommuting allows a full- or part-time employee to work at home while connected to the employer by telecommunications devices such as computers, fax machines, and modems. According to a 1992 study by the U.S. Department of Labor, about 2 million U.S. workers are paid wages or a salary to work at home. Companies large and small are beginning to offer this option to employees who do not have to be present in the workplace and to qualified employees who live too far from the office to make a long commute worthwhile. Major disasters quickly isolate people from their jobs and places of employment. The earthquakes, floods, and hurricanes of the 1990s have highlighted the value of telecommuting—within hours, companies whose physical plants were in ruins were functioning (thanks in large measure to cellular communications) and arranging for alternative means to meet their customers' needs. In the summer of 1994, AT&T announced a telecommuting day, encouraging and arranging for any worker who could to telecommute.

Employee leasing is becoming increasingly popular. According to the Aegis Group, a consulting firm, "there are now more than 1,300 employee-leasing companies and roughly one million leased employees nationwide" (Resnick, 1992). Basically, when a company decides to lease its employees, it simply fires them, allowing a leasing firm to hire them and lease them back to the original employer. All employee costs, including wages, salaries, and benefits, are paid for by the leasing firm. The company that utilizes the employees reimburses the employee-leasing company for all costs and pays a fee for its administrative services. Under leasing agreements, the utilizing company makes most of the personnel and supervisory decisions, getting assistance in recruiting, hiring, and employee evaluations from the employee-leasing company.

The primary advantages of leasing are lower costs for fringe benefits, such as group insurance and worker's compensation insurance, and freedom from the paperwork burdens associated with government reporting requirements. In most instances, the supervisor's responsibilities for leased employees will not change significantly.

Utilization of Teams

Increasingly, businesses are turning to the use of teams—some self-managing, others not. It is common in many different types of organizations to find teams "that recommend things, teams that make or do things, and teams that run or manage things.... Teams are a means to an end. And that end is performance superior to what team members would achieve working as individuals" (Katzenbach, 1992).

As was stated in this chapter's introduction, when supervisors work with and through teams of subordinates, they become team facilitators: They share responsibility with a team for "cost, quality, and on-time delivery of the product. So [supervisors] must train their teams to manage the production process, including work assignments, and to solve problems that crop up along the way, rather than provide solutions themselves" (Klein and Posey, 1986).

Team facilitators make certain that the team has the resources it needs when they are needed, arranges the meetings where information is passed along and ideas are put to use, represents the team's views and concerns to outsiders, and helps resolve disputes between and within teams. To be an effective team facilitator, you must be skilled at presenting your ideas in a group setting, at running different kinds of meetings, at sharing your skills and knowledge willingly and freely, at turning decision making

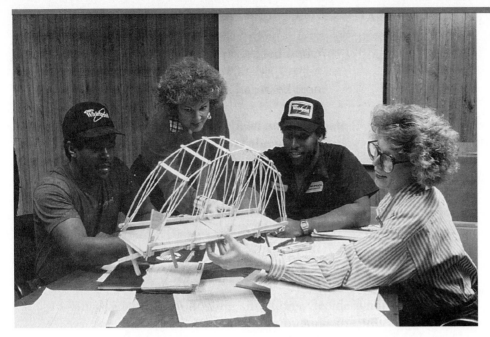

Quality circles at Whirlpool bring together people from all levels to create better products. Involvement in such groups makes workers feel important; in turn, they work harder and produce more.

into a learning experience for all team members, and at taking control in a crisis (Klein and Posey, 1986).

To use teams effectively, people must be prepared to join them and to work efficiently in them. This happens through training and empowerment. Supervisors **empower** their subordinates when they equip them to function on their own, without direct oversight and constant supervision. Empowering others requires supervisors to give their people opportunities to contribute their knowledge and expertise, and to encourage them to take on new tasks and to continuously improve their capabilities. It means allowing them to participate in planning their work, making decisions, and solving problems. In short, empowering others means sharing the traditional roles and responsibilities of the supervisor with subordinates. More will be said on the subjects of teams and empowering subordinates in the Supervising Teams features, beginning in Chapter 2.

empower
to equip people to function on their own, without direct supervision

SOURCES OF SUPERVISORY PERSONNEL

Most employers look for supervisory personnel from one of two sources: existing employees or a list of outside applicants. Most companies would prefer a person with experience because most are not able to spend the time and money required to train someone to be a supervisor. This means that in most companies the person who aspires to become a supervisor—to move from worker to management—must take on the responsibility of

EXHIBIT 1.4

Ten attributes that organizations look for in applicants for management positions.

Source: Reprinted with the permission of *HRMagazine* (formerly Personnel Administrator) published by the Society for Human Resource Management, Alexandria, Virginia.

1. Oral communication skill—effective expression in individual or group situations (includes gestures and nonverbal communications).
2. Oral presentational skills—effective expression when presenting ideas or tasks to an individual or to a group when given time for presentation (includes gestures and nonverbal communication).
3. Written communication skill—clear expression of ideas in writing and in good grammatical form.
4. Job motivation—the extent to which activities and responsibilities available in the job overlap with activities and responsibilities that result in personal satisfaction.
5. Initiative—active attempts to influence events to achieve goals; self-starting rather than passive acceptance; taking action to achieve goals beyond those called for; originating action.
6. Leadership—utilizing appropriate interpersonal styles and methods in guiding individuals (subordinates, peers, superiors) or groups toward task accomplishment.
7. Planning and organization—establishing a course of action for self and/or others to accomplish a specific goal; planning proper assignments of personnel and appropriate allocation of resources.
8. Analysis—relating and comparing data from different sources, identifying issues, securing relevant information, and identifying relationships.
9. Judgment—developing alternative courses of action and making decisions that are based on logical assumptions and reflect factual information.
10. Management control—establishing procedures to monitor and/or regulate processes, tasks, or the jobs and responsibilities of subordinates; taking action to monitor the results of delegated assignments or projects.

preparing himself or herself for such a promotion. This preparation involves finding out what you have already of what you will need and acquiring the rest through your own efforts. Exhibit 1.4 lists the ten attributes that companies look for in applicants for management jobs at all levels. Take a few minutes to study it. Be honest as you decide whether you possess a given attribute or not, and if you do possess it, whether you need to improve on it. Schools can help, and research on your own is also useful. A job change may be the best step you can take to obtain further experience that could be useful in improving a skill or gaining an attribute.

Many employers prefer to hire some or all of their supervisory personnel from the ranks of community or four-year college graduates. After some preliminary training and understudy, these people are installed as functioning supervisors. The practice of hiring all or some of a firm's new supervisors from outside the company takes its toll on the morale of the employees. Personal incentive and the competition for supervisory positions are enhanced, however, since fewer positions are available to be filled by advancing workers. As a result, some workers may begin to pursue a college education, whereas others may be encouraged to complete the advanced training they began years ago. The practice of hiring supervisors from outside the company may also infuse new ideas and approaches into the organization.

A major disadvantage of the practice of going outside the organization for new supervisors fresh from college is that they may lack the first-hand experiences and technical skills needed to supervise the company's workers. "At Union Pacific...all new employees who aspire to a management position must first become a data integrity analyst.... Why the hurdle? Union Pacific carries 13,000 shipments a day on 700 trains running on 19,000 miles of track. Coordinating that massive traffic flow poses a huge data management challenge..." (Richman, 1994). As Jim Damman, national customer services vice president puts it, "we saw that the company's future growth would depend more on the ability of our managers to be masters of technical data rather than overseers of the hourly workers" (Richman, 1994). Inexperienced supervisors may also experience a built-in resistance to their supervision from older, more experienced members of the department who may have been passed over or not considered for the supervisor's position.

Several of your associates may not wish to be promoted to the ranks of management. Some are reluctant to give up the security that goes with knowing their job and doing it well. Others may be convinced that the extra prestige is not worth the extra time, problems, and responsibilities that go along with a supervisory position. In some cases, a worker may be asked to take a pay cut if he or she accepts a promotion to supervisor. This is primarily due to the loss of hourly pay status and overtime pay. Although the cut may only be temporary, it often means a considerable loss of income for the worker.

In addition, the attitude of the company toward supervisors may make many workers shy away from a supervisory role. In far too many companies, supervisors are given lip service as managers but are not treated with the respect, pay, and benefits other levels of management receive.

Instant Replay

1. The supervisor is the only manager whose subordinates are nonmanagement employees called workers.
2. Throughout this text, supervisors are referred to as team leaders or team facilitators.

3. Throughout this text, subordinates may be referred to as workers, team members, or associates.

4. The three most important types of skills for any manager to possess are human, technical, and conceptual. All are required for success, but different levels of management need them to different degrees.

5. Supervisors are responsible to three groups: their peers, their subordinates, and their superiors. Each group represents a source of support, demands on the supervisor's time, and potential problems or challenges for the supervisor.

6. Each organization attempts to define a supervisor's role through the creation of a job description and through the demands that various groups and individuals place on the supervisor. Problems can result from role conflict and role ambiguity.

7. Supervisors as well as other managers represent linking pins, tying two or more organizational groups or units together by their memberships in each.

8. Current trends that affect supervisors include changes in information and technology, the drive for improvements in both quality and productivity, the growth in both highly educated and illiterate adults in the workforce, increasing ownership of American businesses by foreigners, the growing effort to value diversity, shifts in the traditional scheduling and performance of work, and the growing use of teams.

9. Supervisors emerge from two sources: from inside and outside the organization. Organizations prefer to hire those who are ready to move up; in small organizations, this places the burden for training on the individual who aspires to move into management.

Questions for Class Discussion

1. Can you define this chapter's key terms?
2. What are the three essential management skill areas that supervisors must have and apply? Give an example illustrating the application of each skill area.
3. What are the three groups to whom supervisors have responsibilities? Give an example of a responsibility to each group.
4. How do the concepts of effectiveness and efficiency apply to a supervisor's performance?
5. What are the seven current trends in the U.S. economy? How can each affect the supervisor?
6. What are the sources of supervisory personnel for a business?

Incident

Purpose   To discover how many trends discussed in this chapter are part of your current work environment.

Your Task   Answer each of the following as completely as you can using your current or most recent job environment as your model. Where parenthetical choices are given, choose one. In all other questions, written responses are called for. Share your results with your class.

1. I work/have worked in a team. (yes) (no)
2. My team has/had the following basic duties:
3. I am/have been a team leader. (yes) (no)
4. As a team leader my duties are/were:
5. I am/have been a team facilitator/supervisor. (yes) (no)
6. As a team facilitator, my duties are/were:
7. My company employs contingent workers. (yes) (no)
8. The contingent workers used perform the following duties:
9. My job requires/will require technical skills. (yes) (no)
10. My company cares about quality. (yes) (no)
11. My company cares about productivity. (yes) (no)
12. It shows it cares about quality and productivity by:
13. My company is foreign-owned. (yes) (no)
14. The foreign ownership has required me to change by:
15. The dominant culture in my organization stresses:
16. The subcultures existing in my company are based on:
17. Subcultures are: (tolerated) (welcomed) at work.
18. My employer offers these nontraditional work options:

The Cajun Dog

CASE PROBLEM 1.1

The Cajun Dog is a fast-food restaurant owned by Jim Foster and special-izing in unique and traditional treatments of that old American favorite, the hot dog. Jim bought his restaurant about four months ago, and it has become a neighborhood favorite. He employs four high school students, each of whom works no more than four hours each day, Monday through Saturday. Three come in about 4:00 P.M., and one works from about 7:00 or 8:00 P.M. until closing. The workers are high school seniors; after they graduate, Jim wants to offer one of them a full-time position so that he can work fewer hours. Decision time is about two months away, so Jim will have about six months of experience with each of them. He plans to pick the one who demonstrates the best overall performance.

Jim has worked in the fast-food business for about three years and has solid experience in food preparation and counter service with two of the largest chains. He saved his money and at age twenty-six bought his business from a husband-and-wife team who wanted to retire. Before he took over, however, he worked with them for about one month to get the feel of the business. Although Jim had never been a supervisor of others, he felt his experiences had taught him all he needed to know.

Although Jim pays above minimum wage to his part-timers, he has not seen the enthusiasm he had expected from them. They sit idle during slow periods, and he has to hound them to keep them busy. When one or more of them show up late, it usually means a tough time for Jim, and it overburdens the ones who do come in on time. Jim finds it hard to understand why they do not have the same drive he had when he worked in their jobs. In his words, "If I don't stand over them all the time, they let me down. They bring their friends in, but their friends just want to sit around and gab."

When he hired his people Jim spent about three hours with each of them, patiently showing them what he wanted them to do. All of his help have been trained in waiting on customers and preparing the shakes and soft drinks. None of them prepares the food. Jim has reserved this task for himself although two of his people have expressed a strong interest in food preparation.

Jim's management philosophy is simple. He has learned that people should do as they are taught and not deviate from "the method." As Jim puts it, "There is no room for creative counter people and Pepsi preparers. All I ask from my help is that they do what they are told, when they are told, and in the exact manner in which the task was taught. I don't want any back talk. Do it my way or get out." When Jim corrects a person, he usually does it in a personal way, attacking the individual as "lazy" or "stupid." When Ellen, an employee, offered a suggestion for speeding up the flow, Jim blew his stack.

One employee, Ben, is really upset and thinking about leaving. Last week, Jim added two new hot dog specialties to the menu. Unfortunately, he forgot to tell Ben and the others. They only found out about the new items through customers, who seemed pretty irate when Ben told them that the items did not exist.

Questions

1. Which of the attributes from Exhibit 1.4 has Jim failed to exhibit? Give examples from the case to support your choices.
2. Do you think Jim's workers are unique because they work part time? Why or why not?
3. Do you think Jim's background has equipped him to be a successful supervisor? Why or why not?

Kim Tanumi's Ms. Print Shop

Kim Tanumi is about to celebrate her first year as an entrepreneur in the printing business. Her Ms. Print Shop is a franchise that operates in several Midwestern states. She had several years of printing experience before purchasing her franchise and going through the company's extensive training course. She has no experience as a supervisor. Kim supervises her two full-time employees, both recent community college graduates. Karen majored in English while Roger specialized in communications arts.

Although Kim has trained both Roger and Karen to operate and maintain all the equipment she owns, she has performed all the nonmachine tasks. Lately, her business has grown so much that Kim has found this arrangement unsatisfactory. She has decided to expand both their jobs to include taking inventory, ordering supplies, and making deliveries to neighborhood customers—the "busy work," as she calls these duties.

Kim met with both employees two weeks ago and proposed her plans. To her surprise, both employees resisted the changes. They were upset that they had not been consulted while Kim was planning the changes. Both Karen and Roger believed that if their jobs were to expand, they should receive substantial increases in pay and benefits. Roger stated further that he wanted to learn more about the business, not just machine operations. His schooling had given him most of the skills necessary for doing such things as layouts and proofing. He was quite honest about the fact that he would like to own and operate his own small print shop and saw his present position as a natural learning bridge to that end. He wanted experience dealing with customers as well. He has taken accounting courses and wanted to apply this knowledge too. The meeting ended with Kim holding her ground and leaving both employees quite unhappy.

Since the meeting, Karen has quit, and Roger has become an unhappy employee. He has taken on his new duties reluctantly and does not seem to be giving it his best. Kim took over Karen's duties and, after interviewing several people, hired a retired printer, Jesus Morales, who has thirty-five years' experience. Jesus was bored with his retirement, wanted to keep his skills sharp, and was willing to work for slightly more than Karen had been paid. Jesus took over Karen's duties and, in addition, was given supervisory authority over Roger. This further alienated Roger since he felt he should have been given supervisory status over a new hire. Kim had not considered this alternative. Roger has decided to start looking for a new employer in the near future.

Questions

1. What do you think of Kim's use of human skills?
2. How has Kim lived up to her major responsibilities to her subordinates?
3. Using Exhibit 1.2, comment on Kim's use of each role with Roger.
4. Using Exhibit 1.4, what attributes has Roger exhibited that may indicate that he is a good supervisory candidate?

Notes

Bridges, William. "The End of the Job," *Fortune*, September 19, 1994, 62–64, 68, 72, 74.

Brownstein, Vivian. "As the Job Market Heats Up, Can Inflation Stay Cool?," *Fortune*, August 22, 1994, 23.

Business Week. "Learning from Japan," January 27, 1992, 52–55; and *Fortune*, "Japan's U.S. Plants Up 9% in 1991," April 20, 1992, 16.

Business Week. "Managing by Values," August 1, 1994, 46–52.

Chandler, Clay, and White, Joseph B. "It's Hello Dollies at Nissan's New 'Dream Factory,'" *The Wall Street Journal,* July 6, 1992, B11.

Chicago Tribune. "How Many Switches It Takes to Be Viewed As a Job-hopper," September 19, 1994, sect. 6, 5.

Chicago Tribune. "Workers Lack Three R's, Hurting Small Firms, Study Says," June 5, 1992, sect. 3, 3.

Drucker, Peter. *Managing for Results* (New York: Harper & Row, 1964), 5.

Hammer, Michael, and Champy, James. *Reengineering the Corporation* (New York: Harper Business, 1993), 32, 76–77.

Inc. "Asking Workers What They Want," August, 1994, 103.

Johnson, Ross, and Winchell, William O. *Management and Quality* (Milwaukee: American Society for Quality Control, 1989).

Kahn, R. L., Wolfe, D. M., Quinn, P. R., Snoek, J. D., and Rosenthal, R. A. *Organizational Stress: Studies in Role Conflict and Ambiguity* (New York: John Wiley & Sons, 1964).

Katz, Robert L. "Skills of an Effective Administrator," in *Business Classics: Fifteen Key Concepts for Managerial Success, Harvard Business Review,* 1975, 23–35.

Katzenbach, Jon. "The Right Kind of Teamwork," *The Wall Street Journal.* November 9, 1992, A10.

Kirk, Randy. "It's About Control," *Inc.,* August 1994, 25–26.

Klein, Janice A., and Posey, Pamela A. "Good Supervisors Make Good Supervisors—Anywhere," *Harvard Business Review,* November–December 1986, 126.

Lee, William. "The New Corporate Republics," *The Wall Street Journal.* September 26, 1994, A12.

Likert, Rensis. *New Patterns of Management* (New York: McGraw-Hill, 1961), 61.

Miner, John B. *Management Theory* (New York: Macmillan, 1971), 39–48.

Nauman, Matt. "Job Well Done," *Chicago Tribune,* September 18, 1994, sect. 17, 3.

Peters, Tom. "Nobody Knows Nothin', So Go Ahead And Take Those Risks," *Chicago Tribune,* August 29, 1994, sect. 4, 3.

Resnick, Rosalind. "Leasing Workers," *Nation's Business,* November 1992, 20.

Richman, Louis S. "The New Worker Elite," *Fortune,* August 22, 1994, 56–59, 62, 64, 66.

Serwer, Andrew E. "McDonald's Conquers the World," *Fortune,* October 17, 1994, 103–104, 106, 108, 112, 114, 116.

Smith, Deborah. *Temp* (Boston: Shambhala, 1994) 3.

Taylor III, Alex. "GM's $11,000,000,000 Turnaround," *Fortune,* October 17, 1994, 54–56, 58, 62, 66, 70, 74.

The Wall Street Journal. "For College Graduates, a Heartening Word," September 26, 1994, A1.

Van, Jon. "Laptop Leads Cast of Office Offerings but Bosses Must Filter What's Needed from What's New," *Chicago Tribune,* March 17, 1991, sect. 20, 7.

Suggested Readings

Blank, Renee, and Slipp, Sandra. *Voices of Diversity.* New York: Amacom, 1994.

Hammer, Michael, and Champy, James. *Reengineering the Corporation.* New York: Harper Business, 1993.

Hunt, Daniel V. *Quality in America*. Homewood, Ill.: Business One Irwin, 1992.

Kayser, Thomas A. *Building Team Power*. New York: Irwin, 1994.

Kotter, John P. "What Leaders Really Do." *Harvard Business Review* (May–June 1990): 103–111.

Loden, Marilyn, and Rosener, Judy B. *Workforce America*. Homewood, Ill.: Business One Irwin, 1991.

Nuventures Consultants, Inc. *America's Changing Workforce—About You, Your Job and Your Changing Work Environment*. La Jolla, Calif.: Nuventures Publishing, 1990.

Richman, Louis S. "The New Worker Elite," *Fortune* (August 22, 1994), 56–59, 62, 64, 66.

Semler, Ricardo. *Maverick*. New York: Warner Books, Inc., 1993.

Smith, Deborah. *Temp*. Boston: Shambhala, 1994.

2

You
and Your Future

OBJECTIVES

After reading and discussing this chapter, you should be able to do the following:

1. Define this chapter's key terms.

2. Explain how managers can avoid personal obsolescence.

3. List the six steps involved in preparing oneself for advancement.

4. List the five steps involved in planning a career.

5. Explain the importance of a personal code of ethics.

INTRODUCTION

"The notion that you can work for one company and be guaranteed that you will retire from there at age 62 is not so reasonable anymore," says economist Michael Podgursky from the University of Massachusetts (Franklin, 1994). "The new compact between company and worker dismisses paternalism and embraces self-reliance.... The key difference: shared responsibility. Employers have an obligation to provide opportunity for self-improvement; employees have to take charge of their own careers" (*Business Week*, 1994). The economy and industries are changing so rapidly that no company can really know what it will be doing one or more years into the future. The emphasis is on gaining a competitive edge and on reinventing the fundamental processes and organizations through which work is accomplished.

Downsizing, rightsizing, empowering, telecommuting, employee leasing, teaming, decentralizing, and reengineering are all changing the complexion of work and the workplace. All these efforts bring sudden and often painful changes to a company's employees and their careers. Reengineering requires organizations to decide on their core competencies and label their essential processes. These must be continually reexamined and redesigned to keep the firm effective and efficient. Most companies define "their reengineering efforts as simplifying jobs, performing jobs in a logical order, combining jobs and contracting out support work [outsourcing] to other firms" (*Chicago Tribune*, 1994). According to a Pitney Bowes Management Survey of 100 major U.S. companies, "Workers at three-fourths of firms that have carried out reengineering actions were more fearful about losing their jobs.... Likewise, 55 percent of the firms said their employees felt overburdened by their assignments after the changes. [But] "71 percent of the companies said their initiatives led to greater employee productivity, 61 percent reported cost-efficiency increases and 40 percent saw profit increases" (*Chicago Tribune*, 1994). According to *Business Week* (1994), all sectors of our economy are experiencing:

> a workplace that will evolve year after year. Many will find the result both enervating and rewarding. In companies that are flattening hierarchies and, bit by bit, decentralizing decision-making, workers are gaining greater control over what they do; self-direction has superseded the doctrine that workers do only what they're told. High performers are rewarded with higher pay. And flexible human resource strategies can free workers to pursue more fulfilling combinations of varied work, family life, and other interests.

Flexibility training is being stressed by many companies today. The aim is to keep both the company and its employees ready to respond to rapid changes—both planned and unplanned.

Diversity in Our Workforce

Various writers, researchers, and federal government statistics have come up with the following trends and figures for what has become known as *workforce 2000:*

- More female workers. In 1990, about 45 percent of America's workforce was female. In 2000, 50 percent will be. About two-thirds of all new entrants until the year 2000 will be female.
- More working mothers with preschoolers at home. By the year 2000, about two-thirds of all working women will have children under the age of six.
- More single-parent families. Nearly 8 million single mothers care for children under the age of eighteen; nearly 1.5 million single fathers do too. The 25 million households with children under eighteen will grow through the year 2000.
- More dual-career couples. The 42 percent of families with dual-career parents will grow significantly through the year 2000.
- More nonwhites entering the workforce. In 2000, about 25 percent of our working population will be minorities; about 45 percent of the growth in our net new jobs will come from people of color—U.S. born and immigrants.
- More older Americans. Americans age fifty-five or older are about 15.5 million and will increase by 38 percent by 2005.

Work in America is shifting from manufacturing to the service sector at an increasing rate and from the routine, fatiguing, and monotonous to the intriguing, exciting, and challenging. Companies and industries are focusing on total quality management and reinventing themselves as never before. Increasingly, American businesses of all sizes are finding themselves in a global economy with all the uncertainties and challenges that it represents. These changes and challenges mean that you are now, or soon will be, in a world of work that is more demanding and stressful than ever before. What you are willing to invest in your future today will determine where you will be able to go in the future. You must work to guarantee your employability, not job security. Your primary goals should be to commit to a lifelong program of continuous learning, mastering the newest technologies as they come along in order to be ready for future job and career opportunities. This chapter focuses on your future and how you can avoid personal obsolescence by planning for your own advancement and career.

obsolescence
a state or condition that exists when a person or machine is no longer able to perform to standards or to management's expectations

OBSOLESCENCE

Obsolescence exists when a person or machine is no longer capable of performing up to standards or to management's expectations. What choices does management have when confronted with an obsolete person or

Person	Machine
Invest in the person through training and development, and offer incentives for efforts at self-improvement.	Keep the machine and modify it, when economically feasible to do so, to improve its efficiency and longevity.
Tolerate the person and his or her limitations and inefficiencies.	Keep the machine and live with its limitations and inefficiencies.
Tolerate the person, but reduce his or her role in the organization by deletion of duties or demotion.	Keep the machine but reduce its role in production, relegating it to backup or temporary use.
Discharge the person and replace him or her with a better-qualified individual.	Scrap the machine and replace it with a more up-to-date model.

machine? Exhibit 2.1 highlights the alternatives. A person can become obsolete in attitudes, knowledge, skills, and abilities. Obsolescence in any of these areas marks a person as a potential candidate for the scrap heap. Such a person may become too costly to keep or maintain. Exhibit 2.2 is a short quiz to help you determine if you are, or are in danger of becoming, obsolete.

Personal obsolescence can happen quite suddenly. Overnight changes can render an individual's performance inadequate or unnecessary. Corporate reengineering efforts and the shift from vertical layers of management to cross-functional teams have had this impact on workers as well as supervisors and other managers. When a company decides to outsource—send work to outsiders and stop doing it itself—"The best and the brightest employees who did the work often are hired by the outside agency, but the others lose their jobs" (Kleiman, "Human," 1994).

According to Tom Peters (1987), the supervisor's role is changing. In many companies he and others have studied, the traditional first-line supervisor's job has become obsolete. In companies where teams dominate, the supervisor has become a coordinator, facilitator, trainer, coach, and adviser. Candidates for supervisory positions and practicing supervisors receive training in working with and through teams, problem-solving techniques, statistics, participative management, and communications. Their primary duty is to empower others—team members—to do what they do to the best of their abilities. Their primary focus is horizontal—working to improve the flow of work from the beginning to the end of a

EXHIBIT 2.2

Twenty questions to help you assess your degree of personal obsolescence.

*Note that these questions put the burden to avoid obsolescence on you. For every "no" response, you highlight an area where you need a change in behavior. Your "yes" responses pinpoint areas that are keeping you current and growing.

Ask yourself the following questions to determine your degree of personal obsolescence.*

Attitudes

1. Is my mind free from anxiety over personal matters while I work?
2. Do I believe in myself—my knowledge, skills, and abilities—and in my associates?
3. Am I open and receptive to advice and suggestions, regardless of their sources?
4. Do I look for the pluses before looking for the minuses?
5. Am I more concerned with the cause of management's action than with its effect?

Knowledge

1. Am I curious—do I still seek the why behind actions and events?
2. Do I read something and learn something new every day?
3. Do I question the old and the routine?
4. Do I converse regularly with my subordinates, peers, and superiors?
5. Have I a definite program for increasing my knowledge?

Skills

1. Is what I am able to do still needed?
2. In light of recent trends and developments in my company and industry, will my skills be required one year from now?
3. Do I practice my skills regularly?
4. Do I regularly observe how others perform their skills?
5. Have I a concrete program for acquiring new skills?

Abilities

1. Do my subordinates, peers, and superiors consider me competent?
2. Do I consistently look for a better way of doing things?
3. Am I willing to take calculated risks?
4. Do I keep morally and physically fit?
5. Have I a specific program for improving my performance?

process or project and working across functional lines. Exhibit 2.3 contrasts the old traditional role of the supervisor with the new emerging role in team environments.

Again, according to Peters (1987), "There is no more difficult transition in a career than the one from nonboss to boss; the second toughest is

EXHIBIT 2.3
Differences between the old and the new supervisor.

Old—Traditional Role	New—Emerging Role
1. 10–20 subordinates	As many as 75 people reporting directly or through teams
2. Scheduling work	Coach, leader, coordinator, and trainer focusing on empowering team members to schedule
3. Enforcing rules	Creating bonds of mutual trust, enabling others to set and follow their own rules
4. Planning others' work	Enabling others to plan their work
5. Focusing downward	Focusing horizontally, working to speed the flow
6. Transmitting and translating middle-management needs and demands	Transmitting and selling teams' needs upward
7. Issuing orders and giving instructions	Facilitating: getting expert help as required by teams
8. Creating and instituting changes and innovations	Assisting others to be creative and to constantly strive for improvements

to boss of bosses. These passages should be marked by programs commensurate with their significance." Since many organizations lack adequate programs to aid these transitions, the primary responsibility for preparing yourself to move into a supervisory position rests with you. You must take the initiative and work to facilitate your own advancement; you must nurture your own and your associates' quests for continual improvement.

Avoiding Obsolescence

Just as corporations are reengineering themselves, you will have to periodically reengineer yourself and your career. The key, say many authors, is *flexibility*. According to the U.S. Department of Labor statistics, 75 percent of today's employees will require some form of retraining to fit in to the year 2000's workforce. Throughout your working life, you can expect to change your job about six times and have at least three careers. The dean

Continuing education programs improve your chances for advancement and keep you from becoming obsolete. At McDonald's Hamburger University, managers learn about all aspects of their operation to maintain the cutting edge.

of Indiana University's school of business, John Rau, has this advice (Kiechell III, 1994):

> [Focus] along each of three dimensions. On what [is called] traditional content: The classic choices are functions like marketing or finance, but because more companies are thinking of their businesses as processes, perhaps some cut at that—distribution, say, or customer acquisition. Then overlay a concentration on a particular industry or sector—publishing, for instance, or health care. Finally, you will...need process skills—team leadership, team membership, the ability to communicate.

Walter Kiechel III (1994) adds that managers need to be *"specialists—* you must be an expert in something, *generalists*—you must know enough of different disciplines to be able to mediate among them, *self-reliant—* think of yourself as a business of one, and *connected*—you must be a team player. Call them the points of the compass for managerial careers in the new economy."

The emphasis today is on rewarding "teamwork, measurable quality improvements, and employees' acquisition of new skills" (Richman, 1994). Westin Hotels has "identified 14 key attributes employees from housekeepers to hotel managers must have. Besides technical competence, these include a capacity to demonstrate initiative, an ability to communicate clearly, and a commitment to quality" (Richman, 1994). Through careful screening, the hotel chain has found people capable of managing themselves and has reduced employee turnover while increasing customer satisfaction (Richman, 1994). Employees at European Collision Center, an auto repair shop in Massachusetts, constantly learn new skills by returning to school and cross-training. They "take 'ownership' of a car while it's in the shop, staying with it [from] start to finish. No one looks over their shoulders." Customers love what they get, and "traffic has doubled every year for five years" (*Business Week*, 1994).

Perhaps all this is best summarized by author William Bridges (1994) when he states that to survive in the new world of work one must have four essentials (D.A.T.A.):

> The new qualifications are that you really want to do the work (desire), that you are good at what the work requires (ability), that you fit [a specific] kind of situation (temperament), and that you have whatever other resources the work requires (assets).

THE IMPORTANCE OF EDUCATION

The more education one has, the more income and employment security one achieves. The median income (the figure at which there are as many people above the number as there are below it) for U.S. households rises dramatically as the educational attainment of the heads of these households increases. According to U.S. Census Bureau figures, two-year college graduates earn about twice as much as those who only finish grammar school and about one-fourth more than those who only graduate from high school. Average (1992) salaries for high school graduates were $18,737; for four-year college graduates, $32,629; for masters-degree holders, $48,653 per year (Kleiman, "Study Shows," 1994). Lifetime earnings for these groups were estimated at $821,000, $1,421,000, and $1,619,000, respectively (Arndt, 1994).

Education is achieved through various sources: community colleges, colleges and universities, professional associations, on-the-job training, to name but a few. In addition to helping you acquire bachelor's, master's, and doctoral degrees, the courses you can take in individual industries are quite valuable and will improve your chances for raises and promotions. By joining certain professions and professional associations, you become eligible for their various training programs. For information on how they can help you, write to the following addresses:

Academy of Management
P.O. Box 39
Ada, Ohio 45810

The American Management Association
135 West 50th Street

The American Management Association
135 West 50th Street
New York, New York 10020

American Society for Quality Control
310 W. Wisconsin Avenue
Milwaukee, Wisconsin 53203

The American Society for Training and Development
P.O. Box 1443
1630 Duke Street
Alexandria, Virginia 22313

The National Association for Female Executives
127 West 24th Street
New York, New York 10011

Society for the Advancement of Management
126 Lee Avenue, Suite 11
Vinton, Virginia 24179

According to a 1994 survey of 100 college recruitment offices by the Hanigan Consulting Group, a student's "grade point average is the most important factor in determining hiring decisions and salary level.... [S]tudents with grade point averages higher than 3.5 received an average of 3.1 job offers [and] averaged $36,821 annually on graduation" (Kleiman, "Praise," 1994). The commitment to learn and to keep learning must be acquired so that you can continually seek what you need to grow and survive. The Japanese have a word for this commitment: kaizen. According to kaizen, everyone in a company has two basic obligations: maintaining standards and seeking to improve them. Each person employed has to seek steady improvement in his or her personal and working lives (Imai, 1987). Each of us needs to make a commitment to continue our educations and to work toward steadily improving ourselves and our situations.

Planning for Advancement

Your future must be planned if you wish to control it. You start by knowing where you have been and where you are now. Then decide where it is that you want to go. The six steps in planning for advancement are as follows:

1. Take a personal inventory.
2. Analyze your present situation.
3. Set your objectives for self-improvement.
4. Develop your program.
5. Set your program in motion.
6. Evaluate your progress periodically.

EXHIBIT 2.4
Assessment checklist.

Rank each of the following in order of their importance to you

	Rank
Good health insurance and other benefits	___
Interesting work	___
Job security	___
Opportunity to learn new skills	___
Having a week or more of vacation	___
Being able to work independently	___
Recognition from coworkers	___
Regular hours (no weekends, no nights)	___
Having a job in which you can help others	___
Limiting job stress	___
High income	___
Working close to home	___
Work that is important to society	___
Chances for promotion	___
Contact with a lot of people	___

Taking a Personal Inventory   This first step is designed to give you a realistic understanding of your interests, values, and aptitudes. Exhibit 2.4 is a start at assessing interests and values—those states or conditions in life that are important to you. It consists of several psychological and physical conditions found through or as a result of work and its environment. Rank each characteristic listed in order of its importance to you, numbering them from 1 to 15. Your preferences should be used to evaluate your present and potential jobs and employers throughout your job search. All the listed factors were ranked as very important by 50 percent or more of the workers surveyed in a recent Gallup Poll. All are listed in the order of their importance to those surveyed—good health insurance and other benefits ranked number 1, interesting work ranked number 2, and so on (Caggiano, 1992).

Along with your interests and values, you should assess your aptitudes—your ability, talent, or capacity to perform certain mental and physical processes. The aptitudes most frequently measured by employers and used to match applicants to jobs are as follows:

1. Abstract reasoning—the ability to think logically without using numbers or words. Skilled supervisors, technicians, engineers, scientists, and computer programmers must have this ability.
2. Verbal reasoning—the ability to think, comprehend, and communicate effectively through the use of words. Authors, teachers, supervisors, salespeople, and secretaries must have this ability.

3. Mechanical reasoning—the ability to recognize the mechanical principles that govern the use of machines and tools. Supervisors, engineers, mechanics, and skilled craftspersons must have this ability.

4. Numerical ability—the ability to solve mathematical problems and to think in numbers. Supervisors, economists, accountants, designers, and technicians must feel comfortable with numerical reasoning.

5. Spatial relationships—the ability to make things three dimensional and to imagine the shapes and sizes of things. Depth perception and the ability to estimate distances are also part of this aptitude. Supervisors, assemblers, draftspersons, scientists, and technicians share this aptitude.

6. Manual dexterity—the ability to move the hands skillfully and easily. Nearly every assembly operator, craftsperson, technician, artist, musician and their supervisors need this aptitude.

By taking a battery of aptitude tests through your college's counseling office, you will discover which aptitudes you have and what kinds of jobs you would be most capable of handling. Nearly every job demands one or more of these aptitudes from the job holder. Through proper interpretation of the test results, you will learn what kinds of jobs you are best suited for. Failure to assess your aptitudes accurately will prevent you from finding out about any false perceptions you may have of your own abilities.

Analyzing Your Present Situation   Your present situation consists of the resources you have available to spend in acquiring what you need and the view you have toward your present state in life. How much money and time have you available to help you get what you want and lack? How strong is your commitment to improve on what you have? What roadblocks may stand in your way? How happy are you with your present job, income, education, and quality of life? The more you desire to change, the easier it will be to do so. Make use of the supports you have that will aid your efforts to improve yourself and your life: family, friends, your boss, peers, programs at work, and the outside learning facilities available to help. Consider the advice of Ms. Sandy Rowe, editor of *The Oregonian* in Portland, "if you don't have genuine passion for what you're doing, don't do it. Passion for your work helps you through the most difficult times" (Hanson, 1994).

Setting Your Objectives for Self-Improvement   As clearly and precisely as you can, put the qualities you wish to obtain and the skills and abilities you wish to develop into writing. Be specific. Determine which of these you need most urgently, and make them objectives for the short run. Set a time limit by which each is to be procured, and then stick to it as well as you can. Set the remainder of your needs as long-term goals—goals to be achieved within a year or two. Finally, consider the means you wish to use to reach each goal. Be realistic and a little conservative. Do not take on too much at once, or you will only be setting yourself up for a letdown and frustration. Start with the goals you need most urgently, and select the one that appears easiest to achieve. As with a diet, early success is important to both commitment and continuation.

Developing Your Program   The program you formulate should contain the answers to who, what, when, where, why, how, and how much. Break it down into phases, each with specific goals and time limits. Keep it in writing and in front of you so that you constantly remind yourself of the targets you wish to hit. Share its contents with your loved ones: They can boost your willpower. Exhibit 2.5 can help you get started. Complete it, and check on your progress regularly. When you reach one goal, add another.

Setting Your Program in Motion   Begin your execution of the program as soon as it is formulated. If you meet heavy resistance in one or another of its phases, leave that phase, and divert your attention and efforts to another. Then come back to that phase and try again.

Evaluating Your Progress Periodically   If certain goals you have stated appear to be impossible, you may have to abandon them. With each goal you abandon or achieve, establish another in its place. Remember that the program is a continuing effort at improvement and personal growth. Check your progress against the time limits you established. Were you realistic? Are you on course? Share your successes and setbacks with your husband or wife, or with a good friend. Seek counsel from the sources that you feel are best qualified to help. But keep working at your program!

Most large companies offer supervisors and associates many opportunities for growth and development. Programs range from reading materials to college degrees underwritten by company funds. Find out what options are available to you and what the requirements are for taking advantage of each of them. Pick the ones that you and your boss feel will be most beneficial to you for both the short and long term. Be selective, and do not overcommit yourself. It is better to do one or two things splendidly than to do several only adequately.

PLANNING YOUR CAREER

A **career** for our purposes consists of a sequence of jobs that takes people to higher levels of learning and responsibility, usually in a specialty area. As a career progresses, one acquires new skills, skill levels, experiences, and competencies. This series of jobs is often called a **career path.** Career pathing (routing an employee through a series of related horizontal and

career
a sequence of jobs that takes people to higher levels of learning and responsibility

career path
a route chosen by an employer or employee through a series of related horizontal and vertical moves to jobs of ever-increasing responsibilities

The results of my aptitude, abilities, and skills inventories show the following

My Five Greatest Weaknesses   date: _____ 19 _____

1. *Not being up to date enough in my chosen field* _____

2. *Poor at speaking to gruops on my feet* _____

3. *Being unsure of my abilities to use my personal computer to*

   its full potential _____

4. _____

5. _____

What I Want Within 1 Year	How I Intended to Get It	Cost
1. *Keep up to Date.*	*Read the journals in my field regularly, and subscribe to most appropriate one.*	*$25*
2.		
3. *Build my computer skills*	*Enroll in a night course next semester at Wright College.*	*$115*
4.		
5.		

What I Want Within 2 Years	How I Intended to Get It	Cost
1. *Improve my public speaking*	*Enroll in Toastmasters in town*	*$?*
2.		
3.		
4.		
5.		

EXHIBIT 2.5
Sample self-development program in written-out form.

vertical moves to jobs with ever-increasing responsibilities) for supervisors and their associates is becoming more common in many smaller firms but is on the decline in larger ones. Small businesses that are growing fast offer the best career opportunities. Many offer employees less pay and benefits but "greater opportunities for individual growth.... [A]n employee is likely to have more responsibilities in the first three to five years at a smaller company than at a larger one. That's because smaller firms have fewer employees and, thus, typically need workers to take on many tasks" (Szabo, 1994). If you are in a job and career at present, find out what path(s) it leads to. If you find that no clearly defined path has been designated by your employer, the burden will be yours to determine a path with your current employer or with another. You may find that a career path has been set up for you but that it is not to your liking. In such a case, a change in employment may be needed. As we have stated, you can expect several jobs and careers during your lifetime.

Like your future, your career must be planned if you are to control it. Five recommended steps for you to take in planning your career are:

1. Determine your career objectives.
2. Investigate jobs and career paths.
3. Label likely employers.
4. Seek employment.
5. Assess your situation periodically.

Meeting recruiters at job fairs is one of several channels to pursue in your job search. The student in the picture prepared for meeting the Pfizer recruiter by dressing well, having an up-to-date résumé, and thinking out answers to commonly asked questions.

Determining Your Career Objectives

Write a mission statement for yourself, just as any business does. State in writing what you want to achieve and where you want to be over the next one, two, and three years. Start by listing your career goals. State as clearly as you can just what you want from work and what kind of work you want to specialize in over the next few years. Now work backward: List the short- and long-term steps you must take to get you what you want. You will then know what steps are needed to reach your career goals. As you grow in experience and pass through several jobs, you and your circumstances will change.

Investigating Jobs and Career Paths

You may wish to begin this step by looking at the jobs that best match up with your interests and aptitudes. *The Dictionary of Occupational Titles,* published by the U.S. Department of Labor, lists hundreds of jobs and describes what tasks and responsibilities they require. A second publication from the same source, the *Occupational Outlook Quarterly,* speaks to the forecast for hundreds of jobs and career fields. These, along with many privately published reports and periodicals, can help you assess the jobs and career fields that will be in demand in the long term. Check with your college's placement office and with local librarians for a list of useful sources of information. According to the 1994 *Occupational Outlook Handbook* published by the U.S. Bureau of Labor Statistics, between 1992 and 2005, the net new management jobs added in each of the following fastest-growing categories will be:

> *Construction contractors and managers 85,000*
> *General managers and top executives 380,000*
> *Health service managers 135,000*
> *Management analysts and consultants 89,000*
> *Restaurant and food service managers 227,000*

According to the authors of the Bureau's predictions, economists Geoffrey C. Grandler and Kurt E. Schrammel, "Between 1992 and 2005, employment will rise to 147.5 million from 121.1 million" (Kleiman, "Age," 1994)…"[and] 53 percent of all job openings over [that same] period will arise because of the need to replace workers who transfer to other occupations or leave the labor force" (Kleiman, "Know," 1994). Among the occupations cited by the Bureau as having the fastest growth rates are computer engineers and scientists (112 percent), systems analysts (110 percent), and operations research analysts (61 percent).

Various on-campus clubs offer help with investigations. They often feature guest speakers from occupations that are related to the clubs' activities and may sponsor field trips to visit several major employers' facilities. Another good source is campus recruiters, who represent many different employers and who interview applicants and share information about what it is like to work in different areas. Your professors can help too.

There is no substitute for talking in depth with someone who does the kind of work you wish to do. Schools can often put you in touch with experienced people in various areas through their alumni offices. Family and friends can do the same. Private and public employment services can also help by exposing you to the specifics of various jobs and by helping you assess your suitability for certain types of employment. Finally, there are lectures, professional conferences, and professional associations in your community that stand ready to help you research a specific career opportunity.

Labeling Likely Employers

Once you have a specific kind of work and job in mind, you are ready to begin labeling likely employers. What you want to do here is find the specific job that you would like to get with a specific employer. One way to start is to determine if the area you live in is right for you. Is it growing in population, especially in terms of new businesses and job opportunities? Is the area you live in right for you in terms of its climate and the quality of life that it offers? It may be that you should begin researching jobs in another city or state. It makes the most sense to start your search in a place where you want to live and where the opportunities are most numerous.

Keep in mind that over 56 percent of all working Americans work for companies with fewer than 500 employees (Schor, 1994). Small businesses are adding nearly all the net new jobs in our economy and are excellent places to get a career started.

Sources to help you determine where the jobs are that fit your needs include help-wanted ads, private and public employment services, local colleges' placement offices, friends, family, and contacts employed in various companies. Using this last source is often called **networking.** Begin by talking to your closest friends and relatives—people who know you well and have your best interests at heart. Let them know your career objectives, and ask them for help in identifying possible sources of employment. Some companies pay a finder's fee for each new hire recommended by a current employee. You can also network by attending professional meetings and conferences; there you can meet people from different areas and employers and ask them, once they know you, for some job-search suggestions rather than for a job. According to data from the U.S. Department of Labor, more than half of all job holders found their jobs through person-to-person contacts. Keep expanding your professional contacts, and do not expect instant results. It takes time for parties to get to know one another; as relationships progress, so will the payoffs.

networking
using one's friends, family, and work-related contacts to help find employment or to advance one's career

EXHIBIT 2.6

Letter of application to accompany the résumé shown in Exhibit 2.7.

539 Tenth Avenue
Chicago, Illinois, 60600
(Date)

Mr. William R. Johnson
Personnel Director
J & M Electronics
3872 South Wabash
Chicago, Illinois 60615

Dear Mr. Johnson:

Recently I learned, through the Wright College Placement Office, of the expansion of your company's sales operations and your intention to hire several managers for outside salespeople. If a position is currently available, I would appreciate your considering me for it.

I have had progressively more responsible and diverse experience in selling and customer services. I have sold your company's fine products at the retail level and currently manage a sales force of six people.

For your review I am enclosing my résumé. I would appreciate a personal interview with you, at your earliest convenience, in order to discuss my application further.

Very truly, yours,

John D. Jones

Enclosure (Your résumé)

Once you have information about a specific job that looks good, investigate the employer to determine what kind of an environment it offers. If it is an open corporation (one owned by the public), get a copy of its most recent annual report and read it. A visit to the local chamber of commerce can tell you the company's employment history. A scan of local newspapers can reveal specific stories in which the company's plans and accomplishments are discussed. You want to know as much about an employer as you can before you attempt to apply for employment. Every employer has a community history and an image, and you should be familiar with these before you attempt to give a company a voice in your future.

Seeking Employment

With your research in hand, you are now ready to make contact with a specific person at a specific place of employment. Use a letter of applica-

EXHIBIT 2.7
A personal résumé.

John D. Jones
539 Tenth Avenue
Chicago, Illinois, 60600
(312) 555-1345

Job Objective:	To manage salespeople in the electronics field at the whoesale level.
Education:	Two-year degree in marketing from Wright College, City Colleges of Chicago, 1991.
Work Experience:	Retail sales in consumer electronics, Sears, Golf Mill store, 1989–1990.
	Manager, retail sales staff, Electronics Venture, Northbrook store, 1990 to present.
Accomplishments:	Won "Best Salesperson: award for my department 1989, 1992 at Sears, Golf Mill.
	Employee of the Month at Electronics Venture, May of 1993.
	Youngest supervisor of retail sales department in Electronics Venture's history.
Skills:	Fluent in Spanish.
References:	Furnished on request.

tion (see Exhibit 2.6) requesting a personal interview. It should meet the following guidelines:

1. It should be neatly typed using proper grammar, spelling, and sentence construction; it should be signed by hand.
2. It should be on clean bond paper of standard letter size.
3. It should be addressed to a specific individual (with job title), and its envelope should be marked "Personal" or "Confidential."
4. Its wording should be tailored to the company and the position you are seeking.
5. A **résumé** should be enclosed.

Your résumé should contain your personal data (name, address, and phone number); your employment goals; and relevant education, successes, and job experiences. "It should be achievement-and action-oriented....

résumé
an employment-related document submitted by the applicant and containing vital data such as the person's name, address, employment goals, and work-related education and experiences

Don't overlook summer jobs, internships, volunteer activities and life experiences.... [E]mployers are looking for well-rounded individuals who will be able to succeed in various positions in an organization" (Furore, 1994). Use short phrases rather than long sentences: organized the senior prom; raised productivity in my team by 45 percent in six weeks.

Try to keep your résumé to one page, as shown in the sample in Exhibit 2.7. Inclusion of references is optional. Some applicants simply state that they will be happy to supply them on request. A good résumé is short, neat, specific, focused, and uses a consistent style: Capital letters, underlining, indentation, and italics are used sparingly and the same way throughout. Remember that the person you send your letter to will probably spend less than a minute to read it.

The use of computer networks as a way of seeking employment is growing in popularity. Several national online services list both job offerings and personal résumés. E-Span lists current, paid-for job advertisements. "The Internet and commercial on-line services such as Compuserve, Prodigy and America Online,...offer specialized bulletin boards or forums in an array of professions, through which job seekers can use electronic mail to enter their résumés into a database, respond to job announcements and communicate with others in their field.... [S]ome employers say they prefer on-line advertising, finding it to be a relatively inexpensive way to find computer-literate candidates" (Kruger, 1994).

The Job Interview   Your employment interview is your chance to sell yourself and the employer's chance to sell you on a job and an environment. You can prepare for the interview by (1) going over your research, (2) dressing appropriately, and (3) rehearsing your answers to these most often asked questions:

1. Why have you picked our company?
2. Why did you leave your last job?
3. What are your career expectations?
4. What salary and benefits do you require?
5. What are your personal goals for the next year? Three years? Five years?
6. What team and team-building experiences have you had?
7. What are your strongest points?
8. What are your weaknesses?
9. What psychological rewards do you seek through work?
10. Would you object to moving if your job were to require it?

You should have clearly thought-out answers to these questions before you take the interview. When you are stating a weakness, let the interviewer know what you are doing about it. When you are asked for dollar figures, ask the employer what the job pays. Emphasize that you are interested in other things besides money, such as satisfaction and a chance to get your start in a promising career with a fine company.

You in turn need to find out as much about the job and the employer as you can during your interview. Before you can say yes or no to any job offer, you should have the answers to the following questions:

1. What has been the company's recent growth record?
2. What is its reputation as an employer locally, with the people in its community?
3. Does it offer career tracks or promote from within?
4. What are its major products and markets and long-term plans for growth in the future?
5. What have been its greatest successes recently?
6. What is your future boss like as a person?
7. What, specifically, will be your working conditions in the job being offered?
8. What new challenges and opportunities will the job offer you?

You may be asked to interview with more than one person, or you may be asked questions by a group of people. This is especially true if you are seeking a team member or team facilitator position. Teams often have a say in, or the ultimate authority to hire, their members, facilitators, and leaders. You can expect to interview with all a team's members, either individually or collectively. They will be looking to find in you what their team needs. (This chapter's Supervising Teams feature asks you to assess your team player abilities.) You should expect to be asked to solve problems that team leaders, members, and facilitators face and to deal with them quickly. Expect open questions that call for you to explain your thinking. Be certain to seek any information you think you need to make decisions before you give your thoughts.

Take all the things you need to the interview if the interviewer does not already have them. Such items may include the following:

- Social security card and all necessary licenses
- Résumé
- Transcript of grades (if a current student or recent graduate)
- Pen and pencil
- A list of people who have agreed to act as personal references for you
- Names and addresses of previous employers and the dates you worked for them

Various surveys show that the most common mistakes made by job candidates during interviews are as follows:

- Failing to research the company
- Failing to project enthusiasm for or commitment to one's career

SUPERVISING TEAMS

Increasingly, companies are using teams to carry out nearly every function and process at every level in an organization. At Saturn, General Motors' new auto division, "teams of workers manage everything from budgets to inventory control, often without direct oversight from top management." If you haven't already, you soon will find yourself a member of one or more teams and expected to be a team player.

The following quiz is designed to determine if you have the characteristics needed to be a good team member. After taking it, grade yourself with the answer key that follows.

Characteristics	Always	Sometimes	Never
1. I am a good listener.	_____	_____	_____
2. I enjoy the give and take of negotiating.	_____	_____	_____
3. I like working with and through others.	_____	_____	_____
4. I have good communication and interpersonal skills.	_____	_____	_____
5. I trust others.	_____	_____	_____
6. I respect and value the uniqueness in others.	_____	_____	_____
7. I am open to criticism.	_____	_____	_____
8. I can accept responsibility for the behaviors of others.	_____	_____	_____
9. I enjoy continual learning.	_____	_____	_____
10. I like to solve problems.	_____	_____	_____

Key: Give yourself two points for every *Always* response and one point for each *Sometimes* response.

Scoring: 15–20 points—team leader potential
10–14 points—team member potential
Under 10 points—loner

Each *Sometimes* and *Never* response indicates areas where you should seek improvement.

Source: Byrne, John A. "Paradigms for Postmodern Managers," *Business Week,* January 19, 1993, 62.

- Failing to project strengths and skills
- Exaggerating or lying about one's qualifications and capabilities
- Having a poor personal appearance
- Being unclear about one's career goals and aspirations
- Failing to list and describe in detail one's specific achievements

Finally, be ready to relate specific anecdotes and experiences that illustrate skills you have acquired and lessons you have learned about such things as the value of customer service or the importance of quality performances and processes. When possible, place a dollar value on any savings you made possible for an employer. Real-world examples stick with an interviewer and separate you from other applicants (Furore, 1994). Says Norman Maskin, senior human resources representative at Amoco headquarters (Furore, 1994):

> Relatively few people are in the mode of really trying to stress their accomplishments.... Our interview process is based on achievements, and some candidates struggle with that.... We're interested in a person's ability to learn, teamwork orientation and leadership ability. We want to know about circumstances in which candidates found themselves, what they did, and what the results of their actions were.... We want to know the whole story—the steps he [or she] took to achieve an outcome.

Evaluating Your Job Offer   If you get a job offer at the employment interview, be prepared to say no, yes, or can I get back to you? You can turn an offer down if it does not fit your expectations and needs. There is little hope of success for anyone who takes a job just to get one. If the job meets your approval in the following areas, you should probably grab it (Spenser, 1987):

- Does the company think as you do (are they your kind of people)?
- Do you like the people you have met and what you have seen of the work environment?
- Is the job high profile (one where you will be noticed)?
- Would you be willing to stay for at least several years?
- Are the pay and benefits what you want?

Assessing Your Situation Periodically

Every few months, look closely at your job situation. Ask yourself the following questions:

- Have my expectations become reality?
- Is this the job I thought it would be?
- Am I getting from it what I expected to get?

- Do I know where I am on a career path?
- Are the promises made to me being kept?
- Am I keeping the promises I made?

After your first two performance appraisals, you should know how your boss thinks and what he or she is looking for in your performance. Whatever your situation, commit yourself to your job for a minimum of one full year. This commitment gives you time to earn most benefits, to understand the company's niche and future plans, and to adequately assess your future prospects. It also offers the employer a return on the investment made in you; if you quit before this payback occurs, you are placing any referral and your reputation in jeopardy.

The time will come when you need to change jobs. The change may be necessary to aid your professional growth or to get into a more appealing career. Before leaving your present employer, make certain that there are no other positions in the company for which you qualify. Your experience is usually worth more to your present employer than it is to another. You know it is time to move on when doors are closed to you, you hate going to work each day, and your best efforts go unrewarded. But do not quit your job until you find another. It is better to bargain with a potential employer from a position of employment than from one of unemployment.

Tom Peters (1994), author, consultant, and entrepreneur, suggests that all of us need to reengineer our careers periodically. He states that personal renewal comes in two forms: "Big R" and "Little R." What he labels the Big R involves major activities designed to "profoundly [alter] a career...dramatically [shift] perspectives, and [fend] off staleness that most of us don't see overtaking us." Among his recommendations:

You begin a career at the establishment and advancement stage. As you reach the midcareer stage, you will share what you have already mastered with newer members of the firm.

- Take a six-month sabbatical to learn something completely new
- Earn a degree in a new area
- Achieve excellence at something (a hobby, for instance) outside one's major profession
- Take on a lateral assignment to a different geographic or vocational area

Peters believes that unless you have recently made several major accomplishments that move you in new directions, you are not doing enough. "Little R renewal we understand. It's constant improvement [kaizen] and…to be commended. But such activities are a far cry from the Big R" [and often not enough] (Peters, 1994).

CAREER STAGES

Most of us find ourselves making several job and career changes before we find a true commitment for our lives. We will usually pass through four distinct stages during this search. Exhibit 2.8 summarizes these four stages and the emotional needs they help satisfy.

The trial stage includes the planning for self-improvement and career planning phases we have just examined. It includes the experimentation and self-exploration that allow us to decide on goals and a path to achieve them. The second stage, establishment and advancement, allows us to make a commitment to our chosen field. It gives us a sense of competence and confidence. It is a time of growing responsibilities on the job and in our family lives. The midcareer stage establishes our place in our organization and allows us to share what we have mastered with younger and newer members of the company. New and different goals and priorities emerge, along with new jobs and their challenges. In establishment and advancement or midcareer stages, we may decide on—or circumstances may dictate—a career change. By late career, we are more concerned with grooming our successors and with planning for retirement or a new career than in any other stage.

PROFESSIONAL ETHICS

Ethics is a field of philosophy focused on the rightness and wrongness of human conduct in society in light of specific sets of circumstances. It should be considered when contemplating actions that will affect others. Before taking an action, the ethical person will think about the circumstances surrounding the intended action: his or her objectives, possible means available to achieve them, motives for taking the action, and its possible consequences. Our moral and ethical thinking is affected by our personal values and by our experiences. The ethical person will do his or her best to refrain from taking any action that will be harmful to others. Personal beliefs such as "the greatest good for the greatest number" or "do unto others as they would have you do unto them" (the new golden rule) also act as guides for judging the effects of intended actions.

Ethics helps individuals and groups determine what actions are the most beneficial and the least harmful. All of us must, on occasion, take

ethics
a field of philosophy dealing with the rightness and wrongness of human conduct in society

Stage	Task Needs	Emotional Needs
Trial	1. Varied job activities 2. Self-exploration	1. Make preliminary job choices 2. Settling down
Establishment and advancement	1. Job challenge 2. Develop competence in a specialty area 3. Develop creativity and innovation 4. Rotate into new area after 3–5 years	1. Deal with rivalry and competition; face failures 2. Deal with work/family conflicts 3. Support 4. Autonomy
Midcareer	1. Technical updating 2. Develop skills in training and coaching others (younger employees) 3. Rotation into new job requiring new skills 4. Develop broader view of work and own role in organization	1. Express feelings about midlife 2. Reorganize thinking about self in relation to work, family, and community 3. Reduce self-indulgence and competitiveness
Late career	1. Plan for retirement 2. Shift from power role to one of consultation and guidance 3. Identify and develop successors 4. Begin activities outside the organization	1. Support and counseling to see one's work as a platform for others 2. Develop sense of identity in extraorganizational activities

EXHIBIT 2.8

The four stages most careers pass through.

Source: D.T. Hall and M.A. Morgan, " Career Development and Planning." *Contemporary Problems in Personnel,* rev. ed., eds. W.C. Hamner and Frank L.. Schmidt [Chicago: St. Clair Press © 1977]. Reprinted by permission of John Wiley & Sons, Inc., New York.

actions that have negative consequences for some people and groups while they actually help others—an ethical dilemma. When a government taxes one group to help another, some people are harmed to benefit others. When a business decides to stop manufacturing one item and produce a more profitable one, some employees and suppliers are hurt, whereas others benefit.

Many professionals—including lawyers, doctors, and accountants—and many corporations have stated codes of ethics that they are expected to live up to or incur some penalty. Where such codes of proper conduct exist, they are not prescriptive. They try to create boundaries around individuals' freedom to act. One boundary most of us have is a conscience; it helps us know when we are acting properly and when we are not. For most people, the absence of guilt means that they believe they have acted properly and ethically. The decisions that supervisors must make each day have to be considered in terms of some kind of ethical test or code. If they are not, serious personal and legal problems can and will arise for both the supervisor and the employer.

For most managers' positions, there are no clearly defined and published codes of conduct. Consequently, supervisors who do not have a well-formed conscience or who lack a model for thinking ethically are liable to make unethical decisions resulting in serious negative consequences for themselves, their employers, and others. Authors Solomon and Hanson (1985) offer the following guidelines for contemplating the ethical implications of intended actions:

- Consider other people's well-being, including the well-being of non-participants.
- Think as a member of the business community and not as an isolated individual.
- Obey, but do not depend solely on, the law.
- Think of yourself and your company as part of society.
- Obey moral rules.
- Think objectively.
- Ask the question, "What sort of person would do such a thing?"
- Respect the customs of others, but not at the expense of your own ethics.

Management professor Kenneth Blanchard and cleric Norman Vincent Peale, in their book *The Power of Ethical Management* (1988), offer a series of questions that you can use to determine the ethical implications of intended actions:

- Is it legal? Will I be violating either civil law or company policy?
- Is it balanced? Is it fair to all concerned in the short term as well as the long term? Does it promote win–win relationships?
- How will it make me feel about myself? Will it make me proud?
- Would I feel good if my decision were published in a newspaper?
- Would I feel good if my family knew about it?

One final question: Is any gain made by one party needlessly at another's expense? For example, keeping too much change from a cashier at the checkout counter means that the keeper wins at the checker's expense. This is usually a certain sign that the action (keeping too much change) is unethical.

As a supervisor, you have not only ethical concerns but legal ones as well. You are charged to act both ethically and within the law. Just refraining from doing things that are illegal is not enough for a person who has authority over other people and the resources of a company. It may be legal to fire a person you do not like for that reason alone. But is it ethical to do so? What may be the consequences to you, to your associate, and to your company if you do so?

Your reputation is far too precious to waste on hasty, ill-thought-out decisions that fail to consider both the law and ethics. Times will come when you are asked to act in a way that you believe is immoral or unethical. What will you say to a boss who makes such a request of you? Are you prepared to cover up for a derelict employee? Once you are caught in a lie, your integrity is gone, and it is almost impossible to retrieve. Without personal codes of conduct and values we will fight to defend, our integrity will be compromised by our own actions and the actions of others. It is better to leave an environment that is unethical than to remain and become so ourselves. This text's remaining chapters contain additional insights on ethics.

Instant Replay

1. A supervisor, like a machine or a method, can become obsolete in skills and abilities without a continuing program for his or her future development.
2. You can expect to have several jobs and several careers in your working years.
3. Education, both in and outside college classrooms, is a supervisor's best defense against obsolescence.
4. The more formal education a person has, the greater his or her employability, promotability, and earnings become (on average).
5. Planning for personal advancement includes efforts aimed at determining strengths and weaknesses and at building a program for removing weaknesses.
6. Your career is largely in your hands and must be planned for.
7. A supervisor needs a personal method for thinking ethically in order to survive with integrity in any career.

Questions for Class Discussion

1. Can you define this chapter's key terms?
2. How can you avoid personal obsolescence?
3. What are the six steps this text recommends to help you plan for your own advancement?
4. What happens in each step?
5. What are the five steps this text recommends to help you plan your career?

6. What happens in each step?

7. Why do you think it is important for each person to have a personal method for thinking ethically?

Incident

Purpose: To help you determine your personal ethics.

Your Task: Answer honestly the following statements; think about your answers, and decide if you need to think about anything further.

	Agree	Disagree
1. I like to make decisions while considering their effects on others.	___	___
2. If an action I intend to take is legal, I feel it will also be ethical.	___	___
3. If I am not certain about the ethical implications of my actions, I like to talk it over with others.	___	___
4. If my decision will result in a personal gain at someone else's expense, it is unethical.	___	___
5. When I am asked to engage in an action that I believe is wrong, I let others know about it.	___	___
6. If I take an action and then feel badly about it, I believe I have probably committed an unethical act.	___	___
7. When I consider the fact that I am part of a community, I am starting to think ethically.	___	___
8. When I am faced with a decision that has nothing but negative consequences, I try to pick the alternative that has the least serious negative consequences.	___	___

Indecision

CASE PROBLEM 2.1

Juan Gonzales has been working as a bank teller in a small neighborhood bank since he graduated from high school about four years ago. Today, he has just learned that the promotion he was hoping for has fallen through. He lost out to a teller with higher seniority. Since Juan is planning to marry in a few months, he was counting heavily on a promotion and is very disappointed. "It was my chance to get away from customers," thought Juan, "to get away from the routine and to get into management." Juan thought back on the last four years. He has had nearly perfect performance appraisals and has been complimented by his boss on numerous occasions. He decided to have a talk with his boss, Mary.

Mary was pleased to explain the promotion decision to Juan. She told him that the woman who won the promotion had one year more service and excellent evaluations. But more important, she had completed two correspondence courses offered through the company's training department and had enrolled in a third. The courses gave her an edge and much-needed understanding about the things she would be doing in her new job. "With that kind of commitment to progress," said Mary, "the bank had to promote Susan. To do otherwise would be saying that additional education doesn't count for anything."

After work, Juan discussed his unhappiness with his friend, Pete. Although Juan and Pete are about the same age, Pete is already a supervisor of six people in a large savings and loan office two blocks away from Juan's bank.

"What's your secret, Pete? How come you got to management with only a high school education in the same time on the job that I have?"

"It's no secret, Juan. My office employs about twice as many people as your bank, and my office is just one of three in town. People move up faster in bigger organizations, and there are more jobs to bid for. I had my ears and eyes open, and when a promotion came along I bid for it. It took two tries, but I was in the right place at the right time."

"I think my best move would be to get a job at a bigger business and get out of banking. I haven't learned anything new in three years, and I'm getting to the point where I don't want to go to work in the morning."

"Before you make a move, Juan, make sure you know what you want. Remember, your experience is of more value to your present employer than to any other. It has an investment in you."

"All I know is that I don't want to be a teller the rest of my life. I need a change to a job that pays more money—and fast. I'm getting married soon, and my woman makes more than I do."

"You know, Juan, you aren't getting any younger. One difference between us is that I have found my interest. I love accounting and finance, and I'm getting a lot of good training. Next month, I'm enrolling in a night course for my first real look at college-level accounting. The company is paying my tuition and will pick up the tab for an entire college education if I can get that far."

Juan left the conversation with a sinking feeling in his stomach. He began to feel that he was going nowhere fast. On his way home, he stopped at the drug store to pick up a paper. "Maybe there are some jobs in town that pay more," he thought. "I'll start looking around tomorrow."

Questions

1. What career stage is Juan in now?
2. Do you think Juan is ready for a job change? Why or why not?
3. What advice do you have for Juan?
4. What differences exist between Juan and Pete?
5. Is Juan in danger of becoming obsolete? Why or why not?

Hazel's Choice

Hazel Martine is in her last semester at Rock Valley Community College in Virginia. On graduation, she will receive her two-year degree in marketing. At her college's career week, Hazel discovered four possible job opportunities and applied for all of them. She received two positive responses, interviewed for the jobs, and now has two offers for employment.

The first offer she received would require one year of job rotations, along with formal training in the company's management training program. The company is a well-known fast-food franchiser. It would require Hazel to move to at least three temporary residences in as many states during her first year on the job. Her duties would require her to work in at least three separate company-owned outlets. Following her first year's training, a nonmanagement job in advertising would be her first full-time job at the company's headquarters in New York. The company is vague about what the job would lead to in the future. As her interviewer put it, "It all depends on your performance, and on the availability of jobs for which you are qualified. I should tell you that the best jobs go to the holders of bachelor's degrees."

Her second offer is from a local, well-established advertising firm. The company is offering pay and benefits comparable to the first company's. Hazel would go to work immediately as a junior account executive, gaining familiarity with the agency's services and primary customers and seeing advertising campaigns through from start to finish. No travel would be involved. The company has well-established career paths in several areas and places more emphasis on experience than it does on formal education. If Hazel becomes an account executive, her earnings would comprise a salary plus a commission.

Questions

1. What do you think about Hazel's job search efforts?
2. What factors should Hazel consider before making her choice?

Notes

Arndt, Michael. "Study Finds College Costly, But Worth It," *Chicago Tribune*, July 22, 1994, sect. 1, 7.

Blanchard, Kenneth, and Peale, Norman Vincent. *The Power of Ethical Management* (New York: William Morrow, 1988), 27.

Bridges, William. "The End of the Job," *Fortune*, September 19, 1994, 62–64, 68, 72.

Business Week. "The New World of Work," October 17, 1994, 76–77, 80–81, 84–90.

Caggiano, Christopher. "What Do Workers Want?" *Inc.*, November 1992, 101.

Chicago Tribune. "Execs, Workers Clash Over Redefined Jobs," October 11, 1994, sect. 3, 3.

Franklin, Stephen. "Shifting Sands of Job Stability," *Chicago Tribune*, September 15, 1994, sect. 3, 12.

Furore, Kathleen. "Accentuate the Positive," *Chicago Tribune,* July 3, 1994, sect. 19, 2.

Hanson, Cynthia. "What It Takes to Succeed: Advice from 10 Top Achievers," *Chicago Tribune,* September 11, 1994, sect. 6, 9.

Imai, Masaaki. *Kaizen: The Key to Japan's Competitive Success* (New York: Random House, 1987).

Kiechell III, Walter. "A Manager's Career in the New Economy," *Fortune,* April 4, 1994, 68–72.

Kleiman, Carol. "Age Shifts, Computers Affect Job Shift," *Chicago Tribune,* October 2, 1994, sect. 8, l.

———. "Human Resources Gets Outside Help," *Chicago Tribune,* September 25, 1994, sect. 8, 1.

———. "Know Where Jobs Aren't," *Chicago Tribune,* October 9, 1994, sect. 8, 1.

———. "Praise Works Wonders in Improving Morale," September 21, 1994, sect. 6, 5.

———. "Study Shows that College Diploma is Worth Attaining," *Chicago Tribune,* August 1, 1994, sect. 6, 7.

Kruger, Pamela. "On-Line Openings," *Chicago Tribune,* October 17, 1994, sect. 6, 1, 17.

Peters, Tom. "Radical Restructuring to Gain Fresh Perspective Is Necessity," *Chicago Tribune,* October 10, 1994, sect. 4, 4.

———. *Thriving on Chaos* (New York: Alfred A. Knopf, 1987), 299–301, 329.

Richman, Louis. "The New Work Force Builds Itself," *Fortune,* June 27, 1994, 68–70, 74, 76.

Schor, Juliet. "Debunking the Small-Business Myth: Big Firms Still Dominate," *Working Woman,* November 1994, 16.

Solomon, Robert C., and Hanson, Kristine, R. *It's Good Business* (New York: Athenaeum, 1985).

Spencer, Jim. "Analyzing a Job," *Chicago Tribune,* March 18, 1987, 2.

Szabo, Joan. "Offering Careers, Not Just Jobs," *Nation's Business,* June 1994, 56.

Suggested Readings

Blanchard, Kenneth, and Peale, Norman Vincent. *The Power of Ethical Management.* New York: William Morrow, 1988.

Henderson, Verne E. *What's Ethical in Business?* New York: McGraw-Hill, 1992.

Kleiman, Carol. *The Career Coach.* Chicago: Dearborn Financial Publications, 1994.

Loden, Marilyn, and Rosener, Judy B. *Workforce America.* Homewood, Ill.: Business One Irwin.

Semler, Ricardo. *Maverick.* New York: Warner Books, 1993.

Solomon, Robert C., and Hanson, Kristine R. *It's Good Business.* New York: Athenaeum, 1985.

Webber, Ross. *Becoming a Courageous Manager: Overcoming Career Problems of New Managers.* Englewood Cliffs, N.J., 1991.

Management Concepts

OBJECTIVES

After reading and discussing this chapter, you should be able to do the following:

1. Define this chapter's key terms.

2. List and define the four essential elements of any formal organization.

3. List and explain the four steps involved in delegating.

4. Identify the three levels in the management hierarchy, and describe the activities of each.

5. Identify the four major functions performed by all managers.

6. List and explain the six steps in this chapter's decision-making model.

7. Specify the kinds of decisions that require your group's involvement.

8. Explain the value to supervisors of a daily planner and a time log.

INTRODUCTION

Everyone needs to be able to take charge of his or her own life. Each of us must be able to plan our daily activities, control our use of resources, interact with others to get jobs done, and accumulate the resources necessary to accomplish tasks and to reach our goals. Management is both an art and the application of known, proven principles. Through the practice of management, we become better people. All that we share together in this book will help make you a better manager of your finances, social relationships, family, and career and will promote your advancement in life.

DEFINING MANAGEMENT

Management is an activity that uses the functions of planning, organizing, directing, and controlling human, informational, and material resources for the purposes of setting and achieving stated goals. Management is also a team of people that oversees the activities of an enterprise in order to get its tasks and goals accomplished with and through others.

A **manager** is a member of a team of decision makers that gets things done with and through others by carrying out the four management functions or activities. Managers occupy positions of trust and power in a formal organization such as a business.

The term **formal organization** is used here to distinguish our concern from other types of organizations—for example, social or informal organizations. A formal organization is one put together by design and rational plan, such as a business or industrial union. A formal organization is basically the coming together of several people for the accomplishment of stated purposes. The necessary tasks to be performed are identified and divided among the participants. A framework for decisions and control is established.

The four essential elements of any formal organization are as follows:

1. A clear understanding about stated purposes and goals
2. A division of labor among specialists
3. A rational organization or design
4. A hierarchy of authority and accountability

Each of these elements is related to the others. We will look at each of them separately in order to understand all of them better.

Stated Purposes and Goals

Every business enterprise is established to make a profit. How each organization intends to make its profit is stated in its **mission.** The mission

management
the process of planning, organizing, directing, and controlling human, material, and informational resources for the purposes of setting and achieving stated goals; also, a team of people making up an organization's hierarchy

manager
a member of an organization's hierarchy who is paid to make decisions; one who gets things done with and through others, through the execution of the basic management functions

formal organization
an enterprise that has clearly stated goals, a division of labor among specialists, a rational design, and a hierarchy of authority and accountability

mission
the expression in words—backed up with both plans and actions—of the organization's central and common purpose—its reason for existing

states in words—backed up with both plans and actions—the organization's central and common purpose—its reason for existing. It acts as a unifying force, giving all personnel a common purpose and direction. To create a proper mission, two things are needed by top management: a recognition of what the organization does best—its core competencies—and a continuing focus on the future. According to professors and consultants Gary Hamel and C. K. Prahalad (1994), "Our experience suggests that to develop a...distinctive point of view about the future, a senior management team must be willing to spend 20% to 50% of its time over a period of months. It must then be willing to continually revisit that point of view, elaborating and adjusting it as the future unfolds." Both individuals and teams in all parts of the organization need their own mission as well. "A common, meaningful purpose sets the tone and gives teams direction, momentum, and commitment.... A real team needs both a common purpose and specific goals" (Katzenbach, 1992).

Each day, an organization's managers must ask two basic questions: What is our business? What should it be? As time progresses and circumstances change, an organizations' managers must continually reassess where they are and where they want to be. The new challenges and opportunities that occur each day and are likely to occur must be sensed and taken advantage of. This often leads to a redefinition of a mission through top management's statement of its **vision** that outlines where the company wants to go and what it wants to be in the future—how it proposes to change itself. The organization's chief executive establishes a vision for the entire organization. Specific goals and plans for their achievement are set by top management. With these in mind, managers of each division and department establish for themselves both short- and long-range goals and plans required for them to do their parts in achieving the vision. When asked for his vision for Chrysler, chief executive Robert J. Eaton, responded (Taylor III, 1992):

vision
the statement of what kind of company the organization wants to be in the future

> I see us as a full-line manufacturer with more emphasis on niche areas than other carmakers...vehicles from subcompact through large...sport utilities, vans, convertibles, et cetera. I want us to be the premier U.S. auto company with outstanding products, quality, cost, and customer satisfaction and with the necessary return for the shareholder.

A Division of Labor Among Specialists

We live in a world of specialists. In government, the professions, and business, men and women are asked to choose areas in which to specialize so that they can become experts in their fields. Any formal organization is set up to make good use of the special talents and abilities of its people. Each person is assigned tasks that he or she is best qualified to complete

A team of supervisors meets to discuss goals for their firm. After agreeing on their overall goals, each supervisor must decide how his or her own workers will be utilized to meet the goals.

through the application of specialized knowledge. Through the coordination and teaming of these specialists—each of whom contributes a part to the whole job—the entire work of the organization is planned and then carried out.

In many of today's businesses, specialization is achieved by grouping individual experts into cross-functional teams that take ownership of a project or a process—such as designing a new product or improving customer billing. The goals are to save time and money through both incremental (kaizen) and radical (reengineering) change.

A Rational Organization or Design

Formal business organizations must have designs that properly facilitate their missions and activities. It must be tailored to provide for the proper flow of needed information to all individuals, teams, and units. It must allow for the coordination and oversight of essential operations. Above all, it must be flexible enough to met new challenges and opportunities. Chapter 4 has more to say about organizing.

A Hierarchy of Authority and Accountability

hierarchy
the group of people picked to staff an organization's positions of formal authority—its management positions

The term **hierarchy** refers to the number of levels in an organization and the group of people (managers) who are picked to occupy those levels and make all the necessary plans and decisions that allow it to function. Men and women (as both individuals and in teams) possessing the abilities required are installed at different levels throughout the organization. These people constitute the organization's management team. From the chief executive to team facilitators and team leaders, they must plan, organize, direct, and control the many activities that have to take place if the organization's goals are to be reached.

Authority

Authority is the right to give orders and instructions to others and to use organizational resources. Every manager needs authority in order to mobilize resources required to accomplish tasks. Authority allows team facilitators and team leaders to make a decision or take action that affects the organization and its associates. All managers have the authority of their offices or positions. This kind of authority is often called positional or formal authority because it resides in a job or position and is there to be used by the person who holds that job or position.

authority
a person's right to give orders and instructions to others and to use organizational resources

Formal or positional authority is usually described in a formal written document, called a job description, that outlines the specific duties that the position holder is expected to execute. Managers' job descriptions usually give them the right to assign work to subordinates or team members, to oversee the execution of work, to appraise subordinates' and team members' performances, to use various kinds of capital equipment, and to spend specific amounts of budgeted funds. As a supervisor, team facilitator, or team leader, you must act within the limits of your authority and avoid interfering with others' use of theirs.

Giving instructions and having them carried out in a satisfactory way are two different things. Have you ever wondered why two managers with the same authority often get very different results? The essential difference between such managers is their ability to influence others.

Power

Power is the ability to influence others so that they will respond favorably to the orders and instructions they receive. Two managers may have the same authority but not the same power over others. One may be effective, and the other ineffective.

power
the ability to influence others so that they respond favorably to orders and instructions

There are several sources of power. In general, power comes to a person through his or her position (formal job description), personality traits and character (attractiveness to others), knowledge and experience base (expertise), and relationships with other powerful people. Power that flows to a manager from the position held is called legitimate or position power. It consists of the right to punish and reward—sometimes called coercive power. Your attractiveness to others is the basis for friendship and professional relationships. It is usually referred to as your charisma.

Your influence over others because of what you know and are capable of doing is called expert power. Finally, you have influence over others because they see you as a person who is well connected—a person with powerful associates.

All sources of power are important to you if you want to be a truly effective manager. Authority alone is not enough. You must be the kind of person others respect and want to follow. Authority and power make a manager a leader—a person others willingly follow. Chapter 10 has more to say on leadership and power.

Responsibility

responsibility
the obligation each person with authority has to execute his or her duties to the best of his or her abilities

Responsibility is the name given to each employee's obligation to execute all duties to the best of his or her ability. Because all employees have the authority of their job descriptions, they all have responsibility. The concept of responsibility tells us not only that we must perform our duties but also that we must do so in line with the instructions and limits we receive from above. Failure to do our best may bring punishment, denial of rewards, and separation from our jobs.

Accountability

accountability
having to answer to someone for your performance or failure to perform to standards

Accountability is having to answer to someone (your superior or teammates) for your actions or failure to act. Suppose you have a job description that assigns you the duty to prepare a monthly report on the output of your department. Administrative routine dictates that this report be delivered to your boss on the first day of each month. Your authority is in your job description. Your task is the report. Your responsibility is to do the report properly to the best of your ability and to deliver it to your boss by the start of each month. If you begin the report but fail to finish it by the due date, you will have to answer for that failure to your boss. You will have to give an accounting of your progress and accept the credit or the blame. All employees in any organization have duties and, therefore, authority, responsibility, and accountability.

DELEGATION

delegation
the act of passing formal or positional authority by a manager to another

Delegation is the act of passing one's authority, in part or in total, to another. Only people possessing authority over others, such as managers, team leaders, and team facilitators, can delegate. When you accept a duty through delegation from your boss, you accept new authority and the responsibility for it, and you agree to be held accountable for your performance of the new duty. When you as a supervisor delegate authority, you agree to be held accountable for your decision to delegate (the way you have chosen to handle your responsibility) and for the execution of the delegated duty by your subordinate. The act of delegation, therefore, creates a duality of both responsibility and accountability related to the same task or duty and its execution. If this were not so, any manager could pass a tough job to a subordinate and escape from it entirely, with no adverse consequences. But the concept of accountability tells us that giving a task away is a way in which a manager has chosen to execute a task—the way the manager has chosen to handle responsibility for the task. That decision must be answered for.

Consider this example. Suppose you are going away from your job next Tuesday for personal business. You have one task that must be executed during your absence, and you decide to delegate it to a subordinate. You take your day off. When you return, you discover that the task was not performed. Your boss will want to know why, and you will be asked to answer for the failure to execute the task. You, in turn, will want to know what went wrong and why. Both you and your subordinate are accountable for the ways in which you chose to handle responsibility for the same task. But you, as supervisor, shoulder the primary burden of accountability in the eyes of your boss.

Why You Must Delegate

Delegation is a tool that allows you to train team members and associates. By introducing your most capable subordinates to bits and pieces of your job, you get them ready to advance. Unless you have a trained successor to fill your shoes, it will be very hard for you to get promoted. Your boss will not want to create a hole in the operations by letting you move up if it means leaving behind a leaderless group.

Second, by delegating, you can free yourself from time-consuming routines and other duties that might be better performed by subordinates. Until you create some free time for yourself, you will not be able to accept delegation from your boss. Like yourself, your boss wants to meet your need to grow by letting you experience greater responsibilities, thus grooming you for promotion.

Third, delegating empowers your associates. For the majority of people, empowerment adds interest, challenges, and opportunities for growth. By empowering your people, you are making a clear statement about your trust and faith in them. You are helping improve your operations by tapping into their uniqueness and creativity. You will also be aiding their search for job satisfaction by giving them more say and control over their activities and decisions.

Some managers fear the delegation process because they do not want to give up any of their authority. They fear that a subordinate cannot do the job as well as they can or that they will lose control over the execution of their authority once it is in the hands of another. They may fear that once subordinates know their bosses' jobs, they will be a threat to their job security. But fearing the act of delegation is no excuse for not doing it. You

SUPERVISORS AND ETHICS

Juanita Alvarez is a relatively new supervisor at Furman & Associates, a management consulting firm. She was promoted because of her expertise in computer programming—she was considered the best of seven department members—and is now overseeing the work of six former co-workers.

Juanita prides herself on her continuing efforts to stay current in her field, believing that maintaining her expertise is the best way to influence her associates. She is reluctant to delegate high-profile jobs to her associates because she fears they will not be able to do them as well as she can. She is afraid of the consequences that can result from a job poorly done, especially on projects assigned by top management.

Her subordinates are all young, well trained (by Juanita's predecessor), and eager to grow in their fields. All are specialists to some extent, but most recognize that they need a wide variety of programming experiences in order to advance their pay and careers. When asked by her associates for a role in the tougher assignments, Juanita usually turns them down. When asked for assistance on a project, she prefers to give her associates only as much as she feels they need to complete a project.

What are the ethical issues for Juanita and her associates? If you were her boss, what advice would you have for her?

must recognize that you will have no other choice. Your boss expects it, subordinates may demand it, and you will be away from your job at times because of illness and vacations. Keep in mind that delegation frees you from any task that your subordinates can do, helps you identify the subordinates that you can depend on, and lets you spend more of your time on things that only you can do or that you do best. This chapter's Supervisors and Ethics feature deals with delegation.

How to Delegate

Four basic steps are involved in the decision to pass some of your authority to another person:

1. Decide on the task(s), limits, and supports. Spell out in as much detail as is necessary exactly what you want your associate to do, the limits that you are placing on the execution, and the supports you have to offer. (You want Sarah to collate a report, but you do not want her to

staple the pages together or to deliver them to anyone but yourself. You want the task done by the close of business today. You will be available throughout the day in your office if Sarah needs help.)

2. Choose the subordinate. The person you choose may be one in need of the experience, one who is capable of doing the job already, or one who wants exposure to the task. You may want to choose more than one person so that several people get the training or exposure. This will give your people more flexibility and will allow you to be less dependent on any one person.

3. Give the assignment. Let the person know what you want done, the limits, and the supports. You may want to put everything in writing. This is a good idea if you will be away while the person is accomplishing the task. It is also recommended that you tell the person why he or she was picked to do the job. Be honest. Explain why the task is necessary and the kind of results you expect. Ask the subordinate for feedback. Find out if there are any misunderstandings. When the subordinate can restate the assignment and limits accurately and knows how to perform the task(s), you are ready for step four.

4. Stay in touch. Even so-called simple tasks are not so simple when an inexperienced person has to perform them. Keep track of the person's progress by checking with him or her periodically. You may ask for periodic reports of progress if the task is to stretch over several days or weeks.

Part of delegating is making sure your subordinate understands the job. Although you may delegate the work, you are still accountable for its outcome.

When the task is accomplished, let the subordinate know how you evaluate his or her efforts. You may want to reward the person with praise and point out what went well and what could be improved.

What You Do Not Want to Delegate

In general, you should not delegate a task that you do not understand or know how to perform. If you do, you will be unable to offer any support when trouble arises, and you may not be able to evaluate the results fairly. As a supervisor, you should not delegate the authority to punish or reward. People work to please those who have this authority. Delegation should never strip you of these rights and duties. Finally, if you have no one who is capable of taking on the task, you must either get someone ready to take it or keep the task for yourself.

THE MANAGEMENT HIERARCHY

We have concluded that, among other things, managers make up a team of decision makers charged with operating the formal organization of a business. You will recall that one of the characteristics of a formal organization is that it has a hierarchy of authority and accountability. We will now examine this hierarchy.

The simple pyramid shown in Exhibit 3.1 is a basic model for a management hierarchy. In most organizations, this pyramid is divided into three levels: top management, middle management, and the supervisory or operating level of management. As depicted in the exhibit, both the top and bottom levels are rather thin compared to the middle level. This pyramid is typical of a traditional structure often found in government and large organizations in stable industries and stable competitive environments. Companies in other industries and environments will need a different, more flexible structure. We discuss organizational structures in detail in Chapter 4.

Many sole proprietorships and partnerships have only one or two managers who must, out of necessity, direct more than one specialized area. Most sole proprietorships and partnerships are extremely small in terms of both the number of people they employ and the dollars they earn and spend. They cannot afford, nor are their operations complex enough,

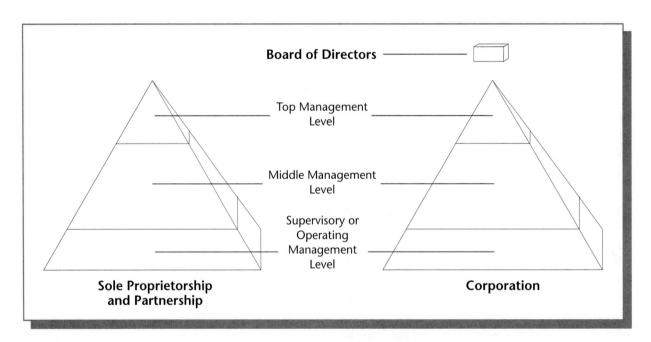

EXHIBIT 3.1
The pyramid of the management hierarchy.

to demand more than one or two levels of management. Managers in small organizations often execute their own plans and direct their own efforts because they lack subordinates or associates.

The examination that follows uses a business corporation as its model. Much of the discussion applies to sole proprietorships and partnerships. Two exceptions: A corporation is the only type of business organization to have a board of directors and to include a secretary (a corporate officer) as a member of its top management.

The Board of Directors

Outside and above the corporate management pyramid is the board of directors, which is represented graphically in the second pyramid in Exhibit 3.1. The board members, who are elected by the stockholders or owners of the corporation, elect their own chairperson. The directors have jurisdiction over the actions of the chief executive of the corporation. They review the major decisions of the chief executive. The board helps decide what the company's business is and what it should be. It formulates company policy—general guidelines for management action at every level when dealing with recurring situations—picks the chief executive, and diagnoses and recommends treatment for business ills in the absence of recommendations from the chief executive. In short, the board of directors is a watchdog for the owners' interests and a tough court of review before which the chief executive's case is tried. The majority of a board's members are full-time executives working for other unrelated and noncompeting companies or industries.

Only in a crisis does the board depart from its role of judge and adopt an executive approach. It may give orders to remove or replace the chief executive in order to bring the firm through a period of difficulties. Only at such rare times can the board function as the top management of the corporation. When the crisis ends, the board quickly returns to its judicial role.

The Top Management Level

Occupying only the small topmost portion of the pyramid, the **top management** level is the location of the chief executive or president and his or her immediate subordinates (vice-presidents or their equivalents). In a sole proprietorship, the owner is usually the chief executive. In a partnership, the role of the chief executive is usually shared between or among the managing partners, each of whom concentrates on his or her own specialty.

In a corporation, the top management is made up of the officers of the company: a president, one or more vice-presidents, a treasurer, and a secretary. Any two (or more) offices may be held by the same person, except the offices of secretary and president.

top management
the uppermost part of the management hierarchy, containing the positions of the chief executive and his or her immediate subordinates

SUPERVISING TEAMS

Many companies have found and are finding that the jobs of chief executive officer (CEO) and board chairperson are just too complex for any one person to handle alone. In today's international business environment, changes come much more swiftly, and decisions must be made more rapidly. Tasks that used to be done sequentially are now being done simultaneously. In 1992, Microsoft, Xerox, and Nordstrom—the retail firm—split their top jobs and created teams at the top.

Xerox now has a corporate headquarters in Connecticut with six top executives. Instead of one chairman and one president, the company now has an executive team headed by Paul Allaire, three operations executives, one head of corporate research and technology, and one head of corporate strategic services.

The old structure slowed decisions and development of products, giving competitors an edge. The new structure eliminates these defects.

At Nordstrom's headquarters in Seattle, three Nordstrom family members share the chairperson's job, and four managers share the presidency (three men and one woman). Long-term strategy is the concern of the chairperson's committee. Day-to-day management is the concern of the four co-presidents. "Like the co-chairmen, the presidents have plenty of spirited, candid debate, they say. They contend that they resolve most disagreements by focusing on what would be best for the customer.... What we have is respect for one another. We have a system where one [person] can veto anything...[we] leave our egos at the doorstep."

Sources: Hwang, Suein L. "Xerox Forms New Structure for Businesses," *The Wall Street Journal,* February 2, 1992, B6; Yang, Dori Jones. "Nordstrom's Gang of Four," *Business Week,* June 15, 1992, 122–123.

The Chief Executive's Role   The chief executive officer (CEO) has several major responsibilities. He or she must articulate a mission, vision, core values (quality, integrity, and employee participation, for example), and guiding principles for the entire company. This chapter's Supervisors and Quality feature highlights Ford Motor Company's mission, values, and guiding principles. These become part of Ford's corporate climate and must govern the actions of its team leaders, facilitators, and associates.

The CEO must also sense when change is called for and initiate the change. Stanley C. Gault, when he became CEO at Rubbermaid, "[I]mmediately reorganized...by centralizing functions like purchasing (to gain economies of scale) and by divesting weak operations. Then he sped up product development, making the company a fountain of new wares" (Nulty, 1994). By continually focusing on the future and reexamining organizational strengths and weaknesses, the CEO is able to develop and initiate major organizational objectives and strategies (grow the company by adding new products, increase market share by cutting costs). The chief executive is the one manager who must be able to observe and comprehend the entire operation. Like the captain of a ship, the chief executive is responsible for his or her own decisions and is accountable for those of all other managers.

The Vice-President's Role   Vice-presidents are the immediate subordinates of the chief executive. In a typical bureaucratic–mechanistic organization, they are charged with the overall operation of the company's functional areas:

- Marketing—sales and all sales-connected activities
- Production—manufacturing and procurement of raw materials
- Finance—managing the company's funds and credit through accounting
- Human resource management—staffing duties

Other business activities, such as engineering, research and development, and purchasing may fall under one or another of these headings, or they may be led by their own specialized members of top management. Further, many companies combine this functional approach with other approaches such as organizing by product or customer groupings. In many companies, vice-presidents are in charge of strategic business units (SBUs). These are often autonomous and organized around product groups or customers served. Such is the case at IBM, Ford, and Xerox.

The vice-presidents must plan, organize, direct, and control the general operation of their departments, units, or divisions so as to achieve their (as well as their company's) stated objectives. Their subordinates are usually middle managers.

The Secretary's Role   The corporate secretary has the following duties:

1. To keep the minutes of the meetings of the stockholders and the board of directors
2. To keep all stock ownership records
3. To act as the custodian of the corporate records and of the corporate seal, which is affixed to all corporate shares and documents as a proof that they are official acts of the company

The corporate secretary may also serve the company in another capacity, such as finance manager, personnel manager, or some other executive position. The job of corporate secretary is seldom a full-time position.

SUPERVISORS AND QUALITY

F ord Motor Company's mission, values, and guiding principles.

Mission

...to improve continually our products and services to meet our customers' needs, allowing us to prosper as a business and to provide a reasonable return for our stockholders, the owners of our business.

Values

How we accomplish our mission is as important as our mission itself. Fundamental to success for the company are three basic values:

- People—Our people are the source of our strength. They provide our corporate intelligence and determine our reputation and vitality. Involvement and teamwork are our core human values.

- Products—Our products are the end result of our efforts, and they should be the best in serving customers worldwide. As our products are viewed, so are we viewed.

- Profits—Profits are the ultimate measure of how efficiently we provide customers with the best products for their needs. Profits are required to survive and grow.

Guiding Principles

- Quality comes first. To achieve customer satisfaction, the quality of our products and service must be our number-one priority.

- Customers are the focus of everything we do. We must strive for excellence in everything we do: in our products, in their safety and value—and in our services, our human relations, our competitiveness, and our profitability.

- Employee involvement is our way of life. We are a team. We must treat each other with trust and respect.

- Dealers and suppliers are our partners. The company must maintain mutually beneficial relationships with dealers, suppliers, and our other business associates.

- Integrity is never compromised. The conduct of our company worldwide must be pursued in a manner that is socially responsible and commands respect for its integrity and for its positive contributions to society. Our doors are open to men and women alike, without discrimination and without regard to ethnic origin or personal beliefs.

How will each of these affect Ford's team leaders' approaches to (1) communicating with associates, (2) making team decisions, and (3) coordinating their operations with other teams?

Source: Peterson, Donald E., and Hillkirk, John. *A Better Idea: Redefining the Way Americans Work* (Boston: Houghton Mifflin, 1991), 13.

The Treasurer's Role   The treasurer has the following duties:

1. To accept charge of, custody of, and responsibility for all funds and securities of the corporation, receiving and depositing all moneys due and payable to the corporation
2. To control all disbursements of company funds
3. To prepare all financial statements, such as the balance sheet and the profit-and-loss statement

The treasurer is either the chief financial officer of a corporation or a member of that staff.

The Middle Management Level

Occupying the middle area of the pyramid, the **middle management** level is the location of all managers below the rank of vice-president and above the operating level. Each functional area has many specific tasks to be performed. Exhibit 3.2 illustrates the hierarchy of a retailer with branch stores. The store's divisional merchandise and branch store managers are not specialists, but all of their subordinate managers are. Each must carry out the operation of a specific part of the store's activities. Like those of all managers, the middle manager's functions are to plan, direct, control, and organize.

middle management
the members of the hierarchy below the rank of top management but above the rank of supervisor

The Operating Management Level

Shown at the bottom of the management pyramid, the **operating management** level is the home for supervisors and foremen. Both direct the work of nonmanagement employees, individually or in teams, called **workers.** If a manager directs the work of other managers, he or she does not belong on this level.

    The supervisor is evolving into a team leader and team facilitator, aiding the efforts of the group he or she heads. Typically, both assist teams by providing the training and support needed by team members. The position of team leader may even rotate on a regular basis, allowing each member of the team who wants to gain experience as a manager to get it. The management of Taco Bell outlets requires team facilitators who earn pay that is connected to the sales and customer satisfaction scores of their outlets. "Today many Taco Bell outlets operate with no manager on the premises. Self-directed teams...manage inventory, schedule work, order supplies, and train new employees [called] crew members.... Regional managers [team facilitators]...are now business school graduates who oversee as many as 30 [restaurant crews]" (Henkoff, 1994). More will be said about the team leaders and team facilitators throughout this text.
    Exhibit 3.1 depicts only the management team. The majority of workers in an organization form the base of the pyramid, the group of people

operating management
the level of the hierarchy that oversees the work of nonmanagement people (workers)

worker
any employee who is not a member of the management hierarchy

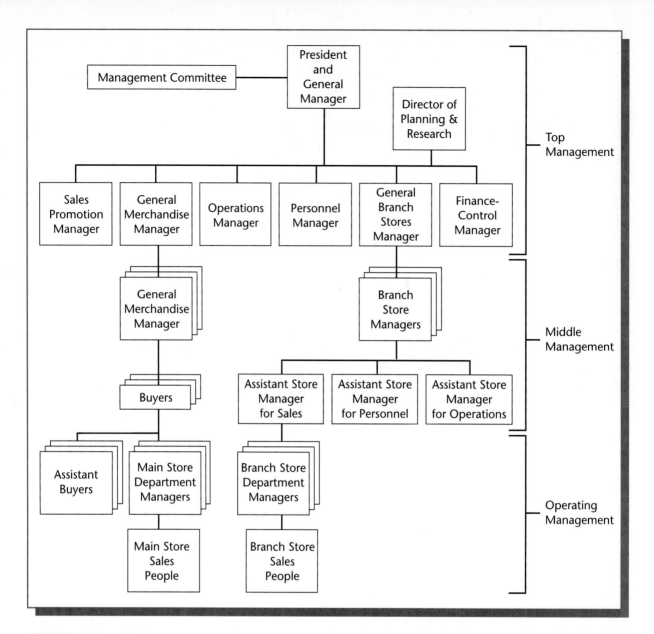

EXHIBIT 3.2

A retail organization showing the three levels of management.
Note: Only the merchandise manager's and the branch store manager's subordinates are shown.

Source: Courtesy of the National Retail Merchants Association, New York, N.Y.

on which managers depend to execute plans and to achieve goals. Exhibit 3.3 shows the complete picture of a typical business corporation.

LINE AND STAFF AUTHORITY

Line authority allows its holder—a traditional manager, team leader, team facilitator—to exercise direct supervision over his or her subordinates. Managers who have line authority can give direct orders to, appraise, reward, and discipline those who receive their orders.

The managers in the organization hierarchy who manage activities or departments that directly influence the success (profitability) of a business

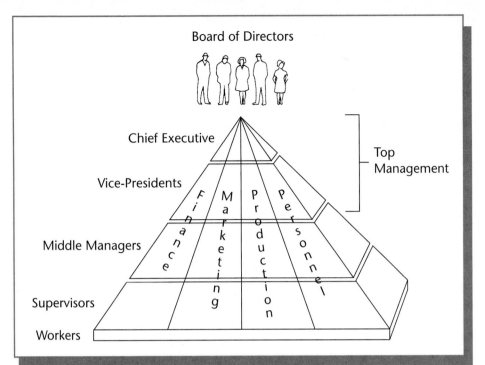

EXHIBIT 3.3
*A corporation's manage-
ment pyramid showing
the functional areas and
the base of workers.*

are called line managers. Their departments make direct contributions toward achieving the company's goals. Since line activities are identified in terms of the company's goals, the activities classified as line will differ with each organization. For example, a manufacturing company may limit line functions to production and marketing, whereas a department store, in which buying is a key element, will include the purchasing department and the sales department in its line activities (Stoner, 1982).

When an organization is small, all positions may be line roles; staff roles are added as the organization grows and as it becomes useful to devote specialists' time to assist the line members in doing their primary jobs.

Staff authority, like line authority, is a kind of formal authority. It is distributed throughout the organization to various managers at any level who advise and assist other managers. Staff managers are specialists who supervise activities or departments that help others achieve the company's major goals. The staff managers' primary mission is to support all other managers who need their specialized knowledge.

The concept of staff is relevant only as applied to the relationships between and among managers. A manager is a staff manager if his or her job is to advise, counsel, assist, or provide service to another manager. You can tell if managers are staff or line managers by observing what their relationships are to the other managers.

Since staff managers are linked to the top of an organization, they receive line authority also. If they have subordinates, they direct, appraise, and discipline those subordinates, just as any line manager does

line authority
a manager's right to give direct orders to subordinates and appraise, reward, and discipline those who receive those orders

staff authority
the right of staff managers to give advice and counsel to all other managers in an organization in the areas of their expertise

with his or her subordinates. When staff managers direct the work of their associates, they are using line authority. But when staff managers give advice or assistance to other managers, they are acting as only staff managers can act.

Exhibit 3.4 is an abbreviated organization chart of a management hierarchy that shows both line and staff positions, as well as the relationships of authority. Note that staff and line managers appear at both the top and the middle of the hierarchy. The broken lines show advisory relationships. The solid lines show the flow of line authority.

Organization charts are just one of several tools used to show the part that each person or section plays in the entire enterprise. They should show the following things:

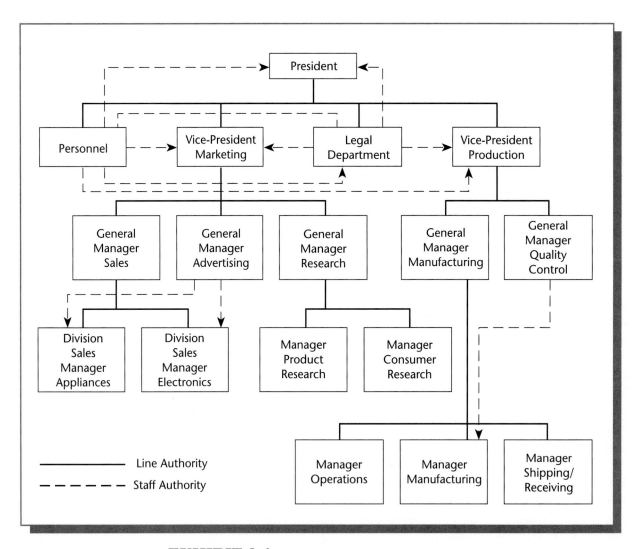

EXHIBIT 3.4
Organization chart showing four staff positions and the flow of both line and staff authority.

- Who reports to whom
- The flow of authority and accountability
- Formal positions of authority and their titles
- Lines of communication
- Lines of promotion

FUNCTIONAL AUTHORITY

Functional authority is the right given to a manager of a department (usually a staff department) to make decisions that govern the operation of another department. Exhibit 3.5 illustrates the flow of functional authority from the staff managers to the other managers in an organization. The lines

functional authority
the right that a manager of a staff department has to make decisions and to give orders that affect the way things are done in another department

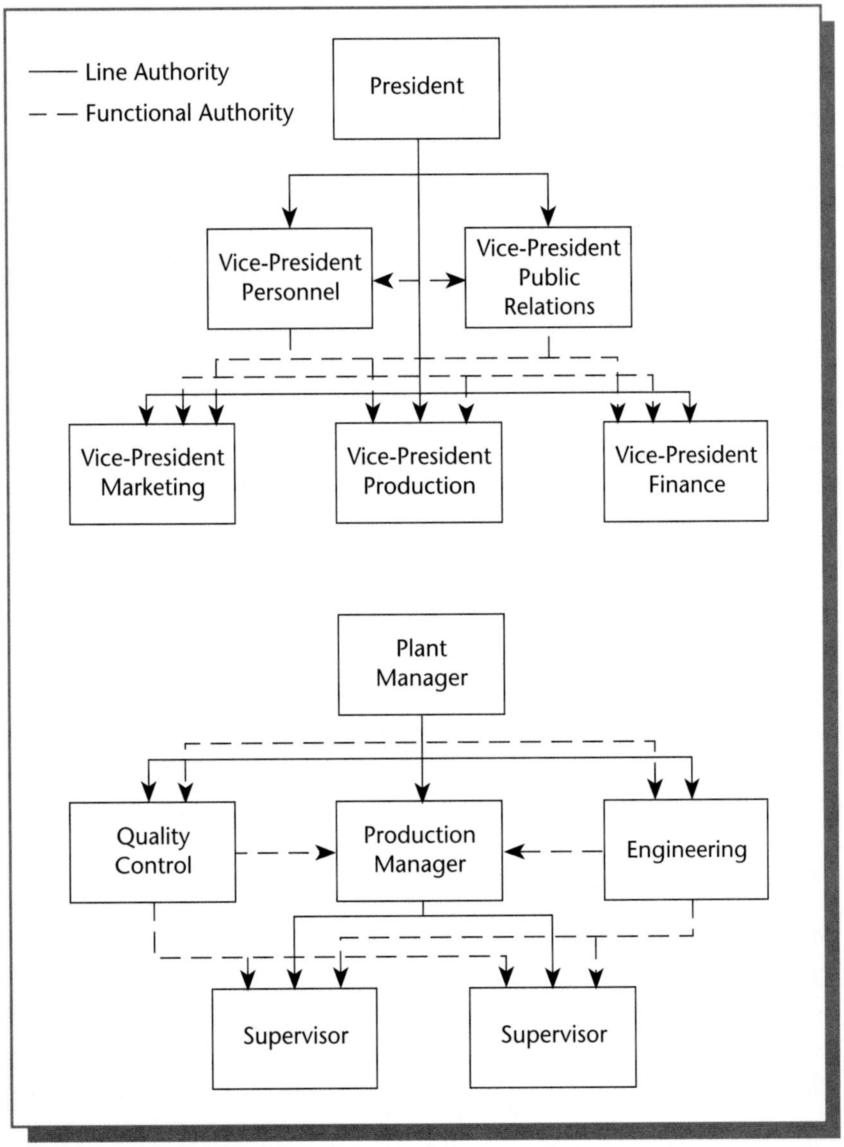

EXHIBIT 3.5
The flow of functional staff and line authority in a manufacturing business.

of functional authority indicate a measure of control by a staff manager over a line manager and his or her people and their activities.

The normal practice (where functional authority is not used) is for a line manager to have complete control over his or her area of responsibility and relative freedom to make his or her own decisions. Staff managers have been installed to help the line as well as other staff managers, but usually only when called on to do so. It is as though the line managers are saying, "Don't call us, we'll call you." Under this arrangement, a staff manager may never be consulted. Line managers must take full responsibility for their actions when acting on staff advice. After all, they could have ignored the advice of the staff manager.

For this and other reasons, many companies make use of the concept of functional authority. This concept holds that if a staff manager makes a decision about his or her area that has application to the area of another manager, the manager of that other area is bound by the staff manager's decision. For example, the payroll department issues a directive stating that henceforth all payroll data from each department must be submitted on a specific form, in a specified way, and by a certain date. If the managers throughout the business wish to get themselves and their people paid on time and in the correct amounts, they had better follow the directive.

Functional authority seems to give a manager many bosses. But does it? Isn't a company merely removing many important, but not essential, areas from a manager's concern in order to promote uniformity and efficiency? When many routine decisions about problem areas are made outside the department, each manager is freed of the responsibility to consider these matters. As a result, the manager has more time to devote to his or her specialized, essential tasks. What is lost in autonomy is more than compensated for by an increase in efficiency and economy in the overall operation of the business.

THE MANAGER'S FUNCTIONS

We will now briefly explore the four major functions of management. By major functions we mean the most important and time-consuming activities common to all managers. These functions consist of planning, organizing, directing, and controlling.

Planning

Planning is the first and most basic of the management functions. Through planning, managers attempt to prepare for and forecast future events. Planning involves the construction of programs for action designed to achieve stated goals through the use of people and other resources. Planning is also a part of the other functions of management: organizing, directing, and controlling. It is the first thing you must do before executing any of these functions.

Organizing

The organizing function determines the tasks to be performed, the jobs or positions required to execute the tasks, and the resources needed to accomplish the tasks and to reach the organization's goals. Organizing is directly related to and dependent on planning.

Directing

The directing function includes the activities of overseeing, facilitating, coaching, training, evaluating, disciplining, rewarding, and staffing. Staffing is concerned with adding new talent to an organization, promoting or transferring people to new jobs and responsibilities, and separating people from the organization. Chapter 11 discusses the supervisor's staffing duties.

Controlling

The controlling function is concerned with preventing, identifying, and correcting deficiencies in all phases of an organization's operations. Through controlling, standards of performance are established, communicated to those affected by them, and used to measure the operations and performances of individuals and the entire organization.

These four functions apply to all managers, but each level of management spends different amounts of time performing each (see Exhibit 3.6). Although top management spends most of its time on planning,

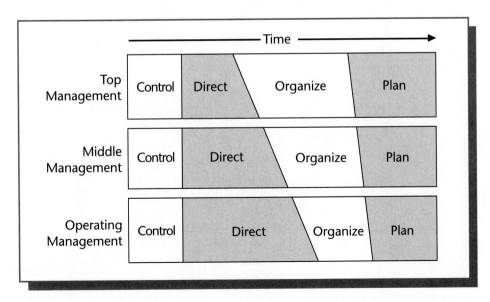

EXHIBIT 3.6
The proportions of time spent on the management functions by the three management levels.

supervisors (operating management) spend most of their time on directing. Chapter 4 explores these functions in more detail from the supervisor's perspective.

Related to the four major management functions are three other sets of activities that are part of each. It is impossible to consider any of the functions without recognizing the need to communicate. *Communicating* (the subject of Chapter 5) is the ability to get your ideas across to others by means of the spoken or written word. It is also impossible to carry out your duties without interacting with others. This fact tells us that a second set of activities is needed to coordinate what you do with others in your organization. By *coordinating*, teams and team members attempt to prevent interference with others. Before, during, and after taking action, you need to promote harmony and mutual cooperation in order to keep your human relationships in good order and to prevent the waste of resources. By keeping in regular communication with subordinates, peers, and superiors, you aid your efforts at coordination. Finally, *decision making* is part of every function as well. Chapter 4 examines coordinating and all four management functions in more detail.

DECISION MAKING

You have been making decisions all of your life. You have already made many today. As a supervisor, team facilitator, and team leader, you are paid to make them to the best of your ability. As we have already seen, you have

Decision making is an important time to involve subordinates. Ask for their opinions. When explaining the decision, take the time to explain why the decision was made.

a responsibility to make them and are accountable for the results. A decision in its most essential form is a conclusion that you reach by making judgments. A decision usually begins in the mind in the form of a question such as "What will I have for lunch?" This question leads to others, such as "What am I in the mood for?" Past experiences and desires come to mind. Different foods are considered, along with certain restraints that may exist, such as the amount of money and time we have available for lunch and the kinds of restaurants we enjoy. Our minds deal quickly with such variables and restraints, and we reach a decision quite easily. In fact, such a decision may already be made for us because some of us are creatures of habit and routine: We eat at the same place so regularly that we don't give it much thought; we just find ourselves at the same place each lunchtime.

What goes on in our minds in deciding where and what to eat for lunch leads us to a process for making decisions. Most of us have a process, but we may never have put it in writing. It's simply there in our minds and serves us each time we try to answer questions and make a decision. What follows is one approach that can help you make difficult decisions rationally. This approach will remove a great deal of uncertainty and will give you a method for problem solving that will help you avoid making many bad or mediocre decisions.

A Rational Model

The rational model in Exhibit 3.7 has six steps. None of them is really new to you, but all are essential and basically easy to take. They simply put what you have been doing all of your life into a systematic framework that will help you make better decisions. We will work through the steps by using an example.

1. *Define the problem.* A problem exists when what you are facing is not as you wish it to be or as it should be. Symptoms are usually the first signs of a problem. Your toaster keeps burning your bread or your television's channels are all snowy.

   Ed, the supervisor of data control, has noticed several computer operators sitting idle and the central computer out of operation. All should be operating. What is the problem? Lazy workers? Broken machines? Without further investigation, Ed will not be certain. He first talks with the operators to discover the source of their idleness. His investigation tells him that a necessary set of figures from the accounting department has not arrived on schedule and that work on the report can progress no further without the figures. What is the problem now? Missing data from accounting? Ed calls the accounting supervisor and discovers that the data were sent over two hours ago. Ed conducts a search and discovers the data on his desk, buried under items that arrived later.

EXHIBIT 3.7

Steps in the rational decision-making process.

1. Define the problem. (The effort here is to define the difference between what is and what should be. Avoid the pitfall of defining symptoms, and go beyond them to their causes.)
2. Identify your restraints. (Your restraints are such resources as time, money, and talent. Anything that limits your abilities to solve a problem as you would like is a restraint.)
3. List your alternatives. (Alternatives are possible solutions. List as many as you can without regard for their good and bad points. Involve the ideas of others if they can be of assistance.)
4. Evaluate your alternatives. (Go back to step two and consider each alternative with your restraints in mind. List the advantages and disadvantages of each course of action.)
5. Decide on the best alternative(s). (Pick one or a combination of two or more that have the fewest serious disadvantages and the most important advantages.)
6. Implement the decision and follow up. (This is the action step that tries out your solution. Learn from the application, and be prepared to fall back to another solution if the one you have chosen does not give positive results.)

Ed started with symptoms and moved to an investigation that led him to the discovery that vital information was getting lost in his own department on his own desk. This discovery tells Ed that his problem is related to the way in which information from outside his office is received and filed. Ed now frames the problem as a question: "How can information flowing to us from the outside be properly handled to avoid losing it?" Having defined his problem, Ed is now ready to proceed to step two.

2. ***Identify your restraints.*** Restraints are limiting factors that affect your efforts to make a decision. Restraints generally fall under several headings, such as who, what, when, and where. Who will be involved in the decision-making process? Is it a decision that needs the group's support and input? If so, the group must be involved in the process. "Who" also asks us to consider who is affected by the problem and whether or not the affected people have a role to play in solving it. What is involved? What resources may be affected and may have to be committed in order to make and implement the decision? Money, time, and other resources will surely be involved in some way. When must a solution be delivered? By what date must a decision be made? Finally, where is the solution needed and best implemented?

Ed has decided that he must make the decision and that the others will simply be informed about it and their parts in it after they give him their ideas about handling the problem. Ed has further decided that few resources will be needed. Time is the primary resource he and others must expend to make a decision. Ed thinks that the "when" is best answered with "as soon as possible" and assigns the highest priority to dealing with the problem. Ed believes the "where" is his office, with its routines and paperwork flow. Ed is now ready for step three.

3. *List your alternatives.* Alternatives are the courses of action that you believe will solve your problem. Alternatives should be developed without criticism, as they are offered and listed. Their merits and drawbacks can be dealt with in step four. In developing your list, be as creative as you can, and seek counsel wherever you think an idea might reside. All of your alternatives should represent possible ways to correct the difficulties you are experiencing.

Ed consulted his workforce, and over a period of several hours, put together a list of four solutions:
   a. Do nothing since this is the first time the problem has occurred. Ed should merely check his desk more often.
   b. Have all incoming work delivered directly to Ed.
   c. In Ed's absence, have all work delivered to his secretary.
   d. Set up a special location for incoming work at the entrance to the office, with a clearly labeled sign directing delivery persons to deposit their items at the designated location.

Ed is now ready to evaluate his alternatives.

4. *Evaluate your alternatives.* This step asks you to look critically at your listed alternatives and to focus on their relative merits and disadvantages. In doing so, you must consider the restraints you have labeled in step two. For some merits and disadvantages, you may wish to assign a relative point value to give either a higher or a lower importance to each.

Ed evaluates his first alternative as follows: The problem is new but could recur. It resulted from the fact that through habit, people have always delivered their items to Ed's desk, not to Ed. Ed checks his desk regularly, but there are blocks of time when he finds it impossible to get back to his office. For this reason, the first alternative (a) is rejected.

Ed realizes that the remaining three alternatives require cooperation from the delivery person in other departments if they are to work. All three would prevent the problem from recurring. The last alternative (d) is advantageous in that no person from his department need be present for the system to work. However, its major disadvantage is that all personnel in Ed's section, Ed himself, or Ed's secretary would have to check the new location regularly for their work instead of getting it directly from Ed as in the past. The major disadvantage to the second and third alternatives (b and c) is that a person must be present. If Ed and his secretary were absent, work would be dropped on a desk, as in the past. The current problem might then recur. Ed is now ready to move to step five.

5. ***Decide on the best alternative(s).*** At this step, the best alternative or combination of alternatives is chosen. The relative merits and disadvantages of each are considered, and the alternative offering the fewest serious disadvantages and the most merits is chosen. Keep in mind that after deciding and implementing, you may find that the problem still persists or that a new problem has arisen. Your efforts will then have to be reexamined and other methods tried. For this reason, you may want to set up a contingency plan and be ready to implement it if necessary.

   Ed has decided to go with his fourth alternative (d). It overcomes what Ed feels is the biggest disadvantage of the other two alternatives: The physical presence of either himself or his secretary is required for them to work. Even though he will have to get outsiders broken in to the new routine, Ed feels that they will cooperate with little opposition. It will take a visit or two from each of them to get them used to the new routine.

6. ***Implement the decision and follow up.*** Without implementation, a decision just sits there and helps no one. Everyone involved in the decision must be informed in advance of their individual roles and responsibilities. They must know what is expected of them, what is new and different, and when things are to change. In addition, they must be committed to their roles in the solution if it is to reap the best results. After the decision is enacted, the results must be monitored.

   Ed has contacted the heads of the various departments that supply his work and has been assured that the new procedure will be made known to delivery persons. Ed has instructed his people to accept no work personally but to direct the delivery to the specially marked area and its receptacles. Both Ed and his secretary will make it a habit to check the delivery area regularly and to distribute the work found there to the proper persons. Ed sets the time when the new procedure will be implemented and arranges to monitor the results.

Common Elements in Decision Making

Most supervisors are new to formal decision making. Before you become a member of management's team, you have specific goals and orders, resources provided by your boss, and a problem solver represented by the boss. You may or may not be consulted when decisions have to be made. But once you become a manager, you soon realize the need to consult with others before, during, and after the period when a decision is made.

Most decisions share the following common elements (Uris, 1986):

- A situation that demands action
- Time pressures created by things getting steadily worse

- Incomplete information
- Some uncertainties that force you to take some risk
- The likelihood of costly consequences if your decision is wrong
- The likelihood of benefits from an effective decision
- The existence of at least two alternatives

Given these elements, you have to gather what input you can from whatever sources are available in the time allotted for your decision. Keep in mind that others may have been down this path before you. Your boss, your peers, and your associates may have the experience and ideas that you lack. Use whatever help you can to avoid as many traps as possible. Your aim is to make the best decision you can given the resources and restraints that exist.

Sharing Decisions

You should involve members of your work group in a decision if they have valuable input to give, if they are going to have to implement it, and if their commitment to the decision is essential to make it work. The decisions you can make alone or without the approval of members of your work group are ones that you can implement alone with satisfactory results. Exhibit 3.8 offers some additional insights into when to involve others in your decisions. Chapter 9 looks in detail at decision making with groups.

1. If time permits discussion and analysis; that is, if you don't have to have the decision immediately.
2. If the decision affects the personal or business lives of the employee(s); at least their input and feedback will help you make a mutually acceptable decision.
3. If the problem you have stems from the behavior of another person, and only that person's corrective action will solve your problem.
4. If you accept final responsibility for a decision that has been given to you and not to the others, but collective discussion would yield a better solution than simply mulling it over on your own.
5. If responsibility for the decision can be shared by the group with no one person's being held liable if a decision that seems right turns out not to work after all.
6. If data available to others are not available to you, or if their expertise will help you solve the problem.
7. If implementation requires group commitment and effort.

EXHIBIT 3.8
When to involve others in decisions that you have to make.

Decisions About Valuing Diversity

Most of us work in a culturally diverse workforce. To prosper in a culturally diverse workforce, you must prepare yourself by valuing your own uniqueness and the diversity in others. Valuing diversity, according to the people who created the term—Copeland Griggs Productions—"means recognizing and appreciating that individuals are different, that diversity is an advantage if it is valued and well managed, and that diversity is not to be simply tolerated but encouraged, supported, and nurtured" (Jamieson, 1991). "Levi-Strauss spends $5 million each year on its valuing diversity educational programs. In 1992, 56 percent of its 23,000 U.S. employees belonged to minority groups.... It supports in-house networking groups of blacks, Hispanics, lesbians, and gay men. A Diversity Council, made up of two members of every group, regularly meets with Levi's executive committee on raising awareness of diversity issues" (Cuneo, 1993).

Here are four guidelines to help you with your efforts to value diversity:

1. Know yourself and your own cultural background. Identify any preconceived notions you hold about others, where they came from, and how they effect your efforts at interactions with others who are different from yourself.
2. Work to identify the negative stereotypes—inflexible sets of beliefs about groups of people, usually obtained through the hearsay of others rather than gained through your own experiences. Once identified, work to release yourself from the constraints they place on your thinking and interactions with others.
3. Get to know your associates at work as individuals. Learn from them about their cultures—their values, customs, and traditions. Attend workshops and seminars on cultural diversity. Read all that you can on the topic. Note the differences as well as the similarities that exist between your culture and those of others with whom you work.
4. Avoid being judgmental. Approach each person as an individual, and seek an understanding of what they value and why. If you are uncertain about how to approach someone, ask him or her how best to do so. In everyday matters, the new golden rule is simply, treat people as they want to be treated. As a team facilitator and team leader, your job is to get the most from all of your associates and team members.

MANAGING YOUR TIME

We all have the same amount of time in each day. The differences between us are in how we use that time. Studies have indicated that most of us waste time on the job through a variety of means. We may make or accept personal phone calls. We may regularly stretch breaks by several minutes. We may fail to plan our work, reacting to things as they come, without giving the work to be done a timetable or priorities. If you often find yourself working late, taking work home, and rushing to meet deadlines, you have a time management problem. People who use time well have enough time for their tasks, are able to train, can take on additional duties, and have time for themselves. Using time well gives us a sense of pride, whereas wasting it gives us a sense of guilt and frustration.

A good way to improve your use of time is to start keeping records of how you use your time at present. Keep a record of your use of time at work by stopping each hour (or after each task is completed) to record how much time you have spent and what you have spent it on. This tactic will let you know very quickly at the end of each day where you wasted time and where you used it productively.

Time Logs

Exhibit 3.9 is one example of a daily time log. It provides an easy way for you to list the activities you perform each day, to record the time each activity took, and to classify each activity as a regular, recurring one or as one that is unexpected and unusual. The regular activities routinely make up a part of each working day: evaluating associates, planning your work schedule, attending planned-for meetings, and preparing regular reports. The unexpected activities include unscheduled visitors (drop-ins), unexpected telephone calls, and crises—problems that have arisen but could not have been foreseen. After a few days, some interesting patterns will emerge. You will have a clear understanding of how you are using time, and you will then be ready to start planning in a realistic way for using it more efficiently.

By dividing your work into categories, you can more effectively execute tasks and assign priorities to them. For example, consider the pile of work on your desk each morning. There is work left over from preceding days, the mail, memos and work generated by others, and various notes that you have left for yourself. Divide this work into three categories: read—file or discard, to be delegated, and must do. The material, when first read, will fall into one of these categories. Memos sent to keep you informed fall into the first category. Work you want others to act on falls into the second. Work only you can do falls into the third. Take the work to be assigned to others, and determine a due date for it based on when it must be completed. Assess your third category from two points of view: how much time each task will take and by what date it must be completed. Then block out the time you will need on your calendar, working ahead as time allows and planning early completions where possible.

Eliminating Interruptions

Your time log will list the unnecessary interruptions that have taken place. The next step is to consider what to do about them. For most supervisors,

REGULAR ACTIVITIES								
Time Spent with Others	Mon	Tue	Wed	Thur	Fri	Sat	Sun	TOTALS
1. Evaluating/praising/disciplining								
2. Attending scheduled meetings								
3. Training/coaching								
4. Making telephone calls								
5. Meals and breaks								
6. Other (specify) _____								
_____								
Time Spent Alone								
1. Reading memos, letters, reports								
2. Preparing reports and correspondence								
3. Planning and scheduling work								
4. Efforts at self-development								
5. Travel time to and from scheduled events								
6. Other (specify) _____								
_____								
UNEXPECTED ACTIVITIES								
1. Receiving telephone calls								
2. Communicating with drop-ins								
3. Attending last-minute meetings								
4. Dealing with unexpected problems								
5. Other (specify) _____								
_____								
Totals								

EXHIBIT 3.9
Daily time log.

(Use this log to keep track of how you spend your time at work, away from work, or both. Use multiples of five-minute intervals and keep track in minutes.)

unexpected phone calls are among the most frequent sources of interruption, second only to unplanned-for visitors who drop by to shoot the breeze or seek your assistance. If you have a secretary, let him or her screen your calls. Calls can be classified as deal with now, I'll get back to you, or leave your message. Ask people to leave brief memos in writing or on your voice mail or e-mail instead of using the telephone. Drop-ins can be asked, courteously, to book an appointment, at a mutually acceptable time and place, so that you will have enough time to deal with their concerns. Social visits can wait for breaks and lunch.

Daily Planners

Exhibit 3.10 is an example of a daily planner that you can use to start getting your use of time at work under control. At the beginning of each year, record the major recurring weekly, monthly, quarterly, and semiannual

EXHIBIT 3.10
Daily planner.

MY OBJECTIVES FOR TODAY: Date:

1. _____

2. _____

3. _____

4. _____

5. _____

ACTIVITIES (who, what, when, where, how)	Starting Time	Ending Time
1.		
2.		
3.		
4.		
10.		

RESULTS:

_____

_____

What to carry over to tomorrow:

_____

_____

_____

(Start by listing your major objectives for the day, in the order in which you wish to accomplish them. Under the Activities section, list the specific tasks you need to perform to reach your objectives and the estimated starting and ending times for each. Complete the Results portion at the end of the day.)

events—regularly scheduled meetings, due dates for projects, deadlines for reports—on the days they occur each month. When you take on any duty with a due date, record that date and then work backward: Mark reminders periodically between then and now to keep yourself conscious of that due date and duty. At the end of each workday, list your objectives for the next—the specific goals or results you hope to have achieved by the end of that day. List them in the order in which you plan to accomplish them, listing things that must be done as your first priority. In the activities section, list the specific tasks, people, events, and other resources required to execute your tasks. At the end of each week, review what you have accomplished, consider the lessons learned about scheduling, and focus on the week ahead. Regard your planner as a living document. You can add to or change your objectives and activities throughout the day as time and circumstances dictate.

Various computer software packages exist that can help you manage your time. Personal information managers (PIMs) offer a variety of features, such as automatic scheduling of appointments, sorting lists, establishing priorities, printing calendars, and reminding you of duties with beeps or on-screen displays. Team facilitators and team leaders should find ManagePro 2.0 for Windows particularly useful since it allows for networking by team members. In Control 3.0 (designed for use on Apple computers) and Lotus's Organizer are other PIMs you may want to consider using.

By using your planners and reviewing them each day, you will learn how realistic your planning of time and activities has been and how you can make it more accurate in the future. When reviewing your daily planner, ask yourself the following questions:

- Did I accomplish all that I expected to? If not, why not?
- Were my time estimates realistic? If not, why not?
- What did I learn about time planning that I can use tomorrow?

It won't be too long before you are blocking out time in your head, as well as on paper, and making better use of it. Then you can eliminate the log and become a regular user of the standard desktop calendar and the appropriate business software.

Using Spare Time

Use your previously unproductive time productively. Time spent traveling to and from work in your car or on a train can be used to catch up on essential, work-related tapes or reading. You can make notes with a notepad and pen, on a portable tape recorder, or with a personal digital assistant (PDA). PDAs allow you to actually write on a handheld computer and offer such conveniences as a pager, address book, fax, and phone. Capture and store your good ideas as they occur. Time spent in an office waiting room can be used productively by simply taking work with you. By doing these things, you will become more accomplished and will look good to others as well as to yourself.

Instant Replay

1. Management is an activity that uses the functions of planning, organizing, directing, and controlling human and material resources for the purpose of achieving stated goals.
2. Management is a team of people that rationally oversees the activities of an enterprise and attempts to get its tasks and goals accomplished with and through others.

3. A manager is a member of a team of paid decision makers that gets things done with and through others by executing the four management functions. Managers occupy positions of formal authority in an organization.

4. Managers work for formal organizations that have clearly stated purposes and goals, a division of labor among specialists, a rational organization or design, and a clearly defined hierarchy of authority and accountability.

5. A person's job description outlines the authority he or she possesses to mobilize the organization's resources.

6. Power flows to a person from two sources: the job he or she holds and the skills, experience, and personality he or she possesses.

7. Authority can be delegated. Responsibility and accountability cannot be delegated.

8. Your decisions should be made with the aid of a rationally prepared decision-making model so that you can consider your alternatives carefully and avoid problems.

9. The management hierarchy consists of three levels inherent in most businesses: top, middle, and supervisory or operating.

10. To be most effective, staff managers may exercise functional authority over many other managers.

11. Managing time is as important as managing a career to a supervisor. Time, like other resources, must be used effectively and efficiently.

Questions for Class Discussion

1. Can you define this chapter's key terms?
2. What are the four essential elements of any formal organization and the definitions of each?
3. What are the four steps you should take when using delegation?
4. What are the three levels of the management hierarchy and the activities performed by each?
5. What are the major functions performed by all managers?
6. What are the six steps in this chapter's decision-making model, and what happens in each?
7. In general, what kinds of decisions require the involvement of your subordinates?
8. How can you use a time log and a daily planner to help you improve your use of time?

Incident

Purpose: To assess the need for diversity training in your organization.

Your Task: Take the following quiz by agreeing or disagreeing, based on your own experiences, with each statement:

1. There is a high turnover among diverse groups. ___   ___
2. There is a lack of diversity at all levels of the ___   ___
   company's hierarchy.
3. Some associates feel isolated from their peers ___   ___
   because of their diversity.
4. One or more diverse groups are the subject of ___   ___
   inappropriate behavior and ridicule.
5. Diversity is not reflected in those with powerful ___   ___
   positions.
6. The company seems to be demanding that diverse ___   ___
   individuals conform to the dominant culture.
7. No programs currently exist that encourage ___   ___
   people to share and celebrate their differences.
8. There have been/are charges of discrimination. ___   ___

CASE PROBLEM 13.1

Who's Responsible?

Ms. Charles, president of SeraRamics, Inc., picked up her phone and dialed 74. Sam Deadwood, vice-president of product development, answered.

"Deadwood here."

"Sam," said Charles, "I have to give a status report to the board of directors in ten days on our new line of housewares. Can you prepare a report filling me in on the details as to when we intend to test-market it and where?"

"You bet, Ms. Charles, I'll put my best man on it right away. You should have the report by the eighteenth, the day before the meeting with the board."

Deadwood pressed his intercom switch.

"Ellsworth here," it crackled.

"Bill, Charles just called and wants a status report on our new line of housewares. She needs the details of the test-market plans. Put together all the details in a report, and give it to my secretary, Betty, to type. Charles needs it by the eighteenth."

"Can do, Mr. Deadwood." Bill Ellsworth walked over to Al Farley's desk. He explained the project to Farley and told him to get the report to Betty by the seventeenth for final typing.

Farley prepared all the data, laid it out in rough form, and took the report to Betty's desk on the morning of the seventeenth. Betty was not there, so he left it in her in-basket.

On the morning of the nineteenth, Charles called Deadwood. "Sam, where is that report you promised me on the housewares line? I'm due at the board meeting in an hour."

"I gave the assignment to Ellsworth, Ms. Charles. I'll check it out right away."

After some hasty phone conversations and checking, the report was discovered on Betty's desk, still untyped. Ms. Charles had to give her report to the board from the rough draft.

Betty had taken a three-day leave of absence on the sixteenth for a family emergency. She was not due back until the nineteenth.

Questions

1. Who is responsible?
2. Who is accountable?
3. How could this situation have been avoided?

Quality Controlled?

CASE PROBLEM 3.2

Juan Avilar was quite upset as he entered Jack Bailey's office on Friday morning. Juan had once again been overruled by Jack's quality control people and in front of his men on the first shift.

"Jack, I've had it with your pushy so-called quality control people. Each time they check my line, they make changes with my people, and I'm the last to know it."

"Easy, Juan," Jack said. "Sit down and tell me all the details."

"I've been over this with you before, and you told me that your people would work with me. Twice this week they have stopped my line and told my people to make changes without seeing me first. Then this morning, while I'm helping Thompson with some routine maintenance, your Silly Sally starts to chew me out in front of my people."

"Just one minute, Juan. If Sally had words with you, I can't believe she would be abusive. I saw her this morning and got her point of view. According to her version, your people were ignoring a change that even you had agreed to about a week ago. She was only reminding you of that agreement, and she wanted to know why the change hadn't been made. Sally tells me that you were the one who was doing the chewing out, not her."

"Sure, go ahead, take her side. I don't know why I expected you'd listen to me. I just want to know who runs my shift—you and your people, or me."

"Juan, you know what the old man said about production and quality control. My people inspect your output at several stages along the line. They're the first to spot trouble, and they must have the power to stop defects."

"Look, Jack, let's get this settled now or I'm going to quit. I know that your people look for defects in my shift's output. I also know that my people aren't stupid. They don't turn out defects on purpose. Nobody wants to make parts that are wrong. All I'm asking is that you stick to the agreement I thought we had. You promised that our people would work through me, not around me."

"That is precisely what Sally was trying to do this morning, from what I can see. She went to you on the line because that's where you were. She asked you about the change that had not been made, and that's when, according to her, you blew your top."

"Ok, forget about this morning. What about the other two instances this week when your people ordered changes made and I was not consulted? My people told me, after they made the changes, that they had been told to do so by QC. Can't you see what that does to my authority?"

"If my people didn't see you first, it was because you weren't around. What do you expect them to do? Should they let defects go on while they try to hunt you down? And how come you are the only shift manager who can't get along with quality control?"

Questions

1. Do Jack's people have functional authority? Why or why not?
2. What should quality control people do when the shift foreman is absent and defects appear?
3. How could this situation have been avoided?
4. Who do you think should be responsible for quality control?

Notes

Cuneo, Alice. "Diversity by Design," *Business Week,* January 19, 1993, 72.

Hamel, Gary, and Prahalad, C. K. "Seeing the Future First," *Fortune,* September 5, 1994, 64, 66–67, 70.

Henkoff, Ronald. "Service Is Everybody's Business," *Fortune,* June 27, 1994, 48–50, 52, 56, 60.

Jamieson, David, and O'Mara, Julie. *Managing Workforce 2000* (San Francisco: Jossey-Bass, 1991), 186–187.

Katzenbach, Jon. "The Right Kind of Teamwork," *The Wall Street Journal,* November 9, 1992, A10.

Nulty, Peter. "The National Business Hall of Fame," *Fortune,* April 4, 1994, 120.

Stoner, James A. F. *Management,* (Englewood Cliffs, N.J.: Prentice Hall, 1982), 310.

Taylor III, Alex. "Chrysler's Next Boss Speaks," *Fortune,* July 27, 1992, 83.

Uris, Auren. *The Executive Deskbook,* 2d ed. (New York: Van Nostrand Reinhold, 1986), 66.

Suggested Readings

Blank, Renee, and Slipp, Sandra. *Voices of Diversity.* New York: Amacom, 1994.

Ellis, Donald G., and Fisher, Aubrey B. *Small Group Decision Making.* New York: McGraw-Hill, 1994.

Gardenswartz, Lee, and Rowe, Anita. *The Managing Diversity Survival Guide.* New York: Irwin, 1994.

Jackson, Terence. *Cross Cultural Management.* Woburn, Mass.: Butterworth-Heinemann, 1994.

Jamieson, David, and O'Mara, Julie. *Managing Workforce 2000.* San Francisco: Jossey-Bass, 1991.

Leigh, Andrew, and Maynard, Michael. *ACE Teams: Creating Star Performance in Business.* Woburn, Mass.: Butterworth-Heinmann, 1993.

Plunkett, Warren, and Attner, Raymond. *Introduction to Management.* Belmont, Calif.: Wadsworth, 1994.

Weiss, W. H. *Decision Making for First-Time Managers.* New York: Amacom, 1985.

Management Functions

OBJECTIVES

After reading and discussing this chapter, you should be able to do the following:

1. Define this chapter's key terms.

2. List and briefly explain the five steps in the planning process.

3. List and briefly define the six principles of organizing.

4. List and briefly explain the five steps in the organizing process.

5. Contrast the bureaucratic/mechanistic organization to the organic organization.

6. List and briefly explain the specific activities that are part of directing.

7. List and briefly explain the five essential steps in the control process.

8. List and briefly describe the three kinds of controls used by managers.

9. Describe five ways in which a supervisor can coordinate his or her operations.

INTRODUCTION

As we stated and briefly defined in Chapter 3, the four major functions of a manager are planning, organizing, directing, and controlling. These represent the major sets of activities performed daily by all managers and autonomous teams. In this chapter, we examine these functions in detail with an emphasis on how you as a supervisor, team facilitator, or team leader can execute each. Planning prepares for the future, whereas organizing establishes a structure through which the decisions you and your people make can be carried out. Directing and controlling put resources and decisions into action and monitor people and processes as well as their results.

Chapter 3 also mentioned three other sets of activities—decision making, communicating, and coordinating—that are part of every manager's and team's daily routines. Chapter 3 presented decision making, Chapter 5 looks at communicating, and this chapter discusses coordinating. All activities are part of the four major functions. You do them, simultaneously, as you perform each.

Although our analysis treats each function separately, keep in mind that all the functions are interrelated and interdependent. For example, planning is at the heart of the other functions; you must think ahead, set objectives, and determine needed resources as the first step in planning, organizing, directing, and controlling.

PLANNING

planning
the management function through which managers decide what they want to achieve and how they are going to do the achieving

You must first decide where you want to go and what you want to achieve before you commit any of your resources to the journey or the quest. **Planning** is the management activity through which managers decide what they want to or must achieve and how they are going to do so. The goals to be achieved may be set by individual managers or teams, or they may be set for them by higher-level managers and teams. Exhibit 4.1 outlines the flow and parts of planning in a formal organization. We will examine each of these parts next.

EXHIBIT 4.1
The flow and parts of planning in a formal organization.

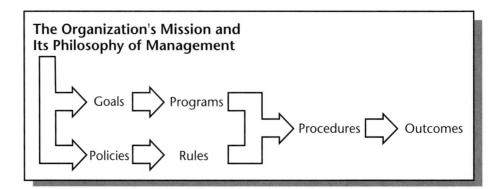

At the Twin Cities Assembly Plant, employee expertise played a major role in the quality of the Splash, a version of the Ford Ranger. Before production began, engineering and manufacturing teams met with truck engineers to find better ways to assemble the Splash. Such teamwork is consistent with Ford's philosophy that "Quality is Job 1."

Philosophy of Management

The ways in which the management of a company thinks about and acts toward people and events that have an effect on or are affected by the business are known as its philosophy of management. An organization's management philosophy is largely determined by the attitudes, values, and guiding principles held by the managers with the most influence—usually top management. It results in general and usually predictable approaches to executing each of the management functions. All managers have a philosophy that affects their thinking and behaviors. Exhibit 4.2 highlights guiding principles formulated by a team facilitator, Frank Pacetta, when he managed Xerox's sales teams at its Cleveland, Ohio, district. Note the emphasis on employees, teamwork, customers, and quality. Says Pacetta, "A statement of principles is a handy guide and summary of where you intend to take your district. I distribute it to all my people, post it in prominent places, and periodically flash it up on the screen if I'm making a pre-

EXHIBIT 4.2
Frank Pacetta's guiding principles at Xerox.

Source: Frank Pacetta with Roger Gittines. *Don't Fire Them, Fire Them Up.* (New York: Simon & Schuster, 1994), p. 114. © by Frank Pacetta, 1994.

- We will achieve the business plan.
- We will satisfy our customer requirements.
- We will treat everyone with honesty, equity, dignity, and respect.
- We will implement and practice the quality process.
- We will establish and maintain high expectations and recognize performance.
- We will lead by example.

- We will all practice teamwork.
- We will strive for open communication.
- We will adhere to Xerox business policies/ethics.
- We will encourage career development.
- We will strive to have representation of minorities in all facets of the business.
- We will all participate in keeping our work environment professional and maintain respect for company property.

sentation with slides and overhead projections" (Pacetta and Gittines, 1994).

Like Pacetta, you have a personal philosophy of management. You have developed, through your experiences, predictable patterns of behavior that are based on your attitudes toward people, your job, your company environment, and your perception of your roles in your company. Your individual ways of approaching people, problems, and events make you unique as a person and as a manager. Your philosophy colors all of your judgments and, therefore, your decisions and their results.

Our values and beliefs about various individuals and groups whose backgrounds are different from our own form our philosophies and affect our ways of thinking about and interacting with them. The major categories through which people differ from one another (or have affiliation with others) are:

- Race—the result of inheritance
- Ethnicity—the result of upbringing
- Languages mastered
- Gender
- Sexual orientation
- Place of birth—native born or immigrant
- Age—young, middle aged, older, or elderly
- Physical characteristics—height, weight, able bodied, physically challenged
- Education earned
- Religious affiliation and beliefs
- Mental characteristics—able or mentally challenged

Equal employment opportunity laws, business practices, and America's population mix bring diversity to the workplace. The job of team leaders and team facilitators then becomes one of creating pluralism—allowing each person to maintain his or her identity and then finding ways to celebrate and effectively utilize the uniqueness of each person.

Mission and Vision Statements

As we mentioned in Chapter 3, every organization needs a mission: The formal statement about the central purpose behind its existence—its reason for being. The corporate vision is the articulation by top management of where the organization is headed and what it wants to commit its resources to achieve, both for the short and long run.

Once these statements have been constructed, all the people in the organization must know about them and subscribe to them. Before you and your associates engage in any activities, make certain that what you plan to do conforms with your organization's vision and mission.

Goals

The objectives that managers decide to work to achieve are known as their **goals.** A typical goal for a company might be to reduce expenses by 10 percent over the next two months. This companywide goal must be translated into divisional, departmental, team, and individual goals with the help of managers at every level. As goals are being formulated, the resources that may be needed to achieve them should be determined. There is little point in setting goals that are beyond the capabilities of a company, group, or individual to achieve.

As a supervisor, many of your and your teams' goals are determined for you by higher levels of management; other goals you set must not contradict those set by higher levels. Your goals determine the parts you and your associates will play in achieving upper management's goals. In addition, your goals (which may require your team members' approval and commitment) must be coordinated with the goals set in other areas of the company to avoid duplication of effort. Once your goals have been determined, they should be precisely stated, communicated, and kept constantly in mind by all concerned until they are achieved.

Two goals you must constantly focus on are to improve quality and productivity. A case in point relates to the quality and productivity achieved by auto industry suppliers. Anderson Consulting, based in Chicago, studied seventy-one parts suppliers "in nine countries [and] found that only 13 were considered world class in terms of quality and productivity and only 3 of the 13 were U.S. based" (Mateja, 1994). According to Anderson Consulting, it is not enough for an auto company to worry only about its suppliers' quality and productivity. It also must be concerned with the quality and productivity of its suppliers' suppliers. The study found that U.S. suppliers averaged 263 defective parts per million but that *their* suppliers produced defects more than seven times that rate. Many manufacturers such as Ford are now working with both groups of suppliers to help them improve their quality and productivity (Mateja, 1994).

goal
the objective, target, or end result expected from the execution of programs, tasks, and activities

Policies

The broad guidelines for management action that have been formulated by members of the top management are known as **policies.** They are based on top managers' philosophies, the company's mission and vision, and attempt to coordinate and promote uniformity in the conduct of the business and in the behavior of associates. In a corporation, the board of directors, usually based on the CEO's recommendations, formulates policies. Policies tell managers what top management wants to encourage or what it hopes to work toward achieving such as promoting diversity and empowerment.

policy
a broad guideline constructed by top management to influence managers' approaches to solving problems and dealing with recurring situations

"Xerox, Johnson & Johnson, and MCI are all noted for their efforts to promote diversity of background and thought among their workers. Nike, Microsoft, and Federal Express [FedEx] are well known for pushing authority down through the ranks and allowing employees plenty of input when it comes to running the business.... Others are learning to give ethnic minorities, homosexuals, and women protection and respect out of a late 20th century defensiveness: In an ever more litigious society, they fear being sued (Mitchell and Oneal, 1994)."

Policies affect your role as a supervisor because you must act within their limits when carrying out your duties. For instance, if your company policy on recruiting and hiring reads like Exhibit 4.3, you had better consider all applicants equally and seek a wide diversity in applicants before you decide to hire.

Rules

rule
a regulation on human conduct at work

Inflexible guides for the behavior of employees at work are known as the company **rules.** They are specific directions that govern the way people should act on the job. Many are prohibitions such as no smoking while on the job or in certain locations; others are simply instructions such as "turn lights off when they are not in use." Rules promote safety and security; they attempt to conserve resources and to prevent problems from arising during the company's operations.

Most rules that govern your area of operations are common to other areas as well. Some may be up to you, as a team facilitator or team leader, or your teams to set. For example, the issue of smoking at work may be handled with a companywide ban on the practice or left up to individual, self-contained work units and teams to deal with. If you have a union to work with, specific work rules will come from the labor agreement. Examples of such rules include break schedules and the assignment of

EXHIBIT 4.3
An antidiscrimination policy.

> There shall be no discrimination for or against any applicant or for or against any current employee because of his or her race, creed, color, national origin, sex, sexual orientation, marital status, age, or handicap or membership or lawful participation in the activities of any organization or union or because of his or her refusal to join or participate in the activities of any organization or union. Moreover, the company shall adhere to an affirmative action program with each functional division's concern with hiring, promotions, transfers, and other ongoing human resource activities.

specific penalties for specific offenses. What's more, various local, state, and federal laws determine rules for the workplace. Such is the case with the Occupational Safety and Health Act discussed in Chapter 16. It is the source of many rules related to both safe and healthful conduct at work.

Programs

Once goals are established for each department or for the entire organization, plans must be developed to achieve them. A **program** is such a plan. It starts with the goal to be achieved (the "what" of the plan); identifies the tasks required; and specifies the who, when, where, how, and how much that are needed. The required people, time allowed, methods to be employed, and dollars that are allotted are all pieces of a program. Most programs are single-use plans. Your budget is but one example. It is created to guide you for a specific period and is replaced by a new one when its time frame expires. Other programs, called standing plans, deal with ongoing activities such as hiring, payroll preparation, and customer service. These must be periodically evaluated and revised as circumstances dictate.

program
a plan listing goals and containing the answers to the who, what, when, where, how, and how much of the plan

Procedures

Procedures are the "how" in programs. They are the ways or methods chosen to carry out the tasks that a person or group must perform to reach a goal. Like programs, some procedures are single use, whereas others are ongoing. New programs may call for the creation of new procedures. Some procedures within your department are left to you and your associates to create and change as necessary. But before you change a procedure, consider who is and will be affected; consult with them before you make the change. The people closest to a task or problem are often the best source of information about it. Exhibit 4.4 shows a company's procedure for handling travel expenses reimbursement.

procedure
a general routine or method for executing day-to-day operations

1. Complete operations form EX-1.
2. Attach receipts for the following expenses:
   - lodging
   - meals (not to exceed $25 per day)
   - transportation (out of pocket only)
3. Have completed form EX-1 signed by immediate supervisor.
4. Forward paperwork to central accounting within five working days of return from trip.

EXHIBIT 4.4
Procedure for travel expense reimbursement.

Outcomes

The main reason for establishing procedures, programs, rules, and policies is to reach goals in an effective and efficient way. The results of efforts to achieve goals and execute programs are called outcomes. In large measure, teams and their facilitators are judged on how effectively they achieve outcomes and on the quality of them. Since most outcomes you are expected to achieve result directly from your associates' efforts, their performances are critical factors in determining your rating as a supervisor, team leader, or team facilitator.

STEPS IN PLANNING

Every manager has an approach to planning that has been developed over time and refined by experience. But just about everyone can improve his or her planning efforts. The five steps shown in Exhibit 4.5 can help you become a better planner. As you read about each in the sections that follow, consider how they are related to the steps in decision making discussed in Chapter 3. After all, planning involves a series of decisions, as do the other management functions. Step one sets your destination. Steps two, three, and four develop your program. Step five keeps track of your progress and evaluates your outcomes. All are related and should be taken in the sequence shown. Each may be affected by people and events outside your jurisdiction and ability to control.

EXHIBIT 4.5
Steps in planning (the planning process).

Step 1: Setting Objectives (Goals)
Establishing targets for both the short and the long term.

Step 2: Determining Your Alternatives and Restraints
Building a list of possible courses of action that can lead you to your goals, and the limits you must live within.

Step 3: Evaluating Your Alternatives
Measuring each alternative's advantages and disadvantages in order to choose the alternative with the fewest serious defects.

Step 4: Implementing Your Course or Courses of Action
Placing your plan in the hands of those who will carry it to completion.

Step 5: Following up
Monitoring the progress, or lack thereof, of your efforts and your subordinates' efforts to achieve the goal.

Step 1: Setting Objectives (Goals)

Your objectives or goals dictate your purposes and direction. They require a commitment of resources to achieve. Each goal you set must be clearly stated, specific, achievable with available resources, measurable, and not in conflict with your other goals and the goals of others.

Some of your and your teams' goals are set for you through the planning of others. Your boss may instruct you to reduce operating costs by 10 percent by the end of the month. How you do it may be left to you to decide. However, most of your goals will require consultation and cooperation with others, such as the union steward, fellow supervisors, team members, or various staff managers.

Remember the concept of reengineering? What is rapidly evolving in many companies is the concept of **stretch targets**: "gigantic, seemingly unreachable milestones...which require big, athletic leaps of progress on measures like inventory turns, product development time, and manufacturing cycles" (Tully, 1994). The alternative—incremental progress and gradual improvement—usually mean things improve little by little. But in many industries, "companies now perceive that they must perform far better to prosper—or even, in the long term, to survive.... Companies conclude that traditional ways of doing business are no longer good enough. That's when they reach for stretch targets" (Tully, 1994).

stretch targets
giant, seemingly unreachable milestones requiring leaps of progress

> "Four masters of what may be called the art of stretch management—Boeing, Mead, 3M and CSX—rely on varying degrees on a set of nuts-and-bolts techniques: (1) Set a clear, convincing, long-term goal. Example: earning the full cost of capital. (2) Translate it into one or two specific stretch targets for managers, such as doubling inventory turns. (3) Use benchmarking to prove that the goal—though tough—isn't impossible, and to enlist employees in the crusade. (4) Get out of the way: Let people in the plants and labs find ways to meet the goals (Tully, 1994)."

If you have not yet experienced the need to set or pursue stretch targets, you soon will. See this chapter's Supervisors and Quality feature for a look at 3M's achievements.

Step 2: Determining Your Alternatives and Restraints

Your alternatives are the various courses of action (sets of tasks) that are feasible and available to you to enable you to reach your goals. Together, they make up a program for action. As with your goals, external factors can limit and influence the courses of action available to you. One course of action may be in violation of the union agreement or may exceed your budgeted funds. Company policies and your associates' capabilities can also restrict your choices.

When you know your limits and the restraints placed on you by others and by your situation, you are ready to make a list of possible courses of action. As you construct your list, do not worry about the specifics of each. Make your list as complete as your time and circumstances allow. Do not be afraid to ask others for their suggestions. Tap in to the diversity that exists for new and unique suggestions on how to deal with any issue. Your peers may have faced similar situations in the past, and you can benefit from their experiences. An excellent way to practice your human skills is to consult with peers and associates; you may need their assistance and commitment in order to execute your plans.

Step 3: Evaluating Your Alternatives

Create a list of advantages and disadvantages for each of your alternatives. Consider what each alternative calls for in resources such as time, labor, and materials. Keep your company's mission, vision, values, and policies in mind as you evaluate alternatives. Consider combinations of alternatives. If no one best alternative—one with the least serious defects and best chance for success—emerges from your analysis, consult with your boss. Consider the second best alternative as a fallback position or contingency plan.

Finally, using your conceptual skills and personal code of ethics, consider the impact of your alternatives on your group, on other sections that affect your operations or that your operations affect, and on your company as a whole. You will have to work with and through those other people and sections in the future, so avoid any loss of their goodwill. You do not want to incur any negative side effects that can be avoided.

Step 4: Implementing Your Course or Courses of Action

Having weighed the relative merits and disadvantages of each of your alternatives and having chosen one that has the fewest serious problems connected with it, you are now ready to move from the thinking phase into the action phase of planning. Meet with those who will share responsibility for executing your program. Explain your course of action in detail, emphasizing the limits and means available. Set completion dates for various operations and establish checkpoints between then and now. Explain the help available to all and stand ready to assist them in times of difficulty. Most important, let them know that you want to be kept informed of their progress.

Step 5: Following Up

You chose or helped choose the goals and the courses of action to reach them, so you bear the primary responsibility for execution. Do not rely on your subordinates to come to you with problems. Check with them peri-

SUPERVISORS AND QUALITY

The 3M company, based in St. Paul, Minnesota, has created the Scotch family of tapes; Post-It notes, and a host of other products. For years, it consistently attained its corporate "...goal: deriving 25% of its revenues from products introduced within the past five years." It prides itself on a corporate culture that encourages all employees to become product champions—to spend part of their time each day trying to create new products. By the early 1990s, the company's earnings had flattened out, creeping along well below the CEO's target of an annual 10 percent growth. New products were too similar to existing ones, and too much time was needed to translate new discoveries into new products. Something was needed to shake the troops up.

"In 1991, [CEO DeSimone] unveiled a stretch target: Accelerate innovation to the point where 3M generates 30% of its sales from products introduced within the past four years.... Since new products grow far faster and generate higher [profits] than old ones,...the higher innovation rate would add the necessary octane to 3M's performance." This goal scared nearly everyone. If it was to be attained, all would have to commit to doing things in radically different ways. The company focused its initial efforts on identifying the products under development that had the greatest chance for financial success. In 1992, fifty candidates emerged, and over half of them have been brought to market. In 1994, both sales and profits increased: The former by 6 percent, and the latter by 12 percent.

What caused the turnaround? The stretch target and shakeup in research and development helped, but these were not the whole answer. One product, Never Rust scouring pads, illustrates the remarkable reengineering that has overtaken 3M. The pad contains fibers of plastic containing fine abrasives and represents "the fastest new product introduction in company history." 3M set a one-year introduction schedule for Never Rust, a far more ambitious schedule than it had reached in the past. While manufacturing facilities were being built, marketing teams were preparing advertisements, promotional activities, and TV spots. "Workers started installing production equipment before the windows, bathrooms, or heating. When engineers hit a roadblock, they called on colleagues from all over 3M.... The plant hit full production right on schedule." Currently, the new pad has gained 22 percent of the market that had been dominated by Brillo and SOS.

Source: Tully, Shawn. "Why to Go for Stretch Targets," *Fortune*, November 14, 1994, 148, 150.

odically, allowing yourself and them time to make adjustments and to avoid surprises. Keep track of the progress being made. Various kinds of computer software exist to help you do so. When you find that progress is ahead of schedule, establish new completion deadlines.

Be sure to recognize good performances and demonstrate sincere concern for problems. Keep in mind that delegation transfers authority but leaves you with accountability. Your reputation and success depend on your subordinates' efforts, and you will be needing them to execute your future plans. We are now ready to examine the organizing function.

ORGANIZING

Organizing consists of four primary tasks:

1. Determining and grouping the tasks to be performed.
2. Assigning work to people or people to work.
3. Establishing a framework of authority and accountability among the people who will accomplish the tasks.
4. Allocating appropriate resources to accomplish the tasks and reach the targets.

Planning to organize begins at the top. At the top management level, concern should be for the entire organization. What is the best way to organize given a particular company in a specific industry and competitive

Supervisors in all fields need good organizational skills. Movie directors need to organize both the technical aspects of their operation as well as the actors' performances.

environment? The answer may result in a pyramid type structure (as discussed in Chapter 3) or in a more fluid and flexible structure.

Two contrasting types of organizations exist today: the *bureaucratic* (sometimes called mechanistic) and the *organic*. The bureaucratic/mechanistic organization usually looks like a pyramid or cone, having several layers of middle management. The organic is flatter by comparison and can change its shape more quickly to meet new challenges and opportunities (see Exhibit 4.6).

The bureaucratic/mechanistic organization makes use of several vertical layers of narrowly defined jobs, usually within several functional areas such as production, marketing, finance, and human resource management. It usually concentrates decision making at the top, discourages risk taking and innovation at the lower levels, and depends on specific vertical channels for communications. It is usually quite difficult and time consuming for such a structure to respond to external changes or to change its structure.

EXHIBIT 4.6

Bureaucratic/mechanistic organization structure contrasted with the organic organization structure.

Bureaucratic/Mechanistic	Organic
	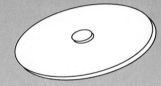
1. Focused on functions	1. Focused on process using cross-functional teams
2. Centralized decision making	2. Decentralized decision making
3. Tall structure, several layers	3. Flat structure, few layers
4. Distinctions between line and staff	4. Both joined in teams
5. Narrow job definitions	5. Wide or no precise job definitions
6. Heavy reliance on rules and procedures	6. Heavy reliance on innovation/reengineering
7. Emphasis on vertical communications	7. Emphasis on horizontal communications
8. Conformity to dominant culture	8. Cultural diversity
9. Emphasis on individuals	9. Emphasis on teams
10. Focus on maintaining stability	10. Focus on change

EXHIBIT 4.7

Three hallmarks of the pizza and network organic structures.

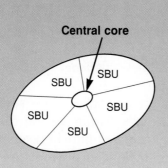 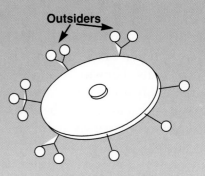

Pizza	Network
1. Autonomous units called strategic business units or SBUs	1. Strong communication links internally and with outsiders: customers, suppliers, and partners
2. Center houses headquarters and various centralized support personnel	2. Focus on core competencies, outsourcing
3. SBUs organized around products, geography, and/or customers	3. Core can be a pizza organization

The organic structure usually focuses horizontally, using a variety of teams whenever and wherever appropriate. See this chapter's "Supervising Teams" feature. Organic structures facilitate cross-functional communications and encourage decision making, innovation, and risk taking at the lowest, most appropriate levels through various means of empowerment. Think of organic structures as "living organisms" capable of changing their shape and purpose as needed to respond to the new and different. Exhibit 4.7 shows two types of organic structures: the pizza, comprising autonomous divisions (called Strategic Business Units or SBUs) served by a corporate core, and the network, designed to include close cooperation with outsiders such as customers, partners, and suppliers.

Both types of organizations have their place under differing sets of circumstances. In general, bureaucratic structures are appropriate in stable industries and noncompetitive environments: Certain utilities—gas and electric companies—and governmental agencies are but two examples. Organic structures work best in unstable, rapidly changing industries and competitive environments such as those in consumer electronics and computer software. More will be said throughout this text about both types of structures.

At every level, the organization structure should facilitate effective and efficient utilization of human resources and service to both internal and external customers. Limits on your abilities to assign work or tasks include the following:

- Existing job descriptions, in writing (which list the duties of people and on which their current levels of pay are based)
- Your skills and your subordinates' technical and human skills levels
- The willingness of your people to accept new challenges and tasks
- The union–management collective bargaining agreement
- Customer needs

Organizing Principles

Six basic principles govern the execution of the organizing function: unity of command, span of control, chain of command, homogeneous assignment, flexibility, and centralization versus decentralization. Each of these principles will help prevent the designer of any organization from falling victim to the most common pitfalls of organizing. Keep them in mind as you plan an organization, evaluate an existing one, or attempt to redesign one.

Unity of Command   Unity of command requires that there be only one individual responsible for each part of an organization. In each organization, each element of the organization should be under one chief. Each individual throughout an organization should have only one boss. This principle helps prevent conflicting orders and instructions and makes control of people and operations easier. At W. L. Gore & Associates:

> A 'product specialist' takes responsibility for developing a product. As it progresses, he or she creates a team, recruiting members from here or there until the team might become a whole plant. By that point the team has broken up into multiple teams, or manufacturing cells. Each member, who can perform most manufacturing processes, commits to performing certain tasks. Each cell has a leader, who evolves from within that cell. The leader is not appointed but achieves the position by assuming leadership which must be approved in a consensus reached through discussion—not a vote (Huey, 1994).

Span of Control   Span of control is a principle based on recognition of the fact that there is a limit to the number of individuals a supervisor, team leader, or team facilitator can manage effectively. Many variables can influence the span of control. Two of these variables are the kind and complexity of the tasks performed by your subordinates and the degree of experience and expertise your associates possess. In bureaucratic structures, the higher levels of the management hierarchy contain the smallest number of subordinates. In organic structures, this principle is usually concerned with how many people should be in a team and how many teams a team facilitator should manage. Jon R. Katzenbach and Douglas K. Smith (1993), consultants with McKinsey & Company, have worked with fifty teams in thirty companies and offer the following counsel:

> Virtually all the teams we have met, read, heard about, or been members of have ranged between two and twenty-five people.... A larger number of people, say fifty or more, can theoretically become a team. But groups of such size more likely will break into subteams rather than function as a single team.... Thus groups much bigger than twenty or twenty-five have difficulty becoming real teams.

Chain of Command   The chain formed by managers from the highest to the lowest is called the chain of command. Managers are the links in that chain. In bureaucratic structures, they must communicate to and through the links as they occur in the chain they are connected to. Links may be skipped or circumvented only when superiors approve and real need to do so exists. In organic structures, command is usually vested in team leaders who head up process, project, or other types of autonomous work teams. These people run their own shows; they "own" their processes and projects and carry within their teams the functional expertise needed to do their tasks.

> Boston Chicken is hiring over 20 people...[and opening] more than one store every business day. "Our 32 regional partners really run our business," says [CEO] Scott Beck.... [T]hese executives are constructing a flat, antihierarchical company based on the power of information.... Using networking software tools such as Lotus Notes and IntelliStore, managers at every level collaborate on team projects like changing menus, solving distribution problems, and planning expansion—all online (Serwer, 1994).

Homogeneous Assignment   Homogeneous assignment is the major reason companies organize by functions as found in the typical bureaucratic structure. Similar or related functions—advertising, selling, and sales promotion, for example—give rise to related problems and require coordinated efforts by teams and individuals with similar levels of experience and expertise to solve them. In organic structures, the focus is on a process such as billing customers or purchasing inventory. In such cases, homogeneous assignment means equipping a team with all needed expertise that bears on each process or project so that it can be managed from its beginning to its end. Hewlett-Packard uses this approach in its all-workers/no-managers

> "...customer-response network: 1,900 technical support staff, mostly engineers. When a customer reports a problem, the call (or electronic message) goes automatically to one of four hubs around the world, depending on the time of day. Operators get a description of the prob-

SUPERVISING TEAMS

With today's business emphasis on decentralization and staying close to customers (both internal and external), the chances are that you and your people already serve on a variety of teams on and off the job. Teams are everywhere: one's family, the folks who run your favorite neighborhood specialty store, and the local church's choir. Most of us have been members of one or more committees or hastily composed groups at work that were created to investigate or solve a problem. Member-ship in a functional group such as the advertising department or the second shift on the factory floor makes us team members in the loosest sense of that term. As a supervisor, you are a member of management's team and a linking pin connecting diverse work groups through the chain of command. The most effective team, however, "is a small number of people with complementary skills who are committed to a common purpose, performance goals, and approach for which they hold themselves mutually accountable." Such "teams are collections of people who must rely on group collaboration if each member is to experience the optimum of success and goal achievement." They plan their work to some degree, usually by setting goals and priorities; have some measure of autonomy in deciding who will do what and how they will do it; and analyze the ways in which the team, its members, their interactions, and the processes are functioning.

As a supervisor, you are a coach. Like any coach, you must be able to study your team's performance with a trained eye, noting any barriers to successful performance and constructing a program to remove or overcome those barriers. It is essential to diagnose the conditions that affect a team—the coach's and team members' abilities as well as the situation they face and its variables—before taking any corrective action. Each team, team member, and the challenges they face will be unique. In future chapters' team features, we will examine team-building activities and how to tell if your teams are functioning properly.

Sources: Katzenbach, John R., and Smith, Douglas K. *The Wisdom of Teams* (Boston: Harvard Business School Press, 1993), 45; Dyer, William G. *Team Building: Issues and Alternatives* (Reading, Mass.: Addison-Wesley, 2d ed., 1987), 4.

lem and its urgency, typing the information into a database and zapping the file to one of 27 centers where it might be picked up by a team specializing in say, operating system foul ups (Stewart, 1994)."

Flexibility Flexibility means that an organization, like Hewlett-Packard, must have the capability of quickly reacting to changing conditions and changing itself to take advantage of new challenges and opportunities. Organic organizations can do both best. Says Paul Osterman, an expert on organization development from MIT, "The market has become far too differentiated and complex for there to be one 'right' way to organize and manage employees" (Richman, 1994).

Once any organization is established, both internal and external changes take place. Managers at all levels must regularly plan to embrace the new and review the organization's relevance and adaptability to changing situations. Most important, an organization's structure is dictated by the operations it exists to accomplish. Attention should be given to the subtle changes worked out by an organization's autonomous units and teams. They often make changes that add greater efficiency and effectiveness to their units and might well do so for the organization as a whole when adopted by others.

Centralization Versus Decentralization Everything an organization or manager does to reduce the importance of an individual subordinate's role leads to centralization of authority. Centralized organizations, like bureaucracies, place the responsibility for decision making at higher levels, concentrating both authority and power at the top.

Everything an organization or manager does to increase the importance of the individual is a move toward decentralization. It places decision authority in the hands of individuals and teams closest to a problem or who manage a process. Decentralization occurs through delegation of authority and empowerment. It speeds up decision making by reducing the number of people and hours needed to make a decision and usually results in an organic organization.

CEO Robert Frey at Cin-Made Corporation, a packaging maker in Ohio, knows the value of decentralization and delegation. His company was losing money and racked by union–management conflict. When unionized workers at one of his plants went on strike, he vowed to never again grant another pay increase. Instead,

> ...he offered to set aside 30% of all pretax earnings as a bonus pool and delegated to the workers—most of them high school dropouts—authority to schedule production, control inventories, choose their own team leaders and screen every new hire. Some were sent out to learn such techniques as statistical process control, which they then taught to teammates. Frey also began giving everyone detailed updates on Cin-Made's finances at monthly meetings. Since 1989, workers bonuses

have added an average 30% to their annual compensation (Richman, 1994).

The trend today in large organizations is to decentralize, to become organic in order to get closer to customers and to respond to rapid changes that occur both internally and externally. Most companies with international operations have found it necessary to give some measure of autonomy to their overseas and specialized operations. Ford runs its European operations from headquarters outside London. Du Pont has shifted "its world-wide electronics operation from the United States to Tokyo, nearer its big base of Asian customers. Du Pont already manages its global agricultural-products operations...from Geneva" (Lublin, 1992).

IBM uses both centralization and decentralization in its new organization. In 1991, the computer giant partitioned itself into over one dozen autonomous divisions. "Simultaneously, IBM created two centrally run entities that took over a host of staff and activities from the newly independent divisions. One...recruits and screens prospective employees. The other...handles benefits processing and other personnel-administration matters" (Lublin, 1992).

STEPS IN ORGANIZING

The organizing process involves a knowledge of many factors, including the skills, knowledge, and abilities possessed by individuals available to perform work; the nature of the tasks to be performed and the best ways to perform them; the principles of organizing; and the five steps discussed here and in Exhibit 4.8.

Step 1: Determining the Tasks to Be Accomplished

The tasks (collections of activities) to be accomplished in your unit will be, in large measure, dictated by current responsibilities and the job design decisions that come to it through the efforts of staff specialists and upper-management decisions. To reach organizational goals, goals will need to be set at every level of the hierarchy. The part that your unit must play in achieving them will be dictated, in part, by decisions at higher levels. Your unit's goals will then dictate the tasks your unit must execute.

Step one illustrates the link between planning and organizing. Planning sets goals, both short and long term, and determines the program needed to reach them. Programs constructed at various levels set forth what is to be done and by whom and determine what resources are to be expended. Tasks must then be broken down into the specific activities required.

Step 1: **Determining the Tasks to Be Accomplished to Reach Planned Goals**
Tasks are identified and included in programs, which then become the specific responsibilities of organizational units to accomplish.

Step 2: **Subdividing the Major Tasks into Activities to Be Performed by Individuals**
Through analysis, tasks are broken down into specific activities which can then be assigned in part or in total to individuals who possess the needed skills, knowledge, and abilities.

Step 3: **Assigning Specific Activities to Individuals**
The skills, knowledge, and abilities needed to execute specific activities are identified, and individuals who possess them are assigned activities. Where existing personnel cannot adequately handle the activities, training, new people, or outside assistance may be required.

Step 4: **Providing the Necessary Resources to Accomplish Activities**
In order to accomplish their assignments, individuals and units may need additional people, authority, training, time, money, or materials.

Step 5: **Designing the Organizational Relationships Needed to Facilitate the Execution of Tasks**
A hierarchy must be designed, or the existing one adapted, to provide the arrangement of authority and responsibility needed to oversee the execution and completion of assignments. The principles of organizing must be adhered to.

Step 2: Subdividing Major Tasks into Individual Activities

Staff specialists can help individual unit supervisors break unit tasks down into specific activities. Existing and familiar tasks usually present no particular problem. Units and unit personnel are already equipped to deal with them. When new tasks are assigned or created, however, an analysis must be done to determine what each will require in the way of personal skills, knowledge, and abilities.

Step 3: Assigning Specific Activities to Individuals

The specific skills needed to perform worker activities can generally be broken down as follows:

- Data processing skills—the abilities to analyze, compile, interpret, synthesize, and compare data or information
- Human skills—the abilities to communicate, instruct, direct, persuade, negotiate, and help people
- Technical skills—the abilities to manipulate, operate, set up, guide, and follow procedures in one's areas of expertise

Once these skills are identified as being a part of an activity, individuals who possess the skills required can be assigned to execute the activity. Workers are matched by their particular skill levels to the activities that must be executed. Conceptual skills are generally not needed by non-supervisory personnel.

Step 4: Providing the Necessary Resources

Additional demands on people and their time may tax them beyond their capabilities. If the activities cannot be absorbed by the existing workforce, new people may have to be obtained, or the work may have to be transferred to an outside source. Where employees do not have the expertise or levels of skills required, additional training may be needed to bring them up to the levels needed. Talent from other areas may be temporarily assigned to assist with the execution of specific activities. Additional funds and authority may be needed to accomplish all the tasks given to a particular individual or unit.

Step 5: Designing the Organizational Relationships Needed

The existing structure of management positions may or may not be adequate to oversee the execution of operations. When it is not, a new design—temporary or permanent—may have to be established. Enough authority needs to be in the hands of those designated to execute the various tasks or to oversee that execution. Everyone involved must have clear knowledge of who is to do what, by what time, and to what standards. The principles of organizing will help you design relationships that can function properly. The end result can be shown in graphic form as an organization chart.

As a supervisor, one of your most rewarding tasks will be training your subordinates to reach their potential. Just as your supervisor once gave you the training to get where you are today, you too have the opportunity to positively affect someone's career.

DIRECTING

directing
the supervision or overseeing of people and processes

Directing may be briefly defined as supervising or overseeing people and processes. It includes the specific activities of staffing, training, offering incentives and examples of appropriate behavior, evaluating performances, rewarding, coaching, counseling, and disciplining. One example of what it means to direct comes to us from theatrical and motion picture directors. These people remove obstacles that may stand in the way of individual and group performances. They attempt, through coaching and by giving examples, to bring out the best performances their actors have to give. Directors are teachers, facilitators, and cheerleaders. So should you be.

Directing subordinates individually and in teams is the most demanding and time-consuming function for all supervisors. If you do it well, your success is practically guaranteed. If you do it poorly, personal and organizational failures will usually result. Your reputation as a supervisor largely depends on your subordinates and the quality of their performances. Their responses to your efforts to direct them will either make or break your career. This is why directing subordinates is the primary focus of this book. All the remaining chapters will help you become an effective director, team leader, and team facilitator.

Staffing

Staffing involves adding new people to the organization, promoting people to higher levels of responsibility, transferring people to different jobs, and separating people from their employment. It is based on human resource planning—the analysis of the organization and its present and future needs for people with particular talents. An inventory of existing personnel is taken to determine who is now at work, what their skill levels are, how long they are likely to remain in the organization, and who among them is qualified for larger responsibilities. Existing personnel are matched to the organization's present and future needs in order to determine what kinds of people will be needed in the future. Through staffing, the organization attempts to provide itself with the proper mix of human talent to accomplish its mission and fulfill its vision. Specific staffing activities are defined as follows:

1. Recruiting is the search for talented people who are or might be interested in doing the jobs that the organization has available. It occurs inside as well as outside the organization. Announcements about job opportunities may be posted on bulletin boards or placed in newspapers or trade journals. Everyone who responds is considered a potential employee until the decision to hire is made. Chapter 11 has more to say about the supervisor's role in recruiting.

2. Selecting screens the potential employees and job applicants to determine who among them is most qualified. Tests, interviews, physical examinations, and records checks are used to eliminate the less qualified. The applicants are narrowed down to the one or more who are most qualified, and eventually a decision to hire one or more people is made. Selection is often considered a negative process because every applicant has flaws, faults, or deficiencies. The people hired have the least serious or fewest deficiencies for the job opening. Chapter 11 discusses the supervisor's role in selection.

3. Placement follows as soon as the person is hired. It involves introducing the new employee to the company—its people, the jobs, and the working environment. The new employee is given the proper instructions and equipment needed to execute the job for which he or she has been hired. Once work rules are explained and co-workers are introduced, the break-in period begins. Chapter 11 has more to say about the supervisor's role in placing and introducing a new person to the job.

4. Promoting involves moving people from one job in the organization to another that offers higher levels of pay and responsibility. Promotions usually require approval by two levels of management and the assistance of the human resources department, where one exists. As a supervisor, your continual concern should be to qualify yourself for promotion and to get one or more of your subordinates ready to take your job.

5. Transferring moves people from one job to another, either temporarily or permanently. A transfer does not usually carry with it an increase in pay or responsibilities. Most transfers are lateral moves;

they facilitate training and are used to move people from one career path to another.

6. Separating people from their employment can be done on a voluntary or an involuntary basis. Voluntary separations include quits and retirements. Involuntary separations include firings (termination due to disciplinary actions) and indefinite layoffs (terminations due to reductions in force, economic slowdowns, and company reorganizations).

Training

Training teaches skills, knowledge, and attitudes to both new and existing employees. It can be provided through classroom and on-the-job instruction. Although the supervisor of each trainee has the primary duty to train, the actual instruction may be done by any person who is qualified to train. Often the human resources department assists supervisors in training by providing training materials or by teaching them how to train their subordinates. In some cases, supervisors delegate the authority to train to an experienced subordinate while retaining accountability for the training. Chapter 12 explores the supervisor's training duties in more detail.

Offering Incentives

Incentives are things or states of being that the company hopes will have a strong appeal to their employees. Those who desire one or more of the incentives offered by their employer will be encouraged to give the kind and quality of performances required to earn them.

Incentives offered to employees vary from one business to another and from one department within a business to another. They all are offered with the intention of helping managers build an effective and efficient organization. Most companies attempt to offer a wide variety of incentives in the hope that they will have something for everyone. The idea is that what may not appeal to one employee as desirable and worth having will appeal to another.

The kinds of incentives most businesses offer include raises, bonuses, promotions, better working conditions, greater challenges and responsibilities, and symbols of status in the organization. Status symbols can be as small as a phone on the desk, as large as an executive suite, or anything in between. Which one, if any, appeals to a given employee at a given time depends on the individual—his or her current level of job satisfaction and financial condition. Chapter 7 looks at human motivation in more detail.

Evaluating

Evaluating requires each supervisor to make periodic appraisals of each subordinate's on-the-job performance. To do this adequately, each super-

"In 1992, Sears, Roebuck & Company was inundated with complaints about its automotive service business. Consumers and the attorneys general in more than 40 states had accused the company of misleading customers and selling them unnecessary parts and services...." Settling these complaints cost Sears nearly $60 million.

Sears was experiencing declining revenues in 1992. The stage was set for the complaints when new performance goals were given to the company's auto center employees along with new incentives to reach them. Minimum quotas for mechanics were increased while their supervisors were given "product-specific sales quotas—sell so many springs, shock absorbers, [etc.] per shift—and paid a commission based on sales. All auto center employees later reported an atmosphere of fear and pressure to perform; jobs and careers were clearly on the line.

"[A]number of organizational factors contributed to the problematic sales practices." Although the company increased both negative and positive incentives, it did not adequately monitor the service centers. "Without active management support for ethical practice and mechanisms to detect and check questionable sales methods...it is not surprising that some employees may have reacted to contextual forces by resorting to exaggeration, carelessness, or even misrepresentation."

What were the "contextual forces" that led to the performance of unnecessary work on customers' vehicles? How would you have handled the pressure if you had been a Sears auto center supervisor?

Source: Paine, Lynn Sharp. "Managing for Organizational Integrity," *Harvard Business Review* (March–April 1994) 107–108.

visor must have precise guidelines and standards to follow. People are rated on the basis of what they were expected to do and how well they did it.

Evaluating employees is done informally each day through routine, regular observations of their work by their supervisors. Formal appraisals are usually done once or twice each year. Supervisors who are not with their people regularly usually find it difficult to rate them properly. Supervisors who do not know themselves well—their own stereotypes and prejudices— often make employee appraisals that are something less than objective or honest. Supervisors who do not know their subordinates as individuals will find it impossible to make honest and fair appraisals.

The primary purpose of employee evaluations is to help people improve their performance on the job and, therefore, their usefulness to their employer and their pride in themselves. Chapter 13 explores the appraisal process in more detail.

Disciplining

Disciplining requires supervisors to act on the knowledge they have about their subordinates' mistakes and shortcomings on the job. Positive discipline demands that employees be informed about and understand the rules that govern their behavior, the standards that govern their output, and the expectations their bosses have of them. The emphasis is on preventing trouble through the creation of an educated, self-disciplined subordinate. Negative discipline is concerned with handling infractions, usually through reprimands or more severe penalties. Chapter 14 deals with the supervisor's duties in this vital area.

Management by Wandering Around (MBWA)

management by wandering around
a leadership principle that encourages supervisors to get out of their offices regularly so that they can touch base with those who affect their operations and those whom their operations affect

Management by wandering around (MBWA) is a principle of management that encourages managers to get out of their offices regularly so that they can touch base with customers, suppliers, and others in their own organizations. MBWA encourages managers to listen, empathize, and stay

Informal encounters with your subordinates are an important part of management by wandering around. Sharing and spreading the enthusiasm of your subordinates is paramount to your own success.

in touch with people who are important to their operations and their mission (Peters and Austin, 1985).

Most supervisors can practice MBWA each time they meet another person at work or make contact with outsiders during their business activities. When you meet customers, interact with them to find out how they like your products and services. If you uncover any complaints or criticisms, take them to the people who should know and can do something about them.

MBWA with suppliers is especially important if your people are receiving unacceptable levels of quality in the resources those suppliers provide. Before most companies' purchasing agents decide on a supplier, they visit various suppliers' facilities and talk with those who will be responsible for creating what they need. If suppliers are making your life and the lives of your subordinates more difficult, practice a little MBWA with them.

Your most frequent use of MBWA will be with your associates. Casual and informal meetings, as well as formal encounters, create lots of opportunities to interact with them. You and they can then catch up on what is happening in your lives. You get a chance to see them in action: to watch and to listen. When people have the opportunity to see firsthand what someone is working on with enthusiasm, that enthusiasm spreads. There is probably no better way to spend most of your time at work than with your people—those who make or break your own reputation and on whom you depend for the execution of your plans and instructions. Most of the activities we examine in later chapters depend on your practice of MBWA.

CONTROLLING

Controlling involves the ability to prevent, identify, and correct deficiencies in the performances of both people and processes. It begins with an assessment of what needs controlling, what types of controls are best (prevention efforts, monitoring ongoing operations, or after-action reporting on a measuring of outputs), and the establishment of various standards for measurement.

controlling
the management function that sets standards that are applied to performance. Controls attempt to prevent, identify, and correct deviations from standards

Standards

A **standard** is a device for measuring or monitoring the behavior of people or processes. Both types can be quantitative, qualitative, or a mixture of the two. Standards set for controlling people include policies, rules, and procedures. Standards set for the control of processes include defining the quality and quantity of expected results at various stages throughout a process and upper and lower control limits that form a boundary around acceptable output. Various measurements and observations are needed at several points throughout the performance of any operation to determine if standards are being met.

standard
a device for measuring or monitoring the performance of people, machines, or processes

EXHIBIT 4.9
The control process in a formal organization.

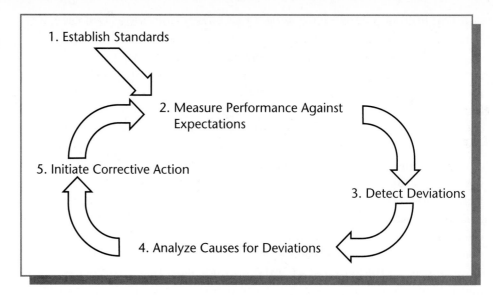

1. Establish Standards

2. Measure Performance Against Expectations

5. Initiate Corrective Action

3. Detect Deviations

4. Analyze Causes for Deviations

The Control Process

Exhibit 4.9 summarizes the control process in any formal organization. Any collection or system of controls should establish standards, measure performances (of people and processes) against those expectations, detect deviations from standards, analyze causes for the deviations (using the problem-solving and decision-making processes), and initiate action to correct deviations from standards.

1. **Establish standards.** Standards answer the questions who?, when?, why?, what?, and how? with regard to employees' performance at work. Qualitative and quantitative standards need to be established wherever key activities (those directly affecting goal achievement) are to take place. People must know their limits and what is expected of them in the performance of their duties.

2. **Measure performance against expectations.** If managers are going to prevent, identify, and correct deviations from standards or norms, they must be able to compare performance to established standards. It is only through comparisons that good or bad, hot or cold take on meaning. For example, the comparison of planned production levels to actual levels of production output will let a manager know if the actual is in line with the desirable.

3. **Detect deviations.** As a result of comparisons, deviations are detected and noted. For example, a worker was supposed to generate fifteen parts per hour for each of the last four hours. The supervisor compares output to this standard and discovers that the worker is five parts short of the goal. To do this, a supervisor needs accurate and timely information about each worker's production output. Both the worker and the supervisor need to know the standard output and how that standard is applied.

4. Analyze causes for deviations. The supervisor has noted the deviation, a lack of sufficient quantity of productive output. An investigation needs to be conducted to determine why the deviation has taken place. Who or what is at fault or not functioning as planned? The decision-making process (Chapter 3) is applied, and possible remedies are determined.

5. Initiate corrective action. Additional training or more explicit instructions and supervision may be called for. Problems with machines, equipment, supplies, or raw materials may call for changes in maintenance procedures, work flow, sources of materials, and more. The objective is to get things back to normal—to turn what is into what should be.

The control process may tell managers or an organization that its standards are inappropriate—either too loose or too strict. Further, the need for additional standards may be uncovered when a supervisor investigates the causes of deviations. New controls may be required to monitor other operations. In 1994, the board of trustees for a Midwestern community college district discovered that its chief financial officer had invested $10 million of college funds in highly risky, speculative, and long-term investments that earned no interest. The board had no control mechanism to prevent the poor decision, so the employee had full authority to do this *without* board approval. The funds are now tied up for several years and probably will lose a significant percentage of their value.

Types of Controls

Preventive controls are familiar to all of us. Safety devices on a machine or firearm to avoid unintentional operation and accidents, a lock on a door to prevent unauthorized entry, safety locks on medicine containers to keep children from opening them, and the various checklists throughout this text are all examples of preventive controls. It is usually better to prevent trouble than to have to deal with it. If all of our problems could be foreseen, organizations would need no other types of controls.

Diagnostic controls attempt to identify trouble when it occurs. Ideally, they should do so immediately. Just as a physician cannot prescribe a treatment for an illness until its cause is identified, a manager needs to know why something has gone wrong in his or her department before taking corrective measures.

Some familiar examples of diagnostic controls are warning lights, meters, and gauges. Personal observation and taking note of abnormal sounds and sights are daily routines that managers use to detect trouble. Once you detect problems, you must identify their causes and deal with them efficiently.

Therapeutic controls are usually automatic in their operation. They are designed to deal with and correct deficiencies once the causes are known. Thermostats that regulate the operation of heating and cooling systems are a good example. A safety valve that opens to release excess steam when the pressure reaches a certain level is another example.

All these controls are necessary to most operations and should form an integrated approach to controlling. No one type is completely adequate. Only through their combined use can a manager effectively control resources and activities. And remember: You can't expect if you don't inspect.

A budget and the budgeting process effectively illustrate the three types of controls. A budget is both a plan and a control. It plans for the expenditure of money that is expected to be available over a fixed period. The people who will be spending the money usually participate in its preparation. They are also bound to follow this money plan once it is approved.

A budget is a preventive control because it prevents (or helps prevent) unauthorized expenditures of funds. It is a diagnostic control because it helps monitor the funds being spent as they are spent and matches actual expenditures against planned expenditures. When budgeted funds prove insufficient to meet required expenditures, an investigation should be made to determine why. If the budgeting process is at fault, changes can be introduced to make it more realistic. Budgets have a built-in therapeutic control. When more money is requested than has been authorized, it cannot be spent without higher approval.

Control Characteristics

Controls may have one or more of the following characteristics (Drucker, 1974):

1. Acceptance by members of the organization who must enforce them and over whom they are enforced. Consultation with and the consent of the governed are hallmarks of effective controls.
2. Focus on critical points that affect individuals' and the organization's abilities to achieve goals. Critical points include essential areas of marketing, financial, production, and personnel activities.
3. Economic feasibility. Controls must be cost efficient—the benefit they give has to be worth their costs of installation and operation. Too much control can be worse than too little. Appropriateness is the key.
4. Accuracy. Controls must provide information about operations and people in sufficient quantity and quality to enable managers to make meaningful comparisons to standards. Too much information can be worse than too little.
5. Timeliness. Information needed for comparisons has to be in a manager's hands in time for him or her to take effective action. Delays in

preparing, gathering, or disseminating information can prolong the occurrence of deviations.

6. Clarity. Controls and their applicability to specific situations must be communicated clearly to those responsible for implementing controls and to those who will be controlled by them.

All these characteristics are important, but a control need not have all of them to do the job it is designed for.

To illustrate these characteristics, we will look at a toolroom situation. Supervisor Fred wants to control the use of his department's tools. He starts by locking them up in a toolroom. Next, he assigns to one person the task of issuing and accounting for each tool. Then he issues an I.D. card to each subordinate and sets up a procedure whereby tools are exchanged for these cards. Finally, he establishes records of the condition the tools are in and fixes responsibility for changes in their condition.

This may or may not be a good control system depending on the circumstances. It may be too expensive depending on the value of the tools he is safeguarding. It may be inadequate and impractical if, in the absence of the toolroom supervisor, no one can get a tool. It may be inappropriate if only one or two workers ever need the tools. In short, all the six control characteristics may be necessary; if any one of them is missing, the controls may accomplish something less than is desired.

Ricardo Semler, head of Semco in Brazil, has established a company controlled by and based on mutual trust and respect between managers and workers or, as he refers to them, associates and coordinators. When he took over the company, it was a traditional bureaucratic organization run by rules, procedures, and manuals. Semler set out to "...create an environment in which others make decisions" (Semler, 1993). In Semler's words:

> We have absolute trust in our employees. In fact, we are partners with them.... We negotiated with our [unionized] workers over the basic percentage to be distributed [in the company's profit sharing plan]...and they hold assemblies to decide how to split it.... Profit sharing has worked so well that once...a union leader argued that too big a raise [for union members] would overextend the company (Semler, 1993).

The company is stripped of barriers that separate, and it is arranged to facilitate learning. Associates in teams run the factory with nearly absolute freedom but recognize that freedom carries responsibilities with it:

> Everyone vouches for his own work, so we don't need a quality control department;...we try to maximize the possibilities and minimize supervision for everyone at Semco.... Before people are hired or promoted to leadership positions, they are interviewed and approved by all who will

be working for them. And every six months managers are evaluated by those who work under them. The results are posted for all to see (Semler, 1993).

Although the company has three levels of management, it maintains a set of concentric circles of coordinators and worker teams to execute most of its tasks. Controlling at Semler is everyone's job, and each person does what is necessary to control his or her own behavior and outputs.

Management by Exception

The recognized principle of **management by exception** applies most directly to controlling. A manager should spend his or her time only on areas that demand personal attention. The routine should be delegated to others, and procedures should be established to deal with it. When exceptions occur, they are usually situations for which there are no precedents. Then the manager's attention is warranted. Where controls reveal exceptions for which there is no prescribed cure, the manager must take action.

The theory underlying management by exception is illustrated in Exhibit 4.10, which identifies a few of the everyday demands on a supervisor's time and tells how the supervisor should handle each of them. Whenever possible, supervisors should delegate routine tasks to their subordinates so as to free themselves for additional tasks they may receive through delegation from their superiors and to enable them to spend more

EXHIBIT 4.10

An illustration of management by exception.

Task	Keep	Delegate	Other
Appraisals of subordinates	✔		
Interviewing applicants for job vacancies	✔		
Handling regular reports to higher-ups		✔	Read before sending
Answering correspondence	Those only supervisors can answer	Those others can do well or better	Read before sending
Attending meetings and conferences	When your expertise is needed	When your input is not required	Have substitute brief you

time on their most important tasks—those that demand their personal attention and expertise. Competent subordinates usually appreciate management by exception because it suggests that the manager has confidence in them.

Management by Objectives

Objectives are goals or targets to be achieved or reached within some specific time. **Management by objectives (MBO)** requires each manager (and sometimes each worker) to sit down periodically with his or her boss and work out goals that can be mutually agreed on. These goals will, when achieved, result in a more efficient and economical operation for a section or department. Such goals can be set only after a clear understanding is reached about what a department's weaknesses are and what its capabilities seem to be. Goals set by any manager must be in line with—not contradictory to—those of his or her superiors and those of departments with whom the manager must coordinate.

management by objectives
a management principle that encourages subordinates to set performance goals that are in line with their unit's and organization's goals and that are approved by their supervisors

If MBO is to work efficiently, those participating in it must set clear, specific, and realistic goals for both the short and long run. Once goals are set, progress (or lack of it) in reaching each goal is monitored by both the person who set the goal and his or her superior. The goal-setter's reputation and performance appraisals will be based in large measure on his or her efforts and success in reaching the established goals.

MBO reduces the need for close supervision by involving subordinates in setting their own sights on specific targets and then having them work out the methods by which each goal is to be reached. In such a system, results are what really matter. In setting goals, each subordinate and his or her superior get to know more about themselves, their individual capabilities, their current operations, and their personal commitments to achieve. Chapter 13 discusses MBO further.

COORDINATING

Coordinating is the managerial task of making sure that the various parts of your organization all operate in harmony with one another. It involves integrating all the details necessary for reaching your goals. Each activity must be executed without interference from other activities in order to have a unified effort in both the planning and the execution phases of every operation.

The coordinating function should happen simultaneously with all the others. Through it, you attempt to foresee potential conflicts or to deal with existing ones. The organization may have to be redesigned for better efficiency, or plans may have to be modified to include a better mix or balance between people and events. Controls may be so rigid that they restrict completion of the work. The direction of subordinates may be so poor that they rebel and resist instructions or work against organizational objectives. Lack of coordination means chaos.

Kinds of Coordination

There are two kinds of coordinating: coordination of thought and coordination of action. You coordinate thought by making certain, through effective communication, that all parties involved in planning an operation have the same concepts, objectives, and overall understanding. You coordinate action by including in your plans for a project the steps to be taken in its execution, the sequence of those steps, the roles that each person must play, and how all the persons involved are to cooperate. As these definitions suggest, coordinating is both an aid to planning and an objective to be realized through planning.

Coordination of thought and coordination of action are best provided for by fixing responsibilities. Each person should have an up-to-date, clear definition of his or her duties in general, as well as of the particular role for each project in which he or she becomes involved. In this way, everyone's efforts are directed toward common purposes with as little wasted effort and overlap as possible. Coordination is the thread that binds an entire operation together. It must be practiced by all managers at every level, both horizontally and vertically.

Coordination Techniques

Organizational units can coordinate their operations through programs, vertical feedback, and horizontal interaction. Programs contain procedures and schedules. Feedback consists of the regular interchanges of information between superiors and subordinates. Horizontal interaction requires teamwork and occurs regularly when individuals and groups from different departments touch base with each other through a variety of means and for a variety of purposes. The larger the organization, the greater the need for these three efforts at coordination. Chapter 5 relates these to organizational communications.

As a supervisor, you can adopt the following measures in your efforts to coordinate your operations:

- Enforcing company policies
- Enforcing departmental procedures
- Regularly meeting with people who share responsibilities for projects
- Practicing management by wandering around—communicating regularly with those who feed you work, those who do your department's tasks, and those to whom you feed work or output
- Using the organization's established lines of authority and channels of communication

EXHIBIT 4.11
A checklist to help you coordinate your activities.

Yes	No	
❏	❏	1. Are intelligent cooperation and mutual understanding exhibited throughout my organization?
❏	❏	2. Are my people cross-trained to keep them aware of the overall operation and the need to cooperate?
❏	❏	3. Are operating procedures in writing understood by those who must follow them, and accessible to those people?
❏	❏	4. Are vertical as well as horizontal communications channels extant, open, and used?
❏	❏	5. Are external activities monitored, interpreted, and integrated, where appropriate, to our operations?
❏	❏	6. Is someone available at all times to execute my role in my absence?

Corrective actions for all "no" responses:

_____

_____

- Sharing information with those who need it through regular routing of bulletins, newsletters, memos, and copies of pertinent documents
- Being available to those who need you; letting people know where you are and how they can reach you both on and off the job
- Rotating responsibilities in order to cross-train your people
- Playing your management roles of liaison, monitor, disseminator, spokesperson, disturbance handler, and negotiator
- Constantly focusing yourself and others on the mission

Exhibit 4.11 contains a checklist to help you coordinate your operations and people.

Instant Replay

1. Planning is often called the first management function because it is a part of every other function.

2. The planning process requires five sequential steps that set goals, construct a program to reach those goals, and monitor the progress and results of that program.

3. Organizing requires managers to determine tasks, break them into activities, identify the skills needed to perform them, and assign them to qualified people.

4. The organizing process requires five specific steps that must be taken sequentially and in line with the basic principles that affect organizing.

5. Directing requires managers to staff their operations and to train, offer incentives and examples, evaluate, and discipline their subordinates.

6. Staffing is concerned with meeting an organization's needs for qualified human resources. It involves human resource planning and development—recruiting, selecting, promoting, transferring, and separating people from their employment.

7. Controlling establishes standards to govern people's conduct and output at work, measures performance and conduct against those standards, detects deviations, finds the causes for the deviations, and implements appropriate remedies.

8. Controls may be preventive, diagnostic, or therapeutic. Plans can set forth objectives, programs, and methods to prevent problems. Diagnostic controls sense deviations and communicate the fact that they are occurring. Therapeutic controls deal with deviations as they occur.

9. Controls should be accepted by those who must use them and should be focused on critical points in vital operations; they must also be economically feasible, accurate, timely, clear, and easily understood.

10. The principle of management by exception tells a manager to spend time on only those matters that demand the manager's personal attention and expertise. Other matters can be delegated or reduced to routines.

11. Management by objectives requires bosses and subordinates to set goals that will become the standards by which their performances are measured. Each employee sets performance goals with which the employee's boss can concur. Timetables are established for reaching each goal, and performances are monitored. Periodic adjustments may be made to the goals or to the methods of achieving them.

12. Supervisors must take measures to coordinate the thoughts and actions of those who affect their operations so as to avoid confusion, waste, and duplication of effort.

Questions for Class Discussion

1. Can you define this chapter's key terms?
2. What are the five steps in the planning process, and what happens in each?

3. What are the six principles that govern the organizing function, and what does each mean?
4. What are the five steps in the organizing process, and what happens in each?
5. What are the major differences between the mechanistic and the organic types of organizations?
6. What activities belong to the directing function, and what is involved in each?
7. What are the five steps in the control process, and what happens in each?
8. What are the three kinds of controls, and how does each function?
9. What are the major ways in which supervisors can coordinate their actions and operations within and outside their work units?

Incident

Purpose: To encourage you to value the diversity in your teams and associates.

Your Task: Perform the exercise described here with your team members and associates.

- Race—the result of inheritance
- Ethnicity—the result of upbringing
- Languages mastered
- Gender
- Sexual orientation—straight, bisexual, gay, or lesbian
- Place of birth—native born or immigrant
- Age—young, middle aged, older, or elderly
- Physical characteristics—height and weight, able bodied or physically challenged
- Education earned
- Religious affiliation and beliefs
- Mental characteristics—able or mentally challenged

Workshops in industry that focus on valuing diversity often begin by asking participants to introduce themselves to each other, using the preceding list. Juan starts the introductions by saying, "I am Puerto Rican by birth and of Spanish heritage; both my parents were born in Puerto Rico. I consider myself young at age twenty-eight and speak Spanish and English fluently. I am a straight male with a high school diploma and two years of college credit toward my bachelor's degree. I am hearing-impaired and a practicing Roman Catholic."

Imagine yourself in this workshop, and write out your own introduction to its participants. Then list the differences and similarities that exist between you and Juan. Which will draw you together? Which seem to form a barrier between you two? Ask yourself what additional information you would like to have from Juan in order to get to know him as an individual. What you have just done must be done by everyone in a workplace if the goal of valuing diversity is to be realized. Next time you and your team or teams meet, consider performing this exercise, and make sure everyone participates. You will be surprised to discover that more conditions that bring people together exist than do those that drive people apart.

CASE PROBLEM 4.1

Remember the Mission

"Another 27 units returned this morning? That makes over 400 rejects this month. What's the reason for the returns?... Yeah. I could have guessed. That damn plastic gear just isn't strong enough. You know, Grace, at this rate we'll eat the whole 2,000 720s by next month.... O.K., I'll be in touch." Phil, the supervisor of the loading dock, hung up his phone in disgust. He began to think about where he was going to put these new returns. He was running out of space and wasn't prepared for the additional workload they represented. "I bet those boys in the plant are shaking now," thought Phil.

The gear problem could be traced to a decision made about four months ago when the model 720 was undergoing design and testing. The computer built the model and printed out the results, and the number crunchers went to work on costing the parts and manufacturing. The numbers were just too high, and a meeting was called to bring them down. All the managers who had anything to do with the 720's design and manufacture were brought together and addressed by the president. She ended her remarks as follows:

> There you have it. We need everyone's input on getting these costs in line. Until we shave another $9.50 per model off the 720, we can't make the kind of profit we need.
>
> I want all of you to give me any idea that will save us money. Remember our mission: We want the most cost-effective products we can produce. We are in business to make profits. That's the bottom line. That's what we are all here to do. Now get cracking, and give me your ideas by next Monday.

After the president left, the managers agreed to attack the biggest cost item first. Within minutes, they focused on the take-up gear—a precision part requiring two separate machining operations. After much debate and without any testing, a decision was made to go with a molded gear in plastic. The savings would be just over $10 per unit. Delighted, they stopped their search. The president approved the change, and the piece was contracted to a regular supplier without any competitive bidding. The supplier was chosen because it had a good track record for on-time delivery and could tool up in two weeks. Since time was running short for startup on the new 720, there was little else the production people could do and still be able to meet their commitments to their dealers.

Just one week after the first of the new 720s were shipped to dealers, complaints and returns began. Several defects were responsible for customer returns, but the biggest problem was the plastic gear. It accounted for 92 percent of the returns received by the company to date. When the earliest returns were pulled apart and examined, the gear's teeth were found on the bottom of the casing. Evidently, if an operator pressed the number key while the machine was still moving in forward mode, the gear would lose some teeth. As designed, the gear was simply not molded in the correct thickness to stand up to the stress. When contacted, the supplier reported that it could not mold the gear any thicker without new equipment.

Another management meeting was called. After considering the options, the president decided to reprint the instruction manual given to operators of the 720s and to replace the broken gears with plastic gears of the existing design. All new machines would be shipped with the new operator's manual, which would call attention to the procedure that broke the gears. Operators were warned as follows: CAUTION: Using the number key while the machine is in forward mode will cause serious damage to the machine.

Questions

1. What do you think about this company's mission statement?
2. How was the decision to cut costs made, and how should it have been made?
3. What do you think of the plan to keep the thin gear and to solve the problem by changing the manual?
4. How could this problem have been avoided in the design phase by using MBWA?

The Typing Pool

CASE PROBLEM 4.2

Linda Grover was promoted to supervisor of the secretarial pool four weeks ago. She had worked as a typist and transcriber for three years in the pool she now supervises. Her promotion was based on her outstanding skills and her ability to regularly finish her work on time. Linda's old position was to remain vacant until budget restrictions were relaxed.

Linda had wanted to be an executive secretary, but no openings were available when this promotion came her way. She still hoped that she could become an executive secretary and planned to apply the moment a position opened up.

In her new job, Linda assigned the work to her people, reviewed it for completeness, and pitched in herself when the group was especially busy. Before her promotion, typing jobs had been assigned on a first-in, first-out basis; each job was given to the first person available to handle it. Because all the people in the pool were skilled at their jobs, the routine seemed to flow out of the unit almost always on time. Since her promotion, Linda has been considering some possible changes.

Many of the more senior members of the pool—four of the six people in the pool—have expressed an interest in certain kinds of projects. Rosa, for instance, likes letters and does them quickly and perfectly. Bob likes statistical and numerical reports with lots of tabulation and tables. Linda met with her group one morning and made the following proposals:

1. All employees were to give her their preferences. When possible, those preferences would dictate assignments.
2. Assignments would be awarded on the basis of seniority and preference.

Linda asked the group to vote on the proposals. The vote was four to two in favor.

Soon after implementing her new procedures, Linda ran into several problems. The least senior people were getting the most difficult work, or so they thought, and were very unhappy. A report that Bob would have ordinarily received went to someone else because Bob was not free to handle it when it came up for assignment. The letters were piling up because Rosa insisted that they wait for her, she being the most senior member of the pool. The work was slowing down, and Linda was getting quite concerned. On several occasions, the least senior people were idle for more than an hour. But this week, Linda was so busy that she was thinking of using overtime for the first time to get the work out. This morning, two reports came back to Linda with serious errors and would have to be retyped. Both were the products of the least senior people.

Linda made some notes and called the two junior members of her department into her office. She showed them the reports that had been returned and asked them what had gone wrong. They had no satisfactory answers as far as Linda was concerned. She told them that from now on, their work would be closely scrutinized, and no work would leave their desks until it was up to their usual high standards.

Linda was depressed. She had hoped the group would be more cooperative. After all, she had their best interests at heart. They had complained that seniority meant nothing, and she had done something about that. She had hoped they would continue to be as good as they had been when she had been one of them. She hoped, also, that her new position would give her more time to relax. Instead, she was working as hard as any of the pool members were. With a sigh, she picked up her phone and dialed personnel.

Questions

1. What planning issues exist in this case?
2. What organizing issues exist?
3. What directing issues exist?
4. What controlling issues exist?

Notes

Drucker, Peter F. *Management Tasks, Responsibilities, Practices* (New York: Harper & Row, 1974), 489–504.

Huey, John. "The New Post-Heroic Leadership," *Fortune,* February 21, 1994, 42–44, 48, 50.

Katzenbach, Jon R., and Smith, Douglas K. *The Wisdom of Teams* (Boston: Harvard Business School Press, 1993).

Lublin, Joann S. "Firms Ship Unit Headquarters Abroad," *The Wall Street Journal,* December 9, 1992, B1.

Mateja, Jim. "A Big Gap Among Makers of Auto Parts, Study Shows," *Chicago Tribune,* November 4, 1994, sect. 3, 1, 5.

Mitchell, Russell, and Oneal, Michael. "Managing by Values," *Business Week,* August 2, 1994, 46–52.

Pacetta, Frank, and Gittines, Roger. *Don't Fire Them, Fire Them Up* (New York: Simon & Schuster, 1994).

Peters, Tom, and Austin, Nancy. *A Passion for Excellence* (New York: Warner Books, 1985).

Richman, Louis S. "The New Work Force Builds Itself," *Fortune,* June 27, 1994, 68–70, 74, 76.

Semler, Ricardo. *Maverick* (New York: Warner Books, 1993).

Serwer, Andrew E. "Lessons from America's Fastest Growing Companies," *Fortune,* August 8, 1994, 42–45, 48–51, 54, 56, 59–60.

Stewart, Thomas A. "Managing in a Wired Company," *Fortune,* July 11, 1994, 44–47, 50, 54, 56.

Tully, Shawn. "Why to Go for Stretch Targets," *Fortune,* November 14, 1994, 145–146, 148, 150, 154, 158.

Suggested Readings

Fierman, Jaclyn. "Do Women Manage Differently?" *Fortune* (December 17, 1990): 115–116, 118.

Howard, Robert. "Values Make the Company: An Interview with Robert Haas." *Harvard Business Review* (September–October 1990): 132–144.

Katzenbach, Jon R., and Smith, Douglas K. *The Wisdom of Teams* (Boston: Harvard Business School Press, 1993).

Kotter, John P. "What Leaders Really Do." *Harvard Business Review* (May–June 1990): 103–111.

Mintzberg, Henry. "The Effective Organization: Forces and Forms." *Sloan Management Review* (Winter 1991): 54–67.

Pacetta, Frank, and Gittines, Roger. *Don't Fire Them, Fire Them Up* (New York: Simon & Schuster, 1994).

Rodgers, T. J. "No Excuses Management." *Harvard Business Review* (July–August 1990): 84–98.

Rosener, Judy B. "Ways Women Lead." *Harvard Business Review* (November–December 1990): 119–125.

Semler, Ricardo. *Maverick* (New York: Warner Books, 1993).

PART II

YOU AND YOUR PEOPLE

Part II contains six chapters about topics that influence or bear directly on the routine relationships between supervisors, team leaders, team facilitators, and their associates.

Chapter 5 is concerned with understanding others and with being understood. Communicating is at the heart of all of your efforts and activities. It is the most basic process performed by every manager in every organization. It is a two-way process governed by specific principles and hindered by specific kinds of barriers; both are examined in detail.

Chapter 6 examines attitudes and how they can be changed. People's attitudes determine how they approach problems, situations, and other people. As a supervisor, your attitudes and your subordinates' attitudes directly affect the success of your unit and people.

Chapter 7 explores the most important theories and models for understanding why people do what they do. It presents the needs all people have in common and what supervisors can do to help their people become and remain motivated.

145

Chapter 8 is concerned with the supervisor's effort to build sound relationships with individuals—associates, peers, and superiors—on the job. At the core of this effort are the need to know each person as an individual; the recognition and appreciation of differences in people; and the practice of the four basic human relations roles of educator, counselor, judge, and spokesperson.

Chapter 9 focuses on the interaction between a supervisor and groups of subordinates. Formal and informal groups are examined along with how they form and how they affect their members.

Chapter 10 covers the various theories and principles that govern the complexities of leading and being perceived as a leader. It explores basic leadership and management styles and suggests when each is appropriate. Supervisors must be able to use each style as dictated by people or circumstances.

Communications

OBJECTIVES

After reading and discussing this chapter, you should be able to do the following:

1. Define this chapter's key terms.

2. List the four major goals of communication.

3. Describe the purposes of a management information system (MIS).

4. List the basic components in the communication process.

5. Outline the steps one should take in planning a communication.

6. List and explain the barriers that can inhibit your efforts to communicate at work.

7. Explain four ways of improving your listening skills.

INTRODUCTION

The importance of communications to you as a traditional supervisor, team leader, or team facilitator cannot be overstated. You must routinely give orders and instructions and relay information and ideas to and from your subordinates, associates, team members, superiors, and peers. Your plans can come to fruition only through effective communications.

communication

the transmission of information and common understanding from one person or group to another through the use of common symbols

Communication is the transmission of information and understanding from one person or group to another through the use of common symbols. **Information** is defined as facts, figures, or words in a usable form—the result of processing data. Information can be conveyed in a nonverbal form by using pictures, charts, colors, objects, gestures, sign language, facial expressions, and body postures. It is usable if it conveys meaning or knowledge—something of use to the receiver (viewer or listener). By **understanding**, we mean that all parties to a communication are of one mind as to its meaning and intent. The understanding that you should seek when receiving a communication is the exact perception of what the other person or group is trying to convey or transmit to you.

information

any facts, figures, or data that are in a form or format that makes them usable to a person who possesses them

Communications can flow downward (vertically or diagonally), upward (vertically or diagonally), or horizontally (left or right). Recalling our previous discussions in this text with regard to organization charts, you will remember that the lines connecting the various blocks of the management hierarchy are, among other things, lines for formal and routine business communications. They are to be used when one manager wishes to share information and understanding with other managers. By using them, managers are helping to plan, organize, direct, control, and coordinate their operations.

understanding

all parties to a communication are of one mind regarding its meaning and intent

GOALS OF COMMUNICATION

All of your communications have as their objective or goal the production of one or more of the following responses:

- To be understood—to get something across to someone so that he or she knows exactly what you mean
- To understand others—to get to know their exact meanings and intentions
- To gain acceptance for yourself or your ideas
- To produce action or change—to get the other person or group to understand what is expected, when it is needed, why it is necessary, and how to do it

All these goals point out the two-way nature of communications: Communications take place between one person or group and another person or group. There must be a common understanding; that is, each person must know the other's meaning and intent. One or both parties may have to ask questions to determine exactly what the other person means. Whether you are the initiator of or the target for a communication, you have the duty to seek common understanding—to be understood and to understand.

When you initiate communication, you should attempt to give the other person or group your exact perception and meaning. Communicating requires a two-way effort. Ideally, all parties to the process should be active participants; unfortunately, this is not always the case. Consider a teacher's instructions to the class: "Put your name at the top of a blank sheet of paper." Without questions, the students begin to write. But what does the teacher want them to do? Should they use a pen or pencil? Will any size or color paper do? Should they print or write? Should they put their first names first or their last names first? The point is that without further instructions, they will not be certain of the teacher's intentions until they seek additional information from the teacher.

Before you can listen attentively to another person, the area surrounding you must be free of distractions. Both parties must concentrate on the ideas and offerings under discussion, clearing their minds of anything that could interfere with the exchange. After someone speaks to you, try rephrasing what the person has said. Put what you think the person said into your own words, and ask if that is an accurate restatement. Rephrasing is important because it forces you to listen for meaning as well as to words. You may restate a person's words verbatim and still not understand his or her underlying meaning. Once you understand the words, try next to understand what the person intends as well. We examine techniques for effective listening later in this chapter.

PLANNING COMMUNICATIONS

No matter to whom or why you feel the need to communicate your ideas, planning must precede the act of communication. The following checklist will serve you well as a sequential list of questions to answer as you prepare to communicate:

1. Is this communication really necessary? Will whatever I want to communicate improve the present situation? If you have no clear answer to these questions, proceed no further until you do.
2. What are the objectives I wish to achieve by communicating? Do I want action? Understanding? Acceptance?
3. What are the essential facts? Do I know them, and (more important) am I able to express them properly?

4. Are my thoughts outlined? Whether your outline is mental or written, keep it brief and to the point.

5. Have I considered my receivers? What are their needs, and how can I sell my message to them? Do I know their backgrounds and frames of reference for this message? What about our relationship? Have I included the why in the message?

6. Have I chosen the right symbols? Whether words, pictures, or some other symbols, are they correct for this communication? Remember that words take on meaning both from the context in which they appear and in the minds of the people involved in the communication process.

7. How should I communicate this message? Face to face? In writing? If in writing, should I use a memo? A letter? Have I time for formal channels, or should I go directly to my intended receivers?

8. When should I communicate? Am I aware of the time element and the receptiveness of my receivers? When will the environment be most free of anticipated disturbances?

9. Have I allowed for questions? Will I be able to judge my receivers' reactions, and will they be able to seek further information from me if they want to? How will I be sure my message has been received and properly interpreted?

THE COMMUNICATION PROCESS

There are six major components or variables in the communication process: the **transmitter** (sender), the **message** (the sender's feelings, intent, ideas, and their meaning), the **direction** (flow of the message), the **medium** (the message carrier), the **receiver** (intended audience), and the **feedback** (efforts by either sender or receiver to clarify the meaning and intent of a message—to seek a mutual understanding). The interaction and mix of these can cause effective or ineffective communications—the transmission of understanding or a failure to do so correctly. Exhibit 5.1 summarizes the communication process.

The Transmitter

As this chapter points out, the effort to communicate is quite complex. Before you attempt to engage in it, you must be certain of the purpose(s) you wish to achieve. What goal do you want to accomplish? Who should receive your message? What is the best way (in person or in writing) to communicate the message? Only after you answer these and related questions will you be ready to outline your thoughts and convey them to others. When you lack the depth of knowledge necessary to communicate, additional research and analysis will be needed. Equally important to the

transmitter
the person or group that sends a message to a receiver

message
the ideas, intent, and feelings that you wish to communicate to a receiver

direction
in communication, the flow or path a message takes in order to reach a receiver

medium
a channel or means used to carry a message in the communication process

receiver
the person or group intended by transmitters to receive their messages

feedback
any effort made by parties to a communication to ensure that they have a common understanding of each other's meaning and intent

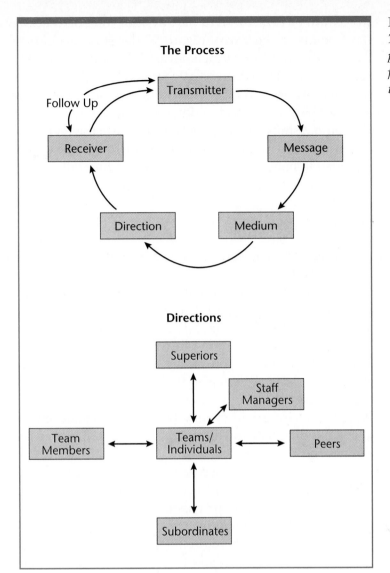

The Process

Follow Up

Transmitter

Receiver

Message

Direction

Medium

Directions

Superiors

Staff Managers

Team Members

Teams/ Individuals

Peers

Subordinates

message's content in ideas is its emotional content and sense of urgency or importance to both you and your receiver. Your attitudes reflect your predispositions toward a subject and will affect the tone of your message. Receivers will know by listening to or reading your messages how you feel about their content. A sense of importance will come through (or not), depending on your feelings about the information.

The Message

Your message consists of your feelings, intent, ideas and their meaning that you want to communicate. What you wish to communicate dictates, in part, your choices regarding the other five components. Your choice of words will be influenced in part by your intended receiver and his, her, or their points of view with regard to the subject matter of your message. How much you have to include, as well as how you will phrase your message, depends in part on what your receiver already knows about the subject and its importance. Abbreviations, acronyms, and slang may be acceptable if your receiver knows what you mean when you use them. Exhibit 5.2 shows a computer and its basic augmentation devices, known as peripherals. A guide to computer memory and a glossary of terms are provided to help translate some of the techno-talk and computerese heard so frequently today.

The Direction

As a traditional supervisor or team facilitator, you will most frequently send your communications in an upward or downward direction. You will be communicating most often with associates, team leaders, or your boss. Both directions carry with them inherent problems. The major problem is that the content of your message will be filtered through and possibly distorted by each person or level that it passes through. People may assume that they know what you intend and will often rephrase the message in their own words as they pass it along to others. Lack of first-hand knowledge or experience with the subject can also cause trouble. The necessary background information may be missing on the higher or lower levels. One solution exists for these problems in the use of feedback, which we discuss shortly.

As a traditional supervisor, team leader, or team facilitator, you use diagonal communication to communicate with staff specialists. Diagonal communication can occur outside formal channels, leaving your boss out of the flow. This is often the case when staff managers possess functional authority. It is wise, therefore, to keep records of all such correspondence and to check with your boss before answering or reacting to staff orders or requests. A simple memo can keep your boss informed of actions that you eventually take. When you are contacted by staff specialists who do not have functional authority, ask them to clear their requests through your boss.

As a traditional supervisor and team facilitator, you use horizontal paths to communicate with peers. As a team leader, you use them to coordinate your team's operations with those of other team leaders. Team members communicate horizontally on a regular basis. You also use horizontal paths to resolve conflicts and mutual problems between and among both groups.

> Ellen Lord, a team leader at Davidson Interiors, a division of Textron in Dover, New Hampshire, found that to keep teams happy, managers must have the patience and presence of mind to act like a parent, teacher, and referee all at once.... [Her] team members in the early days

Glossary

Accelerator board: Speeds up your computer.

Applications: These are the programs that allow you to do work, play games, pay bills, etc.

ASCII: American Standard Code for Information Interchange, pronounced "askee." It allows the accurate transmission of data between different computers.

Bus: A "highway" of wires connecting one part of a computer to another.

Card: A plastic board with electronic parts and connecting circuits. It expands the computer's power.

Coprocessor: Used to relieve the CPU from time-consuming tasks such as math calculations. Allows for faster operations.

Download: To "grab" something from another computer, generally via a modem.

E-mail: Electronic mail. Easier than the Postal Service but not as universal. Yet.

Hz: Hertz, a measure or frequency used to gauge speed. One Hz = one cycle per second. A megahertz (MHz) equals 1 million cycles per second.

Multimedia: Combining text, graphics, sound, video and/or animation in a presentation.

Operating system: Software, like MS DOS, that controls basic computer tasks.

Pixels: The tiny rectangles that compose the image on a TV screen or monitor.

Port: The location where peripherals like printers connect to the computer body.

SCSI: Small computer systems interface, pronounced "scuzzy." A connection used to transfer data at high speeds between the computer and another device, such as a printer or CD-ROM.

Setup

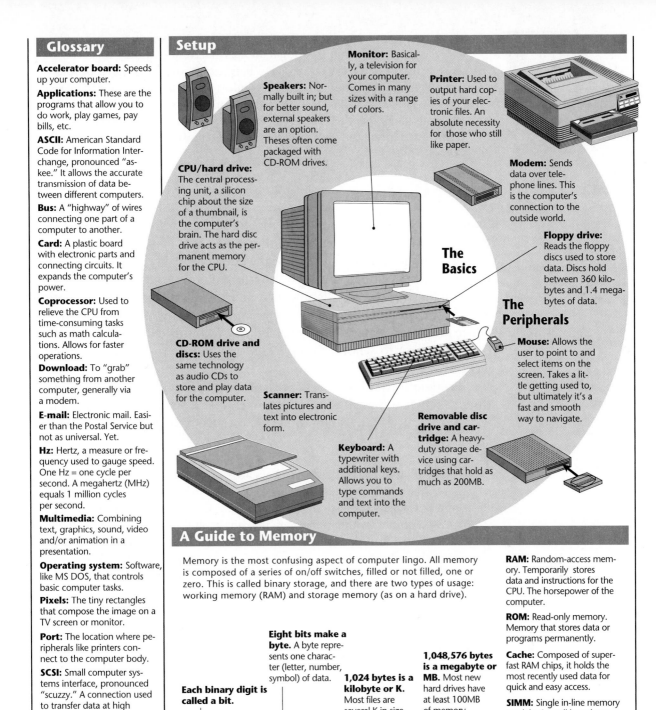

Monitor: Basically, a television for your computer. Comes in many sizes with a range of colors.

Speakers: Normally built in; but for better sound, external speakers are an option. Theses often come packaged with CD-ROM drives.

Printer: Used to output hard copies of your electronic files. An absolute necessity for those who still like paper.

CPU/hard drive: The central processing unit, a silicon chip about the size of a thumbnail, is the computer's brain. The hard disc drive acts as the permanent memory for the CPU.

Modem: Sends data over telephone lines. This is the computer's connection to the outside world.

The Basics

Floppy drive: Reads the floppy discs used to store data. Discs hold between 360 kilobytes and 1.4 megabytes of data.

The Peripherals

CD-ROM drive and discs: Uses the same technology as audio CDs to store and play data for the computer.

Mouse: Allows the user to point to and select items on the screen. Takes a little getting used to, but ultimately it's a fast and smooth way to navigate.

Scanner: Translates pictures and text into electronic form.

Removable disc drive and cartridge: A heavy-duty storage device using cartridges that hold as much as 200MB.

Keyboard: A typewriter with additional keys. Allows you to type commands and text into the computer.

A Guide to Memory

Memory is the most confusing aspect of computer lingo. All memory is composed of a series of on/off switches, filled or not filled, one or zero. This is called binary storage, and there are two types of usage: working memory (RAM) and storage memory (as on a hard drive).

RAM: Random-access memory. Temporarily stores data and instructions for the CPU. The horsepower of the computer.

ROM: Read-only memory. Memory that stores data or programs permanently.

Cache: Composed of super-fast RAM chips, it holds the most recently used data for quick and easy access.

SIMM: Single in-line memory module. A small board containing additional RAM. Boosts the power of the PC.

Eight bits make a byte. A byte represents one character (letter, number, symbol) of data.

1,024 bytes is a kilobyte or K. Most files are several K in size.

1,048,576 bytes is a megabyte or MB. Most new hard drives have at least 100MB of memory.

Each binary digit is called a bit.

1011010010111100101100010101001110100011101000111

EXHIBIT 5.2

The ABCs of computing.

Source: "The ABCs of Computing," in *Computers & the Family,* Special Issue, Newsweek Fall 1994, 14.

sometimes got into fights. A neatnik sitting next to a slob lost his cool. People were becoming emotional about what kind of coffee was brewing in the pot.... [N]o matter how bad it gets you must keep people together and talking until they feel comfortable, a process that can take months. Says she: "We threw all the people in one room and forced them to work together. If people from different functions don't get to know each other, they can't ask favors, and teamwork stalls" (Dumaine, 1994).

The Medium

Your choice of a medium may be dictated by your choice of a receiver. If the receiver is a team leader or team member, oral conversations in person with individuals and teams are usually adequate. Your boss, however, may require written correspondence most often; this is especially when the contents have historical significance and relate to his or her evaluations about your unit's progress. Written communications provide specific evidence for use at a later date regarding just what was communicated, when, by whom, and to whom. Complicated messages are best transmitted in writing.

Some information is best presented in tables, charts, graphs, or pictures. Such visual media can communicate at a glance what would otherwise take many paragraphs to get across. Computer graphics provide a case in point.

> At...Boeing in Seattle,... researchers are developing head-mounted displays that put computer graphics to uses that are...helping workers do complex wiring or place the perfect rivet.... Cables connect the headset to a computer, which generates the image and changes it when the worker turns or proceeds to a new task; a magnetic or ultrasonic receiver on the helmet helps the system track its position...so the wearer sees a diagram superimposed on whatever he's working (Sprout, 1994).

Different media have different effects on receivers. Most people are used to seeing company bulletins, memos, and newsletters because they are routinely used to carry information. As a result, these media lose their ability to capture people's attention and gain their interest. They are read casually, if at all, and may be set aside during busy times to be read at a later date. Further, using two or more media either sequentially or simultaneously can add emphasis and help ensure that reception takes place. Overuse or improper use of such markings as "urgent" or "for your immediate attention" can cause them to become routine and worthy of no great concern. Unusual media should be used to carry only unusual messages.

It is important to use the technology at hand in your organization as it best applies to your purposes and needs. Of particular note are e-mail, voice-mail, voice-messaging, networking, and groupware software packages. E-mail allows others to access your computer mailbox and leave a written message. Voice mail allows someone to leave a spoken message. Voice messaging allows you to send and access your messages through the use of a touch-tone phone and a voice-mail system such as:

> ...Cleveland-based Voice-Tel...Mailbox holders...use a local number to gain access to the system.... The provider's computer instantly recognizes who's calling and which pool of seven-digit-number mailboxes...that caller connects to. When the link is established, the caller can dial around the network as in a typical...voice-mail system—except that with messaging, the other mailboxes can be scattered across the continent, and users can play phone tag all day without incurring long-distance charges (*Inc.*, "Voice," 1994).

Networks focus horizontally connecting "...people to people and people to data" (Stewart, 1994). Through groupware such as Lotus Notes, users of networks share information from a common database—information is entered into a database that can be accessed by anyone in need of it. Filtering is eliminated. "Interdepartmental problem-solving teams form spontaneously [providing] easy links across functional boundaries..." (Stewart, 1994). Groupware allows for teleconferencing and networking between individuals and teams. All may focus on the same problem, information, or situation simultaneously and interact with one another directly.

Growing in popularity are a host of online computer services, accessible through computers and their modems, that allow the sending and receiving of information over telephone lines.

> By dialing up mass-market online services such as Prodigy, America Online, and CompuServe or business-oriented services such as Dialog, Data-Star, and Dow Jones News/Retrieval, computer users can quickly and affordably access the latest market data or stock quotes, shop for office equipment and supplies, get free technical support from leading hardware and software vendors, and even book a flight to Tokyo (Resnick, 1994).

For a quick summary of the latest online computer buzzwords, see Exhibit 5.3.

The Receivers

Just as you must know yourself—your feelings and attitudes about your subject—so too should you know your receiver's. Your own experience tells you that some subjects are received with more enthusiasm and interest than others. Some subjects touch off emotional responses and can inhibit reason and understanding. Try to determine your receiver's prior knowledge and predisposition toward the subject about which you wish to communicate before you attempt to do so. Delicate subjects, such as those requiring reprimands or punitive measures, are best handled in person,

EXHIBIT 5.3
Online computer buzz-words.

Source: Resnick, Rosalind. "Hitching a Ride into Cyberspace," *Nation's Business,* July 1994, 67.

Online Computer Buzzwords

Here are some terms you're likely to come across in exploring online data services:

Bulletin Board System: A bulletin board system (often called a BBS) is similar to an online service but is usually much more limited. At last count, there were more than 50,000 bulletin boards nationwide, most of them run by hobbyists who offer electronic mail (e-mail), file-transfer capabilities, and free or low-cost software programs free of connect-time charges.

Online services such as Prodigy and CompuServe offer bulletin boards, too, on a wide variety of personal, professional, and computing topics.

Communications Software: Just as you need a word-processing program to type a letter and a spreadsheet program to track your accounts receivable, you need special communications software to use your modem.

Almost all leading programs have two features: an automated dialing directory similar to the speed dial on your telephone, and the ability to send and receive text and data files (known in the online world as uploading and downloading).

Some programs are multipurpose, allowing you to dial up any number of online services and electronic bulletin boards; others are front-end programs that make it easier to dial up and navigate a specific online service.

Modem: Like a foreign-language translator, a modem is a device that converts the digital 0's and 1's produced by your computer into analog sound waves capable of being carried over conventional phone lines. In the world of high-tech electronics, computer-to-telephone translation is called modulation, while telephone-to-computer translation is called demodulation. Thus, the name modem was derived.

Modems come in two varieties: internal modems, which attach to a card inside your personal computer, and external modems, which plug into the computer's serial port.

Online Service: Online services offer a gateway to the world of electronic information. By dialing the service with your computer and modem, you can access online bookstores, libraries, newspapers, encyclopedias, bulletin boards, clipping services, department stores, travel agencies, and banking services.

You can also send electronic messages and data to people thousands of miles away for the cost of a local phone call. And, unlike stores and libraries, which close in the evening, online services are always open.

Real Time: Time when you are engaged in an actual conversation, but you are talking electronically with someone via a modem rather than face to face.

one on one, and in private. By knowing your receivers well and anticipating how they are likely to view your message, you can tailor your message's words, tone, and method of delivery to fit the circumstances.

Of note here also are the growing number of telecommuters (teleworkers) being used by governments and such businesses as IBM, AT&T, Du Pont, American Express, and Pacific Bell. This practice is growing because of the Clean Air Act pressures to reduce work-related vehicle use, the efforts of many companies to downsize and trim their overhead costs, and the lost productivity due to commuting times.

Telework centers—or telebusiness centers—have been established throughout the [United States] to keep workers closer to home, thereby reducing their commuting to and from distant offices. Telecommuters use the centers to hold client meetings, do paperwork, complete reports, or make telephone calls. Work space ranges from cubicles to private offices, which can sometimes be leased for as short as an hour. The centers are equipped with computers, modems, copiers, printers, and sophisticated phone services. Other services include videoconferencing and secretarial support (Maynard, 1994).

Based on teleworkers' experiences in Denver's city and county governments, teleworkers are "...at least as productive at home as they were at the office.... Teleworkers abide by managers' rules...because they don't want to jeopardize their job situations" (Maynard, 1994). Laptop computers have made many more people eligible for this role. And for many workers, a daily physical presence at work is really not necessary.

The Feedback

Feedback allows both the sender and receiver to discover if they are of one mind as to the meaning and intent of a message. The primary burden rests with the receiver. When you consent to receive a message, you consent to engage in feedback efforts with the sender; you must make certain that you both have a similar understanding. It is in your own best interest to do so. When a receiver engages in feedback, he or she becomes a sender; the sender then becomes a receiver and should engage in feedback. If the receiver does not engage in feedback, the sender must do so. Asking a receiver to restate a message in his or her own words is a good start. Anticipate where misunderstanding might take place, and quiz the receiver about those areas. Only when both sender and receiver have the same understanding has communication taken place.

The word *feedback* has other meanings in communications: Giving people, individually and in teams, reactions to (praise, constructive criticism) and measurements of their performances. The latter is often referred to as **scoreboarding,** which is an effort to:

> ...set up a game designed to change [a] situation. It has an easily measurable goal [usually quantifiable].... It has rules that everybody understands. At the end there's some kind of payoff for a win.... Teach everybody to track [the] numbers. Show employees how what they do affects the figures. Then put up a big scoreboard and watch what happens. Oh, yes—pass out bonuses if employees hit monthly or quarterly targets (Case, 1994).

scoreboarding
providing feedback on individual and team efforts to reach goals

More will be said in later chapters about scoreboarding. It has the power to energize people and gain their commitments to a project.

COMMUNICATIONS BARRIERS

The essential ingredients in the communications recipe are the transmitter, the message, the direction, the medium, the receiver, and the feedback. If any of these ingredients is defective in any way, clarity of meaning and understanding will be lacking. Communications barriers can arise that will spoil these ingredients and, therefore, the communication process. What follows are seven major barriers to successful communications.

Uncommon Symbols

Words, like "feedback," take on meaning only in the context of the message they compose. Facial expressions can be misinterpreted. Gestures viewed out of context can take on entirely different meanings than were intended. Every child knows the blank expression that his or her slang expressions can evoke on the face of a parent. Every employee knows the discomfort and confusion that can arise when the boss exhibits unfamiliar or contradictory behaviors.

Example: Sally, the supervisor of a data-processing section, has an established pattern of communication. Each morning on entering her section, she greets each of her seven associates warmly and inquires about their well-being and work. Today, she entered the office and went straight to her desk, ignoring all of her subordinates. What do you think might happen in the minds of her subordinates? What might the impact of her behavior be on today's work output?

Communication problems arise when a message in one language must be translated into another. Translating is becoming increasingly necessary for many team leaders, team facilitators, and their companies. According to the U.S. Census Bureau and the 1990 census data, over 19.8 million foreign-born people were living in the United States, an increase of over 5 million since 1980. Spanish-speaking immigrants are the most numerous—some 22 percent of the total—with the largest numbers coming from Mexico. About 9 percent were from Asian nations, including South Korea, Vietnam, and China. The states experiencing the largest concentrations of foreign-born people are Texas, California, Florida, and New Jersey. The city with the greatest number of foreign-born residents is New York City.

Translating any language into another can create problems of interpretation. Consultant and author, Robert M. March (1992) comments on Japanese managers in their American-based companies:

> The connotations of a number of words and phrases translated from Japanese into English can vary greatly and lead to misunderstandings and worse…. Moreover, although the Japanese may speak English, it is still a Japanized English, and their knowledge of local idioms or slang is likely to be minimal, especially in countries like the USA and Australia, where everyday male business speech is replete with local color.

The European Community's translation service offers the following examples of literal translations of messages on signs that, after translation into English, did not come across exactly as their originators intended (Goldsmith, 1992):

- From a Swiss restaurant menu: "Our wines leave you nothing to hope for."
- From a bar in Norway: "Ladies are requested not to have children at the bar."
- From a furrier in Sweden: "Fur coats made for ladies from their own skins."
- From a doctor in Rome: "Specialist in women and other diseases."

Many companies that experience an influx of foreign-born employees have created English as a Second Language (ESL) programs that utilize teachers from neighboring schools. "Northeastern Products Company, a division of Campbell Soup Company, established an on-site ESL program to meet the needs of Hispanic and Asian employees, who represented 36 percent of its workforce" (Jamieson and O'Mara, 1991). Ore-Ida Foods in Idaho, a division of the H. J. Heinz Company, sponsors voluntary ESL classes and offers a tuition aid reimbursement program that covers the expense of Spanish classes (Jamieson and O'Mara, 1991).

You might want to consider the advice of one supervisor in California who leads a number of Spanish-speaking team members:

> I soon realized that if we were to avoid problems in communications I had to stop trying to have them translate their words into English. Since my company does not have language training and only a few of my subordinates speak any English, I bit the bullet. I learned enough Spanish in my spare time through an adult education class to enable me to communicate effectively with my team members. My team members appreciate my efforts and kid me about my broken Spanish. But we have helped each other with our languages and have become a more productive team.

Improper Timing

Unless the receiver is in the right frame of mind and tuned in on the proper channel, he or she will not hear your message. The sender can be upset, agitated, or improperly prepared to communicate. Sometimes the need for the message is too far removed from its transmission, or the message gets delayed in transmission and arrives too late to be effective. We all know the regrets that go with speaking in haste while we are in the heat of emotion or not thinking clearly. When we are distracted, we may hear words but not their intended meanings.

Example: Charlie is upset because of a personal problem with his wife. He has been thinking about it on and off since his arrival at work two hours ago. His team leader approaches him and begins a detailed explanation of a task he wants Charlie to perform before leaving today. Although Charlie is clearly distracted, he nods assent throughout the instructions. What might happen? What should the team leader have done?

Atmospheric Disturbances

The atmosphere or environment of your communications should be as free as possible from noise—any thing or condition in the physical environment that interferes with the transmission and understanding of information. Such conditions as static on the telephone line, the din of machines on the shop floor, and the simultaneous conversations of people in groups create background noise that inhibits communication. When people must shout to be heard or receive too many messages at one time, they experience noise. When noise exists, you must either remove it or relocate your effort to communicate to an environment more conducive to the process.

Example: A team leader had no sooner begun to interview a job applicant in her office when the phone rang. After handling the call, she resumed the interview. Five minutes later, a change in shift occurred, creating noise and confusion outside her office. How successful do you think this interview was for either person?

Improper Attitudes

Unfavorable predispositions toward the subject, the sender, or the receiver will interfere with understanding. In fact, they may provoke emotional and harmful responses in place of the desired ones. A poor attitude in the sender or the receiver will confuse rather than clarify.

Example: One of your subordinates, Shirley, comes to ask you again today if she has gotten the pay raise you recommended for her two weeks ago. She has been asking you about it for the past five days, and you have told her that, as soon as you know, you will tell her. Since you have not heard anything yet, you answer her tersely, "No! Now don't bother me!" Have you created problems for yourself by such a response? How do you think Shirley will react?

Communication problems caused by language can be alleviated through education. Some companies offer on-site ESL (English as a Second Language) courses, like this one at Ore-Ida Foods. Ore-Ida Foods also offers tuition reimbursement for those willing to learn Spanish.

Communicating in a noisy environment interferes with the transmission and understanding of information.

Background Differences

A lack of similar backgrounds in the sender and the receiver with respect to education, previous experiences, present environment, and even gender may hinder receptiveness to a message and prevent a proper reaction to it. Deborah Tannen (1994), author and professor, notes that the majority of men and women, "learn to speak particular ways *because* those ways are associated with their own gender. And individual men or women who speak in ways associated with the other gender will pay a price for departing from cultural expectations." When a newcomer attempts to give advice to the old-timer, the latter may react with irritation. These and many similar situations arise every day at work and usually interfere with communication efforts.

    Example: Allen, age twenty-five, is being trained by Arthur who is about to retire. Arthur is teaching Allen his job. While certain established procedures are being discussed, Allen recommends a change he feels will speed things up. Instead of evaluating Allen's proposal, Arthur shuts him off by stating, "Who's the expert here, you or me? This is the way I have always done it, and it works." What do you think will be Allen's reaction? What are the potential negative effects for the company?

    Communicating with people who differ significantly from you can be a challenge. One big problem is that most of us group people and use labels for them—Hispanics, blacks, whites, Asians, career women, handicapped, and so on. These labels can separate people and may be offensive to those to whom they are applied. The key to communicating with others is to determine what they want you to do and how they wish to be addressed—what they feel comfortable with—and to avoid generalizations and stereotypes.

Two examples serve to highlight the importance of personal communication with a boss, subordinate, or peer. When you ask a member of the Navajo people, "How are you?" you are implying that that person has been sick. This question is not an everyday greeting. It is an inquiry about how a person is doing on the road to recovery. In like fashion, a tendency you might have to ask a differently abled person if he or she needs help can be viewed by that person as an insulting expression of doubt about his or her ability to function independently. Most people with physical limitations will ask for assistance if they need it. They want to be treated like anyone else—on an individual and personal level.

Workshops with the physically challenged yield the following tips for communicating with handicapped subordinates or team members:

- Treat them with the respect and trust due to any employee or co-worker
- Ask them what they need to succeed, and empower them with the needed items, assistance, or conditions
- Don't expect anything less from them than you would expect from ablebodied subordinates in the same job
- Don't wait for them to experience problems in their physical environment; be proactive and seek to identify and to remove barriers to their mobility and productivity

Educate yourself on the attitudes and problems typically encountered on the job by people facing physical challenges. One supervisor who had a subordinate with impaired hearing took the time to learn sign language, and now communicates in this way or in writing with that person. Another supervisor quickly realized that her vision-impaired subordinate's productivity could be improved with the simple addition of a large magnifier lens affixed to a flexible arm attached to her desk. It greatly enhanced the readability of the text she had to work with.

Sender–Receiver Relationships

Potentially conflicting functional relationships, such as between line manager and staff manager or between engineer and accountant, can hinder communications. Suspicion on the part of one about the other's intentions or doubt about his or her ability to communicate about the other's specialty can block the transmission of information. Unequal positional or status relationships, such as between supervisor and subordinate or between skilled worker and apprentice, can cause one to tune out the other.

Example: A production supervisor is told by the chief personnel officer (who has functional authority over enforcing the labor–management collective bargaining agreement) that the production section will be reorganized into autonomous teams and that he is being assigned to training for a team leader position. Since the production manager resents being told by an "outsider" that she will have to learn to share authority with former subordinates, the supervisor resists the training assignment and begins to plot to sabotage the efforts at team building. What are the possible consequences? How could they have been prevented?

Nonquestioning Associates

Without conflict and discomfort, little meaningful change occurs in people and organizations. The saying "If it ain't broke, don't fix it" is often an excuse to maintain the old, familiar, and comfortable ways of doing things and may cause teams and their leaders to wait too long before reexamining the what, why, and how of their performances. A total quality-management philosophy demands that all persons and their organizations commit to continual and often radical efforts to improve. It requires a commitment to a never-ending journey.

In everyday organizational life, there are those who promote and those who object to change. Resistance, no matter what its motivation, is to be expected and helps promoters become aware of any flaws in their thinking—anything they may have overlooked that could spell disaster. When you and your team members propose the new and different, you should welcome disagreements and arguments both for and against proposals. When you don't receive any, you should suspect that you are surrounded by yes men and women. "If your [associates] haven't been disagreeing with you very much or very hard, you may need to do a bootlicking reality check. You may even need to reexamine your organization's incentive structure" (Norton, 1994).

Beware, also, of those among your associates who make proposals that they believe will please you and agree with yours. Such people rarely report unpleasant developments and may act to hide them from your view. According to research by economist Candice Prendergast at the University of Chicago, "...companies unwittingly create a culture of yes men [and women] when they rely on subjective performance evaluations of workers...the more the worker's pay is tied to the manager's opinion of [the worker], the more powerful [the worker's] incentive to say what the manager wants to hear" (Norton, 1994).

Example: This story is told about the founder of a company who held a meeting with his team facilitators to discuss a radical reorganization plan. The meeting went something like this:

> *Founder:* I trust all of you have read my proposal?
> *Team facilitators:* Responses and nodding of heads in the affirmative.
> *Founder:* Do you have any questions or objections?
> *Team facilitators:* Silence and nodding of heads in the negative.
> *Founder:* This meeting is adjourned and will reconvene when you all have both.

All barriers have the same effect on communications: Something less than a mutual understanding results. Knowing that these barriers exist is half the battle. The other half is working to tear them down or to minimize their effects.

MANAGEMENT AND INFORMATION

All managers and their teams exist to make decisions. To make them, they need a steady flow of many kinds of information. Information originates with data (raw facts and figures), which are then gathered, analyzed, and placed into appropriate formats. This information can then be delivered to those who need it. Specialized departments and activities exist in most larger organizations to accomplish these activities.

Management Information Systems

In most large businesses, a systems approach is needed to manage the inflow, processing, and outflow of both data and information. A management information system (MIS) is a formal organizational effort to make information of the right quality available to all decision makers. An organization's MIS should provide usable and needed information to the right people, at the right time, in the right amount, and at the right place. It may or may not use computers.

Designing an MIS begins with conducting a study or survey to determine who needs what kind of information, when, and in what quality and form. Information users help determine how the system will operate and what it will generate. Both users and data processors must cooperate to ensure that the system produces only what is needed—no more and no less—at a reasonable cost.

Author, research director, and professor Thomas H. Davenport (1994) offers the following insights for users of any MIS:

- Managers would rather get information from people than from computers.
- To make the most of electronic communications, employees must first learn to communicate face to face.
- The willingness of individuals to use a specified information format is directly proportional to how much they have participated in defining it or trust others who did.

Davenport adds that an MIS should be "human centered"; it should focus on how people use information rather than on hardware.

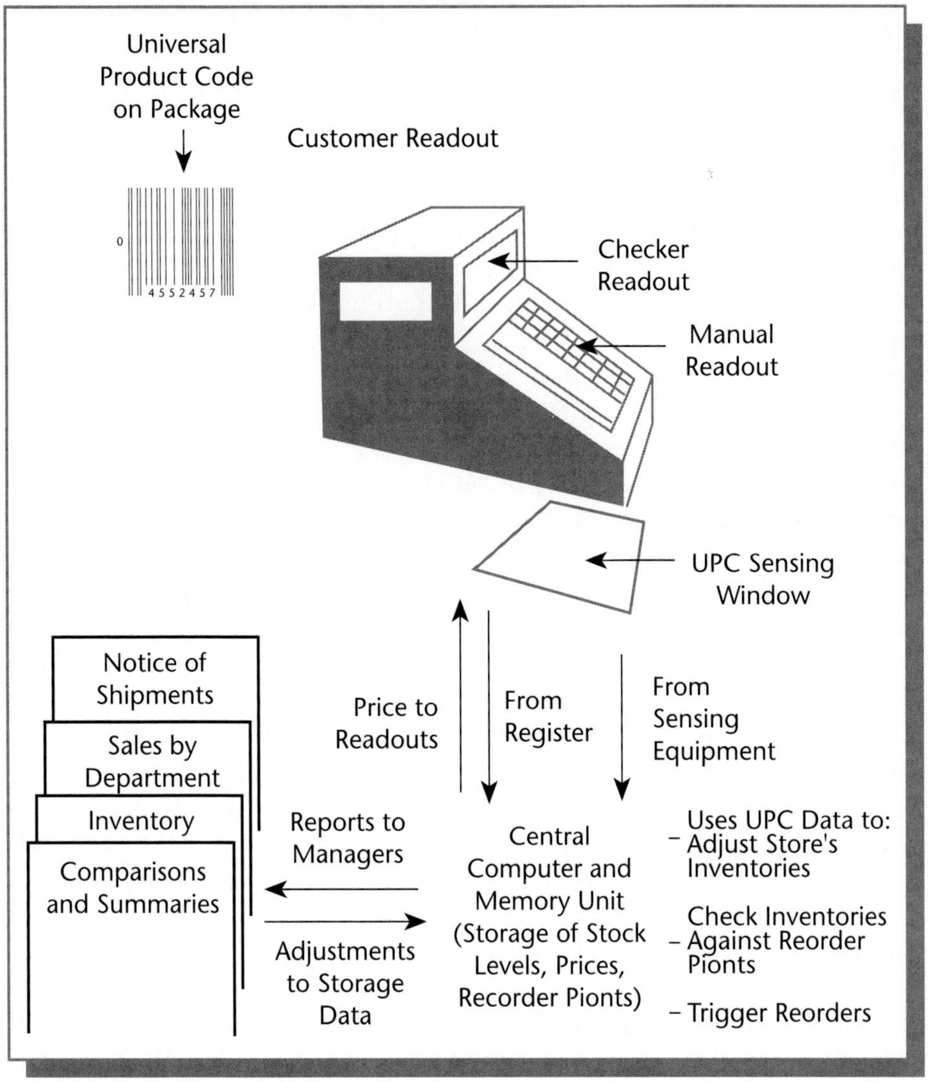
Universal
Product Code
on Package
Customer Readout
0
4552457
Checker
Readout
Manual
Readout
UPC Sensing
Window
Notice of
Shipments
Sales by
Department
Inventory
Comparisons
and Summaries
Price to
Readouts
From
Register
From
Sensing
Equipment
Reports to
Managers
Adjustments
to Storage
Data
Central
Computer and
Memory Unit
(Storage of Stock
Levels, Prices,
Recorder Pionts)
Uses UPC Data to:
- Adjust Store's
Inventories
- Check Inventories
Against Reorder
Pionts
- Trigger Reorders

EXHIBIT 5.4
The part of a chain store's MIS that uses electronic sensing and computerized data processing to assist in checkout, inventory control, and accounting procedures.

One example of an MIS that uses computers (a CIS) is found in many supermarket chain stores. Their checkout lanes are equipped with cash registers and electronic sensing equipment linked directly to a central computer. Most items in these stores' inventories have data stored in the universal product codes (UPCs—the panels on the products that contain solid black lines and numbers below them). The UPCs are sensed at the checkout counter, and the data they contain are sent directly to a computer. Exhibit 5.4 summarizes such a checkout system. It is only one part of the chain's MIS but a vital one. It provides both data and information to the checker, the customer, and the store's and the chain's managers. The UPC data are needed to keep track of the store's inventory and sales, to assist in consolidated purchasing by the chain, and to carry out the routine accounting activities for both the store and the chain.

The Supervisor and the MIS

As a traditional supervisor, team leader, or team facilitator, you are part of your organization's MIS. Whether it is a formal, planned system using sophisticated computers and software or not, you send data to it and receive information from it. After you determine your information needs, you should consult with MIS specialists about meeting these needs. Once methods are in place, you should review them regularly.

Are you receiving too much information, information in the wrong form, outdated information, or not enough information? If so, take action now to improve your situation. Stop the flow of unneeded information. Help create a flow of information you lack. Let those who generate your information know how well they are meeting your needs. You are one of their customers, and they exist to satisfy their customers. If your organization lacks an adequate MIS, investigate what you and your peers can do to create one.

Communicating with Associates   You communicate with subordinates, team members, and team leaders most often and for many reasons. They want to know what you expect from them. They expect and need information from you on their progress, successes, and shortcomings. You should pass memos, bulletins, and reports from others to them on an as-needed basis. Your practice of management by wandering around (MBWA) allows you ample opportunity to find out what is on their minds, what they are feeling and thinking about, and how you should rate them and their performance. Their activities and goals must be coordinated with those of your other subordinates.

Communicating with Peers   Your peers consist of all managers who are on the same level of the company's hierarchy as you are. Touching base with peers regularly allows you to build friendships, share information, coordinate operations, and teach as well as learn. Open and honest communication with peers builds the type of teamwork and mutual commitment to values, goals, and strategies so essential to good working relationships.

Communicating with Others   Others you must communicate with regularly include your boss, staff managers, and outsiders such as customers and suppliers. The boss wants to be kept up to date on your progress and on that of your section, without having to ask for updates. He or she wants to know what your goals are and what information and help you need. Staff people want to be consulted so that they can share their expertise. They need to know your progress on problems they have been asked to help you solve. They want to find you receptive to their suggestions and assistance.

In all of your communications, you should recognize two principles: (1) that you have the right to be heard and understood and (2) that you

The task of leading a team regularly requires a constant focus on cooperation, interaction, and on occasion, personal sacrifices. The leader must focus on what is best for the team *and* the customers it exists to serve. Team leader Gail A. Smith found that although she and her team members liked telecommuting and it provided "comfort and economy," it was not what was best for her clients. After trying to run her team of interactive training software people from her home as telecommuters, Gail soon discovered several reasons why continuing the practice would have led to failure:

- The need to "team." Easy, quick access by each team member to all other team members was vital to problem solving.
- Client expectations. Quick responses to customers was essential. Not working together increased response times.
- Focus. Too many distractions existed at home for her.
- The need for speed. Gail helped found the company, and it had to move quickly to capture markets. Working together in one location proved to be the best solution.

Her crew of seven now operates out of a crowded space, the solution she believes will allow her team and company to succeed.

Source: Smith, Gail A. "When Not to Work Out of the Home," *Nation's Business,* July 1994, 10.

must respect the same right for others. Self-esteem and respect for others are the most essential attitudes of supervisors, team leaders, and team facilitators (Weiss, 1986).

COMPUTERS AND COMMUNICATIONS

"Since 1987, we've added over 130 million information receptacles. Americans now possess 146.6 million e-mail addresses, cellular phones, pagers, fax machines, voice mailboxes, and answering machines—up 365% from...1987" (Tetzeli, 1994). IBM has some unique applications for the computers it uses. An IBM computer can dial a repair office when it is in need of fixing. Its electronic bulletin board connects computer dealers across the United States so that they can find out about price changes

John Yeh, president of Integrated Microcomputer Systems, never lets his speech and hearing impairments get in the way of communication. He has used his nonverbal skills to build a highly successful company.

and other news. All 20,000 IBM repair people carry handheld computers to send messages to and from the home office through a network of 1,000 radio towers across the nation. By networking its computers, IBM gives its people everywhere access to data stored at many locations (Lewin, 1987).

America's largest and most successful retailer is Wal-Mart, which also includes Sam's wholesale outlets. Before he died, Sam Walton saw to it that Wal-Mart's stores and managers were connected to his companies' suppliers. Through interfacing computer networks, store managers track sales by inventory item, rarely run out of stock, keep in touch with suppliers, keep tabs on the progress of orders, and allow suppliers to tap in to their computer memories. Such instant communication and monitoring allows the organization to respond to any trends and changes in consumer preferences within a few hours. Stores can communicate with the home office, each other, and their suppliers with the touch of a few keys on their computer keyboards. Vendors stay on top of the trends that may be developing and are able to respond to the buyers' needs within hours.

Computers can make work faster and more efficient. They can eliminate paperwork, make information flow more freely, put information into more useful forms, and reduce costs. Unfortunately, they can also create more stress for the people who use them. As with so many other things, the manner in which computers are used can mean either that work will be more efficient or that it will be more tedious. If people are not taught how to use their computer technology properly, they will fear and misuse it. If people see computers as another way that management can keep track of them and monitor their work, they may resent management.

What is developing in many companies is a managerial workstation—one equipped with several systems that can increase the efficiency and productivity of managers at every level:

- Portable computers—laptops and palmtops—with built-in modems to allow telephone linkups between them and others. Many managers have portable offices in their cars that carry their computers, telephones, modems, fax machines, and printers.
- Teleconferencing through either cable or satellite communication links allowing people in different locations to see, hear, and speak to one another. Xerox research people use videoconferencing to link them no matter where they happen to be.
- Problem-solving sessions with members seated around a table and simultaneously typing their input into their networked (with or with-

out cable connections) computers. Boeing employees—engineers, designers, machinists, and manufacturing people—used IBM's TeamFocus software to create, in fifteen electronic meetings, a standardized control system for complex machine tools used in several of their plants (Kirkpatrick, 1992).

- Computer software that allows voice-activated commands for physically challenged employees, enabling a computer to "learn" the operator's vocabulary and execute commands without keyboard input. Allstate Insurance companies have such aids for their physically challenged employees.

If this equipment looks and sounds strange to you, it won't for long. Do what you can now to become familiar with how you and your company can put these and many other innovative methods and tools to use in managing your tasks, people, and information more effectively.

SPOKEN COMMUNICATIONS

All successful managers have two basic qualities in common: the ability to think logically (analyze and problem solve) and the ability to communicate effectively. The most frequently used form of communication for a supervisor is oral. The ability to express yourself effectively through the use of spoken words is the most important tool at your disposal.

Effective speaking is much more than knowing correct grammar. You must have a clear purpose in mind, know your audience, and be certain of the type of response you wish to receive. Your way of talking to Juanita is probably different from your way of talking to Elle, even though your subject is the same with both. Elle requires key concepts cemented to several application examples (a kind of show and tell), whereas Juanita requires that you link your message to her experiences.

As you speak, watch your listeners' facial expressions and body language. Give your listeners time to ask questions. If they do not, ask some of your own in order to check their understanding and keep their attention.

Tailor your message to your audience. Choose your words carefully. Use the minimum number of words possible to get your point across. Be honest and open, and your message will be welcomed. Stick to the facts, and leave out the personal opinions. If your listeners ask for more information than you have, do not bluff. Tell them you will get it and give it to them as soon as you can; be sure to do so.

Basic Ingredients

An effective oral presentation to individuals or to groups usually contains three stages: the introduction, the explanation, and the summary. All three parts have a definite purpose and specific ingredients. Our primary focus here is on communications between individuals alone or in groups.

The Introduction   The introduction or beginning of your oral presentation should attempt to do three things: (1) get the listener's attention, (2) arouse interest, and (3) introduce the subject matter and purpose of the communication. The introduction can enable you to gain the listener's attention through a number of devices: a statement designed to startle or amaze, a quotation from a famous source, an anecdote or story with a moral or lesson, or a question that will be answered later in the oral communication (see Exhibit 5.5). To convey the subject matter and the purpose of the communication, you as speaker can simply state what you intend to talk about, why the communication is necessary, and what goals and responses you have in mind. To obtain and keep the listener's interest, you need to say why the communication is necessary and how the message will affect your listener. An effort should be made to relate the oral presentation and the words you choose to your listener's experience, job, or special interests.

The Explanation   The explanation follows the introduction and should also be well organized. It will be well organized if it flows logically from one key point to another. To make sure that it does, you must identify the key points or ideas; you must group them in a sequence that makes sense; and then you must present them in that sequence to your listener.

EXHIBIT 5.5

Guide to planning your oral presentation.

Introduction

- Gain the listener's attention
- Arouse the listener's interest
- Introduce your purpose
- Introduce your idea

Explanation

- Develop your idea with logic and examples
- Link your idea to the listener's interests
- Use language your listener will understand
- Keep it brief and on track
- Use illustrations and graphics whenever possible
- Invite questions when and where appropriate

Summary

- Restate your idea and its advantages to your listener
- Call for questions and be prepared to ask some of your own to check on the listener's understanding of the topic
- State the specific actions you desire and are calling for

Transitions from one point to another should be thought out, and they should carry your listener logically from one point or idea to the next. Emphasis should be used to help your listener define in his or her own mind what the key points are and why they are worth knowing and remembering. Some devices for adding emphasis include repetition, voice tone and inflection, specific wording such as "this is really important," visual aids, and specific questions. When speaking, use these devices to fix important ideas in your receiver's mind.

The Summary   A summary may occur at any stage in an oral presentation where it might be helpful to restate important points you have been making. Frequent summaries aid the memory and add emphasis. Any oral communication should be concluded with a comprehensive summary of all the key ideas, as well as of the responses expected from your listener. This final summary is your opportunity to reemphasize major points, to clarify the message through questions, and to leave a lasting impression with your listener. It should restate the goals and actions expected as a result of the communication in a way similar to how they were first stated in your introduction.

The Informational Meeting

An informational meeting is used to disseminate various kinds of information to all of your people or to certain groups of them. Usually, you will use the lecture format to communicate information about such topics as status reports on work (scoreboarding), new projects or programs in progress, or the interpretation of changes taking place elsewhere in the company that will affect your department and its members.

Many teams hold such meetings fairly regularly since they feel it offers them an excellent opportunity to relate to their teammates and communicate with them efficiently with relatively little time and effort. It is easier to say things once to all those affected than to try to reach each individually. In addition, items of interest that accumulate daily can be assembled and dispensed with before they become dated or too numerous to handle efficiently in a single informational session.

Informational meetings promote cooperation among group members by fostering individual growth, by keeping people informed, and by giving people the reasons behind changes that will be necessary in the future. Informational meetings work best when they permit the supervisor and group members to accomplish the following purposes:

1. Keep informed about what is going on in all areas of the company and in their division, department, or section.
2. Obtain observations and information from people outside their group—for example, from higher management authorities, guest lecturers, or consultants.

3. Report on decisions and changes that have been made or will be handed down from a higher level of the hierarchy.

Employees benefit greatly from such meetings. Their time is efficiently utilized, they get a chance to relate to one another, and they understand more fully how each part contributes to the whole. They are reminded that they are members of a team and are kept informed and up to date on individual and group progress (or the lack of such progress). Although the format is usually a lecture, time should be set aside for questions so that misunderstandings can be cleared up as early as possible or be entirely avoided. Exhibit 5.6 points out a number of things to think about before you decide to hold such a meeting.

Using the Telephone

One of the greatest business machines is the telephone, but probably no other machine is misused so often by so many people at work. How many times have you called and been answered by a simple "Hello?" The lack of identification of a person or a place forces you to ask for that information and wastes time. There is a proper phone etiquette for both the caller and

EXHIBIT 5.6

Guide to planning your meetings.

- Be certain that one is absolutely necessary
- Forewarn all who must attend well in advance; have those who cannot attend send a substitute
- Notify all who are invited, in advance, about the meeting's purpose, starting time, ending time, and place
- Reserve required facilities and equipment; arrange for qualified movers and operators to be on hand as needed
- Prepare notes for the meeting, and rehearse your presentation
- Prepare and distribute the written outline of the meeting's proceedings (agenda)
- Start the meeting on time
- End the meeting once the purpose is achieved or at the scheduled ending time (even if purpose is not achieved)
- Gather input from all people in attendance
- Keep the meeting on its agenda
- Record significant contributions
- Summarize the meeting's results before and after adjournment
- Make certain that all participants know their new roles or the changes that arise from the meeting
- Follow up on the results of the meeting

SUPERVISING TEAMS

As a supervisor, you often find yourself a member of various committees and task forces and will form some of your own. Committees deal with such issues as safety and health, quality and productivity improvement, and the resolution of specific problems facing your work unit. Research has shown that people enjoy serving on such teams when the groups have the following characteristics (all of which have some connection with effective communication):

- Everyone is clear about the group's purpose and goals and their roles as members in it.
- Members have mutual respect for one another and are willing to listen to each contribution.
- Pertinent materials are distributed to all members before the meeting, allowing time for preparation.
- Only those who have something significant to contribute are invited to attend.
- The environment is shielded from interference from outside, whether that interference is from other people or from environmental conditions that add noise—anything that interferes with the transmission and understanding of information.
- An accurate record of each meeting is kept and distributed to those affected, and contributions are attributed to individuals.
- Recognition and rewards are given to those who make sound and useful contributions.
- Members periodically evaluate the effectiveness of the group, noting achievements and areas in need of improvement; members then go to work on making changes.

Consider this a checklist for more productive meetings and groups. Remember that unless people feel committed to a group and its purposes, they will be less than effective participants.

Here is what Sam Walton, founder of Wal-Mart, said in his biography about the importance of communicating with partners and employees:

> Communicate everything you possibly can to your partners. The more they know, the more they'll understand. The more they understand, the more they'll care. Once they care, there's no stopping them.... Listen to everyone in your company. And figure out ways to get them talking.... To push responsibility down in your organization and to force good ideas to bubble up within it, you must listen to what your associates are trying to tell you.

Source: Walton, Sam, with Huey, John. *Sam Walton: Made in America* (New York: Doubleday, 1992), 247–248.

the receiver. Although specifics vary from one company to another, a uniform way to make and to answer a call should be followed by all company personnel. If you have no prescribed procedures, the following tips should prove useful.

When calling, identify yourself and determine who the person is that you are speaking to. Keep a pencil and paper handy to jot down names, numbers, and other bits of information as you receive them. If the first person contacted is the one you want, state your purpose and inquire if your call is being received at a convenient time. If it is not, set a time with him or her for a return call, and determine who will make it. If the time is right, make your call as brief as possible, and close the call with a sincere statement of thanks. Remember that phone calls usually represent an interruption in someone's day and, as such, can catch him or her unprepared or at an awkward moment. Keep in mind that your voice represents yourself and your company to others. Business calls are no place for emotional or discourteous remarks.

When you receive a call, identify yourself and your position in the company, and make certain that the caller does the same. Determine the caller's purpose, and decide if you are the best person to handle the call. If the time is not convenient, arrange for a callback, including who will do it and when. Keep a pencil and paper handy for taking notes.

Listening

Nearly one half of your working day as a supervisor and about 90 percent of your class time as a student are spent in listening (Nichols, 1982). Most of what you know and believe you have learned by listening to others. Your business and academic success depends as much on listening as it does on writing, speaking, or reading. Listening attentively will allow you to respond intelligently to what you hear, but this requires your conscious effort.

The speaker's goal is to be understood. The listener's goal is to understand and to listen with understanding. This means that as a listener, you should attempt to see the expressed idea and attitude from the other person's point of view—to sense how it feels to the speaker and to accept the speaker's frame of reference in relation to the subject (Rogers and Roethlisberger, 1975). Few people can do this well, and that is why so few people are good listeners.

Studies done at Columbia University and at the University of Minnesota have proved that we operate at a 25 percent level of efficiency when listening to a ten-minute talk (Nichols, 1982). Pidgeon Savage Lewis, Inc., of Minneapolis conducted a study of the communicative efficiency of 100 business and industrial managements and found that 37 percent of information passed from the board of directors to vice-presidents was lost. By the time the information had been relayed to foremen and supervisors,

SUPERVISORS AND QUALITY

The commitment to total quality in products, services, and processes has become a tradition in many companies, but it seems that some have lost their focus on the real purpose for their commitments: satisfying customer needs. A case in point is Varian Associates, Inc. The scientific equipment producer focused on reengineering itself and achieved remarkable results. Improvements were made in nearly every area but at a price: "Obsessed with meeting production schedules, the staff in [the] vacuum-equipment unit didn't return customers' phone calls, and the operation ended up losing market share. Radiation-repair people were so rushed to meet deadlines that they left before explaining their work to customers. And Varian is not the only company to discover that obsessed employees, while achieving improvements to company operations, can alienate customers."

"...[Q]uality that means little to customers usually doesn't produce a payoff in improved sales, profits, or market share. It's wasted effort and expense...."

Instead, managers are trying to make sure that the quality they offer is the quality their customers want." Businesses are discovering that unless their customers perceive that they are benefiting somehow, there will be little financial payoff. The result of these revelations has taught companies to get closer and stay close to their customers. Some invite them to serve on product development teams. Others continually ask for feedback to identify failings and additional ways to meet their needs. Hampton Inns tried a money-back guarantee to customers who were unhappy with any product or service, regardless of the reason. "With everyone from maids to front-desk clerks empowered to grant refunds, employee job satisfaction climbed steadily. Turnover at the chain fell...and the program brought in an additional $11 million [in 1993]."

"Listening to customers is the easy part. Doing what they want without spending into oblivion can be difficult." The new focus: improving quality while satisfying customers at a reasonable cost.

Source: Greising, David. "Quality: How to Make It Payoff," *Business Week,* August 8, 1994, 54–59.

70 percent had been lost. Workers ultimately got 20 percent of what had been initiated by the board (Nichols, 1982).

Most of us speak at from 100 to 125 words per minute, but most of us can think at between 400 and 500 words per minute. This difference allows us time to criticize and to let our minds wander off on tangents while listening (Nichols, 1982). Our criticisms can be of the speaker, the delivery, or the content. Being critical, judgmental, approving, or disapproving of a speaker's message takes us away from our primary goals: to perceive the other person's point of view, to know how that person feels, and to understand what the frame of reference is. Wandering off on mental trips during listening shuts down our hearing and perceptions.

Barriers to Effective Listening   Many things (including our own attitudes) stand in our way when we attempt to listen to another person. Here are the major barriers to effective listening:

- Wanting to talk more than we want to listen
- Not being in the right (rested and alert) frame of mind
- Prejudging what the speaker is going to say, based on what we know about the speaker's knowledge of the subject, experience, and point of view; that is, failing to keep an open mind
- Letting the speaker's less-than-perfect delivery turn us off to the ideas and words
- Taking exception to a speaker's remarks as they are made and thus not listening to what follows those remarks
- Allowing events and those around us to distract our attention from the speaker
- Labeling the speaker on the subject dull or boring
- Dealing only with the speaker's facts and not listening for the speaker's emotional content
- Tuning out the speaker because he or she disagrees with what we "know" is right
- Making assumptions about anything we are not certain of—filling in the blanks with what we think the speaker or writer means rather than seeking to determine exactly what he or she means

Exhibit 5.7 is a short quiz to help you determine how effective your listening efforts are. In addition to taking this quiz yourself, you should encourage your subordinates or team members to take it. The maximum score is 30. A rating of 24 or more indicates that you are an above-average listener. A score of 18 to 23 is average. Below 18, your listening skills need improvement.

Active Listening   Active listening is "listening and responding in a way that makes it clear that the listener appreciates both the meaning and the feelings behind what is said" (Rogers and Farson, 1990). Here are two examples of the process (Rogers and Farson, 1990):

Directions: Read the questions below and rate yourself according to the following:

> Always . . . . 3 points
> Usually . . . . 2 points
> Rarely . . . . 1 point

	Choices		
1. Do I let speakers send their messages without interrupting them?	3	2	1
2. Do I take notes, recording the most important points made by a speaker?	3	2	1
3. Do I try to connect the speaker's points with my past experiences to help me remember them?	3	2	1
4. Do I try to restate the speaker's points to make certain that I understand them?	3	2	1
5. Do I give the speaker my undivided attention, blocking out any noise or distractions?	3	2	1
6. Do I keep my emotional reactions to the speaker in check, not allowing them to distract me?	3	2	1
7. Do I keep my emotional reactions to the speaker's message in check, not allowing them to distract me?	3	2	1
8. Do I keep listening even if the message is boring or uninteresting to me?	3	2	1
9. Do I try to get at the speaker's intended meaning by listening "between the lines" of the speaker's words?	3	2	1
10. Do I formulate questions to ask the speaker that will clear up any unclear messages in the speaker's words?	3	2	1

EXHIBIT 5.7
Measuring your listening skills.

1. *Employee:* Don't you think my performance has improved since the last review?
   Supervisor: It sounds as if you think your work has picked up over these last few months?

2. *Employee:* Just who is responsible for getting this job done?
   Supervisor: Do you think you don't have enough authority?

Active listeners leave a door open for a person to continue to tell what is on his or her mind. In the two instances just presented, the supervisor answered the employee's question with a question to draw the employee out and to get a deeper insight into the problem or at least the employee's perception of it. Active listeners follow these guidelines:

- They think with people and respond to their needs
- They avoid passing judgment, either positive or negative
- They listen for total meaning—both for content and for feelings
- They respond to what a person is really saying. For example, if a subordinate came to you and said, "I've finished your assignment," your response should be different from if the statement was "Well, I've finally finished your damn assignment!" (Anderson, 1984).

Keep in mind that listening is not a passive activity. It requires mental alertness and manipulations. Use every opportunity to seek clarification of the speaker's subject, feelings, and frame of reference. Questions are the key. Of course, when you have the information and understanding you need, questions are no longer necessary.

WRITTEN COMMUNICATIONS

Probably the most difficult form of communication is the written form. Yet nothing will mark you more clearly as a poor manager than an inability to write your thoughts effectively and correctly. Your written communications may be around a long time and will put you on record for future reference. A badly written, poorly constructed piece of writing can discredit you as nothing else can.

Just what is good writing? It is writing that transmits an idea or information clearly to the intended reader in accordance with the rules of grammar and proper sentence construction. Before you put your thoughts into writing, you should satisfy four criteria: (1) have something specific that must be communicated; (2) have something that is best stated in writing; (3) have command of language fundamentals, such as proper punctuation and spelling; and (4) have a specific reader in mind.

Effective writing, like effective oral presentations, must accomplish several things. It should especially be gauged to accomplish the following purposes:

- Command the reader's attention. Something in your writing or its appearance has to get the reader to read.
- Arouse interest. The writing's appeal must be aimed at the reader's specific interests. The "what's in this for you" should be up front. A benefit can be promised, or a potential loss or cost can be cited. Tailor your message to a specific reader or reader interest.

- Specify the action called for. The basic purpose of most business correspondence is to get a favorable response or an acceptance from the reader.

Written summaries and reminders make effective follow-ups to oral communications. The combination of the two forms of communication helps add importance and emphasis to key points, prevent misunderstandings, and provide evidence that communication about a subject has taken place. If you are a regular computer user, use your word processing software to help you prepare professional written messages. If you are not, learn about the many uses of word processing and how it can help your written communications.

Effective writing amounts to talking on paper or a computer screen. Effective writers make their points clearly, using ordinary language that is familiar to the people they are trying to reach. Your writing should read well—sound good to the ear when read aloud. As you write, say what you are writing to yourself. When polishing your writing, read it aloud to catch any awkward phrases or sentences, any disconnected or unclear thoughts. When you write, you have complete control over the message. Consequently, if your communication is less than effective, you have only yourself to blame (Weiss, 1986).

Mechanics

Writing effectively is not easy. But you can make it a lot less difficult for yourself if you lay a proper foundation before you try to write. First, you should have a specific objective in mind. Next, you should gather your facts (this may involve searching your files or consulting with others). Then, you should make an outline—that is, a simple breakdown of your major points. Expand each major point by writing beneath it the minor ones that you wish to use to support it. You can use a sequence of numbers, letters, or both to identify major and minor points. Use whatever system is comfortable for you. Then arrange your points in the order best suited for a logical presentation.

Although much of your writing will be done with little or no research, it may sometimes be necessary for you to research a problem before you write about it. When you have to do research, remember the sources of information available to you: your own files, library indexes, individuals in your own section or unit, and higher authorities. You may want to use 3-by-5-inch file cards to record information. When you have completed your research, test the results by drawing conclusions from what you have learned and recorded. You should be able to prepare an outline from your conclusions.

Practice using simple, familiar, and concrete words. In reviewing your writing, be sure that you clearly understand the words you have used.

Then ask yourself the following questions: "Will my readers understand my words? Will they get the same meaning that I do from them?" With some words, there is little danger of any misunderstanding. For example, the word *book* means much the same thing to all of us. Other words, however, may have wide differences in meaning for various people. Consider, for example, the term *implement*. A farmer would probably think you meant a plow, but in business memos, the word means "to carry out a policy or a plan." If you have any doubt about a word, find another word that you are sure will be understood to carry the meaning you intend. If your readers must continually stop to ponder the meaning of your words, they will lose track of what you are telling them.

If you want your written communications to have impact, use short sentences. Professional writers know that writing is easier to read and remember if most of the sentences and paragraphs are brief. You should not use short sentences all the time, however, because such writing tends to strike readers as choppy and monotonous. Try to alternate a long sentence with one or two short ones, and try to keep sentences to fifteen or twenty words.

In preparing your paragraphs, try to limit each of them to a single topic. As a rule, start each paragraph with a topic sentence that tells what the paragraph is about. Use transitional devices to tie both your sentences and your paragraphs together. The final sentence in a paragraph can either emphasize the points you wish to get across or lead the reader to your next subject.

The introductory paragraphs tell what the writing is about. The paragraphs that make up the body of a communication state the writer's case (facts, figures, and so on). The closing paragraph or paragraphs recommend an action or summarize the important points of the paper. Once you are convinced that you have said what you want to say in the way you want to say it, stop writing.

Exhibit 5.8 shows an actual memo (memo A) sent by Jane, a middle manager, to her subordinate managers. Read it first, and then read memo B, which is a suggested improvement. Do you believe that memo B carries the basic message intended by the author of memo A? Which memo would you prefer to receive if you were one of Jane's subordinates?

Writing Letters

Unlike memos and reports, letters are sent to outsiders. Like phone calls, they represent you and your company to customers, vendors, government officials, and others. Before you write the letter, consider the following:

* Can I identify my reader and his or her interests?
* Have I a central purpose clearly in mind?
* Is a letter the best way to communicate?
* What style, of the approved styles I have to work with, is best?

MEMO A   (Date)

TO: ALL SECTION SUPERVISORS

The newly designed personal data sheet—Form 14A—has a necessary, essential, and vital purpose in our organization. It provides the necessary and statistically significant personal data required by the personnel department to be kept on file for future references regarding promotions, transfers, layoffs, and more.

During our recent relocation efforts from the rented facilities at Broad Street to our present location here at Cauley Boulevard, files were lost, damaged, or misplaced, necessitating the current request for replacement of vital personal data on each and every manager in this department. It is also the company's policy to periodically update personal data on file through periodic, personal perusal of one's own records—updating and adding new information as required and deleting obsolete or outdated personal data on file.

Therefore, please complete the attached personal data sheet at your earliest possible convenience but no later than Thursday, May 14, and return it to me by the close of the business day on the 14th.

                                                        Jane Barton

MEMO B   (Date)

TO: ALL SECTION SUPERVISORS

Attached is our company's revised edition of the personal data sheet. Please fill it out completely and return to me no later than the close of business on Thursday, May 14. Thank you.

                                                        Jane Barton

As you write the letter, consider the following:

- What is the person's name, its correct spelling, his or her job title, and his or her current address?
- How can I say what I must in as brief and clear a way as possible?
- Have I outlined my thoughts to flow smoothly and logically?
- Have I linked my ideas to my reader's interests?
- Have I been courteous?
- Have I checked the spelling and grammar I have questions about?

EXHBIBT 5.9

The four basic types of organizational grapevines. 1. The single-strand grapevine: A tells B, who tells C, who tells D, and so on. This type of grapevine tends to distort messages more than any other. 2. The gossip grapevine: A informs everyone else on the grapevine. 3. The probability grapevine: A communicates randomly, for example, to F and D. F and D then continue to inform other grapevine members in the same way. 4. The cluster grapevine: A selects and tells C, D, and F. F selects and tells I and B, and B selects and tells J. Information in this grapevine travels only to selected individuals.

Source: Samuel C. Certo, *Principles of Modern Management*, 4th ed. (Boston, MA: Allyn & Bacon, 1989), 337.

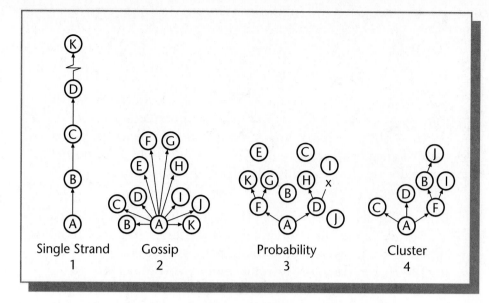

When you are satisfied that the letter represents your best effort (others you trust may help you make this decision), send it. If it called for a response within a certain time and that time is past, follow up on your correspondence in the most appropriate way.

Getting Help

If you need help in the area of communications, get it. A course at your local college can improve your spoken and written communications. The results will be well worth your investment of time and money since you will harvest the benefits for the rest of your life.

There is a saying: "Nothing is ever written, only rewritten." From the time you pen the first few words of your message, you will probably want to revise or rewrite your thoughts. From the rough draft to the finished communication, you will be polishing, tightening up, and filling in. Keep a dictionary handy. Do not be afraid to refer to a basic grammar text either. Remember that your words carry your reputation.

THE GRAPEVINE

grapevine
informal channels at work that transmit information or misinformation

Transmission media or channels of communication can be formal or informal. Formal channels are those specifically set up for the transmission of normal business information, instructions, orders, and reports. The organization chart of a business outlines formal channels. Informal channels—the **grapevine**—are not specifically designated for use in the dissemination of information, but they are used for this purpose by nearly every employee (see Exhibit 5.9).

Informal channels exist because of the natural desire of employees to be in the know and to satisfy their curiosity. Because employees mix and socialize frequently during and outside their normal working relationships, they speculate and invent "information." The less they know about something, the more they invent. At coffee breaks, during lunch, or at social events, people often share things they have heard and seen even though they may not have a complete story to tell.

The grapevine will often give managers a clue about what is bothering their people and where the need for immediate or future action lies. Although it is generally a means by which gossip and rumors about the company are spread, managers should be tuned in to it. Do not, however, use the grapevine for disseminating orders or instructions to your people. It is no substitute for formal channels.

Gossip can sometimes serve you in your role as a supervisor by acting as an early warning system. When you hear a rumor, ask yourself what you would do if it were true. Gossip also alerts you to where the leaks are and who may be letting confidential communications get into circulation.

To prevent the grapevine from yielding a crop of sour grapes, satisfy your people's need to know what is happening in their department by applying the following rules to your daily situation:

1. Tune in on their informal communications.
2. Combat rumors and gossip with the facts.
3. Discredit people who willfully spread improper information.
4. Be available to and honest with your people.
5. Know when to remain silent.

By applying these rules, you create in your subordinates a feeling of confidence about what is true and what is not true. You also strengthen your personal reputation as a source of sound information, and you foster better morale and cooperation. As a result, you can lessen resistance to change and soften its impact.

Instant Replay

1. Communication is the transmission of information and a common understanding from one person or group to another through the use of common symbols.
2. A common understanding is achieved when both the sender and the receiver know each other's ideas, attitudes about the ideas, and frames of reference.
3. The major goals of the communication process are to be understood, to gain understanding, to gain acceptance for yourself or for your ideas, and to produce action or change.
4. A management information system (MIS) is a formal method for making accurate and timely information available to management to aid the decision-making process and the execution of management and organization functions. Computers are making all kinds of communications more effective and efficient.
5. The major components or variables in the communication process are the message, the transmitter, the direction, the medium, the receiver, and the feedback.
6. Communication barriers act to interrupt the flow of information and understanding or to inhibit it from taking place. Communication efforts should be planned with the barriers in mind in order to eliminate them or to minimize their effects.
7. Delivering a speech or a lecture usually involves the use of an introduction, an explanation, and a summary.
8. Listening takes up nearly one half of our days. It is a skill that can be learned and improved by anticipating a speaker's next point, by identifying the speaker's supporting elements, by making mental summaries, and by adopting a tailored approach to note taking.
9. The grapevine consists of the transmission of information or misinformation through informal channels in the working environment.

Questions for Class Discussion

1. Can you define this chapter's key terms?
2. What are the four major goals behind the effort to communicate? Which do you think are part of every effort to communicate?
3. What does a management information system do for (a) managers and (b) the organization?
4. What are the basic components of the communication process? How might the choice in one category influence the choices in others?

5. You are getting ready to communicate to your subordinates about a change in a safety procedure. What should you do before you attempt to relay your message?
6. What are five barriers to effective communication? Can you give an example of each from your experience?
7. How can you improve your listening skills and your ability to retain more of what you hear?

Incident

Purpose: To help identify several common computer-user symbols to denote emotion.

Your Task: Decode the listed smileys by writing your interpretation of each in the spaces provided. Then invent one or two of your own. (To read these examples, rotate the page 90 degrees to the right.)

Smiley	Meaning of Smiley
:-)	_____
;-(	_____
'-)	_____
:-@	_____
:-#	_____
____	_____
____	_____

(Key: from top to bottom: basic happy smiley; crying, unhappy smiley; winking smiley; screaming smiley; my lips are sealed smiley)

CASE PROBLEM 5.1

MIS or Mess?

"Have a seat," said Linda Presley, the management information center director of Wohl, Inc., a Calgary-based manufacturer.

Patty Hutton pulled a chair close to Linda's desk.

"We have a problem. The shop supervisors are complaining that they are not getting the production information they need on time. Wesley stopped by this morning to let me know that their daily status reports arrive from three to four hours after the start of each shift. What she and the other supervisors need is a report within the first hour."

"Look, Miss Presley, we can only give them data that comes from their data. They don't send the information my people need until well after each shift ends. Then we have to process it through the central computer and print it."

"Patty, I don't want to hear any excuses. You have been warned before about this, and you promised that you would cure the problem. Why haven't you?"

"Miss Presley, I investigated the matter and sent a standard interoffice memo to all the supervisors. I told them that if I was to help them, they would have to help me. I detailed what I needed and when. So far, only two of the six supervisors have responded with any change in their behavior. Some of the reports I get are almost illegible. When my people have to waste time trying to unscramble their scribblings, it affects the time it takes to generate their reports."

"Well, the matter has come to the attention of Briggs, the plant superintendent, and he has spoken to me about this on more than one occasion. I don't want to have to explain your failures to him again. Do you understand me?"

"What do you suggest I do, Miss Presley?"

"Get Briggs and those supervisors off my telephone and out of my office. I'm getting a little tired of taking heat for your failures. If you can't resolve this simple situation, maybe someone else can."

Patty got up from her chair, visibly upset. She turned and walked to the office door.

"I resent your personal attack on me and my people. We work hard and have managed to satisfy every other demand that management has thrown our way. I'm getting frustrated, along with my people, at the failure of so-called management people like those supervisors to follow simple instructions. We have far more important people to serve and much more important data to generate."

Before Linda could speak, Patty Hutton was out the door and slamming it.

"I'll fix her," said Linda to herself. She picked up her pen and began to write a memo to the personnel director. She also wrote a record of the encounter in the form of a "memo to file."

"I've got to start building my case," thought Linda.

Questions

1. What barriers to effective communication do you see from Patty's position?
2. What are the goals of this communication?
3. Why have the four supervisors failed to respond to Patty's requests?
4. What were the problems that the meeting was intended to deal with? What are the problems at the end of the case?
5. How could Linda have handled the meeting better?

Memo Mumbles

Professor Ian Wilson is the chairperson of his college's business department. His faculty members work three basic shifts: morning, afternoon, and evening. Because of this split in work times, Professor Wilson has decided to conduct the regular monthly faculty meeting at two separate times—one in the early afternoon and one in the early evening. Both meetings will have the same agenda. Professor Wilson wrote the following memo to his faculty:

MEMO

TO: All business faculty

DATE: 4/7

FROM: Professor Wilson

SUBJECT: Regular monthly faculty meeting

1. Our regular meeting this month will be held in two sessions, both with the same agenda—on April 27, Tuesday, and April 29, Thursday. The meeting on the 29th will be held at noon in room 901. Day faculty will attend. The evening faculty will attend the meeting on the 27th at 5 P.M. in room 109. Faculty meeting agenda will follow.

2. Faculty with a preference may attend either meeting.

On the morning of the 27th, Wilson placed an agenda on each faculty member's desk. At the 5 P.M. meeting on the 27th, two faculty members arrived twenty minutes late, missing some vital information. After the meeting, Wilson asked them why they were late. Both said that they had waited in room 901 for ten minutes and then returned to the department office and discovered their mistake.

After the meeting on the 29th, Professor Wilson noted that three of his faculty members had not attended either meeting. One, a day faculty member, simply forgot about the meeting. (His agenda was buried under student homework papers.) The other two members told Wilson that they had gone to room 109 at 5 P.M. and waited twenty minutes. When the rest of the faculty failed to appear, they went to the cafeteria to have supper. Both assumed that the meeting had been canceled.

Questions

1. What went wrong in the communication process?
2. What communication barriers exist in this case?
3. As department chairperson, what would you do to make certain that your faculty members attended a meeting?

Notes

Anderson, Carl R. *Management Skills, Functions, and Organization Performance* (Dubuque, Iowa: Wm. C. Brown, 1984), 202.

Case, John. "Games Companies Play," *Inc.,* October 1994, 46–47.

Davenport, Thomas H. "Saving IT's Soul: Human-Centered Information Management," *Harvard Business Review* (March–April 1994), 122.

Dumaine, Brian. "The Trouble with Teams," *Fortune,* September 5, 1994, 92.

Goldsmith, Charles. "Look See! Anyone Do Read This and It Will Make You Laughable," *The Wall Street Journal,* November 19, 1992, B1.

Inc., "Voice Mail Versus Voice Messaging—Here's the Difference," August 1994, 110.

Jamieson, David, and O'Mara, Julie. *Managing Workforce 2000* (San Francisco: JosseyBass, 1991), 87.

Kirkpatrick, David. "Here Comes the Payoff from PCs," *Fortune,* March 23, 1992, 93.

Lewin, Mark. "IBM: There's Message in High-Tech Madness," *USA Today,* June 8, 1987, 10E.

March, Robert M. *Working for a Japanese Company* (New York: Kodansha International, 1992), 92–93.

Maynard, Roberta. "The Growing Appeal of Telecommuting," *Nation's Business,* August 1994, 61–62.

Nichols, Ralph G. "Listening Is Good Business," in *Readings in Management,* ed. Max D. Richards (Cincinnati: South Western Publishing, 1982), 111.

Norton, Rob. "New Thinking on the Causes and Costs of Yes Men (and Women)," *Fortune,* November 28, 1994, 31.

Resnick, Rosalind. "Hitching a Ride into Cyberspace," *Nation's Business,* July 1994, 66–68.

Rogers, C. R., and Rarson, R. E. "The Meaning of Active Listening," in *Active Listening* (Chicago: Industrial Relations Center of the University of Chicago, 1990), 3.

Rogers, C. R., and Foethlisberger, F. J. "Barriers and Gateways to Communication," in *Business Classics: Fifteen Key Concepts for Managerial Success* (Cambridge, Mass.: *Harvard Business Review,* 1975), 45.

Sprout, Alison L. "Reality Boost," *Fortune,* March 21, 1994, 93.

Stewart, Thomas A. "Managing in a Wired Company," *Fortune,* July 11, 1994, 44.

Tannen, Deborah. *Talking from 9 to 5* (New York: William Morrow, 1994), 15–16.

Tetzeli, Rick. "Surviving Information Overload," *Fortune,* July 11, 1994, 61.

Weiss, Donald. *How to Be a Successful Manager* (New York: Amacom, 1986), 33.

———. *How to Write Easily and Effectively* (New York: Amacom, 1986), 49–50.

Suggested Readings

Axtell, Roger E. *Dos and Taboos of Hosting International Visitors.* New York: John Wiley & Sons, 1990.

Gootnick, David E., and Gootnick, Margaret M., eds. *The Standard Handbook of Business Communication.* New York: The Free Press, 1984.

Kaumeyer, Richard A., Jr. *How to Write and Speak in Business.* New York: Van Nostrand Reinhold, 1985.

Konsynski, Benn R., and McFarlan, F. Warren. "Information Partnerships—Shared Data, Shared Scale." *Harvard Business Review* (September–October 1990): 114–120.

Lucas, Henry C. "Utilizing Information Technology: Guidelines for Managers." *Sloan Management Review* (Fall 1986): 39–47.

March, Robert M. *Working for a Japanese Company.* New York: Kodansha International, 1992.

Mensching, James R., and Adams, Dennis A. *Managing an Information System.* Englewood Cliffs, N.J.: Prentice Hall, 1991.

Tannen, Deborah. *Talking 9 to 5.* New York: William Morrow, 1994.

———. *You Just Don't Understand.* New York: Ballantine Books, 1990.

Weiss, Donald. *How to Make an Effective Speech or Presentation.* New York: Amacom, 1987.

———. *How to Write Easily and Effectively.* New York: Amacom, 1986.

Managing Change and Stress

OBJECTIVES

After reading and discussing this chapter, you should be able to do the following:

1. Define this chapter's key terms.

2. Explain how people form their attitudes.

3. List and briefly explain the four basic steps you can take to change a person's attitude.

4. List and briefly explain six techniques available to change people's attitudes.

5. List six causes of stress on the job.

6. List six ways of coping with work-related stress.

INTRODUCTION

The United States is presently engaged in an economic battle for the survival of its major industries and for the preservation of their market shares in major markets at home and abroad. We are facing major competitive threats from all of our trading partners and from the developing nations, where labor is relatively cheap. Customers that we used to call our own are being enticed by foreign competitors that deliver better, cheaper, higher-quality goods and services at lower costs. U.S. companies in every industry are changing and innovating—embracing ever-increasing technologies and forging alliances with foreign partners and even competitors to become more responsive to their customers.

Many U.S. industries are responding to the challenges of foreign producers by:

- Increasing their use of automation and computer-driven machines and processes
- Redesigning jobs to put more decisions into the hands of those who know the work best, creating teams and hands-on managers
- Reducing the ranks of middle managers and cutting back on jobs that do not contribute directly to profits and production
- Introducing new and renewed efforts at controlling costs and improving both quality and productivity
- Reengineering their structures and processes for greater efficiency and effectiveness

Efforts at improving quality must start with the commitment of top management in each business and spread to every employee. "Engineers, designers, marketers, administrators, and the production workers on the line have to work together to ensure quality, and they all have to know that they are critical to the process" (Pennar, 1987).

People are the key to better quality and productivity. People are the most valuable resource in any organization's efforts to survive, grow, and prosper. The attitudes, values, and beliefs that people bring to work and that are formed at work influence them in either a positive or a negative way. Without the commitment of each person to produce to the best of his or her abilities, a company's efforts will yield less than satisfactory products and services.

ATTITUDES, BELIEFS, AND VALUES

This chapter looks at attitudes, beliefs, and values that influence a company's output and rewards. It examines how they form and how they influence individuals in the workplace. It discusses how you as a supervisor can influence individuals to become or to remain good producers. Finally, it offers advice on how you can manage change and stress in yourself and in others.

Attitudes

An **attitude** is a person's manner of thinking, feeling, or acting toward specific stimuli. Attitudes—the feelings people have toward things and other people—determine people's readiness to respond favorably or unfavorably to other people and to events. Two fundamental attitudes you should have as a supervisor are respect for yourself and respect for others. Without belief in yourself and in the value of others, you cannot create or maintain a positive, productive environment in which people, including yourself, can give their best and feel a true commitment to quality work (Weiss, 1986).

"A dynamic relationship exists between behavior and attitudes. Generally, people try to keep them consistent with each other, so that if an attitude is changed, behavior will also alter to correspond. It also turns out that changing behavior can influence a change in attitude" (Bittel and Ramsey, eds., 1985). Examples abound at the Toyota-GM assembly plant (NUMMI) in Freemont, California. The training, employee commitment, and emphasis

Your workers' attitudes will be a direct reflection of your attitude toward them. The worker pictured here receives a pat on the back and words of encouragement from his supervisor. Wouldn't you work harder knowing your supervisor really cares about you?

Motorola is famous for its emphasis on quality, productivity, and innovation. Its best plant in its Land Mobile Division is in Penang, Malaysia. It is decorated with scoreboards touting a variety of performance statistics and slogans to boost morale. "Opened 20 years ago as a cheap assembly shop for pagers, the facility now has an all-Malaysian research and development team of 200 engineers who help develop next-generation two-way radios and cordless phones."

Among the plant's keys to success are its reliance on employee suggestions for improvement (41,000 in 1993 alone), a firm commitment to cooperation through teams, and each associate's willingness to take the initiative "to identify and act on problems that hinder quality and productivity." Workers are rewarded for spotting trouble and fixing it. Careful screening of applicants (basic command of mathematics, English, and science is a must) leads to selections based on individuals' attitudes toward working in teams. New employees work under the guidance of skilled ones and partake in forty-eight hours of training a year.

Paramount in all employees' efforts is a continuing drive to stay competitive with other company production units. "Just as the Penang plant had its origins as a source of cheap labor, the workers' fear is that Motorola someday could shift work to an even cheaper locale. So managers are...looking for ways to boost efficiency even further. Says Managing Director Ko: 'I constantly tell them that we will lose out to other places if we aren't cost competitive.'" Judging by one worker's performance, Marina Osman, the plant has few worries. She is a member of the "100 Club," a group of employees who have recommended 100 or more "cost-saving ideas and had at least 60% of them implemented." Says Osman, "'I'm one of the family here,...I want to do what is best for the company.'"

Source: Engardio, Pete, and DeGeorge, Gail. "Importing Enthusiasm," *Business Week, Special 1994 Bonus Issue,* "21st Century Capitalism," 122–123.

are on quality and teamwork; team members and team leaders walk like they talk. The attitude of one team leader, Lee Ledbetter, is that team leaders work for the team members, not the other way around. "Communication between workers and managers and among the workers is the key to NUMMI's success. Good products and a good process are important...but it's the ability to correct mistakes, to stop the line that makes for top-quality cars" (Nauman, 1994). The employees know that they will not be disciplined for pointing out problems but may well be for not doing so. Team members, like Kenton Kinler, want it this way: "'We need different avenues to channel out our ideas [on how to increase efficiency and enhance quality].... Through the [problem-solving circles] and team meetings, we're allowed to do that'" (Nauman, 1994).

Motorola has a worldwide reputation for quality. It believes that "In the business wars of the coming decade,...the most crucial weapons will be responsiveness, adaptability, and creativity. To develop those attributes, Motorola is gearing up a new campaign built around lifelong learning.... The goal is a workforce that is disciplined yet free-thinking" (Kelly and Burrows, 1994). The company has experienced steadily rising productivity and quality since 1987 through a continuing commitment to teams, empowerment efforts, and training: It spends on average 4 percent of its payroll to give each employee at least forty hours of training each year (Kelly and Burrows, 1994). Its training efforts extend to its suppliers as well. "Symbolic of the commitment is Motorola U., with headquarters in Schaumburg, Ill., 14 branches from Tokyo to Honolulu, and a budget of more than $120 million. Courses designed by 'instructional engineers' cover such topics as critical thinking, problem-solving, management, computers, remedial English, and how to run a robot" (Kelly and Burrows, 1994).

Beliefs

Our work experiences and the people we have worked with have created changes in us at various stages in our lives. Our experiences have taught us our individual sets of beliefs. A **belief** is a perception based on a conviction that certain things are true or are based on what seems to be true or probable in one's own mind. This latter kind of belief is often called an opinion. Beliefs shape our attitudes, and our attitudes, when made known to others, display our beliefs.

When you are confronted with people or concepts not already part of your experience, you are usually not predisposed in any specific way toward them. You lack definite attitudes, opinions, and beliefs about them. It is at this point that you are most open and impressionable about the new contacts. Initially, you try to make your own observations, gain some insights, and draw your own conclusions. This is the normal process by which we form new attitudes. Friends or associates can influence us to some degree depending on how true and useful we feel their attitudes are. Your attitude toward a source of information determines whether you

belief

a perception based on a conviction that certain things are true or probable in one's own mind (opinion) accept that source's conclusions, wholly or in part, or reject them. In forming new attitudes, we refer to our existing attitudes.

Think back to the time when you were seeking employment with your present employer. Why did you decide to apply to that company rather than to other companies? If you had no prior experience with your present company, you probably relied on its reputation, as relayed to you by others whose beliefs and opinions you respected. A friend may have suggested that you apply because he or she worked there and liked the company. You were willing to put your future in the hands of an employer on the basis of another's attitude and your attitude toward that person. As a new applicant, you made your own observations during the selection process and got answers to specific questions. Your beliefs about your new employer were taking shape, and when you accepted the job, you had probably formed a positive set of attitudes toward both your employer and your new job. Your attitudes, therefore, had a definite influence on your behavior. They will continue to do so.

William A. Jenkins, vice-chancellor of administration at Vanderbilt University in Nashville, states: "I believe people want to be productive. I don't believe people wake up in the morning and say, 'I'm going to do a bad job today.' They want to do well, which means the university will do well. I call it 'Service with Enthusiasm.'... Employees are happy when they feel a sense of involvement and with that comes commitment" (Kleiman, 1994). Jenkins believes that it makes financial sense to make and keep employees happy—they are more productive, which translates into increased profit—and this belief influences his behavior as a manager. He celebrates his associates' successes with regular meetings that help to maintain open communications with them. Here are a few of his recommendations for managers to follow for making their associates happy (Kleiman, 1994):

- Keep associates informed
- Establish trust
- Walk in your associates' shoes
- Listen to your associates
- Acknowledge and celebrate your associates

Values

One set of beliefs that we all have is our values—activities, conditions, and objects that we feel have merit or worth in our lives. Values include judgments about what is right and what is wrong (our ethics). Values are often expressed as wants and as things worth working hard for, both to obtain and to keep. Having a high-paying job and working for an employer whom you admire and respect are examples of values. The four top values of 3,300 *Working Woman* readers are (1) liking their work, (2) having good benefits, (3) feeling productive, and (4) having good pay (McHenry, 1994).

Like attitudes, values are learned throughout life. Usually, values are more difficult to change than attitudes are.

People and organizations are often quick to make assumptions about a person's or group's values based on their ethnic or racial background, religious affiliation, place of birth, gender, or age. Individuals with varying sets of values have almost always worked side by side in U.S. businesses, especially in large metropolitan areas. One thing is certain: As people change, so too will their values. People experiencing deprivation may value its elimination above all. People undergoing stress may value its removal. Our experiences and circumstances help shape our values. "When managers accurately understand the values in a particular work force, they can guide the organization to appropriately motivate and reward employees" (Jamieson and O'Mara, 1991).

Authors and experts on cultural diversity, David Jamieson and Julie O'Mara (1991), have run workshops and seminars for many years. Their clients, who work in and with diverse workforces, "were asked to identify work-related values that they believed were most important to the majority of people in their work forces now and that would continue to be important in the near future.... Nine values stand out, having been identified by the majority of the respondents." These are:

1. Recognition for competence and accomplishment
2. Respect and dignity
3. Personal choice and freedom
4. Involvement at work
5. Pride in one's work
6. Lifestyle quality
7. Financial security
8. Self-development
9. Health and wellness

Although no one worker or group of workers may have all these values, they all should be considered when you take any action that can have an impact on one or more of your subordinates. It is essential for each supervisor to get to know each subordinate and his or her values. The more diverse your workforce, the more diversity there will be in the values employees hold. One major challenge for all managers is to balance the majority's values "with the need to recognize and value individual differences" (Jamieson and O'Mara, 1991).

PEOPLE'S ATTITUDES ABOUT WORK

Herb Kelleher, CEO of Southwest Airlines, hires people with a sense of humor and "...who have to excel to satisfy themselves and who work well in a collegial environment. We don't care that much about education and experience, because we can train people to do whatever they have to do. We hire attitudes" (Peters, "Fountain," 1994). Colleen Barrett, an executive vice-president, says her airline is looking for the following traits: "listening, caring, smiling, saying 'thank you' and being warm…" in all applicants (Peters, "Fountain," 1994). Southwest has had over twenty-one straight years of profits. Kelleher believes in firing a customer before an employee: "The customer is frequently wrong…. We write them and say, 'Fly somebody else. Don't abuse our people'" (Peters, "Fountain," 1994). "Such belief—and actions—make Southwest one of the ten best places to work in America according to "The 100 Best Companies to Work for in America" (Peters, "Fountain," 1994).

The Work Ethic

People's attitudes about work—their **work ethic**—can be grouped into three areas: the importance of working, the kind of work a person chooses or is required to perform, and the quality of the person's individual efforts while performing work. Your attitudes in each of these areas will affect the attitudes you hold in the other areas. Your attitudes may change or be reinforced depending on the experiences you have had and will have in seeking employment, in carrying out your work, and in receiving rewards from working. As a supervisor, team leader, and team facilitator, you can influence the experiences of your associates and, therefore, help shape their attitudes about work and their individual work ethics. Chrysler Corporation is "…looking for workers who show not only aptitude, but the right attitude. Teamwork is a must, along with the ability to use math, computers and statistics to identify, analyze and solve quality and cost problems—without shouting for a supervisor" (Muller, 1994). Although it has no requirement that applicants have high school diplomas, nearly one fourth of its Windsor, Canada plant's third shift (600 people) have a college degree. Like NUMMI, Chrysler needs teams of empowered individuals committed to quality and productivity improvement to stay competitive.

Author and professor David J. Cherrington reports in his book, *The Work Ethic: Working Values and Values That Work*, that significant differences exist between and among different age groups and between men and women with regard to their work ethic. Older workers tend to have more positive attitudes toward their work and quality of performance than do younger workers. More men than women work primarily for money, whereas the reverse is true when it comes to seeking personal satisfaction from work. There are exceptions of course, but as a supervisor, you need to be aware of your own work ethic and the work ethic of each of your associates so that you can work to improve the negatives and to take advantage of the positives. You need to know why people are working for you and your company, what they think of their work, and the quality of their performances. Only then can you understand them as individuals. Generally speaking, the more positive a per-

work ethic
people's attitudes about the importance of working, the kind of work they choose or are required to do, and the quality of their efforts while performing work

son's work ethic, the more valuable that person is as an employee and as your associate.

THEORIES X AND Y

A professor of management at Massachusetts Institute of Technology, Douglas McGregor constructed two theories that attempt to summarize the two prevalent yet opposing sets of attitudes adopted by managers today with regard to human nature and motivation (McGregor, 1970). **Theory X** portrays a somewhat traditional view that unfortunately all too often underlies a manager's behavior:

Theory X
a set of attitudes traditionally held by managers that assumes the worst with regard to the average worker's initiative and creativity

1. The average person has a natural dislike for work and will try to avoid it.
2. The average person has to be threatened, controlled, coerced, and punished to give a fair day's work.
3. The average person avoids responsibility, lacks ambition, and needs constant direction.

Judging from a recent survey of 301 companies in several industries, Theory X is alive and well.

[It] found roughly 20 million Americans may be electronically monitored on the job. Just over 40 percent of the companies polled said they searched employee E-mail, 28 percent said they looked at network mail and 15 percent said they peered into voice mail (*Chicago Tribune*, "Bosses," 1994).

The International Labor Organization, a United Nations agency, found that workers in industrialized countries are steadily losing their privacy as technological advances allow bosses to monitor them extensively—and often secretly.... Big brother is watching the workplace, with more and more employers using computers, cameras, listening devices and telephones to keep tabs on their workers... (*Chicago Tribune*, "Bosses," 1994).

Theory Y
a set of attitudes held by today's generation of managers that assumes the best about the average worker's initiative and creativity

Theory Y, on the other hand, is an attempt to apply what is now known about the majority of people in light of recent research on human behavior and motivation. Theory Y states the following propositions about the average person:

1. The average person desires work as naturally as he or she does play or rest.
2. The average person is capable of controlling and directing himself or herself if committed to achieving a goal.
3. The average person is committed to a goal on the basis of the rewards associated with it and its achievement.

4. The average person desires responsibility and accepts it willingly.
5. The average person possesses imagination, ingenuity, and initiative.
6. The average person is intellectually underutilized in the average industrial setting.

A team leader or team facilitator who adopts this set of beliefs about his or her associates will take an entirely different approach in relationships with them than would a manager who adheres to Theory X. The Theory Y manager will assume the best and expect no less from each individual, while also demanding the best from himself or herself. According to management consultant and author, Tom Peters ("Nobody," 1994): "Front-line people have been secretly champing at the bit for decades: Give them the same information the boss gets. Give them access, at any time, to any kind of training they desire. And then let them have at it. 'They' will respond." Julia M. Garcia and her ten team members run one of Frito-Lay's twenty-three potato-chip teams (Zellner, 1994):

> [They] are responsible for everything from potato processing to equipment maintenance. To help them devise ways to produce and ship chips more efficiently, Garcia and her teammates receive weekly reports on cost, quality, and service performances [scoreboarding] and are kept abreast of the team's ranking in relation to Frito's 22 other potato-chip teams nationwide. Garcia's group, at the top of Frito's rankings for more than a year, also determines crew scheduling and even interviews potential employees for the department—once the sole domain of management.

Countless companies have had similar experiences once they tapped the inherent diversity and willingness to do good in most human beings. Look around you at work. You will probably find many examples of men and women, both in and out of management, who are putting forth a mediocre effort. This often is the result of their managers' expecting nothing more from them. Subordinates learn to give what is expected. A mediocre subordinate is usually the reflection of a mediocre manager.

THEORY Z

The early 1980s brought a sharp focus on management practices and techniques as exhibited by Japanese managers. Aside from Japan's unique culture and relatively homogeneous population, several major differences exist in the attitudes held by American and Japanese managements. In Japan, input from workers and managers at every level is sought before decisions are made. Supervisors and middle managers seek the input of their subordinates before deciding issues. Japanese workers generally feel more loyalty to their employers than do their U.S. counterparts. These attitudes of loyalty are built, in large measure, on a set of factors shown in Exhibit 6.1. **Theory Z** is a blend of the factors listed under the type J orga-

Theory Z
a set of approaches to managing people based on the attitudes of Japanese managers about the importance of the individual and of team effort to the organization

Type A (American)	Type Z (modified American)	Type J (Japanese)
Short-term employment	Long term employment	Lifetime employment
Individual decision making	Consensual decision making	Consensual decision making
Individual responsibility	Individual responsibility	Collective responsibility
Rapid evaluation and promotion	Slow evaluation and promotion	Slow evaluation and promotion
Explicit, formalized controls	Implicit, informal control with explicit, formalized measures	Implicit, informal control
Specialized career path	Moderately specialized career path	Nonspecialized career path
Segmented concern	Holistic concern, including family	Holistic concern

EXHIBIT 6.1

Characteristics of three types of organizations.

Source: W. G. Ouchi and A. M. Jaeger, "Type Z Organization: Stability in the Midst of Mobility," *Academy of Management Review*, vol. 3, no. 2, April 1978, 305–314.

nizations. This theory is characterized by high motivation and productivity from workers and is the result of high levels of trust and commitment to workers from their managements (Ouchi, 1981). Corporations in the United States have benefited from the Japanese approach to industrial management and have borrowed many of its concepts.

THE SUPERVISOR'S ATTITUDES

Exhibit 6.2 illustrates the attitude situation for workers and for management. Depending on your attitudes, you fit into one of three locations in the diagram. Before and during the initial stages of training of workers to become supervisors, team leaders, or team facilitators, the workers' attitudes place them to the left of center, in the prolabor area. The major job of supervisory training programs is to change the trainees' attitudes toward and their conceptions of management. If the program is successful, it will lead to a shift in the trainees' attitudes toward the center line—the fence between prolabor and promanagement attitudes.

The center line or fence is the awkward yet mandatory position for most supervisors, team leaders, and team facilitators because of their unique roles as spokespersons for both labor and management. They are concerned most directly about the welfare of their subordinates and associates and at the same time must share and fortify management's author-

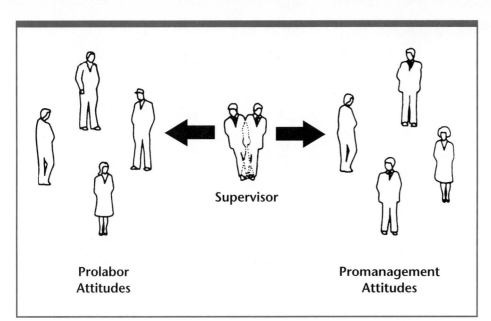

Supervisor

Prolabor
Attitudes

Promanagement
Attitudes

ity. Needless to say, this fence straddling can be uncomfortable and demanding at times, but it is necessary nonetheless. Truly, supervisors, team leaders, and team facilitators are positioned between the needs of their subordinates and associates and the needs of their superiors.

As any one of these managers, your attitudes should be in harmony with your company's policies and your understanding of sound management principles and practices. You should be willing to question your own attitudes whenever you observe contrary ones in either a peer, an associate, or a superior. Try to be objective in determining which are the better attitudes to hold. Maintaining an open mind and being receptive to the new and different will stimulate your growth and improve your knowledge and understanding of yourself and your position.

Beware of accepting the attitudes or opinions of others as your own. We all have a tendency to fill a void in our knowledge by the quickest means available, but this can be a dangerous practice. When you first became a supervisor, you may have heard from your boss or predecessor, "Watch out for Al; he's a sneak." or "You sure are lucky to have Agnes; she's a peach." Dismiss these "insights" and wait to form your own attitudes and opinions through your personal observations. What subordinates or superiors were like with your predecessor and what they will be like with you are almost always different.

The Pygmalion Effect

George Bernard Shaw's play about an English flower girl in the slums who is groomed to become a lady of English society was called *Pygmalion*. The Broadway musical *My Fair Lady,* later made into a film, was based on Shaw's play. From these, we have deduced what has become known as the

The Pygmalion effect, or self-fulfilling prophecy, was portrayed in My Fair Lady. *Professor Higgins attempts to transform a lower-class flower girl (played by the late Audrey Hepburn) into a lady by treating her like one. In this climactic scene, the former flower girl who learned to believe in herself as a lady, fulfills the prophecy: she has indeed become a lady. What could your subordinates accomplish with your belief in them?*

Pygmalion effect: Assuming the best about people will often result in their giving their best; assuming less will often yield less in their performance. In short, people learn to give what they are expected to give. Students and trainees often learn in accordance with what their teachers and trainers expect of them.

One real tragedy of Theory X is that it is a self-fulfilling prophecy about people. If a manager really believes what this theory holds about subordinates, he or she will treat them in an authoritarian and suspicious manner, threatening them and exercising close control. New employees who have something new and creative to offer will soon learn that their ideas, initiative, and drive are not respected or rewarded. They will learn to behave in the ways the boss expects. Soon the employee will adopt the what's-the-use attitude that this boss assumed existed from the beginning. Then the boss can smile and say, "See, I told you so." What Theory X does not say, but implies, is that a small minority of people possess the attitudes, values, and beliefs necessary to manage others.

Research done by J. Sterling Livingston (1979) and others has given us the following insights into the Pygmalion effect and the supervisor's impact on subordinates:

1. What a manager expects of subordinates and how he or she treats them largely determine their performance and career progress.

2. A unique characteristic of superior managers is their ability to create high performance expectations that subordinates fulfill.
3. Less effective managers fail to develop similar expectations, and the productivity of their subordinates suffers as a result.
4. Subordinates more often than not appear to do what they believe they are expected to do.

You should have little doubt that you as a supervisor can help or hinder a new person's ability to adjust and to succeed in your company's environment. Your attitudes will soon shape those of your subordinates. They will look to you for respect, guidance, and example. What you expect from them and what you exemplify each day will determine their attitudes and reactions toward you and toward their own work.

Problem Supervisors

Without realizing it, some supervisors may be the primary cause of an employee's difficulties. Through their actions or lack of action, supervisors can and often do influence their subordinates' behavior. Supervisors have the ability to aggravate their subordinates' difficulties and to put them off balance. A supervisor can confront subordinates who are on the edge of trouble and either help them steer clear of it or push them into it. Like a parent or older brother or sister, the boss should be someone to look up to for a good example and good advice. Your people are very conscious of your behavior and read into it guidelines for their own behavior.

A few thoughts about perception are needed here. One person's perception of another person is a unique thing. Perceptions of people come from several sources, including what we see them do or hear them say, what we learn about them from others, and what we think about them based on our experiences and beliefs.

How your people perceive you—what they think of you as a person and a boss—is very important to you. You need to recognize that although you are one person, you are seen and heard by many others. Your observers are all unique individuals with different attitudes, values, and experiences. Each will observe you at different times and under different circumstances. Therefore, each person's perception of you will be unique and unlike any other. Consider the checklist in Exhibit 6.3. If some of the questions sting you a bit, you could be a cause for unhappy and poorly performing subordinates. With every yes response to the items, you are sowing seeds of trouble in your relationships with subordinates. Without positive perceptions of you, your subordinates will not have the trust and respect for you that they should. You will lack power to influence them by means other than threats and punishment. In short, you will lack leadership ability.

Questions	Yes	No
1. Do I like to control my people with threats?	_____	_____
2. Do I like to keep them a little off balance and insecure?	_____	_____
3. Am I unpredictable in my behaviors and dealings with them?	_____	_____
4. Do I make promises that I do not or cannot keep?	_____	_____
5. Do I betray confidences?	_____	_____
6. Do I issue conflicting orders and instructions?	_____	_____
7. Do I forget to compliment them for work well done?	_____	_____
8. Do I discipline them in public?	_____	_____
9. Do I carry a grudge?	_____	_____
10. Do I play favorites?	_____	_____
11. Do I take my subordinates for granted?	_____	_____

EXHIBIT 6.3
What you are doing that influences your subordinates' perceptions of you.

YOUR SUBORDINATES' ATTITUDES

Your people have attitudes about their work, the company, and you as their boss. When you first take office in your new job as a supervisor, your people will adopt a wait-and-see attitude about you and your abilities. They are, for the most part, open and objective, waiting for evidence on which to base their opinions. The attitudes they will eventually adopt about you are almost entirely within your power to mold. The attitudes they already possess toward other things are hidden from view and will take some time to uncover. These were formed in an environment and through experiences of which you were not a part. Nevertheless, their attitudes will surely influence their performance, their output, and the reputation of the department. Your success and theirs are linked directly to attitudes—both yours and theirs.

One of the most important tasks for managers (and particularly for supervisors) is to identify improper or unacceptable attitudes—attitudes held by subordinates that interfere with their rendering better-than-average or average performances. Once these attitudes are uncovered, managers must begin the demanding task of changing them in order to bring their people to a greater realization of their potential and their departments to a higher state of effectiveness.

Good Attitudes Versus Bad Attitudes

We all have a tendency to label things good or bad. Such a label is based on our own individual points of view. Good attitudes serve us well, whereas bad ones cause us trouble. Once we recognize an attitude as the source of problems, we are encouraged to change it. We consider our good attitudes to be proper, and we consider our bad attitudes to be improper. But problems arise when we label other people's attitudes. First, we attempt to determine the other person's attitudes through observations of the person's actions or words. Second, we may be quick to label another person's attitude bad or improper simply because it differs from ours.

As a supervisor, you need to understand your attitudes and those of your subordinates, and you need to discover why you and they have these attitudes. Labels are not important. The key questions are: Do I know what attitude that person has? Do I know why the person has it? Is the attitude a source of problems to me as a supervisor or to the person as an employee? The attitudes you must attempt to change in yourself and in your subordinates are those that are sources of problems.

Suppose, for example, that as a supervisor in a machine shop you observe a subordinate named Joe not wearing his safety goggles while operating a grinding wheel. Safety regulations tell him to wear safety goggles while grinding. You remind him to wear them, and he agrees to do so. Ten minutes later you pass him again; he is not wearing his safety goggles. At this point, you may ask yourself why. The question should have been asked earlier. If it had been, the second infraction might have been prevented. The answer to the question lies in the worker's attitude toward wearing safety goggles. He believes that his attitude is a proper one, or he would not behave in this manner. As his supervisor, you do not hold the same attitude because you believe his behavior is improper. Your tendency is to label his attitude bad or improper. At this point, the dialogue might go as follows:

> *Supervisor:* Joe, you know we have a shop rule about wearing safety goggles, don't you?
> *Joe:* Yeah, I know the rule.
> *Supervisor:* Do you want to lose an eye?
> *Joe:* Nope.
> *Supervisor:* Didn't I tell you a few minutes ago to wear your goggles?
> *Joe:* Yep.
> *Supervisor:* Well, why don't you wear them, then?
> *Joe:* The strap's too tight. It gives me a headache.

The lesson should be obvious. People believe their attitudes are adequate, and their behavior reflects this. Until they see a need for change or can be shown an alternative that gives them better results, they have no incentive to change. Joe was willing to accept a risk to his eye in order to avoid a headache. Why he did not complain without being asked is another problem. If he has to buy goggles out of his own money, he may be reluctant to buy another pair. If the company furnishes them, the storeroom may be out of Joe's size. There could be a dozen reasons. The point is what is the person's attitude, and why does the person have it? When you know the answers to these questions, you can begin to change the attitudes that are the sources of the problems.

UNCOOPERATIVE ATTITUDES: WHY PEOPLE RESIST CHANGE

Cooperation means working together to reach common objectives or goals. If you are the kind of supervisor this book is trying to develop, you will have minimized your problems and found little resistance to overcome. The primary barrier to cooperation, therefore, is yourself—your weaknesses, inadequacies, and failure to offer a good example. Look first at yourself and your management practices before you accuse others of wrongdoing. If you can honestly say that the barrier to cooperation lies outside yourself, the remainder of this chapter should prove helpful to you.

At the core of a person's noncooperation is his or her lack of motivation to cooperate. This means that the person has no desire at present to do so. It falls to you, therefore, to attempt to provide the climate and incentives that will foster a spirit of cooperation in each of your people. As a rule, people are unwilling to cooperate for either of two kinds of reasons: personal or social.

Personal Reasons

Individuals may be unwilling to cooperate with you or their fellow workers because they see no personal advantage in doing so. They may not understand the changes you propose in your operations, and they may fear the implications of such changes to them in their jobs, status, pay, or future. How well people accept changes may be contingent on how well changes have been introduced in the past. They can remember what happened at that time, and they will assume that similar results will occur this time. If a change was handled well in the past, the gate remains open for new changes. If not, you can anticipate resistance or opposition to the change. On the other hand, people may resist changes because of the personal advantages they can keep if the changes are thwarted. For example, if people know their jobs well and are successful at them, they have job security. They are using tried and proved methods, and feel no need to make an effort to learn something new. Thus they have no need to alter their present routines.

Most of us have a built-in fear of change. This fear seems to grow as we advance in years and experience. Nearly all such fear is based on ignorance—not knowing what the changes might mean to us and to our position. We have seen people displaced through advances in technology. We have seen old and traditional skills and crafts eliminated. A change in methods may be viewed as a criticism of our present performance, especially when the change is enforced from outside our department. The supervisor is an initiator, translator, and implementer of change. As such, he or she must plan for change, communicate the need for it effectively, and show subordinates the advantages that will accrue to them as a result of adopting the change. In short, the supervisor must point out the need for and advantages of cooperation and must remove any attitudes that stand in its way.

Social Reasons

As you are well aware, most people in a business do not work by themselves. They are probably members of both informal and formal groups. Changes proposed or suspected may give rise to a fear that the worker's social relationships may be upset, either by the loss of his or her present associates or by the need to find new ones.

An individual may be in favor of a change because he or she can see personal advantages in the new development. The group to which he or she belongs, however, may be against the change. What then can the individual member of a group do? He or she can either adopt the group's viewpoint about the change and risk difficulties with the supervisor or favor the change and risk expulsion from the group.

CHANGING THE ATTITUDES OF SUBORDINATES

A supervisor can bring about a change in a subordinate's improper attitude or behavior through a four-step process. After you have observed improper behavior by a subordinate, or after you have heard an improper attitude expressed by a subordinate, you should take the following steps:

1. Identify the improper attitude or behavior.
2. Determine what supports it—opinions and beliefs (root causes).
3. Weaken or change whatever supports it (root causes).
4. Offer a substitute for the improper attitude or behavior.

Consider the following example, contributed by one of my students: Mike was a supervisor of thirty assemblers in an electronics plant in Chicago. It was his practice to turn each new employee over to an experienced worker for training until the new person adjusted to the job and became capable of meeting both quality and quantity standards on his or her own. One day, Mike hired a young, recent immigrant from India named Ehri. Ehri was placed under the direction of Dave, an experienced and willing worker-trainer. Once he was on his own, however, Ehri's production was marked by an unacceptable level of rejects.

Step 1: Identifying the Improper Attitude or Behavior

When you determine that a subordinate's behavior is improper, you must look for the attitude behind it and state it in precise terms.

Mike went to Ehri and observed him at work. Ehri was working at an almost frantic pace. Mike assumed that this was the reason for the large number of rejects and asked Ehri to slow his pace and concentrate on quality, not quantity.

Often, just by investigating the action, showing concern, and giving corrective instructions, you will be able to solve the problem. The worker may realize at that point that his or her behavior is unacceptable and change it to meet the demands of the supervisor. This did not happen with Ehri.

Mike had failed to identify the attitude that supported the fast pace of work. Instead, he simply identified an action, which he attempted to stop with orders and instructions. He had dealt with the symptom of an attitude, not with the opinions or beliefs that were causing the problem.

Step 2: Determining the Root Causes

On the basis of your investigation and analysis, see if you can spot the roots of the attitude—the primary beliefs that both support and feed the attitude in the employee's mind. The best way to do this is to get the employee talking about his or her true feelings.

Some frequent root causes that support and nurture incorrect attitudes include the following:

- Group pressures
- Faulty logic
- Misunderstood standards
- Previous supportive experiences

Mike thought the problem had been ended. After all, when a supervisor lays down the law, especially to a new worker, the subordinate should respond. Ehri's production, however, continued to yield an unacceptable number of rejects. Next, Mike and his boss both talked with Ehri. They again emphasized quality and included an implied threat that unless the situation reversed itself, Ehri's job was in jeopardy. But still the problem persisted.

Mike had not uncovered the root cause. Even though he was armed with the additional authority of his boss, Mike was still treating a symptom of the attitude. He had not yet uncovered the attitude and its root causes.

Finally, it occurred to Mike that the problem might have originated in Ehri's training. He approached Dave and related the problem of too much quantity and too little quality. After stating that Ehri's job was at stake, he asked if Dave knew how this situation might have evolved. Dave became somewhat embarrassed, and on further questioning, Mike discovered that Dave had told Ehri that quantity was all management really cared about, regardless of what they said to the contrary. Mike had finally struck pay dirt. He now knew what Ehri's attitude was and the root cause for it—misunderstood standards.

Step 3: Weakening the Root Causes

Once the root causes are known, they can be analyzed and their vulnerabilities noted. A program of action can then be constructed to change beliefs systematically through the use of reason. One way is to point out flaws in the employee's assumptions or changes that have taken place to weaken those assumptions since they were formed.

Mike instructed Dave to go to Ehri and explain that he had been misinformed. Dave apologized to Ehri and made it clear that he had only been kidding about quantity over quality.

Dave had the reputation of being a practical joker, and he really had meant no harm by what he did. He was only taking advantage of a novice who was naive to the ways of a skilled worker like Dave. Ehri had a language difficulty with English and tended to take things literally. Thus he had been easy prey for a joker. Dave felt certain that once Mike talked to Ehri, Ehri would realize that he had been had. When Dave understood that Ehri had not responded to Mike's talk, he was most eager to help correct the problem.

Step 4: Offering a Substitute

Dave had no trouble persuading Ehri to change his thinking because Ehri had received quite a bit of pressure by that time. Once Ehri realized (as a result of the statements of both Dave and Mike) that his attitude was based on misinformation, he became a superior worker.

You may be able to change behavior by constant harping and criticism, but like the action of water in wearing away rock, it may take too long a time and leave some noticeable scars. In general, people will change only if they see that the attitudes they hold are no longer worth keeping. Threats and orders usually only suppress a natural and observable behavior and drive it underground. The person becomes sneaky and does what you say only when you are there to police your order. When you are absent, his or her old behavior pattern resurfaces. The fact that you do not agree with or accept this behavior is usually not enough. You must identify the attitude, find its roots, and get the individual to question his or her own position. Only then will you be able to initiate a permanent change in that person's behavior.

TECHNIQUES FOR CHANGING ATTITUDES AND INTRODUCING CHANGE

Fortunately, there are many tried and proven methods for changing attitudes, reducing resistance to change, and instilling a desire to cooperate. These methods depend on your understanding of the previous chapters and your ability to apply the knowledge they contain. There are six basic techniques at your disposal for introducing changes and resolving conflicts:

- Force-field analysis
- Effective communications
- Persuasion techniques
- Participation techniques
- Training programs
- Organizational development activities

Force-Field Analysis

force-field analysis
a method for visualizing the driving and restraining forces at work within an individual so as to assess what is needed to make a change in a person's attitudes

Kurt Lewin, a social psychologist, has given us the research in human relations on which **force-field analysis** is built. It is a useful device for visualizing the situation you face when you attempt to overcome resistance to change in your subordinates.

There are two types of forces within individuals with regard to any issue affecting them at any given time: driving forces and restraining forces. Driving forces encourage us to change, whereas restraining forces encourage us to resist change. Whether we are predisposed toward a change in a negative way or in a positive way depends on the nature and quantity of these forces. If there is a balance between them, we are in a state of inertia. If a change is to take place, driving forces must outweigh the restraining ones, the restraining ones must be reduced, or a combination of these must take place. Exhibit 6.4 illustrates this concept.

To understand more clearly this type of analysis, let us consider an example. Assume that you want one of your workers, Barbara, to work

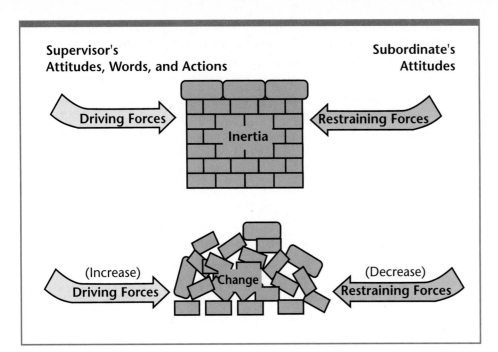

over a coming holiday. Since overtime is a voluntary situation in your shop, Barbara has a choice. Let us assume that you have asked her, and she has refused. The situation might appear as follows:

Driving Forces

1. She will receive additional pay at overtime scale.
2. If she works, she will please you.
3. Working over the holiday is better than being idle.

Restraining Forces

1. She has no immediate need for extra pay.
2. She wants to be with her family.
3. She prefers time off to extra pay.

At this point, there appears to be a standoff. You cannot order her to work, so you must try to weaken her restraining forces or add to the driving forces. Before attempting to do either, be sure that you see the situation as she does. Assuming that the forces listed represent a true picture of her conception of the situation, and that she understands the driving forces that are present, let us see what you might do to change her mind.

In view of the restraining forces, the easiest step is to increase the driving forces. You might be able to get her best friend at work to come in over the holiday. Once Barbara knows that someone she respects and admires has agreed to help out, she may too. In addition, you could let her know that the reason you have asked her is that you really need her and her abilities. If she is the best person for the work to be done, let her know you feel that way. You can also appeal to her group loyalties by explaining that the team needs her for a successful performance rating and that without her it stands a good chance of falling below expectations. In other words, the reputation of her group, either formal or informal, will be tarnished without her unique contributions.

If you are a leader in Barbara's eyes, you may get her to work overtime by putting your request on a personal basis such as, "Barbara, can you work overtime this Monday? I really need you." But not all managers are leaders, nor are all of them leaders to all of their subordinates. You should not try these steps unless you are sincere. We are not talking here about playing games with people or their feelings.

You can change a person's mind and his or her prior attitude toward an idea or a suggestion if you manage to change his or her perception of a situation. This means that you must attempt to perceive the situation as the other person does and then go to work on the forces. You will not always succeed, but the effort is worth making if the change you are trying to make is important to your department.

Effective Communications

Chapter 5 dealt with the fundamentals of successful communications in general. Everything contained in that chapter is essential to every manager. Unless you have open channels with your people, peers, and outside specialists, you will have no real chance of winning their cooperation. To overcome fears, attitudes, and the lack of motivation to change, you must employ effective communication techniques. Regardless of the form of communication you use, you must lay the groundwork for change and get its advantages across to your people before you can expect them to go along with you. Remember that your goal is to get your particular understanding of a situation into their minds. To do this, you must listen to and observe them.

Persuasion Techniques

Each of the following persuasion techniques works well in certain situations. Which one you choose depends on your understanding of the people and events involved in the particular situation you face. Become familiar with all of them so that you will always carry with you one or more techniques that can be applied to any set of circumstances.

1. Give your subordinates the reason behind the proposal. Let your people know why the change is necessary. Put it in their terms, and tailor your message to each individual.
2. Show them how. Explain how the change will affect them, how it will help them, and how it will be implemented. Appeal to their individual needs.

You will find that you must often use persuasion techniques to get your subordinates to cooperate. Always remember to put yourself in your subordinates' shoes. Treat them the way they wish to be treated.

3. **Tell them the truth.** If the change will be painful, let them know it. If they are to be displaced, assure them that the company will either relocate them or retrain them for new positions. Do not lie to them or kid them. They will respect your integrity and remember it in the future. See Exhibit 6.5 for an example on how to gain a person's acceptance of more work with no increase in pay—a continuing reality in today's downsized organizations.

4. **Try a compromise.** It is not always possible to give a little or meet them halfway, but when you can, do so. You may not have foreseen all the possibilities, and maybe they have some good points on their side. Often the method is not as important as the results you expect of them.

5. **Give them an example of a past accomplishment.** Tell them about similar situations and the positive results that were obtained. Explain how each person benefited as a result of the change.

6. **Plant a seed.** Give them an idea, and let it germinate. In advance of the change, converse with them about "How nice it would be if..." or "Have you guys thought about...." Then nurture that idea with the proper care and feeding. Your subordinates may come to you with the very suggestion you anticipated. Even better, they may think it is their own idea.

7. **Ask them questions.** Ask your subordinates the kinds of questions that, if they are honest with themselves, will yield support for a change or remove the cause of a possible conflict. Properly presented, these questions will lead them to the predisposition you favor.

It's a fact of today's downsized corporate life: At some point, most managers will need to ask an employee to take on more work without raising her pay. The secret to running this negotiation smoothly is to make the employee see what's in it for her. Since the alternative may be unemployment, you can even present the increased work load as good news. Point out that while others are losing their jobs, she's making herself more valuable to the company. If she's already a prized employee, see if you can reward her increased productivity through other means—a better title or larger office, training in new skills, more vacation time. If she's not that essential, you should just get across the point that this is a take-it-or-leave-it deal. (The manager's words are marked in green; the employee's, in black.)

ICEBREAKER   I've just come from a daylong strategic-planning meeting, and I have some reassuring news to give you.

PITCH   I'm sure you've probably heard rumors about the company's plans to reduce expenses by downsizing. Our department will have to do its share, but fortunately not through layoffs. I was able to convince the brass that we could cut costs by becoming more efficient. They've decided to eliminate a position in international sales instead, and let us handle the work.

WORK-LOAD OBJECTION
So that means more work for us. Will we have to stay late every night? I've signed up for a computer class on Wednesdays at 6:30.

FINANCIAL OBJECTION
Well, then, I hope I can expect a heftier paycheck to go along with these extra responsibilities?

NO OBJECTION   OK.I know times are tough, so I'll be a good soldier and do my share. What's involved in the new setup and schedule?

DIFFICULT SITUATION   I know this is difficult, but we'll all have to adjust. I'll be as flexible as possible. Why don't you come in an hour earlier on the days you have class, and I'll make sure you're able to get out of here on time.

LONG-TERM OUTLOOK   I'm afraid there *won't* be any additional money, since the point of all this is to save. But in the long term, we'll have an opportunity to show what we can do and increase our skills. That will only help in the future, either here or someplace else.

PAY FOR PLAY   Well, that may not be a problem for people who don't have any family responsibilities, but I've got a lot of expenses. Will there be future rewards in my paycheck? And when can I expect them?

GET REAL   Look, there are folks at this company who'll no longer *have* paychecks. If you don't feel you can pitch in at this crucial period, perhaps you'd better evaluate how important this job is to you.

YOU'RE NEEDED   I know that it's important to be adequately compensated. Right now, though, the company really needs us to pick up the slack. Maybe in three months we can see how it's going and come up with some other way to recognize your hard work.

EXHIBIT 6.5
Convincing associates to take on extra work without extra pay.

Source: Adapted from Stephen M. Pollan and Mark Levine, "Adding Work Without Pay," *Working Woman,* October, 1994, p. 73.

8. Offer them a choice. The choice you present is not whether to do something or reject it but rather when or by whom it will get done.

9. Offer them a challenge. Put the idea as a goal to be reached or a standard to be surpassed. Present the change as a test of their team's abilities and skills. Turn the event into a game or contest—a way of probing their potential.

10. Make them a promise. If possible, give them your promise that if the idea is not successful or does not yield the desired results (given an honest effort), you will retreat from your position and withdraw the directive.

11. Try making a request. Instead of ordering compliance and being autocratic, ask them to cooperate. You will be amazed at what a difference requests make in a person's attitudes. This technique especially appeals to the individual who feels insulted by demands but who bends over backward to meet an appeal for help.

12. Give them a demonstration. Show them by your own performance what the new system calls for, how it will work, and how it will benefit the group or individual. Introduce the change with a planned and carefully executed tryout, and the doubts will fade in the light of reason. Seeing is believing.

13. Involve them in the decision. Using a problem-solving session, get them into the problem with both feet. State the dimensions of the problem, and then lead them in reaching a consensus.

Before you decide on any one of these suggestions, put yourself in your subordinates' shoes. Identify with their attitudes, and set your course to meet their restraints and increase their drives. By finding the supports for their resistance and weakening those supports through logic and facts, you will pave the way for their acceptance of a substitute.

None of these persuasion devices, however, is a substitute for proper management or leadership. In fact, their success or usefulness depends on your being the best person and the best manager you can be. Only then can the potential of your people be released and fully utilized.

Participation Techniques

As we have seen throughout this chapter, people have a need to be in the know about the things that affect them. Managers must use various means to involve their people in decision making and to allow them to participate more fully in the work of the department.

The first device for employee participation open to managers is their formal authority. By delegating it to the more responsible members of their groups, they go a long way toward exposing their subordinates to the complexities of their jobs and toward developing them and their potential. How much a manager gives away depends on many things. Is he or she allowed by the boss to delegate? Does the manager have subordinates who are responsible enough and good enough at their jobs to handle new responsibilities? Has the manager paved the way for delegation through proper training, appraisals, and human relations? All these are essential questions that must be answered before managers can give away any of their duties.

Related to delegation is the formation of worker teams to assist in identifying and solving problems. "At a time when companies are looking for ways to streamline operations and cut costs, managers...have gotten measurable results that show the best answers can come from asking those who know best—the workers" (Narisetti, 1992).

Although we discuss problem-solving sessions in detail in Chapter 9, this chapter's Supervising Teams feature tells about one company's successes with worker-run problem-solving teams.

The third method of enlisting participation depends on the style of supervision you adopt toward your subordinates. The democratic and spectator styles promote a feeling of shared responsibility and a voice in what affects people. Each of these styles places a solid trust in the workers and makes the supervisor more dependent on them. The workers know this and usually act accordingly. No one wants to betray the trust of another. For the most part, people want to live up to the expectations others have of them, provided that they have the abilities and skills to do so. Chapter 10 explores in some detail different styles of management and their advantages and disadvantages.

All these methods are effective if the necessary prerequisites exist. They give workers a much-desired voice in the decision-making process. If these tools are used properly, a manager cannot help winning support from the majority of his or her subordinates.

Training Programs

Training programs are formal ways in which you and your organization can teach employees skills, knowledge, and attitudes that they need to perform their present tasks. When you teach one of your subordinates how to operate a piece of machinery, you impart the information he or she needs to understand the machine's performance capabilities. Through practice, the operator gradually gains the manual dexterity required for efficient operation of the machine. Finally, you impart the proper attitudes about safe operation, proper operating procedures, and appropriate maintenance by the operator. You teach it all simultaneously and with equal emphasis. Chapter 12 covers training in greater detail.

organizational development
a planned, managed, systematic process used to change the culture, system, and behavior of an organization to improve its effectiveness in solving problems and achieving goals

Organizational Development Activities

Organizational development (OD) has been defined by the Conference Board, a nonprofit research group, as "a planned, managed, systematic process [used] to change the culture, systems, and behavior of an organi-

Reynolds and Reynolds Company has achieved significant improvements in one of its plant's methods, quality, and productivity through two primary efforts: forming worker-run problem-solving teams and implementing cross-training. The company is a manufacturer of business forms and computer systems. One of its plants, in a suburb of Dayton, Ohio, repairs computer systems components. The plant was having problems coordinating between repair and distribution units. The forty-five non-union employees seemed, at times, to be acting at cross purposes. The managers in charge of repair and distribution decided to form a five-person team comprised of volunteers—"two employees each from the distribution and repair sides and one from internal engineering." The team's first goal was to improve formal communications.

The team began with a meeting of all nonmanagement employees. Suggestions were made and criticized. Workers worried that management might not approve of their ideas and that membership on teams might hurt their individual performance ratings. Over the following months, the team members sent their ideas to supervisors, and the team decided to rotate its membership, allowing others who wanted to a chance to serve. Among the time- and money-saving ideas that were generated were proposals to cross-train repair persons so that they could vary the kinds of repair work they performed, prepare weekly schedules specifying which products were to be repaired, and share information through a network with all technicians.

The results have been truly significant. Parts repaired per month have risen from 4,800 to 6,500. Backlogs on orders have been reduced from 5 to 1.3 percent. Waiting time for parts repairs has gone from two weeks to one day. The need to handle returned parts more than once has been eliminated. All these improvements were accomplished without increasing the workforce and with minimal investments in capital equipment. It took supervisors a while to see the importance of letting the workers take ownership of problems, but the bottom-up approach to solving problems has proved its worth at Reynolds and Reynolds.

Source: Narisetti, Raju. "Bottom-Up Approach Pushes Plant's Performance to the Top," *Chicago Tribune*, November 29, 1992, sect. 7, 13.

zation in order to improve the organization's effectiveness in solving problems and achieving its objectives." This process involves efforts in education and training that eventually affect everyone in an organization.

Organizational development requires an organization to identify its strengths and weaknesses, define its objectives, identify its problem areas, establish OD goals, set up programs for achieving its OD goals, and evaluate the progress made toward improvement. Outside consultants and experts usually conduct research into the organization's operations and recommend and teach the implementation of OD programs for change. If OD efforts are to succeed, the commitment of top management to them is essential. Organizational changes, if they are to be lasting, must begin at the top.

OD Goals　Organizations that adopt organizational development programs must set specific goals for their entire operation and its various divisions and subunits. The total organization may have the following goals: (1) to improve the overall performance of the organization's productivity, profitability, and human resources and (2) to improve the organization's efforts at communicating, promoting intergroup cooperation, and preparing for and coping with change.

As a supervisor, your goals will be influenced by those of your boss and your unit or division. One goal might be to reduce waste and scrap by 10 percent. Another might be to improve the communication skills of the personnel in your department. Specific programs can then be designed to accomplish your goals.

OD Programs　OD programs include those designed to assess employee attitudes, to improve employee cooperation, and to build team spirit. A few commonly used programs are quality circles, joint labor–management committees, and training programs of various kinds. Quality circles are groups of workers or managers who come together regularly on a voluntary basis to discuss mutual problems and possible solutions to them. Labor–management committees work to reduce conflict and to promote common interests in such areas as reduction of waste, removal of health and safety hazards, and reduction of employee turnover. Chapter 9 examines working with these groups and others in more detail. Training programs can be designed to improve skills, communications, teamwork, and just about anything else the company wants to improve. OD programs and activities may be designed and conducted by the company or by outside agencies.

OD activities need your commitment if they are to succeed. You, like all the managers above you, must be committed to them, and you must be willing and able to sell them to subordinates who will or must participate in them. Remember that OD is an organization-wide effort to control and to introduce change. Change can mean security for those who know it is coming and are prepared for it. It can mean insecurity for those who do not. You can do a great deal to reduce insecurity and stress among your people if you and your subordinates are willing participants in your organization's efforts to control its evolution.

STRESS

Changes, the passage of time, and threats (real or imagined) perceived by employees can cause stress among organization members. **Stress** occurs in people when they face situations that they are powerless to deal with or uncertain of what to do about. All of us experience stress on and off the job. When we attempt to learn new skills, meet new people, or are asked to chair a committee or run a meeting, we are usually somewhat uncertain about exactly what we should do. When we face a series of stress-inducing activities or situations, such as role conflict or role ambiguity, our peace of mind and our health can suffer. Among the most serious health threats associated with stress are migraine headaches, depression, skin problems, ulcers, high blood pressure, and heart trouble. People who face continual stress such as air-traffic controllers, physicians, and surgeons can become victims of chronic depression that sometimes leads to dependence on drugs.

stress
worry, anxiety, or tension that accompanies situations and problems we face and makes us uncertain about the ways in which we should resolve them

With today's emphasis on cost-cutting, layoffs, outsourcing and exporting jobs, and reengineering, workers and managers are facing several new realities in their workplaces, all of which are sources of stress. People working for U.S. corporate giants such as IBM, Sears, and General Motors have discovered that job security is no longer a reality. Employees need corporate incentives and programs to enable them to retrain for the several job and career changes that may become necessary. And according to UCLA's Institute of Industrial Relations, although harsh economic conditions have made it necessary to cut costs and have made workers more willing to accept givebacks, "each new cut undermines credibility in those companies that try to manage on the basis of mutual respect" (Franklin, 1992). According to John Simmons, a consultant on employee involvement plans, workers feel betrayed and less willing to contribute since their employers worry more about cost-cutting than they do about increasing worker responsibilities (Franklin, 1992).

The International Labor Organization (ILO) of the United Nations issued a report on stress around the world in 1993 entitled "Job Stress: The Twentieth Century Disease." In it, the ILO states that job stress is rapidly increasing around the world and is affecting nearly every job category. The ILO report indicates that in the United States about $200 billion is lost "annually from compensation claims, reduced productivity, absenteeism, added insurance costs and direct medical expenses for related diseases such as ulcers, high blood pressure and heart attack" (*Chicago Tribune*, "World," 1993). The leading causes of stress are usually identified as workplace monitoring, conflicting personal and job demands, difficult co-work-

SUPERVISORS AND ETHICS

Companies with their backs against the wall, either economically or competitively, often turn to what has become known as a "no-brainer" solution—they cut jobs. According to an American Management Association survey of 713 major U.S. companies, "one out of four...said they planned to cut their work forces in the coming year [1995], the highest such figure ever recorded by the survey." But if history repeats itself, about twice that number will actually do so. These cuts are often followed by, or the result of, efforts to reengineer organizations and their processes. AMA research also shows that continuing layoffs are becoming corporate policy in America.

What have been the results? About one third experience gains in productivity; less than half experience higher profits. But "86% of the surveyed companies reported a decline in employee morale after layoffs." Survivors are left with added workloads, higher levels of stress, and uncertainty about their futures.

Continuing efforts at downsizing raise several ethical issues. What about the burdens created for those who remain? Might there be a connection between some of the people being separated and their eligibility for company pensions? Finally, does an employer have an obligation to save some employees through retraining for the new jobs created through reengineering? AMA research indicates that "as companies lay off workers they are increasingly adding workers in different jobs...."

Source: Franklin, Stephen. "No End to Cuts, But What Are Firms Learning?" *Chicago Tribune,* September 27, 1994, sect. 3, 1, 5.

---

ers, machine-paced work, too much work, uncomfortable environmental conditions, low wages, the lack of control over one's job, incompetent supervisors, and fear of losing one's job. According to Debra J. Lerner of the New England Medical Center (Kotulak and Van, 1994):

> Job strain, broadly defined as being responsible for doing a lot of work with little control over how it's done, not only can make people sick, it can also make them feel lousy about their lives. A national survey of 1,319 working men and women found that job strain was associated with lethargy on and off the job, a decreased social life, and more depression.... Previously job strain had been associated with an increased risk of heart disease and other physical ailments.

Working Woman magazine surveyed its readers and discovered that 71 percent were experiencing stress linked to inadequate pay and "working long hours" (McHenry, 1994). In a Pitney Bowes Management Services survey of 100 major U.S. companies (*Chicago Tribune,* "Execs," 1994):

Workers at three-fourths of firms that have carried out reengineering actions...[defined as] simplifying jobs, performing jobs in a logical order, combining jobs and contracting out support work to other firms...were more fearful about losing their jobs.... Likewise, 55 percent of the firms said their employees felt overburdened by their assignments after the changes. At the same time, 71 percent of the companies said their initiatives led to greater employee productivity, 61 percent reported cost-efficiency increases and 40 percent saw profit increases.

Coping with Stress

Some stress is healthful. It gets us motivated and raises our energy levels. But excessive stress has to be recognized and the causes eliminated or brought under control.

Both organizations and individuals recognize the need to manage the stress in their environments and lives. Stress can and does cause both physical and psychological harm. Courts and juries are awarding significant damages to employees who suffer both kinds of harm due to stress. The workers' compensation boards of many states will let workers recover damages for psychological injuries arising out of physical ones. Managers at every level of an organization have a legal duty to identify causes of stress, to work to reduce their impact on employees, and to identify and try to help employees who have trouble handling stress.

If you have a subordinate or team member who is having difficulty handling stress on the job, meet with that person to construct a stress-coping and stress-reduction program of action. If the cause seems to be inability to perform duties, training may be the cure. If the stress comes from other sources, your company may have in place an employee assistance program (EAP) that can help. Many organizations have the following types of EAPs to assist their employees:

- Facilities for exercise, such as health club memberships, jogging tracks, exercise instruction, and weight-training rooms
- Courses to teach people how to handle stress through such means as meditation, proper nutrition, time management, conflict management, substance abuse, and communications workshops
- On- or off-site confidential counseling opportunities to explore such stressors as financial, drug, marriage, and psychological problems
- Flexible work schedules, job sharing, daycare, and telecommuting to accommodate individual needs
- Time off for coping with family and other emergencies

The 1993 Family and Medical Leave Act requires unpaid leave for up to twelve weeks for employees who have worked for a covered employer for at least one year and for 1,250 hours over the previous twelve months for any of the following:

1. To care for the employee's child after birth or placement for adoption or foster care
2. To care for the employee's spouse, son or daughter, or parent who has a serious health condition
3. For a serious health condition that makes the employee unable to perform his or her job

Bryan E. Robinson, author, psychologist, and teacher, recommends the following techniques for "combating an out-of-control work life" (*Chicago Tribune*, "Bringing," 1994):

- Make a conscious effort to slow down the pulse and rhythm of daily life—eating, talking, walking, and driving.
- Learn to say no when you are overcommitted and you have a choice about new assignments.
- Delegate work to competent people.
- Avoid unrealistic deadlines or self-imposed time limits on important tasks.
- Build time cushions into your schedule. One way is to allow more time for each appointment during your day.
- Avoid making important decisions in haste. Take time to think about them carefully.

Psychologist Jude Miller adds that people can cope with stress by "being assertive and clarifying problems appropriately with coworkers or supervisors—and get out of the building and walk once a day" (*Chicago Tribune*, "If," 1994).

In addition to taking these steps, try getting enough rest, and eat a proper diet to build up your resistance and stamina. Try to play as hard as you work, and separate your work from your family and social life. Getting better control over your use of time can create free time where you had none before. Improving your communication skills can prevent problems and make up for others' lack of these skills. Management by wandering around puts you in regular touch with others who may have good advice and experiences that you lack. This chapter's Incident feature contains a checklist to help you identify the stress-inducing conditions that exist in your workplace.

Technostress

With today's highly technical society, a new kind of stress is emerging: technostress. The introduction of new machines and technology often brings new stressors to an organization and its people. Managers need to plan for the selection, introduction of, and adaptation to new machines and equipment to reduce the stress on employees as much as possible. People need to be consulted and trained before any new equipment is

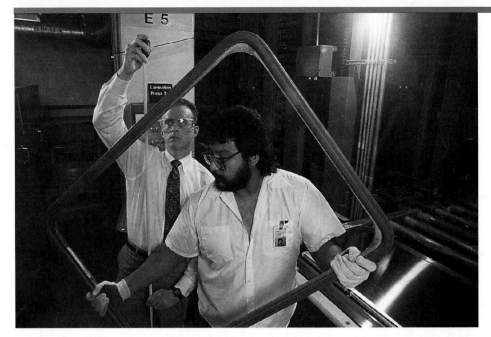

The physical stress of repetitive work can be alleviated with the help of ergonomics. Here an ergonomics consultant observes a worker. By learning how the worker does his job, the ergonomics expert can make modifications to reduce stressful movements.

introduced. With new technologies come new demands on both associates and supervisors. All may fear higher quotas, reductions to the workforce, and being asked to learn new skills. Supervisors fear underutilization of equipment and morale problems that can result from the improper introduction of equipment.

Coping with Technostress

Technology in the office has brought about a number of stressful conditions. Many high-tech machines make noises that, over time, can become extremely annoying. Copiers, printers, video display terminals (VDTs), and fax machines are but a few examples. Improper training in how to use such equipment puts people under stress as well. Improper arrangements of office equipment and workstations add to physical discomfort and emotional distress.

Various kinds of adverse health effects have emerged with the introduction of computers and computerized workstations. The most harmful effects are operator fatigue, eyestrain, exposure to radiation and electromagnetic fields, and carpal tunnel syndrome. This last-mentioned effect is the result of repetitive wrist–hand, hand–fingers motions, such as those made by a computer data entry clerk. These repetitive movements irritate nerves and tendons causing pain, numbness, and swelling. Properly designed workstations and properly trained operators can help eliminate and counter these harmful effects.

For help with office and workstation arrangements, consider the services of an architectural interior designer. Pay attention to the complaints of people who must use the equipment and spaces. Interior office design professionals are practitioners of ergonomics: the successful blending of people, equipment, and machines. See Exhibit 6.6 for a guide to proper VDT operator posture and workstation design. Additional advice from the federal government's Occupational Safety and Health Administration (OSHA) for avoiding these problems includes the following:

- Positioning equipment to avoid glare from windows and overhead lights on VDT screens
- Using adjustable screens with adjustable contrast and colors
- Using detachable and adjustable keyboards (height and tilt)
- Establishing breaks in place: operators refocus their eyes for several minutes each half hour
- Establishing regular hourly breaks, allowing operators to move away from their workstations

Several cities have passed or are considering legislation that implements most if not all of these guidelines.

If you and your employees face continual stress, your attitudes about work, your employer, and your co-workers are bound to be affected. Since stress is a result of uncertainties, you can usually do various things to give your people more certainty. Training is one way to give people the level of skills and the knowledge of procedures that are lacking and may be causing their stress. Unqualified individuals may be transferred to jobs that

EXHIBIT 6.6

Ergonomic arrangements of VDT furniture and equipment and proper posture for the operator

Source: Kemper National Insurance Companies

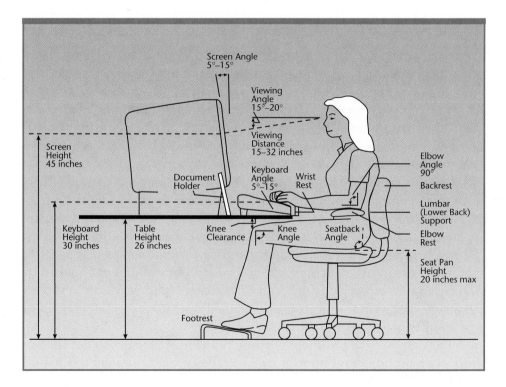

they can handle. Professional help may be available through your company's human resources office, your company's health and workers' compensation insurers, and various EAPs such as trained counselors, psychiatrists, and drug interdiction programs. These can help people cope with their stress and the results of it more effectively.

Instant Replay

1. Our experiences help shape our individual beliefs.
2. Our beliefs help shape our attitudes.
3. When supervisors observe improper attitudes or conduct in subordinates—attitudes or conduct that prevents average or above-average performance—they must act to change them.
4. Changing attitudes requires us to identify the attitude that needs changing, determine the supports for it, weaken those supports, and offer a substitute and sell it.
5. Techniques for changing attitudes include force-field analysis, effective communications, persuasion techniques, participation techniques, training programs, and organizational development activities.
6. Stress is worry, anxiety, or tension that accompanies situations and problems we face and causes uncertainty about the ways in which we should resolve them. Stress can distract us from our work, adversely affect our attitudes, and injure our health unless we learn to cope with it or to remove it from our workplace.

Questions for Class Discussion

1. Can you define this chapter's key terms?
2. How do you form an attitude about a person, place, or thing?
3. What kinds of attitudes held by workers need changing? How would you go about changing a subordinate's attitude?
4. What are the six techniques or tools described in this chapter that can help you change your own or other people's attitudes?
5. What are six major causes of stress in the workplace?
6. What are six ways in which a person can cope with work-related stress?

Incident

Purpose: To identify stressors—those elements listed but not present in your working or school environment.

Your Task: Read the checklist that follows, and mark those items that you find in either your work or school environment. (You may evaluate both or only one environment.)

		Present	Absent
1.	Open communications exist between and among managers and workers.	___	___
2.	Employees are adequately trained before taking on new tasks.	___	___
3.	Employees are adequately recognized and rewarded for achievements.	___	___
4.	Employees are trained in how to handle stress.	___	___
5.	Employees' privacy is respected.	___	___
6.	Employees are encouraged to take risks.	___	___
7.	Employees are notified in advance of pending changes.	___	___
8.	Employees believe, on average, that their pay and benefits are fair.	___	___
9.	Employees are aware of and encouraged to take advantage of EAPs.	___	___
10.	Major reorganization or reengineering has not taken place in the recent past.	___	___
11.	Major reorganization or reengineering is not planned for the near future.	___	___
12.	The work climate or environment is pleasant to work in.	___	___
13.	Employees may work flexible hours and schedules.	___	___
14.	In general, employees feel that enough employees exist to perform work.	___	___
15.	Employees have access to and are trained to use the technology they need.	___	___

CASE PROBLEM 6.1

Burdens

As Peter approached Patricia he noticed that she was deep in thought. "Mind if I take a few minutes?" asked Peter.

"Oh, sorry, I was a million miles away. Pull up a chair."

"I won't take much time, Pat. I just need your help. The Townsend report is going to be late this week because I can't get the figures I need from production control. I have asked those people for the numbers about six times, and they keep assuring me they will send them. Can you put a bug in their ears to hurry the data along?"

"I'll call them today and see what I can do." Just then Pat's phone rang, and she picked it up. After a few minutes of mostly listening, Pat hung up and turned to Peter with a worried look on her face. "Pete, I know you are swamped with work now that your department has been reduced by three people, but Sarah needs your help. You are the only person left who understands the computer program for inventory control. She inherited the job that Walters vacated and can't seem to get the program to operate properly. If you could get her started and go over things with her, I think that she will be able to carry on. She learns fast and...."

Peter interrupted Pat. "If you want me to help another department, I will; but you had better give me more time for my regular work. Since last month's cutback, my people have been experiencing about a 20 percent increase in their workloads. Al is threatening to quit, what with all these new demands on him. By the way, rumor has it that more cuts are due. Will my department get any? I'm down to muscle now. Any more cuts will take out bones."

Patricia assured Peter that no more cuts were coming and watched as he shuffled off to Sarah's office. She looked at the pile of papers on her desk and sighed. Another week of twelve-hour days lay ahead for her, with no relief in sight. She thought back over the last few weeks, mentally listing her problems. After last month's cutbacks, her department had been merged with two others, and she had become a middle manager. Her staff was now about 80 percent of what it had been, and her workload had more than doubled. The new computers were more of a problem than a blessing for her at present. The only people who really understood how to use them effectively were either laid off or moved to other areas. Peter was one of two people she had had to promote to head the new departmental structure, and she had not trained them to become supervisors. They were both in trouble now, and she had to do much of what they should be doing. She picked up her phone and canceled her lunch date. "Looks like another lunch of coffee at my desk," she thought.

Questions

1. What sources of stress is Patricia experiencing?
2. What sources of stress is Peter probably experiencing?
3. What would you recommend to them as ways of coping with their stress?

Conflicting Views

CASE PROBLEM 6.2

"You're from the old school," said Rita. "A little change never hurt anyone. You know the old saying that the only thing certain is change itself."

"Well," countered Gayla, "I believe that changes should be kept to a minimum and that conflict should be eliminated entirely. I don't want to go through another month like this last one. Don't you remember how so-called good friends were fighting with each other over such silly things as wastebaskets and the color of desk blotters?"

Rita and Gayla were discussing the recent move from their rented quarters to the company's newly constructed regional office. Personnel and sections from three rented facilities were now in the process of taking over the new facility. Rita's group of sixteen people was the first to arrive and had its pick of spaces. Gayla's group was the last to arrive; its members found themselves on the third floor, overlooking the parking lot, and occupying offices everyone else had rejected.

When Rita's people arrived, they were asked to visit the stockrooms in the basement to pick their desks, file cabinets, desk sets, and other accessories by marking the tags on each item with their names and sections. After Rita placed her people in their offices, she had asked each of her subordinates to stake out a specific area or cubicle. Once each person had chosen a spot, Rita requested that the items chosen from stock be delivered and set up.

Things were a little different for Gayla and her group, however. When they arrived at the end of last month, there were just enough chairs, desks, desk sets, and so forth to equip each person's workstation. The stations were already set up on the third floor, in the rear quarter of the building. Exposures were north and east. The northern view was of the parking lot and the rear of a wholesale warehouse. The eastern view was of a busy interstate highway that ran parallel to the building about 100 feet away.

Needless to say, Gayla's people were complaining and moaning from the first day. The northeast corner of the top floor would mean cold winters, and the views were about as depressing as one could imagine. When Gayla's people found out that the others who had come ahead of them had been able to choose their own office furnishings, they really got upset. Gayla was having a very tough time trying to get her people to settle in and get productive. It did no good to explain to them that they were last because their lease had been the last to run out. Everyone suspected that higher-ups had it in for Gayla and that they were paying the price with lousy facilities. When reminded by other workers that their previous rented facilities had been considered better than anyone else's, Gayla's group members became somewhat defensive.

Over the last two weeks, Gayla was told by Rita and two other supervisors that her people were trying to swap wastebaskets and blotters with others in the building. In one instance, one of Gayla's people tore up a blotter and kicked a large dent in the wastebasket that belonged to a person who would not swap with her. What had been intended as good-natured kidding was being taken by the third-floor group as insulting remarks and conduct. Gayla sensed things were getting out of hand.

Questions

1. What do you think about the way in which this company handled change?
2. Conflict can arise from competition between individuals and groups for scarce resources. What are the causes for conflict in this case?
3. What attitudes seem to be creating both stress and conflict?
4. What can the supervisors do to change them?

Notes

Bittel, Lester R., and Ramsey, Jackson E., eds., *Handbook for Professional Managers* (New York: McGraw-Hill, 1985), 421.
Chicago Tribune. "Bosses Keep Close Watch on Workers," August 7, 1994, sect. 7, 8.

———. "Bringing Your Work Life Under Control," September 19, 1994, sect. 4, 3.

———. "Execs, Workers Clash Over Redefined Jobs," October 11, 1994, sect. 3, 3.

———. "If You're Reading This, Odds Are Good That You're Stressed," November 21, 1994, sect. 4, 3.

———. "World Faces Epidemic of Job Stress," March 23, 1993, sect. 1, 3.

Franklin, Stephen. "For Workers And Their Employers, It Was a Wonderful Life." *Chicago Tribune*, December 22, 1992, sect. 3, 3.

Jamieson, David, and O'Mara, Julie. *Managing Workforce 2000* (San Francisco: Jossey-Bass, 1991), 27–29.

Kelly, Kevin, and Burrows, Peter. "Motorola: Training for the Millennium." *Business Week*, March 28, 1994, 158–159.

Kleiman, Carol. "Helping Employees Work Happy." *Chicago Tribune*, October 30, 1994, sect. 8, 1.

Kotulak, Ron, and Van, Jon. "Job Strain Sickens People And Also Demoralizes Them." *Chicago Tribune*, November 6, 1994, sect. 5, 4.

Livingston, J. Sterling. "Pygmalion in Management." *Harvard Business Review on Human Relations* (New York: Harper & Row, 1979), 181.

McGregor, Douglas. "The Human Side of Enterprise," in *Classics in Management*, Harwood F. Merrill, ed. (New York: American Management Association, 1970), 461–475.

McHenry, Susan. "Jobs We Love to Hate." *Working Woman*, November 1994, 12.

Muller, Joann. "Assembling a New Auto Worker." *Chicago Tribune*, May 29, 1994, sect. 8, 1.

Narisetti, Raju. "Bottom-Up Approach Pushes Plant's Performance to the Top." *Chicago Tribune*, November 29, 1992, sect. 7, 13.

Nauman, Matt. "Job Well Done." *Chicago Tribune*, September 18, 1994, sect. 17, 3.

Ouchi, William G. *Theory Z: How American Business Can Meet the Japanese Challenge* (Reading, Mass.: Addison-Wesley, 1981); and Pascale, R. T., and Athos, A. G. *The Art of Japanese Management* (New York: Simon & Schuster, 1981).

Pennar, Karen. "America's Quest Can't Be Half-Hearted." *Business Week*, June 8, 1987, 136.

Peters, Tom. "'Fountain of Youth'—And Low Fares." *Chicago Tribune*, September 26, 1994, sect. 4, 5.

Peters, Tom. "Nobody Knows Nothin', So Go Ahead, Take Those Risks." *Chicago Tribune*, August 29, 1994, sect. 4, 3.

Weiss, Donald. *How to Be a Successful Manager* (New York: Amacom, 1986), 8–9.

Zellner, Wendy. "Team Player: No More 'Same-ol'—Same-ol'." *Business Week*, October 17, 1994, 95–96.

Suggested Readings

Beer, Michael, Eisenstat, R. A., and Spector, Bert. "Why Change Programs Don't Produce Change." *Harvard Business Review* (November–December 1990): 158–166.

Brod, Craig. *Technostress: The Human Cost of the Computer Revolution*. Reading, Mass.: Addison-Wesley, 1984.

Choate, Scott. *Your Guide to Corporate Survival*. Clearwater, Fla.: CC Publications, 1991.

Fisher, Shirley, and Cooper, Gary L. *On the Move: The Psychology of Change and Transition*. New York: John Wiley & Sons, 1991.

Gordon, Edward E., and Ponticell, Judith A. *FutureWork—The Revolution Reshaping American Business*. New York: Praeger Books, 1994.

Helmstetter, Shad. *You Can Excel in Times of Change*. New York: Simon & Schuster, 1991.

Kinkhead, R. W., and Winokour, D. "Navigating the Seas of Cultural Change." *Public Relations Journal* (November 1991): 14–16.

Osborne, R. L. "Core Value Statements: The Corporate Compass." *Business Horizons* (November–December 1991): 27–34.

"Quality: How to Make It Pay." *Business Week* (August 8, 1994): 54–59.

Human Motivation

OBJECTIVES

After reading and discussing this chapter, you should be able to do the following:

1. Define this chapter's key terms.

2. List and give an example of each of the five common needs that humans share.

3. List and give an example of each of Herzberg's maintenance factors.

4. List and give an example of each of Herzberg's motivational factors.

5. Describe the contingency theory of motivation.

6. Describe the expectancy theory of motivation.

7. Describe the reinforcement theory of motivation.

8. Describe the equity theory of motivation.

9. Discuss the concepts of quality and productivity and what supervisors can do to promote improvements in each.

INTRODUCTION

People are the most complex, difficult-to-manage resource that any business has. All of us are constantly changing and growing. Each day we are a little different from the way we were the day before. We bring our hopes and ambitions to work, along with our problems and defects. Most of us want our jobs and careers to provide us with many things. Some of us view our jobs as a source of the money we need in order to live the kind of life we feel is important. Some of us want a challenge, work that we can take pride in, and a sense of progress and accomplishment.

Most employers recognize that their employees are complex creatures who expect more than a paycheck from their employment. Employers know that dissatisfied, unhappy workers are generally poor performers. They know that satisfied workers often produce above the standards set for their jobs. Knowledgeable employers recognize, therefore, that it is in their best interests to attempt to provide their employees with the kinds of satisfaction they seek on the job.

This chapter explores the common human needs we all share and their relationship to our behavior. It introduces you to popular theories on human motivation and describes what you and employers can do to help others get more from their jobs than simply a paycheck. Finally, it links motivation with the all-important concepts (defined in Chapter 1) of quality and productivity.

MOTIVATION DEFINED

motivation

the drive within a person to achieve a goal

Motivation is the drive within a person to achieve a goal. It is an internal process that takes place in all human beings, influenced by their perceptions and experiences as well as external variables. People are motivated by a variety of causes that can and do influence their behaviors. For example, Jamal's wife is expecting a baby. Consequently, he has become very eager to work all available overtime hours to earn more income. Maria is asking for additional duties from her supervisor and has returned to school to get herself qualified to earn a promotion. But as soon as both people achieve their objectives, their behaviors will usually cease to be motivated by these objectives.

As a supervisor, team leader, or team facilitator, your primary responsibility is to influence behaviors in order to create more effective and efficient operations and employees. You have the authority to influence the motivation of your subordinates and team members by tailoring your approaches and the rewards available to each when you are coaching, counseling, and training. You control, to a great extent, the design of the physical and emotional environments in which you all perform your duties. You must maintain an environment that supports your subordinates' motivated behavior.

Worker recognition enhances self-esteem. Here, a supervisor at Xerox presents a service award based on length of service. The presentation is held in front of co-workers to enhance self-esteem.

As author and consultant Tom Peters puts it: "The average person, age 18 or 58, comes to the workplace fully endowed with motivation. Our primary roles as 'leaders' is to clear the silly B.S. out of the way—and let the troops get on with the job" (Peters, "To," 1994). Lou Holtz, head coach at Notre Dame, adds: "'It's not my job to motivate players. They bring extraordinary motivation to our program. It's my job *not* to demotivate them" (Peters, "Managers," 1994). Terry Neill, a management consultant with Anderson Consulting, believes that "Genuine empowerment…is not the things you do to or for people: it's the impediments you take away, leaving room for folks to empower themselves" (Peters, "Managers," 1994).

This chapter examines six basic, interrelated theories about motivation—why people do what they do. All will help you visualize and interpret the causes behind your own and your subordinates' behavior.

HUMAN NEEDS

When people work for subsistence-level wages, as most Americans did until the late 1940s, they concentrate on surviving. Their primary concern is for employment that will give them the money to furnish themselves and their families with the necessities of life—food, clothing, and shelter. They live in fear of losing their jobs and, therefore, tolerate nearly any kind of working conditions and environment. People who observed the industrial economy of the United States in the early years of the twentieth century found little joy in its workers' hearts. Many companies and their managers believed that people worked primarily for money, and they were partially correct in those beliefs. Theory X (Chapter 6) had many disciples.

The Hawthorne Studies

Since the 1920s, businesses have studied their employees in efforts to find out more about them—why some work well and others do not, why some last only a short time on the job and others stay for many years. Most of the ideas you read earlier and will read in this chapter have come from studies made by businesses and social scientists. Probably the most important study—one that launched intense interest about and research into employee behavior and motivation—was the Western Electric Company's study in the 1920s. In 1927, engineers at the Hawthorne Plant of the Western Electric Company near Chicago conducted an experiment with several groups of workers to determine the effect of illumination on production. When illumination was increased in stages, the engineers found that production increased. To verify their findings, they reduced illumination to its previous level—and, again, production increased. Perplexed, they called in Elton Mayo and his colleagues from Harvard to investigate.

The First Study The Harvard researchers selected several experienced women assemblers for an experiment. With the permission of these workers and the records of their past production, management removed the women from their formal group of assemblers and isolated them in a room. The women were compensated on the basis of the output of their group. Next followed a series of environmental changes, each discussed with the women in advance of its implementation. For example, breaks were introduced and light refreshments were served; the women received no direct supervision as they had before, only indirect supervision from several researchers in charge of the experiment; the normal six-day week was reduced to five days, and the workday was cut by one hour. Each of these changes was accompanied by an increase in the group's output (Mayo, 1945).

To verify the assumptions that the researchers made, the women returned to their original working conditions: Breaks were eliminated, the six-day week was restored, and all other conditions that had prevailed before the women were isolated were reinstated. The results were that production again increased!

In the extensive interviewing that followed, Mayo and his group concluded that a team spirit had been created, quite by accident, when management singled out these women to be the study group and then consulted with them before making each change. The women felt that they were something very special, both individually and collectively. Their isolation as a group and their proximity at work provided an environment for the development of close personal relationships. The formal group had been transformed into an informal one—a clique.

The Second Study To test the researchers' findings, a new group of workers was selected and isolated. This time the researchers chose a group of men. Several of them were involved in wiring equipment, whereas others soldered the wired connections. Two inspectors were part of the group and approved the finished jobs. An observer was on hand throughout the working day to record the men's work and reactions.

Several important events happened in this formal group. The men eventually split into two separate informal cliques. The basis for the split was that one group felt its work was more difficult than the other's. Its members adopted a superior attitude. This left the remainder of the workers to form another clique. Both cliques included wirers, solderers, and an inspector. Each group also engaged in setting standards of output and conduct. The members of the group that considered itself superior mutually agreed on production quotas. Neither too little nor too much production was permitted, and peers exerted pressure to keep fellow group members in line. As intergroup rivalry developed, the output of the other group began to decline. The superior group became superior in output also, which caused additional condescending behavior and a still greater decrease in morale and output in the other group. The workers who produced the most in each group were excluded from their group if they did not conform. Even though each man was to share in a bonus based on the formal group's total output, informal group conflict resulted in a decline in production.

These two experiments revealed that people work for a variety of reasons—not just for money and subsistence. They seek satisfaction for more than their physical needs at work and from co-workers. For the first time in our industrial history, clear evidence was gathered to support people's social and esteem needs.

A Hierarchy of Needs

The Hawthorne studies and many more that followed have given us a much wider view of why people work and what they expect from work. A well-known psychologist, Abraham H. Maslow, identified five universal **human needs** that act as fuel for our internal drives to change or achieve. Exhibit 7.1 shows this hierarchy of needs as levels or steps in an upward progression from the most basic to the highest psychological need (Maslow, 1970).

The Needs-Goal Model of Motivation

Human needs provide the basis for our first theory of motivation. Our definition of motivation—the drive within a person to achieve a goal—tells us that motivation is an internal process. It is something we do within ourselves, not something we do to others. The term *drive* in our definition denotes a force that is fueled by human needs common to all of us. These needs, both physical and psychological, provide motives for our actions and behavior. To achieve our goals, we must take actions. Our actions

human needs
physiological and psychological requirements that all humans share and that act as motives for behavior

Self-Realization Needs	Job-Related Satisfiers
Reaching your Potential Independence Creativity Self-Expression	Involvement in Planning Your Work Freedom to Make Decisions Affecting Work Creative Work to Perform Opportunities for Growth and Development

Esteem Needs	Job-Related Satisfiers
Responsibility Self-Respect Recognition Sense of Accomplishment Sense of Competence Sense of Equity	Status Symbols Money–as a Measure, for Some, of Self-Esteem Merit Awards Challenging Work Sharing in Decisions Opportunity for Advancement

Social Needs	Job-Related Satisfiers
Companionship Acceptance Love and Affection Group Membership	Opportunities for Interaction with Others Team Spirit Friendly Coworkers

Safety Needs	Job-Related Satisfiers
Security for Self and Possessions Avoidance of Risks Avoidance of Harm Avoidance of Pain	Safe Working Conditions Seniority Fringe Benefits Proper Supervision Sound Company Policies, Programs, and Practices

Physical Needs	Job-Related Satisfiers
Food Clothing Shelter Comfort Self-Preservation	Pleasant Working Conditions Adequate Wage or Salary Rest Periods Labor-Saving Devices Efficient Work Methods

EXHIBIT 7.1

A. H. Maslow's hierarchy of human needs, shown with job-related satisfiers that companies can provide to meet each need.

toward achievement are efforts, both mental and physical, that we feel are necessary to attain our goals.

Our goals may be tangible or intangible. We may want a new car or a job with higher status. The specific forms our goals take are a result of our personal makeup and desires at given moments in time and are shaped in part by our experiences, individual perceptions, and current environments.

According to the needs-goal theory of motivation, a person who is motivated is in a state of unrest because he or she feels or believes that something is lacking—the goal. It is the unfulfilled need that creates the state of unrest. And since our needs can never fully be satisfied, we are continually setting goals. It is in our nature to want more—to continually strive to progress, to improve our conditions, and to acquire something new.

Exhibit 7.2 illustrates the needs-goal motivation process. As you study the figure, keep in mind the following assertions about human needs and motivation:

- The unsatisfied need is the strongest motivator
- People can be influenced by more than one unsatisfied need at any given time
- Needs can never be fully satisfied: They may cease to motivate behavior for a time, but they can and will return to act once again as motivators
- People who seek satisfaction in one need area and do not find it will experience frustration and may try to compensate by overemphasizing another need

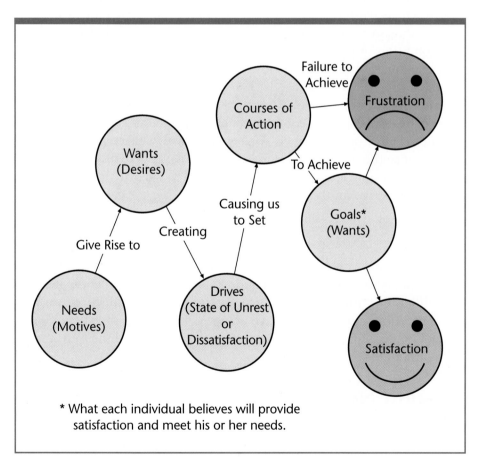

EXHIBIT 7.2
The motivation process in which needs act as motives for human behavior.

- The perception of what we need at any given time is shaped in part by our experiences, by external influences on us, and by our capabilities to change our situations

Physiological Needs

Physiological or bodily needs are at the base of the needs hierarchy. These are the needs for adequate food, clothing, and shelter and the instinct for survival. Unsatisfied physiological needs can influence behavior, whereas satisfied physiological needs are not motivators. For example, when we are hungry, we desire food of a type and in a quantity necessary to satisfy our hunger. Once we have eaten our fill, our hunger dissipates and no longer motivates our actions. New needs surface and take over as motives for our actions. But as we all know, hunger will return.

Safety Needs

The second level of human needs—safety needs or physical security—is our next concern. Having satisfied our physiological needs for the moment, we are concerned about providing for their satisfaction in the future. Once we have achieved an economic position that provides the means necessary to secure our physical maintenance, we want to protect this condition. A person who gets a job is anxious to keep it. He or she is concerned with preventing its loss and the accompanying loss of the ability to provide for physical needs. The person may, as a result, join a union to gain this kind of security. He or she may take out insurance as protection against economic losses from illness or accident. Like his or her physical needs, the person's need for security will weaken as a motive for actions once the individual reaches an adequate degree of satisfaction. But if his or her job is threatened, the need for security may once again become an active motivating force.

Social Needs

With the satisfaction of safety or security needs can come the desire to satisfy social needs. These needs include a desire for human companionship, for affiliation with people and groups, for love and affection, and for a sense of belonging. Once we have achieved a measure of satisfaction that we feel is adequate, our social needs begin to wane, and the fourth level of need stimulates our behavior.

Esteem Needs

The need for esteem is two-sided. First, we have a desire to be appreciated for what we are and for what we have to contribute—to be respected by others. Second, we need to have a feeling of self-esteem—to know we are worth something to ourselves and to others. We need a positive self-image. From this need comes the desire for praise and for symbols that reflect our self-approval and others' appreciation of our efforts. We seek prestige and status positions among our peers. We behave in ways that are pleasing and acceptable to others whose opinions we value. We wish to master the tasks given us, thus becoming competent performers. We want fair and equitable treatment from others.

Self-Realization Needs

Finally, our need for self-realization (sometimes called self-actualization) takes over when we achieve some measure of satisfaction in the previous four levels. We begin to experience a need to fulfill our potential and to be creative. To some, this means striving for higher levels in company management and obtaining the added authority and prestige that such positions provide. To others, it means being the best machinist, computer programmer, violinist, or supervisor that they have the potential to become. The need for self-realization causes a person to pursue interests and knowledge for their own sake and for the joy of the pursuit.

All these needs are common in all of us to some degree. At any given moment, one or more of them are active, while the others lie dormant. When we feel satisfied in one or more areas, those areas will cease for a time to motivate our behavior. What is enough satisfaction for some, however, may be too little or too much for others. In general, no need is ever completely satisfied, and none can ever cease completely to be a motivator. It is the unfulfilled need that is the strongest motive for human behavior.

SUPERVISORS AND HUMAN NEEDS

What does all this mean to you as a supervisor? A major goal for every organization is to help individual associates reach their goals while they help the organization reach its. You know that our common needs provide the motives for human behavior and that each person is a unique individual with personal goals that may be quite different from those of his or her peers. As a supervisor, you are in a unique position to assist your subordinates and to provide them with some of the satisfactions they are seeking. You can be most helpful with regard to their safety, social, and esteem needs, as we shall now see.

Concerning your subordinates' needs for safety and security, you are probably the one who initially provided them with their training. When your subordinates joined your department, chances are that you received and welcomed them. You assessed their strengths and weaknesses and got to know as much about them and their abilities as possible. Then you determined their specific needs for training so that they might improve their performance and skills. What you were doing was providing them with the knowledge, skills, and attitudes they would need to keep their jobs. You were increasing their sense of security and helping them remove some of their initial fears. You taught and enforced safety on the job (the focus of Chapter 16). Your actions helped them achieve a measure of satisfaction for both their physical and safety needs.

You helped your subordinates with their need for affiliation when you introduced them to their new jobs and work groups when they first arrived. Your effort to know them has made you aware of their individual needs for affiliation and has enabled you to identify workers who are satisfied and those who are frustrated with regard to their social needs. If you were doing your job, you went to work on the problem of those who needed more social contacts and were not experiencing them; you did all you could to help the isolated individuals gain acceptance by fostering a team spirit among your subordinates and by making them all feel part of a larger group. The process of turning individuals into team players is difficult and time consuming. People need to learn a variety of skills to make the transformation, and teams are not for everyone or for every task. But where they do apply and when they function properly, they provide satisfaction for team members' need for affiliation as nothing else at work can.

In regard to your subordinates' esteem needs, you have several key roles to play. In your appraisals, you are providing your people with the raw material they need to help them know themselves and improve. You are also giving them an accurate assessment of how they rate with you and with the company. You can pass out praise if they deserve it and note the specific areas they must work on to gain your continued praise and acceptance. You also have authority that, if delegated, can enrich their feelings of importance and give them a way to learn certain aspects of your job. They know that this is an important sign of your faith and confidence in their abilities. You know that if you are to advance, you must know your boss's job, and if they are to advance, they must know your job. Each day you may receive suggestions from your people. If they are good, use them and give the credit to the source of each suggestion. If they are not suited to the operation, tell the subordinate the reason.

Various incentive systems are used by companies to gain suggestions and provide recognition to their creators. "Modern of Marshfield, a furniture manufacturer in Wisconsin,...set up a suggestion program...named 'colleague of the month'" (*Inc.*, "Motivation," 1994). Winners are chosen by a committee of previous winners and rewarded financially. The "colleague of the year wins a trip for two to a fancy locale" (*Inc.*, "Motivation," 1994). Silicon Graphics, Inc. has an "Off-the-Wall Award" (Austin, "Motivating," 1994). "The point, according to its creator, senior vice-president of administration Ken Coleman, is to 'reinforce what's really important to our business: It's OK to be wacky and different, because the only real strategic weapon we have that can't be copied by our competition is our people'"

(Austin, "Motivating," 1994). These are but a few ways to help your people and your operation improve.

A major difficulty may arise if you attempt to discover which of the five need levels is a conscious concern to each individual subordinate at any given time. This is difficult knowledge to gain because when you observe your people, you do so in a fragmented way. You see them at work under the influence of many forces from within and outside the company. Even if you know each of your people well, you can be fooled by your observations. In observing the actions of others, we seldom see the motives for them. You, like your associates, tend to play roles at work that mask your true feelings and motives. Yet every supervisor, team leader, and team facilitator concerned about his or her job and associates must attempt to determine what needs are most important to them. This knowledge will allow you to provide some incentives that could trigger a greater effort or contribution by subordinates. They, their teams, and your reputation will benefit by their improved performance.

ACCOMMODATING DIVERSITY

Is there a difference between what men and women seek to achieve from working? Researchers from *Inc.* magazine claim that differences between what men and women want from work are insignificant. What seems to matter more than gender is the differences people have in their levels of formal education. According to Rosalind C. Barnett, a researcher for Wellesley College's Center for Research on Women, "Men and women find similar aspects of the workplace rewarding and problematic" (Caggiano, 1992).

An international consulting firm, the Wyatt company, found in its survey "that employees who thought their employer's policies helped balance work and family responsibilities were far more likely to feel a commitment to their company as more than 'just a place to work' than those who thought otherwise (62 percent versus 13 percent)" (Caggiano, 1992). The Chivas Regal Report on Working Americans asked workers what would give them a feeling of success. The largest group—62 percent— chose a "happy family life" (Caggiano, 1992). According to authors Patricia Aburdene and John Naisbitt (1992), a wife-and-husband team, younger women and men will both keep working toward a better balance between their work and families. Companies will gain the best from their people and improve their productivity when they help their employees do this with such quality-of-work-life programs and policies as flexible scheduling, job sharing, leaves of absence, and day care.

According to the U.S. Labor Department's 1992 report, the numbers of female and minority managers increased significantly in U.S. companies along with the shrinkage in the differences between men's and women's salaries between 1981 and 1991. Women now earn about 73 cents for every dollar earned by men in similar jobs, up from the 60+ cents of the early 1980s. The growth is due in part to a decline in men's earnings and the continuing movement of women into what traditionally had been male occupations. Finally, the 103rd U.S. Congress, seated in January 1993, contained more women and members of minority groups than any other Congress in America's history.

MAINTENANCE AND MOTIVATION

As a further help in understanding motivation, let us examine the contributions of Dr. Frederick Herzberg, whose work on motivation in business demonstrated some applications of Maslow's hierarchy of human needs. Herzberg and his associates found that two sets of factors must be provided in the working environment to promote motivation.

Maintenance or Hygiene Factors

maintenance factor according to Herzberg, a factor that can be provided by an employer in order to prevent job dissatisfaction

First, there is a set of factors they labeled **maintenance factors** or hygiene factors. These conditions or factors are extrinsic—not connected to the work we do—and will not cause employee motivation in the great majority of people. But a lack of them can cause dissatisfaction, thus preventing or inhibiting motivation. These environmental conditions, provided in the right mix (from each employee's personal point of view), can only prevent dissatisfaction and remove barriers to motivated behavior. The best a business can hope for by providing these factors is that the average employee will put forth an average commitment in time and effort at his or her job.

Herzberg (1975) identified five maintenance factors:

1. Economic—wages, salaries, fringe benefits, and the like
2. Security—grievance procedures, seniority privileges, fair work rules, and company policy and discipline
3. Social—opportunities to mix with one's peers under company sponsorship at parties, outings, breaks, and the like
4. Working conditions—adequate heat, light, ventilation, and hours of work
5. Status—privileges, job titles, and other symbols of rank and position

Regarding economic factors, money was viewed by Herzberg as a maintenance factor because, for the majority of people he and his researchers worked with, it is extrinsic to one's job and is of little help in satisfying our higher-level psychological needs—esteem and self-realization. It cannot make people who are working in a job they hate, or under conditions that hurt psychologically or physically, work with a personal commitment to excel. Money or the promise of it can motivate us in the short term (as economic incentives such as bonuses and suggestion awards indicate), but once obtained, it ceases to motivate. When people feel that they have enough money (for each of us this is an individual perception), they cease to seek to acquire more.

The quest for money often masks a search for what money cannot buy. "If your workers are complaining about their pay, it's usually a sign that something else is missing.... People will work for less (not less than a fair wage...) if they enjoy their work and feel as if they're being treated fairly" (Caggiano, 1992). Money cannot offer most of us intrinsic satisfactions—those directly connected to work and the performance of it. According to author, professor, and psychologist C. J. Cranny (Caggiano, 1992), "the most important factor in creating an atmosphere that workers find satisfying is whether employees find their work 'intrinsically interesting.'" This can only happen through what Herzberg called motivation factors.

Motivation Factors

Motivation factors, the second set of factors, are intrinsic—directly related to the work we do—and provide the incentive to make a better-than-average commitment, for the great majority of us, to our efforts. Motivation factors provide the means by which individuals can achieve greater job satisfaction. When provided in the proper quantity and quality, they have the potential to satisfy employees' needs and cause an increased commitment of time and energy by them. Herzberg (1975) identified seven motivation factors:

motivation factor according to Herzberg, a factor that has the potential to stimulate internal motivation to provide a better-than-average performance and commitment from those to whom it appeals

1. Challenging work—The average person wants to view his or her job as offering an avenue for self-expression and growth. Each person needs something to tax his or her abilities.
2. Feelings of personal accomplishment—The average employee gets a sense of achievement and a feeling of contributing something of value when presented with a challenge that he or she can meet.
3. Recognition for achievement—The average employee wants to feel that his or her contributions have been worth the effort and that the effort has been noted and appreciated. Money awards, for some, help here.
4. Achievement of increasing responsibility—The typical employee wants to acquire new duties and responsibilities, either through expansion of his or her job or by delegation from the supervisor.
5. A sense of individual importance to the organization—Employees want to feel that their personal presence is needed and that their individual contributions are necessary. Higher-than-average compensation can help here for some people.

6. Access to information—Employees want to know about the things that affect them and their jobs; they want to be kept in the know.
7. Involvement in decision making—Today's employees desire a voice in the matters that affect them and a chance to decide some things for themselves. They need freedom to exercise initiative and creativity.

These factors, unlike the common human needs they help satisfy, need to be designed into the structure and operations of a business. When companies make the commitment to empower employees, they give individuals and teams the authority to make their own decisions, solve their problems, and achieve greater control over their work. In short, associates and colleagues achieve greater autonomy—a key motivating factor in Herzberg's research. A 1993 Gallup Poll discovered that associates feel empowered when they have the authority to (*Inc.*, "So," 1994):

- Stop work in progress to correct problems (NUMMI workers have this authority)
- Intervene on a customer's behalf (Marriott associates have this power, as shown in the Supervisors and Quality feature that follows)
- Rework a product or redo a service (Motorola employees have this duty)
- Make an exception to procedures (autonomous teams have this ability)
- Replace merchandise or grant refunds (most discount chains grant their store managers this power)

Some employees do not desire all or even a few of these factors and the opportunities they represent. This may be true because, for the moment at least, they lack ambition and do not feel the need to change. Still others, because of mental or emotional limitations, may lack the potential to take advantage of these factors and to master higher job responsibilities. For those who, in the manager's opinion, can take advantage of these factors but for the present do not do so, some standards and goals must be set to prod them to keep growing. The manager should make it clear to these employees that more is expected of them and that they can receive more rewards in return for an increased effort. In short, the supervisor, team leader, or team facilitator must try to get such employees oriented toward making progress, both for themselves and for the company.

A recent Gallup Poll asked workers how important various characteristics of the job were to them. It discovered an interesting and nearly equal mix of Herzberg's maintenance and motivation factors. Among the major characteristics listed as "very important" were (Caggiano, 1992):

1. Over three fourths of those surveyed listed good benefits, interesting work, and job security (in this order).

SUPERVISORS AND QUALITY

Motivated service associates are the key to customer satisfaction in most businesses, especially the hospitality industry. No one knows this better than the committed and enthusiastic employees of Marriott International's Schaumburg Marriott in Illinois. Tony Prsyszlak, a community college graduate, is a prime example. He greets guests as they arrive: "But please don't call this gregarious 23-year-old a doorman. He is now a multitalented 'guest service associate'—GSA, for short." Prsyszlak is just one of five GSAs who can handle your check-in; all wear several hats—doorman, bellman, front-desk clerk, and concierge. And all are self-managing. The GSAs are a select few—10 percent of the applicants who show the necessary flexibility and steadiness under pressure.

More than ever before, "companies are scrambling to hire, train, and hang on to ordinary mortals who can perform feats of extraordinary service.... [I]n an era of flattened hierarchies and heightened expectations, [what is needed are] people who are resilient and resourceful, empathetic and enterprising, competent and creative—a set of skills, in short, that [were] once demanded only of managers." To find these extraordinary people takes patience and careful screening, considering not so much formal education and experience as "personality and psychology." Once found, these valuable human beings must be carefully trained and empowered. After an initial eight hours of training, all new hires are given a "buddy" or mentor to help them through their next ninety days. Refresher training is provided at the end of each month. The results of Marriott's new approaches have led to more motivated associates, delighted guests, and a decline in employee turnover.

Source: Henkoff, Ronald. "Finding, Training & Keeping the Best Service Workers," *Fortune*, October 3, 1994, 110–111, 114, 116, 118, 120, 122.

2. Sixty-two to 68 percent listed the opportunity to learn new skills, one week or more of vacation time, working independently, and recognition from co-workers (in this order).
3. Fifty-eight percent listed regular hours, having a job in which they could help others, and limits to job stress.
4. Fifty-two to 56 percent listed high income (eleventh on the list), working close to home, work that is important to society, chances for promotion, and contact with many people (in this order).

For subordinates who have the potential and the drive to achieve something greater, supervisors have a duty to provide a work environment

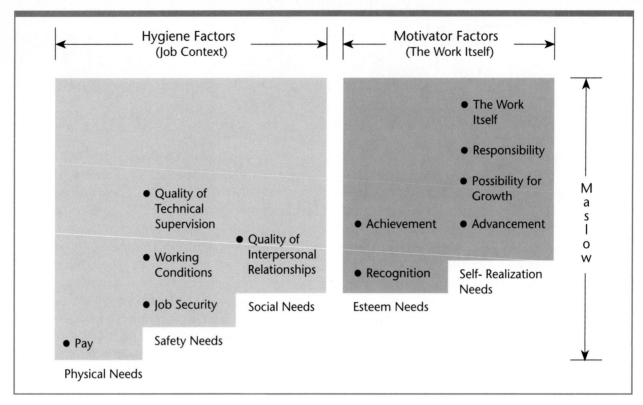

EXHIBIT 7.3

Integration of Maslow's needs hierarchy with Herzberg's maintenance–motivation theory.

Source: Warren R. Plunkett and Raymond Attner, *Introduction to Management*, 4th ed. (PWS-Kent Publishing Company, 1992), 351.

that contains the motivation factors. If they are made available, like different kinds of fine foods on a buffet, the "hungry" people in any group will select among them according to their needs.

Exhibit 7.3 integrates Maslow's and Herzberg's needs theories. Hygiene or maintenance factors generally help us satisfy our physical, safety, and social needs. Motivation factors generally help us satisfy our esteem and self-realization needs.

THE CONTINGENCY THEORY

John J. Morse and Jay W. Lorsch (1975) have built on Douglas McGregor's Theory Y and Herzberg's motivation and maintenance factors with their theory of motivation called the contingency theory. Morse and Lorsch conducted research to determine how the fit between an organization's characteristics and its tasks relates to individuals' motivations. They found that an organization—task fit affects and is affected by the quality of task performance and by individuals' feelings of competence.

The contingency theory has four basic components (Morse and Lorsch, 1975):

1. Among people's needs is a central need to achieve a sense of competence.
2. The ways in which people fulfill this need vary from person to person, depending on how the need interacts with other needs and on the strengths of those other needs.
3. Competence motivation is most likely to be fulfilled when there is a fit between task and organization.
4. A sense of competence continues to motivate people even after competence is achieved.

All of us want a sense of competence—to be thought of as competent and to perceive ourselves that way. According to Morse and Lorsch, people performing highly structured and organized tasks perform better in organizations that use formal procedures and employ managers who adopt McGregor's Theory X approach. People performing unstructured and uncertain tasks perform better in organizations that exercise less formal control over workers and employ managers who adopt McGregor's Theory Y approach. Our need for a sense of competence is never completely satisfied because new challenges and tasks eventually face us and must be mastered. Real satisfaction comes from producing a continuing series of achievements, each reinforcing our sense of competence (Morse and Lorsch, 1975).

The contingency theory tells supervisors, team leaders, and team facilitators to tailor jobs to fit people or to give people the skills, knowledge, and attitudes they will need to become competent in the jobs they are to be given. Both tasks and people must be analyzed before appropriate fits can be made. Controls on workers and their managers' approaches to them must be appropriate for the tasks being executed and for the psychological needs of the employees.

As a supervisor, you can use the contingency theory when you are seeking new people, looking for someone who is right for a new task, or delegating your formal authority. But you must know your people well—their needs, strengths, and goals—if you want to make the proper decisions when assigning work. You need to know what kinds of reward go with each task. Then you are ready to match people to work that they are capable of doing, thus giving them (or reinforcing in them) a sense of competence. You can tailor your supervisory approach to fit the needs of each person, watching and controlling some more than others. You can provide the instructions and training they need to become or to remain competent. As George M. C. Fisher said when he was CEO of Motorola: [to build a] "...globally competitive organization,... 'You make sure people are empowered and have the tools, training and education to get the job done, and then you get out of their way. It may be simple, but it works'" (Austin, "Motivating," 1994).

Maslow's needs, Herzberg's set of factors, and the contingency model can help us understand how individuals' needs affect their motivation. We are now ready to examine two additional theories that relate to the modification of human behavior at work. Both the expectancy theory and the reinforcement theory help explain what you and your organization can do to "engineer" subordinates' behavior by identifying why people choose their behaviors. Both theories help explain how individuals' perceptions, influenced in large measure by external stimuli, lead them to select a course of action aimed at achieving a personal or a company goal.

THE EXPECTANCY THEORY

The expectancy theory of motivation is related to all the other theories discussed in this chapter. It focuses largely on the individual perceptions of people in an organization that wishes to use the theory. Simply stated, the expectancy theory holds that people will do what their supervisors want them to do if all the following conditions exist (Bittel and Ramsey, 1986):

1. People know, as precisely as possible, what performance or behavior they are being asked to give (how they will be graded).
2. They perceive themselves as being capable of giving the performance or behavior.
3. They strongly desire the reward that is being offered by their supervisor or organization.
4. They perceive that the performance or behavior, once given at the specified level of quality, will bring the desired reward to them fairly quickly.

According to the expectancy theory, when training a subordinate in a task, you must communicate exactly what, how, when, and where you want it done. Reaffirm that the worker understands what to do before delegating the task.

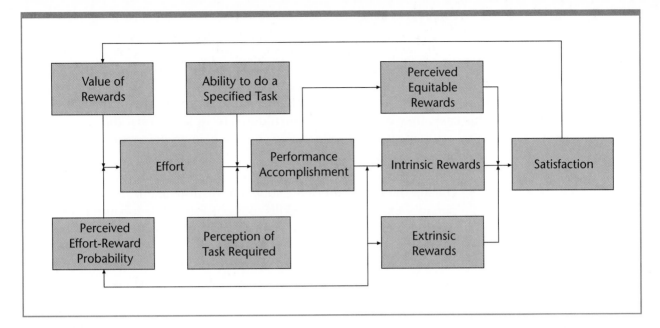

EXHIBIT 7.4

The Porter–Lawler motivation model, illustrating the expectancy theory of motivation.

Source: Porter, L., and Lawler E., III. *Managerial Attitudes and Performance* © 1968, Richard D. Irwin, Inc., Homewood, Ill., 165. Reprinted by permission.

As a supervisor, you can influence conditions one, two, and four most directly. Condition three—the individual's perception of the desirability of the reward—is largely beyond your ability to influence in any meaningful way. We look next at the ways in which you can influence employee perceptions (see Exhibit 7.4).

The Performance

Unless you facilitate teams or lead one, you must spell out in as much detail as possible what you want people to do. Your subordinates must have a clear understanding of the task, the standards that will be used to grade their performance, and the level of quality expected. When facilitating teams and leading them, team leaders and team members have a say in all these things. And when they are autonomous teams, they must wrestle with these issues regularly. Such teams work out their own goals, priorities, procedures, standards, and they evaluate their progress regularly.

When delegating, according to the expectancy theory, you must communicate to your subordinate exactly what you want done, how you want it done, when you want it done, and what limits (if any) may affect the subordinate's performance. Then and only then can the person know what he or she is being asked to do.

Capabilities

Once your subordinates or teams know what is to be done and they perceive themselves as capable of giving the performance, they will next consider the appropriateness of the reward being offered. But what happens when the person or group feels incapable of giving the performance? In this case, they or it will likely turn down or at least resist the assignment. Here are some ways of influencing your associates' perceptions about their capabilities to perform:

- During the hiring process and when forming teams, try to match the persons' experiences and skills to the needs of the job and team. This means that you must know in detail the tasks that must be performed.
- With an existing employee or new hire, provide, through training, the skill levels needed for a task before assigning or asking the person to perform it.
- Try to redesign the job your subordinate has so that he or she will be asked to perform only those tasks that the person feels capable of performing. This may require you to increase or decrease tasks and responsibilities for a subordinate. Only when a person has self-confidence and a feeling of competence is he or she willing to tackle bigger and more demanding tasks.
- When job redesign is not possible or not appropriate, a transfer or promotion may be called for. People who have mastered their jobs and are becoming bored with them cannot be expected to give high-quality performance until their jobs make greater demands on them or offer them greater rewards.

When you have a subordinate who knows what is being asked of him or her, feels capable of performing to the level expected, strongly desires the reward being offered, and is assured that delivering the performance will elicit the reward, you should have a motivated, willing employee.

Rewards

A few words are in order here about what rewards you or your organization can offer and how to link them to performance. The usual rewards are increases in pay, increases in authority and responsibility, and praise. Intrinsic rewards—those noted in Exhibit 7.3 and called motivators by Herzberg—can be offered to employees through delegation, transfers, and promotions. Just be certain that rewards are given to high performers and not to employees who deliver less. If a person works hard, delivers what is called for, and gets no significantly greater reward than that received by mediocre performers, you will have one unhappy, soon-to-lose-motivation employee on your hands. This is one reason companies are shifting their compensation focus to rewarding results, not simply seniority and increases in the cost of living.

Second, make sure that the performance being rewarded is under the complete control of the employee and not dependent on some factor over which the person has no control. If this is the situation, and if the person believes that the way in which he or she is being evaluated is fair, rewards can stir people out of complacency and into a motivational state.

A few words of caution are in order. Keep in mind that people, jobs, and the organizations in which they exist keep changing. So too will the perceptions that people have about everything and everyone around them. Today's motivated employee may be lazy next week. People who showed no interest in new challenges and growth last month may suddenly become motivated by the desire for these rewards. Finally, though you may think a subordinate is perfectly capable of giving a high-quality performance, your perception is not what really matters; it is the perception of the person whom you want to help motivate that counts.

THE REINFORCEMENT THEORY

The reinforcement theory has its foundation in B. F. Skinner's behavior modification theories (Skinner, 1969). This theory encourages appropriate behaviors by focusing on the consequences of those behaviors. Simply stated, behaviors an organization and its managers want repeated should be rewarded; behaviors they do not want repeated should be punished. If a manager or a company wants to modify employee behavior, both timely and appropriate rewards and punishments should be provided.

Positive reinforcement helps teach and emphasize a company's core values—what it believes to be essential to effective and efficient operations. At Andrews Moving & Storage in Ohio, the core values are "Customer satisfaction, integrity, recognition of employees, and the pursuit of growth" (*Nation's Business*, 1994). After circulating these to all employees, a committee of managers and workers was created to address employee concerns. What emerged from its monthly meetings was a mutual pledge, signed by managers and workers: Top management pledged "to providing the highest level of customer service, supporting employees' efforts, and treating all employees equitably. Workers who signed...agreed to provide the best possible service to customers, support fellow employees, contribute new ideals, learn new techniques, and be receptive to change" (*Nation's Business*, 1994). Signing the pledge was voluntary, but all 225 employees did so. It is reaffirmed and resigned each year. It has led to continual efforts to improve by all and has fostered a feeling of teamwork.

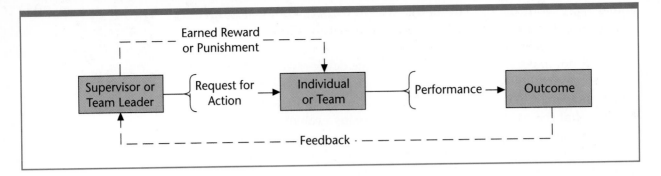

EXHIBIT 7.5
The reinforcement theory in action.

Positive reinforcements should occur as soon as possible after the desired behavior has occurred. Good performance can be rewarded through praise, pay increases, promotions, and special favors within a manager's power to dispense. Through the practice of positive reinforcement, rewarded behavior tends to be repeated.

Negative reinforcement attempts through fear and punishments to discourage repeat performances. People learn what not to do, but not what they should do. Negative reinforcements may include denial of privileges, reprimands, and loss of pay or opportunities. As with positive reinforcement, the quicker the punitive action occurs and the more appropriate it is, the greater will be its impact (see Exhibit 7.5).

Certain performances need no reinforcement. Actions that are undesirable but have small (if any) consequences may often be ignored. Temporary, nonserious misbehavior may simply be noted and go unpunished. Supervisors are often required to make a judgment about the cause of the behavior and the intent behind it. Most people lose their tempers now and then, and all of us make minor mistakes fairly regularly. Save your punishment for serious offenses, and punish people in private. Pass out your rewards publicly and as often as you can to help celebrate positive contributions.

As a supervisor, team leader, or team facilitator using this theory, keep the following points in mind:

1. People learn what is expected of them through warnings and trial and error. Keep your people aware of what is expected and of the consequences for failing to meet expectations.
2. Rewards and punishments must be tailored to the behavior they are intended to reward or punish. Consider the consequences, intent, and seriousness of the results of the punishments or rewards.
3. Don't reward mediocre or poor performance.
4. Don't punish inconsequential instances of misbehavior or positive behaviors.
5. Don't fail to reward behavior you want repeated.
6. Don't fail to punish behavior you want eliminated.

A *Fortune* magazine article on why companies fail points out that some leaders fail to walk like they talk. They will emphasize in words certain concepts and then contradict them with their actions. "They preach the importance of teamwork—then reward individuals who work at standing out from the crowd. They encourage risk taking—then punish good-faith failures…. Corporate leaders can scuttle a reengineering effort quite quickly if they pump up their own bonuses and order a new fleet of company jets while telling the troops to tighten belts" (Labich, 1994). When your walk contradicts your talk, your associates label you a hypocrite and take their example from your walk.

THE EQUITY THEORY

Our final theory considers motivation from each person's unique perspective. The equity theory holds that people contribute, or withhold their contributions, based on an individual perception of their equity ratios. People compare what they contribute (their input) to what they receive from their employers (their outcomes). Outcomes divided by inputs yield a psychological perception of the equity or fairness they receive at work. If you perceive your equity ratio is in balance—psychologically speaking as 1 to 1—you have no reason to be dissatisfied with how you are being treated. If you perceive the ratio as out of balance—1 to 1/2, or 1 to 2—you are either unmotivated (you have a disincentive and may withhold contributions) or motivated (you feel the need to raise your contributions).

What matters in this theory is how people perceive their ratios, not how you as their manager or facilitator perceive them. When people lose their enthusiasm and appear to be slacking off, consider their perceptions of their equity ratios. What is behind their unmotivated behavior? What perceptions are they holding that are interfering with their abilities to give their best? Sit down and discuss their perceptions with them. Ask if they believe anything in the working environment is unequitable or unfair. Quite often you will find a misconception or that they are being influenced by other unmotivated people or untrue information. In such cases, you must do what you can to remove their feelings of inequity, restoring them to a 1 to 1 or greater ratio.

MANAGING MOTIVATION

In Chapter 6, we discussed the importance of employees' beliefs, attitudes, and values. These affect how they perceive their world and the demands that are made on them. What all of us look for in a job is a fit between what we want from work and what our organizations want from us. The closer the fit, the more likely it is that we will find job satisfaction and the means to achieve our personal and professional goals. As Herzberg's theo-

SUPERVISORS AND ETHICS

Reengineering preaches that you can tinker with and fine-tune existing systems and processes just so long before a replacement is required. Instead of continually replacing and rebuilding components of existing systems, companies must continuously focus on redesigning their structures and processes—adopting newer, faster, more efficient models for nearly everything they do. But what good will this do if you leave fearful, unmotivated employees in its wake?

"In too many companies, reengineering is corporate code for firing about a third of the work force. And it's not something you do once and for all. It is a tool, and a powerful one, for reshaping your company continuously." Reengineering, "executed ruthlessly,...can corrode the esprit de corps vital to teamwork. Listen to US West's Jerry Miller, whose team of billing clerks in...Minnesota, got downsized out of existence:... 'When we first formed our teams, the company came in talking teamwork and empowerment and promised we wouldn't lose any jobs. It turns out all this was a big cover. The company had us all set up for reengineering. We showed them how to streamline the work, and now 9,000 people are gone. It was cut-your-own-throat. It makes you feel used.'"

But it does not have to work this way. The Allina company in Minnesota operates over one dozen not-for-profit hospitals. It began its reengineering efforts by focusing on changing worker attitudes and creating mutual trust between union employees and management. A team of management and union people was created and empowered to make changes. "For instance, it found a way to close one of Allina's hospitals without leaving employees stranded. The team set up an employment center that placed 95% of the closing hospital's employees elsewhere in Allina or in other companies. Not only did this gesture raise morale generally and save the company $8 million in severance costs, but more important, it also showed that management was serious about working with labor."

Source: Austin, Nancy K. "What's Missing from Corporate Cure-Alls," *Working Woman,* September 1994, 19; Dumaine, Brian. "The Trouble with Teams," *Fortune,* September 5, 1994, 92.

ry tells us, job satisfaction comes from the work itself, not from things external to it. Without job satisfaction, we will find it difficult if not impossible to become or to stay motivated—to give our best effort to our performance at work.

Employees become dissatisfied for a variety of reasons. They may enter a job expecting too much. Often employers are not as honest as they should be about what a worker will find in the way of satisfactions once he or she is on the job. They often oversell a job and its potential benefits. People are sometimes hired for jobs that are too difficult or too easy. Applicants for employment are often desperate and take the first job offer that comes their way because they need money. Once on the job, people find boredom, unsafe conditions, inadequate training, and uncooperative co-workers. All these situations add up to problems for the new employees and their employers. Most job dissatisfaction can be prevented, but both employees and employers have to work at prevention.

Quality

In Chapter 1, we defined quality and noted its link to the customer or user of a product or service. Quality, in the final analysis, is measured by the ability of a product or service to meet the needs of the internal or external customer. An internal user may be any person or group in the company who receives output from another employee or group. "Every company must please a whole series of customers, depending on the business—wholesalers, shippers, retailers, independent distributors.... Former Ford Chairman, Red Poling, often found chatting up dealers, was among the more high-profile proponents of sensitivity to multiple customers" (Labich, 1994). Exhibit 7.6 highlights four major dimensions of quality.

When a company decides to emphasize quality, it must adopt a total quality management (TQM) approach. Robert Costello, engineer, General

---

1. **Performance characteristics.** A product's operating features and the final outcomes that they produce.
2. **Users' Perceptions.** The ways in which a product feels, looks, and performs—its fit and finish.
3. **Useful life.** The length of time that the product can be expected to deliver performance that is in line with user expectations.
4. **Serviceability.** the manufacturer's willingness and ability to furnish quick and reliable repairs—how well the producer backs up the product and its users in their time of need.

EXHIBIT 7.6
Dimensions of quality.

Motors executive, and Undersecretary of Defense for Acquisitions, built on the work of many quality experts who preceded him when he defined TQM in 1988 as (Hunt, 1992):

> a strategy for continuously improving performance at every level, and in all areas of responsibility. It combines fundamental management techniques, existing improvement efforts, and specialized technical tools under a discipline structure focused on continuously improving all processes.... Increasing user satisfaction is the overriding objective.

The TQM approach begins at the top of an organization and requires the commitment of time, energy, and resources to planning, training, setting objectives, measuring performance, and continually pursuing perfection. "Partial understanding of and involvement in quality can produce only partial success or total failure.... The only chance for a quality process to truly succeed is for a company to simultaneously attack all the issues: leadership, participation, and measurement" (Townsend and Gebhardt, 1992).

The Japanese word *kaizen* has the meaning and intent of TQM—it means a never-ending quest by every member of an organization to improve people and processes. Everyone must be committed to and participate in the effort to improve quality. Your job as a supervisor is to instill this concept into your people and teams. Make kaizen your personal philosophy. Unless you and your people see quality as your responsibility, TQM will not work. In the end, your own career, job security, and your company's survival depend on being competitive against products and services from producers around the world.

Motorola is a quality leader in America. The multibillion-dollar electronics giant and winner of the Malcolm Baldridge National Quality Award in 1988 pursues six-sigma quality—3.4 defects per million items produced. When that goal is achieved, the company will keep implementing efforts to improve. Its participative management program (PMP) places all employees below the top management level in teams, each engaged in constant efforts to reduce defects and cycle times—for existing products, the time from order receipt to shipment; for new products, the time from conception to delivery. Teams and team members are rewarded for their successful efforts (Hart and Bogan, 1992). Motorola recognizes, as do other quality leaders such as Ford, Xerox, and UPS, that TQM is a never-ending journey, not a destination.

High-quality products and services are created by providers who are in close touch with their customers—they know what they want and need. These producers design quality into their end products and processes and set precise performance standards for all of their component parts. From the product design teams to the engineering and production teams, concern for quality dominates the efforts of all concerned. Once the suppliers are chosen (in part for their reputations for and commitment to quality) contracts are drafted, and close contact is maintained to ensure that all the parts produced meet the standards set for them. Chrysler used this approach in the design, testing, and building of its current LH line of cars. It had cross-functional teams—with members from marketing, production, and design, as well as vendors—working on the projects from beginning to end.

In this chapter's Supervising Teams feature, you will see that Honeywell used the same approach—creating a cross-functional team to facilitate communications and participation at all levels of the organization.

Productivity

Productivity was defined in Chapter 1 as the measurement of how much input is needed to produce a given amount of output. It is usually expressed as a ratio between these two variables, yielding a productivity index (PI). By dividing units of input into units of output, a PI can be calculated for most clerical or production activities. Inputs may be tons of materials, hours of machine time, dollars of invested capital, or hours of labor invested to produce the output. Outputs are the units realized through the investment or application of inputs. To illustrate, assume that you invested three hours of concentrated effort into producing six reports for your boss. Your productivity index would be 6 divided by 3 for a PI of 2, or 2 to 1. Two units of output (reports) have been produced for each unit (hour) of input. The value of such indexes is in their comparisons over time. By continually calculating a PI for each of your people, teams, and operations, you can measure the progress or setbacks that occur.

The Quality, Productivity, Profitability Link

Quality and productivity are two sides of the same coin. Improvements that lead to better quality must also lead to increased productivity. When this occurs, profitability—the amount of money earned that stays in the business when all the bills are paid—will increase as well, thus assuring the continued existence of the organization. W. Edwards Deming—the man who taught Japanese companies and many in America much of what they know about quality—believes that when quality improves, costs decrease. Companies have less need to scrap materials and rework their outputs. With less waste and fewer mistakes, productivity improves through the more efficient use of resources. Customers are satisfied, markets expanded and captured, more jobs are provided and companies ensure their futures. "Continual reduction in mistakes, continual improvement of quality, mean lower and lower costs. Less rework in manufacturing. Less waste—of materials, machine time, tools, and human effort" (Walton, 1986). Deming calls this his "chain reaction."

SUPERVISING TEAMS

Instead of beginning at the top to improve both productivity and quality, the Honeywell Company began its efforts to improve productivity and quality at the bottom. This was a mistake. Prior to the early 1980s, its executives had been the key decision makers, and workers "were rarely encouraged to show initiative." Since that time, management has introduced worker teams focused on quality and lower-level management teams focused on problems in communications, career development, and quality of working life. Sharing decision authority was limited to these low-level teams, which "had no clear reporting relationship to the formal organization, and their charters [reasons for existence] and operating procedures were vague."

Richard J. Boyle, vice-president of marketing and business development at Honeywell, decided to establish and chair a steering committee (composed of senior people from key functional areas) to expand decision sharing to the middle and upper levels of his operations. The committee's job was to ensure that better two-way communications took place and that results from the task and prob-lem-solving teams would be used in ongoing operations. The committee became a "coupling mechanism for the entire business unit." Boyle's team eliminated previous reporting relationships. His people got better at coordinating and consulting, while he received better reports and results. Outside experts were asked to help the steering committee members establish priorities and evaluate progress toward objectives. The committee used the employee relations department as a coordinating and support group for various lower-level teams.

The committee's efforts, along with the elimination of such status symbols as reserved parking and dress codes, helped create a more open organization—one more receptive to change. Employee involvement now exists at all levels at Honeywell, with more decisions being made at lower levels. Boyle admits that this takes extra time and can lead to less-than-optimum decisions. But it reinforces employee commitment to shared decision making. "The results, both in quantifiable terms of improved productivity and in less measurable terms of work climate and quality of innovation, have been very positive."

Source: Boyle, Richard J. "Excerpts from Wrestling with Jellyfish," *Harvard Business Review,* November–December 1992, 14.

Quality circles bring together workers into teams aimed at solving problems or improving quality. Involvement in quality circles generally leads to greater self-esteem and production for workers.

Most efforts to improve quality will also help increase productivity. As with quality improvements, productivity gains begin with a commitment from top management to make improving productivity a priority. The efforts required must be funded. Everyone must be committed to making these efforts work. Goals need to be stated and people and corporate environments shaped to take on the new challenges and changes required. Standards must be set, gains and losses measured, plans created, tools and techniques chosen and used, and people rewarded for their efforts.

Productivity can be improved by producing the same number of outputs with fewer inputs or by increasing the outputs with the use of the same or reduced amounts of inputs. Either way, the costs connected with the production effort should fall, yielding a more efficient and effective use of resources. People are a main ingredient in the constant search for improvements in productivity. The more motivated and satisfied the individuals, the more productive they are likely to be. On the other hand, people suffering from job stress and job dissatisfaction tend to produce less than their opposites.

A look at the symptoms typically exhibited by dissatisfied workers and managers should tell you how they affect productivity in a negative way. The typical symptoms are tardiness, absenteeism, delayed work, shoddy work, time lost to gripes and complaints about their stations in life, and actual efforts at theft or sabotage to destroy company property or to simply vent their frustrations on their employer's assets. Over time, dissatisfied employees may become emotionally and physically ill, further reducing their productive capacities. If they decide to leave their source of dissatisfaction, they will cost their employers the funds needed to find and train replacements. Time will be lost to production through turnover, and those who remain will probably be overburdened with the work left undone by the departing employee.

The Property and Casualty Division of United Services Automobile Association puts its philosophy about productivity this way (Belcher, 1987):

> Productivity improvement isn't just working harder, it's working smarter. It means devising a method to get the best return on our investment in people, facilities, equipment and other resources.... Improving productivity...means finding better ways to do more with the resources we have.... In short, we need to provide quality products through distribution systems which are customer-convenient and operator-efficient.

Note that the company, though discussing productivity, makes clear references to quality.

People are both the causes and the cures for problems in quality and productivity. Without well-trained, capable, and committed employees with the proper attitudes, company efforts will not bring improvements. Today's emphasis on empowering workers requires them to be proficient in the four Rs—reading, 'riting, 'rithmetic, and responsibility. Ritz-Carlton hotels empower all employees, without higher approval, to "spend up to $2,000 to fix a guest's problem. ...[Its] new focus on employee involvement has helped cut turnover from 80% to 45%, saving nearly $12.5 million" (Austin, "What's," 1994). When you and your company give people more authority, you are asking them to think and decide more—to depend more on their own abilities and judgment than they have in the past. "As long as you let everybody in on the facts—budgets, cost data, customer-satisfaction feedback—these independent decisions will usually be good ones" (Austin, "What's," 1994). Exhibit 7.7 gives you some suggestions to help you and your people improve your organization's quality, productivity, and profitability.

Quality of Working Life

quality of working life
a general label given to various programs and projects designed to help employees satisfy their needs and meet their expectations from work

Quality of working life (QWL) has been defined by the American Center for the Quality of Working Life as "any activity which takes place at every level of an organization which seeks greater organizational effectiveness through the enhancement of human dignity and growth" (*Chicago Tribune*, 1983). The two major goals of QWL—making working life better for individuals and making the company more effective—are accomplished through a variety of programs in most major companies. Each organization needs to define what it means by QWL and to decide which of the available programs it wants to use throughout its various units. "The result of providing a high quality working environment is increasing employee

1. Be committed to improving quality and productivity and constantly demonstrate your commitment in every action you take.

2. Be certain that you have permission from your boss, and that your subordinates are prepared to share your decision-making authority, before you attempt to do so.

3. Once you have defined a problem, seek suggestions from subordinates closest to the problem about how to solve it. Diverse people yield diverse suggestions.

4. Give your people all the information they need and the reasons for changes in routines and procedures before you attempt to make them; you need their cooperation and support to make the changes effective and efficient.

5. Whenever possible, show and demonstrate rather then simply tell people why changes are necessary.

6. Keep the trust and respect of subordinates and do what you can to break down any barriers to effective communication and cooperation.

7. Encourage your people to look for ways to improve everything they use and do and to share their ideas with you and their coworkers. Then reward them when they do so.

8. Let subordinates and team members know why quality and productivity are important to them and their organization. Explain and demonstrate with real examples the costs of poor quality and lagging productivity—for example, how a defective product lost a customer and wasted resources.

9. Make it clear that each person is accountable for quality and productivity gains. Make employee quality and productivity improvements part of each employee's regular evaluations.

10. Share productivity and quality improvements with other supervisors and get them to share their discoveries with you. Learn from your and their past efforts, both the successes and the failures.

EXHIBIT 7.7

Suggestions for improving both quality and productivity in your operations.

commitment, satisfaction, and feeling of empowerment. These in turn lead to improved productivity" (Schuler, 1995).

Typical QWL programs include a variety of EAPs, training programs, team building activities and the utilization of teams, labor–management committees, flexible work schedules, pay for performance and growth, and any other attempt by a company to "give employees greater opportunities to participate and a larger say in decision making" (Schuler, 1995). These programs are most effective when every manager, team leader, and team facilitator is committed to their success and when those they are designed to serve play a meaningful role in their design and implementation.

Worker Participation Techniques

Many organizations have discovered that the best way to improve operations is to empower employees, both individually and in teams. "To empower people is to make them virtually autonomous, to inform them, to invest them with authority and then trust them to use it" (Austin, "What's," 1994). Giving people access to needed information is vital to making empowerment succeed. Many companies use a variety of techniques to do so: general information-sharing sessions, various kinds of scoreboarding activities, company newsletters, computer training in shareware and networking, business games, and committees for dealing with a variety of work-related issues.

Quality circles are one device that enlists teams to improve working life as well as product quality. A University of Southern California study of America's 1,000 largest corporations "found that 65%...used such groups [in 1993]. Professor Ed Lawler [USC] says that quality circles are losing appeal because they operate parallel to work processes rather than within them. In other words, they're good for solving minor quality problems, but because they don't accompany changes in the way work is done, they can't spark quantum leaps in productivity" (Dumaine, 1994). In most companies, quality circles operate at the supervisory management level and are staffed with volunteers. Meetings are held regularly (weekly or monthly) and focus on one or two problems that are the most important at the time. Priorities are often assigned to problems by the supervisors or team leaders in charge of the section affected. Supervisors may or may not attend the sessions depending on how the company has decided the circles should function. The results of each session are made known to participants and nonparticipants alike. Progress is noted and credit given to those responsible for it.

job rotation
movement of people to different jobs, usually for a temporary period, in order to inform, train, or stimulate cooperation and understanding among them

Job Rotation   **Job rotation** moves people to different jobs, usually on a temporary basis, to give them additional experience, understanding, and challenges. It is most frequently used to cross-train people and to give them a better appreciation for the importance of jobs and their interrelationships. Employees who participate in job rotation are usually more valuable to themselves and to their employers because they can perform competently in more than one job. From this, supervisors gain more flexibility and can deal with absences more effectively.

Job rotation helps get people ready for promotions or transfers. It may mean that the worker gets more pay for the time that he or she works in a different job, and it usually means that time will be lost to production while the person is learning the new job. It is a useful tool for improving the morale of some people but not for all. To some, job rotation may represent a threat to their sense of security and competence.

job enlargement
increasing the number of tasks or the quantity of output required in a job

Job Enlargement   **Job enlargement** increases the number of tasks a job includes or the amount of output expected from the job holder. It does

At a Japanese-style training camp for executives in Malibu, California, workers learn company dedication by singing their company song.

not increase the number of responsibilities or the level of personal involvement the job holder experiences. It usually requires people to do more of the kinds of tasks they are already doing regularly. It is most useful for people who are suffering from having too little to do. Since job enlargement can add challenges for some, it can aid motivation and spark a renewed interest and enthusiasm for work. And for some, a sense of competence can arise from being able to produce more, both in quantity and quality.

Job Enrichment   Today, manufacturers are turning many highly specialized, hazardous, and routinized assembly-type tasks over to robots. For human workers, the emphasis now is strongly on **job enrichment**—enriching a job by providing the job holder with variety, deeper personal interest and involvement, greater autonomy, and an increased amount of responsibility and challenge.

job enrichment providing variety, deeper personal interest and involvement, greater autonomy and challenge, or increased responsibility on the job

Maytag, the home appliance manufacturer, has worked wonders on employee efficiency with numerous experiments in job enrichment. Some workers assemble entire components that were previously designed to be a team effort. Volvo, the Swedish car manufacturer, has small teams of workers who assemble entire automobiles. Texas Instruments, a precision scientific instruments company, has involved its workers not only in additional duties, such as testing and inspecting their output, but also in planning their work by setting their own quality and quantity goals. General Motors, in its new Saturn Division, makes extensive use of both robots and job enrichment techniques. Workers work in teams, master and perform several jobs, and assemble entire components.

In general, the opportunity for enrichment presents itself on nearly every highly refined and routinized job. The question then becomes, "Do the people working these jobs desire enrichment?" For many, the answer is a surprising no. A large number of production-line workers prefer their repetitive, specialized tasks. Their reasons are many. Some do not want a challenge and the additional effort it represents. Others are working to their capacities with their jobs the way they are and could not adjust to more duties. Still others do not like the new responsibilities or the ways in which their jobs were, are being, or will be enriched. A number of companies that embarked on job enrichment as the best answer to the blue-collar blues found that many more difficulties were created than eliminated. Consequently, they have dropped their wholesale attempts and have become much more selective in their approaches. Job enrichment is not the ultimate solution to job dissatisfaction, sagging production, employee absenteeism, and employee turnover.

Instant Replay

1. Industrial studies have shown that people are stimulated to action by five basic human needs and rewards, outcomes, or incentives offered by their employers.
2. The Hawthorne studies of the 1920s demonstrated the social and esteem needs that people have and the natural tendencies of workers to form their own groups or cliques.
3. Abraham Maslow ranked human needs in a hierarchy that progresses from physical needs through four psychological needs. Each has the power to act as a motive for human behavior.
4. Managers and their organizations have the power to assist employees in their search for satisfaction in every need category.
5. Frederick Herzberg identified two sets of factors that can either prevent dissatisfaction or promote motivation in employees. These are called, respectively, maintenance factors and motivation factors.
6. The contingency theory of motivation holds that all of us desire a sense of competence. That desire can be met by organizations and managers who tailor jobs, job assignments, and supervisory approaches to fit individuals' needs and capabilities.
7. The expectancy theory of motivation holds that people will work to exhibit the behaviors an employer or boss expects if they know what the reward will be, are certain that the reward is forthcoming, want the reward, and have or perceive that they have the capabilities required.
8. The reinforcement theory states that behavior that is desirable will be repeated if rewarded and that undesirable behavior can be discouraged by providing punishment for it.
9. The equity theory of motivation states that an individual's perception of the ways in which he or she is being treated at work is what counts.

Inputs are measured against outputs to determine if equitable treatment exists.

10. Productivity and quality go together. Efforts to improve one must also act to improve the other. Efforts to improve both must never end.

11. Quality of working life (QWL) involves programs and projects to help employees satisfy their needs and fulfill their expectations about work. It is part of organization development and uses such approaches as job rotation, job enrichment, and training programs.

Questions for Class Discussion

1. Can you define this chapter's key terms?
2. What are the five needs we humans have in common? What are some examples of satisfactions that are available to us through our work?
3. What are the motivation factors identified by Dr. Herzberg? What is their purpose in an organization?
4. What are the maintenance factors identified by Dr. Herzberg? What is their purpose in an organization?
5. What is the contingency theory of motivation? Does it apply to your life?
6. What is the expectancy theory of motivation? How has it been demonstrated in your own experience?
7. What is the reinforcement theory of motivation? How has it worked in your own experience?
8. What is the equity theory of motivation?
9. What can supervisors do to promote improvements in both quality and productivity?

Incident

Purpose: To assess the motivational climate at work for both you and your subordinates.

Your Task: Take the following quiz. Tally your responses as follows: for each yes response, 2 points; for each no response, 1 point. A score of 14 or higher indicates that you work in a highly motivating climate. Let your subordinates or team members take this quiz. The results may help you create more stimulating environments and jobs for subordinates.

	Yes	No
1. My boss knows me as an individual.	___	___
2. I have access to the people and information I need to perform my job.	___	___
3. Company incentives exist that encourage my intellectual growth.	___	___
4. I have served or am now serving on a team.	___	___

	Yes	No
5. I have taken advantage of one or more company EAPs.	___	___
6. I am proud of my company and share that pride with outsiders.	___	___
7. I receive regular feedback on my performance at work.	___	___
8. My company allows me time to deal with family and personal problems.	___	___
9. I would recommend my company to outsiders as a great place to work.	___	___
10. My pay is linked to my performance.	___	___

CASE PROBLEM 7.1

Julio's Place

Since his promotion to supervisor of menswear at his uncle's store, Julio has been puzzled by shifts in performance by his two salespeople. Chester has dropped to second place after nearly one year as the best salesperson. Since Chester's fall, Roger has become the top salesperson, but his sales volume has yet to reach the average sales that Chester used to generate when he was on top.

Before his promotion four months ago, Julio worked side by side with Chester and Roger. All were supervised by Julio's uncle, Pedro. Over the two years Julio was a salesperson, he had never earned the top spot. Although he liked selling, he liked handling stock and creating displays better. Julio now performs these duties, and he assumed that Chester and Roger would continue to perform as they had when he worked with them. He is at a loss to understand why Chester has seemingly lost his ability to sell.

Chester is thirty, four years older than Julio and two years younger than Roger. He has worked for Pedro for five years, and for the last two years, Chester has been pursuing a two-year college degree in marketing. He married last year, and his wife works as a bookkeeper. She is now earning, for the first time, more than Chester. Until about three months ago, Chester was a ball of fire. He was the first person to report to work, opening the store on many mornings and full of enthusiasm for his work. He was a never-ending source of ideas about how to stimulate sales. He was aggressive, practically attacking customers and always eager to help. Pedro used to call him "a tiger waiting for his prey." But all this has changed. Julio practically had to force Chester to wait on two customers yesterday.

Roger has worked for Pedro for about ten months. He has a dream of owning his own clothing store one day. He wants to get all the selling experience he can and is saving his money like a miser. Since Chester and Roger earn over half their income with commissions on sales, Julio has worked out a system whereby they share customers who do not request either Chester or Roger. When a new customer enters the store, the two salespeople take turns waiting on them. But Chester now seems content to let Roger wait on every customer who enters. Thus Roger's earnings have increased at the expense of Chester's.

Pedro has expressed his unhappiness with the decline in sales and with the decline in Chester's performance. He has asked Julio to "do something quick." Julio is worried because he is not certain what to do. His talks with Chester have been disappointing, to say the least. Julio finds Chester unwilling to discuss any problems. He is evasive and gets angry when the subject of his decline is mentioned. In his discussion with his uncle this morning, Julio said the following: "I don't know what else I can do with Chester except fire him. I want to get rid of the problem, too, but I'm not able to motivate him. You promoted me knowing that I'd make a better manager than a salesman."

Pedro answered Julio: "You are the manager now, and you must deal with this problem. You cannot fire Chester. He has a loyal following of scores of customers. We may lose them if we lose him. Now deal with this problem. Use your experience and college training in business. I want results. If you expect to run this business when I retire, you better learn how to deal with poor performers."

Questions

1. What does Chester's decline tell you about human motivation?
2. What theory of motivation seems to fit Roger best? Why?
3. If you were in Julio's position, what would you do?

Differing Opinions

CASE PROBLEM 7.2

Two middle managers were discussing how they might better motivate their subordinate managers. Doris feels that the most important "carrot" she can offer is a significant raise and increases in the cash value of fringe benefits. Frances holds that recognition in several forms is the best way to stimulate high performances. She believes that if people know what she expects from them and what the rewards for meeting those expectations will be, they will respond. The keys, Frances believes, are to set high standards, be available to help, and offer quick rewards for high-quality performances. In Frances's words, "Nothing stimulates high performance so effectively as a pat on the back, a letter of commendation in a manager's file, and praise from higher-ups in writing. Without these," Frances continued, "no person is going to get promoted."

"Frances, you are naive," said Doris. "Words are pretty cheap, and our people know it. Words, without the backing of money rewards, can't motivate anyone. I have tried praise, but in the case of Thomas Monroe, my newest subordinate, money did the trick. When Tom came on board last year, we had to hire him at the top end of his pay spread. I told him this in his interview. He knew that it would be at least twelve months before he could receive a decent raise. For the past ten months, he has been a mediocre performer. But since then, with his review approaching, he has become my star performer. If that doesn't prove my point, nothing will."

"Well," said Frances, "one case doesn't prove the rule for me. I have some experience in motivation, too, and it tells me that I am right, at least as far as my people are concerned. Most of my subordinates want to move up. We are fortunate to have a growing company with new branches opening up each year. Without my recommendation, my people know that they are going to stay where they are."

"Most of my people live for the here and now," said Doris. "Cash in hand or just out of reach is the ticket. Those who don't work for money are few and far between. The promise of a promotion won't pay today's bills, and it sure won't work to motivate new people. Most of my subordinates have only been here a few years. Most came up from various parts of the company. They know if they please me I will be generous. That's the secret to my reputation as well. When they look good, I look good."

At this point, Jeff Bradley came over. He had overheard their conversation and asked if he could join them. Frances said of course he could join them and asked if he had any opinions about motivating subordinates.

"I'm no expert on the subject," said Jeff, "but I have had six years' experience as a manager and about five before that as a worker in two different companies. My basic philosophy is that people have different needs and expectations from work, and the better you can help them meet those needs and satisfy those expectations, the better they will perform for you." Jeff went on to tell them about one of his subordinates. "With Helen Aegis, punishment seems to work the best. I had talked with her on numerous occasions and until I took action to discourage her negatives, she didn't respond. But she is a widow and has two kids. The last thing she needs is to lose her job. She's a great performer now that she knows that my bark has a bite. Helen needs a job, and as long as she performs to the standards I set, she knows she'll have one."

Questions

1. Do you think that Doris is correct? Why?
2. How is the reinforcement theory demonstrated in this case?
3. What theories of motivation is Frances demonstrating?
4. What does this case reveal about human motivation?

Notes

Aburdene, Patricia, and Naisbitt, John. *Megatrends for Women* (New York: Villard Books, 1992).

Austin, Nancy K. "Motivating Employees Without Pay or Promotions," *Working Woman*, November 1994, 17–18.

———. "What's Missing from Corporate Cure-Alls," *Working Woman*, September 1994, 16–19.

Belcher, Jr., John G. *Productivity Plus* (Houston, Tex.: Gulf Publishing, 1987), 27.

Bittel, Lester R., and Ramsey, Jackson E., eds., *Handbook for Professional Managers* (New York: McGraw-Hill, 1986), 586–589.

Caggiano, Christopher. "What Do Workers Want?" *Inc.*, November 1992, 101.

Chicago Tribune, "Quality of Work Life Becomes Movement of the '80s," November 30, 1981, sect. 4, 1.

Dumaine, Brian. "The Trouble with Teams," *Fortune*, September 5, 1994, 86–88, 90, 92.

Hart, Christopher, and Bogan, Christopher. *The Baldridge* (New York: McGraw-Hill, 1992), 129.

Henkoff, Ronald. "Finding, Training and Keeping the Best Service Workers," *Fortune*, October 3, 1994, 110–111, 114, 116, 118, 120, 122.

Herzberg, Frederick. "One More Time: How Do You Motivate Employees?" in *Business Classics: Fifteen Key Concepts for Managerial Success*. Boston: *Harvard Business Review*, 1975, 13–22.

Hunt, Daniel V. *Quality in America* (Homewood, Ill.: Business One Irwin, 1972), 74.

Inc. "So This Is Empowerment?" July 1994, 96.

———. "Motivation the Old-Fashioned Way," November 1994, 134.

Labich, Kenneth. "Why Companies Fail," *Fortune*, November 14, 1994, 52–54, 58, 60, 64, 68.

Maslow, Abraham H. *Motivation and Personality*, 2d ed. (New York: Harper & Row), 1970.

Mayo, Elton. *The Social Problems of an Industrial Civilization*. Boston: Division of Research, Graduate School of Business Administration, Harvard University, 1945, 68–86.

Morse, John J., and Lorsch, Jay W. "Beyond Theory Y," in *Harvard Business Review on Management* (New York: Harper & Row, 1975), 377–378.

Nation's Business. "Innovation Starts with High Goals," February 1994, 9.

Peters, Tom. "To Be the Best You Can Be, Forget about the Boss," *Chicago Tribune*, December 5, 1994, sect. 4, 2.

———. "Managers Need Surprise Tactics, Front-Line Thinking to Rout Competition," *Chicago Tribune*, October 3, 1994, sect. 4, 5.

Schuler, Randall S. *Managing Human Resources*, 5th ed. (New York: West Publishing Company, 1995), 9–10, 676–677.

Suggested Readings

Adler, Paul S., Riggs, Henry E., and Wheelwright, Steven C. "Product Development Know-How: Trading Tactics for Strategy." *Sloan Management Review* (Fall 1989): 7–17.

Berry, Leonard L. "Five Imperatives for Improving Service Quality." *Sloan Management Review* (Summer 1990): 29–38.

Garvin, David A. "How the Baldridge Award Really Works." *Harvard Business Review* (November–December 1991): 80–95.

Gellerman, Saul W. *Motivation in the Real World*. New York: Dutton, 1992.

Hunt, Daniel V. *Quality in America*. Homewood, Ill.: Business One Irwin, 1992.

Juran, J. M. *Juran on Planning for Quality*. New York: The Free Press, 1988.

Kayser, Thomas. *Team Power*. New York: Irwin, 1994.

Kennedy, Carol. *Instant Management*. New York: William Morrow & Company, 1991.

Nelson, Bob. *1001 Ways to Reward Employees*. New York: Workman Publishing, 1994.

"Quality: How to Make It Pay." *Business Week* (August 8, 1994), 54–59.

Reichheld, Frederick F. "Zero Defections: Quality Comes to Services." *Harvard Business Review* (September–October 1990): 105–111.

Walton, Mary. *Deming Management at Work*. New York: G. P. Putnam's Sons, 1990.

Building Relationships with Individuals

OBJECTIVES

After reading and discussing this chapter, you should be able to do the following:

1. Define this chapter's key terms.

2. List and briefly explain the six purposes of human relations.

3. Describe the application of each of the four human relations roles to the relationship between a supervisor and his or her subordinates and peers.

4. Describe how a middle manager's job is different from a supervisor's job.

5. Describe how a supervisor can create and maintain good human relations with his or her boss.

INTRODUCTION

This chapter explores how you as a supervisor can build good working relationships with each individual with whom you must work. Relating successfully to others is the key to your growth and advancement. From solid individual relationships will come the cooperation and assistance you and others at work need to reach your goals.

The development and maintenance of sound on-the-job relationships with associates, peers, and superiors is referred to as **human relations.** From the moment you first meet another person at work, a relationship begins. How you relate to each person with whom you must work is largely up to you to determine. The quality of your interpersonal relationships, however, will determine just how effective and efficient you will be. None of us works in a vacuum. We all must depend to some extent on others.

Much of what this chapter examines is related to the contents of Chapters 1, 5, and 7. It will carry over to all the remaining chapters in this text as well, for sound working relationships are at the heart of building teams, leading, staffing, training, appraising, and disciplining.

human relations

the development and maintenance of sound on-the-job relationships with subordinates, peers, and superiors

GOALS OF HUMAN RELATIONS

The wide range of ages, differing backgrounds, and lack of similar experiences so often found among workers make the task of building sound human relations difficult for associates, team leaders, team facilitators, and the traditional supervisor. After a brief look at the goals of human relations, we examine some major roles you must play to build relationships on the job. Keep the following goals in mind as you approach the task of building sound human relations:

- To provide what help you can to enable each individual to achieve the measure of satisfaction he or she wishes to achieve on the job
- To increase each individual's contribution of intellectual effort, commitment to the company and to his or her job, and quantity and quality of output
- To foster a spirit of cooperation between yourself and your subordinates and peers and between yourself and your boss
- To provide what help you can to enable each individual to be himself or herself while on the job
- To know and understand each individual as an individual
- To approach and supervise each associate as an individual

Enabling Workers to Be Themselves

A 1992 survey of 131 U.S. human resource managers indicates that workplace diversity is a common concern. The survey, conducted by a business research group, the Conference Board, examined how companies are dealing with diversity. It discovered that increasingly, management sees it as strategically important—affecting the entire organization and its long-term future, a "major challenge," and "part of good management." Many respondents believe that workplace diversity gives their organizations a competitive advantage in the marketplace (Randle, 1993).

Tactics used to foster diversity include company policies, sensitivity and consciousness-raising programs for employees, committees and task forces, training programs, and one-on-one coaching and counseling programs. Many companies have an executive in charge of creating and maintaining a diverse workforce. One example is Nathanial Thompkins, Baxter International Corporation's director of diversity management. At Baxter, an Illinois-based healthcare company, the focus has been on changing the company's culture and systems, followed by training and information sharing. All its efforts are designed to change the ways the company deals with people and how managers and others think about people in order to give employees access to opportunities (Randle, 1993).

Tom Peters (1992), management author and lecturer, asks a question: "Wouldn't a corporation that could exploit the uniqueness of each of its 1,000 employees (or 100 or 10,000) be phenomenally powerful?" Consider it—1,000 sets of skills and unique approaches, 1,000 sets of ambitions and creative urges, all complementing each other. Apple, the computer giant, asks its people to commit to its vision while they are with the company. In return, it gives them the opportunity to express themselves—their curiosity and creativity—and to grow through a variety of experiences. At Oticon, Denmark's hearing-aid maker, all employees are members of one large "talent bank that effectively organizes itself to create and tackle whatever projects need doing" (Peters, 1992). Those who cannot gain support for their ideas, find a project and create a team to complete it, or find a project team where they are welcome will not be on the payroll for long.

A diverse workforce makes demands on supervisors that a homogeneous one does not. When a subordinate, peer, or boss has one or more identities that we do not share, "we are likely to relate to this person based on the stereotypes that we associate with the individual's [religion,] affectional orientation, age, ethnic heritage, gender, physical abilities/qualities, and/or race" (Loden and Rosener, 1991). While working to overcome these stereotypes, you must also try to perceive individuals as they perceive themselves—as members of diverse groups that influence their attitudes and, therefore, their behavior on the job. Diversity trainers, consultants, and authors, Renee Blank and Sandra Slipp (1994), remind us that, "All workers want to succeed on the job and be accepted by the organization,

SUPERVISORS AND ETHICS

Mainstream American culture still dominates many working environments and leads to difficulties in developing relationships and getting the best from those with differing cultural backgrounds. The following contrasts should help you become aware of and value more effectively the individuals with whom you must work. Consider which perspective accurately reflects you and which are found in your associates. Then think about the possible conflicts that can arise or have arisen between people with any of these differences.

Mainstream Culture	*Other Cultural Perspectives*
1. Emphasis on individual performance	Emphasis on collective action
2. Emphasis on competition	Emphasis on collaboration
3. Directness in communication	Indirectness in communication
4. Loyalty to company and work	Family and friends take precedence over work
5. Personal assertiveness	Passivity
6. Empowerment of individuals	Reliance on direction from above
7. Time is money; nonrenewable resource	Time is a renewable resource
8. Identity through work	Identity through family and friends
9. Emphasis on task performance	Emphasis on relationships
10. Criticism of performances; placing blame	Concern for saving face

What are the potential ethical issues related to building relationships between people with these differing values and perceptions? What can people with these differences do to enable them to work successfully together in the workplace?

Source: Adapted from Lee Gardenswartz and Anita Rowe, *The Managing Diversity Survival Guide*, New York: Irwin, 1994.

but they also want to maintain their own senses of identity and have their special perspectives and assets acknowledged and appreciated."

Authors and lecturers Marilyn Loden and Judy Rosener (1991) believe that "most people want more authentic, honest, and respectful relationships with others than they presently have." Exhibit 8.1 contains their findings about what will enable people with diverse backgrounds to interact more effectively and comfortably. As their contacts increase and

EXHIBIT 8.1

What people of diverse backgrounds want from their relationships and their organizations.

Source: Marilyn Loden and Judy B. Rosener, Workforce America! [Homewood, IL: Business One Irwin, 1991], 76–78.)

Younger and Older Employees Want:
- More respect for their life experiences
- To be taken seriously
- To be challenged by their organizations—not patronized

Women Want:
- Recognition as equal partners
- Active support of male colleagues
- Organizations to proactively address work and family issues

Men Want:
- The same freedom to grow/feel that women have
- To be perceived as allies, not as the enemy
- To bridge the gap between dealing with women at home and at work.

People of Color Want:
- To be valued as unique individuals, as members of ethnically diverse groups, as people of different races, and as equal contributors
- To establish more open, honest working relationships with people of other races and ethnic groups
- The active support of white people in fighting racism

White People Want:
- To have their ethnicity acknowledged
- To reduce discomfort, confusion, and dishonesty in dealing with people of color

- To build relationships with people of color based on common goals, concerns, and mutual respect for differences

Differently Abled People Want:
- Greater acknowledgment of and focus on abilities, not just on disabilities
- To be challenged by colleagues and organizations to be the best
- To be included, not isolated

Physically Able-Bodied People Want:
- To develop more ease in dealing with differently abled people
- To appreciate abilities—in addition to understanding disabilities
- To give honest feedback and appropriate support—without being patronizing or overprotective

Gay Men and Lesbians Want:
- Recognition as whole human beings—not only as sexual beings
- Equal employment protection—like all other groups have
- Increased awareness among straight people regarding the impact of heterosexism in the workplace

Heterosexuals Want:
- Increased awareness of lesbian and gay issues
- A better understanding of the legal consequences of being gay in America
- More dialogue about heterosexist issues with lesbians and gay men

grow more open, people begin to value and appreciate each other's diversity. Keep these findings in mind as you develop your relationships with others at work.

Communicating Supportively

All of your efforts at developing sound human relations involve communicating by both words and actions with your associates and those outside your immediate sphere of influence. The ways in which you communicate can cause others to be open and honest or closed and defensive. If your words and deeds are supportive of the feelings and efforts of others, you encourage open and honest two-way communications. This two-way communications process should firmly bridge your relationships with your associates, peers, and superiors. According to authors Blank and Slipp (1994), all managers must:

- Convey clearly [their] expectations for the work unit, while recognizing group differences in communication and perspective
- Provide feedback [on performances] often and equally to all members of the workforce
- Openly support the competencies and contribution of workers from all groups
- Become comfortable asking questions about preferred terminology or interactions
- Confront racist, sexist, or other stereotypic or discriminatory behavior

Take the short quiz in Exhibit 8.2. Any "rarely" responses indicate a need to improve your communications efforts.

DEVELOPING SOUND WORKING RELATIONSHIPS WITH SUBORDINATES

As we stated in earlier chapters, your success as a manager is directly related to and dependent on the performance of your subordinates. Your reputation is in their hands since it is a product of their efforts. Your future therefore depends in large measure on how well you are able to relate to them and to promote in them a desire to excel. According to Blank and Slipp (1994), "...it is you, the manager, who ultimately holds the key for releasing the full potential of each person in your work unit." With this recognition should come a personal commitment to do what you can to help all of your associates and teams toward a complete realization of their potential. The ideal on-the-job relationship between yourself and

EXHIBIT 8.2

	Usually	Rarely
1. I make time to listen to my people's problems.	____	____
2. I greet my people warmly and sincerely express my interest in their well-being.	____	____
3. I give my people the information they need to perform effectively.	____	____
4. I encourage my people to come to me with their ideas and suggestions.	____	____
5. I am slow to criticize any idea given to me and try to look for its good points first.	____	____
6. I use humor when it is appropriate in my chances to communicate.	____	____
7. I share any praise I receive when part of it is due to the efforts of my subordinates or team members.	____	____
8. I take the chance, whenever possible, to talk with my people, one on one.	____	____
9. I express sincere interest in my people's families, inquiring as to their health and well-being.	____	____
10. I consider my people's feelings and circumstances before attempting to judge or criticize their actions.	____	____
11. I take every opportunity to compliment people for any job that is well done.	____	____
12. I give quick feedback to my people on all matters that are of importance to them.	____	____
13. I try not to keep those waiting to see me waiting too long.	____	____
14. I offer explanations for my actions and decisions.	____	____

your subordinates will be the end result of your understanding, mastering, and executing the four fundamental roles of the supervisor. These roles relate to and depend on one another. It is every team leader's, team facilitator's, and supervisor's duty to initiate and maintain these relationships. Specifically, the four relationships are defined as follows:

1. Educator—a builder of skills and developer of potential
2. Counselor—an advisor, director, cheerleader, and coach
3. Judge—an appraiser, mediator, and dispenser of justice
4. Spokesperson—a message carrier for both associates and superiors

Your Role as Educator

Your role as an educator is usually the first one you play in relation to a new associate. Before the new person arrives, you have made an assessment of what training he or she will need in order to adjust to his or her duties. This initial training is vitally important; it communicates the manager's expectations, standards for performance, and the skills, knowledge, and attitudes required in the individual. Through training, organizational members discover what the company stands for (its core values) and are united by them. "...[P]eople bring their best to their work only if they can involve their whole selves. They must feel free to talk about the things they are passionate about, to explore opposing points of view. These discussions create deeper relationships if people feel connected by a shared desire to have their organization succeed. Leadership that relies on such characteristics as relationship building, trust, nurturance, intuition and letting go is the leadership of the future" (Wheatley, 1994). Training, when properly planned and executed, does much to remove the initial fears we all have as we begin something new. It convinces trainees of our interest

In your role as educator, you must demonstrate your commitment to helping your subordinates reach their potential. After your training sessions, workers should understand what is expected of them and how they can achieve it.

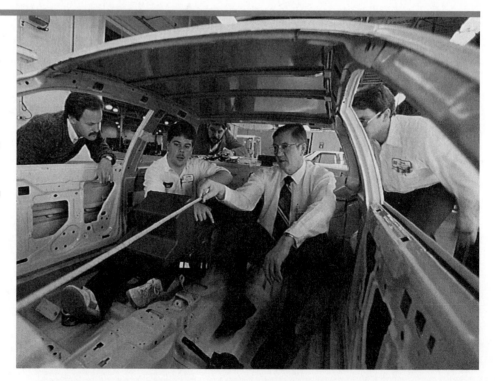

SUPERVISING TEAMS

The decision to create teams in the workplace is not made lightly. Teams are not for every company and not appropriate for many tasks. Route salespeople and executives' secretaries are not candidates for team membership. The primary question to ask is: Can the purpose for which a team is being considered be best accomplished by a team? If it is "...a team purpose as opposed to a broader organizational purpose or just one individual's purpose (e.g., the leader's)..." a team that is carefully constructed and given the training and time needed to weld as a unit may be the answer.

"For best results, members should have...a clear, shared understanding of the task to be done and...a strong personal desire to complete the task." They will also need the "right mix of...technical or functional expertise,... problem-solving and decision-making skills,... [and] interpersonal skills" required to investigate and analyze problems and implement solutions. Finding the right mix of skills usually means finding the right mix of people—those who possess what is needed or those who can acquire them in a reasonable amount of time. The result will usually be diversity in membership with the corresponding differences in approaches to reaching solutions. Then the team members must be encouraged and allowed "...to invest the time early in the process to plan their task, build teamwork, and acquire the knowledge they need."

Sources: Katzenbach, Jon R., and Smith. Douglas K. *The Wisdom of Teams* (Boston: Harvard Business School Press, 1993), 47–48, 62–63; "Setting Up Successful Company Work Groups," *Nation's Business,* August 1994, 10.

in and concern for them. They should emerge from training with a clear understanding of what is expected of them and how they are supposed to achieve it. Through training, a team leader, team facilitator, and supervisor demonstrate their commitment to helping trainees experience successful performance and reach their potential.

There is a second phase to your role as an educator. You will recall from Chapter 4 that we included in our definition of directing the element of educating. We stated there that to educate meant to foster subordinates' intellectual development. "Enlightened employers like General Electric, Motorola, and Allied Signal have discovered that a key ingredient for getting employees to acknowledge and embrace organization change is compensation.... [T]hese companies reward teamwork, measurable quality improvements, and employee's acquisition of new skills. 'Getting the rewards right and steadily raising the goals [stretch goals] is how a company communicates its values and direction to its work force'" (Richman, 1994). You set an example for your associates when you seek personal growth through additional formal education and company programs; you exemplify your commitment to your company's emphasis on education. This just might be the incentive your associates need to continue their formal education or take advantage of company-sponsored programs that foster self-development. Acquiring portable skills is the best way to ensure your employment security.

The reality in today's downsized businesses is that fewer people are left to do more work. One answer to this dilemma is to adopt the latest in information technology. Through training and empowerment, more workers—individually and collectively—are taking on what used to be managerial activities. "Although information technology is altering work patterns for all employees, the changes are greatest at the lowest levels of the organization.... Workers have to think like managers, understand the business implications of what they do, and master new technologies.... That means managers must spend more time instilling commitment to the task and finding ways to measure results..." (Treece, 1994). With these new requirements comes the need for team leaders and team facilitators to (Treece, 1994):

- Instill commitment in subordinates rather than rule by command and control
- Become coaches, training workers in necessary job skills, making sure they have resources to accomplish goals, and explaining links between a job and what happens elsewhere in the company
- Give greater authority to workers over scheduling, priority-setting, and even compensation
- Use new information technologies to measure workers' performance, possibly based on customer satisfaction or the accomplishment of specific goals

Through empowerment and training, workers must (Treece, 1994):

- Become initiators, able to act without management direction
- Become financially literate so that they can understand the business implications of what they do and changes they suggest
- Learn group interaction skills, including how to resolve disputes within their work group and how to work with other functions across the company
- Develop new math, technical, and analytical skills to use newly available information on their jobs

By understanding your role as an educator, mastering the knowledge and skills you wish to teach others, and executing this role in accordance

SUPERVISORS AND QUALITY

"**A**re you tenacious? Do you have the technical skills to run the business and produce the product? Do you believe in your own ability?" These are questions, the answers to which indicate a person's ability to become an entrepreneur. Successful business startups are the product of passion and perspective, according to the director of the University of Southern California's Entrepreneur program, Jon P. Goodman.

Entrepreneurs have several traits that any supervisor, team leader, and team facilitator would do well to acquire. Empowered teams and work groups need inspired leaders and members. Such people demonstrate a true commitment to a vision and values. They then keep their associates focused on both and inspire them to produce quality outputs.

Entrepreneurs see problems as opportunities, crises as challenges, and failures as learning experiences. They "...have imagination, the ability to envision alternative scenarios.... Successful entrepreneurs act out of choice. They are never victims of fate." When you adopt these perceptions, you become a role model for others. Your enthusiasm and commitment will become infectious, leading to the ability to inspire others to give quality performances.

Source: Goodman, Jon P. "What Makes an Entrepreneur?" *Inc.*, October 1994, 29.

with established training principles and procedures (Chapter 12), you are well on your way toward promoting your own success by fostering success in others.

Your Role as Counselor

Think back to encounters you have had with school counselors throughout your formal education. What was it they were trying to do for you? Why did the school feel they were necessary? Their advice was usually related to school and general growth-and-development problems common to most students. If the counselors were doing their jobs, they wanted what was best for you. They tried to get to know you and your individual needs, aspirations, and desires. They listened to you and, in turn, hoped you would listen to them—to their advice on how realistic your thinking was. Sometimes they suggested solutions to your problems. If they were wise, they did not suggest solutions to personal or emotional problems,

To be effective in your role as counselor, you must practice empathetic listening. When you have discussions with subordinates, do more listening than talking.

but they may have instead suggested that you talk with a specialist—an authority better equipped than they to help you in that particular area. In case you have not guessed, this is also a description of how you should play your role as a **counselor** to your subordinates.

A. A. Imberman (1969), a management consultant, states that there are two tests that employees use to judge their supervisors:

counselor

the human relations role in which a supervisor is an advisor and director to subordinates

1. Is the supervisor aware of me? Can I turn to him or her for friendly help? Will he or she listen to me?
2. Will he or she do something about my problem?

If the answers to these two questions are yes, the workers view their boss as a good one. By the first question, the employees really want to know if the supervisor knows them personally. Does the supervisor know about their ambitions and their family and individual needs? By the second question, they ask if the supervisor is willing to help. Notice that the workers are not asking for the boss to come up with a solution every time they present him or her with a problem. They only want the boss to try. Doing something can be as simple as being available to listen to them. We all know the release that accompanies talking out a problem with a sympathetic listener. We often reach our own solution after or during such an experience. Sometimes we are not really looking for a solution because we know that only we ourselves or time can provide it, as in the case of a family argument or illness. Of course, job-related problems are something else. If it is within your power to solve the problems or recommend solutions, do so. If the problems must be resolved at a higher level, see that they are referred there and that the disposition or decision is relayed to your subordinate. Even if the results do not satisfy the individual, you have tried to help. You have done the best you could, and a subordinate will know it. You will have passed a major test.

Staying Aware   To get to know your people in depth, you should interact with each of them daily and meet informally, face to face, at least once a week for twenty to thirty minutes. These counseling or coaching sessions allow you to accomplish several things:

- Get to know each person as an individual
- Periodically update your knowledge about each of your subordinates
- Pinpoint personal and business-related problems that you may be able to help resolve
- Find out how each subordinate is doing on the job
- Show your concern for each subordinate's growth and improvement

Many supervisors ignore counseling until a problem arises. Then they call a hasty conference and belittle, berate, or chew out the subordinate who is in trouble. Very soon subordinates get the message that the only time they see or hear from the boss is when he or she is unhappy or upset about their performance. Some supervisors claim that they do not have the time or that the time spent on counseling could be better spent on other things. The plain fact is that if supervisors do not counsel their people, they will have plenty of fires to put out and very little time for counseling. But if they invest the time necessary to touch base with each person periodically, they will be able to spot trouble coming and thus prevent many problems that later might require corrective measures or hastily called sessions to deal with the difficulty.

Doing Something   If you are going to do something about a subordinate's problem, you should conduct a formal interview. The four basic principles that apply to a problem-centered coaching interview are described in the following extract (American Hotel & Motel Association, 1976):

> The first principle of successful coaching is to get your subordinate involved. The more active a part the subordinate can take in appraising the problem for himself, and in outlining possible courses of action, the more committed he will be to the solution. And, the more enthusiastically he will work for its success.
>
> The second principle is that you encourage him to participate actively in the interview. Your role in the coaching interview is not to tell your subordinate what to do or how to do it, but rather to help him develop

for himself a plan of action for dealing with the problem at hand. You can raise key questions which will help him find a solution, but don't lead him by the hand unless it is absolutely necessary.

The third principle is to make sure you both understand the meaning of what is being discussed and said. The only sure way of doing this is to get your subordinate to express his views in his own words. You should restate those views, in different words, to see if you can reach agreement. Otherwise, the two of you could come away from the coaching conference with entirely different ideas of the issues discussed and decisions made.

Finally, the fourth principle is to force yourself to do more listening than talking. Even if you say relatively little during your meeting, the interview can prove of considerable value—provided you listen. If he is upset, you give your subordinate a chance to let off steam. You also give him an opening to try out his ideas on you for a change.

As a link between training and coaching, consider these observations from three experts on team development (Wellins, Byham, and Wilson, 1991):

Good coaches don't solve a [person's or] a team's problems; they help individuals solve their own problems.... The key is to develop skills and confidence simultaneously during training.... [B]y coaching individuals through the possible steps for handling the problem effectively, the [coach] offers help without taking responsibility for action. This is the soul of empowerment because it creates a sense of ownership. The effective leader helps individuals and teams look at their problems and determine appropriate alternatives. Employees will feel empowered only if they solve problems themselves. Most importantly, the next time a problem comes up, they will be better able to deal with it.

An analogy can be drawn between the supervisor's role in the motivation of subordinates and the director's role in bringing out the best in actors. A director knows that, like a supervisor, he or she cannot motivate an actor to put on a superior performance. The director realizes that motivation comes from within, and that certain limitations exist in and around every actor that can interfere with a superior effort. But the director knows that he or she can do much to provide the climate and incentives for the actor that can spark an inner drive to excel. He or she may remove distractions that might interfere with an actor's concentration. He or she can make certain that the actor has done the necessary homework and learned the lines. The director can confer with the actor to find out how the actor perceives the role. The director is able to set the stage with props and lighting that will allow the actor to perform to the best of his or her ability. Lastly, throughout the rehearsals and the performances, the director offers advice and criticism. This coaching and sincere concern are often the spark the actor needs to give a superior performance. By sensing the actor's needs, strengths, and weaknesses, the director can tailor advice and direction to bring about a commitment to excel within the actor.

Supervisors must get to know themselves well, and they must get to know their subordinates in depth. Having committed themselves to these tasks, they will find that they are able to build sound human and working relationships with their subordinates. Supervisors should be able to tailor their approaches with an eye to the needs and responses of each subordinate.

Your Role as Judge

Playing judge successfully involves being proficient at four important tasks:

1. Enforcing company policies and regulations, as well as your department's procedures and rules
2. Evaluating each subordinate's performance
3. Settling disputes between your people and teams or between your people, teams, and yourself
4. Dispensing justice

Enforcement   To enforce company policies and regulations, you must first be aware of them. You have to know what they say, as well as their proper interpretation. Then you must see to it that they are followed by both your subordinates and yourself. Finally, you must be certain that they are not violated by your section's procedures, practices, and rules. Consistency of enforcement is the key to gaining acceptance of company policies and management decisions.

You must follow a similar procedure with regard to your department's procedures and practices. Do people know about them? Do they understand them? Are they following them? All these questions are usually answered through various controls you design into your operation. Proper induction and training should go a long way toward ensuring that the department's procedures and practices are properly interpreted and utilized.

Evaluation   Evaluating subordinates is one of your most important and time-consuming tasks as a supervisor. Appraising your people involves making judgments about their performance and their attitudes. Using established standards for each job, you must make an objective and honest evaluation of each person's output and individual contribution to the department. Is he or she meeting production standards? Is he or she correcting or trying to correct deficiencies noted in previous appraisals? Are his or her attitudes proper, or are they interfering with his or her efforts and those of other workers in the department?

Appraisals take place daily. In routine visits with your people, you have an excellent opportunity to note their successes and question their deficiencies. This will allow you to catch an error when it first appears and take corrective action to prevent its recurrence. At the same time, you are letting your people know regularly how they stand with you. Your being with them routinely gives them the opportunity to ask questions and to clear up misunderstandings. When the time finally rolls around for the formal semiannual or annual review, there should be no surprises. You have kept your people informed on a daily basis.

With regard to attitudes, your appraisals each day blend nicely with your role as a counselor. Much of appraising has to do with counseling. When your observations tell you that a worker's attitude causes a deficiency in his or her output or conduct, try to find out why he or she harbors it. Chapter 6 contains helpful information on attitudes and how to change them. You will recall that it is only when people see their attitude as improper that they are willing to reject it. Chapter 13 probes more deeply into the specifics of the appraisal process.

Settling Disputes   Part of your role as a judge is to act as a peacemaker. People problems are the most persistent and frequent problems you have to deal with each day. Inevitably, two or more individuals or groups of subordinates will do battle with each other. It would be best if these battles could be prevented, but that is not always possible. Sometimes the causes are hidden from your view and only surface under stress with an open display of hostility.

When you witness such disturbances, begin an investigation to uncover the causes on both sides. Analyze your evidence, and make a decision. Try to avoid treating the symptoms, but concentrate your energies on the disease. When you have reached a conclusion about the merits on both sides, confront the participants with your findings. Work toward a reconciliation that will not leave any scars as lasting reminders of the battle. Avoid any emphasis on who was at fault (chances are, both sides share the blame), but point out why the problem got started and how it can be avoided in the future.

Conflict between team members and teams is another source of concern for team leaders and team facilitators. Sources of conflict include disagreements over members' or teams' roles or authority, perceptions of unequal treatment, stereotypical thinking about diverse members, and competition for scarce resources. Your job is to manage conflict by creating "...a climate in which healthy debate can occur" (Holt, 1993). People who find it hard to work together can be reassigned. Members and groups can hold meetings to determine their own solutions, redefining their purposes or ways of interacting. "The best management solution to conflict is to eliminate or minimize opportunities for interference between conflicting parties. This may be done through rules, procedures, policies, or penalties for infractions" (Holt, 1993).

Dispensing Justice   Justice, in this connection, means seeing to it that each of your subordinates gets what he or she deserves. When they are doing a good job, they deserve your praise. When they break a rule or violate a procedure, they must be shown the error of their ways. Rest assured that people want to know the bounds that limit them and their activity. Once these limits are explained, people expect them to be enforced and usually anticipate some admonishment for each of their infractions. This admonishment may simply be a verbal warning, but in the case of repeated offenses, it may take the form of some other disciplinary action.

Improper or unacceptable conduct on the job cannot be tolerated. To prevent it, your company installs you as its chief enforcement officer in your department and gives you power to discipline violators. It provides you with policies and regulations, while you provide your department with procedures and rules. When these preventive devices fail, corrective measures must take over.

To many, discipline simply means punishment. This is the negative side of a much broader concept. The positive side is the one that emphasizes informing organization members ahead of time about the limits that surround acceptable conduct. It places the emphasis on self-control and mutual trust. When new employees are hired, you should inform them of the rules on the very first day, and you should make it clear to them what constitutes acceptable behavior and performance and what does not. When you take over a section as its supervisor, promptly inform the members of the standards you will enforce and the expectations you will have of each member. When infractions occur, take action. To do otherwise would ultimately undermine your formal authority and your integrity. You will find that it is much better to start out tough than to try to become so later. It is an unpleasant and difficult duty to discipline people for infractions of a rule that you failed to make clear to them.

When punishment is necessary, you must be certain that it fits the offense. Quite often, when dealing with unionized workers, the manager's disciplinary powers are limited by the union contract. Be certain that you have the power to take a specific action before you do so. And keep in mind that subordinates expect you to act equitably—to be impartial and fair. Chapter 14 deals in more detail with the tasks encountered in disciplining.

Your Role as Spokesperson

Your superiors expect you to represent management's point of view adequately to your subordinates. You are the only manager who can translate management's plans into action. Your boss, in particular, is counting on you to defend and to reinforce management's position. But you must be a spokesperson for your work group as well.

You must realize that you are (or should be) a fountainhead of timely and accurate information to your people. They look to you for an inter-

In your role as educator, you must demonstrate your commitment to helping your subordinates reach their potential. After your training sessions, workers should understand what is expected of them and how they can achieve it.

spokesperson

the human relations role through which a supervisor represents management's views to workers and workers' views to management

pretation of the events they witness. They expect you to help them separate fact from fiction and truth from rumor. Their need to be kept informed demands that you prepare them in advance for changes. They look to you as their **spokesperson**—backing them up either when they are right or when they are wrong because they executed your orders. If they believe that a policy or regulation is unfair, relay their feelings to those in a position to change it. You can do much to protect your people from harassment and from getting shortchanged. Just as you hope for their loyalty, they need yours.

As a team leader or team facilitator, your spokesperson role involves interacting with staff to acquire the appropriate support your team or teams require; networking with outsiders such as internal and external customers served, internal or external suppliers (to resolve problems with their support); gathering needed information and other resources from external sources; arranging for cross-training to expand individuals' and teams' skills and understanding of the needs and functions of others; and keeping higher authorities informed of your team's or teams' progress.

You must respect the confidences of both your superiors and your subordinates. Just because your people request an answer to a question, and you know the answer, is no reason you should give it. Information given to you in private with a request for your silence must be respected. If you betray a confidence, you will soon find yourself on the outside of the group, looking in.

There are times when your employees seem to know more about future events than you do. This is natural, and this situation may be explained in part by the grapevine. If they ask for a clarification or verification and you cannot give it, do not bluff. Admit your lack of accurate information, and assure them that you will try to get it. Then be sure to deliver.

If you properly execute your role as spokesperson, your superiors and your subordinates will learn to trust you and to rely on you more in the future. This will strengthen your relationships with them and will promote harmony and cooperation in your department. Take the quiz in Exhibit 8.3 to help you assess how well you are playing your four human relations roles with subordinates.

MAINTAINING YOUR RELATIONSHIPS WITH SUBORDINATES

So far we have discussed how to build a sound relationship with your individual subordinates. How can you preserve it once you have established it? The answer lies in persistence. When we talked about personality formation, we agreed that it was a continuous process. So it is with on-the-job relationships. Like any other living thing, human relations need constant attention. Each day brings about changes in the parties involved, so that what worked well yesterday may not today. Recognition of this dynamic aspect of people and their relationships dictates the need for maintenance.

Maintenance of your relationships with subordinates can be compared to the situation of gardeners who wish to keep their gardens in a healthful and beautiful condition. They have plans for the care and development of the gardens. There are schedules for feeding, for pruning, and for preventive measures such as spraying and weeding. Their daily observations tell them about the gardens' state of repair and keep them in touch with each plant and its present state of health. What precedes all this is a genuine love for gardening and a commitment to a program for maintaining the gardens. So it must be with your human relations efforts. Establishing a sound relationship with each person is only a beginning. If the relationship is to grow and be mutually beneficial, maintenance must be scheduled and performed.

FRIENDSHIP

There is a distinct difference between the relationship between supervisor and subordinate that this chapter advocates and the relationship between two people called friendship. At the base of sound human relations are common interests (effective and efficient operation of the department, for

EXHIBIT 8.3

*A short quiz to help you
assess how well you are
playing your human
relations roles with sub-
ordinates.*

	Usually	Rarely*

Educator Role

1. I make certain that my actions do not contradict my words and instructions. ____ ____

2. I carefully construct a program for training my people, being certain to set specific objectives. ____ ____

3. I make certain that my people have the information and resources they need to do first-class work. ____ ____

4. I assign work to people based upon their willingness and their abilities to perform it. ____ ____

5. When I find an attitude in a subordinate that is interfering with the performance, I work on changing it. ____ ____

Counselor Role

1. I make time for anyone who wishes to see me about a personal or work-related problem. ____ ____

2. I make certain that any counseling I do is in private and free from interruptions. ____ ____

3. I give the person seeking my help my undivided, sincere attention. ____ ____

4. I recognize that I cannot solve every problem and should not try to give people all the answers. ____ ____

5. When I cannot help someone solve a problem, I will try to refer them to another person with more expertise. ____ ____

*Each "rarely" response indicates that you need to improve your conduct.

example), mutual respect, and a concern for the other person's welfare. This is or should be true about your relationships with your friends, as well. But you should try to prevent a true friendship from emerging out of sound human relations with your subordinates.

If you allow a friendship to form between yourself and a subordinate, you do so at your own expense. How easy is it to give orders to a

EXHIBIT 8.3
(cont.)

	Usually	Rarely*

Judge Role

1. I look for causes behind any failures by my people to meet the standards set for their performances. ____ ____
2. I withhold any criticism until I have all the facts and am aware of all the circumstances surrounding an issue. ____ ____
3. I try to discipline without emotion. ____ ____
4. I recognize that circumstances should temper any approach to discipline. ____ ____
5. I know that it is better to forewarn and to forearm subordinates about the expectations I have or the organization has for them than it is to have to punish people for failing to meet standards. ____ ____

Spokesperson Role

1. I take seriously every complaint or gripe I hear from subordinates. ____ ____
2. I listen carefully to subordinates' suggestions and ideas and try to use them. ____ ____
3. Any problem my people give me that I cannot solve will be taken to a higher authority for resolution. ____ ____
4. When my people experience success, I make certain others higher up hear about it. ____ ____
5. I try my best to accurately reflect management's points of view, defending them and enforcing its decisions. ____ ____

friend? Do you appraise your friend's performance and freely offer criticism to him or her? How about the times when you have to pass out an occasional dirty job? Would you consider your friend objectively as a candidate for it? You cannot form friendships with all of your subordinates, so aren't you opening yourself to criticism about playing favorites?

Your honest answers to these questions should alert you to the inherent dangers of friendship with subordinates. The subordinate you befriend is open to criticism, too, and his or her relationships with his or her peers may be in jeopardy. Choose your friends from among your peers.

GETTING ALONG WITH STAFF SPECIALISTS

Probably dozens of times each week you come across the effects of staff specialists on your department. A good percentage of the forms and reports you generate are destined for their desks. The advice and service you receive at the press of a button or the twist of a dial can save you hours of agony and independent research. These people form an invaluable group of counselors on professional matters. Do everything you can to take advantage of their labors and to foster a cooperative and receptive atmosphere. At times, they may appear to you as prying eyes or fifth wheels. But over the long run, your success as a supervisor—as well as that of all other managers—depends on your seeking and using their advice. And as the concept of functional authority suggests, you may have no choice.

DEVELOPING SOUND HUMAN RELATIONSHIPS WITH PEERS

peer
a person with the same level of formal authority and status in the organizational hierarchy as you have

Your **peers** are all the other managers who are on the same level of the management hierarchy as you are. You work more closely with some than with others, but situations can change rapidly in business. The most important reasons for establishing good human relations with your peers are these:

- To know and understand them as individuals
- To approach and cooperate with them as individuals
- To provide what help you can to enable them to achieve the measure of satisfaction they desire from their jobs
- To foster a spirit of cooperation and teamwork among your peers
- To tap their diverse funds of knowledge, skills, and experience

Your success as a manager is linked to your peers and what they think of you as a person and as a supervisor. Your personal and professional reputation with them is important for a number of reasons. If they think highly of you, they will be drawn to you and be willing to associate with you.

They will freely expend their time and energy on your behalf and help you with advice. How you measure up with them and how they react when your name is mentioned are factors that may influence your boss as well. When your boss looks at his or her subordinates—you and your peers—for someone to delegate responsibility to or to train for a higher position, he or she cannot help comparing you to them. If you cannot get along with or are avoided by your peers, your boss will know it.

Your peers represent an enormous pool of talent and experience that is yours to tap and contribute to if they view you in a favorable way. For this reason, if no other, it is to your advantage to cultivate their friendship both on and off the job. In many ways, you need each other, and all of you stand to benefit from a partnership or alliance based on mutual respect and the need to resolve common problems.

If you are off in your own little world and are unwilling to share your knowledge and know-how, you deny yourself the advice and experience they stand ready to give. You may be branded as uncooperative or antisocial and destined, at best, for a career as a supervisor. Higher positions have no need for isolates. You will find, if you have not already done so, that the more you give of what you have, the more you will receive from others.

Your Role as Educator

The two-way nature of your role as educator includes assisting your fellow supervisors in their growth and development, as well as enlisting their help on your own behalf.

You have a great deal to give your peers. You have talents and skills that may be developed to a greater degree in you than in some of them. You have knowledge about human nature, your job, and management in general that can be beneficial to others. You have attitudes and a personality that can be the basis for friendship and that can sustain a fellow supervisor when he or she needs it most.

Most people have experienced the joy that comes with sharing what they have with others. Parents know the pleasure they receive when they give of themselves to their children. They have seen the delight when they show their children how to do things and when they help their children develop their skills and increase their knowledge. Do you remember the fun you had when you took a friend for a ride in your new car? Can you recall the enjoyment you felt when you helped younger, less experienced people solve a problem that was so difficult for them and yet so easy for you?

Besides the momentary joy you feel when you share your knowledge and your tricks of the trade, you get something much more lasting: a good reputation. Psychologically, all of your peers who profit through your efforts on their behalf are in your debt. They may not always show overt appreciation (and you should not always expect it), but they will find it hard not to reciprocate, to share what they have with you. When you need a favor, a bit of advice, or a helping hand, your colleagues will respond when and if they are able to do so.

Your peers' advice and know-how cannot be found in books. In a relatively short span of time, you will receive (if you are wise enough to ask) what might take you years to discover on your own. Which is easier and more fun: reading about how to do something difficult or having someone who knows how to do it show you how it is done? Your peers probably feel the same way about this as you do.

If you know yourself well, you know your strengths and weaknesses. Where you are weak, a peer may be strong, and vice versa. The more peers you know well, the greater the quantity of help available to you. Give what you have, and take advantage of what others have to give. Do not bury your talents, and do not let others bury theirs.

Your Role as Counselor

Counsel is a mutual exchange of ideas and opinions. Counselors are people to whom you go for advice and to try out your ideas. They provide you with guidance and a plan in the absence of one of your own. The key to counseling your peers is empathy—the intellectual and imaginative understanding of another's feelings and state of mind. From this develops a mutual respect and appreciation.

As with subordinates, just being available and favorably predisposed toward your peers may give them what they need at precisely the moment they need it—a sympathetic ear. By listening to others who have difficulties, you provide emotional first aid. By responding when asked and when qualified to do so, you may give people the support they need to resolve their difficulties.

When a friend asks you for advice and you have empathy for that person, speak your mind freely. Without empathy (which usually means without friendship), you should confine your guidance to work-related matters. Steer clear of personal advice unless you know the person well.

A few words of caution are in order. It is one thing to be asked for your opinion and quite another to give it without being asked. You do not want a reputation as a buttinsky, so avoid any counsel unless it is solicited.

We all have known the value of being on the receiving end of good counsel. An interested, sympathetic advisor and friend not only can temper our views, he or she may resolve our difficulties as well. When we consult a friend, we are either looking for answers we think he or she possesses or seeking a shoulder to lean on. The value of either cannot be measured, but it is tremendously helpful, nevertheless. Our counselor brings a certain neutrality and objectivity to bear on the issue that we are powerless to muster on our own.

For the give and take of counseling between friends and associates to work, we must have communications channels open to the left and to the right. Do your best to avoid arguments and displays of temper with your associates. Do not burn any bridges so that you cannot return to a pleasant relationship once a momentary storm passes. If for a time you alienate a peer, stand ready to apologize when you have been in the wrong. Be quick to forgive a colleague who has injured you. You do not have to call all of your peers your friends, but you should not call any of them enemies. By sharing the successes of others, you enrich the returns to them. By sharing the sorrows of others, you capture their friendship. So it is also when they reciprocate.

Your Role as Judge

Closely allied with the counseling role in human relations with your peers is the role of judge. You have four specific duties to attend to: enforcement, settling disputes, evaluation, and criticism.

Enforcement   The duty you have to enforce company policies and regulations affects your peers as well. There is an urgent need for all supervisors to be uniform in both the interpretation and the application of these policies and regulations. You probably have experienced the unhappy situation that results when one supervisor is lenient and another is severe. Imagine a situation in which you are trying to get your workers to arrive and leave on schedule, whereas the supervisor in the adjacent department allows his or her people to come and go as they please. How much more difficult has this supervisor made your job? Where two managers interpret or enforce the same regulation or policy in different and conflicting ways, a wedge is driven between them. This wedge acts as a barrier to both communication and cooperation. Managers at every level must agree with and work parallel to each other if they are to act in a united and effective way.

Settling Disputes   Where you find yourself at odds with a peer over an interpretation of policy or of how to enforce a rule, get together with that individual and work it out between you. Quite often, your duties overlap those of another supervisor. A meeting and a polite discussion are all that are usually required to resolve the difficulty. If you two cannot work the matter out, get together with your boss and his or hers. Do not let the conflict continue any longer than necessary. Take action as soon as you are aware that a problem exists.

Periodically, you may be called on by circumstances to serve as a peacemaker. For example, two of your associates are engaged in an argument, and their emotions have taken over. As a witness to the dispute, you may be able to intervene with a calmness and logic that the others lack. Do so when you find yourself in such a situation. It does managers no good to squabble, especially in public. Workers read all kinds of things into such events. You may save a friend or associate from the embarrassment of making a fool of himself or herself.

Evaluation   Study your peers for an understanding of their management techniques. All of them have their unique characteristics and methods. Hold your standards up to theirs, and see how they compare. Where you discover significant differences, make every effort to determine which is the better set to follow. Both your and their techniques could prove to be inferior to yet another set of standards.

Your peers make excellent working models to observe and evaluate. Try out your theories and applications on your associates, and get their reactions to them. Watch how they handle themselves in difficult as well as routine matters. Test your attitudes against theirs, and see if you can refine your viewpoints and pick up some of their methods.

Criticism   When you observe a peer engaged in improper or forbidden conduct, you owe him or her a bit of friendly correction. You and your fellow supervisors are a team of managers who must not work at cross-purposes if you are to succeed. When one of your number engages in unauthorized and harmful activities, he or she hurts all other supervisors. Others, especially workers, who observe a supervisor's improprieties draw conclusions that inevitably harm his or her reputation and yours. You are all in this together.

When a peer's actions and objectives are contrary to yours, you must confront him or her with your observations. Let him or her know, in a tactful and sincere manner, what you know. After all, if you know what he or she is up to, it is quite likely that others—including the boss—do too. Of course, you must still discuss the matter in private. You may find more often than not that a peer is unaware that he or she is doing anything wrong and will appreciate your drawing attention to the matter.

You, in turn, must stand ready for constructive criticism yourself. We all need it occasionally and, in fact, stop growing without it. Contentment and smugness creep in, and a false sense of security takes over. We begin to believe that we are consistently right and gradually close our minds to the new and different.

The strongest kind of friendly correction you can exert is your own good example. By promoting the things you believe in and by opposing the things you believe to be wrong, you take a stand and exhibit principles for others to see and admire.

Do not go looking for the problems and failings of others. But when you discover them, you have a duty to alert the other person. A friendly warning or a few words of counsel to let the manager know that he or she may be on thin ice are all that is called for.

We all tend to cover for a friend or peer in trouble. If you do, you may gain a few temporary benefits. But in the long run, you stand to lose far more than you could ever gain. You will identify yourself as an ally of improper conduct and demonstrate wholly unacceptable attitudes for any manager to hold. You do not hold a position of power and trust in order to shield your friends from earned discipline. That would constitute an inexcusable abuse of your position. Nor should you punish; that is a superior's duty. You need not inform on a peer since, in time, things have a way of surfacing and getting to those who should know. But do not compromise your own position of trust and personal integrity to help anyone. You will only be hurting yourself. You have too much to lose for too long.

Your Role as Spokesperson

You owe loyalty to your peers but only when they are in the right. Allegiance to someone is a precious gift, not to be given lightly. It must be earned as well as respected. Loyalty implies mutual trust and confidence. When they are not mutual, they cannot persist.

You should never spread a rumor about anyone. But when you hear one, it is your job as a spokesperson to refute it if you can. If you cannot, ask the other person to substantiate his or her statement. Inquire about the source. The person will know what you are thinking—that he or she is spreading gossip. When this bit of gossip relates to a peer, let that individual know its content and its source.

When an untrue rumor pertains to you, and you view its content as serious (all attacks on your character are), defend yourself. Trace it to its originator, and confront that individual with your knowledge. Control your temper, but make your point as forcefully as you feel is necessary. Then bury the incident, and try not to carry a grudge. If a rumor is minor and not related to your character, let it go. You do not have the time to track down all rumors, nor should you try to do so.

Respect legitimate demands for your silence, as is the case when conversing about personal matters with a friend. Information revealed to you by a peer that pertains to him or her alone should not be a topic of conversation with others. If you reveal a secret or break a confidence, your peer is sure to find out about it. What will happen to your reputation then?

The role of spokesperson also pertains to spreading good news or praising the ideas, contributions, and accomplishments of your peers. Giving credit where it is due and expressing your appreciation for benefits received, especially in public, is a pleasant duty one manager or friend owes another.

When you receive information from a peer, such as orders or instructions, be sure that you verify its content. If you act on it without doing so, you may be in for a shock. He or she may be passing along secondhand data, and much accuracy can be lost in handling and translation. Be certain when you relay information from the boss to a peer that you preserve its original form and intent. If what you received was written, pass it along in the same format.

Finally, remember that you are also a spokesperson for your subordinates. When another supervisor interferes with them or their work, make it clear to the other person that you resent the interference. Such an action challenges your authority. You must shield your subordinates and yourself from outside interference and conflicting orders or instructions.

COMPETITION WITH YOUR PEERS

Keep in mind that although you should maintain good relations with your peers and develop cooperation with them (as suggested in Chapter 6), you are still in competition with them. In much the same manner as a professional athlete, you have to maintain a balance between individual displays of talent and ability and the need for team play. All great athletes achieve their greatness in this way. You must be willing to take a back seat now and then and let another manager's talents come through. If you hog the ball, you do so at the expense of team play. Eventually, you will find that the ball stops coming your way.

Just remember that your reputation and performance evaluation are primarily in your subordinates' hands. Only secondarily do your peers play a part. If you are wise, that part is yours to write, produce, and direct. You have the ability to influence it through your human relations efforts and through interactions with your peers.

The best way to maintain good human relations is to develop yourself into the best person and manager you have the potential to become. You will gain both rational and charismatic power in so doing, which will draw people to you. In giving what you have and drawing on what others have to give, you will build bonds of friendship and strengthen your reputation with your peers.

Use the checklist shown in Exhibit 8.4 as a guide to evaluate your human relations efforts in dealing with your peers. Any "rarely" responses indicate a need to make an adjustment.

GETTING ALONG WITH YOUR BOSS

Before we get into specifics about your relations with your boss, a few words are in order about your boss: how your boss's job resembles yours and how it differs from yours.

Since you are a supervisor, your boss is a middle manager. He or she is accountable for your actions. Your boss is similar to you in that he or she is both a follower and a staff or line manager. He or she executes all the functions of management and is evaluated on the basis of his or her subordinates' performances. Your boss, like yourself, must develop sound

	Usually	Rarely*
1. I carry my own weight.	___	___
2. I lend a hand when and where needed.	___	___
3. I have the best interests of my peers in mind.	___	___
4. I am loyal to my peers.	___	___
5. I respect the privacy of things told to me in confidence.	___	___
6. I refrain from engaging in negative gossip.	___	___
7. I share my expertise and experiences with peers.	___	___
8. I try to earn the respect of peers.	___	___
9. I show my peers common courtesies and respect.	___	___
10. I share information with peers.	___	___
11. I avoid passing the buck.	___	___
12. I am a team player.	___	___
13. I defend my peers' actions in their absence.	___	___
14. I do not bear any grudges.	___	___
15. I try to avoid making any enemies.	___	___

*Any "rarely" responses indicate a need to improve.

working relationships with subordinates, peers, and superiors. He or she probably served an apprenticeship as a supervisor, so you can probably count on him or her to understand your situation.

Compared to a supervisor, however, a middle manager has more differences than similarities. As the following list shows, your boss has a number of duties and interests that are unlike yours. Your boss:

- Directs the work of other managers
- Exhibits strongly promanagement attitudes
- Spends more time on planning than on any other function
- Spends less time with subordinates
- Spends more time with peers and superiors
- Is more of an advisor than a director
- Has more freedom of action and flexibility
- Has more information and a broader perspective

- Is less concerned with procedures and practices (tactics) and more concerned with planning and programs (strategy)
- Is more concerned with tomorrow than with today
- Is more concerned with the causes of management actions than with their effects

As to the last item on this list, a supervisor and his or her subordinates often evaluate a management decision on the basis of its effect on them. This is quite natural and to be expected: What affects your people adversely or is the cause of gripes or worse is always of great concern to you. But the way you react to management decisions reflects on you and your potential to take the duties of a high position.

Suppose that higher management has recently reduced the plant budget for overtime. This decision is translated at your level into less overtime for the department and less income for the workers. Your people see this decision as it affects them—as a reduction in their potential earnings. If you and they have grown dependent on overtime or see it as necessary to current operations, your section may be in for some trouble. Your boss was in on the initial decision. He or she knows the reasons for it and the management objectives it was designed to achieve. For instance, a decision to reduce overtime expenses may conserve income, allow your company to price its line more competitively, and reduce overall expenses. Your boss is concerned with these matters because they affect him or her more directly than your problems do. The boss sees all these objectives as being logical and sound and supports them. Once the reasons behind a decision are known to you, you should support the decision as strongly as your boss does. Give what facts you can to your subordinates to soften the blow. Emphasize that the conservation of income may prevent layoffs and save jobs. You must be flexible enough to meet rapidly changing situations such as this. Add to this flexibility a readiness to adjust to situations as they are, not as you would like them to be.

YOUR BOSS'S EXPECTATIONS

Primarily, most middle managers expect their subordinate managers to be loyal followers. Your boss, like yourself, needs the respect and support of subordinates. He or she must be able to count on your willingness and ability to enforce company policies and standards. He or she is relying on you to carry out decisions with the proper attitude. You must not let him or her down. In the eyes of your subordinates, the boss's reputation is as important to them as your own. They have a right to believe that they have good leadership—that you and your boss consistently exercise good judg-

The same principles of supervision that you apply to your subordinates will be applied to you by your boss. Treating your boss with the same respect as you expect to be treated will help win your boss's confidence.

ment. Do not let any of your actions or remarks jeopardize your boss's reputation.

Your boss expects you to get along well with your peers and with the company's various staff specialists as well as with your subordinates. If you are able to resolve your disputes on your own, without arguments and displays of temper, you are demonstrating resourcefulness. By developing and maintaining a cooperative spirit, you open the channels through which aid and advice will flow. Initiative is an extremely important characteristic for any manager to possess. Are you the kind of manager who waits for orders or instructions before acting? Do you need something to be in writing before you implement a change? If you do, you lack this essential quality. We are not talking here about assuming anything: that is always a dangerous practice. But when you have the authority to act in a situation and you know what must be done, you must not be afraid to respond. Unless you are completely at a loss about what you should do, you should act. You will not always be right or pick the best method, but you will not appear paralyzed either. If you wish to make progress, you must be able to perceive what is needed and, when you have the power, see that the need is satisfied. Don't forget that besides your boss, your peers and the company's staff specialists stand ready to help.

Finally, your boss expects you to keep him or her informed. Share your knowledge about essential operations with your boss. Nothing can injure you quite as effectively as for the boss to be surprised—to find out about something secondhand. The boss hates surprises where you and your people are concerned. You can make your boss look awfully stupid if you fail in your duty to keep him or her abreast of developments. Share what information you have with the boss, without betraying any confidences.

WINNING YOUR BOSS'S CONFIDENCE

If you meet your superior's expectations, you are well on your way toward gaining his or her confidence. In addition, try to learn from your mistakes. Each error you make has a lesson or two for you. Study your errors to avoid repeating them. Whatever else you do that demonstrates an effort at self-development should be brought to your boss's attention. The courses you take in school and recent articles or books you have read that have been helpful in your work are all worthy topics of conversation with your boss.

Consider the following courses of action. See if you agree with the thousands before you who have tried them and found them to be of great benefit.

Finding a Better Way

Five magic words on methods improvement have served many supervisors and those aspiring to supervision well. All are related to kaizen and reengineering:

- Combine
- Eliminate
- Rearrange
- Reexamine
- Simplify

When you look at a plan, program, procedure, or practice with these words in mind, you have an essential tool for evaluating them. Nothing is as valuable on your personnel record as the initiation and discovery of a better way to do something. The time, effort, and money that can be saved are important, but the effect on your reputation and career is even more important. Just be certain that the idea is yours before you take credit for it. Where help was received, credit should be given to that individual.

As a manager, you should give methods improvement a high priority. No matter how smoothly an operation is running, there is usually room for improvement. Turn your attention to the costliest operations first. That is where you stand to realize the greatest savings. Then systematically work your way through the rest of your operations. Do not keep your successes to yourself. Share them with your peers and superiors. Others can profit from your innovations.

Keeping Your Promises

A can-do attitude is great if you really can do what you promise. Before making a promise, be as certain as possible of the resources at your disposal and the limits on your operations. If, in your best judgment, you have what it will take to get the job done, commit yourself and your people to the endeavor. It is better to be a little bold than to be too cautious. If circumstances change dramatically for reasons beyond your ability to foresee, let your boss know. He or she will understand, and adjustments can be made. If you should have known about or suspected the changes, your reputation will suffer. Try to avoid going out on a limb that is too weak to support you.

Speaking Positively or Not at All

Whatever the topic of conversation and wherever it takes place, be sure that what you say is positive. There is a temptation to engage in gripe sessions and to put the other person down. Such displays are clearly negative and completely without redeeming qualities. If your gripe is justified, reveal it to those who can act on it. If the person you wish to criticize is a subordinate, approach him or her in private, and keep it constructive. No one, especially not a boss, benefits from associating with a person who is always negative. Few activities are as futile as gripe sessions. Names are dropped and things are said that all too often you later wish you could retract or forget. If you have nothing positive to say, you are better off saying nothing.

Constructive criticism, whether of an individual or of an idea, is not negative, and you are perfectly right to engage in it as long as the environment is correct. When an argument is put forth that favors a course of action and you see a disadvantage to it, you must air that point if the advocate of the proposal fails to do so. When the boss or anyone else puts forth a proposal in your presence, he or she wants your honest reactions. Loyalty demands that you do your best to prevent a person from making a mistake or suffering some humiliation when and where you can. Do not refuse a subordinate, a peer, or a superior such aid when you have it to give.

Taking a Position

You are a thinking human being and a member of management's team. But you must be a contributing member—one who carries his or her own weight and stands ready to help teammates. If you want the respect of others, you must have convictions. These convictions or beliefs tell others what you are and where you stand. Your character and principles are demonstrated when you take a stand on an issue. Before you do, however, make sure that you think it through and anticipate the possible drawbacks, as well as your supportive arguments. Then prepare your defense.

When you take your stand and find it untenable, do not be reluctant to yield to superior forces. Bullheadedness is not a quality that endears you to anyone. Be reasonable. You want to be thought of as a person of principle—as a man or woman who thinks things through and fights for what he or she believes in. The corollary to this is equally important: You must oppose things you believe to be improper or wrong.

Involving Your Boss in Major Decisions

Just as you stand ready to help a subordinate or peer with a problem, your boss stands ready to help you. The boss's time is too valuable to be expended on trivial matters, so reserve your requests for assistance to the critical items.

Most middle managers have regular meetings for both individual and group discussions. Others maintain an open-door policy, relying on their subordinates to bring in their problems. You should know and adjust to your boss's approach.

When you have a problem with which you have wrestled but to which you have no certain solution, set up a meeting with your boss, explaining in advance what you wish to discuss. Assemble your research and facts. Construct a list of alternatives you have considered. Then be sure to report to the meeting on time.

During the meeting, follow the advice of the catchword KISS (Keep it Short and Simple). You want the maximum benefits from the shortest possible time. What the boss wants most is to see that you have considered the matter and given it your best effort. He or she will not make your decisions for you, except when you have reached an impasse. Even then, most bosses offer only suggestions and direct your attention to additional items you may have overlooked. That method may be a little frustrating, but the learning experience is invaluable to you.

Each contact you have with your boss should be as professional as you can make it. Be yourself, but be prepared.

OBTAINING SOME OF YOUR BOSS'S AUTHORITY

It is your job to know yourself well and to seek self-improvement. It is your task through human relations to know and approach your subordinates, peers, and superiors as individuals. Fundamental to your relationship with your boss is getting to know him or her well—his or her needs and ambitions, strengths and weaknesses. You can learn from a strong boss. You may be able to help a weak one. The boss, like you, is probably looking for subordinates who can attend to time-consuming details and assume routine tasks. By delegating them, the boss creates time for more important tasks—the ones he or she alone must tackle. Your boss is also gaining time to devote to taking on a larger portion of his or her boss's duties, thus training for advancement. So it goes from supervisor to chief executive. Through delegation, each trains another. While providing for a subordinate's growth and progress, the boss helps ensure his or her own advancement. A manager who has not trained a subordinate to move up may be unable to move up. The manager who will not grow or help others grow is generally not a manager for long. His or her lack of mobility acts as a ceiling on those with ambition and ability below. A manager's failure to grow may mean the company's loss of promising young talent.

When you have proved to your boss that you are worthy of his or her respect and confidence, the delegation of duties to you will begin. You will get details and routine tasks at first. If you handle them well, you can look forward to increased responsibilities, with the challenges they represent. The increased duties may become yours permanently, enlarging your job description and serving as justification for increases in pay and status, and a possible change in title.

If your boss is reluctant to delegate, you should urge him or her to do so. First, you must free yourself from your details and routines in order to make time available. Then go to your boss with time on your hands and a plea for additional duties. If you have your eye on specifics, let the boss know what they are and why you feel qualified to take them. Here again, take a stand; then sell it and defend it. You may not be successful at first; old habits die slowly. But you have planted a seed, and a good manager will not let it die. Your boss will be disturbed by your idleness and impressed by your initiative. If you persist, the boss will respond.

Do not assume any of your boss's duties or anyone else's without consultation. There is a tendency for a bright and eager young supervisor to spot something that needs doing and do it. This is fine as long as you have jurisdiction over the matter. But when the duty you perform belongs to another, you are guilty of grabbing power from that person. This will be interpreted to your disadvantage. After all, how would you react if a peer or subordinate took on your responsibilities without first consulting you?

Do not get yourself into a position where your boss becomes too dependent on you. If the boss views you as indispensable, he or she may consciously or unconsciously restrict your chances for advancement. He or she will fear losing you, through promotion or transfer, and the corresponding upsetting of the status quo this may represent. Your best defense is to train a successor. When the opportunity arises and the time is right, you can then point with pride and confidence to that subordinate as your logical and well-trained successor.

YOUR EXPECTATIONS
OF YOUR BOSS

Besides mutual respect and trust—which are prerequisites for a working relationship—your boss should provide you with the following:

- Constructive criticism
- Fair evaluations
- Essential guidance
- A constant flow of necessary information
- Recognition for jobs well done
- An appropriate management style
- Training for growth and development
- A good example

Where one or more of these items is lacking, look first at yourself for the cause. Something in you or your performance may be missing. If you do not give respect or loyalty, you have none coming. If you do not respond well to criticism, you may not receive it. If you do not think your boss's evaluations of your performance are fair, why did you accept them without protest? You may not be receiving guidance because you have not asked for any. Is the guidance you seek really essential? If you do not get information, maybe it is because you cannot keep a secret or have no need to know. If no recognition is due you, you will not receive any. Do not expect recognition for simply doing your job. If your boss's management style with you is not to your liking, have you discussed it with him or her? If your boss will not delegate, have you enough time to take on the additional duties? Have you asked your boss for more things to do? You may find, as many management students do, that the more you learn about management principles and practices, the more critical of people in authority you become. If this is happening to you, do not be alarmed. You are experiencing what all children growing up experience: the realization that the adult who occupies a position of trust and authority is really just a human being. As children realize this, they must search for a new understanding and relationship with their parents. No longer are children content with blind obedience; no longer can they accept instructions or orders without knowing the reasons behind them. They are becoming critical and questioning and are now armed with standards on which to base their questions and criticism.

The beauty of all this is that you will now know when something goes wrong and why. How you react to your new knowledge and act on it determines whether you remain always a freshman or become a senior and graduate. Knowledge is power, and power needs controls on its use. As you are maturing, you will discover flaws where you saw none before. An inadequate manager often provides a better learning situation than a real professional does. When things run smoothly, you often do not know why they do. But when things go sour, you have a chance to ask and determine why.

That goes for your mistakes as well as for those of the boss. Your analysis of your boss's shortcomings can prevent them from plaguing your own efforts. Most of the cases in this book (and in every other management text) portray managers with flaws and inadequacies for just this reason.

According to a recent study by professors and psychologists Robert Hogan and John Morrison of the University of Tulsa, the average subordinate thinks that managers he or she works with are competent between 60 and 75 percent of the time. In another study done by Personnel Decisions Inc. of Minneapolis, a human resource consulting firm, 56 percent of the 800 people surveyed thought their bosses were "top-notch"; only 8 percent thought that their bosses treated them unfairly (Winokur, 1991).

Exhibit 8.5 is a short evaluation form you can use to rate your boss. Only you can decide if you want to keep the results of your rating confidential.

EXHIBIT 8.5
Rate your boss. Photocopy this evaluation form and see how you feel toward your present boss.

1. I think my boss really cares about me and my progress because:

   _____

   _____

   _____

2. I think my boss is (pick one or more)
   a. hardworking ____ b. compassionate ____
   c. a good role model ____ d. a good decision maker ____
   e. a good planner ____ f. fair ____ g. a team player ____
   h. competent ____ i. enthusiastic ____
   j. other (please specify)

   _____

3. The thing that really bugs me about my boss is:

   _____

   _____

4. The one thing I need from my boss and am *not* getting is:

   _____

5. If I were in my boss's job, I would do the following things differently:

   _____

   _____

6. The lessons I have learned by studying my boss are:

   _____

   _____

   _____

   Now, what are you going to do about all this?

Instant Replay

1. Human relations involves the development and maintenance of sound on-the-job relationships with subordinates, peers, and superiors.
2. The wide range of ages, backgrounds, and experiences found in workers makes the job of building sound human relations difficult for both workers and their supervisors.
3. Supervisors must relate to people at work by perceiving them as they perceive themselves—as members of diverse groups that influence their attitudes and behaviors.
4. Building human relationships requires you to play four fundamental roles: educator, counselor, judge, and spokesperson.
5. As an educator, you share your knowledge, skills, and experiences with others.
6. As a counselor, you provide advice, service, direction, and a sympathetic and empathetic ear.
7. As a judge, you evaluate the performance of subordinates, enforce company and departmental rules and standards, settle disputes, and dispense justice.
8. You win your peers' respect by lending a hand when and where you can and by being a friend.
9. As a spokesperson, you represent subordinates to higher authority and management to subordinates.
10. You win your boss's respect and confidence by meeting his or her expectations of you and by playing your roles as they are prescribed.
11. You learn your boss's job by creating time in which to execute some of the boss's tasks. Just as you train your replacement through delegation of your formal authority, so too does your boss train his or her replacement.

Questions for Class Discussion

1. Can you define this chapter's key terms?
2. What are the six major purposes of human relations?
3. How should a supervisor play the four basic human relations roles with subordinates? With peers?
4. How is a middle manager's job different from a supervisor's?
5. What is involved in creating and maintaining a good working relationship with one's boss?

Incident

Purpose: To help you identify cultural differences between yourself and others.

Your Task: For each aspect of culture listed, record a summary statement for yourself and another person at work or in your class who you know well and is different from you in some major way. Then discuss the similarities and differences that exist with the other person.

Aspect of Culture	You	Another
1. Importance of being on time		
2. Command of the English language		
3. Openness to meeting new people		
4. Conversational style		
5. Age		
6. Educational background		
7. Work ethic		
8. View on importance of family		
9. Gender		
10. Favorite foods		
11. Willingness to conform		
12. Respect for others		

Looking Ahead

CASE PROBLEM 8.1

As the last of his subordinates said goodnight, Mike took pencil in hand and began to think about next week. He started with a mental review of the completed projects and then turned his attention to the unfinished ones. Starting with Monday's column, he began to block out time for unfinished business. After about thirty minutes of intense thought and a careful review of his notes, Mike grabbed his coat, turned off the shop lights, and left for the day. Here is what his notes showed for Monday (all first names mentioned belong to Mike's subordinates; all surnames belong to other managers):

Monday

1. Work on Henry's personal problem—see at 8 A.M.
2. Check on Suzie's progress with the backlog of shipments. 8:30 to 9:00 A.M.
3. Talk with the old man about late data—got to get the info from him faster to meet reporting deadlines. 9:30 to 9:45 A.M.
4. Meet with Wilson to coordinate enforcement of safety procedures—he isn't enforcing—setting a bad example. 10 to 11 A.M.
5. Meet Harry for six-month review—notes in file. 11 to 11:30 A.M.
6. Lunch with Perkins from Personnel—new job description for Machinist 2 classification. 11:45 to 12:30 P.M.
7. Update shipping reports 12:30 to 1:30 P.M.
8. Introduce Billy to new maintenance procedures on no. 14—maintenance due by Tuesday P.M. 1:45 to 2:15 P.M.
9. Check with payroll about Friday overtime. 2:15 to 3:00 P.M.

10. Place orders for restocking—do with Al and Bert so they know procedures. Pick one for the task next week. 3:00 to 5:00 P.M.

Questions

1. Which of the items on Mike's list affect his relations with subordinates? Which role will he likely play with each subordinate?
2. Which of the items on Mike's list affect his relations with peers? Which human relations role will he likely play with each peer mentioned?
3. Which of the items relate to staff specialists?
4. Which of the items relate to Mike's relations with his boss?

CASE PROBLEM 8.2

People Problems

The new employee in finance is not working out. "She doesn't know the computers or the programs," said Trish, project accountant. "I don't know what you people are doing down there in personnel but you should not have hired Cathy Burstun."

"Calm down," replied Mark. "We sent you Cathy because she met all the key points on the job specification you gave me. Now you seem to be saying that she needed to have qualities you didn't mention before."

"Mark, you know that we use the IBM PCs in the office, so why didn't you check her out on them?"

"Trish, your job description does not specify any brand of computer and the job specs call for—and I quote—'a familiarity with financial operations on computer'—unquote."

"What's the date on that specification?" asked Trish.

"It's dated March 1994."

"Well, there's the problem. You have been working off an obsolete document. It should specify IBMs. We have had them for nearly a year."

"Trish, I'm not a mind reader. The specification you sent should have shown the IBM on it, and the program knowledge should have been spelled out in detail. Can't you make do with Cathy? She's bright, has financial experience, and with a little training she should do fine."

"Hey, Mark, I haven't the time or the budget to teach her how to use a computer and its software. We have been handicapped without Cathy, and we are worse off now with her. She can't do anything we need done if she can't perform on the computer."

"Do you want me to try for a replacement? If you do, get ready for another two or three month's delay. She was the best of twenty people we looked at."

"I don't know what else we can do. I guess you had better start right now. I'll give Cathy what work I can until you find me what we need."

Cathy arrived at Trish's office about noon and pulled up a chair next to Trish's desk. "I've scheduled your physical for Saturday the 19th at 10 A.M. at Wilson General Hospital. Can you be there then?" asked Trish.

"That will be all right. Is that all?" asked Cathy.

"No, Cathy. It is not all. I feel it is my duty to warn you that we are looking for a replacement for you as we speak. As we found out yesterday, you know your way around computer printouts, but you do not know how to use a computer or our financial programs. We have neither the time nor the budget to get you trained. Therefore, unless you get yourself trained in a hurry, all we can do is to give you some basics like filing and proofing to fill your day. I'm not sure about your pay yet. I've asked Mr. Tyson to see if we can pay you the same rate."

Cathy looked shocked. She didn't know what to say at first. Finally, she collected her thoughts and spoke. "I do know my way around a computer. I worked with Apples in school and on my first job. I think with time and a little practice, I could master the IBM and learn its programs. Are you telling me that I'll have to do this alone and at possibly a lower rate of pay?"

"I don't know anything about Apple computers, but I do know that you can't get paid for work you can't do," Trish said. "Your job requires the use of the IBM PC, and you are unable to use it."

"Fine. Now I know where I stand. Is there any hope that I can stay on if I manage to learn the computer and its operations before you find a replacement?"

Trish thought a moment. "You are free to try to learn, but I won't be able to let you try on company time. If personnel finds someone before you're able to perform, I'll have to go with a new person."

Questions

1. How has Trish handled her four human relations roles with Cathy?
2. How has Mark handled his working relationship with Trish?
3. Do you think it was wise to do what Trish is planning to do? Why?

Notes

American Hotel & Motel Association, Educational Institute. Training and Coaching Techniques. East Lansing, Mich., 1976, 75.

Blank, Renee, and Slipp, Sandra. *Voices of Diversity* (New York: Amacom, 1994), 192–195.

Holt, David H. *Management Principles and Practices,* 3 ed. (Englewood Cliffs, N.J., 1993), 497.

Imberman, A. A. "Why Are Most Foreman Training Courses a Failure?" *Bedding* vol. 96, no. 6, July 1969, 40–41.

Loden, Marilyn, and Rosener, Judy B. *Workforce America!* (Homewood, Ill.: Business One Irwin, 1991), 62.

Peters, Tom. "Tapping Worker Curiosity Can Electrify Company," *Chicago Tribune,* October 26, 1992, sect. 4, 6.

Randle, Wilma. "Firms Coming Face-to-Face with Diversity Issues," *Chicago Tribune,* January 12, 1993, sect. 3, 1, 5.

Richman, Louis S. "The New Work Force Builds Itself," *Fortune,* June 27, 1994, 70.

Treece, James B. "Breaking the Chains of Command," *Business Week, Special 1994 Bonus Issue,* "The Information Revolution," 112–113.

Wellins, Richard S., Byham, William C., and Wilson, Jeanne M. *Empowered Teams* (San Francisco: Jossey-Bass, 1991), 175.

Wheatley, Margaret J. "Quantum Management," *Working Woman,* October 1994, 16–17.

Winokur, L. A. "Well, They Say There Are Lies, Damn Lies, Statistics and Bosses," *The Wall Street Journal,* January 10, 1991, B1.

Suggested Readings

Apgar, Toni, ed. *Mastering Office Politics.* New York: National Institute of Business Management, Inc., 1988.

DuBrin, Andrew. *Winning Office Politics.* Englewood Cliffs, N.J.: Prentice Hall, 1990.

Fader, Shirley Sloan. "What Your Boss Wants You to Know." *Business Week Careers* (October 1985): 43–45.

Fournies, Ferdinand. *Coaching for Improved Work Performance.* Blue Ridge Summit, Pa.: Liberty Hall Press, 1987.

Kennedy, Marilyn Moats. "How to Manage Your New Boss." *Business Week Careers* (April 1987): 93–95.

Loden, Marilyn, and Rosener, Judy B. *Workforce America!* Homewood, Ill.: Business One Irwin, 1991.

Pacetta, Frank. *Don't Fire Them, Fire Them Up.* New York: Simon & Schuster, 1994.

Quick, Thomas L. *Inspiring People at Work.* New York: Executive Enterprises, 1986.

Robbins, Stephen P. *Training in Interpersonal Skills.* Englewood Cliffs, N.J.: Prentice Hall, 1989.

Schaffer, Robert H. "Demand Better Results—and Get Them." *Harvard Business Review* (March–April 1991): 142–149.

Supervising Groups

OBJECTIVES

After reading and discussing this chapter, you should be able to do the following:

1. Define this chapter's key terms.

2. List and briefly explain the forces that shape a group's personality.

3. Describe the duties of a meeting's chairperson before, during, and after a group problem-solving session.

4. Describe the duties of a group's members before, during, and after a group problem-solving session.

5. List and briefly describe the group-serving and self-serving roles played by members of a group problem-solving session.

6. List the three types of cliques, and give an example of each.

7. Describe how group behavior can be affected by internal group competition—what happens to the winning side and what happens to the losing side.

INTRODUCTION

Each individual has a personality that undergoes constant change through exposure to his or her environment and to new experiences. When two or more dynamic people interact with one another, the process of change in each of them is accelerated. The coming together of two or more people for the purpose of achieving or obtaining some mutual goal or benefit is the basis for the formation of what we call a group.

More specifically, a **group** is two or more people who are consciously aware of one another, who consider themselves to be a functioning unit, and who share in a quest to achieve one or more goals or obtain some common benefit. When we say that the members are aware of each other, we mean that they know something about each other, are clear about why they are together, and recognize the need to cooperate.

Two basic kinds of groups exist in organizations: the formal group that is created by management and the informal group created by the members of the organization. This latter type of group is formed primarily for social purposes and allows its members to congregate with others who share their values and interests. As a supervisor, you must learn to work with both kinds of groups.

Throughout U.S. factories and offices, self-managing work teams have been created and are having a tremendous impact on the quality and productivity of their organizations' output. The value of such teams is flexibility for management and job enrichment and motivation to excel for team members. The role of the supervisor is changing because of the team structure. Supervisors may be elected members of such teams, serving on a rotating basis, or they may become more like coaches than traditional managers. This chapter focuses on how groups form and how you can effectively manage and get along with groups at work.

group
two or more people who are consciously aware of one another, who consider themselves to be a functioning unit, and who share in a quest for common goals or benefits

COLLECTIVE ENTREPRENEURSHIP

Modern companies that have been able to compete successfully in today's economic environment both at home and abroad have one major thing in common: They have managed to create a team spirit in their employees that translates into high levels of innovation, adaptability, and financial success. Employees at all levels come to believe in common goals and in united efforts to achieve them. Talent and energy then are pooled into what Secretary of Labor Robert Reich has labeled collective entrepreneurship (Reich, 1987).

The term *collective entrepreneurship* is derived from the fact that the companies using it no longer focus on one person—the founder or the top executive—as a guiding light. Employees feel a real partnership and commitment to the company's future because they feel that they are the company. Rewards and praise flow to teams of employees, not to individuals. When hard times arrive, burdens are shared by all the employees, and great efforts are made to keep employees on, not to lay them off. Technology is looked on as a means to aid workers and managers, to cut routine, and to give them more opportunities to use their imaginations and insights for their company (Reich, 1987).

For workers, collective entrepreneurship means "accepting flexible job classifications and work rules; agreeing to wage rates linked to profits and productivity improvements; and generally taking greater responsibility for the soundness and efficiency of the enterprise" (Reich, 1987). For managers, collective entrepreneurship means "continually retraining workers for more complex tasks; automating in ways that cut routine tasks and enhance worker flexibility and creativity; diffusing responsibility for innovation; taking seriously labor's concern for job security; and giving workers a stake in improved productivity through profit linked bonuses and stock plans" (Reich, 1987).

> Collective entrepreneurship relies heavily on integrating individual skills into groups:
>
> Over time, as group members work through various problems and approaches, they learn about each others' abilities. They learn how they can help one another perform better, what each can contribute to a particular project, how they can best take advantage of one another's experience.... Coordination and communication replace command and control. Consequently, there are few middle-level managers and only modest differences in status and income of senior managers and junior employees (Reich, 1987).

THE PERSONALITY
OF GROUPS

A group, like the people who compose it, has a personality as unique and subject to change as any individual's. The group's personality is partially a composite of the personalities of its members. We say "partially" because a group is always something more than the sum of its parts. That something more comes about because of the interaction of group members, which creates energy and qualities that may not be possessed by any of the group members or by a majority of them. An example would be a basic training group in the military. Individually, its members may not have the desire or the will to excel and may not know their capabilities. But in group situations, the pressure to conform and the feeling that "If they can do it, so can I" will dominate. If twenty trainees were dispatched on a twenty-mile hike, one at a time at intervals of ten minutes, very few (if any)

All groups—even formal ones—have personalities. Group personalities are the sum of individual personalities, plus the synergy that is created when those individuals work together.

would complete the march. When all twenty embark on the hike together, all will finish, even if their buddies have to carry some of them. Combat units often exhibit tremendous courage that individuals would not show without the support of and the commitment to their comrades.

There is a term for this two-plus-two-equals-five-or-more quality that many groups seem to possess: **synergy** (pronounced sin-er-jee). Common table salt is a chemical combination of two poisons—sodium and chlorine. Alone they are dangerous; together they are beneficial and take on properties that neither has alone. It has been common knowledge for about a century that two horses can pull more than the combined loads each is capable of pulling alone. A team of twelve horses can pull more than twice the load that a team of eight can pull.

The term *synergy* applies to any combined operation or action; thus it can be either positive or negative. Satisfied groups or group members can exhibit greater positive action or forces for change than the individuals within the group could do on their own.

Syntality

Syntality is used by social scientists to mean "for a group what personality does for the individual" (Uris, 1964). Groups develop a syntality through their exposure to the interactions of their members, through the pressures exerted on them, through their experiences, through their successes and failures, and through their commitments to causes or goals. Groups, like people, can be lazy, hostile, or enthusiastic. As a group leader,

synergy

cooperative action or force of two or more elements pulling together that yields a result greater than the sum of the results that could be achieved separately by the elements

syntality

a group's "personality"–what makes it unique

"There is an inherent conflict in considering workforce diversity because of the need to see each worker both as an individual and as a member of a group.... A key to supervising an individual worker effectively is knowing as much as possible about that worker.... [A] worker's membership in a particular group, that is, his or her group identity...is simply another factor—and often an important one—in helping a manager understand an individual employee's behavior and perspective."

Stereotypes exist for both individuals and groups. Care must be taken to avoid identifying an individual through any stereotype based simply on one or more aspects of his or her background, heritage, or group membership. "When group identity is recognized, it is often in terms of stereotypes—categorizing individuals *only* by their group identity—rather than seeing group identity as one part of a complex individual."

Just as people change over time, so, too, do the groups to which they belong. What may have been true about a certain group last year is not true today. Whereas some group members exhibit many of their group's characteristics, others exhibit only a few. Some members may identify strongly with their groups; others may have only a casual affiliation. And most members of any group belong to and identify with other groups, further compounding their uniqueness and complexity.

The only safe harbor for any of us is to try to get to know each person by their walk and talk. The answers to why they walk and talk as they do are found in part in their experiences, inherited traits, and group memberships. Therefore, these become valuable reference points for both understanding each other and for building various human relationships.

Source: Blank, Renee, and Slipp, Sandra. *Voices of Diversity* (New York: Amacom, 1994), 6–11.

you need to assess your group's syntality in order to determine its strengths and weaknesses; then you must provide the kind of leadership it needs at any given time.

One question you can use to assess your group's syntality is "To what extent does the group work with me to achieve objectives?" A hostile group is one that actively or passively opposes your efforts to achieve group goals. "A lazy group is one with insufficient motivation and lack of drive in assisting you to reach designated goals. An enthusiastic group is one that shares your interest in achieving group goals" (Uris, 1964).

If your group is not enthusiastic, ask yourself what it needs or lacks. What is causing it to be lazy or hostile? Possible answers include the following:

- Inexperience—the group is too new, the members unfamiliar with procedures and with each other
- Lack of training—group members lack the individual expertise and skill levels required for solid performance
- Lack of discipline—you lack the power or authority to keep them on target or in line
- Lack of proper guidelines—the goals are unclear, and the authority limits are not understood
- Existence of a problem member—one or more persons in the group tend to be disruptive, uncooperative, at odds with the others
- Existence of a problem group leader—the leader seems to be reluctant to let the group perform, lacks skills needed to guide them, or feels uncomfortable in the role of coach and facilitator of the group

Once you have identified what is missing, you can begin to supply it. Keep in mind that people who are being asked to work in groups for the first time will have the most difficulties—supervisors included. Moreover, "the behavior of individuals is affected by the character of the group to which they belong" (Uris, 1964).

Some groups are quite strong and forceful, achieving what they set out to achieve. Other groups may be weak, lacking the leadership or the will to achieve. The syntality the group exhibits is most directly influenced by the personalities of the stronger members. The strongest member will usually emerge as the leader of the group, or at least as its spokesperson. The strength we mention here is primarily intellectual, and the force is primarily that of each person's will and drive.

It is just as difficult to comprehend a group's syntality as it is to understand an individual's personality. Since we all work in groups of one kind or another, we need to study the behavior of people in groups and the effects of group membership on both ourselves and those we supervise. Attempting to observe and analyze these effects is quite properly a manager's job. You must begin to see your people as individuals who are also group members and therefore subjected to forces that accelerate change in them. This makes your task of knowing each one a little more difficult.

As you might imagine, there are countless groups of many different sizes and descriptions. For our purpose, however, we shall classify groups as either formal or informal.

DEFINING FORMAL GROUPS

formal group
two or more people who come together by management decision to achieve specific goals

A **formal group** may be defined as two or more people who come together by management decision to achieve specific goals. All formal groups are results of the organizing function, through which people are assigned to different tasks and task units. In most cases, we are placed in formal groups by some higher authority outside or at the head of the group. Your company, your department, your shift, and the various management committees are but a few of the many formal groups you encounter each day.

Any individual, especially a manager, may belong to more than one formal group simultaneously. For instance, you are an employee of a company, working in a particular functional division and within a specific department. You are a member, therefore, of at least three formal groups. If you serve on a committee, you belong to a fourth formal group.

Formal groups may be temporary or permanent. An ad hoc committee—one set up to solve a particular problem and dissolved when the solution is determined—is an example of a temporary formal group. Most formal groups in your company are permanent although even whole divisions can be dissolved or merged into others on occasion, as the needs of the business may dictate. Formal groups may be true teams if they consist of "...a small number of people with complementary skills who are committed to a common purpose, performance goals, and approach for which they hold themselves mutually responsible" (Katzenbach and Smith, 1993). "The teams most popular today are of two broad types: work teams, which include high-performance or self-managed teams, and special-purpose problem-solving teams.... While problem-solving teams are temporary, work teams, used by about two-thirds of U.S. companies, tend to be permanent" (Dumaine, "The," 1994).

Every formal group has a leader. The heads of most formal groups are managers who have been installed for just that purpose. The leader of a self-managed team may be elected or appointed by the team's members, and leadership may be rotated among the members over time. Either way, the formal group's leader has varying degrees of formal authority at his or her disposal. Exhibit 9.1 shows a continuum of empowerment. The higher a team climbs on the continuum, the more autonomy it has. Management teams usually have the highest degree of empowerment.

Management Teams

Teams of managers may be permanent or temporary. They usually (Kizilos and Heinisch, 1986):

> make decisions by consensus in areas affecting the entire operation—resource allocation, funds distribution, facility design, budgeting, hiring—subject to the approval of top management.... [A] team effort yields better decisions, protects...from arbitrary or careless actions, and, above all, strengthens team-members' commitment to [the company's] goals.... [A] boss cannot obtain by decree the creativity, initiative, and dedication needed to do a job properly; such allegiance can come freely only from people who have a sense of "ownership" [entrepreneurship] of the organization's goals.

As a manager, you will serve on several teams. The fact that you are a manager makes you a member of management, which is a team of deci-

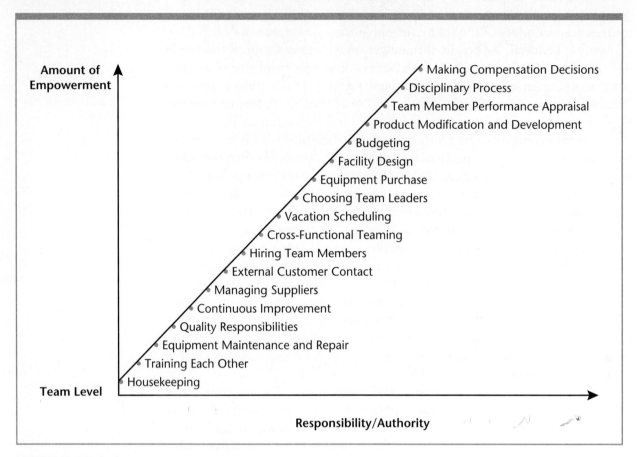

EXHIBIT 9.1

A continuum of empowerment for groups and teams.

Source: Adapted from Wellins, Richard S., Byham, William C., and Wilson, Jeanne M. *Empowered Teams* (San Francisco: Jossey-Bass, 1991), 26.

sion makers. As a traditional supervisor, you head a formal unit within a formal organization—your work group. When you serve on a committee, head a true team, or act as a team facilitator, you are a linking pin, connecting the group with others. You benefit from such connections by gaining a better understanding of others in your organization—how they interact and are interdependent.

The automotive parts supplier A. O. Smith Corporation has created teams that give its seven unions a voice in planning and decision making. It has problem-solving committees on the shop floor, plantwide advisory committees with union representatives, and union officials on the top management strategic planning committee (Hoerr, 1989). Most major corporations have product design teams that include engineers, market researchers, production managers, and representatives from regular suppliers to ensure from the very beginning that a product is created that the consumer wants and that can be built efficiently and with quality. Another kind of management team is the crisis team—a group of managers from various departments that can act swiftly in the face of any crisis the company may face. When not actually dealing with a crisis, it is planning to do so.

According to experts, "the task of setting up work teams among employees should begin at the top" (McKee, 1992). Several preconditions must exist in organizations before they attempt to initiate teams. The first is the expertise needed to form teams in the organization and the willingness to share problem solving with team members. The second relates to the ways in which things get done—procedures, processes, traditions, and habits—and how difficult these will be to change. A third relates to making the commitment in money and time to prepare people for team roles and to continue training efforts. Typical subjects of team training include decision making, how to run meetings, communication skills, handling conflict and change, using quality tools (benchmarking, statistical controls, and scoreboarding), evaluating team and team members' performances, and reengineering concepts and principles. Before GM's Saturn Division produced any cars, "workers got 300 to 700 hours of schooling, covering basic skills such as conflict management and problem solving. That has been followed by ongoing training in specific areas, such as interviewing techniques" (Woodruff, 1993). During 1992, Saturn employees spent over ninety hours—about 5 percent of their time on the job—in training. This chapter's Supervising Teams feature contains a synopsis of Saturn's teams.

Worker Teams

Ideally, you should be concerned with molding your people into a team or group of teams that feels an owner's concern for the organization and its goals. If you have the permission or the order of higher authority to create and manage work teams, you will need a few personal characteristics and skills. A true team leader or facilitator is much more than the head of a group of workers.

Team leaders must have personalities that are both mature and secure. Maturity is required so that emotions can be controlled and responses given by an adult to those who may be less mature. Security is required so that the leader does not fear sharing management authority with others and does not fear being challenged, maybe for the first time. Managers who are new to team leadership have much teaching and learning to do. They must master a participative style of supervision, be willing to teach problem solving and decision making to team members, be proficient in interpersonal skills, and be able to take the time necessary to deal with time delays and possible waste of resources that group approaches often involve. The qualities of patience, tact, and commitment to and enthusiasm for the process are essential. "Typically, a team leader still spends time actually performing various production or service tasks....

SUPERVISING TEAMS

According to research published by *Nation's Business*, several kinds of teams are being created in small and midsized businesses. "Employee teams are managing entire divisions in some companies; in smaller businesses, they are taking on responsibility for everything from housekeeping to product development, from employee discipline to compensation." The significant types of teams that business consultants and owners say can increase quality and productivity in companies are:

Task forces. Temporary committees are created to examine a particular problem or to institute change. At GM's Saturn Division, the fifteen-member machine maintenance team set out to decide the least expensive way to sharpen cutting tools used on transmission parts. They decided that an outside source would be best, thus taking the work away from their own in-house operations. (At Saturn, foremen are called work unit module advisors and are selected through the combined efforts of the division's management and union leaders. Foremen are elected by workers at other GM facilities.)

Quality assurance teams. Quality groups are created to make certain that a company's products and services meet the needs and expectations of customers. A quality assurance group may ask its dealers, clients, and suppliers to serve as group members or consultants; its members maintain constant contact with these people. At Saturn, Annette Ellerby helps her fifteen-member team check electrical systems on the company's subcompacts.

Cross-functional teams. Such teams may be made up of members from various functional groups—marketing, production, finance, and so on—or they may cross-train their members in each other's areas of expertise. Cross-functional teams regularly investigate problems and processes that affect two or more functional areas and work to find mutually agreeable solutions. Their membership and focus keeps shifting as issues are resolved and new ones emerge. At Saturn, "each team regulates personal calls on its phones. Some use an honor system, while others make team members use a personal credit card."

Product-development teams. Product-development teams are a particular kind of cross-functional team. They bring together all functional areas involved with creating new products—engineering, production, research and development, marketing, purchasing, and so on—along with key representatives from suppliers. Saturn uses such teams to create its high-quality, fast-selling models. Demand for its cars is currently outpacing supply.

Sources: McKee, Bradford. "Turn Your Workers into a Team," *Nation's Business,* July 1992, 36–38; Woodruff, David. "Where Employees Are Management," *Business Week, 1992 Bonus Issue,* January 19, 1993, 66.

Setting up your subordinates into worker teams presents new challenges to supervisors, such as mastering the participative style of supervision.

Often the team leader serves as a spokesperson for the team, coordinates team activities with other departments or teams, and devotes time to training new team members" (Wellins, Byham, and Wilson, 1991). Moreover, you need to create an environment in which team members grow and develop by actively participating in the execution of essential tasks. In addition to working out the internal dynamics of your team, you must manage relations between your team and other company units (Klein and Posey, 1986).

Team facilitators (sometimes called team advisors or group leaders) "...frequently play a coordinating and facilitating role. They help teams communicate with one another and serve as a conduit for information that flows from teams to other organizational departments and from these back to the teams" (Wellins, Byham, and Wilson, 1991). See Exhibit 9.2 for a typical day in the life of a team facilitator. As leader of teams, you must learn that your major tasks are to help each team define its goals, set the limits for each team, help obtain the resources each team requires, and mold a cooperative and committed spirit in each team. The team facilitator is a blend of traditional supervisory and middle management responsibilities. Both team leaders and team facilitators often have wide spans of control—numbers of subordinates. "For example, AT&T Operator Services in Richmond, Virginia, moved from a span of control of one leader for each twelve members to one leader for each seventy-two members. As teams mature, it is not uncommon for six or more teams to report to a single group leader" (Wellins, Byham, and Wilson, 1991).

At ABC Rail Products Corporation's Chicago Heights factory, losses were mounting. Managers and union workers were not cooperating. One

EXHIBIT 9.2

A day in the life of a team facilitator.

Source: Wellins, Richard S., Byham, William C., and Wilson, Jeanne M. *Empowered Teams* (San Francisco: Jossey-Bass, 1991), 39.

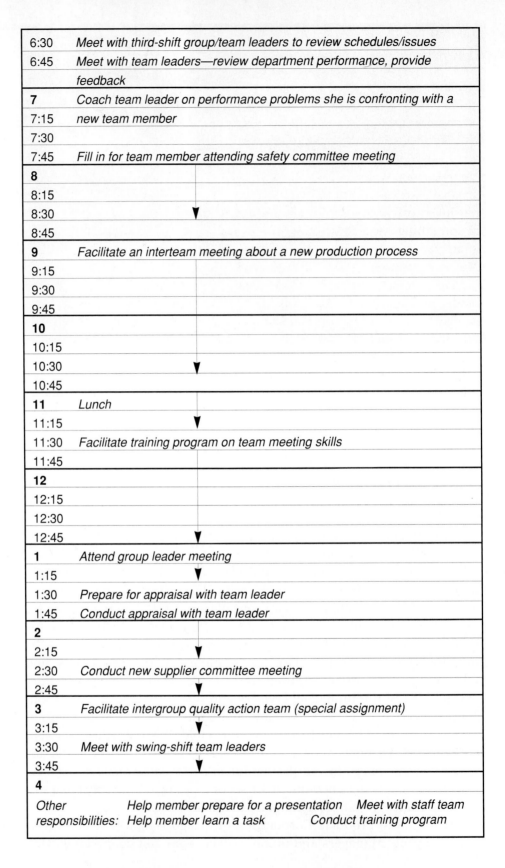

6:30	Meet with third-shift group/team leaders to review schedules/issues
6:45	Meet with team leaders—review department performance, provide feedback
7	Coach team leader on performance problems she is confronting with a
7:15	new team member
7:30	
7:45	Fill in for team member attending safety committee meeting
8	
8:15	
8:30	
8:45	
9	Facilitate an interteam meeting about a new production process
9:15	
9:30	
9:45	
10	
10:15	
10:30	
10:45	
11	Lunch
11:15	
11:30	Facilitate training program on team meeting skills
11:45	
12	
12:15	
12:30	
12:45	
1	Attend group leader meeting
1:15	
1:30	Prepare for appraisal with team leader
1:45	Conduct appraisal with team leader
2	
2:15	
2:30	Conduct new supplier committee meeting
2:45	
3	Facilitate intergroup quality action team (special assignment)
3:15	
3:30	Meet with swing-shift team leaders
3:45	
4	
Other responsibilities:	Help member prepare for a presentation Meet with staff team Help member learn a task Conduct training program

hundred twenty-five jobs were on the line when the chairman and CEO, Donald W. Grinter, met with union leaders: either the two would work to save the plant or it would be closed. Management shared financial data, and union representatives and plant managers met to discuss their options. "Organizational lines began to blur as workers and management formed quality-management teams to address problems as part of a formal total-quality system" (Maclean, 1994). The company worked with vendors to tighten control and quality over supplies, and a new management team was installed. Gradually, the losses diminished, profits returned, and backorders resulted. Says plant general foreman, Bill Dutrizac, "'Now all that inventory is computerized, it's well organized. You ask somebody to do something extra now, they do it'" (Maclean, 1994). Says Don Grinter about the turnaround, "'It was a thousand little things adding up'" (Maclean, 1994).

At Toyota's Georgetown, Kentucky, plant, teamwork is the watchword. "Everything we do here is geared to the team environment—from the way we produce top quality Camrys to the way we solve problems. We do everything together and everybody participates" (*Toyota Today*, 1988), says Alex Warren, senior vice-president. Everyone is expected to reach out and to take responsibility for whatever has to be done. Everyone is accessible to everyone: no walls, no barriers (*Toyota Today*, 1988).

MEASURING GROUP EFFECTIVENESS

Recent research has identified three variables that can be used to determine a group's effectiveness: task interdependence, outcome interdependence, and potency. These three "influence group performance and can be influenced by members and supervisors of groups" (Shea and Guzzo, 1987).

Task interdependence relates to the degree to which a group member is concerned with or involved in the work of other group members. Should the group members be involved with each other as partners or as competitors? Will they have the opportunity to interact infrequently or regularly? Will they feed each other work, or will they work parallel to one another? Quality circles have a high degree of task interdependence, whereas scientists engaged in basic research and development often have a low degree of it (Shea and Guzzo, 1987).

> Outcome interdependence exists when task accomplishment by a group yields consequences that are important to and shared by some or all group members—for example, pay, time off, and recognition. The "outcomes" are bestowed by people other than group members, usually a supervisor or senior manager. They may be rewards or punish-

SUPERVISORS AND QUALITY

The role of team leader on a self-directed work team boils down to being an active participant and facilitator—removing obstacles by providing needed training that allows team members to execute the processes and tasks that accomplish their purposes and goals. Specifically, facilitators' roles include the following:

1. Provide training and tools essential for maintaining and improving quality. Team members should be able to:

- Identify and define internal and external customers' needs and requirements

- Establish quality standards for the team's and team members' performances

- Measure all performances and identify deviations from set standards

- Investigate and remove the sources of deviations from standards

- Make all improvements standard operating procedure until further improvements are made

- Continue to search for evolutionary (kaizen) and revolutionary (reengineering) changes to improve quality

2. Provide training and tools essential for team interaction and collaboration. Team members should be able to:

- Exercise effective communication skills when conducting meetings, resolving conflicts, reaching agreements, and engaging in feedback activities

- Navigate through the various stages of team building successfully

- Appreciate the uniqueness of each team member and value the contributions and participation of each

3. Provide training and tools essential for team members to obtain and improve work-related skills and experiences. Team members should be able to:

- Operate equipment and machinery effectively and efficiently

- Maintain equipment and machinery properly

- Engage in safe work habits and practices

- Execute tasks with effectiveness and efficiency

ments; they may include pay, promotion, skill acquisition, exposure, or survival...[and] do not include any benefits derived from within the group, such as social interaction....

Potency is the collective belief of group members that the group can be effective. This belief depends on group members' sense that they have what they need to succeed—for example, training, skills, talented members, money, time, access to key organization members, and feedback about group performance. Potency tends to be closely linked to performance.... Additionally, task interdependence and potency are linked (Shea and Guzzo, 1987).

For groups to succeed and be effective, they need outcome interdependence, a minimal belief in their own effectiveness (potency), and a degree of interaction that is right for the task (enough opportunities for interaction must be provided). The more successes the group has, the greater its sense of potency. The more meaningful the rewards and the more equally they are distributed, the greater the group's effectiveness (Shea and Guzzo, 1987). These are the hallmarks of a "learning organization," one that "values—and thinks competitive advantage derives from—continuing learning, both individual and collective" (Dumaine, "Mr.," 1994). Here is a case in point. Fred Simon, project manager for the development of a new Lincoln Continental, brought the car to market faster, cheaper, and with less intergroup infighting than ever before at Ford. His engineering teams learned to work together instead of jealously guarding their respective turfs.

> Simon found that the engineers who designed the air conditioning, the headlights, the power seats, and the CD player, all working separately, had each made their component such that when used simultaneously they would drain the car battery.... Because Simon's engineers understood [the value of working in a learning organization] they put their heads together and came up with a solution: Raise the car's idle to increase the battery's charge. Of course, that lowered fuel efficiency, and the engineers in charge of that didn't particularly like making such a sacrifice. The difference this time was that the problem got solved quickly and because it was clear the change was made for the good of the car, no one felt like a loser (Dumain, "Mr.," 1994).

Exhibit 9.3 shows you Douglas McGregor's eleven characteristics of a work team. Use it to evaluate the groups to which you belong.

As a group's supervisor, you need to be a facilitator. You must clearly define the group's goals, listing the essential tasks and the degree of quality you wish to see in their performance. You need to determine what resources will be required, and you need to provide them. You must structure the group, providing enough chances for interaction among and between group members. You must monitor the group and be willing to

1. The "atmosphere" tends to be informal, comfortable, relaxed. There are no obvious tensions. It is a working atmosphere in which people are involved and interested. There are no signs of boredom.
2. There is a lot of discussion in which virtually everyone participates, but it remains pertinent to the task of the group. If the discussion gets off the subject, someone will bring it back in short order.
3. The task or the objective of the group is well understood and accepted by the members. There will have been free discussion of the objective at some point, until it was formulated in such a way that the members of the group could commit themselves to it.
4. The members listen to each other! The discussion does not have the quality of jumping from one idea to another unrelated one. Every idea is given a hearing. People do not appear to be afraid of being foolish by putting forth a creative thought even if it seems fairly extreme.
5. There is disagreement. The group is comfortable with this and shows no signs of having to avoid conflict or to keep everything on the plane of sweetness and light. Disagreements are not suppressed or overridden by premature group action. The reasons are carefully examined, and the group seeks to resolve them rather than to dominate the dissenter.

On the other hand, there is no "tyranny of the minority." Individuals who disagree do not appear to be trying to dominate the group or to express hostility. Their disagreement is an expression of a genuine difference of opinion, and they expect a hearing in order that a solution may be found.

Sometimes there are basic disagreements which cannot be resolved. The group finds it possible to live with them, accepting them but not permitting them to block its efforts. Under some conditions, action will be deferred to permit further study of an issue between the members. On other occasions, where the disagreement cannot be resolved and action is necessary, it will be taken but with open caution and recognition that the action may be subject to later reconsideration.

EXHIBIT 9.3

Douglas McGregor's eleven characteristics of a work team.

Source: Douglas McGregor, *The Human Side of Enterprise*, 232–235. Copyright © 1960 by McGraw-Hill Book Company. Used with permission of McGraw-Hill Book Company.

intervene, when necessary, to offer leadership and coaching. Finally, you must be certain that group perceptions hold that important group outcomes depend on group performance, both individually and collectively (Shea and Guzzo, 1987).

Building a team requires that you give the intended members a "common approach and a common language for addressing management con-

6. Most decisions are reached by a kind of consensus in which it is clear that everybody is in general agreement and willing to go along. However, there is little tendency for individuals who oppose the action to keep their opposition private and thus let an apparent consensus mask real disagreement. Formal voting is at a minimum; the group does not accept a simple majority as a proper basis for action.

7. Criticism is frequent, frank, and relatively comfortable. There is little evidence of personal attack, either openly or in a hidden fashion. The criticism has a constructive flavor in that it is oriented toward removing an obstacle that faces the group and prevents it from getting the job done.

8. People are free in expressing their feelings as well as their ideas both on the problem and on the group's operation. There is little pussyfooting, there are few "hidden agendas." Everybody appears to know quite well how everybody else feels about any matter under discussion.

9. When action is taken, clear assignments are made and accepted.

10. The chairman of the group does not dominate it, nor on the contrary, does the group defer unduly to him or her. In fact, as one observes the activity, it is clear that the leadership shifts from time to time, depending on the circumstances. Different members, because of their knowledge or experience, are in a position at various times to act as "resources" for the group. The members utilize them in this fashion and they occupy leadership roles while they are thus being used. There is little evidence of a struggle for power as the group operates. The issue is not who controls, but how to get the job done.

11. The group is self-conscious about its own operations. Frequently, it will stop to examine how well it is doing or what may be interfering with its operation. The problem may be a matter of procedure, or it may be an individual whose behavior is interfering with the accomplishment of the group's objectives. Whatever it is, it gets open discussion until a solution is found.

cerns.... The best method for coordinating the inputs of managers and employees with different functional skills is to provide simple, common, sensible guidelines and procedures. These guidelines should be used jointly to carry out responsibilities without inhibiting individual contributions" (Bittel and Ramsey, eds., 1985). One typical way to begin is to teach a common approach to solving problems and making decisions. Once the individuals participate in group training sessions and begin to focus on common objectives, they get to know one another, they see the advantages of many minds concentrating on a common problem, and they see the value of compromise and cooperation.

GROUP DECISION TECHNIQUES

Two general categories of groups can help you research and determine solutions: interacting groups and noninteracting groups. The interacting group allows its members to meet face to face and gives them the opportunity to make suggestions, react to each other's suggestions, and synthesize the results. Such meetings are best for evaluating ideas and for arriving at a group solution, but they are not best for formulating ideas (Van de Ven and Delbecq, "The," 1974). Two other kinds of group decision approaches are best for generating new ideas: the brainstorming session and the round-robin method. These two are not interacting approaches because they do not allow for criticism of group members' offerings. After a brief look at the latter two types of meetings, we will examine the interacting group.

Brainstorming

In brainstorming sessions, individuals are given a statement of a problem or issue that requires their input. Members are asked to offer suggestions in the form of ideas or potential approaches that they think will be useful. Wild and unusual ideas are sought since they tend to open new directions of thought and to bring forth more new ideas. The group leader discourages criticisms of the offerings but allows modifications or combinations and lists them as they are put forth. Each person is encouraged to speak out on each item put forth by the group leader. Members are chosen for their ability to offer constructive and meaningful contributions. This technique is used to create advertising slogans, new uses for existing products, new products, and new approaches to existing procedures; it is also used to spark creative thinking and creative thinkers.

Round Robins

A variation of the brainstorming, noncritical group session is the round-robin approach. People are invited to list in writing their contributions on a variety of subjects. The group leader directs the flow of topics and background information and asks each individual to list his or her ideas. All members are exposed to the same input but not to one another's contributions.

The brainstorming and round-robin sessions work best in creating lists of possible solutions for group evaluation from which a final decision is made. The interacting group approach is best used to evaluate alternatives and to obtain a group solution in the form of a consensus (Van de Ven and Delbecq, "Nominal," 1979). The most common kind of interacting group is the problem-solving meeting.

The Problem-Solving Meeting

The **problem-solving meeting** is usually set up and conducted in order to reach a group consensus or a solution to a problem affecting the group. It works best when it uses the discussion format, which allows the members to participate actively under the skillful direction of the chairperson. All the people who are affected by or have information about the problem should be included. Their firsthand knowledge and experience can be of value in both the discussion of the problem—its causes and effects—and the listing and analysis of possible solutions.

problem-solving meeting
gathering to reach a group consensus or solution to a problem affecting the group

One, a few, or all of the following steps for solving problems may be the focus of your problem-solving sessions:

1. Identify and define the problem(s).
2. List possible solutions.
3. Evaluate the positive and negative features of each solution.
4. Choose a solution or solutions.
5. Assign responsibility and authority for implementing the solution(s).

If it is to be successful, the problem-solving session requires a great deal of thought and preparation by the supervisor. By using this type of meeting, you are involving your people in the formal decision-making process of your office. This is not without its hazards.

If you have never included your subordinates in your decision-making process in the past, they may be suspicious of your attempt to do so.

Furthermore, each subordinate brings to the meeting his or her particular interests and attitudes, and each is influenced by his or her informal group. (We discuss informal groups later in this chapter.) The informal group leader will be part of the meeting too, so his or her ideas and attitudes may well affect the quality and quantity of ideas of his or her followers. He or she can inhibit or promote open participation. The meeting, in other words, might be dominated by the informal leader. In a case where two or more informal leaders are present, the meeting might degenerate into a contest of strength. As the formal group leader, you may have your ideas and attitudes challenged openly for the first time. You may be subjected to group criticism for the first time, and you may find yourself pitted against the informal leader or leaders.

All these problems and more can be prevented or minimized by proper planning. The first question you must answer is whether your boss will allow you to share your decision-making authority with your subordinates. If he or she agrees, you must answer another question: What kinds of problems are my people best equipped to solve? The answer lies in part in distinguishing among different categories of problems, as is done in the following list:

- Problems involving the reduction of waste or scrap
- Problems relating to health and safety
- Problems relating to housekeeping
- Problems relating to methods improvement

These problems relate to entire departments, sections, or shifts. By soliciting concrete suggestions and taking advantage of your subordinates' involvement in these problem areas, you will be sharing your authority and enlarging your perspective.

Once you have received permission to involve your people and have determined the kinds of problems they are best able to solve, you are ready to embark on a truly difficult but rewarding effort to win and utilize group participation. Through it, you stand a good chance of changing group behavior by changing the individual and group attitudes of your subordinates.

Dr. Thomas Gordon, a psychologist and management consultant, offers the following observations for group leaders (Gordon, 1977):

1. Once a leader becomes like another member of the group, any tendency for him or her to participate too frequently can be dealt with by the group much more easily than when he or she is perceived as the leader. People feel free to exert some control over the participation of members but are afraid to curb the participation of the leader.
2. The more dependent the group is on its leader, the more his or her contribution will inhibit the participation of other members.

3. A leader's awareness of the potentially inhibiting effect of his or her participation on the participation of the members helps control his or her participation. This awareness encourages the leader to be more alert for subtle signs indicating that group members are inhibited.

GROUND RULES FOR MEETINGS

If the problem-solving session is to accomplish meaningful results, certain rules and procedures must be established and agreed on in advance by all concerned. Imagine playing a sport in which each participant had his or her own set of rules. Chaos would be a certainty. Most sports need an umpire or referee whose job it is to enforce the rules and prevent infractions. This role is yours to play as the supervisor.

Several essential rules are listed in the subsections that follow. Using this listing as a guide while planning and conducting your meetings should prevent most hazards from occurring—or at least prevent any serious conflicts.

Before the Meeting

When you have a specific problem to be solved, communicate it to the group members in advance of the meeting. Be as clear as you can be in defining the problem to be attacked and in specifying the goals you want the meeting to achieve.

Be certain that limits such as time, company policy, and the amount of authority the group will have are clear to the group. Are they empowered only to recommend solutions or actually to choose them? In the latter case, you must delegate some of your formal authority to the group. If you alone have the power to decide, tell them so.

Give your members all the relevant data you have accumulated, to assist them in adopting a realistic point of view. Share your ideas and those of others in management that bear on the problem. Make your members aware of any precedents. Let them know where, when, what, how, and in what order (the agenda) the group will consider the issues.

Reserve the space or room you will need to meet in, gather the aids necessary for conducting the meeting (chalk, flip charts, pencils, paper), and get there a little early to make certain that things are in order. Set specific starting and ending times. Assign seats and prepare name tags when you think it necessary.

Before each meeting, all who have been chosen to attend should be made aware of their responsibilities to prepare for the meeting. Specifically, each member should make the following preparations:

1. Read the agenda, and prepare a list of questions that he or she should answer before facing the group.
2. Gather the information, materials, visuals, and so on that he or she will be responsible for presenting or disseminating to the group.
3. Arrange his or her schedule to avoid being late for the meeting or having to leave early.
4. If a group member should be unable to attend the meeting for any legitimate reason, relay the input expected from that group member to the chairperson.

During the Meeting

Start the meeting promptly, direct the discussion, stick to the agenda and time limits, draw out each member, list the alternatives, and summarize frequently. Maintain order, and keep the meeting on the subject.

During each meeting, the group members have specific responsibilities that should be communicated to them in advance and briefly repeated to them at the start of each session. If the meeting is to be beneficial to all concerned, each member should be prepared to do the following:

1. Be an active participant by listening attentively, taking notes, following the discussions, seeking clarification when confused, and adding input if the group member has the expertise or experience to do so.
2. Promote discussion and input from all members by respecting their right to their opinions and attitudes and by avoiding discourteous or disruptive behavior. (The chairperson should not hesitate to call on quiet members, using specific questions and asking for opinions.)
3. Practice group-serving roles (described in the next section).

From the alternatives listed and analyzed, bring the group to one mind about the best alternative or combination of alternatives to endorse. If the solution is to work, the majority must be behind it. Be ready to compromise in order to break any impasse.

Assign tasks to those affected, if need be, and put the solution into operation as quickly as possible. At the close of each meeting, the participants should be made aware of any specific duties or assignments they will have as a result of the meeting. The chairperson should not allow the members to leave until each of them is clear about his or her new tasks. In addition to the specific duties each person may receive, all participants have the following general obligations:

1. Keep the results and contents of the meeting confidential by not sharing them with anyone or any group that does not have a need to know.
2. Relay decisions and changes to those for whom the group member may be responsible and who will be affected by them.

3. Carry out promises made and assignments received as quickly as possible.

After the Meeting

After a problem-solving meeting, check on the results and on the group reactions. Follow up on individual assignments.

GROUP MEMBER ROLES

At a meeting, members of the group may play several different roles; some of these will be helpful to the attainment of the meeting's goals, whereas others may hinder the group's attempts to achieve success. Two categories of roles—self-serving and group-serving—are available to all members of a group, and chances are that many different roles will be exhibited at each meeting. Exhibit 9.4 summarizes these roles.

Self-Serving Roles

Self-serving roles can have either positive or negative effects on the meeting and on group members. For example, suppose that as a group leader, you block another participant by not recognizing his or her raised hand. If you do so in order to get another person to speak who until then has been withdrawn, you have a positive motive and effect on the group. But if you do so in order to promote your own ideas at the expense of others' (a selfish motive), the action can have a negative effect on the group.

As chairperson, you may decide that it is best to withdraw—that is, become an observer—when one of the members begins to criticize another's suggestions. In this way, a participant may be forced to justify his or her proposal, new information may emerge, and others may be persuaded of the validity of an idea more readily. Why not let a participant tell his or her peers what you want said? Attention getting is the role in which a member focuses attention on himself or herself. He or she may be attempting to get the floor in order to add information or to redirect the discussion to the central point.

Self-Serving Roles	*Group-Serving Roles*
Attention-getting	Coordinating
Blocking	Fortifying
Criticizing	Initiating
Dominating	Orienting
Withdrawing	Researching

EXHIBIT 9.4
Roles played by group members.

Dominating involves pushing a special interest; it may involve blocking by continuing to talk and not allowing another to get into the conversation. Whether these roles go unchecked and exhibit a positive or negative influence is up to the chairperson to determine. Use your good sense and listen intently. Try to get at the motive behind the role a member is playing. If, in your judgment, the motive is positive, let him or her continue; if not, take action.

Group-Serving Roles

Group-serving roles are almost always positive in their effects. No matter who practices them, they attempt to draw members together and shed light where there was darkness. They all promote unity and harmony, and each is essential in order to reach a consensus. They tend to keep a meeting on track, while systematically separating the unimportant from the relevant.

Fortifying is the process by which a member adds encouragement and insights to already aired ideas. It helps elaborate and interpret what has been said. Initiating introduces ideas and major points in order to get the reactions and contributions of group members. Orienting tells the membership where they have been and where they are at present. It may serve to add emphasis or to clarify ideas, and it keeps people from traveling again over the same ground or going around in circles. Researching involves fact-finding and introducing background material pertinent to the discussion so as to remove smoke from people's eyes and substitute facts for fiction.

Observe and label these activities in your group encounters from now on. You will see various positive and negative applications of all these roles in your classes at school, as well as in meetings at work. Study your instructor and the various roles he or she plays. You will pick up some valuable examples of each of these roles, most of which you will be able to use at work when you find yourself a group leader or participant.

PITFALLS

Problem-solving sessions may result in problems if poor leadership results in a violation of the ground rules listed in the preceding section. In addition, several other major pitfalls or traps exist that can cause a meeting to be a sheer waste of time.

The Hidden Agenda

A member's hidden agenda consists of his or her personal feelings toward the subject discussed, the group itself, and the individuals who make up the group. We all have such an agenda whenever we attend a group session, whether with our formal or our informal group. If a proposal or an action is put forth that conflicts with out pet beliefs, we can only try to pick it apart or live with it. People tend to promote (or not oppose) ideas that they feel they can live with and to resist (or offer alternatives to) ideas they feel will mean conflicts, problems, or more effort for them or for those they represent. Often critical remarks toward group members or their ideas are motivated by a dislike or distrust of those persons and their intentions—not their ideas. You must recognize that, as a chairperson, you have the duty to see behind the words and get to the motives. Often, you can nullify the hidden agenda's effect simply by explaining that another person or department does not necessarily have to gain at someone else's expense. What is good for the gander can be, and often is, good for the goose.

An Improper Setting

How many meetings have you attended that were complete disasters because of poor ventilation, bad lighting, or too much background noise? Maybe the facilities were okay when they were reserved, but the timing was wrong for their use. Possibly the room was selected without regard for the number of people who would attend, so many people had to stand or could not even enter the room. I am reminded of a meeting I attended in an industrial firm, at which the central feature was to have been a film. After the projector was started, we realized that the lamp had burned out. So much for that meeting and its organizer.

A Competitive Spirit

Many sessions start out as and continue to be a stage for the display of one member's accomplishments over the others' or of one group's achievements over another's. Competition is fine on the athletic field, but it has no real purpose among members of the team. Watch for the remark that attempts to build one person's reputation at the expense of another's. Nothing can ruffle feathers so quickly or create defensive reactions more effectively. A quick review of the second Hawthorne study should refresh your memory about intergroup competition and its dangers.

Chapter 7 discussed the now-famous experimental studies conducted in the late 1920s at Western Electric's Hawthorne plant. The second study uncovered the formation of two informal cliques—one quite strong and the other somewhat weak. Both influenced their members in significant ways. They offered proof that workers' cliques can be positive or negative factors with respect to company standards, policy, and regulations. If they view management favorably, they are capable of achieving standards of output even higher than management may expect. If they feel negative toward management, the informal group will generate much less production than expected. How workers, individually or in groups, relate to management is largely a result of their supervisor's approach. If he or she practices sound human relations and relates positively to his or her group of subordinates, the supervisor can and does influence the behavior and productivity of the subordinates.

Talkative Members

Have you ever tried to carry on a conversation with someone who only stopped talking to think about what to say next? It is quite a frustrating experience. Your voice only fills the gaps between his or her remarks. Listening is not one of that person's virtues. Members in meetings can quickly fall in love with their own voices and viewpoints. It is the chairperson's job to prevent this. Make sure that everyone has a say and that each person's views are duly noted. Blocking, however, can serve a useful purpose with a talkative member.

Sabotage

Group members who carry on their own conversations while another is speaking, people who attempt to sidetrack the issues, hidden decisions that are made without group consultation: These and similar factors represent efforts to render a meeting useless. The subversive's motivation may be that no decision will enhance the status quo. Disruptive behavior will sour the group and tear down its will to reach a decision or continue the meeting: Interest wanes, and attention slips away. The chairperson must assess the motives and effects of conscious or accidental sabotage and must act to block it or to confront the saboteur directly. The meeting must be pulled back to its proper focus. Exhibit 9.5 gives you some interesting alternatives for dealing with a disruptive group member.

INFORMAL GROUPS

informal group
two or more people who come together by choice to satisfy mutual needs or to share common interests

clique
an informal group of two or more people who come together by choice to satisfy mutual interests or to pursue common goals

Two or more people who come together by choice to satisfy mutual needs or to share common interests are considered an **informal group.** The distinguishing feature between formal and informal groups is the matter of choice. Informal groups are formed because of the mutual social needs of people and because the environment at work favors or at least does not prohibit their formation. Formal groups can also be informal groups, provided that all members freely choose to associate with one another on and off the job.

There are three primary types of informal groups: horizontal, vertical, and random (sometimes called mixed) (Dalton, 1959). These types of informal groups are often referred to as **cliques.** Exhibit 9.6 is an organization chart we will refer to in discussing the three different types of cliques.

1. Try a one-on-one meeting. Schedule a meeting for just the two of you. Confront the person with your observations about how the person is disrupting the group's efforts. Listen for all the reasons and perceptions that unfold. See if you can turn disruptive behaviors around with force-field analysis in the meeting or afterward.
2. Let the group confront the individual. Let the individual face the group members directly. Let the members air their grievances about the problem member's behaviors. Talk about what effects those behaviors are having on the group. Avoid personal attacks. Describe the behaviors that have negative consequences.
3. Place limits on the problem member's participation. Let the group leader prescribe the level of participation allowed. For example, the leader may want to deal directly with the individual after each meeting, not during it. Or the leader may not allow the problem member to participate in group discussions when signs of disruptive behaviors occur.
4. Separate the problem member from the group meetings. Let the individual contribute but on an individual basis, away from the other group members. Assign work that will help the team indirectly.

EXHIBIT 9.5
Some tips for dealing with problem group members.

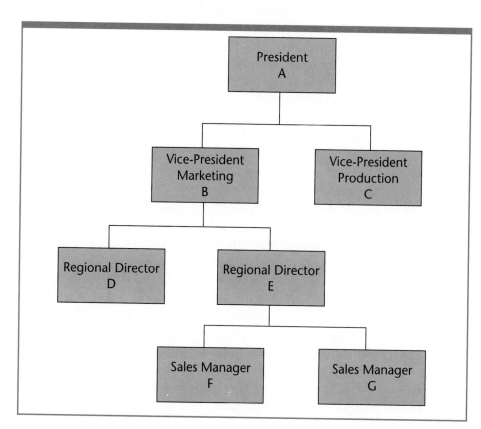

EXHIBIT 9.6
An organization chart.

Horizontal Cliques

A horizontal clique consists of two or more people from the same functional area and on the same level of the hierarchy. In Exhibit 9.6, F and G constitute a horizontal clique, provided that they have chosen one another's company voluntarily on social occasions. D and E would also form a horizontal clique, under the same conditions. B and C would not form a horizontal clique since they represent two different functional areas (marketing and production).

Vertical Cliques

A vertical clique consists of two or more people from the same functional area but different levels of the hierarchy. In Exhibit 9.6, F and E would be an example, as would D, E, and B. If all members of the marketing department formed an informal group, they would also constitute a vertical clique. Vertical cliques involve friendships between a boss and one or more subordinates.

Random Cliques

A random clique comprises two or more people from two or more functional areas. In Exhibit 9.6, B and C would be a good example of this. E, B, and C would also form a random or mixed clique. Whether the members of a random or mixed clique are from the same level of the hierarchy or not makes no difference. If A, the president, is a part of any clique, that clique automatically would be a random one. The reason is that the president is the only manager who oversees all the functional areas of the business. Therefore, he or she does not belong to any one of them but stands alone at that level of the hierarchy.

Your subordinates will usually constitute one or more horizontal or (on occasion) random cliques. Seldom will you find them belonging to a vertical clique. Your analysis of your subordinates' group memberships can help you in your attempts to understand them as individuals and to develop your relationships with their groups.

Let us assume that you have recently become the operating supervisor of the health insurance systems group, illustrated in Exhibit 9.7. You have observed your people and their interactions and have drawn the connecting rings as shown, creating what is usually called a sociogram. Since your subordinates work in proximity to workers in the life insurance systems group, it would seem natural for members of the two groups to mix informally on social occasions such as coffee breaks and lunch periods.

The rings you have drawn encircle the members of the informal groups who most frequently interact socially with one another at work. The numbers in parentheses represent their ages. All the groups represented are horizontal cliques. Even though Ben and Norma are from two different work groups, they are in the same functional area called systems.

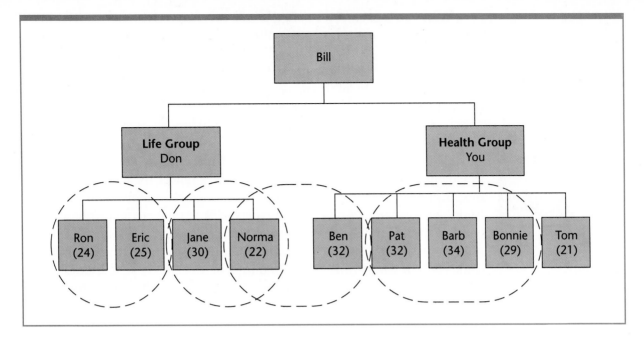

EXHIBIT 9.7

A sociogram showing the informal groupings of members in formal groups.

Now let us see what you have discovered. Pat, Barb, and Bonnie are a clique and prefer one another's company to that of others when they have a choice. This may be partly because they are the only women in the health systems area. It may also be due to the closeness of their ages. More knowledge is needed for a really thorough analysis. You should know their marital status, their individual interests, their backgrounds, and more before you can make any hard and fast conclusions about the nature of their clique.

Ben has chosen Norma's company and vice versa. This is interesting because he has gone outside his section for companionship. Norma is part of two informal cliques. Norma may be an informal leader to either Ben or Jane or both. But again more information would be needed before you could decide for sure. For example, Ben may be romantically inclined toward Norma.

Tom is another situation. He is the youngest member and as such may have little in common with the others. He might be an isolate—a person who wants to belong to one or another of the cliques but is rejected or denied membership for some reason. His age, his personality, his education, or some other factor may be keeping him on the outside. If he is a new employee, he has not had enough time to become accepted or to choose a group to which he might want to belong. He might be a deviate—a person who does not aspire to join or belong to a group. Quite often an isolate will evolve into a deviate if he or she is kept out long enough.

What we have just done in a small way is to observe the social interaction of subordinates and attempt to analyze our findings. If these observations were pursued in greater depth and detail, a better understanding might emerge of why these groups have formed, what keeps them together, and what they mean to you as a supervisor. Such a process will aid you by giving you more direct information about the forces at work on your people and the group influences on their attitudes and performance at work.

Every informal group has a leader. Unlike his or her counterpart in the formal group, the informal leader derives power through the informal means discussed in Chapter 3. The clique members subordinate their wills to one of their number because he or she is a great person to be with or because of the knowledge, skills, and abilities he or she possesses. It is seldom the case that the formal leader of the formal group is an informal leader with a clique of his or her subordinates. This is as it should be. As we pointed out in Chapter 8, a manager's friends should be his or her peers.

JOINING A CLIQUE

Once a new employee is hired, he or she is placed in a specific job, which makes him or her automatically a member of several formal groups that constitute the business enterprise. If the design of work and the working relationships permit them, informal groups or cliques will have been formed as well. The newcomer, like those who have preceded him or her, will naturally desire the companionship of one or more co-workers on a more or less regular basis, both during working hours and while on his or her own time.

The problem confronting the new arrival is that he or she is initially outside the existing informal groups and, although he or she desires membership in one of them, is not certain about which one to choose. He or she needs time to assess the values, attitudes, and reputation of each group. The groups in turn are going to be evaluating the person for prospective membership. In this sense, the new employee is similar to a person seeking admission to a fraternity or sorority. He or she has to look at what it stands for and get to know its members, while in turn, its members look the applicant over.

You as a supervisor can do a great deal for the new employee. If you know your people well and understand their groups, you can do all in your power to help him or her gain admittance to a group of subordinates that constitutes a positive force and will exert a constructive influence on the newcomer. You hope that all the informal cliques in your section are working with management and not against it. But if one or another is not, do your best to steer the new arrival away from that clique and into more beneficial surroundings. We cover this topic further in Chapter 11.

Informal groups often form when workers who share common interests come together as social friends.

Stages of Induction

Before the individual on the outside of a clique can truly become a participating member of the clique, he or she must go through three separate but related stages of induction: (1) observation, (2) transformation, and (3) confirmation.

Stage 1: Observation   Observation is the initial stage we all find ourselves in as newcomers. By necessity, we must remain neutral toward all the informal groups we encounter until we have time to know them. As time goes on, neutrality becomes increasingly difficult to maintain, as we feel pressure from within and from without to make a decision or choice. We may begin a kind of trial membership period, wherein we are invited to participate with a group by one or more of its members. While meeting with each clique, we are somewhat passive and open to group members' opinions and attitudes, preferring to listen rather than to speak our mind.

Stage 2: Transformation   The next step is for us to decide which group we like best. If the group honors our choice, we begin to confine our socializing almost exclusively to the new group. We mask any personal opinions that are contradictory to those the group holds as essential, and we begin to mouth agreement to these essential attitudes. Like a parrot, we begin to remember and repeat the sacred beliefs even though we may not agree with them. Without this stage, we can never really become an accepted member in a strong informal group.

Stage 3: Confirmation   The confirmation stage is complete when we actually abandon attitudes we once held that were in direct opposition to those of the group and adopt the group's values as our own. We give up our individuality while with the group though we may retain it on our own. The group has changed us and our attitudes in much the same way as was discussed in Chapter 6. The difference is that several people may have been at work on us here instead of only one.

From this point on, the group has more influence over our behavior than any other force at work. We now weigh the relative merits of proposals against the group's willingness to accept them. If the group vetoes the action, each member feels bound to support that veto.

Not long ago, a student involved me in the following story. At the start of the business day one Friday, two of George's more able workers presented him with a petition signed by all twenty-six of his subordinates. It requested that the workday begin and end one-half hour earlier. George was quite concerned, since such a request was not in his power to grant, and he felt that the plant manager would not buy the suggestion. Wisely, he refrained from giving an immediate answer but assured the workers that he would consider the matter carefully.

The following week George and I discussed the problem. I asked if he was sure that all the workers really wanted the change. He reiterated that they had all signed the petition. But as we all know, people will sign almost anything—for a variety of reasons. So George decided to interview each worker separately over the next two weeks to determine just how committed each of them was to the proposed change. The results were amazing. Two men were solidly in favor of the change—the same two who had confronted George with the petition and had initiated it. Eight workers were neutral but willing to go along with the others. The remaining sixteen were clearly against it. After George announced his findings, the demand was dropped, and only two people were really unhappy with the decision.

What made the twenty-four other workers sign? The two men were strong personalities, and one was an informal leader of a large clique. Beginning with his clique members, starting with the weakest, the informal leader got one signature after another until nearly two thirds of the workers had signed. The others fell into line when confronted with the sheer weight of numbers. Not wishing to obstruct the will of the majority, the few remaining holdouts also signed up.

GROUP COMPETITION

We have seen that intergroup competition at Hawthorne caused ill will and declining productivity within the formal group. Edgar H. Schein (1970) of the Massachusetts Institute of Technology has added much to our understanding of what happens within and between competing groups. Whether we are dealing with formal or informal groups, the following situation would apply.

What happens within competing groups? Each group exhibits the following behavior:

- Exhibits greater togetherness and cohesion
- Becomes more organized and highly structured
- Expects greater loyalty and conformity from its members
- Willingly accepts autocratic supervision
- Becomes more task oriented and less concerned with the needs of individual members

All these results, at first glance, may appear to be desirable. But as we consider what happens between competing groups, the picture becomes less attractive. In Schein's words:

1. Each group begins to see the other group as the enemy, rather than merely a neutral object.
2. Each group begins to experience distortions of perception—it tends to perceive only the best parts of itself, denying its weaknesses, and tends to perceive only the worst parts of the other group, denying its strengths; each group is likely to develop a negative stereotype of the other. ("They don't play fair like we do.")
3. Hostility toward the other group increases while interaction and communication with the other group decreases; thus it becomes easier to maintain negative stereotypes and more difficult to correct perceptual distortions.
4. If the groups are forced into interaction—for example, if they are forced to listen to representatives plead their own and the others' cause in reference to some task—each group is likely to listen more closely to their own representative and not to listen to the representative of the other group, except to find fault with his presentation: in other words group members tend to listen only for that which supports their own position and stereotype (Schein, 1970).

If this intergroup competition—whether between informal or formal groups—results in one group's emerging as the victor and the other as vanquished, the problems are compounded dramatically. To paraphrase Schein, the winning group behaves in the following way:

- Keeps its cohesiveness
- Tends to become self-satisfied
- Loses its task orientation and reemphasizes individual needs
- Becomes reassured that its self-image must be a correct one and loses the incentive to question its perceptions

On the other hand, the losing group:

- Becomes initially unrealistic about its perception of why it lost, tending to transfer blame to some external cause

- Tends to lose its cohesiveness
- Becomes more dedicated to tasks and winning
- Experiences less intragroup cooperation and less concern for individual needs
- Eventually reexamines its beliefs and self-image and becomes more realistic in its perceptions

It should be clear to you that intergroup competition has more disadvantages than advantages. The loser may improve, whereas the winner declines. This is not to say that competition is wrong—only that competition between groups within a company is dangerous. Competition can be a powerful tool to muster greater output and cohesiveness among your department's members if the enemy is not a group of co-workers but rather some outside force or group. If the thing to be beaten is a standard or a past record of output, the group can muster its forces in a cooperative spirit to excel and exceed its previous record. Like a long-distance runner out to beat the best recorded time for his or her event or to surpass his or her previous best time, groups at work can try and succeed or they can fail with no lasting detrimental effects. To the contrary, they will most likely redouble their efforts and reexamine their operations, and they may seek outside help in the process—a desirable outcome.

OUTSIDERS AND INSIDERS

You are affected each day at your workplace by many factors, some of which are outside your company and some of which are inside it. The same is true for your subordinates.

Outside Factors

When was the last time you went to work with a personal family problem so much on your mind that your performance suffered? Your family is but one of many outside groups that can and do influence your efficiency. Your academic classes in management may be another example. We all hope that you will obtain from your instructor and classmates the means to achieve a more successful performance. But sometimes what you learn will bring you into conflict with your traditional beliefs or with those of your boss, putting you at odds with him or her when you attempt to act on your new knowledge. You may find that you know more about a particular task and the best methods for dealing with it than your boss does. The problem will then be one of your selling your idea to your boss and getting permission to implement it.

Customers and competitors can place demands on the business, in turn directly affecting your operations. Their requests, threats, and innovations may be translated into new products, service methods, or procedures for your department. New schedules of production may be the result, with added pressures and tensions for you and those under you.

Inside Factors

The groups within the company that directly or indirectly affect your performance are your superiors, your peers, and your subordinates. Superiors construct the programs, policies, and regulations that you must enforce and translate to action. Your peers place demands on you for conformity, cooperation, and uniform approaches to problems. They form the nucleus of your friendships and place demands on your time and talents. Your subordinates, as members of your formal groups and as members of their own informal cliques, ask a great deal from you. How you cope with these groups and their demands directly relates to how well you can adjust to tension and frustration. Numerous times you will be faced with conflicts between what you think you should do and what others are asking you to do. Often you must yield completely to the demands of others. On occasion, you must work out compromises. In all cases, however, you are being tested. How strong is your company loyalty? How strong is your friendship? How sincere are you in your commitment to your people? How much do your children really mean to you? Whoever said that life or holding a job was easy?

YOU AND YOUR INFORMAL GROUP

The informal group that you choose or that chooses you will have a dramatic and lasting impact on your reputation and your future. Choose any informal group with the same caution you would exercise when choosing a friend. Pick out the ones that will have the greatest positive effect on your growth and the ones that have the most to offer. As a result, some of their luster and brilliance will rub off on you. You are judged in part by the company you keep. Why open yourself to criticism or end up having to defend your companions or yourself? You do not have to alienate those bent on self-destruction. Simply avoid any permanent bonds or relationships with them. Remain civil but apart.

One of the hazards inherent in membership in an informal group is the restrictions it places on your contacts with others. Once you have reached either the transformation or confirmation stage of induction, you probably have begun to confine your socializing at work to a specific few. In time, you may become rather narrow and cut off from differing opinions. You may be denying yourself the valuable companionship and variety that others have to offer. Do not take yourself out of circulation. Break your routine on occasion, and mix and maintain contacts with others of similar rank. It is foolish to restrict your explorations to the same mountain. After a while, there is nothing left to explore.

COPING WITH SUBORDINATES' CLIQUES

There are seven main principles you should follow to minimize group conflicts and tensions and to maximize group cooperation and contribution:

1. Accept your subordinates' cliques as a fact of life. Just as you belong to one or more, so it is with them. Consider their informal groups as allies and additional forces to be won over and brought to bear on mutual problems. The trick is to learn to work with them—not to fight them or try to eliminate them.

2. Identify and enlist the cooperation of the informal leaders. They represent a force to be reckoned with. Many of them have the potential to be tomorrow's managers. The informal power they have over others can work for you both. Practice sound human relations with them as you would with anyone in your charge. Share with the best of them (whenever you can) some of your formal authority through delegation. They are usually perfect candidates for leadership roles. They are also ambitious people who recognize the advantages that management has to offer.

   Informal leaders are not hard to spot. They are the ones that others like to be with. They are influential with their followers and with other informal groups and their leaders. Informal leaders know the opinions and attitudes of their groups' members and often act as spokespersons for their groups to management. Note who sits with whom at lunch and on breaks. Then note how these people interact—who seems to dominate discussions and settle arguments.

3. Prevent intergroup competition and the occurrence of a win–lose situation. As we stated earlier, groups in conflict tend to tear at each other and to reduce the organization's overall effectiveness. The loser will profit, whereas the winner suffers. Hold out standards to be achieved and surpassed. Use past performance records as targets to hit and scores to beat. These abstract enemies are harder to visualize but easier to beat.

4. Do not force your people to choose between you and their group. If you put it to them on an either–or basis, they will usually pick their group. Their loyalty to and membership in a clique does not have to be at your expense. They can serve both company and group demands. They can be loyal and unopposed to you if you are predictable and loyal to them.

5. Adopt a coach's attitude toward your group(s). Foster a team spirit, and nurture the comradeship that cliques promote. Play fair, and demand that your subordinates do the same. Team players know the value of rules and team play. Enlist their participation as a group, and protect their self-image.

6. Appeal to each group member and to each group's sense of competence. We all have the urge to be good at what we do and to know that others think we are. Give your people a series of challenges that, when met, will give them a sense of accomplishment and pride.

7. Use the traditional and the not-so-traditional levers available to you. Levers are tools that can be used to influence people in specific situations. None is suitable to every situation. Levers such as job assignments, overtime, disciplinary actions, and deserved praise may or may not be within your control, but most of the levers in Exhibit 9.8 will be yours to use. The effectiveness of most of them has to do with your competence in interpersonal and intergroup relations (Sasser and Leonard, 1980). Most are effective when they are used by a person who commands the respect of the people they are used with. This respect comes from the user's skills, knowledge, and demonstrated concern for the group and its members.

By setting goals and helping your subordinates set their own, you will be providing incentives for them to excel and ways for them to build self-respect and confidence. Point out how a poor performance hurts others and makes their jobs more difficult.

EXHIBIT 9.8
Supervisors' levers for gaining group cooperation and compliance.

Source: W. Earl Sasser, Jr., and Frank S. Leonard. "Let First-Level Supervisors Do Their Job." *Harvard Business Review,* March–April 1980, 119–120.

- Use positive reinforcement in the form of incentive schemes, job redesign, and awareness of psychological needs, including peer group acceptance and pride.
- Try negative reinforcement—both the traditional type (write up, fire, suspend) and more indirect means (job reassignment, job redesign, forced overtime).
- Appeal to workers for support on the basis of having gone out on a limb for them or having given over some prerogative to them in the past.
- Appeal to workers on the basis of understanding their position, since first-level supervisors once stood in their shoes.
- Appeal to workers on the basis of previously agreed-on goals and plans for achieving them.

One example of this point involved assembly-line workers on a Corvette assembly operation. They were installing fiberglass parts provided by an outside supplier. These parts had rough edges in their openings that were designed to take dashboard instruments. The rough edges had to be filed clean before the instruments could be inserted. This should have been done by the supplier, not by the assembly-line workers.

To deal with the growing sense of frustration and irritation among their assembly workers, General Motors' supervisors arranged a meeting with the supplier's workers at the GM plant. The workers responsible for the rough-edged moldings witnessed firsthand how their sloppy work affected their counterparts. Moldings quickly began to arrive with smooth openings. All now knew why their work was necessary and what would happen at the other end when it was not done properly.

Instant Replay

1. A group is two or more people who are aware of one another, who consider themselves to be a functioning unit, and who share a quest for a common goal or benefit.
2. Problem-solving meetings may or may not allow for interaction between and among group members. Interaction allows individual group members to react to input from other members.
3. The interacting group works best to evaluate possible alternatives and to obtain a group solution in the form of a consensus.
4. Brainstorming and round-robin sessions work best to construct a list of potential solutions or ideas that bear on the subject under discussion.
5. The roles that group members play may affect the group either positively or negatively, depending on what motivates each group member in the use of each role.
6. Various pitfalls can undermine group meetings and their results. Being aware of them and acting to render them negligible is the job of every group leader or chairperson.
7. Groups that compete experience both positive and negative changes. The most negative feature of intergroup competition is what happens between competing groups: Hostility, lack of cooperation, and outright sabotage can result, eventually bringing both groups down.
8. Supervisors must recognize that informal groups exist and can wield positive or negative powers. Their leaders possess strong personalities and are potential management material.

Questions for Class Discussion

1. Can you define this chapter's key terms?
2. What are the forces that help shape a group's syntality?
3. As a problem-solving group's chairperson, what should you do before, during, and after a session?

4. As a participating member of a problem-solving session, what should you do before, during, and after the session?
5. What are the group-serving and the self-serving roles played by group members in meetings?
6. What are the three types of informal groups described in this chapter? Can you give an example of each from your own experiences?
7. What happens to the winning group in intergroup competition? To the losing group? Between the groups?

Incident

Many people work outside the office and factory. Some, such as outside salespeople, must be with clients and customers regularly. Others work at home, linked to their boss and co-workers by electronic devices, such as a telephone hookup to the company's computer or a fax machine for receiving and sending work, and by telephone for voice-to-voice contacts. The advantages are many to both employee and employer. The employee can stay at home with children in need of day care and avoid the time and expense of commuting to work. The company can operate in smaller spaces, providing less office furniture and equipment. But what about a team spirit linking the telecommuter to his or her co-workers and others at work?

Your Task: List as many ways as you can to include the home-working employees in a group's efforts and activities at work. What would you do to instill the absent employees with a real spirit of teamwork?

The New Kid

CASE PROBLEM 9.1

Most of the draftsmen from design and engineering were assembled, as usual, for their afternoon coffee break. Al, the old-timer of the group, was holding court: "Word is that Mason is being replaced by a woman."

Charles Morrison spoke up. "You're kidding! A woman in our group? That's a first. Hope she's good lookin' and..."

Harris interrupted: "I don't care what she looks like. What's the boss thinking about to hire a woman? No female ever worked here as long back as I can remember. Right, Al?"

"Yeah, but the rumor is she ain't exactly the best candidate for the job. My source in personnel tells me the pressure's on to hire a female, and she was the only one they could find. I hear she's in her twenties, fresh out of school, too."

"What's going on in this company?" asked Harris. "This will be a first for us and the company. No woman ever worked in an all-male job here before. Guess we'll have to watch our language."

Charlie leaned forward, placing his head near the center of the circular table, and whispered something no one outside the group could hear. The group exploded in raucous laughter and table thumping. Then Charlie added: "You know, guys, this new kid could be a problem. We've got a tight group here, and no one makes any waves. I hope we don't run into another Trent. You all remember the trouble he caused."

Al leaned back in his chair, hands clasped behind his head: "Don't worry about another Trent. We took care of that toad good and proper. He isn't a problem now and hasn't been for a long time."

The group continued their conversation for another fifteen minutes and drifted back to their office, thirty-seven minutes after their fifteen-minute coffee break began.

Questions

1. To what kind of informal group do these people belong?
2. In what ways is the power of the informal group illustrated in this case?
3. What diversity issues exist in this case?
4. What should the supervisor of the design and engineering department do to prepare the group for the female addition?

<table>
<tr><td>CASE PROBLEM 9.2</td></tr>
</table>

Claims and Counterclaims

Lee Cannoli joined the Claims Processing Department of the Thomas Paine Insurance Company three weeks ago, and today marked his first full week on the job. Lee is one of fourteen full-time clerks who initially screen customer claims before routing them to an adjuster for final processing. During his first two weeks, he attended a claims-training course and underwent the usual company orientation. For the past five days, Lee has averaged thirty-two claims a day and is quite proud of his progress. His supervisor, Lois Clements, complimented him on several occasions for his output and the quality of his work. Although there is no hard and fast rule about output, Lois made it clear that most new employees were expected to do between twenty and twenty-four claims a day for their first month or so.

Henry Pullman, a fellow claims clerk, approached Lee that afternoon.

"Hi," said Henry.

"Hello."

"I'm Hank Pullman. You're Lee, aren't you?"

"Yes. We met on Tuesday when Ms. Clements introduced me to the other workers. I've been so busy that I really haven't had much time to visit."

"Yeah, I noticed. How many claims do you get through a day, anyway?"

"Well, so far I have been doing between thirty and thirty-two."

Hank winced. "Most of the guys do twenty to twenty-five each day. Looks like you're going to set a record. You make some of us old-timers look pretty slow."

"The claims I'm getting are pretty simple. I've only had a few that took a lot of time."

"But, Lee, if you do thirty or more a day, you are putting the other guys and gals in a bind. Lois will think we're doggin' it. You wouldn't want that to happen now, would you?"

"Gee, I didn't realize I was causing any problems."

"Well, Lee, the other workers are doing the more advanced ones, and they can't work quite as fast on them. You'll find out soon enough when you graduate to the big leagues."

"I don't want to hurt anyone," Lee replied.

"I knew you would understand. Say, some of us are putting together a softball team from the department to compete with the other company teams. Do you play?"

"Heck, I haven't played ball for a couple of years."

"Don't worry about that. It would be a great chance to get to know the kingpins around here. All the best are in on it. Our first practice is tomorrow at Langly Park, just around the corner on Fifth and Greenleaf. About 9:00 A.M. Can we count on you?"

"I'd like that very much. Say, Hank, what does Ms. Clements say about our output? I mean, doesn't she have a quota for us?"

"Claims people are hard to find today. If she gets tough, she knows the workers will leave. Anyway, her boss leaves her alone, and she leaves us alone. Come on, Lee, let's have a cup of coffee. I'll fill you in on this place and who really runs it."

As the two men walked to the cafeteria, Lee thought to himself, "I sure don't want to hurt the other workers.... What the heck, I'll have a little more time to socialize like the others. Hank has been around a long time...he ought to know."

Questions

1. What accounts for Lee's switch from diligent worker to acceptance of a slower pace?
2. Has Lois Clements failed in any way? Is she responsible for what is happening to Lee?
3. Comment on Hank's statement, "I'll fill you in on this place and who really runs it."
4. Which of the three stages of induction into a clique is Lee in at present?

Notes

Robert B. Reich, Bittel, Lester R. and Ramsey, Jackson E., eds., *Handbook for Professional Managers*. New York: McGraw-Hill, 1985, 218.

Bylinsky, Gene. "The Digital Factory," *Fortune*, November 14, 1994, 92–94, 96, 100, 104, 106, 110.

Dalton, Melville. *Men Who Manage: Fusions of Feelings and Theory in Administration*. New York: John Wiley & Sons, 1959.

Dumaine, Brian. "Mr. Learning Organization," *Fortune*, October 17, 1994, 147–148, 150, 154–157.

Dumaine Brian. "The Trouble with Teams," *Fortune*, September 5, 1994, 86–88, 90, 92.

Dumaine Brian. "Why Do We Work?," *Fortune*, December 26, 1994, 196–198, 200, 202, 204.

Gordon, Thomas. *Leader Effectiveness Training: L.E.T.* New York: Wyden Books, 1977, 141–142.

Hoerr, John. "The Cultural Revolution at A. O. Smith," *Business Week*, May 29, 1989, 66, 68.

Katzenbach, Jon R. and Smith, Douglas K. *The Wisdom of Teams.* Boston: Harvard Business School Press, 1994, 45.

Kizilos, Tolly, and Heinisch, Roger P. "How A Management Team Selects Managers," *Harvard Business Review*, September–October 1986, 6.

Klein, Janice A. and Posey, Pamela A. "Good Supervisors Are Good Supervisors Anywhere," *Harvard Business Review*, November–December 1986, 125–128.

Maclean, John N. "Rail Equipment Company Learns ABCs of Success," *Chicago Tribune*, November 6, 1994, sec. 7, 1, 4.

McKee, Bradford. "Turn Your Workers into a Team," *Nation's Business*, July 1992, 37.

Reich, Robert B. "Entrepreneurship Reconsidered: The Team As Hero," *Harvard Business Review*, May–June 1987, 77, 81, 82–83.

Sasser, Jr., Earl W. and Leonard, Frank S. "Let First-Level Supervisors Do Their Job," *Harvard Business Review*, March–April 1980, 119–120.

Schein, Edgar H. *Organizational Psychology*, 2nd ed. Englewood Cliffs, NJ: Prentice Hall, 1970.

Shea, Gregory P. and Guzzo, Richard A. "Group Effectiveness, What Really Matters," *Sloan Management Review* 28 no. 3, Spring 1987, 25–26.

"Teamwork Is the Key," *Toyota Today*, Fall 1988, 4.

Uris, Auren. *Techniques of Leadership.* New York: McGraw-Hill, 1964, 56, 58, 61–62.

Van de Ven, A. H. and Delbecq, A. L. "Nominal Versus Interacting Group Processes for Committee Decision-Making Effectiveness," *Academy of Management Journal* 14, 1971, 203–212. See also Miner, F. C. "A Comparative Analysis of Three Diverse Group Decision-Making Approaches," *Academy of Management Journal* 22, 1979, 81–93.

Van de Ven, A. H. and Delbecq, A. L. "The Effectiveness of Nominal, Delphi, and Interacting Group Decision-Making Processes," *Academy of Management Journal* 17, 1974, 605–621.

Wellins, Richard S., Byham, William C., and Wilson, Jeanne M. *Empowered Teams.* San Francisco: Jossey-Bass, 1991. 135–38.

Woodruff, David. "Where Employees Are Management," *Business Week*, Bonus Issue, January 19, 1993, 66.

"Workplace Diversity: Prepare and Lead Or Postpone and Follow," *Supervisors Bulletin* no. 880, June 30, 1992. Waterford, CT: National Foreman's Institute, 2, 4.

Suggested Readings

Aquayo, Rafael. *Dr. Deming: The American Who Taught The Japanese About Quality.* New York: Carol Publishing Group, 1990.

Boudette, Neal E. "Give Me a 'T!' Give Me a 'E!'" *Industry Week* (January 8, 1990): 62–63, 65,67.

Deutsch, Claudia. "Business Meetings by Keyboard." *The Wall Street Journal* (October 21, 1990): F 29.

Dyer, William G. *Team Building: Issues and Alternatives* 2nd ed. Reading, MA: Addison-Wesley, 1987.

Joy, Louis W., and Joy, Jo A. *Frontline Teamwork.* New York: Business One Irwin, 1994.

Katzenbach, Jon R. and Smith, Douglas K. *The Wisdom of Teams.* Boston: Harvard Business School Press, 1993.

Kayser, Thomas A. *Building Team Power.* New York: Irwin, 1994.

Mosvick, Robert K. and Nelson, Robert B. *We've Got to Start Meeting Like This!* Glenview, Ill.: Scott, Foresman, 1987.

Orsburn, Jack, et al. *Self-Directed Work Teams: The New American Challenge.* Homewood, IL: Business One Irwin, 1991.

Stayer, Ralph. "How I Learned to Let My Workers Lead." *Harvard Business Review* (November–December 1990): 73–76.

3M Meeting Management Team. *How to Run Better Business Meetings.* New York: McGraw-Hill, 1987.

Wellins, Richard S., Byham, William C., and Wilson, Jeanne M. *Empowered Teams.* San Francisco: Jossey-Bass, 1991.

10

Leadership and Management Styles

OBJECTIVES

After reading and discussing this chapter, you should be able to do the following:

1. Define this chapter's key terms.

2. List and give examples of this chapter's eleven principles of leadership.

3. Briefly define the contingency model of leadership.

4. Briefly explain the managerial GRID concept of blending concern for production with concern for people.

5. List and give situations in which each of the four management styles would be appropriate.

6. List and briefly explain four leadership indicators.

INTRODUCTION

In Chapter 3, we defined authority as the right to give orders and instructions. Power was defined as the ability to influence others—to get them to subject their wills to yours. In this chapter, we will see that leadership rests in the use of both power and authority but depends most heavily on power. Although all managers need authority—the ability to punish and reward that rests in their formal positions—manager-leaders need both power and authority. It is possible to be a manager and yet not be a leader. Exhibit 10.1 relates these two concepts. On the left, we find managers with management ability who rely solely on their formal authority—that vested in their job descriptions. On the right, we find people, in and out of management jobs, who possess leadership ability—have power over others from several sources. In the middle, we find manager-leaders—those managers who couple their formal authority with their personal power.

Exhibit 10.2 shows the differences between leadership and management in a different way. It contrasts the traditional roles of a manager with the traditional ways in which leaders handle the same functions. Notice the emphasis given to the leader's role in regard to change. John P. Kotter and James L. Heskett, in their book *Corporate Culture and Performance*, write about ten cases involving companies that went through major cultural changes and the roles that their manager-leaders played in making those changes. Among a leader's primary duties are to sense when change is needed, create a vision of what is needed and a strategy for change, sell both to followers, and see to it that meaningful changes take place. Author John Huey (1994) adds:

> As the power of position continues to erode, corporate leaders are going to resemble not so much captains of ships as candidates running for office. They will face two fundamental tasks: first, to develop and articulate exactly what the company is trying to accomplish, and second, to create an environment in which employees can figure out what

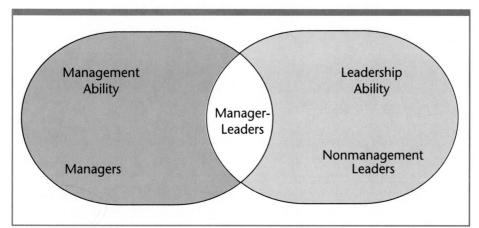

EXHIBIT 10.1
The relationship between managers and leaders.

Management	Leadership
Planning and Budgeting—establishing detailed steps and timetables for achieving needed results, and then allocating the resources necessary to make that happen	*Establishing Direction*—developing a vision of the future, often the distant future, and strategies for producing the changes needed to achieve that vision
Organizing and Staffing—establishing some structure for accomplishing plan requirements, staffing that structure with individuals, delegating responsibility and authority for carrying out the plan, providing policies and procedures to help guide people, and creating methods or systems to monitor implementation	*Aligning People*—communicating the direction by words and deeds to all those whose cooperation may be needed so as to influence the creation of teams and coalitions that understand the vision and strategies, and accept their validity
Controlling and Problem Solving— monitoring results versus plan in some detail, identifying deviations, and then planning and organizing to solve these problems	*Motivating and Inspiring*—energizing people to overcome major political, bureaucratic, and resource barriers to change by satisfying very basic, but often unfulfilled, human needs
Produces a degree of predictability and order, and has the potential of consistently producing key results expected by various stakeholders (for example, for customers, always being on time; for stockholders, being on budget)	Produces change, often to a dramatic degree, and has the potential of producing extremely useful change (for example, new products that customers want, new approaches to labor relations that help make a firm more competitive)

EXHIBIT 10.2
The differences between management and leadership.

Source: Kotter, John P. *A Force for Change: How Leadership Differs from Management* [New York: The Free Press, 1990], 6.

needs to be done and then do it well.... They are confident enough in their vision to delegate.... And they are careful to "model," or live by, the values they espouse.

Chapter 3 pointed out that power comes from one's position. As a manager, you have the right to punish and reward. Power also originates in your personality, competencies, interpersonal relationships, and reputation at work. People look up to authorities who have the expertise they lack. People respect others who are fair and honest. People want to be with and work for others whom they can trust. But trust must be mutual. If you don't trust them, they will find it difficult to trust you. Trust in your people comes from knowing them well—their abilities, goals, and values. You demonstrate it in what you say and do each day. Your behavior at work either earns respect and trust for you or it does not. The example you give sets the tone for your interrelationships and encourages others to use it as an acceptable model for their own behavior. Now-retired vice-president of marketing at IBM, Buck Rodgers (1987), puts it this way:

> The people you're trying to motivate have to believe that you have more leverage in the company than they have. They have to accept you as an authority figure whose influence can help or hurt them…but they must respect you for your integrity and your ability, and that doesn't come with a title—it has to be earned. If your people see you as a person who can get things done—one who will deliver as promised, who can be trusted, and who can be relied on to help them—you are a leader in their eyes and according to their perceptions.

LEADERSHIP

Leadership is the ability to get work done with and through others while winning their respect, confidence, loyalty, and willing cooperation. The first part of our definition is true of management as well. It is the second half of the definition that distinguishes a leader from a nonleader. It is likely that though you may be a leader to some of your subordinates, you may not be to others. The goal is to be a leader to all of your subordinates. Leadership is an art that can be acquired and developed by anyone with the motivation to do so.

All leaders have three limiting factors to contend with. First, they are limited by themselves—by their knowledge, skills, attitudes, and abilities, as well as by their weaknesses and inadequacies in the exercise of their roles. Second, they are limited by the groups over which they have authority—by the level of experience, the skills, the proficiencies, and the attitudes of their subordinates, as individuals and as a group. The ways in which subordinates perceive and interact with their bosses, their jobs, and one another are factors affecting both the quality and the quantity of their output. Finally, leaders are limited by their environment—by the resources and conditions available to them in their efforts to accomplish the assigned tasks and reach the established goals. All these factors undergo almost constant change, which requires the leaders to reassess these factors continually in determining the difficulties to be confronted.

leadership
the ability to get work done with and through others while winning their respect, confidence, loyalty, and willing cooperation

Leadership Principles

What follows are established principles or guidelines that should govern the exercise of your informal and formal authority. These principles, along with your concerted effort to acquire and develop leadership traits, practically guarantee your attaining leadership status in the eyes of your peers and subordinates. Exhibit 10.3 lists eleven principles of leadership.

Each of these principles holds sound advice for you in any leadership position. They serve as concise reminders and as a checklist to which you should frequently refer. They constitute a handy guide to help you assess your practice of management and the exercise of your authority over others. If you understand their meaning and make an honest effort to act in accordance with their wisdom, you can avoid numerous errors and problems.

You should note a similarity between the leadership principles identified in Exhibit 10.3 [and the management skills discussed in Chapter 1: technical, conceptual, and human. Principles one, six, and ten relate to your development and use of technical skills. Principles three, four, five, and six relate to your human skills. Principles seven, nine, and ten relate to conceptual skills. All the traits mentioned earlier relate in some way to each of the principles.

Leadership Traits and Skills

Since the early 1900s, attempts have been made to discover a list of traits that would guarantee leadership status to their possessor. The U.S. Army surveyed all levels of soldiers exiting the service in the late 1940s to determine what traits were possessed by the commanders who were perceived to be effective leaders. Although a list of fourteen traits emerged from the survey, no commander had all the traits listed, and many famous commanders lacked several.

A list of leadership traits and skills appears in Exhibit 10.4. As in the case of the Army's survey, quite a few traits are listed. It is unlikely, there-

EXHIBIT 10.3
Principles of leadership.

Source: U.S. Army.

1. Be technically proficient.
2. Know yourself and seek self-improvement.
3. Know your people and look out for their welfare.
4. Keep your people informed.
5. Set the example.
6. Ensure that each task is understood, supervised, and accomplished.
7. Train your people to work as a team.
8. Make sound and timely decisions.
9. Develop a sense of responsibility in your subordinates.
10. Employ your resources in accordance with their capabilities.
11. Seek responsibilities and accept accountability for your actions.

Traits	Skills
Adaptable to situations	Clever (intelligent)
Alert to social environment	Conceptually skilled
Ambitious and achievement oriented	Creative
Assertive	Diplomatic and tactful
Cooperative	Fluent in speaking
Decisive	Knowledgeable about group task
Dependable	Organized (administrative ability)
Dominant (desire to influence others)	Persuasive
Energetic (high activity level)	Socially skilled
Persistent	
Self-confident	
Tolerant of stress	
Willing to assume responsibility	

EXHIBIT 10.4

Traits and skills commonly associated with leader effectiveness.

Source: Yukl, Gary A. *Leadership in Organizations,* ©1981, 70. Adapted by permission of Prentice Hall, Inc., Englewood Cliffs, N.J.

fore, that any manager-leader would possess all of them. Research has failed to give us a final list of traits that guarantee leadership status to those who possess them.

Employers watch for individual leadership traits in their employees and in prospective employees when they screen them for particular jobs and training programs. Various psychological tests can be used to construct a personality profile of a person. Jobs are often assigned to people who possess leadership traits related to the particular job. Your eligibility for a management job or training program may rest on your employer's assessment of your traits and skills.

Besides psychological tests, your routine performance appraisals, filled out by your boss, often call for the evaluation of specific traits and skills that you may or may not possess. Certain of them may be considered indispensable, whereas others may be a plus but not essential. All the traits and skills listed can be developed and perfected through a commitment to programs designed to do so. Education, training, and experiences can help you acquire them.

Pluralistic Leaders

Leaders routinely rely on a participative leadership style. But leading a diverse workforce calls for a pluralistic leader, one who truly values diversity in the workforce; he or she helps create a work environment that invites everyone's involvement by promoting cooperation and mutual respect (Loden and Rosener, 1991). Here are two suggestions that you can follow to become a pluralistic leader.

First, uncover any barriers. You need to know what problems, if any, exist for the individuals under your influence. Do company policies, customs, rituals, ceremonies, and procedures block their progress? Do they ridicule or ignore anyone's ethnic background or personal condition? If so, what can be done to eliminate the barriers? Are diverse individuals and groups able to communicate and work in harmony with one another? If not, why not? Is your company's management really committed to valuing diversity and empowering women, the differently abled, and minorities? Your own attitudes need analysis as well to determine any biases, values, stereotypes, and actions that inhibit your ability to value and lead people who are different from you. You can use personal interviews, group meetings, an anonymous survey, the results of any companywide survey, or a combination of these to help you.

Second, make personal commitments. You need to have an honest commitment to encourage two-way communication between you and individuals different from you, to gain new knowledge and perceptions, and to better understand each individual for whose working life you are responsible. You must have a personal commitment to eliminating unequal and unfair treatment based on an individual's age, sex, sexual orientation, physical limitations, race, nation of origin, or religion. Make a commitment to train, coach, and empower your diverse subordinates to draw the best from them. "It's not enough to hire for diversity; you must also plan for the development of your nontraditional workers" (Nelton, 1992). When an organization cannot keep its diverse employees, it usually means that they are sending clear signals that success is not possible for them. When management ranks do not reflect worker ranks, the organization sends such a message.

Men, Women, and Leadership

A recent study of 456 executives (355 women and 101 men) reveals some interesting differences between the ways in which both sexes approach the leadership role. Women respondents tend to be interactive—encouraging others' participation, making people feel part of the organization, and making them feel good about themselves and their contributions. The women made frequent references to their efforts to include others by sharing power and information. Interactive leaders "try to instill...group identity in a variety of ways, including encouraging others to have a say in almost every aspect of work, from setting performance goals to determining strategy. To facilitate inclusion, they create mechanisms to get people to participate and they use a conversational style that sends signals inviting people to get involved" (Rosener, 1990).

SUPERVISORS AND QUALITY

According to the Bureau of Labor Statistics (1992), about 15.4 million people age fifty-five or older are in the U.S. workforce. This number will grow by nearly 40 percent through 2005. Older workers bring years of experience and skill to a job and an organization. They also bring stereotypes. Terry A. Barclay heads Operation Able, a Michigan-based nonprofit training and counseling agency for persons age forty-five and older.

According to Barclay, "'The stereotype in our culture is that older workers are resistant to change. The reality is all of us are resistant to change.... I have yet to encounter an older worker who wasn't just as capable as a younger worker of learning a new skill.'"

To bring out the best in every associate, regardless of age, an environment that encourages learning and risk-taking while making people feel secure and valued is a must. Helen Dennis, author of *Fourteen Steps in Managing an Aging Work Force*, observes that: "'An older worker may have more to lose than a younger worker. The chances of finding a comparable job with comparable salary and benefits at age 55 are not high.'" Managing a diverse workforce requires training that encourages people to learn "at their own pace...in a nonthreatening, noncompetitive environment." It also requires supervisors, team leaders, and team facilitators to uncover their associates motives and

goals. "'Sometimes older workers want different things from work than younger ones,'" says Dennis. "'...[T]hey want a chance to be creative, to mentor, to solve problems, to feel they've made a difference. One of the worst feelings is to leave the work force after 35 years feeling like you haven't made a difference. A lot of older workers want to leave a legacy, to pass on their knowledge.'"

Michelle Gaggini, at age twenty-three, practically began her career as a supervisor of older employees. "'Older workers have a lot of experience, often a lot of loyalty. They can offer qualities to the company that younger workers don't have yet.'" To gain their commitment and support, Gaggini tries "'...to give them assignments that make them feel successful, perhaps asking them to lead a group project that will benefit from their experience.'" She avoids making employment decisions based solely on age; such decisions may result in charges of age discrimination.

Instead, she works hard at building their self-confidence and building in chances for early success. To guarantee quality decisions and performances, Gaggini tries a variety of approaches; she consults with and listens to her people. She allows them a certain degree of personal freedom but believes it is important to "'have agreement on the essentials...and harmony on the nonessentials.'"

Source: Cohen, Charles E. "Managing Older Workers," *Working Woman,* November 1994, 61–62.

The men in the survey described their styles as being a set of "transactions with subordinates—exchanging rewards for services rendered or punishment for inadequate performance. The men are also more likely to use power that comes from their organizational position and formal authority" (Rosener, 1990).

Both the men and the women claimed to have an equal mix of traits considered to be feminine (understanding, compassionate, sensitive, dependent), masculine (dominant, tough, assertive, competitive), and gender neutral (adaptive, tactful, sincere, efficient, and reliable). Some men lead with participation and inclusion, and some women lead with the emphasis on exercising their formal authority. Both styles of leading can be effective, depending on the circumstances. "[W]hat is a disadvantage under one set of circumstances is an advantage under another. The 'best' leadership style depends on the organizational context" (Rosener, 1990). Both have much to learn from each other's styles.

Leadership Behaviors

Gary Yukl (1981) and his colleagues have conducted research to develop "meaningful and measurable categories of leader behavior." They have given us nineteen categories of leader behavior, along with definitions and examples (see Exhibit 10.5). These categories clearly label just what leaders do and help us recognize these behaviors in our own daily lives. Since these behaviors are quite specific, they can help you identify what you are doing—or are not doing but could do—to perform your job effectively.

As you study the nineteen categories, rate yourself on how many of them you put to use regularly. Try to link each behavior to the skills and traits in Exhibit 10.4. Then try to relate each to your knowledge of human motivation and to the various theories we examined in Chapter 7. Finally, consider how each ties in with your roles as educator, counselor, judge, and spokesperson.

THE CONTINGENCY MODEL OF LEADERSHIP

Fred E. Fiedler (1974) and others have speculated that the effectiveness of a group or organization depends on two main factors: the leader and the situation the leader and group find themselves in. The leader's authority and power will place limits on his or her ability to get things done through others. Leaders tend to be either task oriented or relationship oriented. Fiedler's situational factors include leader–member relations, task structure, and the leader's positional authority to punish or to reward.

1. *Performance Emphasis:* The extent to which a leader emphasizes the importance of subordinate performance, tries to improve productivity and efficiency, tries to keep subordinates working up to their capacity, and checks on their performance.

   EXAMPLE: My supervisor urged us to be careful not to let orders go out with defective components.

2. *Consideration:* The extent to which a leader is friendly, supportive, and considerate in his or her behavior toward subordinates and tries to be fair and objective.

   EXAMPLE: When a subordinate was upset about something, the supervisor was very sympathetic and tried to console him.

3. *Inspiration:* The extent to which a leader stimulates enthusiasm among subordinates for the work of the group and says things to build subordinate's confidence in their ability to perform assignments successfully and attain group objectives.

   EXAMPLE: My boss told us we were the best design group he had ever worked with, and he was sure that this new product was going to break every sales record in the company.

4. *Praise-Recognition:* The extent to which a leader provides praise and recognition to subordinates with effective performance, shows appreciation for their special efforts and con-tributions, and makes sure they get credit for their helpful ideas and suggestions.

   EXAMPLE: In a meeting, the supervisor told us she is very satisfied with our work and said she appreciated the extra effort we made this month.

5. *Structuring Reward Contingencies:* The extent to which a leader rewards effective subordinate performance with tangible benefits, such as a pay increase, promotion, more desirable assignments, a better work schedule, and more time off.

   EXAMPLE: My supervisor established a new policy that any subordinate who brought in a new client would earn 10 percent of the contracted fee.

6. *Decision Participation:* The extent to which a leader consults with subordinates and otherwise allows them to influence his or her choices.

   EXAMPLE: My supervisor asked me to attend a meeting with him and his boss to develop a new production schedule, and he was very receptive to my ideas on the subject.

7. *Autonomy-Delegation:* The extent to which a leader delegates authority and responsibility to subordinates and allows them to determine how to do their work.

   EXAMPLE: My boss gave me a new project and encouraged me to handle it any way I think is best.

EXHIBIT 10.5
Yukl's nineteen categories of leader behavior.

Source: Yukl, Gary A. *Leadership in Organizations,* ©1981, 121–125. Adapted by permission of Prentice Hall, Inc., Englewood Cliffs, N.J.

8. *Role Clarification:* The extent to which a leader informs subordinates about their duties and responsibilities, specifies the rules and policies that must be observed and lets subordinates know what is expected of them.

> EXAMPLE: My boss called me in to inform me about a rush project that must be given top priority, and she gave me some specific assignments related to this project.

9. *Goal Setting:* The extent to which a leader emphasizes the importance of setting specific performance goals for each important aspect of a subordinate's job, measures progress toward the goals, and provides concrete feedback.

> EXAMPLE: The supervisor held a meeting to discuss the sales quota for next month.

10. *Training-Coaching:* The extent to which a leader determines training needs for subordinates and provides any necessary training and coaching.

> EXAMPLE: My boss asked me to attend an outside course at the company's expense and said I could leave early on the days it was to be held.

11. *Information Dissemination:* The extent to which a leader keeps subordinates informed about developments that affect their work, including events in other work units or outside the organization, decisions made by higher management, and progress in meetings with superiors or outsiders.

> EXAMPLE: The supervisor briefed us about some high-level changes in policy.

12. *Problem Solving:* The extent to which a leader takes the initiative in proposing solutions to serious work-related problems and acts decisively to deal with such problems when a prompt solution is needed.

> EXAMPLE: The unit was short-handed due to illness, and we had an important deadline to meet; my supervisor arranged to borrow two people from other units, so we could finish the job today.

13. *Planning:* The extent to which a leader plans how to efficiently organize and schedule the work in advance, plans how to attain work unit objectives, and makes contingency plans for potential problems.

> EXAMPLE: My supervisor devised a shortcut that allows us to prepare our financial statements in three days instead of the four days it used to take.

EXHIBIT 10.5 (cont.)

14. *Coordinating:* The extent to which a leader coordinates the work of subordinates, emphasizes the importance of coordination, and encourages subordinates to coordinate their activities.

> EXAMPLE: My supervisor had subordinates who were ahead in their work help those who were behind so that the different parts of the project would be ready at the same time.

15. *Work Facilitation:* The extent to which a leader obtains for subordinates any necessary supplies, equipment, support services, or other resources; eliminates problems in the work environment; and removes other obstacles that interfere with the work.

> EXAMPLE: I asked my boss to order some supplies, and he arranged to get them right away.

16. *Representation:* The extent to which a leader establishes contacts with other groups and important people in the organization, persuades them to appreciate and support his or her work unit, and uses his or her influence with superiors and outsiders to promote and defend the interests of the work unit.

> EXAMPLE: My supervisor met with the data processing manager to get some revisions made in the computer programs, so they will be better suited to our needs.

17. *Interaction Facilitation:* The extent to which a leader tries to get subordinates to be friendly with each other, cooperate, share information and ideas, and help each other.

> EXAMPLE: The sales manager took the group out to lunch to give everybody a chance to get to know the new sales representative.

18. *Conflict Management:* The extent to which a leader restrains subordinates from fighting and arguing, encourages them to resolve conflicts in a constructive manner, and helps settle conflicts and disagreements between subordinates.

> EXAMPLE: Two members of the department who were working together on a project were having a dispute about it; the manager met with them to help resolve the matter.

19. *Criticism-Discipline:* The extent to which a leader criticizes or disciplines a subordinate who shows consistently poor performance, violates a rule, or disobeys an order; disciplinary actions include an official warning, reprimand, suspension, or dismissal.

> EXAMPLE: The supervisor was annoyed that a subordinate kept making the same kinds of errors and warned him to make a more concerted effort.

EXHIBIT 10.5 (cont.)

Leadership Personalities

According to Fiedler's contingency model (sometimes called situational leadership), leaders are primarily motivated by their tasks or their interpersonal relationships with their followers. Whether one or the other is an appropriate focus depends on the leader's situation. Task-oriented leaders seek accomplishments that fortify their sense of self-esteem and competence. Relationship-oriented leaders seek the admiration and respect of their followers to meet their social and esteem needs. Both types of leaders need to be able to play both kinds of roles. The task-oriented leader may, as the need arises, adopt the relationship orientation. A relationship-oriented leader may focus on getting the job done when a crisis arises and time is short. But each will then return to his or her former orientation. This flexibility marks a true leader who is destined to achieve higher authority. Not all people have this flexibility (Fiedler, 1974).

The Leadership Situation

According to Fiedler's contingency model, a leader's situation has three variables: the degree to which the leader is or feels accepted by followers, the degree to which the task to be accomplished is structured or defined, and the extent of the leader's power—his or her job description and the influence held over others in the organization. The greater the leader's power and acceptance by followers, and the more highly structured the task, the easier it is for the leader to control a situation (Fiedler, 1974).

The interaction of these variables is shown in Exhibit 10.6. On the bottom of the figure are eight combinations of the three variables, each describing a possible work situation. In position III, for example, the manager enjoys good member relations, the tasks of the subordinates are unstructured, and the leader possesses a strong organizational power base.

On the upper half of the figure are the two orientation styles: employee orientation and task orientation. In position I—where leader–member relations are good, task is structured, and leader position power is strong—the manager should employ a task-oriented approach. In position IV—where leader–member relations are good, task is unstructured, and leader position power is weak—employee-oriented behavior would be more appropriate.

Research into the contingency model shows that task-oriented leaders perform best when they have either high or low concentrations of power, control, and influence over their situations. Relationship-oriented leaders perform best with moderate power, control, and influence. Leaders should be matched to the situation that calls for their favored approach or orientation. Instead, organizations often require managers to adjust to a variety of situations calling for different approaches by managers.

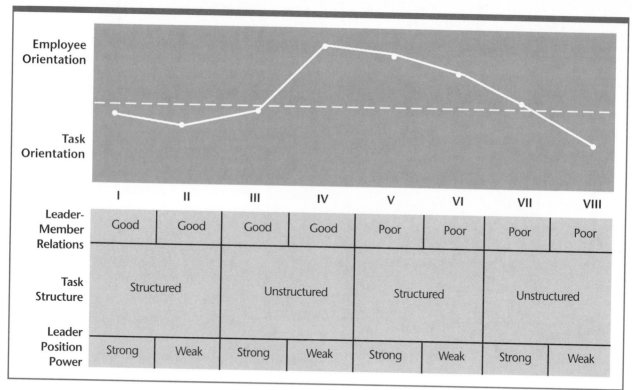

	I	II	III	IV	V	VI	VII	VIII
Leader-Member Relations	Good	Good	Good	Good	Poor	Poor	Poor	Poor
Task Structure	Structured		Unstructured		Structured		Unstructured	
Leader Position Power	Strong	Weak	Strong	Weak	Strong	Weak	Strong	Weak

EXHIBIT 10.6

How the style of effective leadership varies with the situation.

THE MANAGERIAL GRID®

Many studies show that a leader's concern for or focus on his or her subordinates should be balanced against a concern for production or results. In the short run, managers who bow to organizational pressures to get results often achieve the greatest success by focusing on production and ignoring the needs of their subordinates. This kind of crisis management works best to put out fires when time is short. It almost always utilizes the autocratic style of leadership, which we describe later in this chapter.

Research tells us that in the long run, however, the best leadership style is one that attempts to maintain a balance between the needs of subordinates and the demands of the organization for results. Exhibit 10.7 shows the managerial GRID concept developed by Robert Blake and Jane S. Mouton (1975).

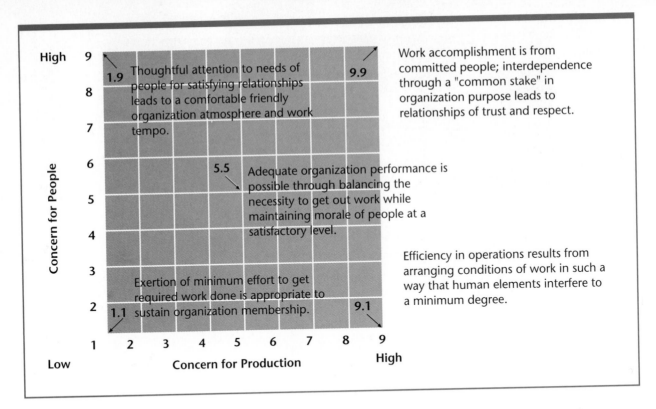

EXHIBIT 10.7
The managerial GRID.

Source: Adapted and reprinted by permission of *Harvard Business Review.* An exhibit from "Breakthrough in Organization Development" by Robert R. Blake, Jane S. Mouton, Louis B. Barnes, and Larry E. Greiner (November–December 1964). Copyright © 1964 by the President and Fellows of Harvard College. All rights reserved.

Position 1.9 on the grid may be described as one in which thoughtful attention to the needs of people for satisfying relationships leads to a comfortable, friendly organizational atmosphere and work tempo. Position 1.1 allows for the exertion of minimum effort to get the required work done and to hold on to the organization's members. Position 5.5 represents a balance between the need to get work accomplished and the need to maintain adequate morale levels. Position 9.1 represents a maximum focus on getting work out and arranging conditions of work so that human elements interfere to a minimum degree. Position 9.9 allows for work to be accomplished by committed people, for an interdependence of workers and management through a common stake in the organization, and for a relationship between leaders and followers that is based on trust and respect (Blake and Mouton, 1975).

Where the leader fits on the grid at any given time is not entirely for him or her to decide. The leader's personality and management orientation, the company's culture and climate, and the competence of the followers all influence placement. Leaders should strive for the 9.9 position but remain flexible enough to adapt to the needs of the followers and the situation.

As Tannenbaum and Schmidt (1973) have pointed out in their excellent article on choosing a leadership pattern, a successful leader knows the forces that influence his or her behavior at any given time and accurately understands himself or herself, the individuals and group he or she is dealing with, and the broader social environment in which he or she operates. The leader can then determine the most appropriate orientation to take and behave accordingly.

The appropriate position for a manager to take at any given time may be dictated by the people and circumstances involved. When time is short and deadlines are fast approaching, a shift to position 9.1 may be called for. With new and inexperienced people who are undergoing training, position 9.1 may again be called for. The key idea under both sets of circumstances is to get work out or get people productive as soon as possible. As time passes and pressures subside, the manager has the opportunity to focus on subordinates as individuals and begin to move toward a 5.5 position. With highly competent, experienced people, a manager can move to a 9.9 position—one in which teams are molded and individuals pool their skills to focus on a goal common to all team members.

As a manager, you will not be in any one position on the grid with all of your people. Some may call for a 1.9 or a 9.1 position today and later may require a 9.9 or a 5.5 position. The real value of the grid is to help you decide, at any given time, what position you are in with regard to an individual or to your entire group of subordinates. Then you must ask yourself if you should be in the position you are in. The theories that follow will help you pick a proper grid position.

MANAGEMENT AND LEADERSHIP STYLES

Four main styles of management are available to you: bureaucratic, autocratic, democratic, and spectator. All but the bureaucratic style are also leadership styles. Each can have either a positive or a negative impact on your subordinates, depending on their characteristics and the situation in which each is used. As we will see, each has its place and, when used appropriately, can help you motivate people and create an environment that fosters both quality and productivity. As a leader-supervisor, you must be able to use all three leadership styles as the need for each arises.

Exhibit 10.8 compares the three leadership styles in terms of the ways in which they use authority. Note that at the left, managers hold most of the formal authority. The manager-leader may announce a decision or ask for feedback on it before it is made final or implemented, but the decision is

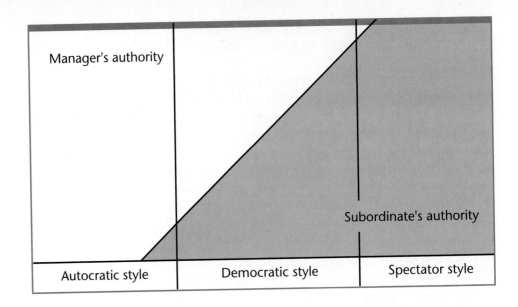

EXHIBIT 10.8
A comparison of the three leadership styles.

Manager's authority

Subordinate's authority

| Autocratic style | Democratic style | Spectator style |

made by the manager-leader. The middle position asks subordinates to play a part in making the decision. They may be asked to help define a problem, to come up with alternatives, to evaluate alternatives, or to do a combination of these. Finally, on the right, subordinates are delegated the authority they need to make their own decisions, individually or through teams.

The Bureaucratic Style

bureaucratic style
a management style characterized by the manager's reliance on rules, regulations, policies, and procedures to direct subordinates

The **bureaucratic style** is typified by the manager's reliance on rules, regulations, policy, and procedures. To him or her, they represent authority and certainty. It is management by the book. Through the exercise of this style, the manager adopts the posture of a police officer religiously enforcing rules and depending on superiors to resolve problems not covered in the manual.

Unlike the other three styles, the bureaucratic style cannot really be a leadership style because managers who practice it are not really directing their people in a personal way. Instead, they are directing them through regulations, procedures, and policies.

Prerequisites There are three major prerequisites for the use of the bureaucratic style:

1. All the other styles must be inappropriate for use.
2. Subordinates subjected to this style must need it.
3. Latitude in decision making and deviations from procedures must be forbidden to the manager and subordinates.

Limitations This style is appropriate for governmental bodies, military services, and nonprofit enterprises such as public hospitals and char-

ities. It has a very small place in businesses, and its use there should be limited to the following situations:

- During the installation of new equipment and operations when the people in charge of an operation are specialists
- In doing research or conducting analytical studies
- In training record-keeping, filing, and other clerical personnel where faithful adherence to set procedures is essential for the success of the job
- In enforcing safety or carrying out strictly routine, highly repetitive operations

If used properly, the bureaucratic approach can be an effective style that has positive effects on people. If used improperly, it can be devastating to anyone with ambition and creativity who is subjected to it.

Employee Reactions   This style does little to build motivation in subordinates. It promotes the formulation of strong work habits that, after a time, become very difficult to change in even the smallest way without strong employee resistance. Employees tend to adopt an indifferent attitude toward their peers and their work. The supervisor becomes rather unimportant to the subordinate and is perceived by them as a watchdog rather than a manager. Workers generally do what is expected of them but little more. There are a number of people, however—both in and out of management—for whom this style represents security, and they respond well to this style for that reason. For most people, however, it is only of value in the special situations listed previously.

The Autocratic Style

autocratic style
a management and leadership style characterized by the retention by the leader of all authority for decision making

Leaders of the **autocratic style** keep power to themselves and do not delegate to their subordinates. The making of a final decision is reserved for the leaders alone. They keep their subordinates dependent on them for instructions, and they allow their subordinates to act only under their direct supervision.

Prerequisites   The necessary prerequisites for using the autocratic style are the following:

1. You must be an expert in the practice of management, as well as in the handling of your subordinates' jobs.
2. Your subordinates must need this approach.
3. You must wish to communicate primarily by means of orders and detailed instructions.

Limitations   In general, you should restrict your use of this style to the following situations:

The autocratic style of management lends itself to situations where you need short-term, high-quantity production out of your staff. Supervising repair and damage from a ruptured storm drain in New York City is one such situation.

- When you are dealing with new employees who are unfamiliar with the tasks and methods they are expected to perform
- When time is short or when there is an emergency situation that does not allow you to explain the reasons for your orders
- When you are directing a stubborn or difficult subordinate who does not respond favorably to requests or to your use of the other three styles of supervision
- When your authority is directly challenged (by putting your wishes in the form of orders, you place your subordinate in the position of either following the orders or being guilty of insubordination)

You should restrict your use of this style of supervision to the situations outlined. If you lack the prerequisites, you cannot use it effectively. Once the situation changes, you should shift to another leadership style. Keep in mind that the autocratic style is both a management style and a leadership style.

Employee Reactions   People subjected to the autocratic style will generally be high-quantity producers but only for the short run. They will tend to be tense and somewhat fearful of you. If the style is used on a person too long—that is, after the need for it has ceased—he or she will become resentful and withhold his or her normal contributions to the job. It is not a style that builds team players or encourages strong ties among the workers. It causes subordinates to become dependent on their leaders.

The Democratic Style

Managers of the **democratic style** adopt a "we" approach to their work and to their subordinates. They play the role of coaches, drilling their teams on fundamentals and sharing decision-making authority with them. They make frequent use of problem-solving meetings, as outlined in Chapter 9. They delegate freely to subordinates who have earned their confidence, as well as to members of the group in general. They attempt to build a strong team spirit and to foster mutual respect and interdependence between themselves as coaches and the members of the team, as well as among the team members and their peers.

This style of supervision often goes by other names, such as the consultative, general, or participative style. It is a leadership style very much in use today.

Prerequisites   The following conditions are needed before you implement the democratic style:

democratic style
a management and leadership style characterized by a sharing of decision-making authority with subordinates by the leader

If you supervise using the democratic style of management, you will share decision-making responsibility with your subordinates. This style works well with highly skilled or experienced workers.

1. You should have your superior's permission to use it.
2. You should be willing to accept a certain number of mistakes and delays in the early stages of its implementation.
3. You should have a personal commitment to this style and a strong belief in its ability to motivate people; once you extend this style to your subordinates, you will find it difficult to shift to a different style.
4. You should have carefully prepared your subordinates by means of initial delegations of some of your authority, and you should be willing to continue to consult with your subordinates on small matters during the early stages of the new style's use.
5. You should have a high degree of patience and the time required for group meetings on decision making and other topics.
6. You should be prepared to accept less-than-optimum solutions to problems.

Some supervisors may feel threatened by this style. If so, they should not attempt to use it or be asked to use it until they have been prepared through training to do so. A worker who has never before been asked for the time of day, let alone an opinion on new procedures, might become quite suspicious at sudden attempts to obtain his or her participation in matters affecting the department.

Limitations   This style is best used in the following situations:

- When your workers are highly skilled or highly experienced at their jobs

- Where time is sufficient to permit participation by your subordinates as individuals or as a group
- When preparing groups or individuals for changes
- When attempting to solve problems common to the group (such as improvement in methods, in safety, or in environmental conditions) and when group support is needed to implement solutions
- When attempting to air gripes or otherwise relieve workers' tensions

Employee Reactions   The great majority of today's workers are educated enough for the democratic style of leadership. Through it they can achieve and sustain a high quality and quantity of output for extended periods. The supervisor who uses this approach is employee centered rather than work centered, and his or her people know it. They appreciate the trust and freedom that the supervisor gives them through the use of the democratic style. Cooperation and group spirit are strongly promoted, and a corresponding boost is given to morale. Under the democratic style, workers tend to understand the contributions of their peers to a greater degree, and they get to know each other better than under the other two styles.

The transition at Levi Strauss & Company's Murphy, North Carolina, plant points out the value of both democratic and spectator styles. The plant moved from a traditional, top-down autocratic style of management to a team-based mix of democratic and spectator styles.

> ...Tommye Jo Daves, a 58-year-old mountain-bred grandmother...is responsible for the plant which employs 385 workers and turns out some three million pairs of Levi's jeans a year.... [Through management training]...two lessons stuck with Daves: 'You can't lead a team by barking orders, and you have to have a vision in your head of what you're trying to do.'... She and her line supervisors have since been converting their plant...to team management, in which teams of workers are cross-trained for 36 tasks instead of one or two and thrust into running the plant, from organizing supplies to setting production goals to making personnel policy. Now Daves and her mostly female management crew get lots of direction from the ranks but much less from above (Huey, 1994).

The results? She and her team have reduced the company's policy manual from 700 pages to 50. Quality and customer-response time have improved, whereas costs and rejects have declined. The transition has not been an easy one. Says Daves, "'sometimes it's real hard for me not to push back and say, 'You do this, you do that.'... Now I have to say, 'How do you want to do this?' I have to realize that their ideas may not be the way to go, but I have to let them learn that for themselves'" (Huey, 1994).

The Spectator Style

The **spectator style,** sometimes called the free-rein style, is characterized by treating subordinates as independent decision makers. The manager or

spectator style
A management style characterized by treating subordinates as independent decision makers

SUPERVISING TEAMS

"In traditional American organizations, it was not unusual for managers and supervisors either to ignore the emergence of...subgroups or to actively discourage this natural process for fear that such groups would constitute cliques whose informal leaders would represent a challenge to formal authority."

Today's supervisors are being taught to encourage the formation of teams and how to transform workers into leaders and members of self-managing teams.

Carl Bramlette, a management professor at Georgia State University, has given us a set of phases that supervisors pass through while moving from the traditional planner, director, and controller focused on individual subordinates to what he calls a "team resource person." The first phase has the supervisor recognizing or forming—on his or her own or through higher management edict—one or more work-unit teams. The supervisor is at the center, managing and initiating, encouraging team member interaction, and beginning the process of sharing "control and problem-solving duties with group members."

The second phase begins as the supervisor moves away from traditional methods of managing and begins to share leadership roles and functions with team members. The supervisor becomes a "coordinator," managing "the group primarily through coordination of their skills and activities, and using their resources as fully as possible." Training and power sharing continue while the supervisor increases contacts with other individuals and teams outside his or her unit or specific teams.

Phase three transforms the supervisor into what Bramlette labels a "team boundary manager," leaving daily decisions and activities in the hands of willing and competent team members. Teams continue to report to the supervisor. "He or she collects data and gives the group feedback on its performance based upon such measures as production, quality, cost, or customer satisfaction." The supervisor acts as a facilitator, getting the resources needed for each team and acting as a mediator between the groups and outsiders. The supervisor may intervene when a group has a problem it can't resolve.

Finally, the supervisor becomes a "team resource person." Teams now have accountability for their own work and determine their own leadership. The team resource person provides any assistance the team may require or arranges for it to be provided by others. Eventually, the team resource person may be phased out.

Source: Bramlette, Jr., Carl A. "Free to Change," *Training and Development Journal,* March 1984, 62–70.

manager-leader develops a strong independent spirit in individual subordinates and teams and relies on their skills, knowledge, experience, and initiative. Subordinates, individually or in teams, perceive themselves to be professionals—that is, experts in their specialties.

The supervisor becomes a facilitator, coach, and consultant. He or she remains available to subordinates and will intervene when asked to do so or when it is deemed necessary. Supervisors are generally physically removed from direct and frequent contact with subordinates, but continue to stay in touch through meetings, reports, and records of output.

This style of leadership is usually the last phase in the evolution of the supervisor's approach to handling subordinates, as both this chapter's Supervising Teams feature and the life-cycle theory of leadership point out.

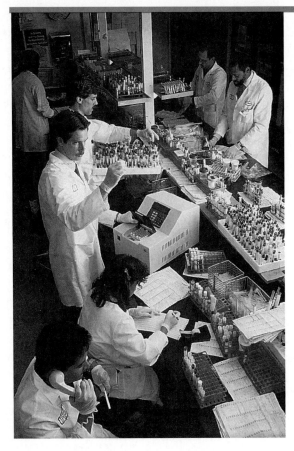

The spectator style of management is useful when your workers are experts in their field and enjoy working independently. Lab technicians are one such example. What could you do as supervisor to motivate such workers?

Prerequisites The prerequisites of the spectator style of leadership are as follows:

1. Since workers are treated as experts, they must be highly experienced and skilled in their crafts.
2. Controls other than direct and frequent observations must be established to monitor the performance and interactions of both individuals and teams.
3. Workers, individually and collectively, must possess pride in themselves and their abilities as well as the qualities of endurance and initiative.

Limitations The use of the spectator style should be restricted, as a rule, to the following groups or situations:

- When you have in your department highly skilled, experienced, and educated personnel
- When you are using outside experts, such as staff specialists, consultants, or temporary skilled help
- When you as the boss are new at your job or lack personal experience in the work being performed by your subordinates

Employee Reactions Workers who work under the spectator style perceive themselves as being in business for themselves; that is, they adopt a somewhat independent air and see their boss as a kind of staff assistant who stands ready to help them if they need him or her. This style generally promotes high levels of individual output for indefinite periods. It fosters pride and morale better than the other styles do. But if the boss becomes too remote or inaccessible, insecurity may set in, along with resulting stress, fears, and frustrations. All the workers are pretty much on their own and strongly feel the need to prove themselves to their boss and their peers. Consequently, people working under this style need constant reassurance that they are performing up to standard and that they are appreciated.

As a supervisor, team leader, or team facilitator, you must be familiar with all four management styles. You will be faced with subordinates, associates, and situations at one time or another that will call on you to use each of these styles.

During the training of a new employee, you should probably rely on the autocratic style, the bureaucratic style, or a blend of the two. Once the newcomer has been placed in his or her job and is performing up to standard, you should switch to one of the other styles of leadership. If you do not, your worker may rebel, and you will have gone a long way toward helping bring about his or her termination.

If you try to use a style that is wrong for a specific subordinate, he or she will probably let you know it. Changes in an associate's attitudes and behavior are the first sign that you may be using an improper style of leadership. Selecting the proper style for individual workers is easy once you acquire some experience as a supervisor, but it may involve a bit of trial and error. Do not hesitate to switch if the style you are presently using fails to get the desired results. And don't forget that a lot of help is available to you through the advice and counsel of your peers and your superiors.

You may not be entirely free to select your own styles of leadership. Your boss may frown on the use of one or another of them. You may feel inadequate in your understanding of how to implement one or more of the styles. Your tendency might be to use the one you feel most at home with on all of your people. This is almost always a mistake. A subordinate who has worked well under a spectator style may, because of changes in his or her job, require an autocratic or democratic style of direction to get him or her through a period of transition to a new assignment. You should stand ready to offer the style each subordinate needs. Only by practice and study can you feel confident enough to use all four styles successfully.

THE LIFE-CYCLE THEORY

People need different styles of supervision and leadership at different times. Paul Hersey and Kenneth Blanchard (1982) have given us a theory of the general evolution in the leadership approaches to employees as their tenure and experience grow. The life-cycle theory, detailed in Exhibit 10.9, shows that the new employee (block 1) needs a high-task focus. As the

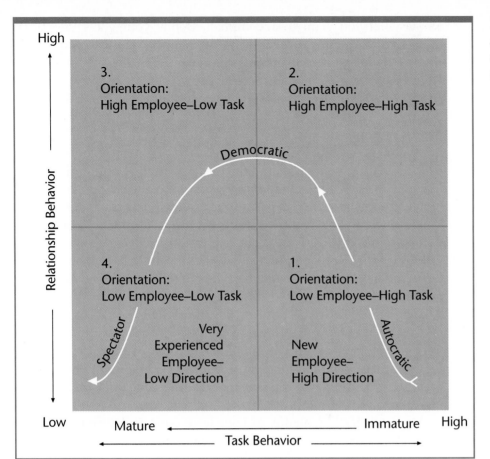

EXHIBIT 10.9
Adaptation of Hersey and Blanchard's life-cycle theory.

employee takes on new knowledge and skills and demonstrates competence, he or she requires a high-employee–high-task focus (block 2). With employees who have matured in both tenure and capabilities, the supervisor can move from a high-direction to a low-direction focus, as required (block 4—the experienced, secure employee) (Hersey and Blanchard, 1982).

THE BASIC STEPS TO BECOMING A LEADER

After many years in marketing management at IBM, Buck Rodgers (1987), reports that there are nine basic steps, as he sees it, to becoming an influential manager-leader:

1. Establish who's in charge. Each person in a unit within an organization must be clear about his or her authority, responsibility, and accountability.

2. Know what you want to accomplish. Define your goals, short and long term. Map out your priorities for each day. Monitor your use of time, and check on your progress regularly.

3. Know what you want each person you manage to accomplish. Set specific goals for a person to achieve, and let that person know the quality of performance expected. Judge performance on achievements, not on style.

4. Let the person know what you expect. Don't let people guess at what you want from them or about how they are doing. Communicate regularly with each individual about what you expect and about what will happen when those expectations are met, exceeded, or not met.

5. Find out what your employee wants for himself or herself. Insist that each subordinate spell out goals, aspirations, and expectations.

6. Find out what your employee expects of you. What is expected in terms of help—more frequent or less frequent contact with you? more responsibility?

7. Take being a role model seriously. Subordinates do as you do more often than they do as you say they should do. Your example provides the psychological and performance models for your group.

8. Expect others to be self-motivated, but don't count on it. People have their peaks and valleys. You may need to intercede on occasion, helping subordinates to improve, grow, and prosper.

9. Understand that the quality of your leadership is determined by the methods you use to motivate others. What you use and apply to others will be used and applied to you. Open, honest, and sensitive communication builds mutual trust and respect.

ASSESSING YOUR LEADERSHIP ABILITY

You can rely on four major indicators as you attempt to determine the effectiveness of your leadership with your people: (1) morale, (2) group spirit, (3) proficiency, and (4) self-discipline. Each of these in turn can be evaluated to help measure the impact you and your methods are having on your formal group members, individually and collectively.

Morale

People's attitudes toward all the individuals, things, and events that affect them at work constitute their morale. Morale can be defined as an individual's state of mind with regard to his or her job, supervisor, peers, and company. It reflects a person's level of involvement in work and appreciation of the people and conditions that he or she must relate to every day. Through the actions and statements of people, you can effectively mea-

SUPERVISORS AND ETHICS

Ray is a traditional supervisor of a toy department in a major chain of discount stores. After the store closed last night, he spent two hours setting up discount signs on various "specials" throughout his department that offered customers up to 25 percent discounts on several very popular items. The discounts he posted were faxed to him yesterday by company headquarters and were to remain in effect for the next seven days.

Shortly after opening the store this morning, one of his cashiers notified Ray that a customer was complaining about the scanner's price not matching the store's sale price for an item. Ray scanned the item and discovered that the new sales price was not recorded. Instead, the older higher price was still in the computer's memory. Ray immedi-

ately told his cashier to honor the sale price and reported his finding to the store manager, Ukare Shimito.

Ukare seemed somewhat unconcerned, dismissing the problem as an "oversight" on her part, and told Ray that the sale price would be entered shortly. She gave Ray this advice: "If the customer discovers a price difference at checkout, honor the sale price you posted by the merchandise."

Throughout the day, Ray was notified of several other price differences by cashiers. All but one was in the store's favor; prices were higher than the sale placards advertised. By closing time, the sale prices still had not been entered into the computer.

What do you think of the store manager's response to Ray? If you were in Ray's position, what would you do now?

sure their morale. If your subordinates are positive individuals who take pride in their work, they reflect favorably on you and your group. If they are absent frequently, fail to attend to their duties, or dwell on negative factors, you can assume that you strike them as less than a leader.

Group Spirit

What are the major attitudes reflected by the members of your formal group and any informal groups associated with it? Are they positive and supportive, fostering teamwork and harmony, or are they negative and destructive? Both individual and group attitudes are shaped in large measure by your human relations efforts. If your group is without team spirit, have you recently voiced your appreciation for its achievements? Are you trying to work with its members and to use their talents? Do you know their needs and values? Do you know your group members as individuals?

Proficiency

How good are you at your job? How good are your subordinates? Are you making an effort to improve both your own level of competence and theirs? Are you aware of any efforts of theirs to seek a higher level of competence? Are you fostering their growth and development? This indicator is tied directly to morale and group spirit. If these are below normal or negative, your subordinates' demonstrated proficiency levels will be too.

Self-Discipline

Can your shop or office function in your absence? Do your people respond promptly and positively to your instructions? Do they accept honest criticism well? Have you had to reprimand more often than praise? Do your people know the reasons behind what they are expected to do? Can they be trusted? If not, what are you doing about these problems?

You can rate yourself by using these indicators at any time. Chances are that your boss is doing so regularly. If you are placing the kind of emphasis that you should on your human relations, you should experience little difficulty in these general areas.

Instant Replay

1. Leadership is based on a person's formal authority and other sources of influence, such as one's personality, skills, knowledge, and personal relationships with others.
2. Not all leaders are managers, and not all managers are leaders. People who can get work done through willing followers who respect them in the process are leaders.
3. Various leaders have various different traits, such as enthusiasm, tact, and endurance. No one set of traits is common to all leaders.
4. Leadership principles offer advice on how a person who wants to be a leader should behave. They are illustrations of a manager's three skills studied in Chapter 1.
5. The contingency model of leadership holds that the effectiveness of a group or organization depends on the leader and the leader's situation.
6. In general, leaders can adopt a focus on task or a focus on people. In some circumstances, they must focus on both. Which focus they adopt depends on their own abilities, their subordinates' abilities, and the situation they face at any given time.
7. The managerial GRID represents the possible positions managers may take with respect to their focus on and blending of their two primary orientations: task and people. Use it to determine where you

are with regard to specific subordinates both individually and in teams.

8. There are four management styles: bureaucratic, autocratic, democratic, and spectator. The last three are also leadership styles.

9. Four ways to assess your leadership effectiveness are to evaluate the morale of your individual followers, their individual levels of proficiency, their levels of self-discipline, and the spirit of the teams you supervise.

Questions for Class Discussion

1. Can you define this chapter's key terms?
2. What are this chapter's eleven principles of leadership? Can you give an example of each from your own experience?
3. What is the contingency model of leadership's basic parts?
4. What does the managerial GRID system attempt to show with regard to leaders?
5. What are the four basic management styles? Which is not a leadership style, and why isn't it?
6. What style of supervision would you use in each of the following situations, and why would you use it?
   a. A new employee with two years' experience in a similar job
   b. An old-timer who appears to be an informal leader of one of the cliques in your department
   c. A neurotic employee, with a good deal of experience, whose neurosis is interfering with his or her job performance
   d. An employee, with many more years' experience than you have, who resents you personally and your authority
7. What are four indicators of how well a person is leading?

Incident

Purpose: To emphasize the differences between leadership and management.

Your Task: Read each listing, and indicate if it is unique to (a) management, or (b) leadership.

1. Creating a vision for the company or company unit   ___
2. Engaging in day-to-day planning   ___
3. Sensing the need for and producing the strategies for change ___
4. Setting the path for reengineering the company or its units ___
5. Setting up an organization structure   ___
6. Controlling and problem solving   ___
7. Inspiring and energizing people to overcome barriers   ___
8. Producing a degree of predictability and order   ___
9. Creating policies and procedures   ___

Conflicts

Peggy Simmons has just been appointed supervisor of the shipping operations at Fantasy Products, a Toronto mail-order operation specializing in unusual consumer products. She has worked for the company in several capacities, but this is her first supervisory position. She is now responsible for five women, three of whom she has worked with as a co-worker in the past. Her section packs and ships orders as they are received from the order-processing department.

Peggy has a reputation with three of her subordinates as a fun person. Betty, Susan, and Ellen have all worked with Peggy in the past and know her to be full of life and a joy to be with. Peggy knows a great many jokes and shares them whenever she can. She joked her way through many of the rush days from November through December. Although she has been known to come late and to leave early on occasion, she worked hard and carefully when she was on the job.

During her first week as supervisor, Peggy tried to remain her old self. But problems began to appear. With the Christmas season just two weeks away, Peggy knew that things had to get better soon if orders were to be processed quickly enough. She sensed a carefree and leisurely atmosphere, which already had caused a backlog of several days' orders. No one seemed to take Peggy seriously.

When Peggy tried to change her approach from "they know what to do, let them do it" to "from now on, it's by the book," Betty was the first to react. In discussions during breaks, Betty made it clear to her co-workers that she felt Peggy was letting power go to her head. Ellen agreed and added that she and the others probably knew what to do better than Peggy did. Susan believed that in a few weeks all the fun would be out of their work if Peggy persisted in rigid work routines and shipping schedules. All three had influence over the other two women because they had been around a long time and had worked with Peggy for several years.

By the end of Peggy's third week, it was clear that a revolt was in the making. Her subordinates seemed to be ignoring her quotas for the day and just smiled at her when she tried to get them to pick up the pace. Breaks seemed to be stretching from fifteen minutes to thirty. When Peggy called Susan aside to talk with her about the problems, Susan was openly hostile and told her that Betty and Ellen were on her side and doing what she was doing, too. Susan demanded to know why she was being singled out for criticism. One day Peggy was absent and returned to find that the shop had fallen nearly two days behind. It was clear to her that the five subordinates had sat on their hands in her absence.

Questions

1. Assess Peggy's leadership using the four measures at the end of this chapter.
2. What leadership traits does Peggy seem to lack? What leadership skills does she lack? (Use Exhibit 10.4 in your answer.)

3. What could Fantasy Products have done to prevent Peggy's current situation?
4. What style of management did Peggy begin with? What style is she attempting to use at the end of the case?

Shock Therapy

Robert Manson is exhausted. He has just returned home from his first day as a trainee at Casa Del Sol, a neighborhood restaurant featuring Mexican cuisine. Bob has been hired to learn the business and eventually to take over its management once the owner, José Morales, leaves to open his second restaurant. After going through his mail and finishing a beer, Bob begins to reflect on the day's experiences.

The first thing that bothered Bob was the fact that José was an absolute dictator. He seemed to be the exact opposite of what his college course in supervision said a manager should be. Bob remembered how José shouted orders and instructions to almost everyone throughout the day. Even during the slack periods between meals, José was making constant demands on his people, Bob included. Not once could Bob remember José asking anyone's opinion or using the word "please." Despite José's approach to management, the restaurant ran like a well-oiled machine. This fact puzzled Bob the most. Why, he thought, weren't the people resentful of José? They all did their jobs efficiently, and not once had Bob heard them complain.

Bob remembered one incident very clearly. A waiter had asked José if he could make a change in a procedure. After listening impatiently to the proposal, José responded as follows, "No good. Just do it like I trained you to, and we will all get along just fine. Everyone here does everything the same, and that's the way it is. You follow?" The waiter nodded and went back to his duties.

Bob was worried that he could not operate the restaurant in José's style. He knew the values of participative management and felt that it was his natural style. He was afraid that he could not adjust to an autocratic style, especially since he believed it was a negative style, to be used when all other styles failed.

During his first day, Bob had studied the restaurant's procedures and questioned the wisdom behind a few of them. Now he felt he could not discuss them with José. He began to think his career in restaurant management would be a short one if he could not adjust to José's methods.

Bob liked José. All the people who worked for José seemed quite happy with their work. José had been civil and even friendly toward Bob throughout the day, but he demanded and got instant reactions from people. The restaurant was a successful business and offered Bob the promise of a very fine salary. José's methods certainly seemed to work, and the place was packed for three meals each day.

How can it be, Bob reflected, that such autocratic methods had produced such good results? Bob begins to search for his text on supervision.

Questions

1. Why does José's autocratic style yield good results?
2. Where would you place José on the managerial GRID? Why?
3. Assess José's leadership ability using the four measures discussed in the text.
4. What advice do you have for Bob?

Notes

Blake, R. R., and Mouton, J. S. "Breakthrough in Organization Development," in *Harvard Business Classics: Fifteen Key Concepts for Managerial Success* (Cambridge, Mass.: *Harvard Business Review*, 1975), 162.

Fiedler, Fred E. "The Contingency Model—New Directions for Leadership Utilization," *Journal of Contemporary Business* vol. 3 no. 4 Autumn 1974, 65–80.

Hersey, Paul, and Blanchard, Kenneth H. *Management of Organizational Behavior: Utilizing Human Resources*, 4th ed. (Englewood Cliffs, N.J.: Prentice Hall, 1982), 88–91.

Huey, John. "The New Post-Heroic Leadership," *Fortune*, February 21, 1994, 44, 48.

Loden, Marilyn, and Rosener, Judy B. *Workforce America!* (Homewood, Ill.: Business One Irwin, 1991), 180–194.

Nelton, Sharon. "Winning with Diversity," *Nation's Business*, September 1992, 18–22, 24.

Rodgers, Buck, with Levey, Irv. *Getting the Most Out of Yourself and Others* (New York: Harper & Row, 1987), 122.

Rosener, Judy B. "Ways Women Lead," *Harvard Business Review*, November–December 1990, 119–125; and Sharon Nelton, "Men, Women, and Leadership," *Nation's Business*, May 1991, 16–22.

Tannenbaum, Robert, and Schmidt, Warren H. "How to Choose a Leadership Pattern," *Harvard Business Review*, May–June 1973, 162–164, 168, 170, 173, 175, 178–180.

Yukl, Gary A. *Leadership in Organizations* (Englewood Cliffs, N.J.: Prentice Hall, 1981), 121.

Suggested Readings

Fiedler, Fred, Chemers, Martin, and Mahar, L. *Improving Leadership Effectiveness: The Leader Match Concept.* New York: John Wiley & Sons, 1976.

Huey, John. "Secrets of Great Second Bananas." *Fortune* (May 6, 1991): 64–65, 70, 72, 76.

Kotter, John P. "What Leaders Really Do." *Harvard Business Review* (May–June 1990): 103–111.

Nelton, Sharon. "Men, Women and Leadership." *Nation's Business* (May 1991): 16–22.

Pagonis, William G. "The Work of the Leader," *Harvard Business Review* (November–December, 1992): 118–126.

Plunkett, Lorne C., and Fournier, Robert. *Participative Management.* New York: John Wiley & Sons, 1991.

Rodgers, Buck, with Levey, Irv. *Getting the Most Out of Yourself and Others.* New York: Harper & Row, 1987.

Rosener, Judy B. "Ways Woman Lead." *Harvard Business Review* (November–December 1990): 119–125.

Schaffer, Robert H. "Demand Better Results—And Get Them." *Harvard Business Review* (March–April 1991): 142–149.

Sellers, Patricia. "Does the CEO Really Matter?" *Fortune* (April 22, 1991): 80–82, 86, 90, 94.

Stewart, Thomas A. "Do You Push Your People Too Hard?" *Fortune* (October 22, 1990): 121, 124, 128.

Yukl, Gary A. *Leadership in Organizations.* Englewood Cliffs, N.J.: Prentice Hall, 1981.

PART III

SHAPING YOUR ENVIRONMENT

CHAPTER 11 SELECTION AND ORIENTATION

CHAPTER 12 TRAINING

CHAPTER 13 THE APPRAISAL PROCESS

CHAPTER 14 DISCIPLINE

Part III includes four chapters directly concerned with how well you as a supervisor will be able to influence the productivity of your subordinates. This section deals specifically with the proper ways to bring in new people, get them ready to perform to standards, appraise their results, and correct their deficiencies. Through the successful application of the principles in these chapters, you will exercise proper leadership to influence the performance of your subordinates directly.

Chapter 11 explains the difficult but regularly needed processes of selection and introduction of new employees. The primary emphasis is on the supervisor's role in hiring and welcoming new people into work groups. Legal restraints and pitfalls are discussed so as to give you the knowledge you need to get the best people and to get them off on the right foot. You will learn what to do, how to do it, and what not to do while executing these two vital activities.

Chapter 12 explores the ways in which you can impart new knowledge, skills, and attitudes to workers. Through training, you give each worker what is needed to perform to standards, to excel, and to stay out of trouble. You enhance workers' chances for advancement and for increased earnings by training them in accordance with certain all-important principles. Along with the principles, various training methods are discussed in order to help you to pick the one that is most appropriate for your training programs.

In Chapter 13, we explore the leader's role as judge—the process through which you evaluate your subordinates' performance. Appraisals help you determine the effectiveness of your training efforts and give you the backup you need to reward and punish.

Chapter 14 examines both positive and negative aspects of discipline. If you are to discipline effectively, you must stress prevention along with efforts to correct individuals. The principles and pitfalls of disciplining subordinates are explored in detail.

Selection
and Orientation

OBJECTIVES

After reading and discussing this chapter, you should be able to do the following:

1. Define this chapter's key terms.

2. Describe the role of the supervisor in the selection process.

3. Describe the assistance normally rendered in the selection process by a personnel or human resource department.

4. List and briefly describe four selection devices.

5. Describe what a supervisor should do to prepare for a selection interview.

6. List and briefly explain four pitfalls of the selection process.

7. List the basic goals of an orientation program.

8. List the basic goals of an induction program.

9. Describe what takes place during a new employee's socialization process.

10. State the five basic questions new employees want answered.

INTRODUCTION

Selection is the personnel or human resource management function that determines who is hired by a business firm and who is not. It is the process by which applicants are evaluated so as to determine their suitability for employment. The basic aim of the selection process is to find the number and kind of employees required by a company to meet its needs for personnel at a minimum cost to that company. Selection begins with a description of the kind of person needed to fill a vacancy and ends with the decision to hire a particular person. When a company is looking for non-management personnel, the person who would supervise the prospective employee should be involved in that person's selection.

According to an Employment Management Association survey of thirty-six firms, "the average cost for [workers, managers] and internal hires in 1993 was $3,207.... The average cost to hire [salaried] employees was $6,504...which equals 14.1 percent of the average salaries" (Kleiman, "In," 1994). Clearly, selection is an important and costly process that, if done badly, can add significantly to a company's inefficiency. It is becoming increasingly difficult to terminate employees because of various state, local, and federal laws that guarantee employment and civil rights. This means that it is even more important to hire right the first time (Kleiman, "Personnel," 1987).

After a new employee has been recruited, interviewed, tested, and hired, you must begin to prepare for his or her arrival and initiation. Some groundwork for this procedure is laid during the selection process. The applicant is informed of the nature of the job, the company's operations in general, and the wage and fringe benefits that go with the job. What remains to be done is the careful planning for and execution of the new employee's formal introduction to the company, the job, the supervisor, and the working environment in depth.

This chapter looks at these extremely important functions from a supervisor's viewpoint. In some companies, the supervisors have nothing much to say about hiring new workers. They are told that new people have been assigned to their departments, and they must accept that decision. This is not as it should be. Therefore, we shall turn our attention to the kind of selection process in which supervisors play a significant role.

ADVANTAGES OF SUPERVISOR INVOLVEMENT

If adequate selection is to take place in a business, the decision to hire a new worker should be made by the person who will become his or her boss. This is because the manager has first-hand knowledge about his or her department, the workforce, and the job that must be filled. He or she is best equipped to assess each applicant's suitability and potential both for performing the duties he or she will inherit and for getting along with the existing workforce. It makes a great deal of sense, therefore, to involve supervisors in the selection process and, in particular, to give them the power to make the final decision to hire a new employee.

When you know that your decision is the final and binding one, you are putting your reputation on the line. Before you pick a person for your department, you will probably look over all the applicants carefully in order to select the best from among the many individuals you interview. Since the person hired is someone you have chosen, you will feel a personal commitment to him or her that otherwise would be missing. You will want him or her to make it because, if this does not happen, it will adversely affect you as well as the new employee. Part of your success and that of your department will be riding on your choice. If you are the department head, you should have a voice in adding new people to it.

In many companies, teams are involved in the selection process. The Supervising Teams feature shows how such companies are sharing or delegating their hiring decisions.

THE SELECTION PROCESS

Exhibit 11.1 outlines the selection process as it occurs when a supervisor and the company's personnel or human resources department work together. In most medium- to large-size firms, the supervisor places a

---

Supervisor

1. Request for a New Worker (Check on availability of up-to-date job descriptions and specifications)

8. Final Interview

   Reject ☐

   Accept ☐

Personnel Department

2. Posting of the Job

3. Recruiting of Applicants

4. Filing of Applications

5. Preliminary Interview and Reference Checks

6. Psychological and Performance Testing

7. Evaluation of Results and Transfer of Records and Applicant to Final Interview

9. Processing of Paperwork and Physical Exam/Drug Testing

EXHIBIT 11.1
A typical selection process involving a personnel or human resource management department and the supervisor of a new hire.

SUPERVISING TEAMS

According to authors Joseph Boyett and Henry Conn, "In Workplace 2000, peers will hire peers. Managers and supervisors and the company personnel department will have much less control over hiring decisions." Current hiring trends show that companies are either sharing the hiring decision with team members—the applicant's peers— or letting their teams take over the entire hiring process.

Both team members and applicants must be prepared for team selection efforts. Training and guidelines must be given to team personnel to ensure that discrimination is avoided. Interviewing skills and techniques must be taught. Applicants must be told about the team selection process and the kind of environment they will be entering.

Interviews and other screening efforts must focus on determining the applicant's attitudes and skills—both technical and social. According to a human resource manager for the Gaines Pet Foods division of Quaker Oats, "Social or team membership skills that are looked for in the interview may include problem solving, idea generation and implementation, and giving and receiving feedback." The team may devise exercises or tests involving one or more applicants and then evaluate performance results. With peers at Gaines Pet Foods "predicting the success of the candidate by making the selection, they make a commitment to helping the new employee succeed."

At Johnsonville Foods in Wisconsin, CEO Ralph Stayer believes in letting his employee teams hire the people they will be working with. His company's teams work for performance bonuses and want to control their membership.

The owners of Professional Salon Concepts in Illinois, Terri and Steve Cowan, have decided to get all employees involved in selection; they now have all twenty employees (called consultants) organized into five teams that do the preliminary interviewing. They determine twenty to twenty-five applicant attributes, and then each candidate is interviewed by each team. Each interview lasts about twenty minutes. The teams rank the applicants; the owners then interview the top-ranked ones. Although the owners make the final decision to hire, the teams have voted for those chosen and are committed to their success. The owners no longer have to sell their choices to their consultants.

Source: Kochanski, James. "Hiring in Self-Regulating Work Teams," *National Productivity Review,* Spring 1987, 153–159; Boyett, Joseph H., and Conn, Henry P. *Workplace 2000* (New York: Plume, 1991), 249–252; Noble, Sara P., ed., *Managing People: 101 Proven Ideas for Managing People* (Boston: *Inc. Magazine* 1992), 15.

request for a new worker with the personnel department as soon as the need for such a person arises. Enough time must be allowed, when possible, to search for, select, and hire a person before the absence of his or her predecessor can create serious problems.

To ensure that both the supervisor and the personnel department know what kind of person they will be looking for, an up-to-date description of the job and its duties must be prepared or kept on hand, along with a detailed listing of the personal skills and abilities required of the job holder. These two documents are called the job description and the job specification, respectively.

Job Description

A **job description** is a listing of the duties (tasks and activities) and responsibilities of a job or formal position in an organization. All jobs you supervise should have such a listing. Reference to this document proves helpful in assigning work, settling disagreements, appraising subordinates, and filling vacancies. Exhibit 11.2 consists of a job description for a secretarial position. You will note that nothing on it deals with the personal characteristics desirable in the job holder. These are detailed in the job specification.

job description
a formal listing of the duties that make up a position in the organization

EXHIBIT 11.2
Job description for personal secretary.

Title: Secretary	Job No. C-10 Grade 4
Effective Date	9-96
General	Perform clerical and secretarial duties involving typing, dictation, correspondence and report preparation, filing, maintaining records, scheduling appointments, distributing mail. Handle confidential information regularly.
Specific Duties	Take dictation in shorthand and transcribe.
	Compose and type routine memos and business correspondence.
	Compile and type routine reports.
	Sort and distribute mail daily.
	Maintain and set up files of memos, letters, and reports.
	Obtain data and information by telephone or personal contact on behalf of supervisor.
	Receive visitors.
	Schedule supervisor's appointments.
	Answer phone and take messages.
	Handle confidential files.
Equipment	Electric typewriter, dictation machine, photocopier, desktop computer, and printer.

Analysis by: _____   Approved by: _____

Job Specification

Exhibit 11.3 shows the **job specification**—a listing of the personal characteristics and skill levels a person must have in order to fill the secretarial position described in Exhibit 11.2. Such factors as typing speed, clerical and secretarial experiences, and formal education are listed. You need this information when selecting someone to fill a job, assigning work, and determining promotions. As time passes, jobs change. So too must their descriptions and specifications. It is standard practice to review and update these documents at least once every two years. If you have them and they are up to date, use them. If this is not the case, you should set about the task of constructing them or bringing them up to date.

Steps two through seven in the selection process (as illustrated in Exhibit 11.1) are usually performed for you by your company's personnel department. Posting the job so that all present employees are aware of it may be required by union contract. Posting allows existing employees to apply for the vacancy and can result in promotions and transfers that will create new vacancies. Recruiting applicants from outside can be done in several ways and usually must include sincere efforts to attract minority and female applicants.

EXHIBIT 11.3

Job specification for the secretarial position shown in Exhibit 11.2.

Title: Secretary	Job No. C-10 Grade 4
Effective Date	9-96
Factor	*Explanation*
Education	High-school graduate or equivalent.
Experience	Secretarial, including stenographic duties and word processing.
Training Period	1 month.
Dexterity	Precise movement of hand and fingers required to operate keyboard at no less than 60 words per minute and take shorthand at 90 words per minute.
Adaptability	Must be able to adjust to frequent changes in duties, such as typing, filing, composing letters, handling telephone.
Judgment	Must be able to follow existing procedures and establish new practices where necessary. Must be able to compose business letters, establish filing systems, and receive visitors.
Responsibility for Losses to Company	Maximum loss possible: $200, due to clerical errors
Contact with Others	Frequent contacts with visitors, vendors, and company managers.
Physical Demands	Lifting requirements: under 10 pounds.
Analysis by: _____	Approved by: _____

After receiving and processing the paperwork that results from steps four through seven, personnel will usually send you two or more applicants for a final employment interview. As a rule, personnel will send you only applicants who qualify for and have the potential to succeed on the job you want to fill. You must pick the person you believe is the best qualified of the applicants you interview. Then you turn the applicant over to the personnel department for final paperwork.

Exhibit 11.4 lists and briefly describes the federal restrictions placed on the selection process. In the discussions that follow, the effects of these federal laws are examined as they relate to each of the selection steps or devices. They may be summarized briefly as follows:

1. It is unlawful for an employer to fail or refuse to hire or to discharge an individual because of race, color, religion, sex, age, national origin, or handicap.

2. It is unlawful for an employer to limit, segregate, or classify an employee or applicant for employment in any way that would tend to deprive the individual of employment opportunities because of race, color, religion, sex, age, national origin, or handicap.

EXHIBIT 11.4
Federal antidiscrimination laws.

Source: Ledvinka, James, and Scarpello, Vida G. *Federal Regulation of Personnel and Human Resource Management* (Boston: Kent Publishing Co., 1991), 30–32. Copyright © by Wadsworth, Inc. Reprinted by permission of PWS-Kent Publishing Co., a division of Wadsworth, Inc.

Law	Type of Employment Discrimination Prohibited	Employers Covered
U.S. Constitution First Amendment	Religious discrimination	Federal government
U.S. Constitution Fifth Amendment	Deprivation of employment rights without due process of law	Federal government
U.S. Constitution Fourteenth Amendment	Deprivation of employment rights without due process	State and local governments
Civil Rights Acts of 1866 and 1870 (based on Thirteenth Amendment)	Race discrimination in hiring, placement, and continuation of employment	Private employers, unions, employment agencies
Civil Rights Act of 1871 (based on Fourteenth Amendment)	Deprivation of equal employment rights under cover of state law	State and local governments (private employers if conspiracy is involved)
National Labor Relations Act of 1935	Unfair representation by unions, or interference with employee rights, that discriminates on the basis of race, color, religion, sex, or national origin	Private employers and unions

Law	Type of Employment Discrimination Prohibited	Employers Covered
Equal Pay Act of 1963	Sex differences in pay for substantially equal work	All employers and labor organizations
Executive Order 11141	Age discrimination	Federal contractors and subcontractors
Title VI, 1964 Civil Rights Act	Discrimination based on race, color, religion, sex, or national origin	Employers receiving federal financial assistance
Title VII, 1964 Civil Rights Act (as amended in subsequent years)	Discrimination based on race, color, religion, sex, or national origin	Private employers with 15 or more employees, governments, unions, employment agencies
Executive Orders 11246 and 11375 (1965)	Discrimination based on race, color, religion, sex, or national origin	Federal contractors and subcontractors
Age Discrimination in Employment Act of 1967 (as amended in 1978 and in subsequent years)	Age discrimination against those over 40 years of age	Private employers with 20 or more employees, unions with 25 or more members, employment agencies
Title I, 1968 Civil Rights Act	Interference with a person's rights due to race, religion, color, or national origin	Persons generally
Executive Order 11478 (1969)	Discrimination based on race, color, religion, sex, national origin, political affiliation, marital status, or physical handicap	Federal government
Title IX, Education Amendments of 1972	Sex discrimination	Educational institutions receiving federal financial assistance
Vietnam Era Veteran's Readjustment Act of 1974, Executive Order 11701 (1973)	Discrimination against disabled veterans and Vietnam-era veterans (affirmative action required)	Federal contractors, federal government

EXHIBIT 11.4 (cont.)

Law	Type of Employment Discrimination Prohibited	Employers Covered
Rehabilitation Act of 1973; Executive Order 11914	Discrimination based on physical or mental handicap (affirmative action required)	Federal contractors, federal government
Americans with Disabilities Act of 1990	Discrimination based on physical or mental handicap (affirmative action required)	Employers generally
Civil Service Reform Act of 1978	Specifically incorporates Title VII, 1964 Civil Rights Act; mandates federal government as "workplace reflective of the nation's diversity"	Federal government
Federal Employees Part-Time Career Employment Act of 1975	Requires increased part-time career employment opportunities	Federal government
Immigration and Reform Control Act of 1986	Discrimination based on citizenship or national origin	Employers generally
Civil Rights Restoration Act of 1987	Discrimination based on race, color, religion, sex, national origin, age, and handicap	Educational institutions receiving federal financial assistance
Civil Rights Act 1991	Permits women, persons with disabilities, and persons who are religious minorities to have a jury trial and sue for punitive damages if they can prove intentional hiring and workplace discrimination. Also requires companies to provide evidence that the business practice that led to the discrimination was not discriminatory but was job-related for the position in question and consistent with business necessity.	Private employers with 15 or more employees

EXHIBIT 11.4 (cont.)

RECRUITING

Two sources of needed personnel exist: internal and external. Internal means of finding people include promoting from within to fill a vacancy, transferring a person from one job to another (usually a permanent job change), recalling a laid-off worker, and using job rotation to fill a vacancy on a temporary basis. Consider posting your employment needs with your company's other divisions and partners.

People currently employed at your company have friends, neighbors, and relatives who might make good employees who are compatible with current employees. But herein lies a problem: Like recommends like. If there is a need to expand the workforce to include more women, minorities, and handicapped people, you will need to look beyond your present workforce for new employees. Moreover, you may be required by management policy or union contract to post the job, letting others who are currently employed apply for your job vacancy.

To ensure an adequate pool of diverse candidates for most vacancies, you must consider outside sources of personnel. Typical external sources include unsolicited applications; employment agencies (both public and private); referrals from existing employees; schools, colleges, and universities; temporary help agencies, unions, and trade associations; and solicitation through help-wanted advertising. This last source may make use of various electronic media to include radio and cable television programs devoted to helping local employers find talent and computerized recruiting services—various on-line bulletin boards and other sources.

minority
according to the
EEOC, a member of
the following groups:
Hispanics, Native
Americans, African
Americans, Asians or
Pacific Islanders,
Alaskan natives

Most companies today have an Equal Employment Opportunity (EEO) policy that states the employer's intent to recruit, hire, train, and promote people in all job categories without regard to race, color, creed, sex, age, country of origin, or handicap. From this policy come the guidelines for specifically recruiting representative numbers of **minority** members and women. Minorities include the groups described in Exhibit 11.5.

Title VII of the 1964 Civil Rights Act requires parties who file discrimination complaints to do so within 180 days of the alleged violation. It provides two basic remedies when discrimination is proved: reinstatement and recovery of lost pay. The Civil Rights Act of 1991 amended the 1964 Civil Rights Act to allow for the recovery of punitive damages if it can be proved that a company engaged in a discriminatory practice with malice or with reckless indifference to the law. Limits placed on these damages are as follows:

- Between 15 and 100 employees: $50,000
- Between 101 and 200 employees: $100,000
- Between 201 and 500 employees: $200,000
- Over 500 employees: $300,000

U.S. Government Titles	More Appropriate References
1. Hispanics, Spanish-surnamed Americans	When people desire it, use their country of origin: Puerto Rican, Mexican, or Chicano/Chicana; people of color
2. Blacks not of Hispanic origin	African American, Caribbean American, Black people, people of color
3. Asians, Pacific Islanders	When people desire it, use their country of origin: Korean American, Chinese American; people of color
4. Native Americans, American Indians	American Indian, Native American, or tribal affiliation: Cherokee, Pawnee, Navajo
5. Alaskan Natives	Native American, Alaskan (never "Eskimo")

EXHIBIT 11.5
Minorities as defined by federal law and EEOC guidelines.

Affirmative Action Programs

When companies have been found guilty of discriminatory practices, do contract work for the federal government (valued at $50,000 or more and the company employs more than 50 employees), or admit that they need to improve their employment record with regard to women and minorities, they develop or are required to develop an affirmative action program (AAP). One important part of an AAP is a stated goal and timetable for achieving the goal of hiring the missing women or minorities. As a supervisor, you may be allowed to hire only qualified women or minorities until the stated goal for your area is reached.

The Supreme Court's Consensus on Affirmative Action

In 1987, the Supreme Court strongly endorsed the affirmative action concept and, according to several Court-watching experts, has now reached a consensus on how affirmative action plans should work. In a 6–3 decision, the Court approved a Santa Clara County (California) Transportation Agency plan that gave a dispatcher's job to a woman even though six men were more experienced. The woman and the men were all qualified for the promotion, but the dispatcher position lacked women job holders. The following seems clear at this writing. For promotions and hiring, affirmative action can be used if (Mauro, 1987):

- It avoids specific numbers of openings for women and minorities
- It avoids hiring or promoting an unqualified woman or minority member over a qualified candidate
- A "conspicuous imbalance" in the representation of women and minorities exists in a job category (or the workforce as a whole)

EEO/Affirmative Action and Valuing Diversity

Equal employment opportunity (EEO) and affirmative action are legal concepts initiated and mandated by the federal government and reinforced by numerous state and local laws. They tend to be quantitative and to focus on the problem of getting employers to build and maintain workforces that are truly representative of the population mix from which they draw employees.

Valuing diversity efforts are purely voluntary, beginning where EEO and affirmative action efforts end. These are proactive efforts designed to bring change and stimulate creativity while creating working environments that welcome and utilize the unique skills of every employee. They seek to truly integrate, not assimilate. Valuing diversity means acceptance and co-existence for different cultures and various ethnic and social groups' values.

Reverse Discrimination

The now famous Bakke *v.* Regents of the University of California case of 1978 dealt with the issue of reverse discrimination. In its review of this case, the Supreme Court of the United States held that race could be used as a criterion in selection decisions, but it could not be the only criterion. Affirmative action programs are permissible when a case of prior discrimination has been established and when an employer has a significant under-representation of minority and female employees (considering the makeup of the labor force the employer has to draw from). "Generally, minority/female promotion or hiring over white males will not be considered reverse discrimination if the company has not met its affirmative action goals" (Pell, 1994).

Recruiting Women

Under current federal and state laws, few jobs can be denied to women. Companies are under an obligation to redesign jobs, where necessary, to allow women access to them. Job specifications can be changed to allow women to hold a job. Schools that train professionals and either receive federal grants or use federal scholarship funds are actively recruiting female applicants. As a result, more and more qualified women are entering what were once male-dominated professions. Companies have even hired unqualified women and minorities and paid for their education and training to meet their affirmative action and equal employment goals. As a supervisor in charge of hiring new workers, you must consider women and seek them from whatever sources you can. It's the law.

Recruiting the Differently Abled

The differently abled in America are those individuals who:

- Have a physical or mental impairment that substantially limits one or more major life activities
- Have a record of such an impairment
- Are regarded as having such an impairment

Two major laws govern the protection of people with such disabilities: the Rehabilitation Act of 1973 (covering firms doing business with the federal government) and the Americans with Disabilities Act of 1990 (covering nearly every firm with fifteen or more employees). Protection is extended to people with current or past physical and mental conditions. Examples of those protected are people with dependency on legal drugs whose dependency does not impair work performance; people with a history of cancer, heart trouble, or a contagious disease, providing that their conditions do not pose a significant risk to co-workers or render them unable to perform their work; and people who have undergone or who now are undergoing rehabilitation for their drug dependencies.

Under both laws, employers must make reasonable accommodations (that cause no "undue hardship") for the handicapped. Jobs may have to be redefined, removing those tasks that the handicapped person cannot perform. Prerequisites such as passing a physical exam may have to be waived when parts of that exam are not job related. Physical facilities may have to be altered to accommodate access by the physically handicapped. Signs in braille and wheelchair ramps are but two examples. According to the Job Accommodation Network, a federal agency (Kleiman, "In," 1994):

> for every dollar spent by businesses to accommodate workers with disabilities, employers are realizing a gain of $30 in benefits.... Among the benefits: the ability to hire or retain a qualified employee; elimination

of the cost of training a new employee; savings in worker's compensation and other insurance costs; and increased productivity. Nationwide, 261 companies reported the average cost of making adjustments for workers with disabilities is $735. The average benefit is $22,065.

For private businesses not engaged in doing business with the federal government, affirmative action to hire the handicapped is not required. Both laws give employers some flexibility in that they do not require toleration of lower performance levels from handicapped employees, and they do not force employment of handicapped persons who would pose a significant threat to the health and safety of others at work.

Under Section 1630.4 of the ADA, employers may not discriminate against a qualified person (one capable of performing a job's "essential functions") with a disability when they recruit, hire, determine pay and benefits, make job assignments, and grant leaves of absence (McKee, 1993). The vague language of this act is gradually being interpreted in specific court cases and EEOC rulings. The EEOC administers the ADA.

Recruiting Minorities

Recruiting minorities usually involves seeking them where they live—in their neighborhoods—if enough likely prospects are to be found to form a pool of applicants. Neighborhood associations, churches, community action groups, state employment offices, ethnic newspapers, and current minority employees should be contacted. And before minorities are introduced to a workforce, the existing workers must be encouraged to cooperate with the company's affirmative action efforts. As with all new employees, every effort must be made to find the best qualified and to ensure their early success on the job. If you have preconceived notions about minority groups, you will have to eliminate them and commit yourself to the successful integration and retention of all qualified employees.

THE SUPERVISOR'S ROLE IN MINORITY HIRING

With the increased emphasis on recruiting and hiring minority members today, you are more likely now than ever before to encounter minority employees in every department of your company. They, like everyone else, expect an even chance for success. They may need extra training to fill any gaps left in their formal education and previous employment experiences. They want and need to be respected and appreciated for their good points and potential. They want to carry their own weight.

Nonminority supervisors must realize that a minority worker may arrive expecting the worst: resentment, rejection, hostility, and isolation.

He or she may tend to read into your actions and words or those of peers more than is in them. He or she may seem hypersensitive. In a way, he or she may be looking for signs of discrimination, as well. What a nonminority worker might brush aside, a minority member may consider an insult or personal attack. Until all of your subordinates feel that they are being treated as individuals, you can expect a measure of discontent.

The human relations roles described in Chapter 8 are even more necessary when dealing with minorities; they may demand additional effort and diligence from you in order to relate successfully to each of them. Keep in mind the new golden rule: Treat people as they want to be treated. Evaluate people on their merits, avoiding stereotypes and generalities. Get to know each person as a unique individual.

There may be a few workers, however, who will try to take advantage of the situation. Some workers will be looking for special privileges. They may want to use the fact that they are women or members of minorities as a lever in attempts to gain favored treatment. This inequity, although clearly understandable, must be prevented. You will suffer most of all through alienation of your other subordinates and their accusation that you are playing favorites.

As supervisor, you play a major role in the success of minority or differently abled subordinates. With the vast majority of the new labor force coming from diverse groups, your company's success rests on your ability to help all employees reach their potential.

Enforce your department's standards of performance and conduct impartially. Let all of your workers know their rights and the avenues open to them if they feel that they have been treated unjustly.

APPLICANT SCREENING PROCEDURES

Steps four through eight listed in Exhibit 11.1 deal with several selection tools or screening devices: the application, the preliminary interview, various kinds of tests, and the final interview. These devices, like recruiting, are governed in some ways by federal, state, and local antidiscrimination legislation.

Your best defense against accusations of discrimination or bias in hiring is to be certain that any employment practice or device adheres to the following (Schuler, 1995):

- It is job-related—it is predictive of success or failure on a specific job
- It is a business necessity—the company must do what it does to provide for its continued existence
- It acknowledges a bona fide occupational qualification (BFOQ)—for example, a licensing or age requirement

- It honors a bona fide seniority system (BFSS)—a seniority system established and maintained that does not have the intent to illegally discriminate

The Application

The application is your primary method for obtaining the key facts about an individual candidate for a job. What it contains and how it is prepared by an applicant can help you weed out unqualified people and avoid wasting the time it takes to interview applicants. An application "should state that your company is an Equal Employment Opportunity Employer and that you do not discriminate on the basis of race, color, religion, national origin, age, sex, [sexual orientation where prohibited by state or local laws], marital status, or handicap," and the application should make it clear that your company hires "at will" (Half, 1985). This last statement indicates that the person is not guaranteed any specific period of employment.

Examine your employer's application form. If it contains any of the inquiries discussed in Exhibit 11.6, your guard should go up. Evaluate the need for each question, and eliminate those that are not closely related to job performance or to predicting success on the job for which the applicant will be considered.

Interviews

interview

a two-way conversation under the control of one of the parties

The **interview** can be defined as a conversation between two or more parties that is under the control of one of the parties and that tries to accomplish a special objective. A conversation is a two-way verbal interchange of ideas and information. Thus an interview is a verbal interchange between two or more persons, and the employment interview is an exchange between you (as a representative of your company) and the applicant. It must be carefully planned and skillfully executed if its special objective is to be achieved.

As a supervisor, you will be using interviews to help instruct your people, to evaluate them and share their evaluations with them, to screen and hire new employees, to solve problems, to gather information, and to sell your subordinates on the need for changes. Interviews demand a quiet environment, a clear understanding by the parties of the special purpose of the interview, and extensive use of open and closed questions (see Exhibit 11.7).

The major purpose of an interview is to get the interviewee talking freely and frankly about all matters that are relevant to the accomplishment of the interview's purpose. The interviewer listens attentively, never interrupts, and usually refrains from expressing opinions or making snap judgments.

Age, Date of Birth? Since state and fedeal laws prohibit discrimination, do not use the answer to this question illegally. Requesting the applicant's age is generally permissible as long as the information is not used for a discriminatory purpose.

Arrests? Since an arrest is no indication of guilt and minorities are arrested disproportionately, this question should be avoided because it is discriminatory.

Convictions (other than traffic violations)? This question is not advisable on a general basis, but it may be appropriate for screening candidates who have been convicted of certain offenses and are under consideration for certain kinds of jobs. The same applies to less than honorable military discharges. If this information is necessary, exercise care in how these records are used in order to avoid possible discrimination.

Available for Saturday or Sunday Work? While employee work scheduling is an important factor, this question may discourage applications from members of certain religious groups. If this question is necessary because of business requirements, indicate that an effort will be made to accommodate the religious needs of employees.

Age and Number of Children? Arrangements for Care? While the intent to these questions is to explore a source of absenteeism or tardiness, the effect is potentially discriminatory against women.

Citizenship? Unless required by national security, this question should be avoided because it creates a potential for discrimination on the basis of national origin.

Credit Record? Own a Car? Own Home? Unless required because of business, these questions should be avoided because of potential adverse effects on minorities or women.

Eye Color? Hair Color? Eye and hair color are not related to job performance and may serve to indicate an applicant's race or national origin.

Fidelity Bond? Since a bond may have been denied for an arbitrary or discriminatory reason, use other screening considerations.

Friends or Relatives? This question implies a preference for friends or relatives of employees and is potentially discriminatory because such a preference is lifely to reflect the demography of the company's work force.

Garnishment Record? Federal courts have held that wage garnishments do not normally affect a worker's ability to perform effectively on the job.

Height? Weight? Unless height or weight is directly related to a job requirement, this question should not be listed on the application form.

Maiden Name? Prior Marriage Name? Widowed, Divorced, Separated? These questions are not related to job performance and may be an indication of religion or national origin. These inquiries

(continues)

EXHIBIT 11.6

Potentially discriminatory inquiries on application forms.

Source: Illinois Department of Employment Security.

may be appropriate if required for identification purposes in preemployment investigations or security checks.

Marital Status? A federal court has held that refusal to employ a married woman when married men occupy similar jobs is unlawful sex discrimination.

Sex. State and federal laws prohibit discrimination on the basis of sex except where sex is a "bona fide occupational qualification" necessary to the normal operation of business.

NOTE: If certain information is needed for postemployment purposes, such as Affirmative Action plans, it can be obtained *after* the applicant has been hired. Maintain this data apart from information that is used in the hiring decision process.

The best general guideline to follow on employment application forms is to ensure that the information elicited is related to qualifications for effective performance on the job.

EXHIBIT 11.6 (cont.)

Open questions usually begin with:	Closed questions usually begin with:
Why	Can
What	Is
When	Do (Does)
Where	Have (Has)
Which	Shall (Will)
Who	
How	

Note: A closed question can be answered with yes or no; an open question cannot be. The opening word in a question determines whether it will be open or closed.

EXHIBIT 11.7
Open and closed question starters.

As an interviewer, you must be certain that you and the person being interviewed are of one mind, that your understanding and his or hers are the same with regard to the purpose of the interview and to what each person means by his or her contribution. While you encourage a free flow of information, you must keep the interview on track and avoid time-consuming meanderings.

The employment interview has two primary purposes: to evaluate the qualifications and suitability of the applicant to fill the job opening and to give the applicant the information needed to make an intelligent decision about accepting an offer of employment, should it be given. Be honest about the working conditions, the chances for advancement, and the type of duties you will expect the new employee to perform. Review the job description and the job specification for the job before you conduct the interview, and have them handy for reference during the interview.

Avoid asking questions that could open you and your employer to accusations of employment discrimination. Exhibit 11.8 gives you precautions to follow when conducting the interview. In addition to these, conduct all of your interviews in the same manner, using the same format, questions, and environment. Some supervisors tape record their interviews so that every word is a matter of record for future reference.

There are two basic kinds of interviews and approaches to interviewing: the directive and the nondirective. The directive interview is planned and controlled by the interviewer. The nondirective interview is planned by the interviewer but controlled by the interviewee.

- **Do ask questions that are job-related or necessary for determining an applicant's qualifications for employment.**
- **Do question candidates in a consistent and uniform manner, regardless of race, sex, national origin, age, or handicap.**
- **Do evaluate applicants on job-related criteria in accord with the actual requirements for successful performance of the job.**
- **Do select the best-qualified individual for the job. If the position is underrepresented with minority group or female applicants, maintain a record of good faith attempts to recruit and consider minorities and/or females for the position.**
- **Do accord special consideration to the disabled and handicapped and Vietnam-era veterans. If feasible,**

consider whatever minor adjustments or accommodations can be made to enable the handicapped to perform the job successfully.
- **Do make reasonable accommodations to the religious observance obligations of employees.**
- **Do not ask any questions of a female applicant that would not be asked of a male candidate (such as inquiries pertaining to child care, marital status, birth control methods, or hindrances to travel or working weekends).**
- **Do not ask questions of one race that would not be asked of another (such as questioning one's ability to work in a location with members of another racial group).**
- **Do not establish a negative tone in the interview in an effort to discourage any applicant from seeking the position.**

(continues)

EXHIBIT 11.8
Major "do" and "don`t" guidelines for conducting an employment interview.

Source: Illinois Department of Employment Security.

- Do not give undue emphasis to the hazardous or tedious aspects of a job, especially if they occur on an infrequent basis.
- Do not inform an applicant that the position is "reserved" or must be filled by a female or minority group applicant because of Equal Employment Opportunity or Affirmative Action obligations or regulations. Affirmative Action is not a license to discriminate against anyone in an effort to compensate for past hiring inequities. A possible exception to this suggestion may occur when a court or regulatory agency has made a finding of discrimination and directs remedial action in the form of specific hiring goals.
- Do not impose additional desirable qualifications beyond the actual requirements of your job opening.
- Do not devise additional testing requirements as part of a preemployment screening procedure unless the testing is job related and properly validated.
- Do not ask the birthplace of an applicant nor require that the appli-

cant submit proof of birth. Since birthplace may indicate a person of foreign origin, it is better to avoid this question than to risk a discrimination charge on this basis.
- Do not ask the citizenship of an applicant. Ask whether the person is a citizen or has a visa authorizing full-time permanent employment.
- Do not ask questions that tend to identify the age of the applicant when age is not related to successful job performance.
- Do not ask a person's religious affiliations.
- Do not ask about an applicant's type of military discharge from general military service. You may ask about job-related experience in the U.S. Armed Forces.
- Do not ask if the applicant has ever been arrested. You may ask if the person has ever been convicted.
- Do not ask questions on the general physical or mental condition of an applicant. You may ask if the applicant has any physical or mental condition that may limit his or her ability to do the job.

EXHIBIT 11.8 (cont.)

directive interview
an interview planned and totally controlled by the interviewer

Directive Interviews   The **directive interview** is based on a format of specific questions set down in advance and followed exactly. The questions should ask for the information the interviewer considers most essential. Here are some examples: "What did you do between your job with the ABC Company and your employment at XYZ, Incorporated?" "Why did you leave the ABC Company?" These questions generally ask for facts and leave little room for the candidate's opinions. The only opinions you should look for are those that directly affect how the person views the job and type of working conditions that he or she will experience if hired.

Generally, the interviewer will ask the set of questions (questions he or she has written down in advance) in the order in which they are listed. Feel free to record the applicant's responses as they are given. Certain questions may be more important than others since they may reveal more valuable information. These questions should be highlighted in some way so that you can make certain not to forget to ask them. You will probably do as much talking as the applicant does since you must both ask questions and supply information. Make sure that the applicant knows the nature of the job for which he or she is being interviewed and that he or she has an opportunity to ask questions too.

This type of interview works best when you are dealing with applicants for routine production or clerical positions. It allows you to obtain the maximum amount of job- or performance-related information in the minimum amount of time.

Nondirective Interviews The **nondirective interview** is also planned, but it is generally less structured and more flexible. Questions are written down, but they are designed to be open or loose in order to allow applicants more freedom in their responses and to reveal the attitudes behind their words. Typical questions that might be asked include the following: "Why did you apply for this job?" "Of the jobs you have held, which did you like best (least) and why?" The object of these open questions is to let the applicants talk so that their aspirations, goals, and preferences can come out.

The interviewer is not bound to a rigid format with this indirect approach. One question can lead to others, with the applicant's responses

nondirective interview
an interview planned by the interviewer but controlled by the interviewee

determining the direction and flow of the interview. Quite often you will find out a great deal from an applicant's detailed explanations and will uncover much more than you would in a direct interview. People left to talk on their own will say more than they normally would because they are not sure how much you want to know. They will seize the opportunity to speak their minds if they are relaxed and encouraged to speak up.

Either type of interview may include an on-the-job performance test if you think it necessary. Such a test is designed to let the applicants demonstrate their ability to run a machine, meet close tolerances, file correspondence, type correct copy, and the like. If this type of test has not already been done by the personnel department, you have an excellent opportunity to do it during or after your interview.

Preparing to Interview   Like any other type of interview—whether for counseling, for sharing your evaluations, or for interrogation and fact finding for disciplinary actions—the employment interview should be held in private and in an environment as free from interruptions as you can make it. Since you usually know well in advance when an applicant is due to report, set aside enough time to do the kind of interview you prefer, and do your homework before the meeting. Read the candidate's application form thoroughly, and consult the comments, if any, from the personnel interviewer. Look over the candidate's test scores, and list any deficiencies that you feel could interfere with his or her successful performance. Prepare a brief checklist of the essentials you wish to cover so that you do not waste time or overlook an important area. Exhibit 11.9 is such a list.

The Applicant	*Present Situation*	*The Job*
Experience	Maturity	Skills required
Strengths	Health	Working conditions
Weaknesses	Sincerity	Hours
Hobbies	Social adjustment	Duties
	Why is he or she here?	Tools/equipment
Previous Employment	Present wage	Special demands/
Reasons for taking	Education earned	hazards
Reasons for leaving		
Work liked best	*Personal Goals*	
Work liked least	Aims and objectives	
Relations with supervisor	Wage requirements	
Relations with peers	Education desired	

EXHIBIT 11.9
A checklist to help you formulate your interview questions.

Conducting the Interview No matter what type of interview you choose, you should observe the following basic procedure:

1. Put the applicant at ease. Keep in mind that the applicant will probably be a bit nervous, so do what you can to eliminate this barrier to successful communications by planning to make him or her comfortable as soon as you meet. A comfortable chair, a quiet room, good ventilation, a cup of coffee, and a smile along with your handshake will go a long way toward relieving his or her tension.

2. Stick with your schedule. If you have planned your questions and prepared an outline to follow, stay with them. Watch the time so that you cover what you must before your time runs out. Both of you may be tempted to wander from essential areas and talk randomly about whatever arises. You have several points to cover, and you do not usually have the luxury of unlimited time. If you do not get what you are there to get, you will have to make a decision on the basis of less-than-complete knowledge about the applicant.

3. Listen. By now you are probably sick of reading about listening, but it is of the greatest importance to the communications process—especially when you are engaged in a discussion. If you do all the talking, you will learn nothing. If you use the time between your questions simply to plan for what you will cover next, you will miss the applicant's answers. If you are not attentive to the applicant, you will shut him or her off. Summarize your thoughts about the applicant periodically, in writing, as time and discussion lags permit.

4. Remain neutral. Retain your impressions and opinions until the end of the interview. Mask your reactions, whether favorable or unfavorable. If the applicant senses your feelings one way or the other, he or she will begin to tailor responses to your reactions. You will receive what you have indicated you want to hear, not what the applicant wants to say. When you disagree with a response, ask the applicant for his or her reasons. Try to uncover his or her way of looking at things. You will gain a perspective on the individual and his or her attitudes that otherwise would be denied to you. As with appraisals, you should not concern yourself with an applicant's opinions that are not related to the nature of the job, to working, or to the working environment. If an applicant's attitudes or feelings are contrary to yours, simply ask yourself if it really matters. Will those opinions keep the applicant from a successful job performance? If not, forget them.

5. Avoid asking leading questions. Questions formulated to lead a person to the answer you want to hear will do just that. An example is "You got along with your boss, didn't you?" If a person answers no, he or she is pretty stupid. These questions simply waste time. They tell an applicant where your values are, but you will not learn the applicant's values.

6. Give the applicant your decision. If you have decided that a person is not right for the job, let him or her know it. It is not fair to keep people hanging or to put them off when you have definitely ruled them out. They have other plans to make and need to know where they stand as soon as possible. If you like a candidate but wish to interview one or two others before you decide, let the applicant know that as well. He or she may be interviewing with several employers and may not be ready to give you a decision either. But give a specific time by which he or she will have your final decision. Then stick to that time limit as best you can. If you delay your decision too long, you may lose your prospect. If you know this person to be the best you have seen thus far and totally qualified for the position you have vacant, offer him or her the job. You have what you need. Further searching may be expensive and may yield no one better. You may be surprised to hear the applicant tell you that he or she is not sure and wishes to examine other opportunities. If you really want that person, set a time by which he or she should give you a definite answer.

During the interview, all you can hope to do is to assess what the person has done and what you believe him or her to be capable of doing. You cannot assess what an applicant will do; you can only gauge his or her potential based on past performances. You should concern yourself most with the person's ability to handle the duties of the job in question. This is the most important consideration.

Tests

Under federal guidelines, tests are any criterion or paper-and-pencil or performance measure used as a basis for any employment decision, including selection and hiring. Such measures include interviews, application blanks, psychological and performance exams, physical requirements for a job, and any other device that is scored or used as a basis for selecting an applicant. All the types of tests you use should attempt to measure only the performance capabilities that can be proved to be essential for success in the job to be filled.

disparate impact
the existence of a significantly different selection rate between women or minorities and non-protected groups

Disparate Impact   Federal guidelines say that selection devices must have no **disparate impact.** Disparate impact exists when a significantly different selection rate exists for women or minorities than for other groups. For example, if an employer hires 60 percent of white males who apply but less than 80 percent of that figure (less than 48 percent overall) of women and minorities, the employer may be open to charges of disparate impact. In order to avoid such accusations, employers need to recruit large numbers of applicants for each employment vacancy to ensure that enough women and minorities are included in the screening process. Accurate records of all those interviewed and hired must be kept.

All applicants whether hired or not must be classified by sex, race, and ethnic group, including whites.

Some screening devices that may lead to disparate impact are educational requirements, height and weight requirements, preference of employer for relatives of existing employees, promotions restricted to current employees, and reference checks. Unless a screening device can be shown to be job related, a business necessity, or a bona fide occupational qualification, it should not be used. A few selection devices have been accepted in most cases. These include state-mandated licensing requirements, language abilities, and apprenticeship training for skilled craft positions.

Validity   **Validity** is the degree to which a selection criterion or device measures what it is supposed to measure. With respect to testing for employee selection, the term often refers to evidence that the device is job related—that the device is a valid predictor of future performance on a job. Two kinds of validity in testing are criterion validity and content validity.

Criterion validity involves the demonstration that those who perform well on the test will perform well on the job. Conversely, those who do not perform well on the test will not perform well on the job. Content validity means that the test is a fair sample of the content of the job. Content validity is built into a test by carefully studying the activities that are called for on a job and then building ways to test for an ability to perform those activities.

An example of validity follows. A state decided to construct a physical exam for the selection of highway patrol officers. It decided to use a standard test given to military recruits. After using the test for a period of months, it went back to see how well the troopers were doing in relation to their test scores. They found little relationship between how well the troopers did on the test and their performance ratings on the job. The test was thrown out as invalid.

To construct a valid physical test, the state decided to study the physical demands made on troopers during the execution of their daily duties. A short run with full weight of equipment was created, and a drag-and-carry test simulating the extraction of accident victims was fabricated. The test was given to recruits but was not used to hire them. After the recruits were selected and had their job performances rated by their superiors, the test results were compared to their ratings. A good relationship was found, and the test was then considered a valid selection device. It simulated with accuracy what physical demands were made on troopers, and the test included major examples of their daily requirements.

validity
the degree to which a selection device measures what it is supposed to measure or is predictive of a person's performance on a job

Drug Testing

Nearly all large companies have had some experience with drug-addicted employees. Drug-addicted workers can and do cause injuries to themselves and to others and damage to property. According to a 1994 survey by the American Management Association, 56.7 percent of "companies with sales of less than $50 million...carry out drug testing on job applicants" (*Inc.*, 1994), up from 32.4 percent in 1990. But the problem of testing all applicants for jobs is a large and difficult one. The expense related to drug testing can run as much as several hundred dollars per administration. Reliable labs must be found to do the testing. There is the problem of taking the samples: Some hold that it is an invasion of privacy; the process requires someone to monitor the taking of samples. There is the additional concern for privacy about the results and what to do with a positive result. Many experts agree that common over-the-counter drugs can lead to a positive test result. Blood and urine samplings together tend to yield the best, most reliable results.

As a supervisor, the extent of your involvement in drug testing will probably be limited to getting the results after the offer of employment has been made and the test(s) given. Offers of employment are usually conditional on successful completion of physical exams and drug tests.

AIDS and Hiring

Acquired immune deficiency syndrome (AIDS) describes a physical condition in which a virus called HIV has crippled a person's immune system. The infected person falls victim to a host of opportunistic diseases and infections, which eventually cause death. Since 1981, when the disorder was first diagnosed, over 150,000 Americans have died from AIDS. About one million Americans are currently believed to be HIV positive—infected with the virus. The majority "are young adults between the ages of 25 and 44, the age category that contains half the nation's workers" (Noble, 1992).

In 1987, the Supreme Court held in a 7–2 decision that simple fear of contagion by any virus—without any medical assessment that the fear is well-founded—cannot justify firing an employee with any contagious disease. Through this decision, those who test positive for HIV and AIDS victims (along with others who suffer from contagious diseases) have been placed under the protection of the 1973 Vocational Rehabilitation Act (which prevents discrimination against the handicapped by schools, governments, and any business doing business with the federal government) and the 1990 Americans with Disabilities Act. The ADA covers public access to public accommodations and employment decisions by private employers of fifteen or more employees. Under its provisions, employers must make "reasonable accommodations" for those with HIV or AIDS. Fear of AIDS is a reality in the workplace requiring education for all employees. Increasingly, companies are finding both people with AIDS and those who test positive for HIV on their payrolls. More and more employers are formulating policies and creating training programs to deal with these issues.

One evening, the plant maintenance engineer contacted the company president at her home and asked if she was aware that employees were using drugs on the job. She replied that she was not and asked how he knew this to be a fact. The engineer replied that he had found drug paraphernalia—syringes, rubber straps, and unidentified pills in various trash containers throughout the work areas. The president immediately contacted the company's attorney and asked for his help.

Together, the president and the attorney worked up a program to deal with possible drug abuse on the company's premises and involving company employees. The program involves three distinct phases: education, testing, and rehabilitation opportunities. It was initiated with a two-hour education session on drug abuse, its affects on the workplace, and its costs in both dollars and human terms. The employees were informed that they would be tested for drugs through urine sampling (the most common form of testing) on the following Monday at a nearby testing lab. Employees were assigned a report-in time and given the entire day off with pay. Persons testing positive were required to enroll in a rehabilitation program before being allowed to return to work. Those refusing to be tested or to join the rehab program were fired after explanations and warnings. Each year, all employees are randomly tested at least once.

This company's policy is typical of a sound approach. It makes no exceptions, it forewarns and offers treatment, and it is not punitive for those who avail themselves of the opportunity to get straight. Its primary motivations are to prevent injuries and losses and to keep good people on the job.

Many companies are adopting the guidelines recommended by the American Red Cross and the National Leadership Coalition on AIDS. Four basic categories that need to be addressed are compliance with laws, nondiscrimination, confidentiality, and continuing education. We will discuss more on this issue in Chapter 16.

Screening by Polygraph

The polygraph, sometimes called the lie detector, was used by 10 percent of U.S. companies to screen job applicants before being banned by a federal law effective December 27, 1988. The Employee Polygraph Protection

Act states that private employers may not require, request, or suggest that employees or prospective employees take lie detector (polygraph) tests, except when conducting in-house investigations. Employers may then request employees to take lie detector tests under strict conditions.

Several companies are marketing honesty tests, which are written and graded by the vendor. The use of such tests is suspect since many have yet to be determined to be valid and reliable. Many states have passed laws to restrict their use.

THE IMMIGRATION REFORM AND CONTROL ACT

The Immigration Reform and Control Act of 1986 requires most employers to hire only American citizens and aliens who are authorized to work in the United States. When you hire, you must verify the employment eligibility and identity of each employee and complete and retain the one-page federal form, I-9. In general, you must complete Form I-9 for persons employed for three days or more (except for employees of temporary employment services and contractors' employees) by the end of the third business day following the hire. For people employed for fewer than three days, you must complete the form by the end of the first day of employment.

Once Form I-9 is completed by both the employer and the new hire, the documents used to verify identity and employability should be photocopied and kept on file with the Form I-9 for three years after the date of employment, or for one year after the date the employment is terminated, whichever is later.

PITFALLS

In employee selection, as in most of your duties, a number of pitfalls may snare you if you are not aware of them. Since there is a strong similarity between appraisals of subordinates and appraisals of applicants, some of the same pitfalls discussed in Chapter 14 apply here as well.

1. The halo effect. This occurs when you let one outstanding good or bad characteristic in an applicant influence your overall assessment.
2. The rush job. If you are inadequately prepared for an interview, how can you find out all you need to know about an applicant?
3. Comparisons. It is not fair to compare, for example, an applicant to someone who has had years of experience on the job. You should ask yourself if the applicant can meet the standards set by the job description. (For example, you have no reason to expect that the new person

can replace right away all the skills of a retiring worker who has had thirty years' experience on the job.)

4. Failure to follow the principles of sound interviewing. After you have completed this chapter, you should have a good grasp of what these principles are.

5. Overselling your company or the job. By overstatements, puffed-up generalizations, and inaccurate or untruthful information, you might be sowing the seeds that eventually frustrate the new person and lead him or her to quit. The person may be taking the job with false hopes and on the basis of your inaccurate promises. He or she will soon discover that his or her mental images do not coincide with the hard realities encountered on the job. Selection is an expensive process. If the person you select stays only a short time, you will have to repeat the whole process all over again. You will have been unfair to both your company and the employee. You will probably be worse off than you were before because of the further disruption to your workforce and production schedules. Your subordinates may begin to suspect that your judgment is not what it should be.

6. Omitting pertinent information. If you leave out some vital facts with regard to the applicant's duties or working conditions, he or she will be forced to make a decision on the basis of incomplete information. If the applicant had known all the facts, he or she might not have accepted the position. Therefore, once they become known, the applicant may decide that you have misled him or her and quit. You may have a tendency to leave out the unpleasant aspects of the job or to skip over them lightly. This can only lead a person to think badly of you and may give rise later to gripes and frustration. Give the facts as clearly as you can, leave out the sugar coating, and be complete in your description of the job.

7. Neglecting sound public relations. By either overselling or omissions, you may be paving the way for a later termination. Moreover, if your decision at the close of your interview is a negative one, and you have not left the person with a good impression about your company and its people, you will be promoting unfavorable public opinion about your organization that could cause a decline in job applicants and even in sales. Treat the applicant as you would a guest in your home. You want to make an honest but favorable impression so that, no matter what happens, when the visit is over both parties will leave with positive impressions.

8. Asking discriminatory questions. Companies can get into major difficulties with federal and state governments if they seek information that is discriminatory on application forms and during interviews. Antidiscrimination laws and the Equal Employment Opportunity Commission (EEOC) guidelines must be obeyed; failure to do so exposes you and your employer to legal actions, fines, and bad public relations that will make it more difficult to conduct business in the future.

9. Hiring friends and relatives who don't qualify. This error can result from putting emotions ahead of logic. Pressures from these two groups can be tremendous and must be overcome so that members of these groups are subjected to the same screening devices and procedures that apply to all other candidates. If you feel that you cannot be objective in hiring, you may have to let other, more objective people make the decision to hire.

PLANNING THE NEWCOMER'S FIRST DAY

Assuming that you have offered the job and the applicant has accepted, you must now begin your planning to welcome the new arrival.

During the interview and after it, you should have a fairly good idea of the need for training that exists. If you know that some training will be needed, begin to map out your plans, and get the program organized in a way that allows you to begin as soon as possible. Prepare your people for the new person by communicating everything you know that is positive and not confidential. Get the work area ready, the passes (if any) on hand, and all the items prepared that he or she will need to get right to work. In short, plan to make that first day a truly positive experience—one that will tell the applicant that his or her decision to work for you was correct.

ORIENTATION

orientation

the planning and conduct of a program to introduce a new employee to the company and its history, policies, rules, and procedures

Orientation includes the planning and conduct of a program to introduce the new employee to the company, including all policies, practices, rules, and regulations that will affect the employee immediately. Orientation programs are usually conducted by members of the personnel or human resource management department and usually occur within the first few days after the new person arrives. The programs may last for a few hours or for a few days, depending on the size of the company, the content of the program, and the number of new employees to be oriented.

Most businesses provide some kind of formal or informal orientation program for their new employees. Approaches range from companywide meetings and small group conferences to the use of printed materials (such as manuals and handbooks) on company policies and procedures. Most orientation programs give employees a broad overview of the entire organization, with a special emphasis on how and where the new person fits in.

As a supervisor, you may or may not play an active role in your company's orientation program. But you must know the specific contents of the program so that you can reinforce its major messages and build on them with your own efforts during induction. You don't want to contradict any of the key points of information given to new employees. If you are in charge of orientation, you will find Exhibit 11.10 helpful since it provides a checklist of the major ingredients in most orientation programs.

Orientation Program Goals

The goals of an orientation program usually include the following:

- To instill a favorable first impression with regard to the company, its products, its leadership, and its methods of operation
- To familiarize the new people with the policies, procedures, rules, and benefits that are initially most important
- To outline in detail the specific expectations that the company has for its employees with regard to on-the-job behavior
- To explain the various services that exist for all employees, identify who staffs them, and describe how one can take advantage of them

The orientation program's goals may be communicated and achieved in small, face-to-face situations or in group lectures and presentations. In many large firms, corporate managers from many levels and departments are introduced and may conduct some of the orientation sessions. This is most often the case when large numbers of new employees are to be welcomed to their new environment. In any case, your company is depending on you to fulfill the promises of its orientation effort in the everyday job setting.

- Employee assistance programs (EAPs)
- Company history, products, and organization
- Pay and benefits (paydays, vacations, holidays, and insurance)
- Work rules (policies and rules governing all employees while on the job and dictating their conduct)
- Disciplinary procedures
- Grievance procedures (union contract if applicable)
- Safety procedures and responsibilities
- Health facilities (what and where located)
- Opportunities for advancement and training
- Social functions and facilities
- Quality-of-work-life programs

EXHIBIT 11.10
Subjects covered in a comprehensive orientation program.

INDUCTION

induction

the planning and conduct of a program to introduce a new employee to his or her job, working environment, supervisor, and peers

Induction includes the planning and conduct of a program to introduce your new person to his or her job, working environment, supervisor, and co-workers. Induction is your responsibility as the new person's supervisor. Planning for it begins as soon as an offer of employment is accepted. Following the final selection interview, you must begin to tailor your induction activities to fit the needs of your subordinate. You must set specific goals and work out a timetable to achieve them.

In Chapter 6, we discussed theories X, Y, and Z and the Pygmalion effect. You will recall that these theories are about assumptions that managers make about their new people and how those assumptions can affect the treatment of new subordinates. You must assume the best about your new people until they prove your assumption to be incorrect. You must have faith in their ability to learn their new responsibilities. You needed that faith to offer them employment, and you will need it to structure your approaches to them during induction and training.

It is essential to get your people started with a positive set of experiences from their first day on the job. A warm welcome and immediate successful experiences will reassure the new person and help remove the anxiety and insecurity that comes with a new job. Induction becomes a very important program that can and does affect the short- and long-term performance of new employees. Induction can give people a proper start or sow the seeds for early failure and employee turnover.

It is important to shield your people from negative initial experiences by introducing them to successful employees and experiences and by keeping the malcontents away from them until they have firmly established their attitudes and mastery over their tasks. You must control their environment by controlling their exposures to it and in it. Keep this in mind as you construct your induction activities and timetable.

Induction Goals

Your induction program can have as many goals as you think proper and can take as long as you feel is necessary. Among the typical induction goals are the following:

- To instill a favorable impression and attitudes about the work section, its operations, and its people
- To remove as many sources of anxiety as possible by helping the new person meet his or her needs for security, competence, and social acceptance
- To design and provide initial experiences that foster motivation and promote early success
- To begin to build a human relationship that is based on trust and confidence

To accomplish these goals, base your planning on them. Your planning should be concerned with the construction of an induction program whose procedures and practices will enable you to achieve each of the aforementioned goals. Determine what specific steps you wish to accomplish and in what sequence you want them to occur. Then determine what resources and facilities you require. In short, you must decide what to do, how to do it, and who to have assist you. You may wish to delegate some of the tasks to your most reliable assistants. Exhibit 11.11 contains a checklist that may prove useful to you as you plan your program.

Making Arrangements

You must contact the personnel department and procure the necessary forms, passes, booklets, and so forth so that they are available on the first

	Yes	No
1. Have you reserved time for proper introductions to coworkers?	—	—
2. Are the tools, equipment, supplies, and other things on hand for the newcomer's first day?	—	—
3. Have you obtained up-to-date copies of the newcomer's job description?	—	—
4. Are needed identification forms and personnel forms available and scheduled to be filled out by the newcomer?	—	—
5. Have you reserved time with others that the newcomer should meet during his or her induction?	—	—
6. Are copies of the company's employee handbook, policy manual, and union contract ready for the newcomer?	—	—
7. Have you planned to give the newcomer a really positive experience the first day?	—	—
8. Have you planned a systematic introduction of the new person's duties to him or her?	—	—
9. Have you talked with the newcomer's coworkers, paving the way for a friendly welcome?	—	—
10. Have you reserved enough time to spend with the newcomer in the first few days on the job?	—	—

Things left to do: _____

_____

EXHIBIT 11.11
Checklist for planning your induction program.

day. As the newcomer's supervisor, you will want to brush up on the forms and content of the booklets so that you can effectively guide the employee through the maze of paperwork and can smooth out the wrinkles that might otherwise interfere with a constructive first impression.

The person's work area must be prepared so that the basic inventory of tools, equipment, supplies, and materials is on hand. It must be put into a clean and polished state of readiness so that the new employee starts off with the standards of housekeeping and maintenance firmly in view. Everything must be in its place and in working order so that there are no surprises waiting for the new person or for you.

Make arrangements for the new person to join one or another of the formal groups of workers in your department. It is a good idea to get someone to act as the new employee's mentor—a guide and tutor who will be available to answer questions and help once you have finished your induction. A mentor should be a volunteer who knows the ropes and whose judgment and abilities you respect. This person can provide immediate acceptance and social companionship on the job and off (during breaks and lunch).

Prior to the new person's arrival, inform the formal group about his or her qualifications. Share all the positive features you know about the new person that are not confidential. Paving the way for his or her acceptance by the group will help shape his or her attitudes. There is much to do, so do not waste time and put things off too long. What happens the first day may make the difference between a successful career employee and one who will quit before long.

If the new employee is in need of training, the details of the training must be thought through and outlined. A training schedule needs to be drawn up, and the goals that the newcomer is to achieve must be established. All the necessary aids and materials have to be obtained in advance, and the people to be involved in the training must be given notice about the parts they will play so that they can prepare for the training sessions by brushing up on the skills they will need to demonstrate. Chapter 12 examines training in more detail.

THE SOCIALIZATION PROCESS

socialization

the process a new employee undergoes in the first few weeks of employment through which he or she learns how to cope and succeed

When people enter a new organization to take up a new job, they go through a number of experiences that familiarize them with their new environment—its people, goals, processes, and systems. **Socialization** is the process through which both the new person and the organization learn about each other. Ultimately, this leads to a contract that both parties can live with. Through socialization, new employees find out what restrictions exist on their freedom, how to succeed and cope, and what place exists for them in the new environment.

After all the new employee's questions are answered, a **psychological contract** forms between employer and employee. It is not written but understood by all concerned, and it summarizes what both expect to give to and get from the other. The terms of the contract evolve as time passes and experiences increase. A sense of fairness or equity must exist between employee and employer: Each must believe that the other is doing his or her part and giving in proportion to what he or she expects to receive (Schein, 1978).

Not all new employees will survive long enough to forge a psychological contract. And after the contract is formed, conflicts can arise in which one person believes that its terms are being violated by the other. During orientation and induction, certain promises may be made and then broken. Such is the case when a job is oversold and puffed up into something it is not. A supervisor can tell the new person to produce at one level—the only one the supervisor says will be acceptable—and then tolerate a lower level of output from the new person or from others.

As you participate in orientation and induction programs and activities, make certain that you know what is and is not likely to happen to the new person once installed on the job. Be honest and sincere, and clear up any misconceptions that you sense the new person has. Don't promise or let your company promise more than you know it can deliver. Now let's return to induction and the specific questions that newcomers have on their minds. How you help them answer these questions will shape their views of the terms of their psychological contract.

psychological contract
an unwritten recognition of what an employer and an employee expect to give and to get from each other

THE FIVE BASIC QUESTIONS

As soon as the new employee arrives, the induction or initiation procedure begins. The typical induction answers the following five basic questions for the new worker:

1. Where am I now?
2. What are my duties?
3. What are my rights?
4. What are my limits?
5. Where can I go?

Where Am I Now?

After greeting the new arrival warmly, you should explain in words and graphic form just where he or she fits into the entire company's operations. By starting with a copy of the company's organization chart, you can move from his or her slot in your department all the way up the chain of command to the chief executive. Explain the jobs performed in your department and in the departments adjacent to it. Name the personalities involved in each, with particular emphasis on those the new employee is most likely to

SUPERVISORS AND ETHICS

Some companies have policies preventing the hiring of the spouse of an existing employee. Others hold that when one employee marries another, one must quit. The decision is often left to the couple, and they know of the policy before they marry. But many companies have no such policies and even encourage the romances between employees through a variety of means. Bill Gates, the billionaire CEO of Microsoft, wed an executive employee in 1993. "The company's Seattle headquarters has at least a dozen married couples who met and courted during their 18-hour workdays. People who work together have, almost by definition, similar backgrounds, talents, and aspirations." According to one chief executive, Orin Smith of Englehard Corporation, "'It's not marriage between employees that causes trouble. It's what leads up to it.'"

A growing body of academic research suggests that sexual attraction between co-workers, whether or not it is acted on, may boost people's productivity on the job. If two employees marry, the company where they work often ends up getting a terrific deal, including higher levels of job commitment from both spouses than from folks whose mates toil elsewhere.

Most remarkable is that nearly three quarters (70 percent) of the CEOs in *Fortune*'s 1994 poll said that romances between workers are "none of the company's business." One study of all male teams and teams with both females and males found that, without exception, the mixed-sex teams were faster and more imaginative at problem solving than the single-sex groups.

There are some possible downsides, however. Over 70 percent of executives surveyed agreed with the following statements:

1. Office romances increase the possibility of favoritism or the appearance of favoritism.
2. Office romances can create an unbusinesslike appearance.
3. Office romances expose the company to the danger of sexual harassment suits.

Over 70 percent disagreed with these two statements:

1. In the long run, office romances inevitably result in problems for the company.
2. When an office romance develops, one of the parties should leave the company voluntarily.

To overcome the appearance of or actual favoritism, companies like Wal-Mart will not allow one sweetheart or spouse to directly supervise the other. And keep in mind that states like Illinois and New York will not allow an employer to punish an employee for doing what is legal outside one's workplace.

Source: Adopted from Anne B. Fisher, "Getting Comfortable with Couples in the Workplace," *Fortune*, October 3, 1994, 138–142, 144.

encounter. Give the newcomer a good idea of how his or her job and department relate to the ultimate success and profitability of the company.

This initial explanation can be followed by a tour of the department and a look at the work area. Introduce the person to his or her co-workers and mentor, and give them a chance to chat. Next, familiarize the new person with the facilities within the department that he or she will need to use from time to time—storage areas, supply room, toolroom, washroom, water fountain, and the like. This is also a good time to point out the bulletin board, time clock, and various signs that are posted about the area. Give the newcomer a chance to ask any questions that relate to what he or she sees. Anticipate the likely problem areas and, if he or she does not get to each of them, be certain that you do.

From the tour of the immediate work area and your department, take a walk through the adjacent areas and explain the functions that go on in each. Introduce the newcomer to people you meet along the way in such a manner as to demonstrate your enthusiasm and pride in having him or her join your operation. Something like this should do the trick: "Bill, I'd like you to meet Howard Kramer. Howard, this is Bill Watkins. Howard has just joined our team, and we are lucky to have him." This gives your new worker a chance to know your true feelings about his or her decision to come aboard. The newcomer will quickly begin to sense that he or she is respected and well thought of, as well as needed. Howard will not remember the names of all those to whom he has been introduced, but he will remember your enthusiastic welcome. When he meets these people later, chances are that they will remember him and exchange a greeting.

During your walk through the company, you should have an excellent opportunity to review the company's history and to reinforce its orientation program. By sharing knowledge of the company, you will give the new person the sense of being an important part of a big operation. There is tremendous value in this since we all like to feel we belong to groups that are bigger and more powerful than ourselves. Review the company's line of products or services, and point out the major events in the company's history that have contributed the most to its present position. Pass on all the positive information you have that is not confidential so that a positive image is created of the company, its people, and its future.

When you tour the cafeteria or lounge area, treat the new arrival to a cup of coffee. Some companies pick up the tab for the first day's snacks and lunch, and some do not. If your company does not, why not pay for the coffee yourself? It is hard to think of a better way to say "welcome." Lunchtime is a good time to visit in a relaxed and personal way and to assess the impact of the morning's events on your new person. It gives him or her a chance to clear up any questions.

A student once told me that he has a simple philosophy about induction and orientation. In his words, "I just treat them like I would an old friend I haven't seen for some time. There's so much to talk about and share that conversation is never a problem."

What Are My Duties?

After you return from your tour, take the new person back to the work area. All the supplies, materials, tools, and equipment needed will be there because you made sure they would be. The area will be clean and orderly, thus demonstrating the standards of housekeeping and maintenance you expect the employee to maintain.

Give a copy of the job description to the new person, and go over each duty. Explain the details implied by the general listing, and check his or her understanding of each. Wherever you can, demonstrate each duty—either by performing it or by giving specific examples.

Issue any passes or identification cards needed for parking, entering the cafeteria, obtaining tools, and the like. Help the newcomer fill out all the necessary forms, which are sometimes a bit confusing and difficult to follow. By answering questions for your new worker, you will be helping to accomplish all the goals of your induction program.

What Are My Rights?

By "rights," we mean receiving what is owed or due each employee. All workers are entitled to receive their wages according to a prearranged schedule. Explain the pay periods and how pay is calculated. Explain fringe benefits such as group life- and health-insurance plans, the company's profit-sharing plan, paid holidays, incentive awards, the suggestions plan, and the like. In particular, communicate the eligibility requirements (where they exist) for each benefit.

If there is a union, be certain to introduce the steward and explain the rights a person has in regard to union membership. Where this is voluntary, say so. Do not give your views about unions. Simply advise the newcomer of what he or she needs to know.

Review the overtime procedures you follow, and explain how workers become eligible for overtime. Go over the appraisal process, and specify what will be rated in it. If there is a union, explain the grievance process and how to file a grievance complaint.

Cover all the areas that you know from experience have been sources of misunderstanding in the area of workers' rights. For instance, workers often confuse sick days with personal-leave days. Be sure that your employee knows the difference and understands the company policy with regard to these matters.

What Are My Limits?

Your first and most important duty regarding discipline is to inform each employee about the limits or boundaries placed on his or her conduct and performance (see Chapter 15). Discipline starts with the induction and orientation of each person. The do's and don'ts that you intend to enforce should be explained, along with the penalties attached to each. Each employee should have copies of the company regulations and department rules.

Pay particular attention to the areas affecting safety. Each worker should know not only the rules but company policy as well. If safety equipment is needed, be sure that it is issued or purchased, whichever is required. Then be certain to emphasize safety throughout the newcomer's training. Instill respect for safe working habits and conduct right from the start. Enforcement then becomes easier.

Where Can I Go?

This question involves the opportunities for advancement that exist for each new person. Explain his or her eligibility for training and advanced programs that increase both work skills and the opportunities for promotions. State the criteria you use for making promotion and transfer decisions. People need to know what is required of them in order to advance. Finally, explain the standards they must meet in order to qualify for a raise.

FOLLOWING UP

Plan a follow-up interview to talk with the newcomer about the first day's experiences and answer any questions that may have accumulated. See if you can get a handle on how he or she really feels.

At the end of the first week, schedule another informal meeting with the new person, and determine if he or she is making an adequate adjustment to the new job. Your personal daily observations should tell you if he or she and the group are getting along and if any personal problems are beginning to surface. Watch for warning signals such as fatigue, chronic complaints, lack of interest, or sudden changes from previous behavior patterns. If you spot any of these signals, be prepared to move swiftly to uncover the causes.

You must be prepared for the possibility that the new person may not work out. He or she may not, despite your efforts and those of the personnel department, be cut out for the type of work that has been assigned. If your observations and his or her responses seem to indicate this, get together with your boss and discuss the matter. You may be able to work something out, such as a transfer to a different job within or outside your section. It may also be possible to redefine duties to compensate for the difficulties. You want to try your best to salvage the new arrival and to avoid costly termination and replacement proceedings.

All you have to do is treat the new person like a guest in your home whom you wish to impress favorably. If you have his or her welfare uppermost in your mind, you will not go wrong. Be honest. Keep the channels of communication open. Through adequate planning, a warm welcome, and a constructive induction program, you will be doing all that you can do or are expected to do.

Probation

Most organizations make it clear to new employees that their first weeks are a probationary period—a period of adjustment for both the new person and the organization—after which a more permanent commitment by both can be made. Most union contracts allow for this and will not extend the protection of the union to a new person until a period of time has elapsed—usually about thirty days. Find out what your company's policy is on this, and let the new person know it.

During the probationary period, you must do your best to ensure that the new person settles in and adjusts as well as possible. If you recommended the new arrival or gave the offer of employment, it is in your best interest to do so. It is during the probationary period that most of the new employee's attitudes about work, the company, you, and the coworkers are formed. During probation, you have the time to note the new person's strengths and weaknesses. Praise the person for the former, and help the person remove the latter. Your opinion of the new person will probably be the deciding factor in confirming or denying continued employment. If the new person works out, you can take pride in the fact that you have played a part. If the new person is let go, you will have to take part of the responsibility for that as well.

Instant Replay

1. A proper selection process involves the supervisor of the worker who will be hired, usually as the interviewer in the final selection interview.
2. Supervisors should make the final selection because their commitment to the success of new employees is vital.
3. People interviewed in a final selection interview should be pre-screened, using proper selection devices, by personnel or the human resource management department.
4. Selection devices include any interview, form, or other instrument that will be weighed or used in making the decision to hire.
5. Selection devices and procedures should not adversely affect minorities and women, and they should have validity.
6. The selection process is both an information-gathering and an information-giving process.
7. Errors in the selection process can be expensive both in fines and court costs connected with discrimination charges and in replacing a person who should not have been selected.

8. Orientation programs are usually conducted by the personnel or human resource management departments and are designed to welcome new employees to the enterprise as a whole.

9. Induction programs are usually conducted by the supervisor of the new employee and are designed to welcome new employees to a specific job, working environment, and peer group.

10. Orientation and induction programs are normally tailored to fit the specific needs of different groups of new employees.

11. Studies show that the first few days on a new job are extremely important and largely determine the future performance and careers of newcomers.

12. The supervisor of a new person, more than any other factor at work, can mean the difference between success and failure on the job.

13. Both orientation and induction programs should be designed to remove sources of anxiety and to help new employees satisfy their needs for competence, security, and social acceptance.

Questions for Class Discussion

1. Can you define this chapter's key terms?
2. What is the proper role for a supervisor to play in the process that will select his or her new subordinate?
3. What will a personnel or human resource management department normally do during the selection process?
4. What are the major selection devices used in a typical selection process?
5. How should you prepare to give a selection interview?
6. What are the major pitfalls in the selection process?
7. What are the goals of a good orientation program?
8. What are the goals of a good induction program?
9. What happens to an employee who passes through the socialization process?
10. What are the five basic questions that new employees want answered?
11. How can you link what you know about motivation to the orientation and induction programs' goals?

Incident

Purpose: To test your knowledge of the application of federal human resource laws.

Your Task: Agree or disagree with each of the following statements. Do not consult the key that follows until you have checked each question.

	Agree	Disagree

1. It is illegal to hire an alien for a job. ___ ___
2. Every employer is required to have an affirmative action plan. ___ ___
3. The Americans with Disabilities Act requires affirmative action plans for HIV- and AIDS-infected individuals. ___ ___
4. In general, screening devices must be approved by federal authorities before they can be used. ___ ___
5. Employers may use polygraph tests during selection activities. ___ ___
6. An I-9 form must be completed before an applicant is hired. ___ ___
7. Affirmative action programs specify exact numbers of people to be hired. ___ ___
8. Women and handicapped people are considered minorities. ___ ___
9. People who have been discriminated against cannot sue for punitive damages. ___ ___
10. Drug testing is not a common practice in hiring. ___ ___

(*Key:* All are false.)

CASE PROBLEM 11.1

Belle's First Job

Ever since the First Trust and Savings Company hired Belle Walker for the summer, she has been a thorn in Kay Farrel's side. As head cashier, Kay is responsible for supervising the bank's eight tellers. Three weeks before Wilma Banks was to retire, Belle was hired as Wilma's replacement, without any consultation with Kay. Kay was openly critical of the way in which Belle had been hired because it was a significant departure from past practices and company policy.

Kay had inquired why exceptions were made in Belle's case but was given only terse and evasive answers. After some checking on her own, Kay discovered what she believed to be the real reason. James B. Walker, Belle's father, is one of the most important merchants in town. He keeps large personal and business accounts at the bank and is a member of its board of directors.

Kay does not have any serious doubts about Belle's ability to become a good teller. Belle is a high school graduate and has been an above-average student for most of her school years. She is a bright and personable young woman and is very good with customers. Her instructor for the first three weeks was Wilma Banks, the best teller at First Trust and Savings Company.

During the first two weeks of training Belle, Wilma mentioned on several occasions that Belle's heart did not seem to be in her work. She would often say she understood but then make some simple mistake when left on her own. She enjoys talking to the customers more than she does handling their banking transactions, and more than a few times they let Belle know this. Belle is also fond of saying that she really does not need this job or the money it pays but wants to work for the experience and to meet new people. She is headed for college in the fall and wants to fill some time.

This week, the first week Belle was on her own, she was unable to balance out at the end of her shift on Tuesday and Thursday. She had a significant excess of cash she could not explain on Tuesday and a shortage of cash on Thursday. Kay is also concerned about Belle's tardiness—another departure from her behavior pattern of the first two weeks on the job. Twice this week she has been late in opening her window. This creates problems for the other tellers, who do not hesitate to let Kay know how they feel about it. When Kay spoke to Belle about her tardiness on Monday, she was assured it would not happen again. But Belle was late again today.

Kay knows that Belle will be around only for another eight weeks and wonders if it is worthwhile to raise the problem about her performance. She has doubts about her boss's willingness to stand behind her in any attempted disciplinary action. He has let her down before, even when a big depositor's daughter was not involved. Kay is afraid, however, that letting things go unchecked might lead to more serious problems in her department.

Questions

1. What special treatment has Belle already received? What are the consequences?
2. Suggest a selection system that might have avoided this problem.
3. What should Kay do now?

Arthur's First Day

CASE PROBLEM 11.2

Michael Henderson was looking forward to Arthur Duffy's arrival. Mike had not had a chance to interview Arthur because of an illness in his family, but from all the reports Mike had received from personnel, Arthur was just the right person to fill the hole in Mike's shop. As Mike was reviewing his orientation program, Arthur appeared in the office. Mike greeted him and asked him to sit down. After some brief words about the weather and the trip to the plant, Mike got down to business.

After a few minutes of conversation, it became obvious to Mike that Arthur knew next to nothing about the company. Mike was also surprised to find out that Arthur had not been tested for his mechanical skills. After a phone call to personnel, Mike discovered that the results of Arthur's physical exam had not yet arrived. This meant that Mike could not put him to work. Irritated, Mike decided to show Arthur around the shop anyway and to introduce him to his co-workers.

Following the tour and the introductions, Mike took Arthur to lunch in the company cafeteria. During the meal, Mike cautioned Arthur about several things. First, Mike told Arthur to stay away from Jackson and his crowd because, Mike said, they were troublemakers and could cause problems for Arthur. Second, Arthur was cautioned not to join the union because, in Mike's words, "the top decision makers around here hate the union. If you join, your chances at a promotion will be shot." Finally, Mike warned Arthur to ignore any deviation from shop rules that he would witness once on the job. "I don't want you to pick up any bad habits," said Mike, "but I don't want you to squeal on anyone either."

When Arthur and Mike returned to Mike's office, a copy of the mechanical aptitude test was there. "Here is the test," said Mike as he handed it and a pen to Arthur. "Just sit here and do the best you can. It's no big deal, but company policy demands that you take it before you can work in the shop. When you're done, just give it to me and take off. I'll see you tomorrow at startup time, and if we have the results of your physical, I'll put you to work in the shop."

While Arthur was taking the test, Mike returned to his pile of papers and proceeded to turn out the work as usual. During the next two hours, Mike entertained two visitors, took and made several phone calls, and disciplined a worker in front of Arthur. When Arthur finally finished, it was after 4 P.M., so Mike left the plant with him.

"Say, what are the hours here anyway?" asked Arthur.

"We start at 8 A.M. and quit at 5 P.M., with an hour for lunch. Any more questions?"

Questions

1. What specific errors in the selection process exist here?
2. What problems exist in Arthur's orientation and induction?

Notes

Half, Robert. *On Hiring*. (New York: Crown, 1985), 67.

Inc. "And Whose Syringe Might This Be?" August 1994, 104.

Kleiman, Carol. "In Brief, this Interview Technique Is a Plus," *Chicago Tribune*, December 14, 1994, sect. 6, 5.

———. "Personnel Office Tasks Growing But Staffing Isn't." *Chicago Tribune*, April 19, 1987, sect. 8, 1.

Mauro, Tony. "Big Boost for Affirmative Action." *USA Today*, March 26, 1987, 1A.

McKee, Bradford. "The Disabilities Labyrinth," *Nation's Business*, April 1993, 18–23.

Noble, Barbara P. "At Work: AIDS Awareness Goes to the Office," *New York Times*, December 6, 1992, 25.

Pell, Arthur R. *The Supervisor's Handbook*. (New York: McGraw-Hill, 1994), 102.

Schein, Edgar H. *Career Dynamics: Matching Individual and Organizational Needs*. (Reading, Mass.: Addison-Wesley, 1978), 94–97.

Schuler, Randall R. *Managing Human Resources,* 5th ed. (New York: West Publishing Co., 1995), 261–262.

Suggested Readings

Allen, Jeffrey G. *Complying with the ADA: A Small Business Guide to Hiring and Employing the Disabled.* New York: John Wiley & Sons, 1993.

Gordon, Edward E., Morgan, Ronald R., and Ponticell, Judith A. *Future Work— The Revolution Reshaping American Business.* New York: Praeger Books, 1995.

Jenks, James M., and Zevnik, Brian L. P. "ABCs of Job Interviewing," *Harvard Business Review* (July–August 1989): 38–39, 42.

Ledvinka, James, and Scarpello, Vida G. *Federal Regulation of Personnel and Human Resource Management.* 2d ed. Boston: PWS-Kent Publishing Co., 1991.

Libbin, Anne E., Mendelsohn, Susan R., and Duffy, Dennis P. "Employee Medical and Honesty Testing." *Personnel 65* (November 1988): 38–48.

Loden, Marilyn, and Rosener, Judy B. *Workforce America: Managing Employee Diversity as a Vital Resource.* Homewood, Ill.: Business One Irwin, 1991.

Nuventures Consultants, Inc. *America's Changing Workforce.* LaJolla, Calif.: Nuventures Publishing, 1990.

Sugiura, Hideo. "How Honda Localizes Its Global Strategy." *Sloan Management Review* (Fall 1990): 77–82.

Tully, Shawn. "GE in Hungary: Let There Be Light." *Fortune* (October 22, 1990): 137–138, 142.

Weiss, Donald H. *How to Be a Successful Interviewer.* New York: Amacom, 1988.

12

Training

OBJECTIVES

After reading and discussing this chapter, you should be able to do the following:

1. Define this chapter's key terms.

2. List at least three advantages that a supervisor receives from training a subordinate.

3. List at least three advantages that a trainee receives from training.

4. List the three basic requirements that a trainer must satisfy in order to train.

5. List the five basic requirements a trainee must satisfy in order to learn.

6. List and briefly describe the seven principles that govern training.

7. List and briefly describe the four parts of the training cycle.

8. List and briefly describe the five pitfalls in training.

INTRODUCTION

This chapter is concerned with how you can help your subordinates acquire new skills, improve their existing ones, and improve their abilities to handle their jobs. The process of training is concerned with improving employees' performances in their present jobs. It helps them acquire the attitudes, skills, and knowledge they need to execute their present duties and the duties that will soon be coming their way.

Training becomes necessary by the very fact that you have subordinates. Whether they are old-timers, newcomers, or a mix of the two, you must continually see to it that they are functioning effectively and to the best of their abilities. If they are not, training is called for. Whether you train or rely on others to help you with training, you are responsible for seeing to it that your people are properly trained.

American corporations spend in excess of $43 billion on training each year (Bureau of Business Practice, 1993). Among the leaders in training are GE, U.S. Robotics, and Motorola; each spent 4 percent or more of its payroll on training in 1993 (Kelly and Burrows, 1994). "Motorola calculates that every $1 it spends on training delivers $30 in productivity gains within three years" (Henkoff, 1993).

THE SUBJECTS OF TRAINING

Training imparts attitudes, knowledge, and skills. It is an ongoing process governed by basic principles and provided by people with the aid of machines and methods specially suited to the subjects to be covered and the persons to be taught. Training, like daily living, increases our knowledge and understanding of the people and things that surround us.

training
the activity concerned with improving employees' performances in their present jobs by imparting skills, knowledge, and attitudes

Attitudes

We have already said much about attitudes, and all of it is related to the training process. You must remember that when you train, you are attempting to instill positive attitudes—either as replacements for improper ones or as useful additions to fill voids in the minds of your trainees. Attitudes are taught primarily through your own example and secondarily through your words. Workers learn an attitude by observing what you do. If you talk about safety but act in an unsafe manner or lightly skip over safety during the training period, your workers will adopt the same casual attitudes. The most important attitudes that you must help form in trainees are those that involve their job and their safety.

Knowledge

Knowledge is the body of facts, ideas, concepts, and procedures that enable people to see or visualize what must be done and why. If trainees can understand the whole job and its relationship to the work of others, they have a better chance to master their own jobs. They must understand the theory (fundamental principles and abstract knowledge) that governs their work before they can adequately perform their own tasks. Then they must (with your help) translate the theory into practice through the training process. Knowing what to do is one thing, but applying the knowledge is the most important thing.

Skills

When we apply knowledge, we are exercising some type of skill: technical, human, or conceptual. Technical skills require muscular coordination—based on knowing what to do, why, and how to do it—that we can use to operate tools, machines, and equipment. Conceptual skills involve mental processes such as those used in problem solving, learning, and communicating (reading, writing, calculating, and imagining).

The best way to teach a skill is to involve the trainees as quickly as possible in performing the skill. Practice and more practice are keys to the successful acquisition of motor skills. Moving from an in-depth understanding of the tools, equipment, or machinery to an actual working knowledge of the trade or craft, the trainees experience a controlled exposure to both the technical side and the manipulative side of their jobs.

Early successes are essential, and you must exercise extremely close supervision so that your employees do not acquire improper work habits and so that you instill confidence as soon as possible. Often you may have to ask the trainees to unlearn certain procedures or habits acquired by earlier experiences before you can substitute the proper methods. This is a difficult and time-consuming task that requires a great deal of patience from both you and your trainees.

Tom Peters (1987), co-author of *In Search of Excellence* and *A Passion for Excellence,* offers several suggestions to managers who want their companies to survive in today's business climate. First, he says, workers must be trained to accomplish the following goals:

- Learn many jobs (twenty to thirty).
- Perform many tasks (maintenance, repair, budgeting, and quality control).
- Perform many skills (problem cause-and-effect analysis, listening, interpersonal dynamics—team problem-solving skills).
- Function as a member of a business team, with team leadership rotating among its members.

Second, he says, managers must be trained and developed to achieve the following ends:

SUPERVISORS AND ETHICS

If companies expect their employees to think and act ethically, they must create "organizational integrity...based on the concept of self-governance in accordance with a set of guiding principles. From the perspective of integrity, the task of ethics management is to define and give life to an organization's guiding values, to create an environment that supports ethically sound behavior, and to instill a sense of shared accountability among employees" (Paine, 1994). Guidance and examples from the top form the foundation of an ethical corporate culture and environment. In addition, training and incentive for fostering ethical behavior are required. Finally, ethical training efforts and results must be audited and either punished or rewarded.

According to Peter Madsen, executive director at Carnegie Mellon University's Center for the Advancement of Ethics, ethics training involves two related areas: compliance training that alerts people to policies, regulations, and laws that establish acceptable behavior within a company and cognitive thinking exercises that develop skills to allow people to think through various "moral mazes" they may be confronted with in the workplace (Human Resources Management, 1992).

Ethics training can take some interesting and unusual formats. Citicorp uses "an ethics board game, which teams of employees use to solve hypothetical quandaries. General Electric employees can tap into specially designed interactive software on their personal computers to get answers to ethical questions. At Texas Instruments, employees are treated to a weekly column on ethics over an international electronic news service" (Labich, 1992). The key seems to be to make ethics training realistic and connected to one's personal situation in life and at work. A company is limited only by its ethics trainers' creativity and imagination.

Sources: Paine, Lynn Sharp. "Managing for Organizational Integrity," *Harvard Business Review,* March–April 1994, 111; Labich, Kenneth. "The New Crisis in Business Ethics," *Fortune,* April 20, 1992, 167, 168, 172, 176; *Human Resources Management: Ideas & Trends in Personnel* 273 (Chicago: Commerce Clearing House, April 15, 1992), 60.

In an effort to improve their workforce, many large companies offer basic education programs. Literacy classes, such as the one shown at Aetna Insurance Company, teach skills workers need to succeed on the job.

- Be better listeners.
- Believe in the virtually unlimited potential of every worker.
- Become true facilitators for the teams they must lead.
- Recognize and pay for productivity increases and quality improvements. Above-average base pay and team-based incentives tied strictly to measurable performance improvement are essential.

The problem is, however, that about 20 percent of current and new employees lack the basic literacy skills they need to succeed in their jobs (Grossman, 1989). According to the American Management Association, 24 percent of major U.S. employers are conducting basic remedial training programs to enable their employees to cope with their present and future job demands (Godin, 1994). R. J. Reynolds invested about $2 billion in automating its factory in Winston-Salem, North Carolina, before discovering that its workforce lacked the reading skills necessary to operate and maintain the new equipment. Of its 6,000 workers, 1,300 had to be put through a basic literacy program. Finally, IBM offered a free college-level course in algebra to its employees but discovered that only 30 out of 280 workers who signed up were able to read and calculate at the twelfth-grade level—a prerequisite for taking the course (Grossman, 1989).

ADVANTAGES OF TRAINING FOR THE SUPERVISOR

Just what do you yourself get out of training a subordinate? What is in it for you? The following are but a few of the many benefits you receive when you train your people properly:

1. You get to know your subordinates. When you are dealing with new employees, you hasten the process of learning about their needs, wants, and potentials. With your other subordinates, you get a chance to update your knowledge of each person, thereby making easier your personnel decisions and recommendations with regard to promotions, raises, transfers, and the like.

2. You further your own career. As your people grow in abilities, proficiency, and reputation, so will you. As each individual increases his or her efficiency and effectiveness, the whole group benefits. As your subordinates look better, feel better, and perform better, they strongly affect your reputation as a supervisor and leader. As we have stated before, your reputation is largely a product of their performance.

3. You gain more time. As a result of training, your people become more self-sufficient and confident. You will find that, as their performance improves, you have more time for the essentials. You will spend less time on corrections and deficiencies and more on planning, organizing, controlling, and coordinating. You may be able to shift from an autocratic style of supervision (so necessary during the training) to a less time-consuming style.

4. You promote good human relations. One of your primary roles in developing good human relations with your people is that of educator. You give them logical reasons to support sound working relationships with you and their peers. They gain self-confidence, pride, and security through their training, which promotes cooperation and respect for you. Many will see you as the cause of their improvement and will rely on you more for advice and direction in the future.

5. You reduce safety hazards. By emphasizing safety rules, procedures, and attitudes through your proper conduct and words, you reduce the likelihood of violations and the resulting accidents and injuries. How tragic it would be to have to live with the knowledge that a subordinate's injury might have been prevented if you had done all that you should have in the area of safety.

ADVANTAGES OF TRAINING FOR SUBORDINATES

Training gives your workers as many advantages as it gives you (if not more), including the following:

1. They increase their chances for success. Through training, workers gain new knowledge and experiences that help reduce the risks of personal obsolescence and increase their value to themselves and to the company. By exposure and practice, workers learn new techniques that enhance their abilities and their enjoyment of work. By

successfully completing training, workers confront change, meet challenges, and decrease fears.

2. They increase their motivation to work. Through successful training experiences and proper guidance, individuals experience a greater measure of achievement. They find ways to reduce fatigue, increase contributions, and expend less effort to accomplish their tasks. These accomplishments tend to fortify a desire to work harder. We all need the security that comes with knowing our jobs so well that we are free to learn new skills and to advance in our careers. We all need a sense of competence.

3. They promote their own advancement. As workers become more proficient, they earn the right to receive additional duties, either through delegation or through a job change. By proving themselves through the learning process, they justify the investment of additional company time and money in their development. They become more mobile members of the organization.

4. Their morale improves. Mastery of new responsibilities inevitably leads to new prestige and importance. This newfound pride can be translated into higher earnings, a greater commitment to the company, and a renewed self-image. As the spirits of group members rise, they can and often do spread throughout the group. Workers see themselves as necessary and more valuable parts of the whole and as greater contributors to the group's success.

5. Their productivity increases. Their output becomes less problem ridden, exhibits less wasted effort and materials, and results in higher-quality production and a greater return to themselves and the company.

Some or all of these benefits will accrue to everyone who takes part in training. The degree to which an individual receives such benefits is a variable that cannot be predicted. But training does tell your people of both your company's interest and your personal interest in their welfare and development. Just be sure to let trainees put their training to use as soon after its completion as possible.

REQUIREMENTS FOR TRAINERS

Ideally, you as the supervisor should plan and execute the essential function of training. This is true primarily because of the many personal benefits available to you when you do. After all, the workers on your team are your responsibility.

There are times, however, when you cannot train subordinates. You may lack either the time or the first-hand knowledge of the job to be taught (or both). In such cases, you may have to delegate the training duties to a subordinate or rely on the various staff specialists your company can provide. Either way, you are accountable for their actions and the results. Therefore, it would be wise for you to assist, when you are able, in the planning of the training and to check up on its execution periodically. Better one ounce of prevention than pounds of cure.

Regardless of who does the training, he or she should meet the following requirements:

- Be willing to conduct the training
- Know the body of knowledge, attitudes, and skills to be taught
- Know how to train—possess a working knowledge of the ways in which people learn, the principles that govern training, and the several kinds of training methods, along with their respective advantages and disadvantages

Every trainer must want to do the best job possible and must recognize that his or her actions and enthusiasm will teach as much as, if not more than, the words spoken during training. Training is an art that can be learned.

Kenneth Blanchard (1987), chairman of Blanchard Training and Development and co-author of *The One-Minute Manager*, believes that a positive relationship with workers is a powerful motivator. "To gain the respect and loyalty of employees, a manager should emphasize the positive aspects of someone's performance and de-emphasize the negative." Such a manager builds a relationship of TRUST with subordinates:

- T stands for time—taking time to provide feedback on performance.
- R stands for respect—respect that grows from relationships based on trust.
- U stands for unconditional positive regard—trainers should have the best interests of trainees at heart.
- S stands for sensitivity—the best trainers learn to anticipate the feelings and needs of trainees.
- T stands for touch—trainees need a pat on the back and a pleasant "Well done!"

Behavior Modeling

The case problems given in this text at the end of each chapter show, for the most part, supervisors in trouble and usually doing the wrong things. Sometimes they simply do not know what to do, and sometimes their attitudes get in the way. Such cases help you spot a failure and search for the causes of it. **Behavior modeling,** on the other hand, teaches attitudes and proper modes of behavior to individuals and groups by involving them in real-life situations and providing immediate feedback on their performance.

behavior modeling
a visual training approach designed to teach attitudes and proper modes of behavior by involving supervisors and others in real-life performances

SUPERVISORS AND QUALITY

Many people consider their coaches from their athletic training days to have been their most valuable role models for training. Coaches continually kept them focused on the fundamentals so essential to play their best. Conditioning kept them in shape and ready to tackle the moves for their sport. Coaches exhibited patience and a detailed knowledge of what the individual needed to expand on his or her potentials. They helped keep each person motivated to give his or her personal best. As author and consultant, Arthur R. Pell uses the word *coach* as an acronym to highlight the typical coach's behaviors:

- **C** hange. The coach must keep people alert to new technologies, new methods, and new approaches.
- **O** observe. The coach must keep observing people to identify what additional training is needed.
- **A** ssess. The coach must assess what has been accomplished and measure it against the desired goals.
- **C** ounsel. An important part of the coach's job is to counsel people individually, commend them for their strengths, and encourage them to improve where needed.
- **H** elp. The coach should help people hone their skills and improve their work by providing training and by recommending courses, seminars, readings, and other sources of learning.

The coach should help the group and each member of the group succeed by encouraging people to do their very best.

Source: Pell, Arthur R., Ph.D. *The Supervisor's Infobank.* (New York: McGraw-Hill, 1994), 123.

The person modeling a behavior can be anyone—supervisor, team leader, team member, or outside expert. By watching a film, a videotape, or live role-playing sessions, supervisors and others are shown proper ways to deal with true-to-life situations. Participants, by watching, discussing, and then trying to apply what they see, can and do experience behavioral changes.

Behavior modeling can be used to teach human relations: how to deal constructively with employee complaints, how to conduct training, and how to do virtually anything supervisors are likely to have to do. Participants in behavior modeling are usually called on to act out what they believe to be proper conduct, given specific situations and persons to deal with. Their performances are usually taped or filmed and then discussed by all concerned on playback.

If your company offers it, this technique can help you learn how to be a better trainer. You can use behavior modeling to help your trainees duplicate behaviors, as well. It is always a good idea to rehearse your training lessons before you attempt to perform for real. Watching yourself on film or listening to your delivery on tape can greatly improve your timing and delivery of vital information.

A variation on behavior modeling is used by some companies in both training and performance appraisal of nonsupervisory employees. Managers videotape or record people during the actual performance of their duties and allow them to review the recordings with or without the assistance of supervisors or co-workers. The tapings are usually done with the permission of the trainee, whether newcomer or old-timer. As one training director puts it, "actors, singers, and dancers usually perform in front of mirrors to polish their crafts. Why shouldn't the same principle hold true for our phone and route salespeople?"

REQUIREMENTS FOR TRAINEES

In general, people who are about to go through training should meet the following requirements:

1. They should be informed about what will be taught and why.
2. They should recognize that they need what is to be taught.
3. They should be willing to learn what is to be taught.
4. They should have the capability to learn what is to be taught.
5. They should see the advantages to them in mastering what is to be taught.

Given trainees who meet these preconditions and a trainer who meets his or her preconditions, genuine learning and meaningful change can take place. Learning theory tells us that without motivation or the incentive to learn, no real learning will take place. When learning does take place, motivated trainees and trainers are the central reason for it. The principles that follow will enable you to design and execute a successful training program.

THE PRINCIPLES OF TRAINING

There are several established and proved principles that you should keep in mind while planning and conducting a training program. These principles should be used as a checklist to make certain that you have not overlooked

When you train your workers, both your technical expertise and attitude are important. Training is a perfect time to instill motivation in a subordinate.

anything important. To help you remember them, they are summarized by the acronym MIRRORS:

- **M**otivation
- **I**ndividualism
- **R**ealism
- **R**esponse
- **O**bjective
- **R**einforcement
- **S**ubjects

These principles are interdependent and interrelated.

Motivation

Unless both you and the trainee are motivated, the training process will achieve something less than is desired. Your **motivation** should come easily since you have much to gain from training. If you delegate to a subordinate, you again should have no problem with motivation because he or she willingly accepted the responsibility. It is the trainee who poses the greatest concern. New employees are usually anxious to get through training successfully so as to gain some level of independence and security. Old-timers may be less than enthusiastic, however.

Remember that training imparts a sense of competence. If people know what is expected of them, believe that they are capable of mastering those expectations, see the rewards that lie ahead, and want those rewards, they will be motivated.

motivation
the training principle that requires both trainer and trainee to be favorably predisposed and ready to undergo training

individualism
the training principle that requires a trainer to conduct training at a pace suitable for the trainee

Individualism

The principle of **individualism** states that the training you prepare and present must be tailored to meet the needs and situations of individuals. To do this, you must know what skills, knowledge, and attitudes the people already possess so that you can start from there in designing your program. By building on what they already know, you can use their experiences as a frame of reference. What is to be added can be linked to their present abilities.

By individualizing your approach, you can adjust the sequence of what is to be taught to fit present conditions most appropriately. For instance, if people already know how to operate a particular piece of machinery that is similar to but not the same as the one they must now operate, begin by pointing out the similarities, and then show the differences or exceptions.

Finally, this principle states that you must vary your presentation of material to fit people's ability to assimilate it. Let the trainees advance at a comfortable rate, and do not give too much at once; you will only frustrate and confuse them if you do.

You are probably experiencing exposure to older employees. By the year 2000, the average worker in America will be thirty-nine years old, and the baby boomers will be reaching their fifties. When older employees go through training, you can individualize your approach by relying on thoroughness rather than speed. Use older employees' backgrounds and experiences as connecting links to the new information or methods. By providing constant feedback to keep them abreast of their progress, you help overcome some of the fear of failure that older workers have when facing the new and different.

Realism

Make the learning process as close to the real thing as you can. In most training situations, you should teach people on the job, using the actual equipment, tools, or machinery that must be mastered. In the case of office or clerical employees, use the actual forms, manuals, procedures, and practices. This **realism** is not always possible because of various limitations. Noise levels may interfere with proper communications; space may not be adequate for proper demonstrations or explanations; equipment or machines may not be available for training use because they are being fully utilized in current production. When you cannot train on the job, or deem it wiser not to do so, set up conditions that are as close to the actual working situation as possible. Use examples and situations that accurately reflect actual problems the worker is likely to encounter. Then move from the simulated conditions to the actual environment as soon as possible.

A medium-size manufacturer in the Midwest was reluctant to purchase and install the latest manufacturing equipment in its plant because it lacked skilled workers who could operate and maintain it. The solution was to find a community college that had the computer-integrated equipment in its facilities and to send a select group to learn the equipment. After the group was trained, the workers returned to train others in the plant on the equipment that was then being installed.

realism
the training principle that requires training to simulate or duplicate the actual working environment and behavior or performance required of the trainee

Response

The principle of **response** reminds you to check on the trainees' receptiveness and retention regularly. Involve the trainees in a two-way conversation. Ask questions and encourage them to do the same. Only by frequent checking can you be sure that lasting progress is taking place.

Response also includes the concept of evaluation. Besides oral questions and answers, you can evaluate or measure the trainees' progress by

response
the principle of training that requires feedback from trainees to trainers and vice versa

SUPERVISING TEAMS

The Springfield Remanufacturing Corporation in Springfield, Missouri, has relied on trained, committed team members since its management bought the company from International Harvester in 1983. The company specializes in rebuilding used engines. But as CEO Jack Stack puts it, "Our real business is education. We teach people about business.... When people come to work at SRC, we tell them 70 percent of the job is disassembly—or whatever—and 30 percent of the job is learning."

Worker training focuses on teaching the basics about how a business operates. Employees are taught how to read financial statements—cash flow, balance sheet, sources and uses of funds—everything workers need to know to keep score and follow the evolution of what Stack calls "the great game of business." Classes and tutorials are offered, allowing people to learn as much as they care to and to advance as far as they wish. The more they learn, the more they realize how dependent they are on one another and the more they understand what is needed for the survival of their company.

SRC gives individuals the responsibility for their own futures and job security. It asks people to think about where they want to go and how things can be done better, faster, and cheaper. By giving employees a share of the profits and making continual training available, SRC is building a flexible, organic organization that can respond rapidly to change and customer demands. The employees feel and act like owners because they have been given the incentives and tools (bonuses, weekly meetings, training, and so on) to do so. The company shares all the information it has with employees. It relies on all its approximately 650 employees to spot what needs doing and to do it. All employees have the same goals and depend on one another to reach them. Thus the whole company acts as one—a team committed to finding the most efficient and profitable ways to run SRC.

Source: Stack, Jack, with Burlingham, Bo. *The Great Game of Business* (New York: Doubleday/Currency, 1992).

conducting performance tests or written quizzes. Use whatever means you believe will yield the information you seek. Involve the trainees in feedback throughout the training process. Share the results of trainees' regular evaluations with them. One member of a corporate training program put it this way: "I like the daily quizzes my instructor gives. They let you know right away how well you have caught on to the material covered. It keeps you on your toes and forces you to review each night. I need this course. It means another twenty-five dollars per week."

Objective

The principle of the **objective** states that trainees and trainers should always know where they are headed at any given point in the training process. As a trainer, you have to set goals for the training program and for each of the individual training sessions you conduct. These must be communicated to the trainees so that they know where they are headed and can tell when they get there.

The trainees' goals are targets to shoot for during each session, as well as throughout the entire program. They should be realistic, specific, and within the trainees' ability to achieve. They tell employees that their training is planned and professional. There will be more about objectives later in this chapter.

objective
the training principle that requires trainer and trainees to know what is to be mastered through training

Reinforcement

According to the principle of **reinforcement,** if learning is to be retained, it must involve all the senses—or as many as possible. When you first explain an idea, you may involve both sight and hearing using a demonstration coupled with an explanation. Then you can let the trainees try out their understanding by repeating the demonstration and explanation in their own words. They will then be using sight, touch, and hearing and will be reviewing the concepts as well. By using frequent summaries and by reviewing key points, you will be practicing reinforcement. By repetition and practice, you lend emphasis and greatly increase retention.

Try to put the knowledge and skills that must be learned to work in a real situation as soon as possible. Studies reveal that we retain about 50 percent of what we hear immediately after we hear it and about 75 percent of what we experience immediately after the event. As time passes without further reference to our knowledge or to the application of our skills, our retention of them diminishes still further. More than one training supervisor knows the truth behind the adage "Tell them what you are going to tell them; tell them; and tell them what you told them."

reinforcement
The training principle that requires trainees to review and restate knowledge learned

Subjects

The principle of **subjects** is two-sided: You must know as much about the trainees as possible, and you must have a mastery of the subject to be taught. By researching and rehearsing before the main event, you will be aware of the likely trouble spots both in the presentation and in the learning of the material.

In determining what you wish to teach—the subjects of your training program—you have several areas to consider. If you are preparing to teach

subjects
the principle of training that requires trainers to know the subject being taught and to know the trainees' needs

an entire job, you will want to consult the job description and its corresponding job specifications. Next, you will need to know what skills and knowledge the job holder has, in relation to what he or she needs. Then you can construct a program to teach the skills, knowledge, and attitudes the new person needs. Be certain that the description of the job accurately outlines the job and its duties as they presently exist, not as they once were.

To determine the subjects to teach to your current subordinates, consult their most recent performance evaluations, your current observations, and the workers themselves. Disciplinary actions and records may point out the need for training. So may the results of exit interviews conducted with voluntarily departing subordinates. Common complaints may signal common problems that can be eliminated, through training, for those who remain employed.

A company recently switched from one brand of computers to another and introduced the use of several new software programs throughout one of its divisions. After a week, work began to fall off in quality. It became obvious to the division manager that many departments were having trouble with the new software. On investigation, the division chief discovered that several supervisors were unable to teach the new software because they had not learned it. Several other supervisors knew the software but seemed unable to teach it to their team members. The division chief got together with the personnel head of training and constructed two courses: training the trainer to train and a course on the uses and applications of the software. In the latter course, help was obtained from the vendor of the new computers. A skilled analyst was dispatched to the company, the course was taught to supervisors and videotaped, and the rest of the troubled workers took the course by watching the video presentation and working along with it.

THE TRAINING CYCLE

Exhibit 12.1 shows the four parts of a successful training effort. Training, like planning, demands that you know your destination before you plan your trip. The first step is to identify where training is needed. Once areas are identified, objectives can be written to specify what is to be taught, under what conditions, and how the learning can be verified. Unless all persons undergoing the training have no knowledge of what is to be taught, a pretest is called for to determine who knows what and to what extent they know it. You can then construct a training plan to answer the questions of who, when, where, how, and how much about the training. The program is then put into action, and the results are evaluated to determine areas that were successful and the need for improvements or repetition of some lessons.

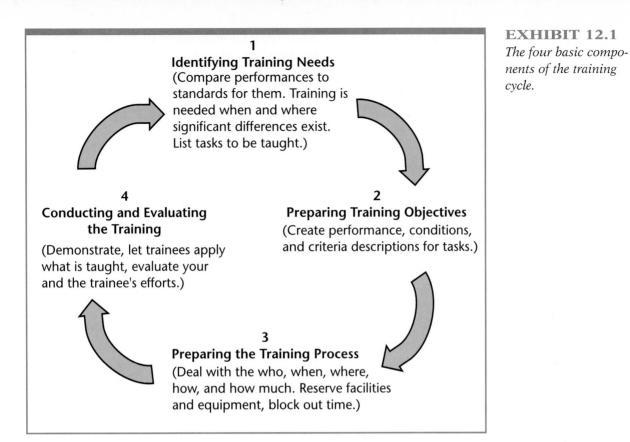

EXHIBIT 12.1
The four basic components of the training cycle.

1
Identifying Training Needs
(Compare performances to standards for them. Training is needed when and where significant differences exist. List tasks to be taught.)

4
Conducting and Evaluating the Training

(Demonstrate, let trainees apply what is taught, evaluate your and the trainee's efforts.)

2
Preparing Training Objectives
(Create performance, conditions, and criteria descriptions for tasks.)

3
Preparing the Training Process
(Deal with the who, when, where, how, and how much. Reserve facilities and equipment, block out time.)

Part 1. Identifying Training Needs

You know that you or your people need training when things are not as they should be. Your efforts at control and supervision should tell you when performances are not meeting expectations or standards. Training is always needed to some degree with the addition of new subordinates to your area. As new equipment is arranged for, people have to be trained to use and maintain it. When new procedures are to be established, people should be warned and taught how to execute them.

Let's assume that you are a restaurant manager faced with the arrival of a new employee who must be trained in your restaurant's methods, attitudes, and skills as they relate to being a waiter. How would you start to determine what should be taught? It would make sense to turn to your copies of the waiter's job description and job specification. You have these, they are up to date, and you have already used them to conduct your recruiting and interviewing prior to your decision to hire. They contain a list of duties and tasks, as well as a list of the personal qualities demanded of a waiter. From each task listed on the job description, you can determine the specific skills needed to execute the task. The task of greeting customers cordially after they are seated by the host requires language and interpersonal skills. The task of serving customers their orders requires manual dexterity and coordination—mental as well as physical. Once you know what types of performance are expected of the waiter, you have the raw material necessary to assess possible training needs. If the new person is experienced, you will probably have to teach your particular restaurant's applications of skills already possessed to some degree.

The day has arrived. Ben, your new waiter, has two years of experience with the job. Your earlier and present contacts with Ben will tell you the areas in which he needs training. After induction, you show Ben the job description and talk through each of the duties with him, making sure to point out any differences that may arise between what Ben has been doing elsewhere and what he will be expected to do for you. Now that Ben is familiar with his tasks, you are ready to try him out on each and monitor his performance. But before monitoring, you must have a clear understanding of each task, of the conditions that surround its performance, and of the criteria by which you will judge the quality of performance. These three items constitute what is called a **training objective.**

training objective
a written statement containing what the trainee should be able to do, the conditions under which the trainee is expected to perform, and the criteria used to judge the adequacy of the performance

Part 2. Preparing Training Objectives

Before you can train or a person can learn, both parties must have common objectives in front of them. These should be in writing to avoid confusion and to ensure mastery. All objectives should state three things as clearly as possible: (1) what the trainee should be able to do (the performance expected); (2) the conditions under which the learner is expected to do it; and (3) how well the task must be done—the criterion or criteria (Mager, 1984). Let's look at each of these in more detail.

Performance   The specific things you want a trainee to do are usually outlined or summarized under the major headings of tasks listed in a job description. But each task may and usually does have a series of minor tasks connected to it. For example, Ben's job description states, "takes orders from patrons." What subtasks or other duties are connected to this one? One might be that the waiter be able to write the orders on a prescribed form in a prescribed manner so that the kitchen people can properly interpret it. Before an order can be taken, patrons need to know what is available. Consequently, menus must be distributed and specials for the day announced. All these subtasks must be understood and stated if they are to be taught. Finally, certain skills are connected with these tasks. They, too, must be identified, described, and (in some cases) taught.

Your immediate concern with Ben will be to decide which tasks he can perform, and you cannot do that until you have listed all the tasks in all of their detail. Before you can train Ben or evaluate how much he already knows, you have to possess a complete list of required tasks, skills, and attitudes.

Objectives usually state the performance needed by using active verbs such as "construct, list, identify," and "compare." These specified behaviors can be observed or evaluated fairly easily. The more specific the duty, the easier it will be to find out if the trainee has mastered it. Stay away from verbs such as "know, understand, appreciate," and "believe"; these actions are far too vague to be taught or evaluated with precision.

Conditions   Objectives should contain a listing of the items needed by the trainee to execute the performance and any limits or constraints that will be placed on performance. In our ongoing example of Ben, the new trainee, you already know that he will need the restaurant's prescribed order forms, a writing instrument, and a knowledge of the kitchen staff's shorthand for taking orders from patrons. But there is a time restraint as well at your restaurant. Ben must take the order within a fixed period after patrons are seated or, if they are undecided at his first visit, he must return to the table within five minutes of his first contact (at which he announced the specials of the day).

When preparing to write the conditions for a task, consider the following questions (Mager, 1984):

1. What equipment will the trainee need and be allowed to use?
2. What resources will be denied to the trainee (equipment, manuals, materials, and so on)?
3. What time restraints should be listed?

Conditions usually begin with the word *given*. For example, "Given the restaurant's order form, a ballpoint pen, and a working knowledge of the restaurant's order shorthand, the waiter should be able to...." Each learning objective at the beginning of each chapter in this text begins with a specification of the conditions that are considered necessary for a student to demonstrate each performance listed. The two conditions are to read and to discuss each chapter. Only then can a student be expected to perform each objective. In a business setting, some objectives may begin with a statement about what will be denied to a trainee. For example, "Given no direct supervision..." or "Without the aid of tools, the trainee should be able to...." Such a condition is understood to exist when you as a student take most of your tests. You understand that you are to answer the questions asked without the aid of notes, texts, or other classroom learning materials unless they are specifically authorized for use.

Each major task listed on Ben's job description can be broken down into subtasks. A performance and condition for each can then be written. For example, the subtasks related to "taking a customer's order" may break down as follows:

1. Visit the table.
2. Greet the customer cordially.

3. Introduce yourself and the specials of the day.
4. Offer to take the customer's order.
5. If the customer is undecided, leave and return to take his or her order.
6. Write the customer's order.
7. Deliver the order to the kitchen.

Each of these subtasks is involved in the major task of taking a customer's order. Each has a condition or two attached to it. Writing your restaurant's policies and procedures into the first performance will give you the following:

1. Visit the table within one minute after the customer is seated by the hostess, armed with the restaurant's order forms, a ballpoint pen, a knowledge of the kitchen shorthand and daily specials, a clean uniform, and a smile on your face.

The performance expected is to visit the customer's table. The conditions surrounding that performance include a one-minute time limit, possession of equipment and knowledge, and a warm and friendly demeanor. Each of the other six subtasks may be given conditions as well. If they are all to be taught together, the conditions in number one will be understood to exist in numbers two, three, four, and six. A new time limit may be required for number five.

The key to writing descriptions of conditions is to be detailed enough to ensure that the desired performance will be executed in the way you as a trainer want to see it. Add as much description as you feel you must to communicate your intent to the trainee. When in doubt, describe. With detailed lists of tasks and their conditions, both you and the trainee can progress in an orderly manner, leaving little to chance.

Criteria   Criteria state the standards that a trainee must be able to meet in order to give a satisfactory performance. When speed, accuracy, and a quality of performance can be stated, they should be made a part of the training objective. In this text, the learning objectives at the front of each chapter do not specify criteria for measuring the adequacy of your performance. That is a job for your instructor to decide. The questions at the end of each chapter ask you to demonstrate your performance in the learning objectives. But the quality, speed, and accuracy factors and what you will be allowed to use while performing them have been left up to your instructor to determine.

Criteria need not always appear in a training objective. Sometimes they are part of the conditions. Ben's first performance required him to visit a table within one minute of the customer's being seated. In this case, the time limit is both a limit and a criterion for evaluating Ben's performance.

Some criteria are best demonstrated or shown. You as a trainer can do this, pointing out the quality of performance you desire through personal demonstrations or by using the behavior modeling techniques of film or videotape. Nothing need be written into the training objective in this case.

As long as you and the trainee know what makes a performance acceptable, you have met the requirement for including criteria in your training objectives. If you cannot find some words or ways to determine acceptability of performance, perhaps you should reconsider its importance to you and to your trainee (Mager, 1984). It may be of such minor importance that it should not be treated formally in training.

Part 3. Preparing the Training Process

You have determined the needs for training. You have identified the tasks to be taught and have written solid training objectives. These answer the questions "Why should there be training?" and "What will be taught?" The rest of your training program will answer questions relating to who, when, where, how, and how much (see Exhibit 12.2).

Who   You answer this question by determining the specific people who will conduct the training and who will learn from it. In our example, you are the trainer, and Ben is the trainee.

When   The answer to this question blocks out specific periods for conducting training. Since you run a busy restaurant, the best times for training are before the doors open to customers, during between-meals times, and after closing.

The Who:	Who will do the training? Who will receive it?
The When:	What times will be set aside for training?
The Where:	What specific physical areas and equipment will be needed to conduct the training?
The How:	In what chronological order will the tasks be taught? What methods of instruction are best for each task?
The How Much:	How much money will be needed to ensure a successful training effort? How much time and equipment will be needed to teach all the objectives?

EXHIBIT 12.2
Checklist to help you plan your training program.

Where   Specific areas must be designated and reserved for training use.

How   In what order will the objectives be taught and by what methods? Priorities and a training schedule must be constructed to guarantee that all items are included in an order of presentation that makes sense to the trainee. Many techniques can be used to deliver your training. Exhibit 12.3 lists the major techniques and specifies where they are most appropriately used. Each has positive and negative features, and one is usually more appropriate than the others for teaching specific performances. All of them can be classified under one of three headings: buddy systems, machine-based systems, and group sessions.

Buddy systems

The buddy system is a person-to-person or one-on-one method of training. It may also be known as the teacher–pupil method or the master–apprentice method. Whatever it is called, this method utilizes one trainer and one trainee; a person who knows the job teaches someone who needs to know

EXHIBIT 12.3
Comparisons of basic training methods.

Source: Al-Malik, Sulaiman M. Unpublished paper. Georgia State University, Winter 1985; published in Byars, Lloyd L., Ph.D., and Rue, Leslie W., Ph.D., *Human Resource Management*, 3d ed. (Homewood, Ill.: Richard D. Irwin, 1991), ©1991, 243–245.

Method	Definition	Strengths	Weaknesses
1. Lecture	Speech by the instructor, with very limited discussions.	Clear and direct method of presentation. Good if there are more than 20 trainees. Materials can be provided to trainees in advance, to help in their preparation. Trainer has control over time. Cost-effective (cheap).	Since there is no discussion, it is easy to forget. Sometimes it is not effective. Requires high level of speaking ability. Requires quick understanding by trainees.
2. Group discussion (conference)	Speech by the instructor, with a lot of participation (questions and comments) from the listeners. Sometimes instructor not necessary; however, a leader is needed.	Good if the participants are small groups. Each participant has opportunity to present own ideas. More ideas can be generated.	Sometimes they get away from the subjects. Some group leaders or instructors do not know how to guide discussions. Sometimes one strong individual can dominate others.

(continues)

Method	Definition	Strengths	Weaknesses
3. Role playing	Creating a realistic situation and having trainees assume parts of specific personalities in the situation. Their actions are based on the roles assigned to them. Emphasis is not on problem solving, but rather on skill development.	Good if the situation is similar to the actual work situation. Trainees receive feedback that gives them confidence. Good for interpersonal skills. Teaches individuals how to act in real situations.	Trainees are not actors. Trainees sometimes are not serious. Some situations cannot be implemented in role playing. Uncontrolled role playing may not lead to any sufficient results. If it is very similar to actual life, it may produce adverse reactions.
4. Sensitivity training (laboratory training)	Use for organizational development. Creating situations and examining the participants' reaction and behavior, then having feedback about behavior. Group members exchange thoughts and feelings in unstructured ways.	Helps individuals find the reasons for their behavior (self-insight). Helps individuals know the effects of their behavior on others. Creates more group interactions.	People may not like information about their behavior, especially if it is negative. May lead to conflict and anger within the group. May not be related or transferable to jobs.
5. Case study	A written narrative description of a real situation, issue, or incident that a manager faced in a particular organization. Trainees are required to propose suitable solution or make appropriate decision.	Cases are usually very interesting. High group discussion and interaction about many solutions, since there is no absolute solution. Develops trainees' abilities in effective communication and active participation. Develops trainees' ability to figure various factors that influence their decision building. Develops trainees' ability to make proper decisions in real-life situations (transfer of learning).	Slow method of training. Often difficult to select the appropriate case study for specific training situation. Requires high level of skills by both trainees and trainer, as the discussion can become boring. Can create frustration on part of trainees, especially if they fail to arrive at specific solution.

(continues)

CHAPTER 12 • TRAINING   **459**

Method	Definition	Strengths	Weaknesses
6. Management games	Giving the trainees information about the organization and its environment; then dividing into teams. Each team is required to make operational decision and then evaluate its decision.	Develops practical experience for the trainees. Helps in transferring knowledge and in applying administrative thoughts. Helps to evaluate and correct the trainees' behavior.	Often, it is difficult to study the results of each team's decision. Some teams may not take it seriously. May be a slow process.
7. Simulation exercises	Same as management games, except a digital computer is used to input information and analyze the team decisions. Results of trainees' actions are evaluated.	Same as management games.	Same as management games. Very costly. Difficult to simulate very complex system.
8. Wilderness training	Several managers meet out of the workplace and live in cabins or tents for up to seven days. They test their survival skills and learn about their own potential—for creativity, cooperation, etc.	People learn limits and capabilities.	Very costly. May not be transferable.
9. In-basket training	Creates the same type of situation trainees face in daily work. Trainees observed: how they arrange the situations and their actions regarding them. Trainees evaluated on the basis of the number and quality of decisions. Used for MD and assessment centers.	Effective for corrective action or reinforcement. Widely used in assessment centers for measuring supervisory potential.	Tendency to be or become overly simplistic.
10. Incident process (problem solving)	Simple variation of the case study method. The basic elements are given to the	Has an immediate feedback from the instructor. Develops supervisory	Requires high degree of instructing skills in forming answers.

(continues)

EXHIBIT 12.3 (cont.)

Method	Definition	Strengths	Weaknesses
	trainee, who then asks the instructor for the most sufficient information that will help him or her in making a decision. The instructor will only give the requested information.	skills in seeking facts and decision making.	
11. Vestibule training	Setting up training area very similar to the work area in equipment, procedures, and environment but separated from the actual one so trainees can learn without affecting the production schedule. Used for training typists, bank tellers, etc.	Fast way to train employees. Trainees can get the most from this method.	Very expensive.
12. Apprenticeship training	Trainee works under guidance of skilled, licensed instructor and receives lower pay then licensed workers.	Develops special skills: mechanical, electronic, tailoring, etc. Extensive training.	Takes a long time.
13. Internship training	According to agreement, individuals in these programs earn while they learn, but at a lower rate than if they worked full time.	More chance for trainees to apply what they have learned. Trainee gets exposure to both organization and job.	Takes a long time.
14. Projects	Like group discussion method. Trainees together analyze data and reach conclusion.	Helps trainees to know more about the subject.	Requires instructor's time to ensure the group is going in the right direction.
15. Videotapes and movies	Recording and producing certain events or situations with clear descriptions in	Tapes can be played of many items to ensure individual's understanding.	Recording and producing has to be done by professionals to get good quality.

(continues)

EXHIBIT 12.3 (cont.)

CHAPTER 12 • TRAINING   461

Method	Definition	Strengths	Weaknesses
	order to cover certain subjects. Can be shown many times, then reviewed and discussed to help trainees understand more fully.	Many events and discussions can be put on one tape. Because length of time is known, presentation and follow-up can be scheduled.	Expensive.
16. Multiple management	Lower- and middle-level managers participate formally with top management in planning and administration.	Helps top management to identify top management candidates. Enhances employees' participation in the organization.	

EXHIBIT 12.3 (cont.)

it. Instruction usually takes place on the job, using the actual workplace, tools, and equipment during regular working hours. When the person doing the training is properly prepared, the buddy system has the following major advantages:

1. It is flexible. Learning can take place in a classroom, in a laboratory, or on the job. Changes can be introduced quickly. The system can be tailored in pace and content to meet the individual needs of the trainee.
2. It allows immediate feedback. The teacher-trainer works directly with the trainee and can evaluate his or her progress or lack of progress personally and quickly, offering corrections and reviews to improve retention and mastery.
3. It is personal. It humanizes the training process and allows for questions and answers, reviews, and additional drills or practices at any time. Personalized corrections may be made, and personalized instructions may be given throughout the duration of training. The system frequently helps the trainees satisfy some of their social needs.

The primary disadvantages of the buddy system are the following:

1. It is costly. The salary or wages of the trainer go to pay for the training of just one trainee during any training sessions. Expensive equipment and machines are tied up and used by only one trainee at any

given moment. The time and talents of the trainer are used by only one trainee per session.

2. It is difficult to prepare for and conduct adequately. If the real advantages of the buddy system are to be realized, the instructor must adequately assess the needs of the trainee, tailor the instruction to meet those needs, and avoid passing along attitudes, prejudices, and shortcuts that differ from what the trainee needs and what management wants taught.

Machine-based systems

Computer-based or programmed instruction methods are referred to as machine-based systems of instruction and training because they rely heavily on a machine to relay information and evaluate trainee responses. Computers, through their video display terminals and programs, and machines that use filmstrips, videotapes, audiotapes, records, and the like can enhance the learning environment and enrich the kind of training that takes place.

All machine-based instruction requires people (1) to prepare the learner and materials, (2) to monitor the training process by keeping track of time and handling questions or making adjustments to the equipment, and (3) to evaluate the progress or lack of progress made by each trainee. This method is more often used to supplement other types of training than to substitute for them. It works well when used to complement the other methods.

The advantages of machine-based training include the following:

1. It is uniform. It ensures that the same material is presented in exactly the same way to each trainee.
2. It is flexible. It can be adjusted, or can adjust itself, to fit the needs and pace of the trainees. It involves the learners in the learning process. It frees trainers for other duties and allows them to handle more than one trainee per session. By periodically checking on each person's progress and by remaining available to each trainee, the trainer will often be able to accomplish other tasks while the machines do part of the instructing.
3. It is inexpensive. Although the materials and machines may be expensive to prepare, install, and keep in repair, these costs can be spread over dozens or hundreds of trainees and over a long time; moreover, such costs can be slowly absorbed as an operating expense through allowances for their depreciation. Vendors of equipment such as word processors and computers often provide machine-based training or trainers and materials free or at a reasonable cost at the time of purchase and before or just after equipment deliveries.

The disadvantages of machine-based training are the following:

1. It is impersonal. Machines cannot fully replace the need for human interaction. They cannot provide the warmth of a smile and a compliment from an instructor for a job well mastered in training. They cannot sense an employee's fear or frustration or the lack of comprehension of a video or verbal message.

2. It requires expertise. Learning materials demand a great deal of money, know-how, and time to prepare. To be economical, they must use materials that will not require frequent changing and will not become obsolete in a short time.

3. It can be boring. For trainees with short attention spans, for those who learn quickly, and for those who already know a significant portion of the material to be mastered, the teaching-machine method of training can become frustrating and boring.

4. It needs to serve many trainees in order to be economical. Computer programs and videotapes cost too much to prepare if only a few trainees are to use them.

Group sessions

Lectures, conferences, and role-playing sessions can be quite effective methods of training more than one person at each session. Lectures present basic principles and individual points of view, and they can be used to introduce, summarize, or evaluate training sessions or performances. Conferences and discussions can inform, solve problems, clarify situations, and help participants critically evaluate their opinions, attitudes, and methods. Role playing helps people act out a situation to what they see as its log-

Most training requires you to interact with employees. But technical training, such as learning new computer software, can be done on computer. When you assign your subordinates to computer-based training, be sure to follow up on a personal basis.

ical conclusions. Participants see one another in different lights and have a chance to evaluate the solutions of others while trying out their own solutions on the group. All group sessions deal with two or more trainees and require expert planning and leadership if they are to be successful.

The major advantages of the group-sessions method are the following:

1. It is uniform. Two or more people are exposed to the same material in the same way at the same time.
2. It is inexpensive. Compared to other training methods, group sessions offer savings in hours and salaries for training purposes.

The major disadvantages of the group-sessions method are the following:

1. It is impersonal. It does not allow for individual differences, individual participation, or close involvement in the training.
2. It magnifies errors. The impact of each mistake or bit of misinformation is magnified by the number of trainees.

Natasha Josefowitz (1985), management consultant and author of two books on management, notes that people have preferred ways of learning and teaching. Basically, we all learn by seeing, hearing, and doing. People who prefer to learn by hearing should be talked through operations and the reasons for them. People who prefer to learn by seeing should be shown the execution of tasks, examples of why they are necessary, and the finished results expected. People who learn best by hands-on doing should be given ample time to perform with you as you demonstrate each operation. But people learn best when more than one of these methods is used in training. Exhibit 12.4 presents a model to help you conduct your training programs.

In designing your training program, try to utilize more than one method of training. For most types of training, a single method will not do. A blend or mix will probably suit your purposes better. When you know what has to be taught and what human and material resources you have available, think about which methods should work best for you and your trainees.

How Much   This question needs two answers. You must determine how much time you will need to teach your performances and how much money you will have to spend. You will need to incorporate your time into your training schedule. You may need approval for spending money that is not already in your budget for training. Needed training equipment and supplies must be ordered ahead of time and must be in place when training begins.

Break the job into learnable units—units small enough to be effectively taught and absorbed in one session. If the units are too big, the trainee will be unable to digest them. It is far better to have less material—

Step 1: Preparation of the Learner

1. Put the learner at ease—relieve the tension.
2. Explain what is being taught, and why.
3. Create interest, encourage questions, find out what the learner already knows about his or her job or other jobs.
4. Explain the why of the whole job and relate it to some job the worker already knows.
5. Place the learner as close to the normal working position as possible.
6. Familiarize the worker with the equipment, materials, tools, and trade terms.

Step 2: Presentation of the Operation

1. Explain quantity and quality requirements.
2. Go through the job at the normal work pace.
3. Go through the job at a slow pace several times, explaining each step. Between operations, explain the difficult parts, or those in which errors are likely to be made.
4. Again go through the job at a slow pace several times, explain the key points.

5. Have the learner explain the steps as you go through the job at a slow pace.

Step 3: Performance Tryout

1. Have the learner go through the job several times, slowly, explaining to you each step. Correct mistakes, and if necessary, do some of the complicated steps the first few times.
2. You, the trainer, run the job at the normal pace.
3. Have the learner do the job, gradually building up skill and speed.
4. As soon as the learner demonstrates ability to do the job, let the work begin, but don't abandon him or her.

Step 4: Follow-up

1. Designate to whom the learner should go for help if he or she needs it.
2. Gradually decrease supervision, checking work from time to time against quality and quantity standards.
3. Correct faulty work patterns that begin to creep into the work, and do it before they become a habit. Show why the learned method is superior.
4. Compliment good work; encourage the worker until able to meet the quality/quantity standards.

EXHIBIT 12.4
A four-step outline for conducting training.

Source: Dessler, Gary. *Personnel/Human Resource Management,* 5th ed., Copyright © 1991, 264. Reprinted by permission of Prentice Hall, Englewood Cliffs, New Jersey.

leaving ample time for review and practice—than to have too much. A good rule of thumb is to attempt to teach no more than three performances in every sixty-minute session.

Part 4. Conducting and Evaluating the Training

When you are finished with your planning, execution begins with the preparation of the training area. Have everything on hand and in working order so that the session can flow smoothly and without interruption. Have the area properly arranged and in the same condition you expect your workers to keep it in. Prepare yourself through rehearsals—trial run-throughs—to check on your timing and command of the material.

Prepare the workers in the following ways:

1. Put them at ease.
2. State the objectives to be achieved during the session.
3. Point out the advantages they will receive from the training.
4. Explain the sequence of the events they are about to follow.

You should stress the fact that when you and the company take the time and make the effort necessary to train workers, it is positive proof of concern for the workers and an expression of confidence in their abilities. Training is costly, and the trainees should know the costs and why management is willing to incur them. If eligibility for training was competitive, let each trainee know of your pride in his or her selection. Let your trainees know that there is no harm in making mistakes. In fact, we learn more by analyzing our mistakes than we do by listening to a teacher who says all the right things. It is by examining our failures or incorrect examples that we discover their causes and can prevent their recurrence.

Demonstrating   During the demonstrating phase of your training presentation, you have the opportunity to show and tell. You can perform as your objective specifies or let experienced help demonstrate the tasks for you. In Ben's case, you may want to call on your trusted and skilled old-timers to do what they do best. Or you may videotape performances and let the trainee view the film, commenting on what is being shown and asking and answering questions. If your trainee has no questions, ask some of your own. Check on Ben's understanding of each critical performance. Remember that training involves communication, and communication requires feedback.

Application   The application phase of training asks the trainee to get his or her feet wet. In this case, Ben will be asked to duplicate the performance that he has just witnessed. You may want to show Ben more than one performance before asking him to repeat it. However, don't try to include too many behaviors before you let the trainee try them out. By mixing the demonstration with applications, you provide the trainee with immediate feedback and highlight both what he or she has mastered and what he or she has not. You will be applying the principle of reinforcement, as well as providing the early and measured successes that are so important to the mastery of performances and the motivation of the trainee. You may be able to videotape the trainee in his or her performance and use the tape in playback to review his or her efforts.

Evaluation   The evaluation phase determines if the trainee has mastered performances and if the training effort was successful. The basic question here is: Can the trainee perform, under the prescribed conditions and to the necessary degree of quality, all the essential tasks taught? Evaluation may take place at any point in a demonstration or during a trainee's application of lessons. Performance tests, written or oral quizzes, and the trainer's own observations are the most frequently used devices for evaluating performances.

Provide trainees with frequent and immediate feedback. Let them know when they are correct, and ask them to spot their own mistakes. Let them examine the product of their efforts and try to find any defects. Once they discover an error, explain, or get them to explain, just how it can be prevented from happening again. Point out how one error—the one just made, for example—can lead to others. Use each mistake as a point for review, and then conduct a critique to summarize the entire lesson.

Through evaluation, you can quickly ascertain the need for reteaching a point. You will also realize just how fast you can place people on their own, free from your strict supervision and control. Put people on their own, but gradually. Do not let them feel that when the training ends, it is sink or swim. Be available to them, and let them know that you are. Simply make your visits and observations less frequent as each person demonstrates an ability to perform to standards. Your follow-up should tell you whether lasting effects have been achieved or whether an individual needs additional training.

There is a technique of great merit in use in different types of apprenticeship programs. The master mechanic or teacher bugs a machine by deliberately planting a problem within it. The student must troubleshoot the item to uncover its problem and then correct the deficiency. This technique may fit your needs, so give it some thought. Just be sure that the bug you plant does not permanently damage the equipment.

TRAINING FOR VALUING DIVERSITY

Training that promotes valuing diversity takes many forms. Workshops and seminars—conducted in-house or at training centers by insiders or outsiders—can bring unique approaches and share lessons learned by others that enlighten participants and stimulate dialogue among them. Advisory teams or committees have been created by many companies to both plan and implement valuing diversity training programs. Mentoring programs assign people to sponsor those who differ significantly from themselves. For example, an African-American female may be assigned to mentor a Korean-American male, while a white male is assigned to mentor a Mexican-American female. Members of specific groups such as gay men and those differently abled can be encouraged to form their own support groups and interact with other diverse groups of employees. These efforts, once begun, usually remain part of annual training efforts and may evolve to take on new challenges.

Within these general approaches is a variety of methods and tools that aid diversity training. Some training efforts let participants listen to presentations from individuals representing diverse groups; others show video or motion picture episodes portraying diverse people in various situations. These then become discussion starters, engaging participants in a give-and-take on the issues presented. A variation on this technique is the interactive video, which stops the action periodically and lets the participants enter the presentation with their own thoughts and suggested outcomes for the situations portrayed. Each episode is a case study or simulation of a real event. Shell Oil Company uses an "interactive video...in which a learner, using a computer terminal interfaced with a videodisc player and a touch screen, works alone through a self-paced lesson" (Jamieson and O'Mara, 1991). Each lesson ends with a list of questions. When incorrect responses are given, the lesson is repeated with different examples. Participants learn at their own pace and at times convenient to them. A division of Procter & Gamble, Folger Coffee Company, uses role-playing exercises to get trainees into other people's shoes. Events are scripted, and participants play roles that are unfamiliar to them.

The main purposes of all these efforts are to learn how our attitudes and perceptions of others form, in what ways people differ from one another, how those differences can give individuals and organizations specific advantages, and how to improve the skills needed to interact with people who differ. As King-Ming Young, head of Hewlett-Packard's Professional Development Group, puts it, "Managers today must demonstrate a larger repertoire of behaviors to get the most out of each employee" (Jamieson and O'Mara, 1991).

PITFALLS

Besides violations of any of the aforementioned principles of training, the following are the major pitfalls:

1. Leaving it to others. By delegating or using the assistance of staff specialists, you may hope that proper training will take place. Since you are not directly involved, you tend to wash your hands of the process and rely on their efforts. Remember that you have accountability and must participate in both the planning and the execution so far as necessary to know what is being done and what goals are being achieved. You will be stuck with the results, so make them as beneficial as possible.

2. Making assumptions. A trainer sometimes makes the mistake of assuming that because trainees were told to read about a concept, they will understand it on their own—or that because the trainer presented the material according to plan, all of it has been assimilated. There is an axiom that bosses would be wise to cite to their subordinates: "When you assume anything, you make an ass out of you and me." Rely on facts and observations that can provide you with the basis for a proper evaluation of the program and its effectiveness, not on assumptions.

3. Fearing a subordinate's progress. Some people fear the successes and increasing abilities of others because they view them as threats to their own security. Have you known a manager who refused to train a subordinate because he or she was afraid that if someone else could do the job, he or she might lose it? Managers may refuse to delegate in order to keep their people dependent on them and may deliberately deny subordinates the chance to advance, fearing that the subordinate might challenge their position. Keep in mind that unless you have a trained successor, you are locking yourself into your present position. Training is the job of every manager who has subordinates. By not doing it, you are neglecting a very important duty. This neglect will be reflected in your ratings.

4. Getting too fancy. Trainers may get too caught up in methods and training aids and lose sight of what it is they must teach. There may be too much flash and too little substance. Have you ever listened to a speaker or lecturer who talked for hours and said nothing? If you have ever seen a fireworks display, you know what this error is like.

5. Substituting training for proper selection processes. Training is not a substitute for proper selection procedures. Selection (Chapter 11) involves trying to produce the best available person to fill a vacancy. It requires skills in such areas as interviewing, testing, and recruiting. Some employers treat selection as an unimportant activity and rely on the training of new employees to impart the skills required to execute a job properly. This is especially true in areas where keen competition for qualified people exists among employers, such as in data processing. But some skills cannot be taught effectively by employers, such as the abilities to read and write effectively in English or any other language. Companies cannot afford to conduct such training and lack the qualified personnel to do so. Selection should make certain that people brought into the organization only lack skills, knowledge, and attitudes that the employer is willing and able to teach.

Instant Replay

1. Training is the supervisor's responsibility. It may be delegated, but the supervisor is accountable for it.

2. Training imparts skills, knowledge, and attitudes needed by trainees now or in the near future.

3. Training benefits you, your trainees, and your employer. Be certain that trainees know what they are to learn and why.

4. You are judged on your performance and on the performance of your subordinates. The better they do, the better you all look to each other and to superiors.

5. Anyone may train if he or she possesses the body of knowledge, skills, and attitudes to be taught; knows and follows the principles that govern training; and wants to train.

6. The training cycle asks you to identify your training needs, to prepare performance objectives, to create a training program, and to conduct the training.

7. The central purpose behind training is to get performances up to standard—to make certain that they turn out as planned.

Questions for Class Discussion

1. Can you define this chapter's key terms?
2. What are three advantages that a supervisor receives when he or she trains a subordinate?
3. What are three advantages that a trainee receives through training?
4. What are three basic requirements that a trainer must satisfy?
5. What are five basic requirements that a trainee must satisfy in order to get the most out of training?
6. What are the seven principles of training, and what does each mean to a trainer?
7. What are the four major steps in the training cycle?
8. What are the five pitfalls that a trainer should be aware of?

Incident

Purpose: To create and conduct a brief training program, following the four basic parts to training as shown in Exhibit 12.1.

Your Task: Create a training program through which you teach another person your way of performing any skill you possess, such as building a model or kneading dough. After you have created your learning objective(s), chosen a method, reserved a location, and gotten a volunteer, write down each step, noting the standards you wish to teach and use to evaluate the learner's performance. Set a time limit, and conduct your training session in class, following the steps outlined in Exhibit 12.4. When you have taught the lesson, evaluate your efforts through the learner's and the class's comments. Don't be surprised if the learner or the class comes up with a better way to do things.

John Paul Jones

John Paul Jones is general manager of the Gier Variety Store in Boston. Bentley Gier founded that store in 1981 and now personally manages another newer store, while entrusting the Boston store to Jones. Jones receives a salary of $25,000 annually and a bonus of 1.5 percent of his store's annual sales. He directly supervises all of his store's eleven employees, ten of whom are salespeople. He regularly pools merchandise orders with Mr. Gier.

The Boston store's annual gross sales amounted to $1.2 million last year, an increase of $65,000 over the preceding year. Both stores carry a wide line of inexpensive household items as well as medium-priced goods in leather, small appliances, and children's wear. Prices range from a few dollars to $200. Since Jones took over the management of the Boston store in 1991, sales have climbed steadily, averaging a 5 percent increase per year.

Personnel has been J.P.'s most frustrating challenge over the past three years. The annual average turnover of sales personnel has averaged 60 percent. Jones has shown a preference for hiring persons of middle age and older. He has attempted to hire experienced salespeople to avoid the need for training, but this has become increasingly difficult.

Sales personnel receive an average hourly wage of $6.50 and work a forty-hour week. Recently, the store has been forced to remain open for twelve additional hours each week to include Sundays. This has caused a rearrangement of work schedules for the experienced staff and has necessitated the addition of two new workers this week, both of whom are inexperienced at selling.

Jones has designed a training program in which the two new employees are assigned to an experienced saleswoman for on-the-job training. The training is to last as long as the trainer deems necessary. A description of the trainer's duties as determined by Mr. Jones is shown in Exhibit 12.5.

Prior to this year, Mr. Jones personally trained each new employee, but lately his duties have become more time consuming. When the two new and inexperienced persons joined the staff, he felt that the new arrangement would be best. He chose the trainer, Blanche Hecker, on the basis of his personal knowledge of her performance and because he considered her to be his best salesperson. She knew the merchandise and had been with the store longer than anyone else. After Mr. Jones talked his proposal over with her (using some salesmanship tactics of his own), Blanche agreed to try the training assignment. Mr. Jones assured her that she would have no difficulties because in his words, "I'll be right here if you need help. Don't hesitate to ask for it."

In designing the program, Jones drew heavily on the years of selling experience that he acquired with Mr. Gier. Both men felt and now feel that unless an employee has to give something for what he or she gets, it will not be appreciated. As a result, the new workers are required to spend one hour each day for a week with Ms. Hecker learning the store's inventory

EXHIBIT 12.5
Sales trainer's duties.

1. Explain the time card and attendance policy to each trainee.
2. Familiarize each trainee with the store's entire inventory.
3. Teach the store's method of pricing goods, and explain the price tag information and coding.
4. Train the trainee to handle cash, credit, and discount sales.
5. Teach basic salesmanship techniques and how to greet customers.
6. Teach register operations and wrapping.
7. Welcome each person to the Gier Team!
8. Instruct each person on the merchandise requisitioning procedures.
9. Compliment the trainees when they are right and criticize them when they are not.
10. Introduce them to the other salespeople and to our store policies.
11. Emphasize housekeeping!
12. Keep the trainees supplied with the supplies they need.
13. Keep Mr. Jones posted on the trainees' progress or lack of progress.

before the store opens. This they are to do with no pay. After the first week's training, the three will return to their normal shift hours, continuing to train on the job.

Blanche Hecker is forty-seven, single, and impeccable in both dress and manner. She has been with the store since 1982 and has established a sales record never equalled by any other employee. She has been in retailing since graduating from high school and has had over seventeen years of selling experience. Although she has never trained anyone before, she has been through the sales-training program offered by H. R. Croft and Company, one of the area's largest department stores.

Questions

1. What do you think are the chances for success of Jones's program? Why?
2. Are Blanche's qualifications adequate for the position of trainer? If not, why not?
3. Analyze the list of Blanche's duties. What is on it that should not be? What has been left off, if anything?
4. To what factors might you attribute Jones's inability to attract trained salespeople?
5. What factors may account for the 60 percent average annual turnover?
6. Which principles of training has Jones overlooked?

Trouble Down the Line

Elwood Orkhurt, plant manager of the Linden Gasket Company's Indiana plant, is quite distressed. In this morning's mail was a letter from Linden's CEO asking for an explanation for the lost account of a valued customer. It seems that an order was shipped a few weeks ago that was 40 percent defective. "Forty out of one hundred gaskets received were unusable and were returned to my office last Thursday," the letter read. It went on: "I need to know as quickly as possible what went wrong on the Simpson order, and I need to have your assurances that something similar will not occur again." Elwood left his office, letter in hand, to begin his investigation.

Elwood began his search with a visit to the shipping office. He found the documents he needed and went to the plant floor. "Let's go into your office, Chuck. We have a problem, and I need your input." Chuck and Elwood entered the operations center and worked their way back to Chuck's office. Chuck shut the door and asked for a further explanation. After Elwood finished and after Chuck read the letter, Chuck spoke.

"Mr. Orkhurt, I think this problem rests with my new foreman, Curt Victor. His shift produced the order in question. From the facts you have given me, I think it's a question of poor judgment. Victor is a hardhead. He wants things his way—been that way since training. He runs that shift with an iron hand. People do what he lets them do and nothing else. Trouble is, he thinks he has an answer for everything. It seems clear to me that the gaskets were too thin and were crushed when Simpson used them because the machines were cutting them with too much pressure. We had a similar problem a few months ago, and it originated with Victor. He authorized the substitution of a gasket material that was too thin to begin with. Seems he ran out of the right gauge and used the next size. It just didn't hold up. Without talking with the parties involved, that's my best feeling."

Elwood told Chuck to talk to everyone on the line who had had anything to do with the order and to report his findings to him by closing time. He left the office in a dark humor. Chuck went looking for Victor.

"Hey, Vic, got a minute?" asked Chuck.

"Sure, what's going on?" asked Victor.

"We have a problem. The Simpson gasket order your shift produced and said was OK for shipping cost us a big customer. It was 40 percent defective. Any thoughts on the matter?"

"Hold on. Those gaskets were ready or I wouldn't have approved them. We produced to specs what the order called for. Always do. We had a little trouble with the tension on one machine but until that was fixed, we didn't continue the run."

"Vic, you didn't substitute materials again, did you?"

"Chuck, I'm no fool. We had that out a while back, and I learn from my people's mistakes. They won't ever do that again. It was a tension problem. The gasket material was being compressed in cutting. We adjusted the machine, tested the adjustment, and ran the order. The test batch was tossed."

Chuck terminated the discussion and went over to the cutting machine they had discussed. Mary was on it, so he asked her about its operations. She indicated that it did compress things on runs and just needed close checking. He asked her if she had worked on the Simpson order, but she said that she was out that day and Nelson had the machine. Chuck went looking for Nelson.

After ten minutes, Chuck finally located Nelson coming out of Victor's work station. Nelson seemed to back up Victor's story indicating that the tension was adjusted and that the order continued without further problems. "Did you check the thickness of the gaskets after the adjustments were made?" asked Chuck.

"Vic told me to keep careful watch on them, so I measured every third one for about half an hour. There were some small variations but not enough to stop the run. Vic looked at the numbers and told me to keep running. To tell the truth, those numbers were just a bunch of numbers to me. Vic told me to keep the run between .005 and .006. I wasn't sure what he meant, but I did measure the gaskets and record the readings I got exactly. Vic looked at those numbers and gave the OK."

Chuck returned to his office and called the shipping department. He discovered that the Simpson order had been returned, and the faulty gaskets were there. He went down to the shipping department after picking up a micrometer and a copy of the customer's specifications. The shipping clerk had unpacked about twenty of the gaskets and piled them on his desk. Chuck applied the micrometer to each gasket, recording his findings for each. He next compared the numbers he got to the thicknesses specified. "Just what I thought," said Chuck to himself. "None of these are the proper thickness. They are all too thin." Chuck went back to Victor and showed him the evidence. Victor seemed amazed.

"Vic, let me tell you what I think happened with this order. I think that after you checked the numbers Nelson gave you following the tension adjustment, you stopped worrying about the tension problem. I think that the run continued, fell out of adjustment, and continued to produce gaskets that were too thin. What do you think?"

"If that did happen, and I'm not saying that it did, you can blame Nelson. It's his job to keep an eye on the tension. He discovered the error in the first place when the machine flattened a gasket so thin that it tore apart when the machine ejected it. That's when he called me over."

"Victor, Nelson tells me that he doesn't understand the measuring process. He said that the numbers he got didn't mean anything to him. And now that I think of it, did you check back to see if the gaskets Nelson ran before the torn one were to specs?"

Victor looked at his feet for a minute and sighed. "That Nelson! He's worthless. Can't do anything right. He didn't say anything about the gaskets before the breakup, so I didn't measure any of them. Damn it. That's his job. I guess we will either have to teach him how to keep track of measurements or let him go. I can't do his job and mine."

Questions

1. Which subjects of training does Nelson seem to lack?
2. Which subjects of training does Victor seem to lack?
3. Which principles of training were violated in this case?
4. What training needs can you identify in this case?

Notes

Blanchard, Kenneth. "Moby Dick Management," *Success!* June 1987, 24.

Bureau of Business Practice. 1993-94 Human Resource Guide. (Englewood Cliffs, N.J.: Prentice Hall, 1993), 201–203.

Godin, Seth, ed. *1995 Information Please Business Almanac and Sourcebook* (New York: Houghton Mifflin, 1994), 289.

Grossman, Ron. "The Three R's Go to Work," *Chicago Tribune,* October 29, 1989, sect. 4, 1.

Henkoff, R. "Companies That Train Best," *Fortune,* March 22, 1993, 62–65.

Jamieson, David, and O'Mara, Julie. *Managing Workforce 2000* (San Francisco: Jossey-Bass, 1991), 83–91.

Josefowitz, Natasha. *You're the Boss!* (New York: Warner Books, 1985), 151.

Kelly, Kevin, and Burrows, Peter. "Motorola: Training for the Millennium," *Business Week,* March 28, 1994, 158–160, 162–163.

Mager, Robert F. *Preparing Instructional Objectives,* 2d ed. (Belmont, Calif.: Pitman Learning, 1984), 21, 51, 86–87.

Peters, Tom "Bosses Must Keep the Ball Rolling to Stay on Top of Their Competition," *Chicago Tribune,* August 10, 1987, sect. 4, 7.

Schuler, Randall S. *Managing Human Resources,* 5th ed. (New York: West Publishing, 1995), 525.

Suggested Readings

Bartlett, Christopher A., and Sumantra, Ghoshal. *Managing Across Borders* (Boston: Harvard Business School Press, 1989).

Clark, Ruth C. "Nine Ways to Make Training Pay Off on the Job." *Training,* 23, 11 (November 1986): 83–87.

Goldstein, Irwin L. *Training in Organizations: Needs Assessment, Development, and Evaluation,* 2d ed. (Monterey, Calif.: Brooks/Cole Publishing Co., 1986).

Hicks, William D., and Klimoski, Richard T. "Entry into Training Programs and Its Effects on Training Outcomes: A Field Experiment," *Academy of Management Journal,* 30, 3 (September 1987): 542–552.

Jones, Gareth R. "Socialization Tactics, Self-Efficacy, and Newcomers' Adjustments to Organizations," *Academy of Management Journal,* 29, 2 (June 1986): 262–279.

Mager, Robert F. *Preparing Instructional Objectives,* 2d ed. (Belmont, Calif.: Pitman Learning, 1984).

Zemke, Ron. "The Rediscovery of Video Teleconferencing," *Training,* 23, 9 (September 1986): 28–36.

———. "What Is Technical Training, Anyway?" *Training,* 23, 7 (July 1986): 18–22.

The Appraisal Process

OBJECTIVES

After reading and discussing this chapter, you should be able to do the following:

1. Define this chapter's key terms.

2. List six major purposes for appraising your subordinates.

3. Explain why clear objectives and standards are needed in order to prepare proper appraisals.

4. List and give examples of three types of appraisal methods.

5. List and give examples of five pitfalls in the appraisal process.

INTRODUCTION

appraisal process
periodic evaluations
of each subordinate's
on-the-job perfor-
mance as well as his
or her skill levels,
attitudes, and poten-
tial

A primary duty for both supervisors and self-managing teams is to execute the **appraisal process,** through which each subordinate or team member's on-the-job performance is periodically evaluated along with his or her skill levels, attitudes, and potential. This process is often referred to as merit rating, employee performance review, or performance appraisal. Regardless of its name, the process is intended to help you, team leaders, and team members fortify interpersonal relationships.

The appraisal process takes place daily as people work side by side. In most organizations, it is formalized—put in writing and made a matter of record—once or twice each year. It provides needed feedback to all employees, letting them know what peers and superiors think of them and their performance. The daily appraisals lay the groundwork for the formal ones, giving the appraisers the knowledge they need to critique a subordinate's or a team member's performance, offering praise for work well done and suggestions for improvement.

GOALS OF APPRAISALS

Here are the major goals of employee appraisals:

- To measure employee performance
- To measure employee potential
- To assess employee attitudes
- To further the supervisor's or team leader's understanding of each subordinate or team member
- To fortify relationships between a supervisor or team leader and subordinates
- To fortify relationships between team members
- To analyze employee strengths and weaknesses—providing recognition for the former and ways to eliminate the latter
- To set goals for the improvement of performance
- To substantiate decisions about pay increases and eligibility for promotion, transfer, or training programs
- To verify the accuracy of the hiring process
- To eliminate hopelessly inadequate performers

If the appraisal process is to accomplish these goals, it must be as objective and accurate as possible. It must reflect an accurate and fair image of the person, in line with company policies and the constraints of moral, ethical, and legal conduct.

Throughout the remainder of this chapter, we examine the appraisal process as it should be executed by a supervisor. If it is performed by team leaders or team members, its goals and principles remain the same. What

is said for the execution of the process by supervisors also applies to appraisals performed by team leaders and team members acting as part of self-managing teams.

WHAT TO APPRAISE

When appraising subordinates, you can focus on their output (results and outcomes of their actions and efforts), on their behaviors (the kind and quality of their activities), or both. The first approach focuses on the end product with quantity (numeric measurements) and quality measures. The second focuses on the way in which work is done and on intangibles such as cooperativeness, initiative, team spirit, and the relative difficulty of tasks being performed. Most appraisal programs try to measure both outcomes and behaviors.

As a supervisor or team leader, you will be appraised on the quality of your behaviors—decision making, planning, communicating, and problem solving—and the outcomes of those behaviors, as well as on the behaviors of your subordinates. For example, your appraisal will consider the amount, timeliness, and quality of work produced by your section or department. Your appraisal, therefore, is partly in the hands of your subordinates and team members. As a team facilitator, you will be appraised by the teams you serve and on how well you aid their efforts.

Exactly what you appraise in your subordinates will be dictated by the forms and approaches your company asks you to use. Look at the forms you will use, and determine how much of them is devoted to

SUPERVISING TEAMS

With the introduction of teams to the workplace, several changes usually occur in the methods used for performance appraisals. A review of business journals yields three generic approaches in use today. One or a combination of them may be just right for your teams.

Peer reviews. Because the nature of teams makes each member dependent upon the performance of other members, members are asked to evaluate the contributions made by each team member and their teams. Peer reviews work best when each member cares about and respects the other members; knows them well; knows how to perform their jobs (is cross-trained); and is taught to make honest, valid, and candid appraisals using precise performance standards. In self-managing teams, members hire, discipline, reward, and separate team members. They must have the authority to act on their appraisals by identifying those in need of help, working with them to help them improve, and, if needed improvements do not occur, separating poor performers from their ranks.

Client reviews. A team's clients are any individuals or groups receiving its output. Clients are found inside and outside the team's department and organization. When clients are not satisfied with a team's output, the team needs to know about it. Different methods exist to gather client input. Team leaders may visit clients regularly each year and interview them, in person or through a written instrument, to gather feedback on their group's performance. Another approach adds the teams' own evaluations of their service to clients and then compares the clients' ratings to the teams' self-evaluations. Each approach can use a variety of standards but must allow all parties to use the same scorecard and scoring system. Typical questions used are "What are we doing well?" and "What are we doing poorly?" and "What can we do for clients that we are not now doing?" The answers provide goals for the future.

Self-assessments. Each team member conducts an evaluation of his or her own personal performance as both an individual worker and a team member. This evaluation can then be compared to peer reviews. Any variances usually require a meeting with the affected parties to gain new insights and understanding of differing perspectives. When disputes and disagreements occur, the team leader or a supervisor may be needed to adjudicate and negotiate solutions.

appraising outcomes and what part of them is concerned with behaviors. Keep this division in mind as you informally evaluate your people each day. The best producers from among your subordinates should be the ones to receive the greatest financial rewards you have to give. Those who demonstrate weaknesses in one or more of their expected behaviors and outcomes should be counseled and scheduled for training to improve their weaknesses.

Standards

Whether you are appraising outcomes or behaviors in your subordinates, you must do so with well-defined, specific, realistic, measurable, and mutually understood criteria or **standards.** You will recall from Chapter 12 that training objectives require such criteria so that both trainer and trainee can tell when a behavior is being demonstrated with sufficient mastery. Appraising people in different job categories may require the use of different factors or criteria. Regardless of the forms you use in your appraisals, be certain that the descriptive words on them have clear and precise meanings to you and to those being rated.

standard
a quantity or quality designation that can be used as a basis of comparison for judging behaviors and outcomes

When you appraise performance, turn to job descriptions and to the training materials developed to teach tasks. The criteria you used in training will allow you to pass informed and mutually understood judgments in discussions with your people. When appraising outcomes or output, be certain that the standards of quantity and quality you use were taught to your people before they are used to appraise them. Keep in mind that standards will vary in proportion to the employee's time on a job and to the training he or she received to perform the job to standard. You should not expect the same output from a new person that you expect from a seasoned veteran. When selecting criteria, consider the following guidelines:

1. Relevance. Standards must relate directly to successful performance on a specific job.
2. Freedom from contamination. When comparing the performance of production workers, for example, the appraiser must allow for differences in the type and condition of the equipment they are using. Similarly, a comparison of the performances of traveling salespeople is contaminated by the fact that territories differ in sales potential. Since diverse employees have diverse styles, the principal factor should be the results they achieve—outputs. You must exercise care to avoid making judgments on the basis of stereotypes, biases, or an employee's deviation from your company's dominant culture's approach.
3. Validity. Employees in each job category must be evaluated by the same standards and methods to avoid discrimination and adverse impact charges.

4. Acceptance. Whatever criteria and methods are used, the system will succeed only if those subjected to it have faith in it and perceive it to be helpful, valid, and fair. If you are stuck with an appraisal system that you and your people do not believe in, get together with your peers who feel as you do and work with higher authorities to change things. If an appraisal system that is in place has no support from either the appraised or the appraisers, it will be worthless and will create negative results for all concerned.

Appraisals and Diversity

The question of whose standards—from a cultural perspective—will be used when evaluating diverse employees is one that companies on the cutting edge of valuing diversity have dealt with. They have discovered that efforts must be made "to distinguish style from substance—so that many styles and approaches can be accommodated without sacrificing effectiveness within the organization" (Loden and Rosener, 1991). They have no "homogeneous ideal"; that standard has led to discriminatory practices that have excluded diverse groups from organizations and positions of leadership, particularly women and people of color. "By shifting the focus away from style to performance results,...organizations are enlarging the range of acceptable behavior for diverse employees while remaining focused on quality performance" (Loden and Rosener, 1991).

While confronting and working to reduce employees' biases and stereotypes through continuous training, new philosophies, policies, programs, and operating procedures—for hiring, promoting, and evaluating employees—are created by organizations to both value and support diversity. These actions change the company's culture to one that accepts (not simply tolerates) the existence of subcultures and taps into their unique strengths and contributions. Recognition is given to the fact that diverse people have diverse needs and expectations. Training can then focus on meeting these and on giving diverse employees the tools they require to survive and prosper—support networks, mentors, skills training, and encouragement for self-development—while encouraging them to be themselves and to act in ways that are comfortable for them and that accomplish the company's goals (Loden and Rosener, 1991).

In many companies, standards for effective performance are created by or with input from diverse groups of employees "who understand the organization's needs and also recognize the untapped talent that those outside the mainstream can offer" (Loden and Rosener, 1991). After all, empowering people means delegating authority and granting autonomy. Once people are trained and equipped to perform their duties, they must be given the latitude to do so effectively and efficiently. Rewards offered for outstanding performance should be varied as well. Just as people work for differing motives, it takes different incentives to entice and satisfy diverse individuals. One size will not fit all.

You as an Appraiser

Before you can appraise your people properly,

1. You must know the job responsibilities of each of your subordinates.
2. You must have accurate, first-hand information about each subordinate's performance.
3. You must have established, bias-free, and clearly understood standards by which to judge both behaviors and outcomes.
4. You must be able to communicate the evaluations to your subordinates, along with the criteria you used to make your judgments (Cherrington, 1983).

If you feel uncomfortable or unsure of yourself when it comes to appraising subordinates, try to determine why. If you do not have enough first-hand knowledge about your people, it may mean that you are not with them enough, fail to accurately record your observations when you are with them, or do not oversee their work as much as you should. If you as an appraiser need training in how to appraise properly, ask for it. Appraisals are far too important to you, to your subordinates, and to your organization to not be done properly.

Unless you oversee the work of self-managing teams, you will usually not share the duty to appraise subordinates. Even with such teams, you will usually appraise (along with the team members' self-appraisals) the performance of the team and its members. With or without self-managing teams, the appraiser has the responsibility to ensure that results are kept confidential and only shared with those who are officially approved to receive appraisal results.

Appraisal the Japanese Way

In Japanese companies, a worker's job description is kept somewhat vague. An individual's responsibilities are not defined with precise clarity for two major reasons: First, workers are taught to take a team and family approach to their work and sections; and second, when something goes wrong, it is considered bad taste to try to find out who made mistakes. Efforts are made to find out what went wrong and how to avoid a similar situation in the future. People pursue the investigation with no fear, and lessons learned by all will help prevent mistakes in the future. No person is held up to ridicule, no feelings are hurt, and no reputations are damaged beyond repair (Morrita, 1986).

Although your organization may want to pin the blame for things that go wrong on a particular person, keep in mind that you will most probably have to continue to live and work with the person who gets the blame. At the same time, that person will have to continue to live and work with you and his or her coworkers. Name calling and blame placing are not the purposes of appraisals; showing a person what went wrong and how to correct a situation are. An appraisal goes well if it rewards the good performances, helps the individuals involved learn from past errors, and points the way toward improvement. Appraisals must tell people how well they are doing and what they need to do to improve.

LEGAL CONCERNS WHEN APPRAISING WORKERS

Federal, state, and local laws deal with employment discrimination. The federal laws listed and explained in Chapter 11 bear to some extent on the appraisal process—in particular, the Equal Pay Act of 1963, the Age Discrimination in Employment Act of 1967, and Title VII of the 1964 Civil Rights Act. Karen Clegg, counsel at Allied Bendix Aerospace and a member of the Commerce Clearing House Advisory Board on Human Resources Management, offers guidelines for avoiding charges of discrimination linked to the appraisal of subordinates. According to Clegg, a good performance appraisal system will (Commerce Clearing House, 1985):

- Be in writing
- Contain specific procedures
- Include specific instructions for supervisors
- Provide for training supervisors in how to evaluate employees
- Utilize standardized forms for related groups of employees (for example, one form could be used for appraising supervisory employees, another for appraising hourly employees)
- Be thoroughly communicated to employees
- Be given at least once each year
- Evaluate specific work behavior, not personal traits
- Be continually monitored by equal opportunity experts for impact on protected groups
- Include reviews of subordinates' appraisals (made by team leaders, supervisors, and others) by persons more senior than the appraisers

360-Degree Review Process

Many companies such as Levi Strauss, AT&T, General Motors, and Chase Manhattan Bank are using a 360-degree feedback and multirater assessment. Such systems usually require you, along with your boss, peers, subordinates, team members, and customers (internal and external) to (O'Reilly, 1994):

fill out lengthy, anonymous questionnaires about you. You'll complete one too. Are you crisp, clear, and articulate? Abrasive? Spreading yourself too thin? Trustworthy? Off-the-cuff remarks may be gathered too. A week or two later you'll get the results, all crunched and graphed by a computer. Ideally, all this will be explained by someone from your human-resources department or the company that handled the questionnaires, a person who can break bad news gently. You get to see how your opinion of yourself differs from those of the [raters].... The results won't necessarily determine your pay, promotions, or termination. At least, not yet. The technique as it's now applied doesn't work well for that.... What's most interesting about [the] feedback...is the huge variety of unpredictable comments—and potential learning—that it delivers. Most people are surprised by what they hear. Only a fraction of managers have a good grasp of their own abilities.

Through this system, rated individuals get a usually objective and diverse look at how others perceive them. People learn of the annoying traits as well as their supportive ones. "Many companies are using feedback for cultural change, to accelerate the shift to teamwork and employee empowerment. Bosses who charged up the corporate ladder by controlling everything and barking like a drill sergeant often get an earful from eagerly critical underlings" (O'Reilly, 1994). When the system was used at Du Pont for providing feedback to some eighty research scientists and support personnel, it strengthened their abilities to work in teams. "Chrysler is experimenting with a 360-degree evaluation process, which means that Chrysler employees will be evaluated by everyone they deal with, including suppliers" (Taylor, III, 1994). The key seems to be to "...pick a small number of shortcomings to fix and decide on a few concrete remedies" (O'Reilly, 1994). Robert D. Rockey, Jr., Levi Strauss's president of North American operations, is evaluated through his company's 360-degree review process involving his superior, peers, and subordinates. Based on the feedback he received, Rockey decided to "loosen up somewhat, to command less, to listen more" (Mitchell, 1994).

APPRAISAL METHODS

Your company is probably making use of one or more of the currently popular methods of appraising workers. Each has advantages and disadvantages. No one method is adequate for any person or group. Which one or combination you may have to use (and which will be used for your own appraisals) is usually decided by company policy. Methods used must be valid, standardized, have no disparate impact on women and diverse groups, be based on current and objective job-related standards, and be conducted in conformance with the preceding legal guidelines.

SUPERVISORS AND QUALITY

Through several 1994 surveys, Wyatt Company, a national consulting firm, finds that bosses "don't listen,...don't give [subordinates] a chance to make a difference on the job and [they] don't help them see where their future might be. 'Companies score low on listening and acting on employee suggestions,'" according to a Wyatt consultant. About two-thirds of surveyed workers say that their bosses don't seek and follow up on their suggestions. About the same number of managers believe they are good at giving workers involvement in decisions that affect them. But only 25 percent of workers agree with them. "Most managers said the biggest barrier to change within their companies is their employees. Most employees said the major problem is their bosses' lack of skills and support."

In what ways do the Wyatt surveys reflect the need for 360-degree evaluation programs? How do you explain the differences between managers' viewpoints and those of their subordinates?

Source: Franklin, Stephen. "Nobody Listens Around Here," *Chicago Tribune,* December 14, 1994, sect. 3, 3.

Ranking or Forced-Distribution Method

You may be required to rank your people from most productive to least productive or from most valuable to least valuable. Often such rankings are based on a normal distribution curve, requiring that no more than a certain percentage of your people fall into one or another of the categories listed. Exhibit 13.1 illustrates a typical ranking approach.

You may be required to make a simple list of your subordinates, ranking one over another on their abilities and contributions. This will force you to say that one man or woman is better as an employee than another.

The major disadvantage of the ranking method or forced-distribution method is that it requires you to compare your people to one another. That might be tolerable if all of your workers perform identical tasks. If they do not, the system requires you to compare apples and oranges. Further, it may prevent a supervisor with a disproportionate number of above-average (or below-average) performers from listing them as such

EXHIBIT 13.1

Percentage-ranking method of worker appraisal.

Instructions to Rater: List your subordinates by their overall rating in one or another of the categories below. Use their complete initials and do not exceed the percentages listed.

Percentage	Category	Subordinate(s)
5%	Superior	GBH
12.5%	Above Average	SAB, RGL
65%	Average	PTC, BCT, LH, NPB, SDO
		LMR, GSW
12.5%	Below Average	
5%	Unacceptable	PBC, TGM

because of the rather arbitrary percentage limits established for each category.

The forced-distribution method can be helpful if used in conjunction with one or more of the other methods. It does force you to make a choice and to picture your people as you may never have done before.

Checklist or Forced-Choice Method

One of the most prevalent methods used in industry today is the checklist method or forced-choice method of appraisal. In it, you are asked to pick the one block and statement that best describes your subordinate's standing with regard to the factor listed. These types of forms work well for summarizing the degrees to which a person has or lacks certain characteristics or traits required. Exhibit 13.2 shows a sample.

Picking the one best choice may be difficult, especially when your workers perform many different tasks that have differing standards of out-

EXHIBIT 13.2

Forced-choice appraisal method.

Factor	Superior	Very Good	Average	Fair	Poor
Quantity of Output	Extraordinary Volume and Speed of Output	Above-Average Output	Expected Output-Normal Output	Below-Average Output	Unsatisfactory Level of Output
	☑	☐	☐	☐	☐

put and that demand different types of skills and experiences. Fitting this type of form to young, inexperienced workers typically puts them at a disadvantage since they appear in a bad light when contrasted to the others. Some way of compensating for these shortcomings should be designed into the system.

Critical-Incident or Narrative Method

The most flexible method, but clearly the most demanding way of appraising workers, is the critical-incident method or narrative method. In this method, the supervisor refers to specific situations that highlight or illustrate a worker's abilities, traits, or potential. Using the essay approach, the rater writes personal observations and comments about both positive and negative occurrences in order to dramatize the particular point under examination. Exhibit 13.3 gives such a description.

This method offers the maximum degree of expression possible for precise and informative evaluations. It is difficult, however, because it demands an in-depth knowledge of subordinates' behaviors and attitudes, which can only come from frequent and regular observations and a recording of the results. It demands that a supervisor be with subordinates daily. Although this is highly desirable, it is not always possible. Many subordinates work physically separated by great distances from their supervisors. Salespeople, construction workers, research people, and staff specialists are a few examples. In their cases, comments from the people they serve may prove quite helpful. This method applies best to managers who are rated by other managers.

EXHIBIT 13.3
Critical-incident or narrative appraisal.

> **Initiative** *Constance requests additional work when she runs out and lends a hand to her less experienced coworkers.*
>
> **Cooperation** *Routinely, she coordinates with coworkers, recognizing that her work is the basis for theirs.*

Behaviorally Anchored Rating Scales

The behaviorally anchored rating scale (BARS) method of appraisal uses statements that describe both effective and ineffective job performance. The statements used are constructed by people who know very well the job that will be evaluated. Statements are created to describe a behavior that the rater is expected to be able to evaluate. The statements then run along a scale that includes degrees of acceptable and unacceptable performance. A point value is assigned to each statement. The rater chooses statements that best describe the ratee's performances and totals the points attached to each. The following three statements illustrate the use of BARS for rating a trainer's punctuality while conducting training sessions:

- The trainer always arrives for each training session before the session is scheduled to begin (5 pts.)
- The trainer usually arrives for each training session before the session is scheduled to begin (3 pts.)
- The trainer infrequently arrives for each session before it is scheduled to begin (0 pts.)

Notice that these statements combine the forced-choice method and the critical-incident method. Such a rating list could also be used by the trainer's supervisor and by the trainees. For each behavior considered crucial to successful performance on any job, statements like the ones shown can be constructed. Input from those who will be rated should be sought during construction of the statements to ensure that a complete list of essential behaviors is included and to help enlist the support of those who will be rated under the BARS method.

Although BARS offers specific behavior statements that can be discussed between supervisor and subordinates, it focuses mainly on a person's activities and not on the results that they lead to. Under BARS, you may find yourself with an employee who performs all the activities well but does not achieve the desired results.

Field-Review Method

The field-review method requires that interviews be conducted between a supervisor and personnel staff assistants (either singly or in groups). Questions—usually requiring a yes or no answer—are asked by the specialists with regard to each of the supervisor's subordinates. The staff aides record the answers and write the formal appraisals. After reading them, the supervisor must either approve them with a signature or disapprove them with comments.

This method was designed to relieve supervisors of the burden of paperwork accompanying the appraisal process. It does require, however, that each supervisor be as completely prepared for the interview as if he or she had to fill out the ratings himself or herself. If he or she is not well prepared, extensive revision and rethinking may have to take place before accurate appraisals can be communicated to each worker.

Scale Method

The scale method combines the ranking and forced-choice methods. The rater must decide where each person stands in relation to his or her peers on the basis of a scale, with or without a specific description to go by. Two types of scales are illustrated in Exhibit 13.4. Some scales may attach a point value to the supervisor's choice, and total points may be used to sum up a worker's standing in his or her group. Once again, supervisors are forced to pick one that may not be exactly what they would or could say if allowed freedom of expression.

All these systems are subjective: They allow the rater to let personal interests, preferences, and prejudices flavor the rating given to each person. Even the critical-incident or narrative method records the situation from the supervisor's point of view and in his or her own words. No system has yet been devised that will completely eliminate this. It is up to you, the rater, to be as objective as you can by making every effort to leave personal bias and personality clashes out of each rating. Your emphasis should be foremost on the subordinate's performance on the job, in accordance with the standards established for that job. Only secondarily are you

EXHIBIT 13.4
Scale method of appraisal.

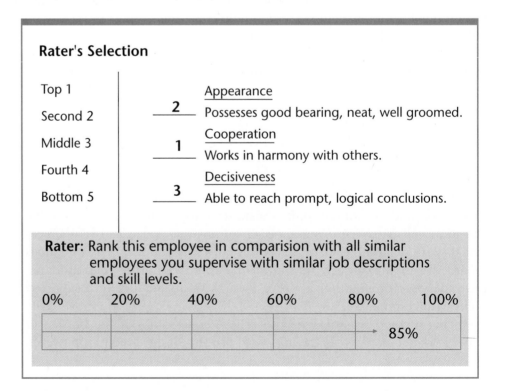

concerned with a subordinate's attitudes and potential. State as clearly as you can what each person did, how well it was done, and what you believe the person is capable of doing.

MANAGEMENT BY OBJECTIVES

In Chapter 4, we introduced you to management by objectives (MBO) as it related to planning. In this chapter, MBO becomes a useful method for appraising the performance of teams, team members, and traditional subordinates. Superior and subordinate(s) determine, through mutual discussions, the goals the evaluated person or persons will work to achieve and strategies required to achieve them. The goals may be related to outcomes, behaviors, or both. Although there are many approaches to MBO as an appraisal method, most managers agree that it is useful because it involves individuals and team members in the determination of what is needed to make themselves and their operations better. Its primary advantage is that people are more committed to achieving goals they have had a role in setting.

Effective objectives have the following characteristics (Schuler, 1995):

As part of the appraisal process, you may need to watch workers perform their jobs. The objective notes you take can be used in your written evaluation.

1. Specificity: Objectives identify acceptable behavior and output.
2. Timeliness: The deadline for completion or attainment is specified.
3. Conditions: Qualifications, boundaries, limits (schedules, policies, resources) should be specified.
4. Prioritization: Objectives are rated by order of importance.
5. Consequences: What can be expected for achieving or not achieving is specified.
6. Goal congruence: Individual and department goals should fit and not conflict.

In a previous chapter, we discussed stretch goals: "...big, athletic leaps of progress on measures like inventory turns, product development time, and manufacturing cycles" (Tully, 1994). Setting and reaching such goals are rapidly becoming ordinary behavior for both individuals and teams in both large and small companies. To leap ahead of competition, incremental changes and gradual improvement are not enough. Part of reengineering demands discarding the old, rethinking everything a company does, and coming up with a whole new effort. Chrysler chose this route with its cab-forward design. "Getting an organization to embrace wrenchingly difficult new goals—particularly in the absence of a crisis—can traumatize employees. Managers who can't stand the relentless new pace quit or get fired" (Tully, 1994). To motivate employees to reach stretch goals, management must be honest (explain the urgency and consequences of not reaching the goal), convince everyone that the goal is possible (point out through benchmarking how others have achieved the goals being sought), empower people to do what they must (let people find their own means), and get out of their way.

Authors and teachers, James C. Collins and Jerry I. Porras (1994), claim that their research shows that long-lasting visionary companies have several traits in common. Among them is the continuous setting and achieving of what they call big, hairy, audacious goals (BHAGs). When President John F. Kennedy set a national goal in 1961 to place Americans on the moon and return them safely to Earth by the end of that decade, he was setting a BHAG. In like fashion, when Sam Walton, founder of Wal-Mart, set the goal to become "a $1 billion company in four years (a more than doubling of the company's size)" (Collins and Porras, 1994), he was setting a BHAG.

Both stretch goals and BHAGs need little explanation, are "clear and compelling and [serve] as a unifying focal point of effort—often creating immense team spirit. [Each] has a clear finish line…is tangible, energizing, highly focused" (Collins and Porras, 1994). When working with your teams and subordinates, encourage them to articulate and strive for such goals. The rewards for doing so are incredible for both the individuals involved and their organizations.

APPRAISING WITH MBO

Approaches to appraising by MBO differ widely. Most involve the commitment of top management to the program, and efforts to introduce MBO begin with top managers learning to use it. Gradually, as the upper echelons gain the expertise they need, MBO is used at progressively more levels. If you do not have the permission of your superior to use MBO, you should not use it.

Exhibit 13.5 outlines a series of distinct steps that can make MBO work for you. It represents only one of many approaches, but it is a comprehensive method that can prevent some of the major problems others have encountered in their early MBO efforts.

Step 1: Setting Goals

As stated earlier, goals are ends or end states that have to do with a person's or a unit's growth and development. If they are to be meaningful, they should meet the hallmarks set forth earlier. They must be set through a dialogue or discussion between superiors and subordinates. They must

EXHIBIT 13.5
*Basic steps in apprais-
ing through MBO.*

Step 1. Setting goals. Ends must be mutually determined through discussions between supervisors and subordinates. Areas for improvement can be determined from past appraisals, current situations, job descriptions, and the rated person's ambitions to improve and gain higher responsibilities.

Step 2. Identifying resources and actions needed. The amount of time, money, and materials required to reach an objective need to be determined. To attain any goal, the efforts of the goal setter and others may be required. Accurate predictions must be made.

Step 3. Arranging goals in priorities. Both the rater and the ratee need to agree as to the importance of each goal and as to how and in what order they should be pursued.

Step 4. Setting timetables. Precise times need to be set for the completion of actions and the attainment of goals. These times will allow formative evaluations on progress to be made and will permit adjustments in either the means or the ends.

Step 5. Appraising the results. The summary judgment as to successes and failures that occurs at this step sets the stage for a return to step one. Thus, the cycle repeats.

be based on the goal setter's recognition of their importance and commitment to their acquisition.

Step 2: Identifying Resources and Actions Needed

Before superiors and subordinates can agree on goals, the means to achieve them must be examined and determined to be within the organization's and the individual's abilities to execute or utilize. Resources include human energy and effort, time, money, and materials. Actions may be required of one person or unit or several. If these are possible and reasonable, success is probable.

Step 3: Arranging Goals in Priorities

Which goal should be worked on first, second, and so on? What end state is considered by both parties to be the most essential? One guideline for answering these questions is the cost in money or lost time that currently exists and awaits a cure. An attack on the most expensive areas of waste or problems could be planned first on the list of objectives. Lesser areas of waste could be attacked simultaneously or at later dates.

Step 4: Setting Timetables

Besides agreeing on priorities, both boss and subordinate must agree on the times by which each goal is to be achieved. Time estimates must be made, and calendars must be prepared for future reference. Dates for completion become guideposts and serve as checkpoints to determine progress and problems. As these dates arrive, boss and subordinate coordinate to determine if any adjustments are necessary. New times may be needed, new or different approaches may be required, or new goals or refinements to the original ones may have to be made.

Step 5: Appraising the Results

At the regular intervals dictated by your company, you and your subordinate meet to discuss the progress and events that have taken place since the last formal evaluation. Your formal appraisal of your subordinates' efforts is not based solely on their goal achievement or lack of achievement. Your appraisals should consider both means and ends (see Exhibit 13.6).

EXHIBIT 13.6
Some additional criteria to consider when appraising with MBO.

In addition to the achievement or nonachievement of a goal, consider the following when evaluating performances:

1. How has the subordinate grown through the effort to achieve the goal or goals?

2. Was the subordinate effective—doing the right things in a proper sequence?

3. Was the subordinate efficient—using only those resources needed and in their proper amounts?

4. Was the individual a help or a hindrance to fellow workers?

5. Were due dates met? Were goals achieved earlier than planned?

6. Were the obstacles met dealt with in the proper ways—some being overcome, some being circumvented?

7. Were the goals easy to achieve or difficult?

8. Is the subordinate getting better at choosing goals and setting priorities and timetables?

SUPERVISORS AND ETHICS

A *Macworld* magazine survey of 301 businesses in 1993 uncovered some disturbing findings about how bosses monitor their employees. Slightly more than 21 percent admitted to "spying" on their employees. Sixty-five percent of managers responding believed that invading an employee's electronic privacy was "philosophically acceptable." Of these, about 22 percent felt it to be "a good tool to verify evidence of wrongdoing," and about 20 percent felt it to be a good way to monitor or enhance employee performance. About two thirds of the companies surveyed hide their behavior from employees.

What do you think about this issue? Should laws forbid such electronic eavesdropping? Do you think there is a difference between your postman reading your mail before it is delivered and your boss reading your e-mail and computer files?

Source: Coates, James. "Computer Privacy? It's Not a Given," *Chicago Tribune,* May 23, 1993, sect. 7, 1.

Each cycle in MBO is time consuming and requires patience and tolerance from both parties. But as the number of cycles increases, so will the proficiency of the parties involved and the accuracy of their estimates. When used properly by people who have been taught to use it, MBO can improve individuals and organizations. It is more difficult to learn and to use with workers than are other kinds of appraisal methods, but it can spark motivation and win commitment to growth and change.

APPRAISING BY COMPUTER

According to 9-5 National Association of Working Women, about 50 million people operate video display terminal (VDT) equipment at work on a daily basis, and about one half of them "are monitored by their employers" (*Chicago Tribune*, "Workers...," 1994). A report by the International Labor Organization, a UN agency, cites a survey by *Macworld* magazine of 301 U.S. businesses that discovered "Just over 40 percent of the companies...searched employee E-mail, 28 percent said they looked at network mail and 15 percent said they peered into voice mail" (*Chicago Tribune*, "Bosses...," 1994). Since 1986, federal law has given "employers the right

Using computers to monitor employees is an increasingly popular trend. The computerized checkouts at markets can objectively monitor the productivity of workers.

computer monitoring
using computers to measure how employees achieve their outputs—monitoring work as it takes place—and to keep track of their total outputs

to listen to job-related calls but prohibits them from listening to personal calls at work" (*Chicago Tribune,* "Workers...," 1994). See this chapter's Supervisors and Ethics feature for more on employer spying.

Computer monitoring measures how employees achieve their outputs—monitoring work as it takes place—in addition to keeping track of their total outputs. It counts such things as the number of keystrokes per minute, the use of individual machines per hour, and the number and kinds of items processed by a sales clerk per customer per hour. Computer monitoring allows employers to rate employees' levels of productivity and to rank them according to how completely and effectively they use each minute of each working hour. By taking averages, new time standards for all kinds of work can be created and used to evaluate individual performances.

Critics of computer monitoring argue that it creates additional worker stress, fatigue, and turnover. Workers fear unauthorized access to and disclosure of highly "personal and private information" (*Chicago Tribune,* "Workers...," 1994). From management's point of view, computer monitoring helps control costs, improve security, increase productivity, and obtain more precise information needed for objective appraisals. Life insurance "industry representatives also contend that some workers like the monitoring because they view it as a way to prove they are doing a good job and see it as protection in the case of disputes with customers" (*Chicago Tribune,* "Workers...," 1994).

The nationwide movements to eliminate annual across-the-board pay increases and to create meaningful pay-for-performance systems of compensation demand specific and quantifiable standards of performance, which computer monitoring can provide. Those who meet and beat fair standards can be justly compensated, whereas corrective and training actions can be taken for those who fall below the standards. Above-average performers need no longer feel ignored or relegated to a par with below-average workers.

Employee-Appraisal Software

Three popular software packages are in use by employers for appraising their employees: Employee Appraiser 2.0, Performance Now! 1.0, and Avantos Review Writer 1.0.

The programs work similarly. Each asks the user to rate an employee in several job areas: Job knowledge, interpersonal skills, customer focus, and so on.... Pop-up advice windows in each package provide short but comprehensive tutorials on human resources. At each step during the review-building process, a manager can click on tips for handling employees' defensive reactions to criticism.... Each...prompts users to support both praise and criticism with examples, and each encourages the managers to enter specifics about their employees during the long stretches between reviews (Stewart, 1994).

ManagePro is a software package intended for managing with MBO. The three employee-appraisal systems will allow ManagePro comments to be integrated into employee reviews. Each of the appraisal packages has various legal and consistency checkpoints built in. You should investigate them for their possible application to your situation.

PITFALLS

Several common types of errors can be made by raters. If you know about them, you can consciously try to prevent them from occurring in your appraisals of your subordinates. Committing any one of them will render your rating inaccurate. Some of the pitfalls discussed here were also discussed in Chapter 11 with regard to rating new applicants and existing employees.

The Halo Effect

One of the errors most frequently committed by raters is known as the halo effect. The rater allows one outstanding positive or negative trait or incident about a person to color the overall rating and image of that subordinate. Because one of your people dresses well and has good manners and bearing, you may tend to let this overshadow his or her other traits or the whole work performance record. Conversely, if the most vivid incident you can recall about a person is his or her commission of a major mistake, you might allow this to obscure his or her many fine qualities. Your formal ratings are supposed to reflect the whole person. You must guard against letting isolated events or appearances dominate your total impression and objectivity toward a worker.

Rating the Person— Not the Performance

There is a strong tendency for a rater to give a person high ratings if the rater and the individual get along and low ratings if they do not. Human nature is such that we perceive in a favorable way people we like most and tend to dismiss those we dislike as worthless persons. A rater's personality and attitudes may clash with those of a subordinate; then, even though that worker's performance and potential are above average, he or she may receive an overall unsatisfactory rating. If you do this, you are not being honest or fair. Your job in appraisals is to rate each person according to his or her performance in a particular job. Unless an individual's personality traits are interfering with his or her work or are a great asset to him or her, there is no reason for you to bring them into the formal appraisal. You may not like an individual, but in fairness you still may have to rank him or her as superior. Leave your personal biases and prejudices out of the picture you paint of the person. Avoid personal attacks.

To keep your actual or potential biases in check, you should avoid the following specific behaviors in appraising subordinates:

1. Stereotyping: choosing to ignore a person's uniqueness and individuality by assuming that any member of a specific group must have the characteristics that conform to a predetermined image of that group's members: Bill is a salesperson, and therefore Bill is...; or Jane is Hispanic, and therefore she is.... Our perceptions of a member of any specific group may or may not be rooted in fact.
2. Projecting: accusing others of the very faults you yourself possess. Examine most of the anger you express toward another person, and beneath it you will find a particular way in which you have played a part in the situation.
3. Screening: noticing only the negative aspects of a person or his or her performance; interpreting events in the most negative way possible; recording only events that support a preformed judgment about a person; ignoring positive contributions.

Rating Everyone as Average

This error, which is often referred to as the central tendency, occurs when you rate everyone as average. You may be tempted to do so because you lack sufficient data to do otherwise or because you see this as the safest, least controversial method of handling your appraisals since you will not have to justify a high or a below-average rating.

Quite often, raters fear that if they rate a subordinate as above average, the subordinate will get a big head and become more difficult to direct or control. Or they may fear that if they rate a person below average, they will face a confrontation at the appraisal interview or criticism from their boss for allowing a poor performance. In other words, supervisors may fear that when they are appraising their people, they themselves are being appraised—that the major purpose of appraisals is to find out how good a boss the supervisor has been and not primarily to evaluate the workers. If you have cause to believe that this is the case where you work, you have a very unfortunate appraisal system. How well your people perform does influence your future. But making out phony appraisals that show them all as average or above average cannot be justified by the facts, and your boss will know it. Simply saying someone is good does not make it so. If you falsify their ratings, your people will know it, too. And if you think it might be hard to supervise an employee who earns a good rating and is told about it, how much more difficult will it be to supervise an employee who feels that you have been dishonest with him or her?

Saving up for the Appraisal

Some supervisors spot a deficiency, record it, and save their discussion of it for the formal appraisal. No criticism should be a surprise to the rated employee; rather, each should have been discussed when it happened. The formal appraisal interview should provide a review of past events that exhibits a concern for preventing the recurrence of past infractions, as well as offering a focus for improvement in the future.

The only safe road to travel is that of integrity. Arm yourself with the facts by careful and frequent observations. Be with your people as often as you can, and make on-the-spot corrections and comments about their work and their attitudes. Let them know where they stand with you regularly. Be open and available; if you are, there will be no shocks or surprises at the appraisal interview. Your informal appraisals will have prepared them for what you will say, they will expect what they receive, and you will have the facts and events to support their ratings.

The Rush Job

Related to most other appraisal errors is the last-minute, hurry-up job of rating that occurs at midnight on the day before the interviews or at lunch or breaks on the day when you must relay the results. Whether you have two subordinates or twenty, you have to give yourself enough lead time for thinking things through and searching your memory and your files for tangible data on which to prepare your case. How would you like it if your boss summed up your past six months at work with a fifteen-minute effort on your appraisal form?

A great deal rides on your formal appraisals. Your people know that it represents in writing your opinion of them and their performances. They know that what you say will directly affect their futures and their earnings. They also know that you go on record with your superiors in these appraisals. Your relationships and credibility are at stake. Do not muff this great opportunity to cement your relations; pass out deserved praise, and build programs for improvement. This should be a task that you tackle with great concern and eagerness. You are laying foundations that will have to support future plans and programs. Make those foundations firm and strong.

Comparisons

If you try to rate a worker by comparing him or her with another, you are making a big mistake. We know that people are unique and dynamic. No two subordinates look alike, think alike, or act alike. Even if your people have the same job, they cannot be compared because their experiences, training, education, attitudes, and skill levels are different. To say that Paul is better than Peter has no meaning unless you know exactly how good Paul is and should be. The questions then arise, "How long has Peter had a chance to be as good as Paul?" and, "Has he the potential to be so?" For these reasons, the ranking and forced distribution methods are not recommended.

The only comparisons that you should make are to the standards that have been established for each job and for worker conduct. You can say that Suzy meets the standards of her job, whereas Helen does not, or that Joe exhibits the cooperative spirit necessary for success in his job, whereas Jess does not. These are not comparisons of one person to another; instead, they are comparisons of each person to the standards and expectations you have for each subordinate in relation to his or her duties.

Not Sharing the Results

We have assumed that whatever your formal appraisal of a worker is, it will be discussed with that worker. To do otherwise defeats the whole purpose behind appraising people—to better their performance individually and collectively. Yet some companies promote systems for evaluating employees that actually prohibit or discourage communicating the results to the rated individuals. They do so because they assume that the daily appraisals have said all that needs to be said or because they see the formal appraisal as primarily a communications device between supervisor and middle manager or between line and staff. This unfortunate perception of the process denies the supervisor and every other manager the opportunity to accomplish all the goals we have mentioned previously. If this situation exists in your company, you must realize how it affects your workers. A sense of fear and distrust is created by this secrecy, and frustration will result from not knowing what the formal reports about a person's abilities have to say. Work for a change in policy if you function under such a system.

Lack of Proper Training

All too often, companies sow the seeds for management failures by neglecting to provide each supervisor with the training he or she needs to appraise people properly. A supervisor who has not been taught how to appraise, how to prepare for an appraisal interview, and how to conduct such an interview will make mistakes that could have been prevented. If you are uncertain about how to do your appraising, seek counsel from your peers and superiors. If the company fails to give you the proper training in this vital area, it will be up to you to fill the gap by yourself. Self-study, conferences with your boss, college courses in personnel management, and management seminars are all good ways to establish or improve your skills in this area.

Lack of Standards of Performance

Unless supervisors have clearly defined and properly communicated standards of performance to refer to as they gather information and make observations of their subordinates, they will not be capable of making and sharing an adequate appraisal. Your people must know what is expected of them. You must know how they perceive their jobs. Unless both the supervisor and the rated employee know these standards ahead of time, the appraisal process and its accompanying interview will yield something less than the goals listed at the beginning of this chapter.

Lack of Proper Documentation

When you attempt to criticize an employee's performance, you must be prepared to give specific information. You must have concrete evidence to back up your observations and criticisms. In noting an employee's tardiness, be specific by giving the dates and the amount of time missed.

Appraisals are used as a basis for decisions about promotions, demotions, raises, and discharge. Federal equal employment opportunity guidelines require you to appraise specific performances that are essential for good overall performance and to document your substantiation for your ratings. You could someday find yourself a party to a lawsuit claiming that you were unfair or discriminatory in your appraisal if you do not justify your ratings.

The Error of Recent Events

Supervisors often find that recent events inordinately influence their judgments about subordinates, especially if they are strongly negative or positive. You must guard against letting the most recent events overshadow those of the previous months. The best defense is to keep accurate records of individuals' performances, recording significant events as they occur. Your appraisal should give equal consideration to all that has occurred over the appraisal period.

THE APPRAISAL INTERVIEW

Your daily contacts should provide you with the facts you need to prepare and support your formal evaluations. The big event for both you and your worker is the appraisal interview, where you both can discuss the judgments you have made. This meeting should occur in private and without interruption.

Three stages are related to sharing the results of your appraisal efforts: preparing for the interview, conducting the interview, and following up on its results.

Preparing for the Interview

The interview should not just happen. It must be planned with the same thoroughness you would apply to the planning of any important event. Then you can foresee and prevent most of the problems and misunderstandings that could permanently damage your relationship (see Exhibit 13.7).

Be certain that you review each rating in detail before you attempt to meet and discuss it with your worker. Even though you wrote it, you probably wrote several others at the same time, and it is amazing how easily you can confuse them in your own mind. Anticipate the areas or individual remarks that might give rise to controversy. Be clear in your own mind about why you rated a person below average on a given point, what led you to that conclusion, and what supports it now. If you have recorded a failure that the person has overcome and is not likely to repeat, be sure that you have so stated on the rating. You do not want to put much emphasis on such a situation, however. After all, most of our learning takes place through trial and error, and we learn best by analyzing our mistakes.

Imagine math students who are first introduced to addition. They receive an explanation of the process and are guided through several examples. Then they are asked to add the numbers 3 and 6. The students try, and they get the wrong answer. The instructor reviews the process and the students' individual application of it to find out where and how they made their errors. When the errors in application are pinpointed, the students try again. This time they get the correct answer. After adding for several days, they master the process and never repeat their original errors. Would you now hold their initial error against them? You would not and should not. The students' more recent performance indicates quite strongly their mastery of the concepts, and they have proved that they will not fall victim to those errors again.

Having analyzed your subordinate's weaknesses as probable points for discussion and questions, construct a list of his or her strong points. Label what he or she does extremely well. Identify favorable personality traits. These represent excellent introductory material to get the interview going. Some managers use what is referred to as the sandwich approach. This technique gives the worker a strength, then a weakness, then a strength, and so on. It tends to soften the blows to a person's ego and to promote confidence in the person being rated. Use whatever approach you feel is best for both you and your worker. Watch his or her reaction, and be ready to adjust your approach as necessary.

1. Evaluators should develop their own style, so they feel comfortable in an interview. If an interview makes the evaluator feel uncomfortable, the employee being evaluated probably will feel uncomfortable too. An evaluator should not try to copy someone else or follow a rigid format if it does not feel comfortable and natural.

2. Both parties should carefully prepare for the interview beforehand. Employees should review their performance and assemble their own information documenting how well they have done. Evaluators should gather relevant information about each employee's past performance and should compare it against the objectives for the period. Lack of preparation for the interview by either party is an obvious indication of disregard and disinterest.

3. The evaluator should clarify the purpose of the interview at the very beginning. The employee should know whether it is a disciplinary session, a contributions appraisal, or a personal development appraisal. In particular, the employee should understand the possible consequences of the interview so that he or she can prepare appropriate responses. For example, an employee's responses during a contributions appraisal can appropriately be a bit guarded and defensive. But in a personal development appraisal, such responses would greatly reduce the effectiveness of the interview.

4. Neither party should dominate the discussion. The superior should take the lead in initiating the discussion, but the employee should be encouraged to express opinions. The superior should budget the time so that the employee has approximately half the time to discuss the evaluation.

5. The most popular format for the interview is the "sandwich" format—criticism sandwiched between compliments. The rationale for this format is that positive comments made at the beginning and end of the interview create a positive experience. The opening compliments should put the employee at ease for the interview. The closing compliments should leave the employee feeling good about the interview and motivated to do better.

6. An alternative format is the problems-recognition-future planning format. This approach is very direct and to the point. The superior begins by saying, "There are _____ problems I'd like to talk with you about: _____, and _____." Each problem is briefly identified at the beginning, before the supervisor discusses the problems in detail. An employee immediately knows what the charges are and does not sit in uncertainty waiting for the next bomb to fall. After the problems have been discussed by both superior and subordinate, the discussion focuses on accomplishments for which the employee deserves recognition. The superior should describe specific actions deserving recognition and be as complimentary as the behavior merits. The interview should not end until the superior and subordinate have discussed plans for future performance. Future goals and objectives should be clarified, and plans for personal development and performance improvement should be discussed.

EXHIBIT 13.7

Guidelines for conducting effective performance appraisal interviews.

Source: Cherrington, David J. *Personnel Management: The Management of Human Resources* (Dubuque, Iowa: Wm. C. Brown Publishers, 1983), 313.

Finally, set down a list of goals or objectives that you would like to see the person set for himself or herself. These should relate most specifically to improving his or her performance and growth. Then determine the possible ways in which he or she might go about achieving each one. For example, suppose that your subordinate has recurring difficulty in making logical and practical decisions. Be ready to get his or her views on how he or she might improve. Have a suggested plan on hand, and recommend that the subordinate follow it if he or she does not have a plan. For every weakness, you should stand ready with a suggestion for improvement. Let us hope that your subordinate will concur. Most appraisal interviews are a mixture of the problem-solving meeting and the informational meeting and fluctuate between directive and nondirective interviews (see Chapter 11). Pick the approach you think best for each individual. Prepare your script carefully, and be prepared to stick to it.

Conducting the Interview

Make arrangements for adequate time and facilities, and ensure that you will be free of unnecessary interruptions. This is time for just you two and should not be interfered with.

Begin the interview by emphasizing that its purpose is to promote improvement in both the individual and the department. Then move into the specifics. Keep it short and to the point.

One good approach is to begin with some rather general questions such as, "Well, Tom, how would you rate yourself on your progress since our last interview?" or, "If you had to appraise yourself for the past six months, what would you say about your performance?" This method gets your subordinate talking and gives you additional insights into his or her way of perceiving things. Moreover, it makes the point that this interview is supposed to be a dialogue and an exchange of points of view. Avoid the lecture format, and get your subordinate's feelings and observations into the open. You should work for mutual agreement and accord.

At some point during the interview, give the worker a copy of the appraisal. Allow him or her time to read it and to understand its contents. Ask him or her for reactions, and take each as a lead into the why behind the rating. With each weakness noted, give a validation of it. Then discuss how it can be overcome. If your subordinate sees no immediate way to attack it, introduce your thoughts on the matter.

Finally, set some specific short-range goals with your subordinate to remedy the list of shortcomings. These should tackle the questions of what should be done, by what time it should be completed, and how each goal should be reached. You will be instilling hope in each person you interview, and more concretely, you will be showing a way out of the present difficulties. Here again is a chance to convince your subordinate of your honest concern for his or her welfare and progress.

Following up on the Results

After the interview and as part of your normal performance of your duties, check on each person's progress toward the goals set in the interview. If Ann said she would brush up on her basic skills, visit with her to see if she has. If Wally said he was going to try a new method, find out how well he is doing. Your people will soon realize, as you do, that appraisals are daily routines that are only periodically summarized through the formal appraisal report and interview. This realization should cause them to give their best regularly and not just at appraisal time. Exhibit 13.8 shows this concept as a cycle that never ends and always repeats itself.

Rewards for Those Who Excel

How much you can do to provide tangible rewards for your people who excel is related to many factors, including the extent of your authority, your control over the purse strings through budget requests, and your boss's willingness to delegate to you. Often, all you can do from a dollar-and-cents point of view is to recommend a fixed amount as a raise. A worker who is near or at the top of the wage rate may only be eligible for a token increase. Until a worker gets a promotion to a higher pay grade, he or she will have peaked out. The incentive to hasten the promotion may be sufficient to impel that person to work at an above-average pace. Or if he or she is trapped by being the least-senior person, it could mean frustration.

You have many intangible awards you can give each person, however: the pat on the back for a job well done; the frequent appreciation you

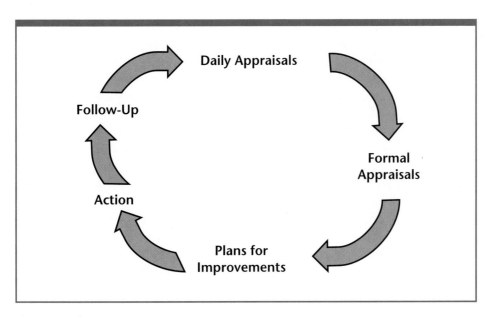

EXHIBIT 13.8
The appraisal cycle.

show each person both in public and in private. Your demonstration of your dependence on each team player goes a long way toward satisfying his or her need for esteem and status. Sending a letter of commendation upstairs for the exceptional contributions your people give when they do not have to, passing over an outstanding performer when some occasional dirty jobs come along, and granting time off if you have the authority to do so can go a long way toward proving to your people that you are aware of each of them and of the value of their individual efforts. Try to make each reward appropriate for the behavior or outcome and timely—following as quickly on the heels of the event as possible. Besides the other things we have discussed, the appraisal process should make you keenly aware of which of your subordinates are carrying the load in your department and just how dependent you really are on them.

 Company celebrations of employee contributions vary widely. Most stage regular events to honor and celebrate jobs well done. Bonuses, certificates of achievement, induction ceremonies, and peer recognition are but a few of the ways in which companies recognize outstanding performances and behaviors. At 3M,

> The company recognizes success not so much by giving shares or bonuses but by holding events where peers cheer peers. Honorees get a certificate and backpat from [CEO DeSimone] and waves of applause. The top awards come once a year, 3M's Oscar night. With considerable fanfare, three or four eminent innovators are inducted into the Carlton Society, a hall of fame for company immortals. Call it corny but it works (Loeb, 1995).

The Hotel Inter-Continental in Miami started a rewards program it calls "It Pays To Do It Right."

> Each month, two of the hotel's 650 full- and part-time hourly employees are recognized for exceptional service. Nominated by guests and managers in two categories, the employee with the most votes in each wins a plaque and $500. Winners are announced at a monthly luncheon that doubles as a pep rally.... At an end-of-year party, the grand-prize car and week's vacation in Europe are raffled off among the 24 monthly winners (Barciela, 1995).

Such celebrations create a climate that encourages excellence by providing a positive reinforcement for the behaviors the organization values. All of us need regular feedback and positive recognition when we do well. Rewards and ceremonies help satisfy employee needs for recognition and security. Says John Hooper, managing director of the consulting and research firm (HR Effectiveness in Oregon): "'Satisfied employees produce satisfied customers, and satisfied customers produce great financial results'" (Barciela, 1995).

Negative Results

Just as your subordinates' appraisals can lead to rewards and tangible improvements, they can lead to negative consequences if warranted. When performance has been judged to be below standard, certain restrictions on privileges, requirements for additional training, and denials of positive benefits may be in order. No raise, no bonus, no promotion, or a possible demotion could be appropriate under management policy or union agreement. In extreme cases where people can but will not perform, termination may result. Let your people know what good and bad effects can follow from their performance appraisals. Be certain that the link between performance and rewards and punishments is clear to each of your subordinates. As with rewards, punishments should be appropriate and timely. Chapter 14 focuses on this difficult area in more detail.

As a summary to appraising and before you begin the appraisal process, review the checklist in Exhibit 13.9. Keep in mind that appraisals can either help or hinder the development of good human relations between you and individuals or groups you supervise. Make the appraisals you perform positive experiences to cement team spirit and individual morale. Lock away any biases you may have, and stick to the facts. Use observable, measurable job-related standards to rate people on their performances and outcomes. Use your appraisal interview to coach and counsel as well as to praise and to criticize.

1. Am I with my people regularly? If not, have I some way of measuring their performance, attitudes, and potential?
2. Do I often let them know how they stand with me? Am I honest when I do so?
3. Do I really know each of my people as individuals? If not, what am I doing about it?
4. Can I detail in writing each of their specific duties? Would my list agree with theirs?
5. Do my appraisals emphasize an individual's performance on the job? Am I using established and approved standards for comparison?
6. Can I back up my opinions with facts? With specific incidents?
7. Have I commented on my subordinates' potentials?
8. Have I planned well to share the results with each person?
9. Have I thought about ways that each can improve his or her rating?
10. Is this rating something I will be proud to put my signature to?

EXHIBIT 13.9

Checklist to help you prepare for the appraisal effort.

Instant Replay

1. Efforts to evaluate subordinates take place daily. Formal appraisals usually take place once or twice each year.
2. The appraisal process is too important for a supervisor to delegate.
3. Appraisals look at a person's personal growth and changes in performance capabilities.
4. Appraisals must be based on known standards and linked to definite rewards and punishments.
5. The many approaches and methods of appraising subordinates all have advantages and disadvantages. All allow for personal bias and subjective judgments.
6. By being aware of the pitfalls of appraising individuals, you can act to prevent their occurrence in your appraisals.
7. The real value of appraisals lies in sharing them with the rated individual. Supervisors get to know their people better and vice versa. Specific problems and achievements can be noted, and plans can be made for improvement.
8. The appraisal process is a cyclical one. As old problems are corrected, new ones appear. Change is inevitable and requires new methods and approaches to routine and special tasks that everyone faces.

Questions for Class Discussion

1. Can you define this chapter's key terms?
2. Why do supervisors appraise their subordinates? What in the process will benefit supervisors? What will benefit their subordinates?
3. Why are clear objectives and standards needed in the appraisal process?
4. Which of the appraisal methods described in this chapter would you as a supervisor prefer to use? Why?
5. What are the major pitfalls of the appraisal process?
6. How often are you appraised at work? How often in your management course? Would you like to be appraised more often? Why?

Incident

Purpose: To experience the difficulties connected with the use of vague, general, usually unobservable traits as rating criteria.

Your Task: Listed here are several traits sometimes used by companies when rating their employees. After each of the traits, write as specific a definition as you can. When you have finished, compare your definitions with those of your fellow students. Then list reasons why rating on the basis of traits is not a valid substitute for rating with clear, observable, job-related standards for work performance.

1. Initiative:
2. Drive:
3. Persistence:
4. Human relations:
5. Promotability:

Keep 'Em on Their Toes

CASE PROBLEM 13.1

Ethan Kress has built his business from scratch. Sixteen years and five stores to manage have given him the confidence to speak his mind about controlling operations. At the New York convention of independent hardware retailers, he did not hesitate to share his methods with colleagues who, like himself, run their own independent operations.

During the first day's lunch break, Ethan and several other entrepreneurs were discussing control of their multistore operations. Ethan explained that he favored a personal approach. He told the group about the visits he made several times each year to his five branch stores. Pretending to be a customer and dressed in his favorite gardening clothes, Ethan would wander the aisles looking for misplaced and mismarked merchandise. He would make mental notes on the orderliness of displays, the cleanliness of the store, the contacts that store personnel had with customers, and the accuracy of checkouts. When his visit was over, he would meet with the store manager and review his discoveries. He took special delight in one particular visit, where he found dirty aisles, a discourteous clerk, and a particular item out of stock. He fired the manager on the spot and promoted the clerk with the most seniority. Ethan stayed with the store as its manager until things were in order again and the new man was able to take over. "I can tell you," said Ethan, "those unannounced visits of mine really keep my people on their toes."

Questions

1. Which appraisal methods does Ethan use?
2. Which appraisal errors appear in this case?
3. Are the standards Ethan uses (a) specific, (b) unbiased, and (c) understandable? Explain.

It's Results That Count

CASE PROBLEM 13.2

Six months ago, Jane Farley set her performance goals in a meeting with her supervisor, Phyllis Johnson. Ten specific goals had been set and were to have been achieved within the six months just passed. Jane had accomplished six of the goals and felt strongly that two more would be reached within the next thirty days. She had begun to view the other two goals as unrealistic given that time and circumstances had changed so drastically since the two were set. As she walked to Phyllis's office, Jane hoped that her supervisor would feel the same way. She would know in a few minutes, when her appraisal interview should begin.

"Sit down, Jane," said Phyllis. "It's that time again. It's been a few months since we last talked about your progress. Let's start with your summary of what goals you have accomplished and which ones remain."

As Phyllis began to review her list of Jane's goals, Jane recited a list of her successes and failures. Phyllis listened intently, making notes throughout Jane's recitation. When Jane had finished, Phyllis began her comments.

"You know how I feel, Jane. It's results that count. You and I agreed six months ago that the ten goals in front of us could and should be accomplished by today. Six of your goals have been reached. That gives you a 60 percent score by anyone's math. Today, you tell me that you need another thirty days for two of your goals. Contrary to your feelings, I do not feel that the last two goals you mentioned are impossible to attain. What I want to know now is, why have you waited until today to tell me of your feelings and failures? When you first realized that your goals were unattainable, why didn't you come to me and discuss it?"

"Phyllis, I honestly thought that I would have eight goals accomplished by today until about two weeks ago. You were on vacation until last week so that would have been the earliest we could have talked. I thought that since we were meeting today, that would be soon enough. We disagree on the possibility of reaching two goals. I think that your budget cuts and the loss of my co-worker, Abrams, have delayed work output enough to make these last two goals impossible until Abrams is replaced and overtime is restored to our section."

"Well, you have not done the kind of job I expected from you. You will be rated below average. The two goals you say you need thirty days more for will be our starting point for your next six month's performance plan. Abrams left five weeks ago, and personnel has not moved to find a replacement. Times are tight, and overtime is not planned for at least the next six months, so you will have to apply yourself more. You may find as others have that eight hours on the job are not enough. If you do, your goals are still the same in number, and extra effort may be required during those eight hours each day or on your own time. Now let's get started on your next set of goals for the next six months."

Questions

1. What do you think of Phyllis's statement, "It's results that count"?
2. Using Exhibit 13.6, how has Phyllis failed in her execution of the supervisor's role in MBO?

Notes

Barciela, Susana. "'Attaboys' Pay Dividends in Work Place," *Chicago Tribune*, January 4, 1995, sect. 6, 5.

Chicago Tribune. "Bosses Keep Close Watch on Workers," August 7, 1994, sect. 7, 8.

Chicago Tribune. "Workers, Bosses Clash on Privacy," October 9, 1994, sect. 7, 8.

Collins, James C., and Porras, Jerry I. *Built to Last.* (New York: HarperBusiness, 1994), 91–99.

Commerce Clearing House Editorial Staff with George S. Odiorne. *Performance Appraisal: What Three Companies Are Doing* (Chicago: Commerce Clearing House, 1985), 31–34.

Drucker, Peter. *The Practice of Management.* (New York: Harper & Row, 1954).

Loden, Marilyn, and Rosener, Judy B. *Workforce America!* (Homewood, Ill.: Business One Irwin, 1991), 161–178.

Loeb, Marshall. "Ten Commandments for Managing Creative People," *Fortune,* January 16, 1995, 136.

Mitchell, Russell. "Managing by Values," *Business Week,* August 1, 1994, 48–49.

Morita, Akio, with Reingold, Edwin M., and Shimomura, Mitsuko. *Made in Japan: Akio Morita and Sony* (New York: E.P. Dutton, 1986).

O'Reilly, Brian. "360 Feedback Can Change Your Life," *Fortune,* October 17, 1994, 93–94, 96, 100.

Schuler, Randall. *Managing Human Resources,* 5th ed. (New York: West Publishing, 1995), 329.

Stewart, Doug. "Employee Appraisal Software," *Inc. Special Technology Issue,* Vol. 16, No. 13, November 1994, 104–105.

Taylor, III, Alex. "The Auto Industry Meets the New Economy," *Fortune,* September 5, 1994, 58.

Tully, Shawn. "Why to Go for Stretch Targets," *Fortune,* November 14, 1994, 145–146.

Suggested Readings

Bernardin, H. John, and Beatty, Richard W. "Can Subordinate Appraisals Enhance Managerial Productivity?" *Sloan Management Review* 28, #4 (Summer 1987): 63–73.

Collins, James C., and Porras, Jerry I. *Built to Last: Successful Habits of Visionary Companies.* New York: HarperBusiness, 1994.

Ewing, David W. *Justice on the Job.* Boston: Harvard Business School Press, 1989.

Longenecker, Clinton O., Sims, Henry P., Jr., and Gioia, Dennis A. "Behind the Mask: The Politics of Employee Appraisal." *Academy of Management Executive* (1987): 183–193.

Nelson, Bob. *1001 Ways to Reward Employees.* New York: Workman Publishing, 1994.

Pecetta, Frank. *Don't Fire Them, Fire Them Up.* New York: Simon & Schuster, 1994.

Pell, Arthur R., Ph.D. *The Supervisor's Infobank.* New York: McGraw-Hill, 1994.

Discipline

OBJECTIVES

After reading and discussing this chapter, you should be able to do the following:

1. Define this chapter's key terms.

2. Differentiate between positive discipline and negative discipline.

3. Explain the role of penalties in the exercise of discipline.

4. List and briefly explain four principles of discipline.

5. List and briefly explain four common pitfalls that can affect a supervisor's efforts at discipline.

6. Explain what it means to be fair when you discipline your subordinates.

7. Describe why supervisors should know themselves and their subordinates well before they attempt to discipline their subordinates.

INTRODUCTION

By **discipline** we mean two distinct and related concepts: education and training to foster compliance with reasonable rules and standards (called positive discipline), and the dispensing of appropriate sanctions for wrongdoing (called negative discipline). Both approaches are necessary to accomplish the primary purpose of disciplinary actions: to promote reasonable and safe conduct at work so as to protect lives and property, and to sustain acceptable performances that promote individual and group success.

Nearly everything we have been exploring since Chapter 1 relates to this chapter. Your human relations role as judge requires you to administer discipline. As a supervisor, you are the person closest to your subordinates and are thus the member of management best suited to deal with them when they become guilty of misconduct or violate rules. You are the person responsible for preparing up-to-date job descriptions and specifications that can be the cause of problems in employee behavior. You play a role in selecting new people. If you bring people into your environment, you should be thinking about how well they will fit into it, and you should help keep potential problem workers out. Your training and appraisals can either prevent problems or be the causes of them. Both can either foster self-discipline and self-control in subordinates or sow the seeds for future performance problems. And most important, what you say and how you act set the tone for employees' behavior at work.

discipline
the management duty that involves educating subordinates to foster obedience and self-control and dispensing appropriate punishment for wrongdoing

THE SUPERVISOR AND DISCIPLINE

Subordinates and team members depend on their supervisors, team leaders, and team facilitators to satisfy many of their needs at work. They expect and deserve to be treated ethically and to have their employment rights respected. Employees at all levels need to know what standards will be applied to their behaviors and outcomes and must be given the training to meet these standards. Finally, all of us need regular feedback on how we are doing and help in our efforts to improve. When superiors fail to help subordinates, others stand ready to do so. Unions, cliques, and lawyers are three such groups.

If subordinates, teams, and team members like their jobs and respect their supervisors, leaders, and facilitators, they have the best reasons for avoiding the need for punitive action. Such workers are bent not on disruption but on construction. When people know that their leaders have their best interests at heart, they will not let them down intentionally.

SUPERVISING TEAMS

When companies use self-managing teams, disciplining members may or may not be part of their duties. Although some discipline their members with subtle group pressures to conform to the group's norms, and others have the authority to pass judgment and deliver punishments, more often than not self-managing teams and their rotating leaders prefer to let traditional managers handle discipline. This is due in part to the personally unpleasant aspects and complex nature of the disciplinary process: It is governed by the law, union agreements, in-house procedures, and the need to carefully document unacceptable performances. All this requires training.

Johnsonville Foods in Wisconsin operates almost entirely through employee teams whose members are responsible for defining their jobs, inspecting their output, scheduling their own production, continuing their learning, and disciplining. CEO Ralph Stayer puts it this way: "We believe discipline is the problem of people who have to work with other individuals, peers. We think any work area should set up its own standards and rules and enforce them. It's part of our overall philosophy. People are in charge of their own areas: setting budgets, hiring, firing, training, and discipline."

Companies that have tried team disciplining have found mixed success. In general, people who are made to feel responsible for their work (those who feel they own their jobs) tend to take more pride in performing their duties. More pride usually means fewer problems with their work and between them and their counterparts. In addition, most people take criticism from their peers with greater reluctance than they do the criticism from their supervisors. (Think about it. Suppose you make a mistake and a team member turns to you and says, "You sure blew it this time. Look at the problem you caused." How would you feel?) Criticism and sanctions given to a person by friends and peers can change behavior, but few such people are willing to discipline each other. Fewer still can be objective, unemotional, and not do lasting damage to relationships while disciplining peers.

Another problem arises when teams discipline their members. It reduces the supervisor's formal authority. This may be appropriate where the supervisor is a facilitator and coach, acting as a supporting agent for the autonomous team. But in general, unless teams or their leaders are responsible for hiring, training, and evaluating team members, they should not have the power to discipline them.

Sources: Stayer, Ralph. "How I Learned to Let My Workers Lead," *Harvard Business Review,* November–December 1990, 72–76; Kiechel III, Walter. "How to Discipline in the Modern Age," *Fortune,* May 7, 1990, 180.

Understanding diversity also comes into play in discipline. When you must discipline Hispanic and Korean workers, don't expect them to look you in the eye. In these and other cultures, it is a sign of respect to lower one's eyes to the ground.

SUBORDINATES AND RESPONSIBILITY

Effective discipline depends on many things, not the least of which is the individual employee's willingness to accept responsibility for his or her work and behaviors. Too many organizations rely on controls outside the individual to enforce compliance to standards and assignments. This is but a statement of distrust in people. There is no real substitute in organizations for its members' self-control and willingness to comply to standards. When individuals accept responsibility for their own efforts, punitive efforts are seldom needed.

Author Peter Drucker (1974) points to three prerequisites that managers at all levels must provide to their people if they expect them to take responsibility for their actions:

- Productive work
- Feedback information
- Continuous learning

These three elements show the link between planning work and doing it. Although planning and execution are separate sets of activities, they can and should involve the same people. MBO is but one example of this. Those who perform tasks are fountainheads of information on how to do them best. They want and need to be consulted and to have their suggestions considered.

In order to take responsibility, your people need accurate and timely information, regular feedback, and occasional guidance. In Drucker's words, a supervisor is a "resource to the achieving worker and his [her] work group...." The proper role for a supervisor includes the following: "Knowledge, information [sharing], placing, training, teaching, standard setting, and guiding" (Drucker, 1974).

A FAIR AND EQUITABLE DISCIPLINARY SYSTEM

As is the case with appraisal systems, unless you and your subordinates view the disciplinary system you must work with as both fair and equitable, it will cause more problems for you than it can cure. You and your company's efforts at discipline must consider a person's dignity, his or her legal rights, and the union agreement where one exists. A fair and equitable disciplinary system has the following characteristics:

1. It has reasonable and needed policies, rules, and procedures that govern human conduct at work. These exist to prevent problems, and they do not violate any federal, state, or local laws.
2. It communicates the preceding information and the consequences that one can expect when guilty of a deliberate violation (forewarns).
3. It has consistent enforcement of rules, policies, and procedures, along with consistent applications of sanctions for infractions.
4. It has progressively severe penalties for repeated infractions by the same party.
5. It places the burden of proving guilt on management.
6. It considers the circumstances surrounding an infraction.
7. It has appeals and review procedures.
8. It has a short memory—it purges memories of wrongdoing after a reasonable time and avoids holding a grudge.

Evaluate the disciplinary system you live with by these standards. If you suspect or know that there are problems, get together with your fellow supervisors and go to those who can change things. You cannot expect to enjoy the respect of your subordinates if you have to violate the preceding standards when executing your role as judge.

The Hot Stove Concept

Professor Douglas McGregor (who gave us Theories X and Y) offers a useful analogy to keep in mind when approaching disciplinary tasks and handing out earned penalties. Called the hot stove concept, it compares the hot stove to the organization's disciplinary system and the burn victim to the employee who has earned punishment. Professor Raymond L. Hilgert from Washington University puts it this way (Kiechel, 1990):

> The first element is advance warning: just as everyone knows that if he touches a hot stove he'll be burned, so should every employee know the rules and work standards. Second, the pain should be immediate: the boss shouldn't wait to respond. Third, discipline should be consistent: anytime you brush up against the stove, you get the message.... Finally, hot stoves are impersonal, and the boss should be too.

Anyone who touches the hot stove will receive the same result. Initially, the victim will feel anger and hostility toward the stove, but normally this reaction is a result of the realization that the angry person is wrong or has acted incorrectly. The anger fades in time, and the victim learns respect for the stove. The victim's behavior will change in the future.

So it should be with your disciplinary actions. They should be immediate when they are earned by wrongdoers. People should not be in doubt that burns will occur when rules, procedures, standards, and policies are violated. Make sure that they know the stove is hot and that it will burn anyone who fails to respect its heat.

An Example   An associate during my beginning teaching days told me about his method for handling cheating in his classroom. He began each new term by defining his policy on cheating. Anyone caught cheating on an exam, project, or quiz would receive a failing grade for it, and his or her parents would be notified to this effect. If a student were caught cheating twice in the same course, he or she would receive a failing grade for the course, and his or her parents would again be notified. For most students, a warning in such clear terms would be sufficient. However, there are always a few people who either do not believe you or who feel that cheating is worth the risk.

When my colleague caught a student cheating, he would simply take up the student's paper and ask the student to see him after class. Before he picked up a paper, however, the teacher would make certain in his own mind that cheating had occurred. When they met after class, the teacher would tell the student what he had witnessed and ask the student to verify his observations. If the student would not admit the offense, the teacher was prepared to let him or her complete the exam. In point of fact, however, my friend was never confronted with this situation. In every case during the five years he used this system, the student readily admitted his or her wrongdoing. In no case, did that student, once caught, ever cheat again.

This method is simple and direct. The teacher practiced it without exception. At no time during five years did this teacher have two students who were caught cheating in the same class. Word got around that this teacher meant what he said. He was a hot stove in action, and the students respected him for it. The honest students felt secure that their hard work and study would pay off and not be jeopardized by the cheating of their dishonest fellow students. The grades in this teacher's class reflected each student's ability and not someone else's. Not once did parents complain about this system. In fact, some of them expressed their complete agreement with it and indicated that they were more involved with their children as a result. Eventually, this teacher's methods were adopted by the school as policy.

One lesson from this story is that you must start out firmly with your people. You cannot afford to be too lenient or permissive. Do not look the other way when you witness an improper situation, but do not go looking for trouble either. You certainly do not want to be accused of spying or setting traps for your people. That is totally improper. Get your subordinate to admit his or her mistake and to accept the penalty. If you get yourself into a swearing match (where it is his or her word against yours), you have a poor case indeed. Get a witness or at the very least an admission of guilt on which to build your case. And remember, criticize the action—not your subordinate as a person.

Progressive Discipline

progressive discipline a system using warnings about what is and is not acceptable conduct; specific job-related rules; punishments that fit the offense; punishments that grow in severity as misconduct persists; and prompt, consistent enforcement

Progressive discipline uses warnings about what is and is not acceptable conduct; specific, job-related rules; penalties that fit the offense; sanctions that grow in their severity as misconduct persists; and prompt, consistent enforcement. Exhibit 14.1 highlights the hallmarks of a progressive discipline system in more detail.

EXHIBIT 14.1
Characteristics of a progressive discipline system.

- Specific rules
- Job relatedness
- Clearly defined punishments
- Punishments that fit the severity of the offense
- Punishments that increase with repeated infractions
- Careful investigation
- Prompt enforcement
- Consistent enforcement
- Documentation of offenses committed and punishments given
- Effective communication of standards and what happens when they are violated
- Effective communication during disciplinary interview
- Disciplinary actions performed in private
- An appeals process established
- Follow-up to prevent recurrence and to cement relations

Managements lose the respect of their employees (and lawsuits in court) when they attempt to enforce vague rules, penalize in an inconsistent manner, fail to follow their own disciplinary procedures, and fail to warn employees of changes and unacceptable conduct. The progressive discipline system is formal; it is familiar to all who are governed by it. It places limits on managers' actions and their flexibility to deal with problem employees. But it must do so in order to be perceived as just and fair. It offers the best defense against accusations of bias and discrimination (Ledvinka and Scarpello, 1991).

POSITIVE DISCIPLINE

Positive discipline promotes understanding and self-control. The primary aim of discipline by any manager anywhere in the organization should be to prevent undesirable behavior or to change it into desirable behavior. You must communicate what is expected of each individual with regard to his or her behavior on the job. This process begins with the arrival and induction of each new employee and continues throughout his or her employment.

The subject of your communications should be the limits placed on each individual by company policies and regulations, departmental rules and procedures, the person's job description, and the union contract (if one exists). By communicating before any infraction occurs the expectations you have of each worker and the limitations under which he or she has to work, you forewarn your subordinate about the type of conduct you want him or her to exhibit while on the job (see Exhibit 14.2). If employees stay within these boundaries, they risk nothing, but if they step outside them, they can expect management to react in certain predictable ways. Once established, these boundaries need to be maintained by regular review of their usefulness and by the judicious application of fair punishments.

Each person is evaluated at work by certain standards and norms. Most situations involving the need for discipline center on a failure to communicate these standards adequately. The need for penalties arises because of an individual's failure to meet one or more of the standards set up to govern his or her performance and conduct.

When employees know their jobs and the standards they must meet, they gain security. They are aware of the degree of freedom allowed and have definitive limits that they know they must not overstep. If they cross one or another of these limits, they know that a punishment will follow the violation.

Positive discipline can be illustrated by a police officer traveling in the flow of traffic in a well-marked, easily identifiable police car. He or she is visible to other motorists, serves as a reminder to obey traffic regulations, and represents a warning that violators will be apprehended and given a penalty. There is nothing sneaky or subterranean about his or her behav-

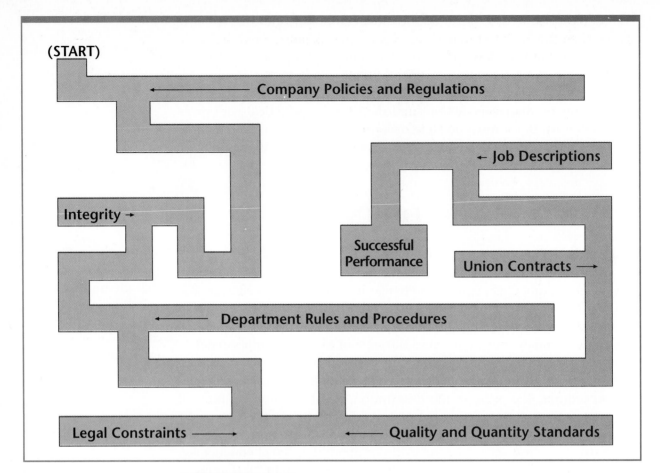

EXHIBIT 14.2

The path to successful job performance is paved with restrictions.

behavior, and the officer's main purpose is to prevent violations from occurring. Contrast this with an unmarked squad car parked out of the view of passing motorists. In this case, prevention is deemphasized, and detection and punishment are emphasized.

One example of positive discipline comes from a Florida company, Tampa Electric. Since 1979, the company has had a procedure it calls a "discipline-making leave day." When an employee below the rank of top management commits an offense or series of offenses that would ordinarily lead to a suspension, the company gives the employee one day's suspension with pay. The employee is given that day to think seriously about whether or not he or she wants to continue to work for Tampa Electric. Since the procedure has been used, 150 leave days have been handed out, and attendance problems have been cut in half. Supervisors who had been reluctant to give an earned suspension now see it as a positive step toward improving conditions (*Success!,* 1987).

Do not leave your people guessing about the limits imposed on them or about their chances of getting caught in wrongdoing and being penalized. Be visible and obvious, and let them have no doubts about your intentions and your punitive powers. You are not trying to trap anyone. Rather you are serving to inform them by your actions and words that you wish to promote reasonable behavior and prevent any unacceptable conduct.

People resent rules that they consider unnecessary or unfair. It is often insufficient to issue prohibitions. People need to know why they cannot do certain things. For example, if employees cannot smoke in department A, the supervisor should explain why they cannot. If your subordinates are not to use company tools at home on a loan basis, tell them why not. Resentment follows from a lack of understanding or a misunderstanding of the need for rules or regulations. Be sure your people have adequate explanations so that their obedience will be based on logic. This procedure should provide an incentive to cooperate.

Legal Concerns

Chapter 11 introduced you to the various laws that govern the hiring and selection processes. The equal employment opportunity laws also affect disciplinary and dismissal decisions. It is unlawful to discipline, deny employment rights to, or fire someone because of his or her race, color, religion, sex, national origin, age, or handicap status. Worker compensation laws from the fifty states prohibit disciplining and terminating employees who make compensation claims. The Occupational Safety and Health Act (discussed in more detail in Chapter 16) protects employees from terminations and other disciplinary actions when they exercise their rights under the act. Labor laws (discussed in Chapter 15) prohibit the disciplining of workers for involvement in efforts to unionize and for engaging in lawful union activities. In addition, some towns and cities have enacted such legislation and laws that prevent discrimination on the basis of one's sexual preference or orientation.

A number of federal and state laws protect **whistleblowers**—employees who make known to authorities the violations of laws and actions committed by their employees that are contrary to public policy (the good of society). It is generally unlawful to penalize individual employees in any way for refusing to engage in or to conduct unlawful activities.

Clearly, every organization needs a specialist in the area of the law and discipline. Check with your personnel or human resource specialists before you decide to take any disciplinary actions.

whistleblower
an employee who makes known to authorities the violations of laws and actions committed by his or her employer that are contrary to public policy

Resolving Complaints

Although Chapter 15 has detailed information on handling employee complaints, a few words are in order here. Complaints should be a warning to you that something is not right for your people. They can be symptoms of deep-seated or long-standing problems with work or its environment. If they are not dealt with in a fair and equitable way, they can lead to employee misconduct. For example, a person's job may be so boring and unfulfilling that she seeks conversations with others at work, disrupting their work and taking her away from her own.

When your subordinate or team member comes to you with a complaint, give it a fair hearing. Show sincere interest, and give the person time enough to say what he or she thinks and feels. Listen without passing judgment. Get the person's perspective. If you can do something to help, do it. If you cannot, find someone who can. Send the complaint or the complainer to another person for assistance. Let people know that you and the company don't want dissatisfied employees.

Some companies have open-door policies that encourage employees to go beyond their immediate supervisor, all the way to the top if necessary. Others have individuals or committees to allow for a fair hearing and adjudication of disputes. See this chapter's Supervisors and Ethics feature for more on alternative methods for resolving complaints. Just be sure that the paths created within your organization are familiar to and used by your people.

Employee Assistance Programs

Programs created to help employees with personal and job-related problems at work are collectively called employee assistance programs (EAPs). A person with a family, health, financial, or stress-related problem may need immediate help. Drug intervention programs offer the addict a way to overcome the addiction and to keep a job. Exercise, diet, and access to medical professionals offer employees a way to handle a variety of problems, which if left unattended, can lead them into disciplinary troubles. People unable to cope with their problems will become problems for themselves and others at work. Some of the symptoms of troubled workers are absenteeism, tardiness, lateness in handling assignments, difficulties in working with others cooperatively, and turnover.

The hospitality industry is one suffering from high rates of absenteeism and employee turnover. Some hotels experience as much as 100 percent turnover in a year. The Chicago Hilton and Towers has reduced its turnover rate to about 38 percent due in large part to its EAPs focused on wellness: smoking cessation, diet, exercise, training in interpersonal relations, and regular meetings with new hires and staff (Kleiman, 1990).

When a subordinate or team member begins to exhibit signs of trouble, heed the following suggestions from several human resource managers (BBP/Prentice Hall, 1993):

- Try to pinpoint the problem. Lack of training? Significant changes in assignments? Changes in the person's personal life? For personal problems, outside expertise may be recommended. Practice your coaching and counseling roles, and talk to the person, one on one.

Alternative dispute resolution systems (ADRSs) include any method used, short of a lawsuit, to settle disputes in the workplace. Favored by federal laws such as the 1991 Civil Rights Act and the Americans with Disabilities Act, they are growing in popularity and used by some of our nation's largest and smallest companies—Motorola, Travel-ers Corporation, and Coors Brewing Company to name but a few. Two reasons for their growing use are that ADRSs are quicker and less costly than traditional law-suits. They may consist of a committee of managers and workers, an outside third party or panel, or a single person—a neutral third party to the dispute—from either inside or outside the firm. They may use a formal procedure or set of procedures as is the case with grievance processing and mediation and arbitration hearings long in use for resolving union–management contract issues and negotiations. (These are discussed in Chapter 15.) In addition to union–management issues, ADRSs deal with accusations of discrimination in employment decisions (promotions, pay, layoffs, and firings), claims of sexual harassment, and disputes over employer evaluations and disciplinary actions. Four major ethical issues accompany the use of ADRSs.

First, whereas some are voluntary, others are not. Mandatory ADRSs exist because of union contracts that build them in and are due to employers requiring new hires to agree to use them instead of litigation. In the first instance, employees have no choice but to use the systems provided to them. In the second, the choice is to take the job, giving up their legal right to sue, or to look for work elsewhere.

The second ethical issue arises through the ways in which ADRSs are administered. In nonunion companies with a mandatory ADRS, management sets up the committee, designates the individuals who will serve as judges (with the potential of over-representation of some groups and under-representation of others), and pre-scribes procedures. Employ-ees may or may not have a say in any of these decisions.

The third issue stems from the facts that, without labor–management contract wording to the contrary, either employees with a complaint or employers will have to pay for the costs of handling complaints. Most employees lack the means to pay the costs of mediation and arbitration provided by outsiders such as lawyers or law firms. Thus they may feel that their only alternative is to live with their problems. When the employer pays, the persons hired to resolve the issues may be more than sympathetic to the employer's views. "Employees in industries, such as securities, that have their own arbitrators say judgments are skewed to favor employers." Employers also profit through savings on various legal fees.

Finally, history teaches that "Employers who win in arbitration generally get lower monetary damages than similar cases tried in federal court and heard by juries." Awards granted may be limited to the actual dollar losses suffered and ignore or refuse to grant monetary awards for pain and suffering—compensatory damages allowed in federal court cases. "The systems succeed so well for employers that they 'virtually eliminate excessive punitive damages [by juries] for reckless employer conduct,' [says] Martin Payson, a partner in the White Plains, New York, office of Jackson, Lewis, Schnitzler & Krupman. His law firm has set up more than 20 such systems."

Sources: Kleiman, Carol. "Unsettling Disputes," *Chicago Tribune,* November 27, 1994, sect. 8, 1; "A Dispute on Company Tribunals," *Chicago Tribune,* December 11, 1994, sect. 7, 8.

Employee assistance programs (EAPs), such as this company-sponsored health club at Mesa petroleum, help reduce worker stress. EAPs help workers deal with personal problems that could otherwise hurt productivity.

- Keep focused on what has changed and what is missing. Concentrate on what is no longer acceptable performance or behavior and on why a change is needed. Explain options, and offer to do what you can to correct problems.
- Check for burnout. People under stress they cannot handle or who work too much can suffer burnout. They may need time away from stressful assignments and conditions to recover their energies and commitment. Options include reassigning work and a leave of absence.
- Consider your own behavior toward the individual. Are you using the proper leadership style? Have you been available for assistance? Have you neglected to give adequate feedback and appraisals?
- Make it very clear that you are concerned for the person's welfare and stand ready to assist in any ways possible to restore the person's performances or behaviors to acceptable levels.

DIVERSITY AND DISCIPLINE

The following guidelines for maintaining a climate that fosters positive discipline apply to any organization and to all people regardless of the gender, religion, race, age, ethnic background, and physical challenges. They are the recommendations culled from the writings of several experts in the area of managing diversity:

- Make certain that every individual knows the standards that will be applied to outcomes and behaviors and why those standards are necessary.
- Make sure that people have the necessary resources to succeed.
- Give each person prompt, objective feedback on his or her performance.
- Tailor rewards and punishments to fit the circumstances.
- Remove any rewards for poor or negative performances. For example, don't give a poor performer less to do and overburden your star performers as a consequence.
- Remove any punishments for positive performances. For example, don't punish people for exercising their authority and initiative when it results in honest failures. Empowering means the freedom to experiment and fail.
- Encourage all employees to respect and value the individuality and uniqueness of each organizational member and the subcultures to which each belongs.

NEGATIVE DISCIPLINE

Negative discipline emphasizes the detection of wrongdoing and punishment. It can become bureaucratic and impersonal, relying heavily on records, rules, and procedures, but it need not be this way. It is often characterized by a lack of trust in subordinates, by demands for blind obedience, and by willful disobedience of rules and regulations by the employees. Many employees play a game with their supervisors when they work in such an environment. They become covert and sneaky in their behavior. They deliberately plot to break rules to see if they can beat the system and get away with it or simply to keep management off balance and irritated. They do so because they resent the approach to discipline taken by their employer and supervisors, and they take delight in frustrating their efforts. They have not developed the attitudes that support a willing compliance with their organization's rules.

A climate in which negative discipline thrives—one in which the need for penalties is frequent—should be examined and restructured to promote willing compliance and positive discipline. Individual counseling is absolutely essential in order to turn the situation around. Human relationships need development, nourishment, and maintenance. Supervisors must initiate and properly play their roles in human relations. Rewards and merit awards should be established for the good performers. The disciplinary system must become more professional and worthy of the respect and confidence of the employees.

negative discipline
the part of discipline that emphasizes the detection and punishment of wrongdoing

Penalties

An important aspect of discipline has to do with penalizing wrongdoers. Sometimes, as with controls, prevention devices and actions may fail; then the need for prompt and fair action takes over. Your power to take action in dealing with infractions is probably limited. Typically, most supervisors can do any of the following:

1. Give an oral warning
2. Issue a written reprimand
3. Suspend a person from the job without pay

Whether you have the powers mentioned here or not depends largely on your job description, your company's policies, and, if your company has a union, the union contract's stand on this issue. Often the union contract will have much to say about your powers to discipline. Be certain that you know the limits placed on your disciplinary powers and that you stay within those limits.

Common Problems

As a supervisor, you will face one or more of the problems identified in Exhibit 14.3 during any given year. Illegal activities may require immediate suspension or dismissal as well as criminal prosecution. Rule violations may be less serious, at least until they become "normal" behaviors for your subordinates. They usually carry the penalty of a verbal reprimand for the

EXHIBIT 14.3
Disciplinary problems supervisors can expect to encounter at work.

Illegal Activities	Gambling; verbal and physical assaults among workers; failing to report physical injuries or intentional damage to property; theft of common property; sexual harassment; possession of forbidden substances
*Rule Violations	Tardiness; leaving early; unexcused absence; unacceptable language; horseplay; excessive break times; minor safety and security violations

*Note: These offenses and violations may be considered minor when they occur infrequently and when their consequences can be considered inconsequential or less than serious by the company and the parties directly involved. Each offense has the potential of becoming serious, however, if left unnoticed and if allowed to be repeated by the same individuals.

first offense, a written reprimand for the second, and a suspension without pay for a third violation. Of course, the person's intentions, his or her work history, and the circumstances surrounding the offense must be considered before any punishment can reasonably be given.

Two of the problems you are likely to run into are absenteeism (most companies say it is their biggest problem) and sexual harassment (a growing concern for many companies). There are some things you should know and some actions you can take with regard to these areas.

Absenteeism People are missing from their jobs for a variety of reasons each day. Some of these reasons mean that you have some work to do to cut down on lost time. If the employee has a legitimate excuse, the first time it happens you may just let him or her know you are concerned. If there is a possibility that the reason will recur, discuss it, and try to prevent it from doing so. Suppose that Jill, a single parent, has not been late or absent in the past. Yesterday, she called in with a request to take the day off because her babysitter was not available. Is this a legitimate reason? Maybe. But it can recur, and Jill should be working on an alternative to her regular sitter.

Sometimes your company may be to blame for absent employees. Suppose your company offers five sick days each year that cannot be banked and if not used are lost. Suppose employees with legitimate gripes are experiencing job-related stress about which the company has done nothing. At some point, the stress becomes too much to deal with, and the employee feels a real need to escape the source of the stress, at least for a time. Finally, suppose your subordinate has come to you with a plea to enrich his job. If you fail to deal with your worker's boredom and loss of motivation, you may have an absent worker in the not too distant future.

Treat all absentees seriously. Talk to each when he or she returns. Keep an eye open for patterns in absenteeism—for example, Jack is always out the third Friday of every month. Be sure that you are setting a good example through your own attendance before you decide to discipline others for poor records.

Stay in touch with all of your people regularly. Greet them warmly when they come in each day. Listen to their concerns, and deal with their problems promptly. Give those who can handle it a bigger say in what they do and how they do it. Through thoughtful delegation, you empower people to become more responsible and to take more pride in themselves and their work.

Sexual Harassment Under Title VII of the Civil Rights Act, **sexual harassment** is unwelcomed sexual advances, requests for sexual favors, and other verbal or physical conduct of a sexual nature when:

1. Submission to such conduct is made either explicitly or implicitly a term or condition of employment

sexual harassment
unwelcomed sexual advances, requests for sexual favors, and other physical and verbal conduct of a sexual nature

Sexual harassment destroys the morale and productivity of victims. You need to be proactive in training subordinates about what conduct is inappropriate, and you must take every complaint seriously.

2. Submission to or rejection of such conduct by an individual is used as a basis for employment decisions affecting that person or third parties

3. Such conduct has the purpose of unreasonably interfering with an individual's work performance or creating an intimidating, hostile, or offensive working environment (Moskal, 1989)

For 1993, 11,908 cases involving sexual harassment were filed with the EEOC. The awards for the injured parties totaled $25.2 million (Duenes and Hermelin, 1994). "…Bettina Plevan, an attorney with [a New York law firm] says her corporate clients who go to trial each pay at least $100,000 in legal fees" (Duenes and Hermelin, 1994). The 1991 Civil Rights Act allows victims to sue for actual and punitive damages. As a supervisor, you could be named in a sexual harassment suit or complaint, making you liable for damages. If you know about a case of sexual harassment at work (see Exhibit 14.4) and fail to take any action, you are liable for the consequences.

Many companies are responding to the need to prevent sexual harassment with training. Some of the programs in use are quite unique and mini-

Examples

- Unwelcome touching, patting, or pinching
- Sexually offensive language, pictures, or objects
- Derogatory, sexually based humor
- Pressure to engage in sexual activity
- Disparaging remarks to a person about his/her gender
- References to an assumed or desired sexual relationship
- Suggestive references about a person's body or appearance
- Unsolicited, unwanted notes, graphics, calls, company, requests for dates
- Obscene gestures

Victim Responses

- Say "no." Sexual harassment is a pattern of behavior that continues after you say "no."
- Don't blame yourself. It's not your fault.
- Don't ignore it. The behavior is likely to continue.
- Do tell someone.

Supervisory Responses

- Confront the perpetrator.
- Report findings to superiors.
- Do not ignore the behavior.
- Follow up on superiors' decisions.

Ideally, you can tell the other person to stop and he or she will. Keep a record of what is going on and what you have done to stop it.

EXHIBIT 14.4
Examples of sexual harassment and what should be done when they occur.

mize a company's legal exposure to charges of harassment. Digital Equipment Corporation provides training that allows trainees to explore the different opinions on what is or is not acceptable conduct. Trainees create their own scenarios that depict what they believe to be harassment. Each is then discussed and analyzed. Du Pont "maintains a 24-hour hot line that provides advice to employees on dealing with sexual harassment" (Campbell, 1993). Many companies use the expertise of outside consultants and conduct workshops and seminars either on or off company premises. According to a 1994 survey by the Society for Human Resource Management, "75% of the 292 companies surveyed say they have implemented some kind of sexual-harassment prevention program" (Duenes and Hermelin, 1994).

You and your company need to take a strong, clear stand against sexual harassment. In addition to prevention efforts, you need to deal with any accusations as soon as you become aware of them. A company policy stating what sexual harassment is and what will be done about it if it occurs must be written and communicated to all employees. There should be a specific procedure to follow in filing a complaint. Anyone who feels the need to complain should be allowed to do so with privacy and dignity. No implied or expressed penalty or fear of retribution should be connected with filing a complaint. See this chapter's Supervisors and Quality feature for additional comments on creating a viable sexual harassment policy.

Before Taking Action

Just what action you take when your subordinates violate rules and regulations should be governed by the following principles:

1. Know each subordinate, his or her record, and the nature and causes of the offense.
2. Know your powers as laid down in your job description; when in doubt, check with your boss and your peers.
3. Check on the precedents, if any, that governed similar situations in the past.
4. Be consistent: If you have given an oral warning on the first minor offense as a general rule, do so in every like case.
5. Consider the circumstances surrounding the misconduct. Was it willful or accidental? Was the person aware of the limits placed on his or her conduct? Is this his or her first offense? Get the facts.
6. If a subordinate has made the same mistake more than once, make the sanctions progressively more severe. Generally, you progress from an oral warning to a written reprimand and eventually to a suspension.
7. Coordinate with the other supervisors on enforcement. Every manager should enforce every policy, rule, standard, and procedure with equal weight and effort. It is better not to have a rule that is unenforced or unenforceable.
8. Be reasonable and fair.

SUPERVISORS AND QUALITY

Companies that care about their employees and their bottom line know that a successful attack on sexual harassment begins with education and preparedness. They are proactive and commit the funds needed to prevent as well as deal with harassment on the job. The costs for the company that experiences sexual harassment and its legal aftermath include:

- Legal fees and damages awarded to victims
- Weakened morale and team spirit
- Injured company reputation
- Weakened employee loyalty to and respect for management
- Reduced quality and productivity
- Absenteeism and employee turnover

The best defense is a good offense. The problem needs to be addressed head on—no denials, no foot dragging. Start with the facts:

- Ninety percent of harassment cases involve men harassing women; 9 percent involve same-sex harassment; 1 percent involve women harassing men.
- Intentional harassment is an exercise of power, not romance.
- Harassment can and does occur in every kind of organization.
- In cases of harassment, it's what the receiver of a behavior thinks about

it that matters, not what the perpetrator thinks.

Next, give guidance through the best means available. Experts teach the following guidelines to men who don't want to offend a woman at work:

- Assume that off-color remarks, comments, and sexual gestures are unwelcome at work.
- Take a person literally when she or he says no.

If you're not certain that your behaviors are acceptable, consider how your spouse, mother, sister, or daughter would feel when witnessing or receiving the behavior you intend.

Now write a policy in line with the following guidelines:

- Start with top management's commitment for both funding and emphasis.
- Get your employees involved in the drafting of a policy.
- Spell out procedures and options for preventing, discovering, reporting, and investigating violations.
- Build in safeguards and protection for all the parties involved.

Finally, when accusations prove founded, follow through with appropriate disciplinary procedures and actions to prevent similar occurrences in the future.

Source: Bravo, Ellen, and Cassedy, Ellen. *The 9 to 5 Guide to Combating Sexual Harassment* (New York: John Wiley & Sons, 1992), 66–67, 110.

530   **PART III • SHAPING YOUR ENVIRONMENT**

Being fair means many things, but the most important aspect of it involves basing your decisions on the circumstances. What may be an appropriate penalty for one party to an infraction of the rules may not be so for another. For example, suppose that you find two of your people in a shoving match; before you can break it up, one of them hits the other. Both people are guilty of fighting, but can you think of reasons justice might dictate for coming down harder on one than on the other? Consider the circumstances and the motives underlying the action you observed. Someone started the fight. Shouldn't that person be dealt with more severely than the person who was provoked? What if one of them had done this before, whereas the other had a clean record? Wouldn't these facts influence your decision?

Being fair does not mean treating everyone the same. You are not a machine that operates automatically or in the same manner with everyone. When we talk about precedents, we mean treating like offenses in a like manner. But the key word is "like." Be careful that what you are dealing with and the people you are dealing with are sufficiently similar to warrant concern for precedents. An old-timer who should and does know better should not receive the same treatment as a new employee. One has learned while the other is learning; one has more responsibility to set a good example than the other.

When you punish, you must look at the person and the circumstances. This does not mean that you do so in order to exercise prejudice or to get even. If you are vindictive or carry a grudge, you are bound to attack people personally. They will know it, even if you do not admit it. You will be basing your actions on a personal dislike for them and not on their actions. As in making appraisals, you must be as objective as you can in order to prevent criticism of your motives or intent. Your job and your reputation are too valuable to risk on immature behavior.

Do not be the cause of your subordinates' mistakes either. Set the example, and let them know you mean what you say. Give them the security that comes with knowing what they must do and why.

A man who audited stores for a large retail chain for over thirty years once told me that, where he uncovered dishonest employees, there was usually a dishonest manager who seemed to encourage them. This type of manager would, on the way out of the store each day, help himself or herself to a handful of peanuts or candy. At other times, such a manager might be too lenient in enforcing rules or regulations or deal weakly with dishonest employees. Honest employees began to resent the extras enjoyed by their peers and decided to get into the action, too. It may start with a pen or pencil, but it may not end until the take reaches some pretty high figures.

Keep in mind that you are not the final voice in matters of discipline. Your company and the union may have procedures providing for review of your decision since matters of discipline are often considered too important to entrust to any one manager. Chapter 15 has much more to say on this matter. If you are wrong, you will be overruled. If not, you should be able to count on your boss for backing. Your subordinates will hear about your disciplinary decisions, too. Do not jeopardize your relations with them by hasty or irrational actions. You could damage your relationships with other workers and their groups if you are unfair. Be sure that you have the facts and that you have put them together properly. Consult with superiors before you act.

Consider the case of a supervisor named John who has given an oral order to a subordinate, Harry. Harry has failed to respond. Orders are intended to provoke an immediate positive response and usually do if they are not overutilized, so John immediately assumes that Harry is being insubordinate. Without any further investigation, John suspends Harry for one week while he and the company decide whether or not to fire Harry. But wait a moment. Aren't there several legitimate reasons Harry could have for not following the supervisor's order? Here are but a few:

1. Harry did not hear the order.
2. Harry was told to do something illegal.
3. Harry was told to perform a task outside his job description or beyond his capabilities or training.
4. John was unclear in his order, and Harry did not understand it.

All these and more could get Harry off the hook. If John goes solely on his observations, without any further investigation, he is likely to make an improper decision and be reversed. In that case, Harry will be back at work, with pay for his time off. Meanwhile, John will have damaged his reputation and alienated Harry, among others. It pays to get the employee's point of view.

Giving the Reprimand

You have studied the case of wrongdoing, gathered your facts, touched bases with experts, and reached the conclusion that disciplinary action is called for. The penalty has been chosen to fit the offense, and you have scheduled a meeting with the offender. Now begins one of the least pleasant parts of being a supervisor. Here are some tips to make that disciplinary session as productive as possible:

- Choose a time and place that ensures privacy and freedom from interruptions.
- Have your facts in writing and your mind clear about the who, what, when, where, and how.
- Be businesslike and serious. The meeting is not the time or place for discussion about anything other than the offense and the consequences of it.
- Take charge of the meeting. Lay out your case with specifics. Get agreement on essentials, and listen for any new information.

- Be clear about the fact that the behavior is in question, not the person.
- Once you have given the reprimand, don't rub it in.
- Try to get a commitment from the offender for improvement and for no repetitions of the offense.
- Both of you should return to your duties.

The Decision to Fire

The decision to fire a person usually rests with the person or persons who have the authority to hire. In most disciplinary cases, this is the course of last resort and should be followed only when all else has failed. Some situations, however, usually demand that the guilty party receive an immediate dismissal. These include the following cases:

1. Gross insubordination such as refusal to comply with a direct, lawful order
2. Drunkenness on the job
3. Willful destruction of company property
4. Serious cases of dishonesty or theft
5. Being found guilty of or pleading guilty to a felony (crime punishable by more than one year in a federal or state penitentiary)
6. Engaging in conduct that is totally unacceptable given the employee's position and responsibilities

Certainly there will be exceptions, even in these extreme situations, and whatever circumstances surround each of these exceptional cases must be considered. It is nevertheless true that a large majority of companies require that the penalty for these infractions be automatic dismissal.

Legal Concerns   Along with employment discrimination laws and the other federal laws already discussed in this chapter, nearly all the states have some laws that restrict an employer's right to fire anyone for any reason. The courts have added to these restrictions. Prior to 1980, the employment-at-will rule from the common law prevailed. **Employment at will** means that both the employer and the employee have the right to terminate the employee's employment at any time, with or without just cause. In 1980, the California Court of Appeals ruled that employers had a duty to deal fairly and in good faith with employees and could be held accountable for discharging employees without having good cause (Bacon, 1989). Since then, more than forty states have allowed exceptions to the employment-at-will rule under specific conditions. Discharged workers can recover losses and regain their jobs by proving that an implied or expressed contract was violated, that an implied or expressed promise of continued employment was violated, or that the firing was contrary to public policy (Bacon, 1989). As a result, employers who wish to retain the

employment at will
the common law doctrine that holds that employment will last until either employer or employee decides to terminate it, with or without just cause

power to terminate employees at will must refrain from making any promises, guarantees, or covenants that may lead the employee to believe that some right to long-term employment exists.

Puerto Rico has created the Discharge Indemnity Act, which details just causes for terminating an employee. It is shown in Exhibit 14.5. Several states are now drafting their own laws using Puerto Rico's act as their model.

PITFALLS

As is the case with the pitfalls we discussed in the previous chapters, the major problems you may encounter when you attempt to carry out your disciplinary duties can be eliminated or at least minimized if you are

EXHIBIT 14.5
Definition of "just cause" in Puerto Rico's Discharge Indemnity Act.

Source: P.R. Laws Ann. Tit. 29, Sect. 185a–185i.

Sec. 185b. Discharge without just cause

Good cause for the discharge of an employee of an establishment shall be understood to be:

(a) That the worker indulges in a pattern of improper or disorderly conduct.

(b) The attitude of the employee of not performing his work in an efficient manner or of doing it belatedly and negligently or in violation of the standards of quality of the product produced or handled by the establishment.

(c) Repeated violations by the employee of the reasonable rules and regulations established for the operation of the establishment, provided a written copy thereof has been timely furnished to the employee.

(d) Full, temporary, or partial closing of the operations of the establishment.

(e) Technological or reorganization changes as well as changes of style, design, or nature of the product made or handled by the establishment and in the services rendered to the public.

(f) Reductions in employment made necessary by a reduction in the volume of production, sales, or profits, anticipated or prevalent at the time of the discharge.

A discharge made by mere whim or fancy of the employer or without cause related to the proper and normal operation of the establishment shall not be considered as a discharge for good cause. . . .

aware of each of them and consciously try to prevent them from interfering with your efforts.

Starting Off Soft

Supervisors, especially those who are new at the job, are apt to associate being lenient with being liked. They sometimes feel that if they look the other way on occasion or mete out less than a deserved penalty for an infraction, they will endear themselves to their subordinates. This is inaccurate. In actuality, their leniency will be the cause of more trouble. If Mary arrives late and you say nothing, she will be encouraged to do it again. So will the others who witness the event and your failure to take constructive action.

It is always easier to start out tough, with an emphasis on the letter of the law. As you gain self-confidence and additional knowledge about your duties and your people, you can shift the emphasis to the spirit of the law as well, tempering your judgment within the framework of your understanding of your people, their personalities, and the group pressures at work on them. This is what is meant by justice. Each person and most events are unique and should be dealt with as such.

If you are soft, those who toe the line will resent you for it. They will see no tangible reward for proper behavior, while they witness some for improper conduct. Your softness will be interpreted as weakness, and you can expect them to test you further to find the limits.

Acting in Anger

How many times have you wished you could take back remarks made to another in anger? If you are like most people, the answer is too often. With emotions influencing your observations and judgment, you will seldom make a sound decision. Too often you will have to back down and apologize for a demonstration of your lack of self-control. Never attempt to discipline while you or the other persons involved are angry.

Count to ten or to one hundred if necessary, but cool down before you decide anything. It also helps to move physically away from the situation and the environment of a wrongdoing in order to regain your composure. Tell the persons involved to report to you in your office in a few minutes. This will give you all time to recapture your composure and reason.

Disciplining in Public

If you have some critical remarks for an individual, pass them along in person and in private. Each person has a reputation to uphold both with you and with his or her peers. He or she has pride and self-esteem, which need protection. He or she does not wish to be subjected to ridicule or embarrassment. It may not be penalties that your people fear but your way of dispensing them. Your methods may make the difference between a constructive and a destructive kind of discipline.

Incomplete Research and Analysis

Let us assume that you see a man stretched out on a packing crate thirty feet away and, because he has his eyes shut, you jump to the conclusion that he is sleeping on the job or, at the very least, goofing off. You should know by now—from your experience and from this book—that appearances do not always reveal the whole truth. Where discipline is involved, it takes more than one observation to make a sound case. Unless you go to the man (preferably with a witness you can count on) and ask him some questions, you cannot really be sure that your observations are correct.

If you intend to penalize someone, be certain that you have a firm case that will stand up to review by a higher authority. Have the details clearly in mind, and make some notes of your observations for later reference. The mind loses certainty and eliminates details with the passage of time between a disciplinary action and the appeal of that action. Answer questions such as who was there and what was said by each. If all you have is a swearing match, you will lose the case, especially when a union is involved.

Exceeding Your Authority

Keep in mind that, like your people, you have limits on your power and conduct. To paraphrase an oil company's slogan, you have "power to be used, not abused." Check with your boss and your peers when you are in doubt about what action to take. There is no legitimate excuse for falling into the trap of exceeding your authority; too many avenues are open to you that can prevent it.

Being Vindictive

The best defense one of your subordinates can have in a disciplinary case is that you are picking on him or her or making a personal attack. Be sure that the reasons behind your action and words are not based on personality clashes or personal prejudice. Put your biases aside, or they will shine through with a neon brilliance for all to see. If you single out one person for disciplinary action, and your methods rest in your personal biases, you will certainly lose your case and will face the wrath of those who must review your actions.

Like your subordinates, you have likes and dislikes. It would not be reasonable to expect you to like all of your people. But you are being paid to serve all of them, regardless of their personal feelings toward you or yours toward them. Unless a subordinate's personality is defective and interferes with his or her performance, you cannot in conscience hold it against that individual. You are not out to win your subordinates over as friends or to socialize with them. It is tough to be fair to those whom we dislike, but if we are to be of service to our company and ourselves, we must make every effort to do so.

Leaving It to Others

Like appraising your people, disciplining them is your exclusive right and duty. You cannot be asked to part with it if you are expected to control and direct your workers properly. Some companies allow the personnel department or some other outside authority to mete out discipline. This reduces the supervisor's role to that of an arresting officer. Your subordinates will soon realize that you cannot punish but can only report violations. As a result, your status will be greatly reduced. This represents a tremendous handicap to a supervisor. Although some managers prefer this arrangement because it releases them from a difficult responsibility, they fail to see that giving up this power makes them impotent and subjects them to additional and needless harassment from above and below.

Even worse than losing disciplinary powers to a higher authority is giving them away to a top worker or straw boss—someone acting with your authority on your behalf. Knowing how difficult it is to discipline properly, how much more likely do you think it is that such people might make a mess of it? Remember, these people are extensions of yourself and, as such, represent you and your other subordinates. Do not give them the power to cause you and themselves trouble. You and only you are responsible for your people and accountable for their actions. If your top worker or straw boss made the wrong decisions, you would have to correct them, thus injuring their already difficult position, possibly beyond repair. Most straw bosses do not want such authority, but if they try to assume it, make it clear to them that they cannot have it.

Failing to Keep Adequate Records

To gain and keep a perspective on each of your people, you should keep records of their performance appraisals, reprimands, peculiarities, and needs. These files will prove quite helpful when you face tough personnel decisions. They also come in very handy when you want to justify your opinions or take specific disciplinary actions.

Instant Replay

1. Both positive discipline and negative discipline are needed if reasonable and safe conduct at work is to be promoted, along with a sense of responsibility for one's work.
2. When an organization or an individual supervisor tolerates a poor performer, the organization or the supervisor cannot, in conscience, discipline anyone whose performance exceeds the poor performer's.

3. The best kind of disciplinary system is one based on the individual employee's sense of responsibility for his or her own work and on each employee's self-control.
4. People need to know what is expected of them and how well or poorly they are doing; they have a right to expect consistent enforcement of necessary rules, policies, and standards.
5. People need to know that good work will be rewarded and that poor performance will earn swift and predictable responses from management.
6. People do not resent punishment that they know they deserve. They do resent being punished for something they did not know was wrong—for not being forewarned.
7. The majority of your subordinates will not need negative discipline if the positive side of discipline has been developed.
8. Discipline is either an easy task or a hard one, depending on how well you have built your relationships with your subordinates and how well you have instilled a measure of self-control in each of them.

Questions for Class Discussion

1. Can you define this chapter's key terms?
2. What is the difference between negative and positive discipline? In what ways are they similar?
3. What is the purpose of punishment in a disciplinary system?
4. What are the basic principles of discipline?
5. What are the major pitfalls a supervisor can fall victim to when carrying out disciplinary functions?
6. What does it mean to be fair when disciplining subordinates?
7. Why should you know yourself and your subordinates well before attempting to discipline or punish them?

Incident

Purpose: To test your knowledge about and ability to spot the existence of sexual harassment in a work setting.

Your Task: After each of the following statements, indicate if you agree or disagree with it. The answers are shown at the end of the exercise. Don't look at them until after you have completed the quiz.

	Agree	Disagree
1. If I don't think I am sexually harassing another person, I am not doing so.	___	___
2. If no complaints of sexual harassment come to a manager's attention, none are occurring.	___	___

	Agree	Disagree

3. Same-sex harassment is not protected under the law. —— ——

4. Fear can keep people who are harassed from complaining. —— ——

5. When a man enters what has been an all-female environment, some behaviors of the women will have to change. —— ——

6. Sexually suggestive visual material, when placed in one's private office, cannot be grounds for sexual harassment. —— ——

(Answers: 1, 2, 3, 6 are "Disagree")

What Should Be Done?

CASE PROBLEM 14.1

After reading each of the following situations, decide what you would do if you were the supervisor. Your options include the following: seeking more information; counseling the person; referring the person to another authority; giving additional training; giving an oral warning or reprimand; giving a written reprimand; or recommending a suspension without pay. You may decide to use a combination of options, and you must give reasons for your choices.

Situation 1. You overhear your subordinates talking about the big pro games coming up this weekend. You notice Wally tearing sheets of paper, writing on them, and placing them in his hat for others to draw out. Several $5 bills are piled on Wally's desk, and Jim and Al are adding to the pile. Company rules forbid gambling.

Situation 2. On your rounds through the shop, you notice that Sally is not wearing her protective gloves. She is at her workstation where she handles sharp-edged sheets of metal, but her machine is not operating. Sally has had two minor injuries in the last six months, and you have warned her twice in the last two weeks to wear the required gear. Company rules state that while at one's workstation, one must wear safety gear.

Situation 3. Your subordinate, Hazel, reports to your office twenty minutes late. She explains that her daughter missed the bus this morning and she had to drive her to school. Hazel has been late three times this month but has always had a different excuse. She has never been late by more than forty minutes and has taken only two sick days in the past twelve months.

Situation 4. Betty arrives in your office crying. She calms down enough to tell you that a worker from another department confronted her in the employee cafeteria and used foul and abusive language to her, embarrassing her in front of several others. Betty claims that she gave the other person no cause to behave the way he did and refuses to tell you who he is.

Situation 5. Bob reports to you to tell you about the theft of a transistor radio from his desk. Bob used the radio at work for several months and always left it on his desk during working hours. Each night he locked it in his desk. The radio disappeared during his coffee break this morning. The radio is old and cost $15 when new. Company rules encourage securing all personal property, unless it is in clear view of its owner. Coffee breaks are routinely taken away from the workstation.

Situation 6. Rita, a co-worker and friend of Ruth's, tells you at lunch that Ruth is being sexually harassed by a supervisor in another department. Both Ruth and Rita are your subordinates, and the supervisor in question is a close personal friend of yours. Both the supervisor and Ruth are married, but not to each other.

CASE PROBLEM 14.2

What to Do About Joe

Frank is worried about his subordinate and chief assistant, Joe. Until rather recently, Joseph Thomson has been an able and willing worker. But the signs of change are too clear to be ignored. About two weeks ago, Frank noticed that Joe was not his regular self. He was losing his sense of humor. When Frank kidded him about something in the past, Joe was quick to fight back with his own brand of kidding. For the past two weeks, Joe has just ignored Frank's efforts at humor or taken Frank's comments the wrong way.

Over the last ten days, Joe has been late to work two times. He has rarely been late more than once a year. He seems tired and drags through the day with little enthusiasm for his work. The work he turns in is up to standard, but the old spirit is gone. Frank asked Joe to take over a special project, and Joe made it very clear that he would if ordered to do so but would not volunteer to do it. Frank was beginning to have second thoughts about continuing to groom Joe to take over for him when he gets his promotion in sixty days.

Frank has tried to talk with Joe about these changes, but Joe is not willing to share his thoughts. Frank has asked around at work to see if he can gain any insights into Joe's behavior but has been unable to discover anything of substance. Against his better judgment, Frank has decided to let his boss, Abel Farley, have a try at getting Joe to talk. After their visit, Abel called Frank into his office.

"Joe didn't say a whole lot, but I think part of his problem is his age. Joe is pushing fifty, and he thinks of himself as an aging man watching the world go by. He mentioned that his youngest child is graduating from college this summer and that he would soon be the only member of his family to not finish college."

"Well, boss, what can we do about midlife crisis?"

"If you aren't happy with his performance, tell him to shape up or ship out."

"I can't fire him for his attitude change. Maybe if I just let him have some time off to get a grip on himself…"

"Frank, why don't you just have a talk with his wife? See if she can suggest anything that might help. It's either that or just ignore his behavior if his work is up to standards."

Frank let things go as they were and found that to be a mistake. Joe disappeared from the office for about an hour and didn't let Frank know where he was going. The last report Joe turned in had to be redone. When Frank went looking for Joe, he found that he had taken his coat and left the office. It was 3 P.M., and Frank became concerned. He called Joe's home, and Joe's wife told him that Joe had come home because he wasn't feeling well. Joe's wife and Frank talked for several minutes, and she told Frank that her husband was worried about his inability to shake his depression. She also told Frank that she thought her husband was "scared to death" about taking over Frank's job. "I'm no psychologist," she said, "but I think he's afraid that he won't be able to live up to your expectations of him."

Questions

1. What do you think about the advice Abel gave to Frank?
2. What diversity issues exist in this case?
3. What should Frank do now?

Notes

Bacon, Donald C. "See You in Court," Reprint of an article from *Nation's Business*, July 1989, 4.

BBP/Prentice Hall. *The 1993-94 Human Resources Guide* (Englewood Cliffs, N.J.: Bureau of Business Practice, a division of Simon & Schuster, 1993), 1238–1239.

Bravo, Ellen, and Cassedy, Ellen. *The 9 to 5 Guide to Combating Sexual Harassment* (New York: John Wiley & Sons, 1992), 51, 67, 110.

Campbell, Linda P. "Examining Workplace Behavior," *Chicago Tribune*, October 20, 1993, sect. 3, 1, 3.

Drucker, Peter F. *Management: Tasks, Responsibilities, Practices* (New York: Harper & Row, 1974), 270–271.

Duenes, Deborah, and Hermelin, Francine. "Sexual Harassment Inc.," *Working Woman*, October 1994, 9.

Kiechel III, Walter. "How to Discipline in the Modern Age," *Fortune*, May 7, 1990, 180.

Kleiman, Carol. "Employee Turnover a Bottom-Line Issue," *Chicago Tribune*, October 21, 1990, sect. 8, 1.

Ledvinka, James, and Scarpello, Vida G. *Federal Regulation of Personnel and Human Resource Management*, 2d ed. (Boston: PWS-Kent, 1991), 315–325.

Moskal, Brian S. "Sexual Harassment '80s-Style," *Industry Week*, July 2, 1989, 24.

Success! "Disciplining Employees with Dollars," April 1987, 25.

Suggested Readings

Bravo, Ellen, and Cassedy, Ellen. *The 9 to 5 Guide to Combating Sexual Harassment.* New York: John Wiley & Sons, 1992.

Campbell, David N., Fleming R. L., and Grote, Richard C. "Discipline Without Punishment—at Last." *Harvard Business Review* (July–August 1985): 162–178.

Ewing, David W. *Justice on the Job.* Boston: Harvard Business School Press, 1989.

Grothe, Mardy, and Wylie, Peter. *Problem Bosses.* New York: Facts on File, 1987.

Leap, Terry L., and Crino, Michael D. "How to Deal with Bizarre Employee Behavior." *Harvard Business Review* (May–June 1986): 18–22.

Ledvinka, James, and Scarpello, Vida G. *Federal Regulation of Personnel and Human Resource Management,* 2d ed. Boston: PWS-Kent, 1991.

1993-94 Human Resource Guide. Englewood Cliffs, N.J.: Bureau of Business Practice, Simon & Schuster, 1993.

Pell, Arthur R. *The Supervisor's Infobank.* New York: McGraw-Hill, Inc., 1994.

P A R T   I V

SPECIAL CONCERNS

CHAPTER 15   COMPLAINTS, GRIEVANCES, AND THE
             UNION

CHAPTER 16   SECURITY, SAFETY, AND HEALTH

Part IV contains an in-depth look at two areas that are of special concern for supervisors: dealing with employee dissatisfaction in both union and nonunion environments and protecting against several different kinds of hazards.

Dealing with worker complaints in a union or nonunion environment is the topic of Chapter 15. It outlines the major prohibitions on union and management conduct as set forth in the most important pieces of federal labor legislation. A step-by-step process is included to help you deal with worker grievances in both small and large organizations. Through the discussion in this chapter, you will find that there are far more factors at work to bring labor and management together than there are to drive them apart.

Chapter 16 covers security of physical facilities, as well as preventing and coping with work-related accidents, illnesses, and injuries. Various steps, checklists, and procedures are outlined and included to help supervisors with these important duties. The essentials of the federal Occupational Safety and Health Act (OSHA) and its inspection procedures are explained in this chapter.

Complaints, Grievances, and the Union

OBJECTIVES

After reading and discussing this chapter, you should be able to do the following:

1.   Define this chapter's key terms.

2.   List the five steps for handling complaints, and comment about what happens in each.

3.   List four prohibitions of the Wagner Act.

4.   List four prohibitions of the Taft-Hartley Act.

5.   Compare the roles of supervisors and stewards in labor relations.

6.   Outline typical grievance procedures for a large organization and a small organization.

INTRODUCTION

This chapter discusses the proper ways of dealing with the complaints of employees. First, we take up how to handle complaints you might encounter in a company where there is no union. Next, we discuss briefly what unions are and why workers join them. Finally, we learn how complaints are handled in a company where there is a union contract.

COMPLAINTS

complaint

any expression of unhappiness with working conditions or on-the-job relationships that comes to a manager's attention

For our purposes, a **complaint** is any expression of unhappiness with working conditions or on-the-job relationships that comes to a manager's attention. Complaints may be based on a worker's assumption that he or she has been treated unfairly or inequitably. Complaints often begin with a worker's perception that he or she has been or is being treated differently from others in similar circumstances.

Complaints may involve (1) objects that can be seen and touched (the switch is broken, or the machine needs adjustment), (2) sensory experiences other than touch and sight (the ventilation is poor in here, or the office is too noisy), or (3) nonsensory situations (my pay is too low, or they do not reward experience around here). Complaints that fall into the first of these categories are easily dealt with by personal observations and inspection. Each complaint is either true or not true and offers little difficulty in resolution. The other two types of complaints are different, however, since they are difficult to pin down and verify.

A complaint may be a symptom of a very different problem from the one it seems to state. The worker may be complaining about his or her level of pay or job classification, but the real issue may be dissatisfaction with the job—even though the worker may feel that more pay or a higher job classification would make the job more bearable. Therefore, even after a careful explanation of why a certain level of pay goes with the labor grade, the worker will remain dissatisfied because the real problem has not yet been dealt with.

Handling Complaints:
A Companywide Systems Approach

Most companies have a recommended or required set of procedures to follow when a supervisor, team leader or team facilitator is confronted with employee complaints. Typically, the first step is to identify the true nature of a compliant and what problem, challenge, or opportunity it poses for an individual or group. This involves getting the facts and differing perspectives from all those affecting or affected by a complaint. Once a complaint is accurately stated, a cause or causes for it—a rule, policy, people prob-

lems, or a change of some kind—need to be discovered. If corrective action of some kind is warranted, the complaining employee is asked what he or she views as an adequate remedy. Alternative courses of action are listed and considered as well, in line with company policies and precedents that may apply to the situation. The persons best situated and equipped to provide a remedy are involved in any solution determination and must see to it that the issues are dealt with effectively. Prompt action is usually called for, and the results must be evaluated to determine if the complaint has been satisfactorily resolved.

Qualities of an Effective Complaint System   Companies that have designed formal complaint systems usually try to make them accessible, safe, and credible. An accessible system gives employees a number of options. Things such as complaint hotlines, personnel counselors, complaint committees, and in-house surveys and suggestion systems are designed and made available. A safe system guarantees anonymous or confidential access to those who can help. It forbids reprisals against complainers and takes punitive action when reprisals do occur. A credible system assures complainers of a fair and objective hearing from truly neutral parties who have power to investigate and to recommend possible sources of action and ways to proceed (Rowe and Baker, 1984).

If a complaint system is to be effective—providing those who have complaints with a safe, credible, and just hearing and an objective resolution—it must guarantee the supervisors of complaining employees that their sensible decisions will be supported by higher-ups and that they will have a face-saving way out of their improper decisions regarding complaints. It must encourage the complainer and that person's supervisor to take up complaints initially and to pursue them jointly to an equitable solution. Finally, it must remove the common sources of fear in employees so that the system will be used and will function properly (Rowe and Baker, 1984).

If employees believe that their complaint will not get a fair hearing, or if they fear the system or the act of complaining or its consequences, they can become negative influences at work. Some turn hostile to management. Others waste time, infect others with negative attitudes, and actively work to harm their companies. Do what you can to remove employee fears and encourage your people to air their complaints. Accept the complaints of employees as a fact of working life and as a chance to mold better employees and working environments.

The Five Functions of an Effective Complaint System Effective complaint systems have the following five functions (Rowe and Baker, 1984):

1. Personal communication with individuals: anonymous and confidential ways to seek accurate information
2. Confidential counseling with individuals: people with authority and professional training who are available to help parties define problems and determine ways to find solutions
3. Investigation, conciliation, and mediation: experts who can help determine facts and encourage the parties to reach agreement on what is needed to resolve complaints
4. Adjudication: a person or group with the powers needed to render a decision or judgment when the parties to a complaint cannot agree on a resolution
5. Upward feedback: people and methods to keep management informed about employee concerns, complaints, and the resolutions of them

Exhibit 15.1 identifies the various people, methods, and devices (structures) used by companies with formal complaint systems to achieve these five functions. Spend time with this table, and identify which functions you can execute and which structures you have available.

Handling Complaints: Developing Your Own Approach

Even if you are not fortunate enough to work in an environment that has instituted the preceding system for handling complaints, you still must

Functions / Typical Structures	Communication with individuals (may be on a confidential basis)	Counseling with Individuals (may be on a confidential basis)	Investigation, Conciliation, and Mediation	Adjudication	Upward Feedback: Management Information
Line supervision	●	●	●	●	●
Personnel/human resources/employee relations	●	●	●	●	●
Multistep appeal systems			●	●	●
Equal opportunity counselors	●	●	●		●
Open-door investigators	●	●	●		●
Ombuds practitioners	●	●	●		●
Work problems counselors	●	●	●		●
In-plant counselors	●	●	●		●
Communications managers	●	●	●		●
Employee coordinators	●	●	●		●
Employee councils					●
Advisory boards					●
Suggestion-processing committees	●				●
Standing working groups			●		●
Jobholders' meetings	●				●
Skip-level meetings	●				●
Managers out on plant floor	●		●	●	●
Question lines (telephone)	●				●
Question boxes	●				●
Question columns in in-house publications	●				●
Attitude surveys					●
Employee audits					●
Employee assistance		●			●
Employee networks	●	●			●
Health and safety committees			●		●
Mentoring systems	●	●			
Nursing and medical offices		●			
Performance appraisal systems	●	●			●
Policy advisory committees					●
Quality circles					●
Product safety and liability committees					●

EXHIBIT 15.1

Typical structures and functions in complaint systems.

*Data usually offered in the aggregate to protect confidentiality and privacy.

Source: Reprinted by permission of *Harvard Business Review.* An exhibit from "Are You Hearing Enough Employee Concerns?" by Mary P. Rowe and Michael Baker, *Harvard Business Review* (May–June 1984). Copyright © 1984 by the President and Fellows of Harvard College. All rights reserved.

deal with them—and more or less on your own. What follows can help you formulate your own approach. Keep in mind that you want to include as many of the aforementioned qualities and functions as you can.

To begin with, your attitude toward the complaints of your subordinates or team members should be to treat them seriously. Your subordinates think that their complaints have merit; they would not bring them to your attention if they believed otherwise. Complaints may come to your attention indirectly through overheard conversations or through uninvolved third parties. In such cases, an investigation is warranted to determine if there is true substance to them. Watch for any sudden changes in established patterns of behavior; these often indicate an unexpressed complaint exists. If complaints are not dealt with as soon as they are discovered, situations worsen and the damage can spread quickly to other persons or teams.

An open-door policy (letting subordinates know that you are available and eager to discuss their problems) can prevent problems from getting out of hand. If your people feel that you care about them, will act swiftly, and have sound judgment, you will find them willing to air their irritations and observations. This can only come about, however, after you have established solid human relations with them individually and in groups. If you hear complaints only through the grapevine, your people are probably fearful and at least reluctant to bring their complaints to you first-hand. This means that they may either distrust your judgment or willingness to hear and deal with their complaints effectively. Find out what is preventing open, honest communications, and then go to work on the problems.

Your four roles of educator, counselor, judge, and spokesperson come into play in handling complaints. As an educator, you teach the essentials for success on the job. Retraining or additional training may be needed to remove the cause of a task-related complaint. As a counselor, you should be experienced enough to know where to send someone with a complaint that you cannot resolve. As a judge of your employees' performances and behaviors, you are able to appraise their efforts, formally and informally, discovering and dealing with their complaints as you do so. As a spokesperson, you can represent the complaining subordinates to higher or outside authorities in order to seek fair treatment of their complaints.

A Recommended Approach

The steps that follow will help you deal effectively with your subordinates' complaints. You should find them useful if your company does not have prescribed complaint procedures.

1. Listen to the complaint. Determine its causes and the complainer's feelings and motives. Be prepared to give the complaining subordinate your undivided attention. If the complainer's timing is not right

for you, set up an appointment as soon as you can for your discussion.

Remain calm. If the complainer is agitated and emotional, you should be the opposite. You cannot counsel effectively unless you are in control of yourself and the situation. Try to uncover what the complainer is thinking and feeling by allowing him or her to verbalize his or her feelings and motives. But avoid passing judgment. What you are after is the other person's perceptions, not your own. Take notes, and reserve your opinions and facts for later in the meeting.

By listening attentively and drawing people out, you may find that what began as the major complaint gradually slips away as the real and underlying issue comes to the surface. When that happens, you will have hit pay dirt. It may be the first time that the workers were able to express what was really on their minds. Gradually, all the facts will emerge in your subordinates' words, and the problem will come into focus. Then and only then can it be intelligently resolved.

Remember that people frequently just want to talk with someone about their problems. By talking, they are expressing confidence in you and showing respect for your opinion. Often, the workers know that the solution to their difficulty is beyond either their control or yours. In discussing such a situation, we often find a clarity and perspective that is almost impossible to discover alone. The workers may come to realize that the problem is not as serious as they originally thought, or they may actually discover a solution as they attempt to explain their views.

2. Get the complainers' solutions. Once your subordinates have talked themselves out, and you feel that you know the real issues, ask them for their solutions. What would they do if they were in your shoes? What do they think would be a fair disposition of their complaint? What you want to know is what they think will make them happy. If it is within your power to grant such a solution, and if you believe it to be a wise one, then do so. If you need more information or wish to check out their side of the story, defer your answer, and give them a specific time for receiving it.

Try to find mutually beneficial solutions that will leave you both better off. Seek a win–win situation where no meaningless compromises are necessary and where no one will have to think of himself or herself as a loser.

3. Make a decision and explain it. Before you can make a decision, you need to consider who is best qualified to make it. If it is yours to make and you have all the facts you need, give your subordinate your decision and the reasons for it. If higher authorities are involved, identify them. If rules, policy, or procedures are involved, explain their meanings and their applicability to the situation. Your subordinate may not receive the answer that he or she was looking for, but he or she will know that you have done your homework.

4. Explain how to appeal. If your workers are dissatisfied with your decision and want to pursue the matter further, tell them how to do so. Let them know whom they should see and how they can make an appointment. If your workers decide to appeal your decision, you should not hold that action against them, and you should let them know that you do not.

5. Follow up. Regardless of the outcome, it is sound management practice to get back to the people who have made a complaint within a reasonable time after its resolution. Assess their present attitudes, and make it clear that you want your people to come to you with their complaints. Be sure you keep a record of any proceedings for future reference.

By being sincere, listening attentively, asking exploratory questions, and acting on each complaint promptly, you will minimize conflicts and reduce barriers to productivity and cooperation.

MAINTAINING A NONUNION ENVIRONMENT

Fred K. Foulkes (1981), professor of management at Boston University's School of Management, has studied the twenty-six largest nonunion industrialized companies in the United States to determine their common attributes, attitudes, and policies. The results are shown in Exhibit 15.2. Together they summarize a strong management concern for employees.

The Honda of America plant at East Liberty, Ohio, does well without a union. Management and workers cooperate for the good of all.

1. A sense of caring. Top management's commitment to employees is demonstrated not only symbolically but also through certain policies and practices. Hewlett-Packard, for example, is committed to job security, innovative training programs, promotion from within through job posting, cash profit sharing, an attractive stock purchase plan, widely granted stock options, and flexible working hours.

2. Carefully considered surroundings. Several situational factors are also important both in fostering an effective personnel program and in encouraging a climate of trust and confidence. These factors include, among others, plant location and size and the handling of sensitive work and particular employee groups.

3. High profits, fast growth, and family ties. Certain financial and ownership characteristics seem to have an important bearing on personnel policies. Most of the companies studied are profitable—some extremely so. Many are high-technology growth businesses, have dominant market positions, and are leaders in their industries. Growth enables them to offer many promotion opportunities, provide full employment, and make profit sharing pay off. Another important company characteristic is close ties between ownership and management.

4. Employment security. Many of these companies attempt to minimize workers' usual nagging uncertainty regarding future employment. . . . methods of weathering peaks and troughs in the work load including hiring freezes and the use of temporary or retired workers. . . . Permitting employees to bank their vacation time can also ensure some flexibility in lean times.

5. Promotion from within. A policy of promoting from within—accompanied by training, education, career counseling, and (frequently) job posting—is most attractive when a company's growth rate opens up many advancement opportunities.

6. Influential personnel departments. Not only are the personnel departments of the companies studied usually extremely centralized, they also have access to and in many cases are part of top management.

7. Competitive pay and benefits. As might be expected, the twenty-six companies in my sample work hard to ensure that employees perceive their pay and benefits policies as equitable. All of them, therefore, compensate their employees at least as well as their unionized competitors do.

8. Managements that listen. The companies studied use a variety of mechanisms to learn employees' views on various matters. Attitude surveys take the temperature of the organization and expose developing employee concerns. Some companies regularly conduct sensing sessions, or random interviews to understand employees' sentiments.

9. Careful grooming of managers. Managers in these companies know that effective management of people is an important part of their jobs. Many of the companies studied avoid bonuses that reward short-term performance. Instead, they emphasize long-term results, including successful employee relations.

EXHIBIT 15.2

Nine common attributes, attitudes, and policies of twenty-six large nonunion industrialized companies.

Source: From Fred K. Foulkes, "How Top Nonunion Companies Manage Employees," *Harvard Business Review* (September–October 1981). Copyright © 1981 by the President and Fellows of Harvard College. All rights reserved.

Managers at every level have more flexibility to try the new and different. There is no adversarial relationship between managers and workers; rather, there is a strong climate of cooperation between the two groups.

LABOR UNIONS

So far in this chapter, we have discussed handling complaints in companies where there is no union. We now shift to companies that are unionized. Before considering complaint resolution in unionized companies, however, we need to take a brief look at unions in the United States.

union

a group of workers who are employed by a company or an industry or who practice the same skilled craft and have banded together to bargain collectively with their employers

A labor **union** consists of a group of workers who are employed by a company or an industry or who are practicing the same skilled craft and have banded together to bargain collectively with employers for improvements in their wages, hours, fringe benefits, and working conditions. Craft or trade unions are composed of workers in the same skilled occupation. For example, the International Brotherhood of Electrical Workers (IBEW) is a union organized to represent skilled craftspersons. Industrial unions include all workers in a company or an industry, regardless of their specific occupations. The United Auto Workers (UAW) and the United Food and Commercial Workers are two examples of industrial unions.

According to figures from the federal Bureau of Labor Statistics, about 15.8 percent of American workers belonged to 247 unions in 1993 (an additional 1.9 percent are covered by union contracts but do not have union membership). This represents a decline of nearly 25 percent in

Workers join unions in an effort to gain bargaining power against management. As the focus of management has changed to become more people oriented, unions have begun to decline in popularity.

union membership—a loss of about 5 percent of American workers from unions' ranks since 1983. Here are the major reasons behind this decline:

- The number of persons working in the traditionally unionized areas (blue-collar or manufacturing jobs) has steadily declined or experienced no growth as the workforce has grown.
- The primary growth areas in our economy contain vast numbers of jobs that are traditionally nonunion.
- Industry jobs have moved offshore and to the South and Southwest, traditionally nonunion areas.
- Workers have shown a trend to decertify their unions, moving from unionized to nonunionized status.
- Many of the foreign-owned companies that have come to America to establish production facilities have created nonunion workforces.
- Enlightened, people-focused enterprises have created work environments built on trust, mutual respect, and genuine concern for the welfare of their employees, removing major causes of why unions form.

Unions are still a force, both political and economic, in our economy. They have achieved some success in replacing their lost blue-collar employees with white-collar, service, and professional employees. Increasingly, unions have become partners with management, working to remove barriers to productivity and to quality. They have done so out of necessity to preserve employment opportunities for their members. They have shown a willingness to trade restrictive work rules and past economic gains for job security.

Employee Associations

In addition to the growing number of white-collar workers in unions, about 2.6 million Americans belonged to **employee associations** in 1993. Salaried and professional employees have traditionally resisted attempts to unionize them, but this reluctance has diminished in recent years. Government employees, nurses, teachers, and university professors have increasingly turned toward collective bargaining through the formation of employee associations. These associations differ from unions primarily because they lack the legal right to strike. Although these groups have occasionally struck in major cities such as New York, Chicago, and San Francisco, they usually do not have the legal right to do so and frequently have been ordered back to work through court orders. According to the AFL-CIO, a confederation of our country's largest unions representing about 13.2 million people, the largest employee associations are the following:

- National Education Association
- New York State Employee Association

employee association a group that bargains collectively with management but has given up or has been barred from the right to strike

SUPERVISORS AND ETHICS

The percentage of American working women in unions is around 14 percent, about what it has been for nearly thirty years. Women are currently poorly represented in the ranks of union leaders and organizers, but some 7.2 million members of the AFL-CIO's 14 million members are female.

A recent report released by a United Nations agency, the International Labor Organization, concludes that women, when given the choice, want to vote for and join unions more than men do. This may be partly because the majority of women are employed in service-sector jobs, which usually pay the least. The report urges unions to organize more women workers and to give them more authority: "Increasing women's leadership at all levels, from the work site to the international presidencies, is the key to realizing the traditional values of unions, women's improvement of their work and home lives, and unions' growth and strength."

Although over the past ten years unions have been most successful in organizing businesses that employ many women, according to Susan C. Eaton, author of the UN report, traditional union leadership has long believed that women were "'less organizable' than men—supposedly because they were not committed [to] long-term [employment] or were not full-time members of the labor force." These assumptions are no longer true.

Eaton believes that unionized female employees find a collective voice through their unions that can be used to create change and deal with key issues such as the glass ceiling (policies and practices that inhibit the advancement of protected groups), the disparity between earnings for men and women in similar jobs, and sexual harassment at work.

Source: Randle, Wilma. "Study Calls on Sagging Unions to Recruit, Promote Women," *Chicago Tribune*, February 12, 1993, sect. 3, 1, 3.

- American Nurses Association
- Fraternal Order of Police
- California State Employee Association
- American Postal Workers Union
- National Association of Letter Carriers
- American Federation of Government Employees

About 40 percent of America's public service employees belong to employee associations. In 1962, President Kennedy signed Executive Order 10988, which required federal agencies to recognize and bargain with the associations that represented a majority of their employees, as determined by secret-ballot elections. Executive Order 11491, issued by President Nixon, further encouraged and improved collective bargaining rights for federal employees. In 1981, President Reagan fired 11,000 air-traffic controllers from our nation's airport control towers for taking a strike action, something they are forbidden by federal law to do. President Clinton signed an executive order in 1994 allowing the federal government to rehire those fired employees.

Replacing Striking Workers   Since 1938, companies experiencing strikes have been legally entitled to replace striking workers with permanent new hires. The practice was not widespread until the 1980s, when Phelps Dodge and Continental Airlines broke their unions by hiring nonunion replacements for their striking employees. In 1989, the Supreme Court ruled 6–3 that striking workers are not legally entitled to get their jobs back once their positions have been filled by nonstrikers. In 1990, Greyhound began hiring replacement drivers even before its negotiations with the Amalgamated Transit Union were at an impasse. After a bitter and long strike, thousands of drivers for Greyhound had no jobs to return to. More recently, Bridgestone-Firestone has engaged in this practice along with the Caterpillar Corporation (1994–1995). The increasing use of this tactic by companies has discouraged several unions from striking, agreeing instead to continue talking once the contract runs out.

Why Employees Band Together

Workers join employee associations and unions for many reasons. They want equity, job security, more pay, and better benefits. By banding together, they improve their bargaining position with employers and are better able to avoid unfair and discriminatory treatment.

Better Bargaining Position   Compared with their employers, individuals have little bargaining power. A company can simply make an offer on a take-it-or-leave-it basis or make no offer at all. The employee is free to say yes or no. The individual's bargaining power rests on his or her ability to refuse to accept an employment offer or to quit when dissatisfied. But where all the employees at a company in a trade or department bargain as one with the employer, the business would have to shut down or operate under severe handicaps if the whole group of workers were to strike.

Fair and Uniform Treatment   Pay raises, transfers, promotions, and eligibility requirements for company training programs can be quite arbitrary without union checks on management's prerogatives. Favoritism and discrimination can influence these decisions, resulting in inequities with little hope for appeal. Unions have increasingly pushed for a greater reliance on uniform published procedures when management makes such decisions; thus, there is a heavy reliance on seniority provisions when management is firing, promoting, and the like. The best man or woman may not always get the benefit, but objectivity will bear on the decision. Workers are constantly trying to protect themselves and their financial futures from insecurity.

One of our most basic needs is for safety and security. Safer working conditions have been brought about through union demands and through state and federal legislation. Fringe benefits such as insurance and pension plans are major examples of unions' quests for greater security for their members.

Union Security Provisions

Unions have fought for years to win recognition from employers. They want to increase their strength by requiring all employees to belong to a union once it is recognized as their legitimate bargaining agent. In an election for certification, a union may win by only a slim majority. Those workers who voted against it may not be willing to join the union voluntarily. To counter this resistance, various types of shop agreements have been formulated and won through favorable legislation and collective bargaining.

With a union shop agreement, all current employees must join the union as soon as it is certified as their legitimate bargaining agent. Newcomers have to join after a specified probationary period—normally thirty days. The majority of union contracts with employers call for a union shop. The union shop is illegal in the twenty states that have enacted right-to-work laws—so named for granting people the right to work with or without membership in a union.

In a modified union shop, employees may elect not to join the union that is representing an employer's employees. Part-time employees, students in work-study programs, and people employed before a specified date may refuse to join. At the same time that the modified union shop is won through collective bargaining, all members who belong to the union must remain members or lose their jobs. Nonmembers at that time may refuse to join.

In a maintenance-of-membership shop, employees who voluntarily join a union must remain in the union during the lifetime of the labor agreement with an employer. The agreement also may provide an escape period during which those who wish to do so may drop their memberships (Chruden and Sherman, 1980).

Employees do not have to belong to the union under an agency shop, but they must pay a fee to the union. The reason for this is that union negotiations benefit all employees—members and nonmembers alike. Since all employees benefit, each should pay his or her share of the costs of winning those benefits.

In an open shop, membership in the elected union is voluntary for all existing and new employees. Individuals who decide not to join the union do not have to pay any dues to the union.

A closed shop requires an employer to hire only union members. This kind of shop is forbidden by the Taft-Hartley Act (described later in this chapter), but it does exist because of hiring practices in many skilled-craft areas. If a construction company needs skilled tradespeople, it will generally contact a union's hiring hall to fill its employment needs.

LABOR LEGISLATION

From Colonial days until the 1930s, unions and employee associations were prosecuted and banned by the courts as illegal conspiracies in restraint of trade. Courts uniformly held, in case after case, that these groups of employees wrongfully interfered with the right of employers to run their businesses as they saw fit. Nearly every employee hired during this period accepted as a condition of employment that he or she would not join a union or engage in union activities. A worker who did join was considered to have breached the contract of employment and was subject to immediate dismissal.

In the 1890s, an additional burden was placed on unions by their inclusion under the provisions of the Sherman Antitrust Act (1890) and related antimonopoly legislation. Courts took the position that unions might be considered monopolistic, and their efforts at collective bargaining were viewed as attempts to interfere with a free-market mechanism. This was the first instance in U.S. history that any federal law dealt with the rights of workers to bargain collectively with their employers. Actually, the Sherman Act did not specifically state that unions were monopolistic, but its wording was so general that unions could be (and were) construed to fall under its provisions. In 1914, however, the Clayton Act removed unions from the jurisdiction of antitrust laws.

Norris-LaGuardia Act (1932)

Further relief came in 1932 with the enactment of the Norris-LaGuardia Act, which severely restricted the use of court orders (injunctions) against organized labor engaged in labor disputes with employees. It also outlawed the use of yellow-dog contracts, by which employees were forced to agree not to join a union. Except in the railroad industry, no laws required an employer to recognize an employees' union or prevented an employer from starting a company union. Employers began to require that new employees join the company union, which was controlled by the management and operated for its benefit. The union leaders achieved for their members only the benefits that management wanted them to.

SUPERVISORS AND QUALITY

In recent years, nonunionized steel-producing minimills (Nucor is but one example) have gradually taken market share from their larger, unionized rivals. They produce speciality products at lower costs with later, more efficient technology and are not saddled with the larger mills' rigid job definitions—about thirty different types—and wages and benefits about $32 per hour. Many unions in several industries have traded wages, benefits, and work-rule changes for a share in corporate ownership. A few, like the United Airlines' unions (except the 17,000 flight attendants), have traded wage and benefit concessions in exchange for equity (in United's case, 55 percent) in their companies. In 1994, the United Steelworkers (USW) "formed what amounts to a joint venture with a New York investment group to buy two high-cost plants that Bethlehem Steel Corp. shut down in 1992. The union agreed to flexible work rules and minimill-like pay scales that are only half what union members make at integrated mills. In return, workers at the new company, called BRW Steel Corp., get a 25% equity stake and two seats on the board of directors—plus 800 jobs...[by 1997]."

USW is currently working on a similar plan to purchase the now closed Sharon Steel Corporation. At BRW Steel, which won't be operational until 1997, wages and benefits will average $16 per hour, and only five job types will exist.

Workers at BRW will have to learn many tasks and will be trained to perform in several jobs. The buyout terms were a bargain—the mills were purchased for about one-twentieth their initial costs—and the states of Pennsylvania and New York are contributing over $50 million in "low-interest loans to modernize them." When up and running, the new company should be able to "undercut its competitors by as much as 25%."

One major problem results for the union with this buyout. The BRW wages and job categories, along with past precedents of givebacks on work rules and linking pay to production, could become the model for bargaining at the larger unionized mills. Says Pennsylvania's commerce secretary, Andrew Greenberg, the union "had to make a leap of faith to embrace the work practices and cost structures of the minimills..." in order to survive as a viable union.

Source: Alexander, Keith L., and Baker, Stephen. "If You Can't Beat 'Em, Buy 'Em," *Business Week*, October 24, 1994, 80–81; Ziemba, Stanley. "Buyout, Demand for Seats Get United Results Off Ground," *Chicago Tribune*, January 25, 1995, sect. 3, 1

The Norris-LaGuardia Act did not attack the practice of blacklisting, nor did it forbid the discharge of employees for union activities. Companies were still in control, and by locking their employees out of their shops (lockouts), they could outlast, in most cases, the workers' enthusiasm for unionization. Since many workers lived on subsistence wages, they could not hold out for very long.

National Labor Relations Act (1935)

As the Great Depression dragged on, Congress began to analyze its causes and soon realized that the mass impoverishment of so many workers had been a significant factor. To achieve a balance of power between labor and management, the National Labor Relations Act (often called the Wagner Act) was passed as one of the measures of the New Deal. It has often been referred to as organized labor's Magna Carta (great charter or birth certificate) because it guaranteed the rights of unions to exist. It gave the individual worker the right to join a union without fear of persecution by his or her employer. In the words of Section 7 of the act:

> employees shall have the right to self-organization, to form, join, or assist labor organizations, to bargain collectively through representatives of their own choosing, and to engage in concerted activities for the purpose of collective bargaining or other mutual aid or protection.

The Wagner Act also listed as unfair practices the following management activities by employers:

- Restraining employees from joining a union
- Contributing financially to or interfering in any way with union operations
- Discriminating in any way against a worker because of his or her union affiliation
- Punishing union members who reported management violations of the act
- Refusing to bargain in good faith with a duly elected union of their employees

The second and third prohibitions are most significant to supervisors. These provisions have been interpreted as forbidding management from making threats or promises of financial gain to employees who are considering union affiliation or who are about to engage in an election to determine a bargaining agent.

The Wagner Act also established the National Labor Relations Board (NLRB), consisting of five members appointed by the president of the United States and empowered to investigate alleged violations of the act and to oversee elections to determine a bargaining unit. Its decisions have the power of law and bind both unions and employers. The Wagner Act was challenged in the courts, but it was declared constitutional by the Supreme Court. It was so prolabor, however, that it eventually had to be amended to curb some of the labor excesses it helped create.

Legality of Cooperative Work Teams   In December 1992, the National Labor Relations Board ruled that the worker–management teams at Electromation Inc. of Elkhart, Indiana, were illegal. The Board voted 4–0 that the company's teams "constitute a 'labor organization' and violate the National Labor Relations Act provision against setting up company-run unions" (Salwen, 1992). This ruling upheld an administrative law judge's earlier ruling that the company's teams were "sham unions." The teams (called action committees) existed in a nonunion environment, consisted of both workers and one or more managers, and dealt with work rules and compensation issues (Salwen, 1992).

The Board's ruling seems to indicate that such teams can be legal when they do not interfere with (in a union environment) or substitute for (in both union and nonunion environments) collective bargaining on such traditional issues as wages, hours, and working conditions. But the issue remains somewhat cloudy and may be further resolved with a case before the Board involving unionized workers in teams at Du Pont Company. The Clinton administration, through Labor Secretary Robert Reich, is committed to keeping cooperative teams legal.

Labor-Management Relations Act (1947)

During the years between the passage of the Wagner Act and the end of World War II, this country witnessed phenomenal growth in union membership and also in abuses of union power. Organized labor grew from about 4 million members in 1935 to about 15 million (35 percent of the workforce) by 1947. Unions were becoming a powerful force and were exercising financial and economic power that was almost totally unchecked. Postwar strikes threatened the economy. Whereas management's hands had been tied, organized labor's hands had not.

Congress again felt compelled to balance the two forces. Despite the protests of labor and a veto of the bill by President Truman, it passed the Labor-Management Relations Act, usually called the Taft-Hartley Act. The act was intended to curb many of the abuses that organized labor had been guilty of in the 1930s. It amended the Wagner Act to include a list of provisions against specific practices by unions:

1. Workers could not be coerced to join or not to join a union.
2. The closed shop was prohibited.
3. Unions were required to bargain in good faith.

Unions are struggling to find a new identity and to adjust their philosophies to meet several challenges: the rise in white-collar (traditionally nonunion) employment along with the decline in traditional union jobs, the threats to their members' wages and jobs from nonunion and foreign competition, and their poor public image. Throughout the 1980s, America's largest unions watched their memberships shrink along with hard-won benefits and wage levels. In response, unions bargained to increase members' employment and job security and gave employers concessions on work rules and monetary issues.

In the 1990s, many unions are shifting from a passive mode and becoming more active. Union leaders realize that they must act in employees' best interests and cooperate to make them more competitive and productive. Lynn Williams, president of the United Steelworkers of America, puts it this way: "When it comes to dividing up the pie, we'll be adversaries. But now we have to grow the pie, and that means working together [labor–management cooperation]." The following methods seem to work and are growing in popularity:

1. Work rules are made less restrictive through collective bargaining—more union members can take on more duties, giving them and management more flexibility.
2. Concessions affect such areas as over-time and vacation pay, not regular wages.
3. Union members and their leadership now approve of joint efforts—teams and committees—designed to improve quality and productivity and to deal with additional issues. Such groups may not be used in lieu of, or as substitutes for, regular collective bargaining, and worker appointments to these groups are usually under union control.

In exchange, unions want more open communication with management, demanding data on costs and profits. Employment security has become the most important issue for the membership, usually guaranteed to some extent for the life of a collective bargaining agreement.

One model for this new labor–management cooperation is the Xerox experience. During the 1980s, the company lost market share to foreign competitors, and it closed factories. Its union, the clothing workers, met with management and set up teams to find ways to improve productivity and quality. It exchanged concessions on temporary workers and on management's right to fire employees (for excessive absences) for member job security during the life of the then-current labor contract.

The results of cooperative efforts have been outstanding. Absenteeism has dropped "from 8.5 percent to 2.5 percent." When 240 jobs were threatened by a proposed closing of a wire harness production facility, workers formed a team that identified means to cut $3.5 million in costs and saved those jobs.

Another team worked up a bid that resulted in the in-house manufacture of parts previously provided by outsiders. These joint union–management efforts have allowed the company to add about 1,700 production jobs and have made Xerox more profitable and competitive.

Source: Nulty, Peter. "Look What the Unions Want Now," *Fortune,* February 8, 1993, 128–130, 132, 135.

4. Complex restrictions were placed on certain kinds of strikes and boycotts. The secondary boycott, by which the union forces an employer to stop dealing with or purchasing from another company not directly involved in a labor dispute, was prohibited. (A primary boycott is the union's refusal to deal with a company with which it does have a labor dispute.) Also prohibited were jurisdictional strikes, which were designed to force an employer to give work to one union rather than to another.

5. Unions could not charge their members excessively high initiation fees.

6. Employers were not required to pay for services not performed (featherbedding).

The Taft-Hartley Act also gives management the right to sue a union for violating collective bargaining agreements. Other provisions require unions to make annual disclosures of their financial records and allow states to enact right-to-work laws "which make union security agreements, such as union shops and agency shops, illegal" (Joel, 1993).

An emergency provision in the Taft-Hartley Act allows the president of the United States, through the attorney general's office, to seek a court order to stop a strike or lockout that threatens the nation's general health or welfare. The court's order can last for up to eighty days. During this cooling-off period, the federal government attempts to mediate the disputes that are separating the parties. The National Labor Relations Board can hold a secret-ballot vote among the striking or locked-out union members after the injunction is sixty days old to see if the company's latest offer is acceptable.

Representation Elections

The National Labor Relations Board (NLRB) has established procedures that must be followed by both management and workers when the latter express their desire to be represented by a union. The certification process (the process of getting the NLRB to certify a particular union as the legitimate bargaining agent for employees) begins when at least 30 percent of the workers sign authorization cards calling for a union to represent them. Then the workers can ask the NLRB to schedule a representation (certification) election.

Once the NLRB determines that the company falls within its jurisdiction (some companies may have too small a sales volume), it must determine how to form appropriate bargaining units. Separate unions may be called for to represent such groups as general service and maintenance workers, office and clerical workers, and technicians. An election for each will then be scheduled and conducted by NLRB representatives. Once the election is held, the results tabulated, and the disputes settled, the NLRB certifies a bargaining agent. The employer is then obligated to enter into negotiations with the certified union toward a collective bargaining agreement. On average, about 3,500 certification elections are sponsored each year by the NLRB, and about 1,500 are won by unions (Franklin, 1993).

The effort by employees to get rid of their bargaining agent (union) works in the same way as the process of obtaining such an agent. Decertification, as it is called, first requires 30 percent of the bargaining agent's members to call for a decertification election. On average, about 420 decertification elections have resulted in the successful shedding of a union each year (Franklin, 1993).

The Supervisor's Role During Representation Elections

Your job is the same as any other manager's during employee certification or decertification elections: Remain neutral and preserve an atmosphere in which workers can express their uninhibited choices. In general, do nothing that is not expressly okayed by higher management. Do not express your opinions—pro or con—toward unions or union membership by your subordinates. Make no threats, and make no promises. Do not give or announce any increases in pay or benefits just before or during representation elections unless the increases are totally unrelated to the election campaigns.

You may point out to workers the economic costs that are connected to union membership. Such costs include the dues paid to support union officers and activities, the costs of processing employee complaints through the union contract's complaint procedures, and the costs connected with strikes that take people off the payroll. You may also point out that both the union contract and its constitution place restrictions on workers. Rules and punishments are prescribed in both.

LABOR RELATIONS

The area of **labor relations** includes all the activities within a company that involve dealings with a union and its members, both individually and collectively. Specifically, two main areas are the most important and time consuming: **collective bargaining** (arriving at a contract that covers workers' wages, hours, and working conditions) and **grievance processing** (dealing with complaints that allege violations of the collective bargaining agreement).

Collective Bargaining

Bargaining collectively—the union representatives on one side of a table, management's representatives on the other—is the traditional way in

labor relations
management activities created by the fact that the organization has a union or unions to bargain with

collective bargaining
the process of negotiating a union agreement that covers wages, hours, and working conditions for employees who are union members

grievance processing
settling an alleged violation of the union–management agreement in accordance with the method outlined in that agreement

which labor disputes are settled and labor–management agreements are formed. Some time before the expiration date of a labor contract, the two groups begin a series of meetings that ultimately lead to the signing of a new agreement. Bargaining may take place on the local level, where only one local union and employer are involved, or on an industrywide basis, where the agreement sets the standard for the industry—as in the automotive and trucking industries.

The usual process involves a specialist in labor relations from the company's labor relations department (usually at the vice-presidential level) and the union's negotiating committee. Both sides employ labor lawyers who are well versed in the most recent developments in labor law and who help them hammer out specific contract provisions and wording.

Both sides bring to the bargaining a list of demands and, in their own minds, assign to each a priority that will become apparent as negotiations develop. Some demands are made merely to serve as trading material. Negotiating involves give and take, so each side must be prepared to bargain away some of its demands in order to obtain others.

Each side attempts to resolve the many minor issues as quickly as it can, reserving the major issues for the final meetings immediately preceding or following a strike. It is then that the pressure for a settlement is greatest. Ultimately, through compromises and trading, a new contract emerges. No one is anxious to be labeled a winner or a loser. Rather, both sides seek to improve their positions and eliminate problem areas that stand in the way of harmony and efficient output. The agreement is then offered to the union membership, who vote to accept or reject it. A simple majority vote is usually required.

The union contract with management spells out in rather precise terms the rights of workers with regard to wages, hours, and conditions of employment. It is a formal written document that both managers and union members must thoroughly understand. It can and does limit management's authority. Both parties must operate within the restrictions it lays down if they are to avoid costly and time-consuming work stoppages and disagreements. As always, outside experts stand ready to help supervisors and union members with interpretations of the contract.

Enforcing the Labor Contract

Enforcement of the terms of the agreement worked out through collective bargaining depends on communication of the contract provisions and of the demands they make on labor and management. Managers—especially those who direct workers—must be made aware of their rights and duties. Copies of the agreement are made available to each manager, along with an explanation that is easy to understand. Any questions that may arise in a manager's mind can quickly be answered by consultation with the personnel department and with labor relations officials.

The union also must make its members aware of their rights and duties. Copies of the contract are distributed to each member, and meetings are held locally to explain the contract's terms. At the plant and department levels, workers may turn to their union representatives for guidance in understanding the contract and in dealing with any alleged violations of it.

The Supervisor and the Steward

The **steward** is first of all an employee and a worker. He or she has the additional responsibilities of a union office because the union members have elected or appointed him or her. Stewards receive release time from work to carry out their duties. Exhibit 15.3 lists the differences and similarities that exist between the roles of supervisor and steward. More points draw them together than keep them apart.

Just as a supervisor is management's spokesperson, a steward is labor's spokesperson. He or she has the duty to represent workers in the

steward
the union's elected or appointed first-line representative in the areas in which workers are found

Supervisors	Stewards
Know the contract	Know the contract
Enforce the contract	Enforce the contract
Look out for the welfare of subordinates	Look out for the welfare of constituents
Are spokespersons for both management and subordinates	Are spokespersons for the union and constituents
Settle grievances fairly (in line with management's interpretation of the contract)	Settle grievances fairly (in line with union interpretation of the contract)
Keep abreast of grievance solutions and changes in contract interpretations	Keep abreast of grievance solutions and changes in contract interpretation
Maintain good working relationships with stewards	Maintain good working relationships with supervisors
Keep stewards informed about management's decisions and sources of trouble	Keep supervisors informed about union positions and sources of trouble
Protect management rights	Protect labor rights

EXHIBIT 15.3
The responsibilities of supervisors and stewards in labor relations.

early stages of the grievance process. The steward must be able to interpret the contract both to the supervisor and to fellow workers if he or she is to carry out the role intelligently. A worker's complaint usually cannot win the union's backing without the steward's consent.

Stewards, like managers, have a difficult and demanding position. They are workers and must conform to company standards or risk disciplinary action. On the other hand, they have the status of elected union officers who, if they wish to retain their posts, must be effective representatives of and counsels to their constituents. They may, therefore, feel a good deal of pressure to push complaints to grievance status, even when their own best judgment says they should not. In circumstances where there are few complaints or grievances, some stewards feel the need to dig for some issues or manufacture some discontent in order to justify their position and to prove that they are serving a useful purpose.

Just how stewards behave is largely an individual matter, influenced in part by their supervisors and by the kind of relationship they have. Where there is room for interpretation, stewards are bound to take the union's view, just as supervisors are bound to accept management's. Therein lies the stuff of which grievances are made.

Handling Grievances

When a worker is dissatisfied with a supervisor's disposition of a work-related complaint, he or she may appeal that decision by filing a formal charge called a **grievance**. All grievances allege that a violation has occurred to one or another of the provisions of the labor agreement. A complaint that is improperly handled can and usually does become a grievance. Managers should consider every gripe about wages, hours, and working conditions a potential grievance. Managers, as well as workers, can and do file grievances.

A grievance is not a personal attack on or an insult to a supervisor; it is a problem to be solved. The first thing you must do is keep calm and listen. Do not start an argument. Grievance discussions can become heated debates, and words may be said that will be regretted later. Grievances that are not properly settled in their early stages can grow into very costly and damaging disputes. Exhibit 15.4 contains do's and don'ts for you to follow while handling a grievance.

If the details of the grievance are not clear to you after you hear the complaining employee's case, ask questions. Find out the what, when, where, why, and how. Find out exactly what the person believes will make him or her happy and what provisions of the labor contract are involved.

Conduct your own investigation to determine whether or not the facts presented to you are complete and true. If they are not or if you are uncertain about any of them, list your questions, and gather the evidence needed to clarify the situation. If you are unsure about the proper interpreta-

grievance
an alleged violation of the labor-management agreement

Do's

- Begin by assuming that every complaint has merit.
- Give the grieving employee your time and listen carefully to each word.
- Identify the specific contractual wording that the grievance alleges was violated.
- Visually check out the location where the grievance supposedly took place.
- Interview every person who may have knowledge of the grievance, the parties to it, the event, the location, and the circumstances.
- After gathering all your facts, check out all past grievances that have a bearing on this one.
- Hold all your interviews and discussions with concerned parties in private.
- Before giving any answer to the grievance, touch base with your boss.
- Give your answer as completely as you can within any time limit prescribed by the union contract.
- Keep written records of all your findings, your interviews, and your answers.

Don'ts

- Settle any grievance outside the terms of the written contract.
- Engage in trading one grievance settlement for the withdrawal of another.
- Engage in bargaining over issues that are not part of the written contract.
- Agree to any changes in the precise wording of the contract.
- Fail to deliver any remedy endorsed by the parties as a settlement for the grievance.

tion or application of the specific language of the labor contract, seek counsel from the labor relations specialists.

If you determine that the grievance is without merit, give the worker and the steward your facts, your (management's) interpretation and application of the labor contract provisions, and your specific reasons for denying the grievance.

Your oral answer to the complaining employee may not be acceptable to him or her or to the steward. If it is not, your involvement may be far from ended. You will probably be given a written copy of the complaint and asked to spell out in specific language the answer you gave orally. You will probably be questioned by various labor relations people and union officials during later phases of the grievance procedure.

If your oral answer is accepted by the complaining employee and the union steward, prepare a written record of the complaint and your disposition of it. Just be certain that the remedy you grant is within your power to give and has your boss's approval.

When writing up a grievance, use the checklist in Exhibit 15.5 to make certain that you have included the necessary information. It often becomes necessary to refer to your written records later, when similar situations arise or when the grievance advances beyond your influence.

Normally, grievances are not put into writing until they progress from the first step to the second. This is especially true in large corporations, where the number of grievances is quite large and where the majority are usually solved at the steward–supervisor level. From this step on, the num-

EXHIBIT 15.5

A checklist to be used when putting a grievance into writing.

1. Who is affected? List the names, numbers, and departments of all workers and management representatives involved.
2. What is it about? Lost time? Pay shortage? Seniority violation?
3. Is it a contract violation? If so, state the clause and how company or union action violates it.
4. When did it happen? Report the exact time or period when the grievance was suffered. If it concerns lost time or retroactive pay, report the exact dates for which time or pay is due.
5. Where did it happen? This is especially important in cases involving a health or safety hazard.
6. Why did it happen? Was the incident simply a clerical error? Was a worker unjustly penalized?
7. What is the demand? What specific action or remedy did the worker and the steward request?
8. Did you obtain signatures and dates? If any written petition was handed in, did you obtain the signatures and dates of the writer and steward?
9. Did you distribute copies to the proper persons? If you prepared a report on the grievance incident, have you made certain that all the interested parties have a copy of it?

ber of people involved increases, as does the need for precise language. Since the complainant and the steward are not present in the later steps, their thoughts and those of the supervisor must be put in writing.

The Grievance Procedure

Where a union and a labor agreement exist, a formal procedure for handling grievances will be outlined and explained in the collective bargaining agreement. Exhibit 15.6 shows typical procedures for small and large unionized companies. The following procedure applies to large organizations:

1. The supervisor meets with the steward and the employee filing the grievance. After the steward has agreed with a worker that the handling of his or her complaint was inadequate and that there is the possibility of an infringement on the contract terms, the steward brings the formal grievance back to a supervisor and attempts to work out a solution.
   Every effort is made in this initial step to resolve the conflict. Both the union and management want to eliminate the time and expense of further discussion and debate.
   If, after hearing them out, the supervisor believes nothing new has been added to change the situation, he or she will stick to the original decision. It is understood, however, that the manager has researched the issue carefully and consulted with the various specialists available before reaching the decision that led to the grievance.
2. The supervisor's immediate superior or a representative from the labor relations department meets with the chief steward. A middle manager, usually with the counsel of a labor relations expert, sits down with the company's chief steward—the person who is in charge of all the other stewards and who speaks on behalf of the union. Issues are examined to determine if any precedents (agreed-to settlements from earlier grievance processing) apply. If no solution can be agreed on, the grievance advances to the next step.
3. The labor relations director or the plant and division manager meets with the union committee members. The union grievance committee usually comprises several stewards, including the chief steward, and one or more representatives from the union local. Costs and time devoted to the problem are increasing, and both sides will want to solve the issues as quickly and as equitably as they can.
4. A member or members of top management discuss the issues with a representative or group from the national or international union that chartered the local union whose member initiated the grievance. If a local independent union is involved that has no affiliation with a national or international union, the local's attorney and business agent will meet with management's representatives.

EXHIBIT 15.6

*Typical grievance proce-
dures for a small and a
large unionized organi-
zation.*

Source: Reprinted with per-
mission of the authors from
*Personal and Industrial
Relations,* 3d ed., by John B.
Miner and Mary Green
Miner. Copyright © 1977
Macmillan Publishing
Company.

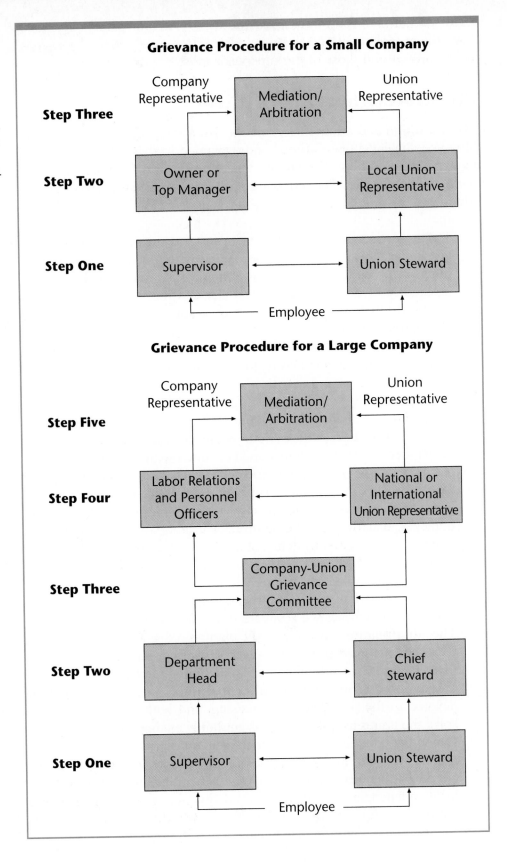

Grievance Procedure for a Small Company

Step Three	Company Representative → Mediation/Arbitration ← Union Representative	
Step Two	Owner or Top Manager	Local Union Representative
Step One	Supervisor	Union Steward
	Employee	

Grievance Procedure for a Large Company

Step Five	Company Representative → Mediation/Arbitration ← Union Representative	
Step Four	Labor Relations and Personnel Officers	National or International Union Representative
Step Three	Company-Union Grievance Committee	
Step Two	Department Head	Chief Steward
Step One	Supervisor	Union Steward
	Employee	

5. Mediation or arbitration is carried out. A neutral third party intervenes, meeting with the personnel involved in the dispute at steps one through four.

Mediation

Mediation brings in the expertise of a neutral outsider who is allied with neither labor nor management. He or she is invited to try to bring the two sides together and, after hearing both points of view, to recommend a solution. The decision is not binding on either party. Often the mediator is a distinguished public official, such as a mayor or a judge, who has a fine reputation and whose insights, wisdom, and power are respected by both sides. He or she usually serves in the public interest, without pay of any kind.

mediation
the use of a neutral third party in a labor–management dispute to recommend a solution to the issues that divide the parties

Arbitration

In **arbitration** a neutral third party is again called in. He or she is a professional arbitrator recommended by the American Arbitration Association (AAA), the Federal Mediation and Conciliation Service (FMCS), or one of the various state agencies set up for this purpose. Arbitrators usually serve with pay. In a typical year, the AAA and the FMCS process about 23,000 grievances through arbitration. About as many grievances are arbitrated through other agencies.

arbitration
the use of a neutral third party in a dispute between management and labor to resolve the areas of conflict

The arbitrator conducts hearings into the dispute, calling witnesses, recording testimony, and in general, conducting the proceedings in much the same manner that a court of law uses to conduct a hearing. It may be quite informal, however, depending on the arbitrator's style. When he or she announces a decision, it is binding on both union and management. Both mediation and arbitration are used to overcome an impasse in collective bargaining as well.

Instant Replay

1. Complaints are serious matters to be dealt with in a serious way. In a unionized organization, complaints can and often do turn into grievances.
2. Handling complaints requires honesty, sincerity, and an open discussion of all the relevant facts and emotions involved. As a supervisor, you must treat them seriously. Your subordinates do.
3. The grievance procedure begins when you and a subordinate or the union steward meet to discuss a formal complaint alleging a violation of a union contract, and you cannot agree on a solution.
4. When you manage in a union environment, you must know your labor agreement's provisions and the results of grievances that act to explain and define its limits.

5. You need to know federal and state laws that regulate your treatment of employees in all matters—not just in labor relations areas.
6. You should develop a cooperative relationship with your steward. You are not enemies or adversaries. Both of you are paid to look out for special interests and to reach accommodations when it is in your mutual interests to do so.
7. Unions exist to serve their members. In many companies, they are a fact of life.

Questions for Class Discussion

1. Can you define this chapter's key terms?
2. How should a supervisor handle complaints in a logical way?
3. What does the Wagner Act prohibit?
4. What does the Taft-Hartley Act prohibit?
5. In what ways are the supervisor and the steward similar? In what ways are the labor relations roles different?
6. Can you outline a typical grievance procedure for a large organization? What might be left out in a small company?

Incident

Purpose: To get a union member's view about his or her union—its benefits and drawbacks.

Your Task: Interview a union member (family member, classmate, friend, or the like) using the following questions and any others you may wish to add. Compare your results with those of your classmates.

1. Why did you join your union?
2. What are the costs—psychological and financial—connected with your union membership?
3. What direct benefits does your union provide you in the following areas:
   a. Wages and benefits?
   b. Working conditions?
   c. Employee assistance, that is, strike benefits?
4. Have you ever had to strike your employer?
5. What were the issues that led to the strike?
6. Does your union contract prescribe a grievance process?
7. What is the process?
8. In general, how would you describe the working relationship between management and the union?
9. What do you think your working life would be like if your union did not exist?

An Intoxicating Experience

Red Hastings entered the break area and noticed Pauline Brown in an animated conversation with her peers. Pauline was talking in a very loud voice that seemed to pierce the air. When she laughed, it felt as though the room's mirror would break. Red thought that her words were slurred and that she looked and was behaving as though she was intoxicated. As Pauline's supervisor, he was concerned. If she was loaded, he thought, she would have to return to the office for an additional two hours of work. Any sloppy work from her could cause his department real problems.

Red sat across the room from her until her break ended and she and her co-workers began to leave. He signaled for her to stay and talk, but she hastily left the area. He followed, only to see her enter the women's locker area. He waited for nearly fifteen minutes until she emerged. Red confronted Pauline as follows:

"You have been drinking, haven't you?"

"I have not," Pauline replied.

"Don't lie to me, Pauline. I watched you on break, and you were a textbook example of a drunk."

"I resent being called a drunk," Pauline answered as she took off at a fast pace to her work station. Red felt that he had smelled the distinct odor of alcohol on her breath as she passed him. Red followed her to the office and watched her carefully for nearly one-half hour. He did not talk with her again but did check her work as she generated it, and it was perfect.

Red was puzzled. Pauline had worked for him for over eleven months, and he had never noticed the kind of behavior she exhibited today. He had many conversations with her and had never smelled alcohol on her breath.

After all the office personnel had left, Red decided to check Pauline's work area. He found a large bottle of mouthwash in her bottom drawer. Its label read "12% alcohol." In her wastebasket, he found a crushed paper bag. As he unfolded it a receipt fell from the bag. It was from the local liquor store and in the amount of $3.79. "Just enough for a pint," he thought.

Red returned to his office to check the company's policy manual. "Just as I thought," he said to himself, "...an employee who reports to work intoxicated can be fired."

Questions

1. If you were Red, what course of action would you pursue if the company had no unions?
2. How might your course of action change if you were Red and worked in a union environment?
3. What alternatives does a company have when faced with an employee with an alcohol problem?

A Minor Change

"They can't get away with this," said Allan, the shop steward. "There's no way I'm going to let this change go through without a fight. We will put all the union's muscle behind this effort to resist drug testing in the plant." Alan was reacting to the new memo circulated yesterday to all plant personnel. It detailed a "minor change" in the company—to conduct random tests of employees who had given management reason to suspect that they were using alcohol or other drugs. The memo was clear that testing would be done at the company's expense and that only workers would be tested. If a positive test result did occur, a second test would be conducted to verify the results of the first. Any employee who refused to be tested would be dismissed.

"Look, Allan," said the plant manager, "management is concerned as our whole society is today about drug-impaired workers and the costs they represent to this company and others. You know about the O'Brien case last month. He was high as a kite; everyone knew it, and he still was allowed to operate the overhead crane. You know what happened as a result. We don't want another case of lost time and medical bills."

"Mr. Munsun," said Allan, "you know that the union is opposed to this testing. It's an invasion of our employees' privacy. The testing has to be done with urine samples, and the figures I have read say that as many as 40 percent of the tests can yield false positives."

"Management is firm on this. Testing was not a program they decided on without much debate. Effective next month, your members will be tested if they give anyone in management cause to suspect that they are using drugs or under the influence of them. You had better get them used to the idea because that is how it is going to be."

The union quickly mobilized its members in opposition to the testing program. The press covered the local union's meeting, and the headlines in the two daily papers let the public know about the company's testing program. Management received many phone calls from community officials and members of the press inquiring about drug use in the plant. The local police chief talked to Munsun and told him that if illegal drugs were found, he wanted to be called in.

In the first week of the drug testing program, two workers refused to be tested and were fired. They filed a lawsuit claiming a violation of their right to privacy and discrimination. One of the workers fired was the best designer in the company with an unblemished record for his fifteen years of employment. His loss threw two major programs into chaos. Within a month, development of a new product was so far behind schedule that it had to be scrapped. This loss led to the replacement of the head designer.

For the first time in the company's history, there was clear evidence that workers had deliberately destroyed company property. Sand was found in a milling machine's oil reservoir. Sand in the machine's oil had caused the failure of its $3,000 motor. This, like the firing of the two employees, did not go unnoticed by the local press.

Plant supervisors and team leaders have all reported an increase in worker-related problems. Many have noted increases in absenteeism and growing negative attitudes in plant employees, labor and management alike. The former plant environment was one of cooperation and mutual efforts aimed at problem solving. The environment now emerging is one of hostility and noncooperation. One supervisor had shifted from participative leadership to autocratic. In his words, "the fellas used to pitch in and respond nicely to requests. Now you have to threaten them with insubordination to get them to respond. It's almost like you're afraid to turn your back to them. Where is all this going to end?"

Questions

1. Why do you think the union has mounted such strong opposition to this program?
2. What assumptions lie beneath the company's testing program?
3. What should management and labor do now?

Notes

Chruden, H. J., and Sherman, Jr., A. W. *Personnel Management: The Utilization of Human Resources* (Cincinnati: South-Western Publishing, 1980), 387.

Foulkes, Fred K. "How Top Nonunion Companies Manage Employees," *Harvard Business Review*, September–October 1981, 90.

Franklin, Stephen. "Arguing Over the Umpire," *Chicago Tribune*, December 5, 1993, sect. 7, 1, 7.

Joel III, Lewin G. *Every Employee's Guide to the Law.* (New York: Pantheon Books, 1993), 326.

Rowe, M. P., and Baker, M. "Are You Hearing Enough Employee Concerns?" *Harvard Business Review*, May–June 1984, 130.

Salwen, Keven G. "NLRB Says Labor-Management Teams at Firm Violated Company-Union Rule," *Wall Street Journal*, December 18, 1992, A12.

Suggested Readings

Caruth, Don, and Mills, Harry N. "Working Toward Better Union Relations," *Supervisory Management* 30 (February 1985): 7–13.

Foegen, J. H. "Labor Unions: Don't Count Them Out Yet!" *Academy of Management Executive*, 3 (1989): 67–69.

Fossum, J. A. *Labor Relations: Development, Structure, Process,* 4th ed. Dallas: Business Publications, 1989.

Freeman, Richard B., and Medoff, James L. *What Do Unions Do?* New York: Basic Books, 1984.

Joel III, Lewin G. *Every Employee's Guide to the Law.* New York: Pantheon Books, 1993.

Kerr, Steven, and Hill, Kenneth D. "The First-Line Supervisor: Phasing Out or Here to Stay?" *Academy of Management Review* 11 (1986): 105–108.

Kochan, Thomas A., Katz, Harry C., and McKersie, Robert B. *The Transformation of American Industrial Relations.* New York: Basic Books, 1986.

McGill, Ann M. *Supervising the Difficult Employee.* New York: Richard D. Irwin, 1994.

Sibbernsen, Richard D. "What Arbitrators Think About Technology Replacing Labor," *Harvard Business Review* (March–April 1986): 8–16.

Tidwell, Gary L. "The Supervisor's Role in a Union Election." *Personnel Journal* 62 (August 1983): 640–645.

Security, Safety, and Health

OBJECTIVES

After reading and discussing this chapter, you should be able to do the following:

1. Define this chapter's key terms.

2. Outline security measures that supervisors can take to safeguard the office and shop from theft by employees.

3. Describe a supervisor's duties in the event of a fire and with regard to fire prevention.

4. Outline procedures open to supervisors to prevent loss from vandalism.

5. Describe the purposes of the Occupational Safety and Health Act.

6. Describe the enforcement procedures and an employer's rights with regard to OSHA inspectors.

INTRODUCTION

As the title of this chapter implies, we are concerned here with the supervisor's duties in the following areas:

- **Security**—protecting physical facilities and nonhuman resources from loss or damage
- **Safety**—protecting people from accidents and injuries
- **Health**—the general condition of a person physically and emotionally, and efforts at preventing illness and treating injuries when they occur

Our focus will be on prevention—the ways in which supervisors and others can head off trouble and minimize damage to their company's human, financial, informational, and material resources. We will explore what supervisors are expected and required to do to help protect these resources. Your duties with regard to security and safety begin with the screening of new applicants and continue every day as you carry out your managerial functions. Keep in mind that supervisors usually have assistance in the areas of safety, security, and health from various staff managers and outside consultants. The larger the company, the more assistance supervisors can expect.

In directing the employees, you can help them avoid accidents and prevent theft through training and discipline. In organizing your department, you can build a structure for preventing accidents and enforcing safety rules. In planning, you can design programs, procedures, and practices that will help carry out management policies and coincide with state and federal safety standards. You can construct effective preventive, diagnostic, and therapeutic controls to deal with safety and security problems. Through effective communications, committee action, and peer-group cooperation, you can ensure the coordination of safety and security efforts throughout the company.

PHYSICAL SECURITY

Each year businesses lose billions of dollars through thefts by customers, employees, owners, and outside criminals. "The International Association of Professional Security Consultants says losses of cash and inventory alone range from $10 billion to $40 billion annually" (Randle, 1995). Thefts of employee property cause suspicion, low morale, dollar losses, and employee turnover. Thefts of a company's assets result in increased costs, lowered productivity, and higher prices for the products and services it has to sell. Keeping their employees' and their own property secure from theft costs employers billions of dollars each year.

Employee Theft

The largest cause of loss to most U.S. businesses is employee theft. "Sixty to 80 percent of all inventory 'shrinkage'...can be blamed on workers, according to Sid Gregory, president of the nationally franchised Triple Check Income Tax Service.... The norm for shrinkage is 2 to 2.5 percent of inventory, although it might run as high as 7 percent in some businesses" (*Chicago Tribune,* "Employees," 1994). The average theft by an employee per incident in 1992 was $513.22, according to Jack L. Hayes International, a consulting firm (Randle, 1995). "In employee surveys conducted by academics and other specialists, as many as 30 percent of workers interviewed admitted stealing from their employers" (Emshwiller, 1992). According to a Chicago testing company, Reid Psychological Systems, "about 17 percent of applicants admit to stealing from a previous employer" (Emshwiller, 1992). The motivations given by thieving employees include rewarding one's self for working the late shift, stealing to support a drug or gambling addiction, staying even in earnings with other employee thieves, and helping friends and loved ones through a financial crisis.

Employees steal time, money, company assets, and secrets. For money and other motives, employees steal vital information about product designs, marketing plans, customers, finances, and research projects. This information in the competition's hands can do great harm. According to the consulting firm Ernst & Young, "more than half the country's businesses are likely to have suffered financially because of information losses stemming from inadequate computer security measures. And at least some of the financial losses have exceeded $1 million per occurrence..." (Ziemba, 1994). Only 58 percent of senior managers consider computer security to be very important. "Those who do consider computer security to be very important tend to be in the banking and insurance industries..." according to an Ernst & Young survey (Ziemba, 1994). Losses of vital information also occur when managers talk too much or to the wrong people, through improper disposal of waste paper, and uncontrolled access to information by visitors and suppliers.

Electronic thieves working from within a business steal billions of dollars each year through a variety of schemes. Computer criminals can siphon money from business accounts into their personal accounts; they can create phony charges from nonexistent vendors and then authorize payment of those charges. Computer theft is committed by programmers, computer operators, clerks, bank tellers, executives, and disgruntled or fired employees. Losses to computer thieves tend to be much larger than losses to conventional thieves.

Two recent problems have surfaced in regard to electronic security: the computer virus and the bugging of facsimile machines. A **computer virus** is a rogue computer program (usually planted by a disgruntled employee or a computer hacker) that can erase or ruin files, thus destroy-

computer virus
a rogue computer program that can reproduce itself endlessly or cause other havoc, such as destroying stored data

ing vital information. It usually hides in computer software until triggered by routine computer uses or by the arrival of a specific time. In January 1990, an infamous inventor of a computer virus was found guilty of unleashing a virus that crippled a nationwide network of thousands of computers. A 1986 federal computer fraud and abuse law was used to convict the former graduate student, resulting in a five-year jail sentence and a $250,000 fine (*Chicago Tribune*, "Invader," 1990).

Facsimile (fax) machines use telephone lines or cellular networks to transmit printed copy. It is possible to tap into these machines by making a secret connection with the telephone lines of the party whose fax messages are to be intercepted or by monitoring cellular calls. Readily available equipment is sold through most electronics stores (Cullison, 1990).

Cures   For controlling theft by employees, a "corporate policy and guidelines are the first lines of defense...experts say" (Rochester, 1987). August Bequai (1987), a Washington, D.C. attorney and author specializing in computer crime, offers five major tips for prevention:

1. Put out the word: Managers must warn employees that the company frowns on computer crime, whether it be theft of a floppy disk or information from a database, and that it will prosecute offenders. When a crime occurs, you have to make good on your word.
2. Name a contact: Employees should have somebody to talk to if they suspect crimes. If you don't have a security director, you should. He or she must be a high-level person reporting directly to the CEO or chairman.
3. Create a code of ethics, and give every employee a copy: State explicitly what the company regards as computer crime and what it regards as unethical. Tell employees these actions are grounds for dismissal or prosecution.
4. Educate top management: Studies have shown that when the top executive understands the use and abuse of computer systems, employees commit fewer crimes.
5. Institute data security: There should be at least three levels of security. Passwords should be changed every thirty days. Don't leave access codes and passwords lying around.

In addition to the use of various types of tags and coded strips to detect merchandise leaving facilities in unauthorized ways, a new tool will soon appear in all kinds of organizations to keep track of assets:

> Sensormatic Electronics Corp. of Deerfield Beach, Fla., and Texas Instruments recently announced the development of a technology that allows companies to track assets, vehicles and even workers. Unlike current asset-tagging systems,...[the new system] will track assets as they move through a building.... [It uses] an FM signal to identify mov-

ing objects and people as they pass through or over detectors. Sensormatic plans to use the system for security and access-control at the 1996 Summer Olympic Games in Atlanta (*Chicago Tribune*, "Keeping," 1994).

Since computers emit radio waves when they are used, computer facilities can be made safer with walls and windows that prevent radio waves from leaving. More than fifty makers of computers and allied equipment now make leak-proof models; these cost about 30 percent more than their leaking counterparts (Hillkirk, 1987).

Since many businesses depend on an unfailing source of electricity to keep their offices and operations going, backup sources in the form of generators and batteries are important. Burglar alarms and fire alarms are often computer controlled, as are the machine tools and physical environments of many labs and workrooms. Power failures can cause loss of data and essential life-support systems. As a supervisor, you may have to enforce backup copy rules to avoid the loss of data. Let your computer users know the importance of copying important data onto a second disk and putting it in a secure place.

Your job may also entail enforcing procedures designed to control who accesses and uses data. Security software, passwords, and access codes are but a few of the readily available and inexpensive solutions to computer security. Access to any database can be limited in several ways to keep unauthorized personnel from viewing or working with them. Several manufacturers have produced software and devices that work as a defense against computer viruses and the bugging of fax machines. Several virus scanners are available, and they are upgraded regularly to help detect new viruses. Some software packages contain virus detection programs and can even remove viruses. Newer fax machines use encoding systems to defend the information transmitted. They scramble messages, making them unreadable to hackers. Check on your office's computer and fax security systems. They may be badly behind the times and leaking valuable information.

Regardless of policies and procedures, all security efforts and programs depend on personnel at all levels for their implementation and use. The quality of enforcement ultimately depends on what employees perceive to be the company's response in backing up informants and enforcers and in dealing with thieves. Ideally, all employees should be taught that theft prevention and detection depends on their cooperation as individuals and as a group.

Selection and Prevention

Preventing crimes committed by employees begins with the selection of each new employee. In most companies, supervisors are involved in the selection of new employees, as they certainly should be. During the screening process, both the supervisors and members of the human resource department should be alert for telltale signs of a potentially dishonest employee (see Exhibit 16.1). In addition to this list of clues, you should check the applicant's lifestyle for any hints that the person is living well above his or her level of income. Be certain, when conducting orientation activities, that all new employees know your company's policy on and penalties for dishonesty. Further, many security experts recommend insuring an organization against employee theft through the purchase of fidelity bonds for all those employees who will have access to large amounts of money or valuable goods.

Ask for and verify a recommendation from the applicant's most recent employer. This precaution will not always uncover a person with a history of theft or willful destruction of company property, however, because many employers simply ask an employee caught stealing to

EXHIBIT 16.1

Some warning signs of a potentially dishonest applicant.

1.	Gaps in employment	Be sure to fill in these gaps during the employment interview.
2.	Criminal record	A criminal record check must be job related. Don't hire anyone who has a criminal conviction that will bear on the job to be filled.
3.	Lies on the application	Significant falsehoods on an employment application signal falsehoods to come.
4.	Frequent job changes	Changes that indicate the person does not know what he or she wants (no focus or common ground connects the past jobs) usually predict a short tenure with your organization.
5.	Financial problems	A strong focus on money issues by the applicant may mean overextension and temptations to profit at others' expense.
6.	Overqualified	Someone seeking a job for which he or she is overqualified may be on a search for a temporary, stopgap job just to make ends meet.

resign. They often do not fire such an employee or prosecute him or her in the courts because they do not want to air their dirty linen in public or admit to themselves that they have hired a thief. Few employers pass negative information about a former employee on to a potential new employer because they fear being accused of violating that person's civil rights and having a lawsuit filed against them for defamation of character. In addition, courts have been notoriously lenient toward white-collar criminals, who have often received only small fines or jail terms of less than a year following conviction for thefts amounting to thousands of dollars in cash or goods.

To prevent losses from employee dishonesty, the Council of Better Business Bureaus (1992) recommends watching for the following warning signs:

- Accounting personnel who fail to keep their records and billings up to date
- Complaints by customers who claim their statements are inaccurate
- Employees who regularly ask for pay advances, turn down promotions, or fail to take vacations
- Employees who seem to be living a more expensive lifestyle than their pay would permit
- Slow collections and the writing off of an unusual number of bad debts

Office Security

Most companies have on their premises tangible assets to protect such as office machines and equipment, as well as valuable, highly sensitive information. To protect these assets, some basic, common-sense approaches work well alongside sophisticated and sometimes quite expensive equipment.

The biggest problem in protecting office equipment, machines, and sensitive information involves preventing access by unauthorized personnel. People must be separated into two groups in the minds of office supervisors: those who belong and those who do not.

It should not be possible for someone to enter an office without being screened at the entrance. To make this screening process easier, many offices have only one entrance; it is usually the only nonfire exit as well. Someone such as a receptionist should be on hand at all times to greet visitors from the moment the office is opened until it is closed for the day. People who have no legitimate reason to go farther should not be allowed to do so. People admitted beyond the reception area should have a specific destination. In the case of messengers and delivery people, the receptionist should accept the parcel or message or should request that the addressee come forward to receive it if a specific signature is required. Parcels should be checked into a central cloak room or, if this is not prac-

tical, should be periodically spot-checked by security personnel. Briefcases, packages, lunch pails, and similar objects can easily be used to carry company property or sensitive information out of an office.

The protection of the employees' personal property can be best achieved by alerting people to the ever-present dangers of loss and theft. Office personnel should be asked to keep their valuables with them or safely locked away. A purse or a pocket calculator left on a desk is just too big a temptation for some people, whether strangers or regular employees. Advise your people to take their valuables home after work, especially when the office is to be left unoccupied over a weekend or long holiday period (when a burglary or fire is most likely to occur). Unfortunately, warnings are not enough for some people, and losses are almost certain to happen.

When a theft occurs, an investigation is called for. It should involve security people if they are available. Use any experience to remind people that losses have occurred. There is nothing quite so effective as an actual loss to drive home the need to safeguard one's own property. Exhibit 16.2 gives a short security checklist to follow at the end of each day. Whoever is in charge of securing the office should refer to such a list before leaving.

Shop Security

Shop or plant security has some definite parallels to office security. Again the prevention of access by unauthorized personnel is the biggest problem standing in the way of safety and security. Controls can be exercised over people who enter the area in similar ways. Personal belongings can be

EXHIBIT 16.2

*Daily security checklist
for closing an office.*

Daily Security Checklist

1. File cabinets locked. ☐
2. Safe locked. ☐
3. Personal valuables secured. ☐
4. Windows locked. ☐
5. Machines off and secured. ☐
6. Night lights on. ☐
7. Nonessential lights off. ☐
8. People out. ☐
9. Doors secured. ☐
10. Alarm on. ☐

Remarks: _____

_____

_____

Date: _____ **Time:** _____

Checklist completed by: _____

secured in employee lockers or checked with the company's security personnel on entering the plant or shop.

But there are some related problems that go along with plant and office security. Besides protecting property and information from theft, you must be concerned with the prevention of vandalism and fires.

Vandalism is generally considered to be wanton or willful destruction or damage to another's property. Sometimes it is done by disgruntled employees and sometimes by outsiders. Whoever does the damage, some simple precautions can help prevent or minimize losses.

To begin with, control over and security for all equipment, machines, tools, and other expensive pieces of company property should be the responsibility of specified people. Portable pieces of equipment should be issued only on request and should be returned by the persons to whom they were issued. The responsibility for levels of maintenance should be associated with the operator and the maintenance department so that each item will be properly cared for and its condition checked periodically. Any

vandalism
wanton or willful
destruction or damage to another's property

damage or changes should be reported immediately, their causes determined, and blame or responsibility (financial and otherwise) fixed.

Physical facilities must be kept clean and under observation at regular and irregular intervals. Storage areas require extra security measures if they contain sensitive or highly valuable materials. Illumination of inside and outside areas helps avoid trouble and unwelcome visitors. Closed-circuit television, guards, proximity devices, and alarm systems are popular but expensive prevention and detection measures. Locks, however, remain the primary means of security used by any business firm; they cannot prevent trouble or vandalism if they are not used properly. Locks and guard routes should be changed periodically. Finally, remind subordinates that damage means costs to them and to the company in time and money. Damaged equipment and facilities are unavailable for production. This often means lost revenues and wages.

Shoplifting

According to the National Retail Foundation and others, 25.2 percent of inventory losses are due to shoplifters (Emshwiller, 1992). For 1991, retailers reported shoplifting losses totaling $2.1 billion (Randle, 1992). According to the consulting firm of Jack L. Hayes International, in 1992 retailers lost an average of $64.24 per incident (Randle, 1995). We all lose because stores must raise prices and spend money to prevent thefts by customers. For 1991, retailers reported spending $308 million for increased store security (Randle, 1992). The Small Business Administration reports that a retail theft is committed every five seconds and costs each American about $150 per year (Council of Better Business Bureaus, 1992). When stores raise their prices, they become less competitive. Dollars lost to theft and spent on security are not available to make businesses more productive and profitable.

Cures   Most experts agree that training employees to look out for shoplifters can and does cut such losses. Such training also reminds employees that the company is serious about theft prevention. Mass merchandisers have reduced their losses through spending on employee training.

As a supervisor of retail salespeople, you can train your people to never leave a customer alone or out of sight long enough to pocket merchandise. You can train your people to catch credit card thieves and users of invalid credit cards by teaching and enforcing proper clearance procedures. Finally, you can enforce antitheft procedures such as keeping display cases locked and displaying one item to one customer at a time.

Your employer has other remedies and prevention measures to offer as well. Rewards can be paid for catching shoplifters and for recovering stolen or void credit cards. Store detectives can be used to pose as shoppers and, along with closed-circuit TVs, monitor shoppers. Tagging merchandise with price tags that self-destruct when tampered with or with tags that only store personnel can remove also helps. Some stores have tags that trigger alarms when the customer leaves the store—indicating that the tag, which should have been removed at purchase, has not been removed. Checkpoint Systems Inc., an electronic security firm in New Jersey, manufactures electronic circuits that set off alarms at exits. Such circuits are quite small and can be built into a product's packaging or affixed to a piece of paper and inserted into a product. Target Stores, a Midwestern mass merchandiser, has installed the Checkpoint system in about one fourth of its stores. It paid for the cost of installation within one year through loss prevention (Reitman, 1990).

Cub Foods in Colorado Springs had a big shoplifting problem until it created and installed two cardboard cops in its aisles. Each is a 6-foot stand-up photograph of a real cop in uniform. The figures are placed in aisles that have experienced losses to shoplifters. Since their installation, shoplifting is down 30 percent. According to Bob Demetry, loss-prevention manager at the store, the figures remind would-be shoplifters of what the consequences can be (Hagedorn, 1990). Wal-Mart's famous senior-citizen "greeters" became a fixture in its stores when it became obvious that they reduced store losses to shoplifters.

In addition to these, the Council of Better Business Bureaus (1992) recommends the following deterrents and devices to protect your business:

- Make everyone leaving the store pass through a checkout lane.
- Reduce the number of exits. Unguarded exits can be converted into emergency exits with noise alarms. Unused checkout lanes should be closed and blocked off.
- Make displays symmetrical and organized to make it easier to notice when an item is missing.
- Keep high-cost, high-risk items in locked displays, behind the counters, or on chains.
- Require all packages brought into the store by customers to be checked.
- Be alert for the following: a group of shoppers entering together, then splitting up; customers lingering in one place, wandering aimlessly, and handling lots of merchandise; a customer who creates a distracting situation—he or she may be creating a diversion for an accomplice who will steal while shop personnel are distracted.

Fire Prevention

According to the National Fire Protection Association, public fire departments fought nearly 2 million fires in 1992. These fires killed 4,730 people and caused about $12.3 billion in property losses (*The American Almanac: 1994–95*, 1994).

Although you are not expected to be a professional firefighter, you are expected to minimize the risks of a fire starting in any area over which you have control. The job is not yours alone. You must have the support of management, your peers, and your subordinates. Without their cooperation, your efforts will be ineffectual.

Most fires result from carelessness and can be prevented. Piles of rubbish, oily rags, the improper use of smoking materials, and flammable liquids represent hazards whose potential harmfulness people with good common sense should recognize. Proper training of personnel in fire prevention and in how to extinguish various kinds of fires can go a long way toward reducing and eliminating fire hazards. A concern for fire prevention begins with the initial training of each new employee and continues to be reinforced by fire prevention programs throughout the year.

Every department should conduct regularly scheduled inspections. All of your people represent potential causes of fires, just as they also represent detection and prevention devices. All employees should be made to feel that fire prevention and detection depend on them personally. Such attitudes are instilled through actions and words and by responding in a positive way each time a subordinate tells you about a potential fire hazard or takes time to remove one. Exhibit 16.3 shows a sample fire prevention checklist.

Be certain that all pieces of fire-fighting equipment such as extinguishers and hoses are visible, accessible, and in proper working order, and make sure that you and your people know where they are and how to use them. Different kinds of fires require different kinds of fire-fighting equipment. The wrong type of extinguishing agent—such as water used on a grease fire—can spread the fire and increase the likelihood of injuries and property damage. Periodic but unpredictable fire drills will prepare your people for the worst and will reinforce proper evacuation procedures and routes.

If and when a fire occurs, you have three jobs to do in a hurry:

1. Get your people out of danger.
2. Call the fire department.
3. Fight the fire if you know how to and have the proper means and training to do so without putting yourself in jeopardy.

PROTECTING PEOPLE

Protecting people from illness, accidents, and injuries is not only smart business—it is required by law as well. By law, a business is responsible for injuries suffered by its employees if the injuries occur during or arise as a result of the employee's employment.

accident
any unforeseen or unplanned incident or event

An **accident** is defined as any unforeseen or unplanned incident or event. Damage to people or property need not occur to have an accident.

Fire Protection

	OK	Needed
1. Are portable fire extinguishers provided in adequate number and type?	☐	☐
2. Are fire extinguishers inspected monthly for general conditions and operability and noted on the inspection tag?	☐	☐
3. Are fire extinguishers recharged regularly and properly noted on the inspection tag?	☐	☐
4. Are fire extinguishers mounted in readily accessible locations?	☐	☐
5. If you have interior standpipes and valves, are these inspected regularly?	☐	☐
6. If you have a fire alarm system, is it tested at least annually?	☐	☐
7. Are plant employees periodically instructed in the use of extinguishers and fire protection procedures?	☐	☐
8. If you have outside private fire hydrants, were they flushed within the last year and placed on a regular maintenance schedule?	☐	☐
9. Are fire doors and shutters in good operating condition?	☐	☐
Are they unobstructed and protected against obstruction?	☐	☐
10. Are fusible links in place?	☐	☐
11. Is your local fire department well acquainted with your plant, location, and specific hazards?	☐	☐

12. Automatic Sprinklers:

Are water control valves, air and water pressures checked weekly? _____

Are control valves locked open? _____

Is maintenance of the system assigned to responsible persons or a sprinkler contractor? Who? _____

Are sprinkler heads protected by metal guards where exposed to mechanical damage? _____

Is proper minimum clearance maintained around sprinkler heads? _____

EXHIBIT 16.3
Sample checklist for fire prevention.

Source: *OSHA Handbook for Small Businesses.*

Workers who slip on a wet floor but do not suffer any injury are still victims of an accident.

Although accidents are usually unforeseen, many are not unforeseeable. Planning and safety programs can and do yield significant decreases in accidents. Through the three Es of accident prevention established by

SUPERVISORS AND ETHICS

According to a book published by the National Safe Workplace Institute (NSWI), "...some 111,000 acts of workplace violence occur nationwide each year—about 425 per workday." Northwestern National Life Insurance conducted a survey and believes "that 2.2 million Americans were attacked at work [from October 1993 through September 1994] and that another 6.3 million were threatened." One of NSWI's authors, Dennis Johnson, claims the violence is due in large measure to "...an over-stressed population; a surfeit of guns; fractured families;...and a spreading multiculturalization and gender revolution in the work force, both of which contribute to the number of scapegoats for anger as well as to mixed signals and differing values that can spark conflict." Workplace liability lawyer, Garry Mathiason, adds, "20% of all workplace incidents that involve physical injury can be attributed to some type of romantic entanglement. Most often, the victim is a woman."

Workplace assaults and actions that can evolve into violence (stalking, verbal abuse, and employer-directed animosity) are becoming a growing concern and represent millions of dollars in actual and potential liability for employers and employees alike. A convenience store in Texas was held liable for $4.5 million in the case of a murdered employee. The court said that it failed to provide adequate security for the employee. An employment agency in California was held liable for $5.5 million in the death of a winery worker. She was stabbed to death by an employee with a history of violence and a criminal record; the court said that an improper background check was made.

Workplace violence is often "preceded by a string of unheeded warning signs: Some traumatic event, like a layoff or a financial crisis, disrupts the person's life, followed by a period of almost paranoid brooding and escalating, often increasingly specific threats." Companies can take and are taking specific actions to prevent workplace hostilities from escalating into violence. Among the options are:

ergonomics
concern about the design of work sites, machines, equipment, and systems to minimize stress and job-related injuries

the National Safety Council—engineering, education, and enforcement—the probability of accidents can be reduced, and their severity can be minimized. Engineering has to do with **ergonomics**—how to design work sites, machinery, equipment, and systems to minimize stress and injury on the job. Education means teaching people what they need to know to prevent illness, injury, and death. Enforcement means making rules, regulations, and procedures work to that same end. We will discuss more about the three Es of accident prevention later in this chapter.

- Taking a firm policy position that states workplace threats, intimidation, and acts of violence will not be tolerated and will be punished.
- People who have court orders restraining their activities must notify the company of their existence.
- People who cannot get along must be physically separated and not allowed to interact on the job.
- All employees, especially supervisors, must notify proper authorities when they witness or discover serious or potentially serious situations.
- Potential problem areas—break areas, locker rooms, and parking lots are kept under surveillance, and a properly trained security staff is on call to deal with problems.
- EAPs—psychiatric counseling, for example—are in place, and everyone knows how to take advantage of them.
- A specific team is in place and trained to intervene and detect problems early on.

- Violence-prevention–dispute-resolution training is provided by consultants or other experts.
- In-depth screening to identify violence-prone individuals is conducted as a routine for screening new applicants.
- Better lighting, having guests sign in, not allowing people to work alone or in isolated surroundings, firing violent employees, and requiring people with demonstrated tendencies toward volatile behavior to get help as a condition of continued employment all further reduce the invitation to violence.

Du Pont is one of several companies that has taken a firm stand and developed policy and programs to deal with these issues. It developed its Personal Safety Program for employees in 1986. It includes workshops on rape prevention, sexual harassment, domestic violence, and abuse of power in the workplace. "Employees have access to a 24-hour hotline staffed by Du Pont volunteers as well as...counselors who can arrange medical and legal assistance."

Source: Dunkel, Tom. "Newest Danger Zone: Your Office," *Working Woman,* August 1994, 36–41, 70, 72–73.

Illnesses, Injuries, and Deaths

According to Joseph A. Dear, the director of the Occupational Safety and Health Administration (OSHA), "'Every five seconds, a worker gets injured enough to need medical attention. And work-related illnesses cost businesses $115 billion each year'" (Kleiman, 1994). In 1992, according to the U.S. Department of Labor, there were 6.3 million job-related injuries (more than one third of which required recuperation away from work) and 6,083 work-related deaths (Franklin, 1994). Repetitive stress injuries, such as carpal tunnel syndrome—a malady affecting the wrists and forearms of those who repeat the same motions throughout the day—increased by 25 percent in 1992 [to 90,000 cases, most of whom were women] (Kleiman, 1994).

Again according to Joseph Dear, "'Every day, an average of 17 workers are killed [on the job]'" (Kleiman, 1994). The causes of death on the job in 1992 were as follows: transportation accidents (40 percent), assaults and violent acts (20 percent), contact with objects and equipment (16 percent), falls (10 percent), exposure to harmful substances (10 percent), and fires and explosions (4 percent) (Franklin, 1994). The U.S. Centers for Disease Control and Prevention reports "that during the 1980s, the U.S. averaged 760 on-the-job murders annually—about three per workday" (Dunkel, 1994). Murder was the leading cause of death in the workplace for women (43 percent) in 1992. Forty-one percent of women who died at work were murdered each year, on average, during the 1980s. The numbers for murdered men for these periods were 18 percent and 10 percent, respectively (Dunkel, 1994). The emotional and dollar costs connected with these numbers are huge: the pain and suffering by stricken employees and their families, lost wages and productivity, medical bills, insurance premiums, and the increased costs in other areas that companies and individuals must incur to survive and cope with their losses.

Although each working environment is unique, each has certain hazards and types of accidents that can be identified and removed or neutralized so that they cause a minimum amount of damage and human suffering. Federal (OSHA) studies over the years have found the following basic elements in workplaces that have good accident prevention programs and records:

1. The top manager assumes the leadership role.
2. Responsibility for safety and health activities is clearly assigned.
3. Possible accident causes are properly identified and either eliminated or controlled.
4. Appropriate safety- and health-related training is instituted.
5. An accident record system is maintained.
6. A medical and first-aid system is ready for possible use.
7. Continued activity is designed to foster on-the-job awareness and acceptance of safety and health responsibility by every employee.
8. People are forewarned about and told how to cope with the hazards they must face on the job.

Regardless of the size of your organization, all these elements can be used to prevent work-related accidents and possible injuries and illnesses.

When followed, this eight-point approach to safety and health in your company will reduce human misery and losses in dollars and hours. You can begin in your own area by identifying present hazards; taking responsibility for enforcement of standards, rules, and procedures; teaching safety and practicing it; and developing regular routines for all of your subordinates.

Warning Signs   Many symptoms exist in the workplace to let you know that you have a problem or will have one in the future. Some obvious signs are accident and injury statistics, employee illnesses that are linked to the workplace, and absentee figures related to these. A company can analyze accident statistics, looking at categories of accidents (accidents to the eyes or fingers, for example) to determine if safety programs of a particular category or type are required. Not-so-obvious signals include labor turnover, excessive waste or scrap, increases in the number of near misses that could have caused injuries or property damage, and the pending receipt of new equipment and new employees (these last two signal a need for safety training).

A rising concern for most employers is the presence of indoor pollution in the plant and office. What has become known as sick-building syndrome (SBS) may be caused by one contaminant or by several acting in concert. Many indoor locations are chemical and bacterial nurseries, trapping such contaminants as asbestos, radon gas, formaldehyde, carbon monoxide, cigarette smoke, and fungi and bacteria of all sorts. Currently, more than 65,000 chemicals are used or manufactured in workplaces in the United States with about 1,500 new ones introduced each year. Only about 10 percent of these are tested by the Environmental Protection Agency. Of these, about 2,000 have been identified as leading to occupational diseases if exposures are high enough (Goozner, 1990). Indoor air pollution has become a larger problem as more structures are built or renovated to become more energy efficient. Exhibit 16.4 gives you some advice on avoiding or cleaning up indoor pollutants.

The symptoms exhibited by those in a polluted environment include redness and tearing of the eyes, congestion, nose bleeds, difficulty with breathing, tiredness, headaches, runny noses, and other flulike symptoms. A study by the Walter Reed Institute of Medical Research in Washington concluded that absenteeism increases about 50 percent in poorly ventilated buildings. Conversely, when buildings are cleaned up, absenteeism and productivity improve, according to environmental consultant Laurence B. Molloy (Rice, 1990).

AIDS in the Workplace

According to the Centers for Disease Control and Prevention in Atlanta, 1 in every 250 people 18 years of age and older (over 1 million citizens) has the AIDS virus—HIV—and every 13 minutes, another person is infected. The virus spreads through sexual contact, contact with infected needles or blood, and from infected pregnant mothers to their fetuses. Over time, most people infected with the virus will develop AIDS. AIDS results from a weakened immune system that allows the body to fall prey to a variety of illness. With the lack of knowledge about the virus and AIDS, workplaces and their employees are ill-prepared to deal with an HIV-positive employee and one with AIDS symptoms. Employers

Before Moving to New Quarters

1. Check the site history. What have been the past uses for the premises? Who have been the tenants/owners?

2. Check with the neighbors. Ask them if there have been any pollution problems in the past with your proposed location and the immediate area.

3. Check with the local city hall. What have been the past zonings for the property? Has there been any problem with the occupants or the facilities?

4. Check the building's plans. Track down the construction drawings and specifications for building materials to spot hidden problems like foam insulation or asbestos.

5. Have the duct work inspected. Look for mold, fibrous particles, humid conditions, and general state of repair and efficiency of operation.

6. Get a certification of habitability from the owner. Get the landlord or seller to guarantee in writing that the premises are not contaminated.

Dealing with Your Existing Pollution

1. Get reliable help. You need professionals to search and to cure most problems. Find an expert to inspect the premises.

2. Give smokers their own ventilation system or restrict use of the premises to nonsmoking.

3. Provide some means for periodic venting. Periodically air out the indoor areas.

4. Keep all duct work clean and dry. Bacteria and fungi grow in dark, moist places.

5. Remove and avoid installing anything that gives off unpleasant, irritating odors. An unpleasant smell generally means complications down the road.

6. Provide lots of plants to absorb carbon dioxide and odors. They give off oxygen as well.

EXHIBIT 16.4

Avoiding and dealing with indoor air pollution.

must have an AIDS policy and offer an ongoing educational effort to deal with this epidemic.

In their search for guidelines, many companies have taken advantage of a variety of volunteer speakers' programs, such as those offered by the HIV Peer Network in New York, and have adopted as policy the guidelines developed by the Citizens Commission on AIDS of New York and New Jersey. Among these are:

*   People with HIV-positive status and AIDS sufferers are entitled to the same rights and opportunities as people with other serious or life-threatening illnesses.

- At the very least, all policies should comply with all relevant laws and regulations, such as the Americans with Disabilities Act (ADA), which protects all persons with AIDS and HIV from discrimination.
- Employers should provide up-to-date information and training on risk reduction for employees.
- Employers should protect the confidentiality of employee medical records.
- Employers should provide education programs for all employees before any problems arise in the workplace.

A manager's kit is available from the Centers for Disease Control and Prevention in Atlanta; it includes posters and pamphlets with guidance on dealing with AIDS in the workplace. Their AIDS Hotline is 1-800-342-AIDS. Additional information can be obtained from your local chapter of the American Red Cross or the Equal Employment Opportunity Commission's ADA Hotline at 1-800-669-EEOC.

Drugs and Employees

Employees whose performances are affected by dependency on alcohol or other drugs are a danger to themselves and to others. They are usually incapable of delivering satisfactory levels of output, and they can cause all kinds of losses to their employers. The drug-dependent employee may steal from the employer or from fellow employees to get the money needed to support his or her habit. Small mistakes can become major problems and can lead to accidents, injuries, and worse. According to the U.S. Department of Labor:

- Seventy percent of all illegal drug users are employed either full- or part-time (over 10 million employees).
- One out of every twelve full-time employees reports current use of illicit drugs.
- One in every ten people in the United States has a problem with alcohol.
- Substance abusers are less productive, miss more workdays, are more likely to injure themselves or someone else, and file more workers' compensation claims than others.

To determine if your organization, unit, or team has a substance abuse problem or the potential for developing one, the U.S. Department of Labor suggests the following:

- Look at the statistics on such things as absenteeism, accidents, property losses, security breeches and workers' compensation claims. Compare them to the past and to national, state, local, and industrial averages for your type of business.

SUPERVISORS AND ETHICS

For many years, one of the fringe benefits of working in a brewery was to drink your company's products on the job during lunch and on breaks. The Adolph Coors Company of Golden, Colorado, was such a company until 1994 when one of its employees was killed on company property after smashing his car into a utility pole. He had a blood-alcohol level "three times Colorado's legal limit at the time...." At the request of the deceased's family and with input from its employees, Coors developed a new policy that allows employees to drink after work in eating areas. "'Consumption is to be modest. By that we mean, not to exceed two 12-ounce beers for half an hour after work,'" according to a company spokes-person. "The company also plans to beef up educational programs for employees on alcohol use.... Coors, the nation's third-largest brewery, is the last major U.S. brewery to ban on-the-job beer consumption." Many breweries continue to give their employees free cases of beer each month or to allow them to purchase cases at a discount.

What is your feeling about the new policy? What about allowing employees to purchase or take home free beer each month?

Source: Chicago Tribune, "Coors Halts On-Job Drinking After Worker's Death," October 7, 1994, sect. 3, 3.

- Consult will all organizational members to get their observations and sense of the extent of the problem. Employees should be part of the investigation and help formulate policy and corrective measures.
- All employees can play various roles to achieve and maintain a workplace free of substance abusers.

Five Steps to a Workplace Substance Abuse Program   Because substance abuse tends to be a hidden problem, many organizations have decided to proceed on the assumption that there may be individuals in the workplace who have or are developing a problem with alcohol or other drugs. The U.S. Department of Labor recommends the following five-part program that includes:

1. A written substance abuse policy
2. An employee education and awareness program
3. A supervisory training program
4. Access to an employee assistance program (EAP)
5. A drug testing program, as appropriate

Step one creates a clear commitment to creating and maintaining a workplace free of substance abuse. It states what is expected from employees and what will be done when the policy is violated. Since no two companies and their situations are exactly alike, your company's policy should be tailored to fit its needs and values. An effective policy should:

- State why it is necessary and what it is trying to encourage and prevent.
- Define what constitutes an infraction, and describe the consequences.
- Recognize that substance abuse is treatable, and identify company or community resources where employees with problems can obtain help.
- Describe the responsibility of an employee with a substance abuse problem to seek and complete required treatment.
- Assure employees that participation in assistance programs is confidential and will not jeopardize employment or advancement, but that participation will not protect employees from disciplinary action for continued unacceptable job performance or rule violations.
- State the company's position on drug testing and, if testing occurs, the consequences of a positive test result.

Exhibit 16.5 is one model for developing a substance abuse policy.

Step two requires companies to inform employees about drug and alcohol abuse and their effects on the company's safety, security, health care costs, productivity, and quality. Companies must explain their policies and how testing and assistance programs will be utilized. To be truly effective, an education and awareness program must be an ongoing one, not just a one-time effort.

Step three requires supervisors, team leaders, and team facilitators—those most directly responsible for enforcing the policy—to learn how to detect performance problems that may indicate substance abuse. Their responsibilities must be fixed and explained in line with the substance abuse policy. Although supervisors at every level are responsible for observing and documenting unsatisfactory work performance or behavior, they are not responsible for diagnosing substance abuse or treating substance abuse problems. They need to know the signs that may accompany substance abuse and what to do when they observe them. For example, supervisors may be required to counsel employees and refer them to an assistance program, a company physician, or drug testing program.

Step four specifies the way or ways for dealing with substance abuse. It may be a company-sponsored or community-based effort to help employees confront and deal with their problems. Providing access to a substance abuse EAP is a clear commitment by a company (and its unions) that it wishes to save valued employees and help them remain or once again become effective performers. With or without a company or union EAP, all employees should have the ability to inform co-workers about alcohol and other drugs, confront users with their unacceptable

EXHIBIT 16.5

*Sample drug abuse poli-
cy statement.*

Source: President's Drug
Advisory Council, Executive
Office of the President.

COMPANY
LETTERHEAD

DRUG ABUSE POLICY STATEMENT

(Company Name) is committed to providing a safe work environment and to fostering the well-being and health of its employees.
That commitment is jeopardized when any (Company Name)
employee illegally uses drugs on the job, comes to work under their
influence, or possesses, distributes or sells drugs in the workplace.
Therefore, (Company Name) has established the following policy:

(1) It is a violation of company policy for any employee to
possess, sell, trade, or offer for sale illegal drugs or otherwise engage in the illegal use of drugs on the job.

(2) It is a violation of company policy for anyone to report
to work under the influence of illegal drugs.

(3) It is a violation of the company policy for anyone to use
prescription drugs illegally. (However, nothing in this
policy precludes the appropriate use of legally prescribed
medications.)

(4) Violations of this policy are subject to disciplinary action
up to and including termination.

It is the responsibility of the company's supervisors to counsel
employees whenever they see changes in performance or behavior
that suggest an employee has a drug problem. Although it is not the
supervisor's job to diagnose personal problems, the supervisor should
encourage such employees to seek help and advise them about available resources for getting help. Everyone shares responsibility for
maintaining a safe work environment and co-workers should encourage anyone who may have a drug problem to seek help.

The goal of this policy is to balance our respect for individuals with
the need to maintain a safe, productive and drug-free environment.
The intent of this policy is to offer a helping hand to those who
need it, while sending a clear message that the illegal use of drugs
is incompatible with employment at (Company Name.)

> If your company is subject to the requirments of the Drug-Free
> Workplace Act of 1988 (by nature of a grant/contract with the
> Federal Government) you should add the following statement to
> your drug policy:
>
> > As a condition of employment, employees must abide by the
> > terms of this policy and must notify (The Company) in writ-
> > ing of any conviction of a violation of a criminal drug
> > statute occurring in the workplace no later than five calen-
> > dar days after such convicion.

work behaviors, provide referral information, and support those who are becoming drug and alcohol free.

These four steps must occur before drug testing can be initiated. Although drug testing of new applicants for jobs is rapidly becoming the norm with many employers, routine drug testing for existing employees is an issue loaded with controversy and affected by union contracts and various laws. Organizations doing business with the federal government are covered by the Drug-Free Workplace Act of 1988 and must certify that they provide a drug-free workplace, have a substance abuse policy, conduct ongoing drug-free awareness programs, require all employees to notify their companies of any criminal drug statute conviction, notify the federal government of such a violation, and impose sanctions for an employee convicted of drug abuse violations in the workplace. The U.S. Department of Transportation (DOT) requires drug testing of employees in safety-sensitive positions and drug abuse awareness education for supervisors and employees. In the federal government, routine, random drug testing has been the rule in the armed services for military and some civilian employees since the early 1980s. DOT began urine tests for drug and alcohol use during annual physicals about the same time and began random testing of air-traffic controllers, aviation and railway safety inspectors, electronic technicians, and employees with top secret clearances in 1987.

State and local laws tend to limit drug testing of employees. For example, a Connecticut statute allows random testing only in certain highly restricted circumstances. But when drug testing is used selectively and in sensitive work settings and testing is done in ways that collect, safeguard, and test samples properly, the courts have been able to endorse it. The U.S. Department of Labor suggests asking the following questions before testing employees for drugs:

- Who will be tested? (Only applicants? All employees?)
- When will testing be done? (After all accidents? When an employee behaves abnormally? As part of a routine physical? Randomly?)
- For which drugs will testing be done? (Only for illegal drugs? For prescription drugs that may affect work performance? For alcohol?)
- How frequently will testing be done? (Weekly? Monthly? Annually?)
- What test will be used, and what procedures will be followed? (How will specimens be collected, identified, and tracked? Will a physician with appropriate training interpret results?)
- What action will be taken if an applicant tests positive? (Refer employees to counseling and treatment after first positive but fire after second?)
- What precautions will be taken to protect an individual's privacy and the confidentiality of test results?

Various organizations and hot lines exist to give you more information and help you create a drug-free workplace and an employee assistance program. Here are several that you will find eager to help:

According to the Secretary of Health and Human Services' 1990 report, smoking costs America over $52 billion each year in health-care costs and lost productivity. Smoking-related diseases cost each American $221 a year, largely in health-care and insurance costs. In 1992, the Environmental Protection Agency (EPA) issued a report calling passive tobacco smoke a human lung carcinogen and linking it to lung cancer and other illnesses. As a result, legal experts are predicting an increasing number of legal actions to include:

- More workers' compensation claims from employees who work or have worked in a smoking environment
- Lawsuits against businesses by customers who have been exposed to others' smoke in public areas such as restaurants and bars

Although various state and local governments have enacted legislation that restricts smoking in areas with public access, including businesses, lawyers are now urging their clients to go beyond legal mandates to protect themselves.

In response to this, businesses are taking action to avoid legal liability or to at least limit it in the future. The question of what to do with smokers and for nonsmokers is one that can be dealt with by management edict. Such is the case at Raytheon, where plant managers can set their own rules. In the company's Massachusetts headquarters, employees may smoke in their offices, smokers' lounges, and the smoking section of the company's cafeteria. The Perini Corporation in Massachusetts provides separate facilities with independent ventilation systems for smokers. Other companies force their smokers to smoke outdoors.

In some companies, workers decide, unit by unit, how to handle the issues. In work-unit and self-managing teams with a mixture of smokers and nonsmokers, the issue is a team decision usually requiring a consensus. One supervisor in Chicago let his work unit make the decision after briefing them on the EPA's 1992 report. "They decided as a group [three smokers, seven nonsmokers] that whatever decision was arrived at had to keep people from being exposed to smoke against their wills." The group wrestled with the problem for several days. Smokers met informally off the job. Both groups were reluctant to take a hard stand. The issue was resolved when the smokers agreed to smoke only outdoors. "The key to making our rule stick was getting everyone involved in setting it."

Finally, some companies (like Ford Motor Company and the Blackwood/ Formall Corporation in Tennessee) have gone smoke free, banning smoking from company premises. Blackwood goes one step further, however. It bans smoking by employees both on and off the job. Any employee hired is given ninety days to quit and signs a no-smoking pledge. Roger Blackwood, owner of Blackwood/ Formall, says that smokers are absent 80 percent more than nonsmokers and believes that owners can be sued for not providing a smoke-free work environment. He's not taking any chances.

Sources: Chicago Tribune, "Company Posts No-Smoking Sign-On or Off Job," July 16, 1989, sect. 8, 1; Felsenthal, Edward. "EPA Report Sparks Antismoking Plans," *The Wall Street Journal*, January 7, 1993, B1, B3.

- The National Clearinghouse for Alcohol and Drug Information: 1-800-729-6686
- The Drug-Free Workplace Helpline: 1-800-843-4971
- The National Association of State Alcohol and Drug Abuse, Drug-Free Workplace Project: 1-202-783-6868
- 800 Cocaine: 1-800-COCAINE
- The American Council on Alcoholism Helpline: 1-800-527-5344
- Alcoholics Anonymous: 1-212-686-1100
- Narcotics Anonymous: 1-818-780-3951

Family Leave

In February 1993, President Clinton signed the Family and Medical Leave Act. It affects employers—businesses, nonprofits, and governmental units—with fifty or more employees by granting their employees up to twelve weeks unpaid leave for the birth or adoption of a child; caring for a spouse, child, or parent; or taking care of one's own illness. During the leave, the employer must guarantee that the employee will be able to return to the same or a comparable job. If employees have healthcare benefits, they must be continued during the term of the leave. Employers may apply employees' accrued sick leaves to the leave period and may exempt members of their 10 percent highest-paid group and those employees who have not worked at least a year or at least 25 hours per week or 1,250 hours during the past 12 months. Employees must provide thirty days' notice to their employers for foreseeable leaves (O'Brien, 1993).

The Supervisor's Role

Nearly all efforts at promoting safety and identifying and getting help to the troubled worker depend on you as a supervisor. Safety programs, regulations, procedures, and committees need your input and enforcement efforts to work effectively and efficiently. Exhibit 16.6 outlines your role in efforts at safety promotion and enforcement.

Many sources of help are available to you for identifying problem areas and for taking corrective actions. Exhibit 16.7 lists the most important areas to consider when conducting your investigations. You may be able to add areas of importance to it based on your own working environment. When you have identified the hazards, you are ready to set up and implement controls to prevent, eliminate, or deal with each of them. These controls get rid of a hazard or effectively eliminate or restrict its potential to cause harm. Dangerous machines can be eliminated or fitted with proper safeguards. Operators can be thoroughly trained and drilled in the safety procedures required. Personal protective gear can be purchased, issued, and checked regularly to see that it works and is being used correctly. Access to hazards can be carefully controlled by restricting it to those who are aware of and equipped to deal with hazardous situations.

The Safety-Minded Supervisor:

1. Takes the initiative in telling management about ideas for a safer layout of equipment, tools, and processes.

2. Knows the value of machine guards and makes sure the proper guards are provided and used.

3. Takes charge of operations that are not routine to make certain that safety precautions are determined.

4. Is an expert on waste disposal for housekeeping and fire protection.

5. Arranges for adequate storage and enforces good housekeeping.

6. Works with every employee without favoritism.

7. Keeps eyes open for the new employee or the experienced employee doing a new job.

8. Establishes good relations with union stewards and the safety committee

9. Sets good examples in safety practices.

10. Never lets a simple safety violation occur without talking to the employee immediately.

11. Not only explains how to do a job, but shows how and observes to ensure continuing safety.

12. Takes pride in knowing how to use all equipment safely.

13. Knows what materials are hazardous and how to store them safely.

14. Continues to "talk safety" and impress its importance on all employees.

EXHIBIT 16.6

Typical profile of a supervisor with low accident and injury rates.

Source: U.S. Department of Labor.

Your role as a supervisor is crucial in spotting troubled workers who need special assistance and in getting them started on a program designed to meet their needs. Look for warning signs such as changes in an employee's routines and behaviors. Increases in an employee's tardiness, absenteeism, ineffectiveness, or need for disciplinary action may signal that the employee has a personal or drug-related problem. Employees who suddenly isolate themselves from fellow workers and who become argumentative with their peers are asking for help.

When you think you have a troubled employee on your hands, let him or her know what you think, and recommend or refer the person to those in your company who can help. If drug use is suspected, your company should have a policy that is in line with your state's laws. A mandatory physical examination or drug test may or may not be approved in your state. Your company's medical department will work with the individual or refer him or her to an appropriate agency for treatment. Failure to comply with the company's directives may leave the employee subject to discipli-

Processing, receiving, shipping, and storage—Equipment, job planning, layout, heights, floor loads, projection of materials, materials handling, storage methods.

Building and grounds conditions—Floors, walls, ceilings, exits, stairs, walkways, ramps, platforms, driveways, aisles.

Housekeeping program—Waste disposal, tools, objects, materials, leakage and spillage, cleaning methods, schedules, work areas, remote areas, storage areas.

Electricity—Equipment, switches, breakers, fuses, switch boxes, junctions, special fixtures, circuits, insulation, extensions, tools, motors, grounding, NEC compliance.

Lighting—Type, intensity, controls, conditions, diffusion, location, glare and shadow control.

Heating and ventilating—Type, effectiveness, temperature, humidity, controls, natural and artificial ventilation and exhausting.

Machinery—Points of operation, flywheels, gears, shafts, pulleys, key ways, belts, couplings, sprockets, chains, frames, controls, lighting for tools and equipment, brakes, exhausting, feeding, oiling, adjusting, maintenance, lock out, grounding, work space, location, purchasing standards.

Personnel—Training, experience, methods of checking machines before use, type clothing, personal protective equipment, use of guards, tool storage, work practices, method of cleaning, oiling, or adjusting machinery.

Hand and power tools—Purchasing standards, inspection, storage, repair, types, maintenance, grounding, use and handling.

Chemicals—Storage, handling, transportation, spills, disposals, amounts used, toxicity or other harmful effects, warning signs, supervision, training, protective clothing and equipment.

Fire prevention—Extinguishers, alarms, sprinklers, smoking rules, exits, personnel assigned, separation of flammable materials and dangerous operations, explosive-proof fixtures in hazardous locations, waste disposal.

Maintenance—Regularity, effectiveness, training of personnel, materials and equipment used, records maintained, method of locking out machinery, general methods.

Personal protective equipment—Type, size, maintenance, repair, storage, assignment of responsibility, purchasing methods, standards observed, training in care and use, rules of use, method of assignment.

EXHIBIT 16.7
Typical scope of a self-inspection program.

Source: *OSHA Handbook for Small Businesses.*

nary measures and termination. You need to keep your people aware of the help that is available to them, and your company should have an ongoing educational program to expose employees to the dangers of drug abuse. Whatever programs your company provides should guarantee confidentiality to all who take part in them. This encourages voluntary compliance and helps avoid possible legal problems later on.

THE OCCUPATIONAL SAFETY AND HEALTH ACT (1970)

OSHA
the federal agency called the Occupational Safety and Health Administration

In 1970, Congress passed the Occupational Safety and Health Act, which created the **Occupational Safety and Health Administration (OSHA)** "to assure so far as possible every working man and woman in the nation safe and healthful working conditions to preserve our human resources." The law, which became effective in April 1971, applies to all employers engaged in any business affecting commerce and employing people. Its terms apply to all the states, territories, and possessions of the United States (and, beginning in 1995, apply to federal government employees). OSHA "has a $300 million budget, 2,300 employees and the power to fine violators. OSHA's regulations are spelled out in a 1,300-page book" (Kleiman, 1994). The law does not apply to working conditions protected under other federal occupational safety and health laws such as the Federal Coal Mine Health and Safety Act, the Atomic Energy Act, and the Migrant Health Act.

According to OSHA, each employer has the duty to furnish employees a working environment free from recognized hazards that cause or are likely to cause death or serious physical harm. Each employee has a duty to comply with safety and health rules and standards established by the employers or by OSHA. Administration and enforcement of OSHA are vest-

Supervisors of workers in hazardous situations need to make sure their employees understand the job and are properly protected. Safety of workers is foremost.

ed in the secretary of labor and in the Occupational Safety and Health Review Commission, a quasi-judicial board of three members appointed by the president. Research and related functions are vested in the secretary of health and human services, whose functions will for the most part be carried out by the National Institute for Occupational Safety and Health. The institute exists to develop and establish recommended occupational safety and health standards; to conduct research and experimental programs for developing criteria for new and improved job safety and health standards; and to make recommendations to the secretaries of labor and health and human services concerning new and improved standards.

Occupational Safety and Health Standards

In general, job safety and health standards consist of rules aimed at preventing hazards that have been proved by research and experience to be harmful to personal safety and health. Some standards—such as fire protection standards—apply to all employees. A great many standards, however, apply only to workers engaged in specific types of work, such as handling flammable materials.

Various safety and health standards have been issued by OSHA and are available to you through your company or from one of the many local OSHA offices in major cities around the country. Exhibit 16.8 shows a representative OSHA regulation. All help define protective measures or ways in which to deal with an identifiable hazard. We will discuss the activities of OSHA in more detail at the end of this chapter.

1910.151 Medical Services and First Aid.

(a) The employer shall ensure the ready availability of medical personnel for advice and consultation on matters of plant health.

(b) In the absence of an infirmary, clinic, or hospital in near proximity to the workplace which is used for the treatment of all injured employees, a person or persons shall be adequately trained to render first aid. First-aid supplies approved by the consulting physician shall be readily available.

(c) Where the eyes or body of any person may be exposed to injurious corrosive material, suitable facilities for quick drenching or flushing of the eyes and body shall be provided within the work area for immediate emergency use.

EXHIBIT 16.8
Sample OSHA standard dealing with medical services and first aid.

Source: General Industry Standards, USDOL-OSHA 2206.

It is not enough to warn and instruct employees about safety hazards. Supervisors must also enforce instructions and remove or eliminate hazards. Supervisors who ignore company or OSHA safety rules and standards can cause a doubling of the OSHA-prescribed penalties if accidents are the result of such behavior.

All employers and supervisors are obligated to familiarize themselves and their subordinates with the standards that apply to them at all times. Any person or business adversely affected by a government standard may challenge its validity by petitioning the U.S. Court of Appeals within sixty days after the new standard is imposed. Variances from standards may be granted to employers if extra time is needed to comply or if an employer is using safety measures as safe as those required by federal standards.

Compliance Complaints

Employees who believe that a violation of a safety or health standard exists that threatens them with physical harm may request an inspection by sending a signed written notice to the Department of Labor, which, in turn, should provide a copy to the employer. The names of the complainants will not be revealed to the employer. If the department finds no reasonable grounds for the complaint and a citation is not issued, the complainants will be notified in writing. Employee complaints may also be made to any local OSHA office. Complaining employees may not be persecuted in any way by their employers.

Since the Whirlpool Corporation *v.* Marshall case in 1980, workers have had the right to refuse a job assignment or to walk off the job "because of a reasonable apprehension of health or serious injury coupled with a reasonable belief that no less drastic alternative is available." This wording and other words in the Supreme Court decision have been interpreted to mean that workers may refuse to perform work that constitutes a clear and present danger, in their minds, to their safety. Employers are not required to pay workers who do not perform such work, but they may not reprimand them in any way.

OSHA Inspections

Since October 1981, OSHA may only target for regular inspection visits firms with ten or more employees, firms with below-average safety records, and firms with complaining employees. Since the 1979 Supreme Court decision in Marshall *v.* Barlow's, Inc., employers do not have to admit OSHA inspectors who do not have a search warrant. But all companies (except those with ten or fewer employees) must keep OSHA-required accident and illness records and records on employee exposure to potentially toxic materials or other harmful physical agents. Since August 1987, 59 million workers have had the right to demand information about hazardous chemicals at their work sites. They can demand to know the identities and compositions of chemicals that they are exposed to at work.

When OSHA compliance officers (inspectors) call, they may be on a routine inspection, or they may be responding to an employee's complaint. In the latter case, the inspectors need not limit their visits to the complaint. Other areas may be investigated as well.

An OSHA inspector may ask the supervisor or any person in charge of an area to accompany him or her on an inspection, or the inspector may conduct the inspection alone. Employers do not have an absolute right to accompany inspectors. If permissible, it is a good practice for any supervisor to tag along on any inspection that involves his or her work area. You may spot violations that the inspector does not, and you will be present to give explanations and to make on-the-spot corrections of minor problems.

OSHA inspections consist of an opening conference between the compliance officer and the employer, an inspection tour, and a closing conference. At the closing conference, the compliance officer reviews the findings and may issue a citation stating the standard(s) violated and specifying a time limit for correcting each violation. Citations for most violations are usually sent by registered mail from the area director of the OSHA office. Citations must be posted in a prominent place until the violations they cite are corrected. Fines may be assessed for failing to post the citation, for removing it prematurely, or for exceeding the time limit mentioned in the citation for correcting violations. When an employer feels that a citation is unfair or incorrect, it may appeal the citation within fifteen working days after receipt.

On-Site Consultation

OSHA has developed a free on-site consultation service that is available to any employer on request. An OSHA consultant will visit a business and tour the facilities, pointing out what operations are governed by OSHA standards and how to interpret them. If violations are found, they are pointed out, and suggestions are offered on how to correct them. No citations are issued, but—as part of the decision to accept a consultation—the employer must agree to eliminate, within a reasonable time, all hazards discovered.

STATE PROGRAMS

When the Occupational Safety and Health Act was passed in 1970, many states already had their own state safety laws. Some of these laws were criticized for their weak standards, ineffective administration, and lax enforcement. Others were considered quite acceptable. The federal safety law offered states the opportunity to develop and administer their own safety and health programs, provided that the states could demonstrate that their programs were "at least as effective" as the federal program. State safety and health programs have to be approved by OSHA.

To obtain approval from OSHA, a state must demonstrate that its standards for safety and health are adequate and that it is capable of enforcing them. A state is given a three-year probationary period to demonstrate that it has adequate standards, enforcement, appeal procedures, protection for public employees, and trained safety inspectors. About half of the states have developed and are administering their own safety and health programs.

Workers' Compensation

Prior to 1910, workers were injured frequently on the job. Their lost wages and medical bills were usually their own problems unless they could prove in a court of law that their employers were the sole force or cause of their injuries. If a worker contributed in any way to the injury suffered or if a worker knew his or her work to be dangerous, the employer could usually avoid legal responsibility for damages.

workers' compensation
federal and state laws designed to compensate employees for illnesses and injuries that arise out of and in the course of their employment

Workers' compensation insurance programs compensate employees for medical and disability expenses, as well as for income lost because of an illness or injury. They are state mandated and may be either elective or compulsory. Under elective laws, a company may provide the protection the law requires on its own; it insures itself against worker claims. But employees or their families would then be free to sue the employer for damages for injuries, illnesses, or deaths. "Large employers that self-insure pay these claims out of the corporate kitty, while smaller concerns typically purchase insurance..." (Fefer, 1994). If a worker suffers an illness or injury on the job, he or she can file a claim with the state's compensation board. Benefits are paid to individuals according to schedules containing fixed maximums that may be awarded by compensation boards.

Under compulsory workers' compensation laws, every employer within the state's jurisdiction must accept the application of the law and provide the benefits required. When the company provides the protection required by law through workers' compensation insurance, the employee who suffers an injury or illness may not sue.

The cost of workers' compensation insurance varies, depending on a company's history of worker claims. The more claims filed against a company, and the more benefits paid by an insurance company, the greater the premium charged for workers' compensation protection. Most businesses, therefore, try to insure workers' safety through the latest in equipment devices and work safety rules—not only to protect their workers from injury but also to protect their profits from the drain of insurance premiums and self-insurance funds.

OshKosh B'Gosh, a maker of overalls, had a routine inspection from OSHA and received a citation. Plant operations were at the root of a growing number of cumulative trauma disorders (CTDs) such as carpal tunnel syndrome. According to Pat Hirschberg, the plant's safety chief, "the directive to fix the problem 'was the best thing that could have happened to us'" (Fefer, 1994). A committee was created "to inspect every aspect of production and uncover the sources of injury. It found that most of the worker's problems arose from small, awkward motions that required force and were highly repetitious" (Fefer, 1994). Operations created abnormal use of fingers, wrists, and hands, and neither tables nor chairs were adjustable. The committee presented its findings and recommendations to senior management and convinced them to make several changes: Special equipment was designed by engineers to facilitate production operations; job rotation was introduced to vary employee activities; training was instituted to teach proper equipment adjustment and work positions; and workers were encouraged to bring their concerns to management so that changes could be made. The results:

EXHIBIT 16.9
Regulatory model of the workers' compensation system.

Source: Ledvinka, James, and Scarpello, Vida G. *Federal Regulation of Personnel and Human Resource Management,* 2d ed. (Boston: PWS-Kent, 1991), 193.

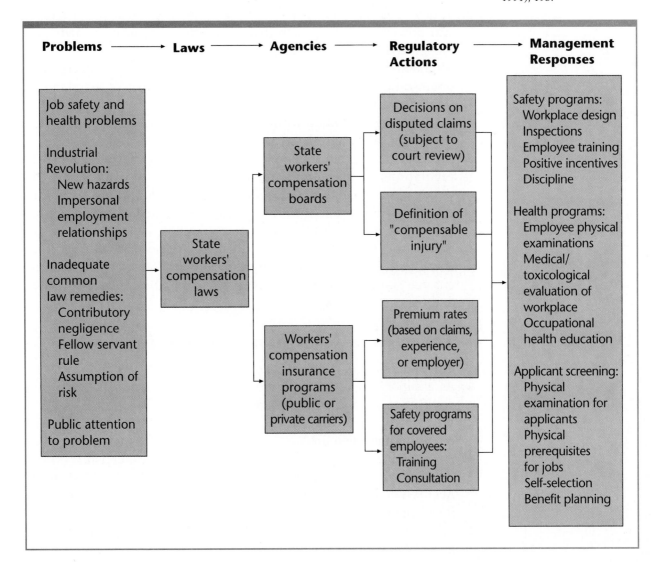

The number of claims jumped by a third when the program was introduced, as people began to pay attention to symptoms they might previously have ignored. But because these ailments were caught in the early stages, they never became costly or severe. [Workers' compensation] claims eventually retreated as the company's prevention strategy took effect. [In 1993] comp costs for the firm were down from 1992 by a third, or $2.7 million. That sum alone more than covers the cost of the company's long-term safety investment... (Fefer, 1994).

For some additional insights, see this chapter's Supervisors and Ethics and Supervisors and Quality features as well as Exhibit 16.9 (note, in the exhibit, the "Management Responses" portion in particular).

Instant Replay

1. The security of your company's and subordinates' assets is partly your responsibility.
2. Your people depend on you and the company's policies, programs, and procedures, along with their own efforts, to protect them from recognized and recognizable hazards.
3. Although safety and security are everyone's legitimate concern, your organization depends on you and its other managers for planning, implementing, and enforcing proper programs.
4. Engineering, education (training), and enforcement are the keys to successful safety and security efforts.
5. Since 1971, over 40 million working Americans have depended on regulations and enforcement inspections provided by the Occupational Safety and Health Administration, along with their employers' efforts and their own actions, to make the workplace a less hazardous environment.
6. Supervisors who really care about safety and security listen to their employees, look for hazards, fix responsibility for safety and security, enforce standards and procedures, and discipline violators of safety and security policies.

Questions for Class Discussion

1. Can you define this chapter's key terms?
2. As a supervisor, how would you go about the task of safeguarding your office or shop environments?
3. What are a supervisor's duties with regard to fire prevention? With regard to fighting a fire?
4. How can a supervisor act to prevent losses from vandalism?
5. What are the major purposes of the Occupational Safety and Health Act? When did it become effective in enforcement efforts? How does it enforce its regulations?
6. What are an employer's rights with regard to OSHA inspectors? In general, how does an OSHA inspector conduct inspections?

Incident

Purpose: To acquaint you with the help available from public and private sources for creating a drug-free workplace.

Your Task: Using the telephone numbers included in this chapter, contact three sources, and request their free materials. Summarize the materials, and present your summary to your class. Together with classmates, create a policy for your school or company.

Safety First

"Our regulations clearly state that employees may not walk off the job or refuse to perform a job just because they think it is unsafe," said Amy Price, the personnel manager of Hadley Products Company.

"That's right," said Andy Prachak. "As the foreman out in that yard, I know what those men go through every day. I don't blame Ed for wanting safer conditions. But I draw the line at open protests and insubordination to get them."

Rick Sczebo, head of the union's grievance committee, interrupted. "You two are talking about firing Ed for leaving a hazardous job. You ought to be grateful Ed hasn't complained to OSHA about conditions out in that yard. There have been two serious injuries already, due mainly to the company's refusing to fix known hazards. Does someone have to be killed or permanently injured before people do something about safety?"

"Don't cloud the issue, Rick," said Amy. "We are talking about a serious breach of discipline. If we let Ed get away with a clear case of insubordination, Andy will have to suffer for it for a long time to come. Ed was given a direct order to finish stacking those skids with his forklift. He refused and left the yard before quitting time and without a pass. What's worse, he refused in front of three other workmen who heard Andy's order."

"Look, Amy, this is not a case of insubordination. Andy will be the first to tell you that Ed is a good worker. Right, Andy?"

"Right, one of the best. That's why I'm shocked at his leaving like he did. It just wasn't like him."

"Well," said Rick, "that ought to tell you how bad things must have been in Ed's mind. You were asking him to risk his life and limb. As the grievance says, and I quote Ed's words, 'Those skids were broken and piled in a dangerous way. They were stacked badly and were already too high. When the foreman told me to add another layer, I knew they would be too unsteady to stay up for long. I wasn't going to put my buddies and myself in any more danger by adding another layer.'"

"You see," Rick continued, "Ed saw a clear danger and acted the way any normal person should. He refused to carry out a stupid order that never should have been given in the first place."

"Now see here," said Andy, "I resent that. If Ed thought the job was that dangerous, why didn't he tell me what he thought? He didn't explain anything until he wrote that grievance in response to his firing. All I know is that I don't want him back in the yard. He's fired now, and if he's rehired, I'll quit."

"Wait a minute, Andy. Let's not lose our heads here," said Amy. "Let's have a cup of coffee and relax a minute. I'll get some. Be back in a minute."

Amy left the room. Andy and Rick glared at each other through a long silence. Then Rick spoke up.

"The union tells me that any worker can leave his job if he believes there is a real danger of death and serious injury."

"Well, what your union doesn't say is what OSHA cases have said: that a worker can leave only when the company knows about the hazards and refuses to do anything about them. Ed never told me what he thought. I'm not a mind reader."

Amy returned with three steaming cups of coffee for two steaming employees. Amy spoke as she set the cups down. "What's it going to take to settle the case, Rick?"

"Amy, what the union wants is to correct the bad conditions out in the yard as soon as possible and to reinstate Ed with back pay and seniority. If we don't get some action soon, we're going to call in the OSHA inspectors."

"If you do," replied Amy, "you could shut this place down with violations. Your members would be out of a job for Lord knows how long. You know how government red tape can foul things up. Let me propose a compromise here. If it's OK with Andy, we will get started on a safety program and fix the problems your boys think are the most serious ones. Give us a list, and we will do as much as we can as fast as our budget will allow. Second, we will bring Ed back with no back pay for the two weeks he's been fired and give him his seniority minus those two weeks. What do you say, Andy?"

"OK, if that's the best we can do."

"What do you say, Rick?"

Questions

1. Comment on the union's and the company's views of OSHA.
2. What are the central issues in this case?
3. If you were the union's spokesperson, how would you answer Amy's suggested compromise?
4. Comment on the supervisor's view of the importance of safety versus the importance of maintaining discipline.

CASE PROBLEM 16.2

The Rumor

The first shift was on a break in the employee cafeteria, and its members were discussing a rumor circulating throughout the plant.

"Have you heard the latest?" asked Chuck.

"You mean about Hansdorf?" asked Fran.

Wally from the other end of the table put his finger to his lips and leaned toward the others. "Hansdorf is HIV positive. Seems there is more to him than meets the eye. Shawn from accounting says that he tested positive on the last random drug test he took about a month ago."

Fran reentered the discussion. "I thought those tests were confidential. What the hell does the company do with the results, post 'em on the bulletin boards?"

Chuck laughed and shook his head. "You people are naive if you think the bad results are kept secret. The real problem is what are we going to do about drug tests that test for more than drugs?"

"Yeah, but what about working around Hansdorf? He's on the shift before ours. Do those guys know that he's got AIDS?"

"AIDS!" shrieked Jill. "You mean that someone in the plant has a death sentence?"

"Hold on, people," cautioned Ray. "Being HIV positive doesn't necessarily mean a person has AIDS. I read that about a million Americans are HIV positive, and no one can say for sure who will develop AIDS."

"We better find out if Hansy has any close friends on our shift," said Chuck.

"Hey, let's not go on a witch hunt, you guys. Cool it. He works in the same plant, and he's not sick. It's not our problem," said Fran.

"Look, I'm not working in a place that has people with AIDS all around me. We better get the union in on this, and let's get rid of Hansdorf," said Jill.

"Don't sweat it, Jill. Women can't get AIDS and besides, you don't get AIDS through casual contact anyway."

The group continued talking about the situation and vowed that the union steward, Rudy, should be contacted. Two of the participants indicated that if the rumor was true and Hansdorf really did have AIDS, maybe the plant was an unsafe place to work.

Questions

1. What training needs can you identify in this case?
2. What diversity issues exist in this case?
3. What do you think about the ways in which management is conducting its employee testing program?

Notes

The American Almanac: 1994-1995 (Austin, Tex.: Reference Press, 1994). 219.

Bequai, August. "Ethics, Education Key to Crime Prevention," *USA Today,* June 8, 1987, 8E.

Chicago Tribune. "Employees Top Shoplifters," December 19, 1994, sect. 4, 3.

Chicago Tribune. "Invader of Computer Network Is Convicted," January 23, 1990, sect. 3, 1.

Chicago Tribune. "Keeping Tabs on Assets, Workers," December 12, 1994, sect. 4, 3.

The Council of Better Business Bureaus. *How to Protect Your Business from Fraud, Scams, and Crime* (White Plains, N.Y.: The Benjamin Company, 1992), 177–178.

Cullison, A. E. "Fax Machines an Open Book to Hackers," *Chicago Tribune,* September 9, 1990, sect. 7, 11B.

Dunkel, Tom. "Danger Zone: Your Office," *Working Woman,* August 1994, 38–41, 70, 72–73.

Emshwiller, John R. "Businesses Lose Billions of Dollars to Employee Theft," *The Wall Street Journal,* October 5, 1992, B2.

Fefer, Mark D. "Taking Control of Your Workers' Comp Costs," *Fortune,* October 3, 1994, 131—132, 134, 136.

Franklin, Stephen. "Remembering Workers Killed, Injured on the Job," *Chicago Tribune,* April 29, 1994, sect. 3, 1, 2.

Goozner, Merrill, "Job Diseases Remain a Major Cause of Death," *Chicago Tribune,* August 31, 1990, sect. 1, l, l4.

Hagedorn, Ann. "It's Why Employees Don't Want the Boss's Portrait on the Wall," *The Wall Street Journal,* November 29, 1990, B1.

Hillkirk, John. "They're Plugging the Leaks in Our Computer," *USA Today,* June 8, 1987, 8E.

O'Brien, Timothy L., Gupta, Udayan, and Marsh, Barbara. "Most Small Businesses Appear Prepared to Cope with New Family-Leave Rules," *The Wall Street Journal,* February 8, 1993, B1.

Randle, Wilma, "Survey Finds Shrinkage in Shoplifting," *Chicago Tribune,* November 23, 1992, sect. 4, 2.

———. "When Employees Lie, Cheat or Steal," *Working Woman,* January 1995, 55–56, 76.

Reitman, Valerie. "Alarm Sounded on Shoplifting," *Chicago Tribune,* January 28, 1990, sect. 7, 12.

Rice, Faye. "Do You Work in a Sick Building?," *Fortune,* July 2, 1990, 87.

Rochester, Jack B. "Insiders Lead the List of Electronic Thieves," *USA Today,* June 8, 1987, 8E.

Ziemba, Stanley. "Study Finds Lax Computer Security Is Costing Business," *Chicago Tribune* November 20, 1994, sect. 7, 5.

Suggested Readings

Council of Better Business Bureaus. *How to Protect Your Business from Fraud, Scams, and Crime.* White Plains, N.Y.: The Benjamin Company, 1992.

Hammer, Willie. *Occupational Safety Management and Engineering,* 3d ed. Englewood Cliffs, N.J.: Prentice Hall, 1985.

Ledvinka, James, and Scarpello, Vida G. *Federal Regulation of Personnel and Human Resource Management,* 2d ed. Boston: PWS-Kent, 1991.

National Safety Council. *Supervisor's Safety Manual,* 5th ed. Chicago: National Safety Council, 1975.

———. *Fundamentals of Industrial Hygiene,* 2d ed. Chicago: National Safety Council, 1979.

Rice, Faye. "Do You Work in a Sick Building?" *Fortune* (July 2, 1990): 86–88.

U.S. Department of Labor. *What Works: Workplaces Without Alcohol and Other Drugs,* 1994.

Appendix

HOW TO PRESENT A CASE IN CLASS

Getting the Facts

1. Read the entire care through.
2. Before reading the questions that follow it, ask yourself where the problems lie. If you have no clear insights, reread the case. Recall that the case appears in conjunction with a chapter in the text. The major purpose of a case is to dramatize an incident within which you can apply the knowledge you have gained from that chapter and the ones preceding it.
3. Read all the questions following the case. Consider each in a sequence that you feel makes the most sense. Use your experience to help you resolve each issue. Where you read about a person taking action, ask yourself, "What will be the effect of that action on the people in the case?"
4. Where a question calls for your opinion, back it up with specific examples from your own experiences when possible.
5. When you feel that you cannot answer a question without additional information, try to read into the case and between its lines. Look for clues that will allow you to deduce or create what is probably true from what you are given. Most cases give you symptoms rather than a disease. Try to get under the surface of the wording. This will become easier for you with each new case.
6. Make notes on your answer to each question. Quote from the case and cite specific references from the chapter(s) that relate to the case.

Presenting the Case in Class

1. Start with a capsule summary of the facts as you see them. Identify the key persons in the case and put their names and titles on the blackboard so that you can refer to them as you speak.
2. When answering each question, be as specific and factual as you can. State your decision and give the audience the benefit of your research and analysis. Cite your references and quote from the case to prove a point. Let the class know where you are when you do so, so that they can follow your argument.
3. Keep in mind that there is no one right answer to the case's questions. There are many wrong ones, however. You are far better off to base your conclusions on the facts than to guess. You can expect the greatest resistance and objections from the class when you state decisions that required deductions or assumptions. If you can show the group your logic, they will probably accept your reasoning. Be prepared for different sets of assumptions—possibly as valid as yours—with the corresponding different conclusions. Allow time for questions. If you are stuck, defer the answer to a classmate or volunteer.

Glossary

accident any unforeseen or unplanned incident or event

accountability having to answer to someone for your performance or failure to perform to standards

appraisal process periodic evaluations of each subordinate's on-the-job performance as well as his or her skill levels, attitudes, and potential

arbitration the use of a neutral third party in a dispute between management and labor to resolve the areas of conflict

attitude a person's manner of thinking, feeling, or acting toward specific stimuli

authority a person's right to give orders and instructions to others and to use organizational resources

autocratic style a management and leadership style characterized by the retention by the leader of all authority for decision making

behavior modeling a visual training approach designed to teach attitudes and proper modes of behavior by involving supervisors and others in real-life performances

belief a perception based on a conviction that certain things are true or probable in one's own mind (opinion)

bureaucratic style a management style characterized by the manager's reliance on rules, regulations, policies, and procedures to direct subordinates

career a sequence of jobs that takes people to higher levels of pay and responsibility

career path a route chosen by an employer or employee through a series of related horizontal and vertical moves to jobs of ever-increasing responsibilities

clique an informal group of two or more people who come together by choice to satisfy mutual interests or to pursue common goals

collective bargaining the process of negotiating a union agreement that covers wages, hours, and working conditions for employees who are union members

communication the transmission of information and common understanding from one person or group to another through the use of common symbols

complaint any expression of unhappiness with working conditions or on-the-job relationships that comes to a manager's attention

computer monitoring using computers to measure how employees achieve their outputs—monitoring work as it takes place—and to keep track of their total outputs

computer virus a rogue computer program that can reproduce itself endlessly or cause other havoc, such as destroying stored data

controlling the management function that sets standards that are applied to performance. Controls attempt to prevent, identify, and correct deviations from standards

counselor the human relations role in which a supervisor is an advisor and director to subordinates

cultural diversity the co-existence of two or more cultural groups within an organization

delegation   the act of passing formal or positional authority by a manager to another

democratic style   a management and leadership style characterized by a sharing of decision-making authority with subordinates by the leader

directing   the supervision or overseeing of people and processes

direction   in communication, the flow or path a message takes in order to reach a receiver

directive interview   an interview planned and totally controlled by the interviewer

discipline   the management duty that involves educating subordinates to foster obedience and self-control and dispensing appropriate punishment for wrongdoing

disparate impact   the existence of a significantly different selection rate between women or minorities and nonprotected groups

diversity   differences in people and groups that serve to both unite and separate them from others

employee association   a group that bargains collectively with management but has given up or has been barred from the right to strike

employment at will   the common law doctrine that holds that employment will last until either employer or employee decides to terminate it, with or without just cause

empower   to equip people to function on their own, without direct supervision

ergonomics   concern about the design of work sites, machines, equipment, and systems to minimize stress and job-related injuries

ethics   a field of philosophy dealing with the rightness and wrongness of human conduct in society

feedback   any effort made by parties to a communication to ensure that they have a common understanding of each other's meaning and intent

force-field analysis   a method for visualizing the driving and restraining forces at work within an individual so as to assess what is needed to make a change in a person's attitudes

foreman   a supervisor of workers in manufacturing

formal group   two or more people who come together by management decision to achieve specific goals

formal organization   an enterprise that has clearly stated goals, a division of labor among specialists, a rational design, and a hierarchy of authority and accountability

functional authority   the right that a manager of a staff department has to make decisions and to give orders that affect the way things are done in another department

goal   the objective, target, or end result expected from the execution of programs, tasks, and activities

grapevine   informal channels at work that transmit information or misinformation

grievance   an alleged violation of the labor-management agreement

grievance processing   settling an alleged violation of the union–management agreement in accordance with the method outlined in that agreement

group   two or more people who are consciously aware of one another, who consider themselves to be a functioning unit, and who share in a quest for common goals or benefits

health   the general condition of a person physically, mentally, and emotionally and efforts at preventing illness and treating injuries when they occur

hierarchy   the group of people picked to staff an organization's positions of formal authority—its management positions

human needs   physiological and psychological requirements that all humans share and that act as motives for behavior

human relations the development and maintenance of sound on-the-job relationships with subordinates, peers, and superiors

individualism the training principle that requires a trainer to conduct training at a pace suitable for the trainee

induction the planning and conduct of a program to introduce a new employee to his or her job, working environment, supervisor, and peers

informal group two or more people who come together by choice to satisfy mutual needs or to share common interests

information any facts, figures, or data that are in a form or format that makes them usable to a person who possesses them

interview a two-way conversation under the control of one of the parties

job description a formal listing of the duties that make up a position in the organization

job enlargement increasing the number of tasks or the quantity of output required in a job

job enrichment providing variety, deeper personal interest and involvement, greater autonomy and challenge, or increased responsibility on the job

job rotation movement of people to different jobs, usually for a temporary period, in order to inform, train, or stimulate cooperation and understanding among them

job specification the personal characteristics and skill levels that are required of an individual to execute a job

labor relations management activities created by the fact that the organization has a union or unions to bargain with

leadership the ability to get work done with and through others while winning their respect, confidence, loyalty, and willing cooperation

line authority a manager's right to give direct orders to subordinates and appraise, reward, and discipline those who receive those orders

linking pin key individual who is a member of two or more formal groups in an organization, thus linking or connecting the groups

maintenance factor according to Herzberg, a factor that can be provided by an employer in order to prevent job dissatisfaction

management the process of planning, organizing, directing, and controlling human, material, and informational resources for the purposes of setting and achieving stated goals; also, a team of people making up an organization's hierarchy

management by exception a management principle asserting that managers should spend their time on those matters that require their particular expertise

management by objectives a management principle that encourages subordinates to set performance goals that are in line with their unit's and organization's goals and that are approved by their supervisors

management by wandering around a leadership principle that encourages supervisors to get out of their offices regularly so that they can touch base with those who affect their operations and those whom their operations affect

management skills categories of capabilities needed by all managers at every level in an organization

manager a member of an organization's hierarchy who is paid to make decisions; one who gets things done with and through others, through the execution of the basic management functions

mediation the use of a neutral third party in a labor–management dispute to recommend a solution to the issues that divide the parties

medium a channel or means used to carry a message in the communication process

message the ideas, intent, and feelings that you wish to communicate to a receiver

middle management the members of the hierarchy below the rank of top management but above the rank of supervisor

minority according to the EEOC, a member of the following groups: Hispanics, Native Americans, African Americans, Asians or Pacific Islanders, Alaskan natives

mission the expression in words—backed up with both plans and actions—of the organization's central and common purpose—its reason for existing

motivation 1. the drive within a person to achieve a goal. 2. the training principle that requires both trainer and trainee to be favorably predisposed and ready to undergo training

motivation factor according to Herzberg, a factor that has the potential to stimulate internal motivation to provide a better-than-average performance and commitment from those to whom it appeals

negative discipline the part of discipline that emphasizes the detection and punishment of wrongdoing

networking using one's friends, family, and work-related contacts to help find employment or to advance one's career

nondirective interview an interview planned by the interviewer but controlled by the interviewee

objective the training principle that requires trainer and trainees to know what is to be mastered through training

obsolescence a state or condition that exists when a person or machine is no longer able to perform to standards or to management's expectations

operating management the level of the hierarchy that oversees the work of nonmanagement people (workers)

organizational development a planned, managed, systematic process used to change the culture, system, and behavior of an organization to improve its effectiveness in solving problems and achieving goals

orientation the planning and conduct of a program to introduce a new employee to the company and its history, policies, rules, and procedures

OSHA the federal agency called the Occupational Safety and Health Administration

peer a person on the same level of authority and status as another

planning the management function through which managers decide what they want to achieve and how they are going to do the achieving

policy a broad guideline constructed by top management to influence managers' approaches to solving problems and dealing with recurring situations

positive discipline the part of discipline that promotes understanding and self-control by letting subordinates know what is expected of them

power the ability to influence others so that they respond favorably to orders and instructions

problem-solving meeting gathering to reach a group consensus or solution to a problem affecting the group

procedure a general routine or method for executing day-to-day operations

productivity the amount of input needed to generate a given amount of output

program a plan listing goals and containing the answers to the who, what, when, where, how, and how much of the plan

progressive discipline a system using warnings about what is and is not acceptable conduct; specific job-related rules; punishments that fit the offense; punishments that grow in severity as misconduct persists; and prompt, consistent enforcement

psychological contract an unwritten recognition of what an employer and an employee expect to give and to get from each other

quality the totality of features and characteristics of a product or service (or process or project) that bear on its ability to satisfy stated or implied goals (requirements of producers and customers)

quality of working life a general label given to various programs and projects designed to help employees satisfy their needs and meet their expectations from work

realism the training principle that requires training to simulate or duplicate the actual working environment and behavior or performance required of the trainee

receiver the person or group intended by transmitters to receive their messages

reengineering the total rethinking of what an organization should be doing and how it should do it

reinforcement The training principle that requires trainees to review and restate knowledge learned

response the principle of training that requires feedback from trainees to trainers and vice versa

responsibility the obligation each person with authority has to execute his or her duties to the best of his or her abilities

résumé an employment-related document submitted by the applicant and containing vital data such as the person's name, address, employment goals, and work-related education and experiences

role ambiguity the situation that occurs whenever a manager is uncertain about the role that he or she is expected to play

role conflict a situation that occurs when contradictory or opposing demands are made on a manager

role prescription the collection of expectations and demands from superiors, subordinates, and others that shapes a manager's job description and perception of his or her job

rule a regulation on human conduct at work

safety efforts at protecting human resources from accidents and injuries

sanction negative means, such as threats or punishments, used by superiors or the organization to encourage subordinates to play their roles as prescribed by superiors or the organization

scoreboarding providing feedback on individual and team efforts to reach goals

security efforts at protecting physical facilities and nonhuman assets from loss or damage

selection the personnel or human resource management function that determines who is and is not hired

sexual harassment unwelcomed sexual advances, requests for sexual favors, and other physical and verbal conduct of a sexual nature

socialization the process a new employee undergoes in the first few weeks of employment through which he or she learns how to cope and succeed

spectator style A management style characterized by treating subordinates as independent decision makers

spokesperson the human relations role through which a supervisor represents management's views to workers and workers' views to management

staff authority the right of staff managers to give advice and counsel to all other managers in an organization in the areas of their expertise

standard a device for measuring or monitoring the performance of people, machines, or processes

standard (in appraisals) a quantity or quality designation that can be used as a basis of comparison for judging behaviors and outcomes

steward the union's elected or appointed first-line representative in the areas in which workers are found

stress worry, anxiety, or tension that accompanies situations and problems we face and makes us uncertain about the ways in which we should resolve them

stretch targets   giant, seemingly unreachable milestones requiring leaps of progress

subjects   the principle of training that requires trainers to know the subject being taught and to know the trainees' needs

supervisor   a manager responsible for the welfare, behaviors, and performances of non-management employees (workers)

synergy   cooperative action or force of two or more elements pulling together that yields a result greater than the sum of the results that could be achieved separately by the elements

syntality   a group's "personality"–what makes it unique

team facilitator   a supervisor in charge of teams but working outside them

team leader   a supervisor working in a team and responsible for its members

Theory X   a set of attitudes traditionally held by managers that assumes the worst with regard to the average worker's initiative and creativity

Theory Y   a set of attitudes held by today's generation of managers that assumes the best about the average worker's initiative and creativity

Theory Z   a set of approaches to managing people based on the attitudes of Japanese managers about the importance of the individual and of team effort to the organization

top management   the uppermost part of the management hierarchy, containing the positions of the chief executive and his or her immediate subordinates

training   the activity concerned with improving employees' performances in their present jobs by imparting skills, knowledge, and attitudes

training objective   a written statement containing what the trainee should be able to do, the conditions under which the trainee is expected to perform, and the criteria used to judge the adequacy of the performance

transmitter   the person or group that sends a message to a receiver

understanding   all parties to a communication are of one mind regarding its meaning and intent

union   a group of workers who are employed by a company or an industry or who practice the same skilled craft and have banded together to bargain collectively with their employers

validity   the degree to which a selection device measures what it is supposed to measure or is predictive of a person's performance on a job

vandalism   wanton or willful destruction or damage to another's property

vision   the statement of what kind of company the organization wants to be in the future

whistleblower   an employee who makes known to authorities the violations of laws and actions committed by his or her employer that are contrary to public policy

work ethic   people's attitudes about the importance of working, the kind of work they choose or are required to do, and the quality of their efforts while performing work

worker   any employee who is not a member of the management hierarchy

workers' compensation   federal and state laws designed to compensate employees for illnesses and injuries that arise out of and in the course of their employment

Index

working relationships with, 276–89
  maintaining, 289
Sullivan, Richard, 21
Summary, oral presentations, 171
Superiors, supervisors' responsibilities to, 11–12
Supervising teams, 56, 78, 119, 173, 258, 279, 322, 378, 396, 489, 514, 563
Supervisors:
  attitudes of, 200–204
  attributes of, 28
  definition of, 4
  and discipline, 513
  effectiveness of, 12
  efficiency of, 12
  and ethics, 59–62, 74, 167, 220, 254, 274, 317, 383, 428, 441, 495, 523, 556, 598
  of groups, 313–52
  and human needs, 239–41
  as linking pins, 16–17
  personnel sources, 27–29
  problem supervisors, 203
  Pygmalion effect, 201–3
  and quality, 80, 175, 193, 245, 326, 363, 419, 446, 530, 560
  responsibilities, 8–12
    to peers, 10–11
    to subordinates, 8–10
    to superiors, 11–12
  roles of, 12–16
    changes in, 39
    role ambiguity, 15
    role conflict, 14–15
    role performance, 15–16
    role prescriptions, 12–14
    role sanctions, 16
  selection involvement, advantages of, 394–95
  and staff specialists, 292
  and stewards, 567–68
  traditional behaviors of, changes in, 4
  trends affecting, 17–27
    education, 21–22
    foreign ownership of American business, 22
    information/technology, 18–19
    quality and productivity improvement, 19–21
    use of teams, 26–27
    valuing diversity, 23
    work schedules, 24–26
  See also Managers
Supervisor-subordinate friendships, 289–92

Supervisor-subordinate relationships, 276–89
  counselor role, 281–85
  educator role, 278–81
  judge's role, 285–86
  spokesperson role, 287–89
Supervisory personnel, sources of, 27–29
Synergy, 316
Syntality, 316–18

T

Taco Bell, 81
Taft-Hartley Act (1947), 4, 559, 562–64
Tampa (Fla.) Electric, discipline at, 520
Tannen, Deborah, 161
Target Stores, and shoplifting, 589
Task forces, 322
Task interdependence, 325–27
Tasks:
  determining, 121
  and planning, 121
  subdividing into activities, 122
Teacher-pupil method of training, 458–63
Team advisors, See Team leaders/facilitators
Team leaders/facilitators, 4, 26–27, 106, 321–23, 332–33
  maturity of, 321
  and performance, 249–52
  relationship between managers and, 357
  requirements, 26–27
    personality, 321–23
  responsibilities of, 326
  schedule of (example), 324
  spokesperson role, 288–89
  supervisors as, 327–28
Team members, conflict between, 286
Teams, 37
  cross-functional teams, 322
  decision to create, 279
  and empowerment, 27
  of managers, 319–21
  product-development teams, 322
  purpose/goals of, 69
  quality assurance teams, 322
  supervising, 56, 78, 119, 173, 258, 279, 322, 378, 396, 489, 514, 563, 602
  and supervisors, 26–27
  task forces, 322
  team facilitators, 26–27

Technical skills, 6–7, 123
Technology, 18–19
Technostress, 222–25
  coping with, 223–25
Telecommuting, 25–26, 27, 37
Teleconference, 168
Telephone, 172–74
Telework centers, 156
Tests:
  and disparate impact, 416–17
  drug testing, 417–18, 601–3
  validity of, 417
Texas Instruments:
  ethics training at, 441
  and job enrichment, 263
  and tracking of assets, 582–83
Theft, employee, 581–83
Theory X, 198, 233, 247
Theory Y, 198–99, 247
Theory Z, 199–200
Therapeutic controls, 132
Thompkins, Nathanial, 273
3M:
  rewards program at, 506
  and stretch targets, 113
360-degree feedback and multi-rater assessment, 21, 484–85
Timeliness, as control characteristic, 132–33
Time logs, 95–96
Time management, 94–98
  daily planners, 96–98
  interruptions, eliminating, 95–96
  spare time, using, 98
  time logs, 95–96
Title VII, Civil Rights Act, 484
Top management level, 77–81
  chief executive's role, 78–79
  secretary's role, 79
  treasurer's role, 81
  vice president's role, 79
Total quality management (TQM), 255–57
  definition of, 256
  kaizen, 256
Toyota, 20
  Georgetown, Kentucky plant, 325
  GM assembly plant (Freemont, Calif.), 192–94, 197, 244
Trainee requirements, 447
Trainer requirements, 444–47
  behavior modeling, 445–47
Training, 126, 438–76
  advantages of:
    for subordinates, 443–44
    for supervisor, 442–43
  application, 467